PROGRAMMING LANGUAGES

PROGRAMMING LANGUAGES

Herbert G. Mayer

MACMILLAN PUBLISHING COMPANY
New York
COLLIER MACMILLAN PUBLISHERS
London

Printed in the United States of America.

Macmillan Publishing Company
866 Third Avenue, New York, New York 10022

Collier Macmillan Canada, Inc.

Library of Congress Card Cataloging Information

Mayer, Herbert G.
Programming Languages.

Bibliography: p.
Includes index.

1. Programming languages (Electronic computers)
1. Title
QA76.7.M39 1987

Printing: 1 2 3 4 5 6 7 8 Year: 7 8 9 0 1 2 3 4

ISBN 0-02-378295-1

Contents

Preface

No human investigation can be called true science
without going through mathematical tests;
and if you say the sciences
which begin and end in the mind contain truth,
this cannot be conceded,
and must be denied for many reasons.
First and foremost because in such mental discourses
experience does not come in, without
which nothing reveals itself with certainty.

Leonardo da Vinci (Treatise, fol. 6)

If you have built castles in the air,
your work need not be lost;
that is where they should be.
Now put the foundations under them.

Henry David Thoreau

This text was written for students taking a course in programming languages at the junior, senior, or first-year graduate level. The course is typically the one in the computer science curriculum designed for CS 8 in the ACM curriculum. Consistent with these guidelines, this text is designed to give students an appreciation for the quality of certain programming languages, to make them aware of recurring flaws in programming language design, and also to familiarize student programmers with subtle aspects of programming, especially those that can cause hard-to-track errors, or "bugs."

No attempt has been made to cover all languages exhaustively, or to cover one language in detail. Rather, the text emphasizes specific constructs and design concepts in order to ensure that the students understand language constructs and considerations unique to a specific language. Programming languages are compared by showing how each approaches and solves the same problem. With simple problems pretested on commercial compilers, students see correct, real-world language situations.

Even though very few of us will actually design programming languages that will be widely used and accepted, students can profitably use ideas and problems discussed in this book to write better programs. Knowledge in the art of designing programming languages is also helpful for extending an existing language. When we take a language and add specific features, we should carefully weigh each construct for merit, compatibility with available language elements, and consistency in language style. Of course, this task sounds much simpler than it is.

Designing a new programming language is even more difficult. One of the reasons for the existence of so many horrible, unfriendly, and inconsistent languages and user interfaces is the gross underestimation of the complexity of this design task. Every creator of a text editor, for example, is in some sense also the creator of a language. User and text editor communicate via a language both understand. We call this the user interface. Often designers take the task of user interface definition too lightly. As a result, many software packages, in particular, operating systems, display incredible user unfriendliness.

How to Read This Text

This book was written so that the readers with different interests in programming languages can select their particular subject of interest. For example, a reader who wishes to study only parameter passing can do so by selecting just Chapter 10, "Parameters." Another reader, mainly interested in Ada but who wishes to know more than parameters, can select the Ada section in each chapter. The combination of these selective strategies is also helpful for quick reference; the reader who wishes to learn how If Statements are constructed in Modula-2 can focus on the Modula-2 section in Chapter 7 "Conditional Statements." We hedge some hope, however, that there will be readers at the other extreme, those who read the complete text and enjoy it.

Chapters 1, 2, and 3 provide a historical and technical introduction to programming languages. Since student's bring uneven backgrounds and skills to this course, these chapters are designed to help put students on more-or-less the same level. For example, many students will not have studied Ada, in which case they should be directed to Appendix B, "Very Elementary Introduction to Ada." Chapter 4 enables students to familiarize themselves with the programming languages discussed in the book through short sample programs. Chapters 5 through 13 cover various syntax components in detail, with numerous examples. These chapters help students develop an understanding of the primary syntactic elements. Chapters 9, 10, and 11 form a trilogy of chapters covering parameter passing, procedure calls, and recursion. Instructors may find these chapters important to assign and cover as a group.

Chapters 15 through 18 cover those topics that are explained differently in each language, and instructors should find this a very important section of the text. Chapter 19 covers concurrent programming, a topic essential for understanding the design and function of "monitors" and "kernels" for systems with just one processor. Chapter 20 introduces Prolog, the first true Logic Programming Language that has the potential of bridging the gap between humans and machines by finally raising the machine's level of communication.

The languages discussed include Ada, Fortran, Pascal, PL/1, Modula-2, and Prolog. Certain selections need a brief explanation. Ada is heavily promoted by the U.S. Department of Defense and will likely be the most widely used language for large-scale "embedded" applications through the next decade. Pascal and Modula-2, among others, will become the most popular programming languages on smaller systems including personal computers, because these languages are simple enough to be comprehensible without extensive training. Pascal should continue to be used as a general purpose language, and Modula-2 should take over the difficult and thus far hardware-dependent area of systems programming. Prolog, now quite popular in Europe and Japan, should become increasingly popular in the United States, especially in artificial intelligence applications.

Acknowledgements

My students at San Diego State University who used earlier versions of this text in lectures on "Programming Languages" have substantially improved the contents by their constructive criticisms and contributions in class. At the beginning of each semester we established the following pact: students would earn extra credit toward their grade for each error and programming bug they discovered in my notes. Many students received excellent grades!

Jeff Bryan of Hewlett Packard in San Diego provided valuable suggestions for improvement. Numerous reviewers contributed helpful suggestions from the earliest stages of the manuscript to final copy: Stephen Allan, Colorado State University; John Conery, University of Oregon; Shepperd Gold, University of Houston; Andrew Oldroyd, Washington University; Viswa Santhanam, Wichita State University; and Mary Louise Soffa, University of Pittsburgh.

Bill Price of Burroughs ASG gave me access to his library of delightful literary treasures, where I found the "Man or Boy" example in the Algol-60 bulletin. More importantly, Bill helped me identify highly judgmental comments throughout the manuscript, especially in reference to Cobol. Bill's direct involvement in the definition of the Pascal standard and his wide understanding of the principles of programming language design provided me with access to extensive background information that enriched this text. His many contributions are greatly appreciated.

Special thanks go to my wife Mary. Her consistent style checking converted many of my original class notes into coherent English. Since she is not a computer expert, I had to explain technical points to her verbally, which she then rephrased into proper English.

Herbert G. Mayer
Portland, Oregon

Für Meine Eltern

Eva und Herbert Mayer

1

Background

Finally a whole theory of abstract complexity,
applying to the most general imaginable programming systems
and measures of complexity in terms of resource use
has been developed, providing important new insights,
such as the hopelessness of complete optimization
in general purpose programming systems.

Michael Machtey, Paul Young
An Introduction to the General Theory of Algorithms

A Programming Language is a tool
which should assist the programmer
in the most difficult aspects of his art,
namely program design, documentation, and debugging.

C. A. R. Hoare
Hints On Programming Language Design

First let's start with a definition of programming languages. The primary function of programming languages is to let the user communicate with the computer via a common interface. This interface can be a very low level machine language, or a language of higher level, which the computer does not understand directly. High level programming languages allow the man-machine communication on a higher, more convenient level than the one that is native to the machine. Programming languages together with their compilers span the gap between low level, binary instructions that machines understand and the higher level on which people express their thoughts.

In this chapter we provide the reader with two different kinds of background information that will support the more detailed and specific discussion in the following chapters. The historical development of computer languages as we know them today is closely connected with the history of computers on which the languages were originally hosted. Since the use of computers and programming languages are so closely interwoven, we include a brief description of the development of computers followed by a short discussion of the major programming languages as they made their first appearance.

Another very different kind of background information is also included. This is an introduction to the *Backus Naur Form (BNF)* for expressing language rules. It should help the programming student master a widely used and very explicit "metalanguage" with which to discuss other languages more clearly and succinctly. In the same section we present the so-called *rail road diagrams*, or syntax diagrams, as a more intuitive means of representing syntax rules.

1.1 Brief History of Computers

[J. Presper] Eckert and [John W.] Mauchly did not themselves invent the automatic electronic digital computer, but instead derived that subject matter from one Dr. John Vincent Atanasoff.

Judge Earl R. Larson
Court Ruling Oct. 19, 1973

Except for the ancient abacus, the oldest artificial computing devices are the Arithmetic Machine built by Blaise Pascal around 1643 and the Four Function Calculator of Gottfried Wilhelm von Leibnitz, introduced about twenty years later. These fairly simple mechanical boxes do not have a stored program and need no programming language. Pascal documented his "computing box" in a letter to the chancellor, dated 1645, when he was barely 22 years old. An outstanding reference for this subject is Pascal [1963].

The earliest "relatives" of programs and programming languages are paper tapes and punched cards as developed by Bouchon, Falcon, and Jacques in the period from 1710 to 1750. Storing information on continuous paper cards was perfected at the beginning of the next century by Jacquard. These tapes held complex, digitized instructions of intricate patterns for weaving looms.

At the same time, around 1810, Charles Babbage started building the Difference Engine. Babbage never finished the Difference Engine, since he discovered a more efficient way of computing data mechanically; this discovery resulted in the design and partial construction of the Analytical Engine in 1835. This work too was never completed because, again, he thought of another, more efficient way of processing data. So goes the tragic story of this genius, whose only fault was to have been born a century too early. His prime programmer was Augusta Ada, Countess of Lovelace, daughter of the poet Lord Byron. In recognition of her pioneering scientific achievement, the new ANSI standard programming language is named Ada, thus also paying a late tribute to her employer, Babbage.

At the turn of the 20th century Herman Hollerith founded the Tabulating Machine Company. His mechanical tabulators were used to speed up the counting and sorting of punched cards for the U.S. Census Bureau. In Europe punched paper cards are still called Hollerith cards.

From 1937 to 1940 John Atanasoff at Iowa State University built the first functional electronic digital computer. He is the genuine first American builder and inventor of an electronic computer, even though he is not often granted proper credit for his outstanding achievement. While he was "speeding across the wintry Iowa landscape in a mind-clearing midnight drive," he figured out several principles essential to building computers, Shore [1984].

Some of these principles, representing a breakthrough in technology, are the use of the base 2 instead of 10, the use of a charged condenser for a memory, and the use of a logic system rather than an enumeration system. Atanasoff communicated these ideas to John W. Mauchly when they worked together at the Naval Ordinance laboratory during World War II. The ideas did not fall on deaf ears.

In the early 1940s J. Presper Eckert and John W. Mauchly started building a monstrous machine, known as ENIAC (Electronic Numerical Integrator and Calculator), which was finally completed in 1946. This machine ran successfully for the U.S. Army Ballistic Research Labs until 1955. Later Eckert and Mauchly formed the Univac corporation, a computer manufacturing firm still competitive today after many changes of ownership. A trial between Univac (Sperry Rand) and Honeywell over who invented the first computer ended in 1973 with the surprising official court ruling that "Eckert and Mauchly did not themselves invent the automatic electronic digital computer, but instead derived that subject matter from one Dr. John Vincent Atanasoff."

In 1944 Howard Aiken at Harvard University completed the Mark-I, an electromechanical calculator. The Mark-I was much slower than the ENIAC due to its relay switching elements; a typical multiplication took over 4 seconds. Like in the ENIAC, the actual program instructions were not stored in the Mark-I's memory as data that could be processed.

At the same time, toward the end of World War II, Konrad Zuse began building his second generation of electromechanical computers in Germany. Zuse was not as fortunate as Aiken, since the establishment at the time did not find his work worthy of continued funding, and the destruction of World War II severely impaired his project.

Earlier in 1936 Konrad Zuse had started building his electromechanical computing machines in Europa. His first experiments predated the ingenious ideas of Atanasoff, but Zuse apparently did not proceed with the speed and clear vision of his American inventor-colleague. By 1945 he had successfully built a working relay computer, the Z4, but due to the war he had to move with his Z4 prototype to the quiet, small German town of Hinterstein. The Z4 was hardly working then. What was worse, Zuse had difficulties getting spare parts, and his staff of about a dozen workers was scattered over the country. Since he had practically no equipment available for repairs, hardware development came to a standstill, and Zuse's attention shifted toward programming language design.

The inability to execute programs on his defunct machine liberated Zuse in some sense from considerations and compromises that could have made his programming language machine dependent. The outcome of this was a programming language concept that remained unparalleled for more than a decade. Zuse's "Plankalkül" language included a mechanism for data structures such as multidimensional arrays, and varying strings, which were so powerful that he was able to express sophisticated programs. These programs included connectivity tests for graphs, algorithms for floating point arithmetic, and sorting functions. Zuse had even designed a rudimentary chess program in "Plankalkül." *Plankalkül,* a German word creation, means something like "Programming Calculus."

Astonishingly, Zuse had hardly any impact on the continuing development of computers and programming languages, even though some of the designers of Algol-60 knew of his work. The more interested reader is referred to Knuth and Pardo [1974], a rare jewel about the history of early programming languages.

The third great scientist, who like Atanasoff and Zuse can be called the father of today's computers with stored programs, is John von Neumann, mathematician and chief consultant for the EDVAC machine (Electronic Discrete Variable Automatic Computer). A peculiar characteristic of von Neumann's machine that is different from present computers is the absence of an address register. Computing successive addresses was achieved by modifying the address operands of machine instructions, which means the code was self-modifying. Years after the EDVAC, machines were still being designed with a self-modifying code, but nowadays this architectural concept is regarded as extremely risky and of questionable value. The one criterion of von Neumann machines that is common to all present computers is the stored program.

The first programmable computers "*spoke*" only machine language. Machine language is unmnemonic, unreadable, and extremely tedious to work with. The step to symbolic assembly language was a gigantic one, and once assembly languages became popular, powerful macro assembly languages evolved.

This brings us to the state of programming today. With the macro assemblers of the past, it was actually possible to develop programming policies that let assembly language source programs resemble the higher level languages of today. But despite this positive development of macro assemblers, higher level languages have almost completely replaced the machine oriented languages. Some farsighted companies have even established the policy that the systems implementation language be high level. This policy was actually initiated by Burroughs Corporation with its extended Algol for the B5000 series. This was quite an extreme act in 1960 and demonstrates courage and vision. This idea was picked up by Hewlett-Packard in the HP3000 series, by NCR for its IRX systems, and many other computer corporations.

The current trend in the development of computers is to bring machines closer to the ideal of a "thinking automaton." Fifth generation computers, under development now, take a different path from the conventional, von Neumann type machines. The new generation is capable of making what appear to be logical deductions or inferences. At the base of these new "inference engines" is a higher level of intelligence. Due to a more advanced architecture of the new systems, their average number of logical deductions per time unit is as high as the number of primitive instructions executed on von Neumann type machines. In other words, while the speed of operation remains constant, each operation does substantially more than on earlier generation machines.

1.2 Brief History of Programming Languages

Fortran

Fortran (FORmula TRANslator) was designed in 1956. At first it was looked upon very suspiciously by programmers, who were accustomed only to machine and assembly languages. Some of the less farsighted professionals speculated that the inefficiencies caused by the automatic translation process could never compete with their own ingenious ways of saving a bit here and a microsecond there.

But it turned out that the language designer and compiler writer John Backus was even more ingenious. In anticipation of this suspicious attitude, he designed an excellent optimizing compiler for Fortran. The implementation took about 18 man years. In fact, the Fortran compiler was not only the first higher level language compiler, but was also the best optimizing compiler for many years to come.

Over the years Fortran developed into Fortran-II, Fortran-IV, Fortran-66, and Fortran-77; the latter two became standard programming languages. The compilers for Fortran-IV on the IBM-360 and, even more, on the CDC-6000 systems are extremely efficient optimizing compilers, following and even exceeding the high standard set by Backus in 1965. Since, originally, the design of Fortran was oriented toward a particular target machine, the IBM-704, the language syntax contains various idiosyncrasies peculiar to that machine. From a pure programming language design standpoint this is a cardinal sin; but seen in the historical context, from an era when programming language research had just started, it is quite forgivable.

Lisp

The bright and shining star between Fortran's efficiency and Algol's coming elegance was Lisp. Developed in the late 1950s, it is still one of the most used of the old, "classical" programming languages. Lisp's design was motivated by the need of Artificial Intelligence (AI) researchers for an appropriate language. Ever since, Lisp has been successful in this special field. Today, however, Lisp is being gradually replaced or at least challenged in AI applications by Prolog.

There are very few language constructs in Lisp. Lists are the sole data structure, and the only operations are function invocations, conditional expressions, and recursion. Even iteration is achieved via recursion in Lisp. Lisp is one of the very few "functional," as opposed to "procedural," programming languages. A procedural language requires the user to express, step by step, how to perform an action. In a functional language the programmer merely specifies what has to be done, the translator figures out how. Most Lisp implementations are interpreted. There is no compelling reason for this other than that the first implementation was interpretive. It ran on an IBM 704, the same machine that hosted the first Fortran compiler.

Basic

Basic is the most used language on microcomputers today. The name is an acronym for Beginner's All Purpose Symbolic Instruction Code. Basic was designed by Thomas Kurtz and John Kemeny at Dartmouth College in 1963 to 1964 as an easy-to-learn, interactive language. The original language was fairly primitive; it had only single-character variable names, which, consequently, allowed no more than 26 variables per program. Similar to Fortran, Basic uses Goto Statements as the main way of changing the flow of control in programs.

Larger programs are, therefore, hard to comprehend and maintain. Over the years Basic has grown more sophisticated. Some implementations even include real-time processing extensions. Most Basic implementations are interpreted rather than compiled and include a line-oriented text editor.

More sophisticated Basic programming environments, particularly on Hewlett-Packard small computers, allow both interpreted and compiled Basic. This way the user has both choices of fast program development and fast running programs. In the development stage a user can test and verify a program's functionality. After the program can be trusted to run reliably, it is submitted for compilation, resulting in an object code that executes fast compared to the slow interpreted version.

Algol-60

Algol was first defined in 1958 as an improvement over Fortran. It was redesigned and improved further, and the final, official report, written in the revolutionary, concise BNF form, was completed and published in 1960—hence the suffix of Algol-60. Algol-60 was probably one of the most ingenious language definition efforts in the early days of programming languages, but paradoxically it never gained widespread acceptance. One can speculate that Algol-60's main flaws were the omission of IO and to a lesser degree the costly parameter passing method "By Name."

Cobol

The same year, 1960, brought a fabulous language, Cobol (COmmon Business Oriented Language), heavily supported by the U.S. government, and in fact required by government offices for computer purchases. This may help explain its wide use today in spite of the fact that Cobol has no clean, logical modules with the facility to pass parameters. Its wordiness is also sometimes misconstrued as being "self-documenting."

Cobol can be used advantageously for certain types of applications, such as those involving the processing of dollars and cents. Also file processing and handling of character string data are advanced in Cobol. For most other applications Cobol is not appropriate. If used anyway, it can make the programming task more difficult than it should be. However, Cobol was a pioneer in defining target-independent IO and in designing structured data. Other milestones set by Cobol are scaled decimal arithmetic and machine-independent data specification. Much of the pioneer spirit that created Cobol's better parts can be attributed to Captain Grace Murray Hopper. Her early ideas in high order language development were quite revolutionary.

APL

APL was designed during the late 1950s by Kenneth Iverson at Harvard University, but the first implementation was not available until the early 1960s. APL is unusual in several respects. It provides a large class of built-in operations that can all be applied to scalars and to arrays of scalars as well. Thus A*B yields an array, if either A or B is an array. Generators are special in APL, yielding vectors. If we let G be an APL generator, then G5 produces the vector of integers 1, 2, 3, 4, 5. All APL operators have the same priority, and multiple operators in one expression are evaluated from right to left. This may be overruled only with explicit parentheses, thus encouraging some effort toward writing readable programs. Overall, however, APL programs strike the novice as being extremely unreadable.

Algol-W

In the mid 1960s Algol-W was developed as an improved successor of Algol-60. It was Niklaus Wirth's contribution toward Algol-68, another spin-off from Algol-60. Even though Algol-60 and Algol-W are not compatible, they are closely related. Algol-W is block structured and recursive. Parameters, however, are no longer passed by name.

The For Statement was redesigned with an implicitly declared local control variable, whose scope is that of the For Statement. We shall find this same principle much later again in Ada.

Jovial

Jovial was one of three languages born out of the effort to improve Algol-60. The other two were Algol-W and Algol-68. Jovial is the acronym for "Jules' Own Version of the International Algorithmic Language." Jules Schwarz's modifications and extensions to Algol impressed the U.S. Air Force so much that it chose Jovial as its preferred, standard language.

Since then Jovial has spawned various dialects, all recognizable as belonging to the same family but quite incompatible with one another. The most widely known version at the current time is J73, documented in Christensen and Willett [1980], eventually to be replaced by Ada. Jovial J73 has benefitted from modern programming language development by including type declarations and enumerative type objects. One of the more bizarre syntax rules in Jovial is the requirement of declaring all subroutines after their referencing statements.

PL/I

PL/I, introduced in 1966, was intended as a replacement for all previous programming languages. To make this possible, it includes features from all other languages. Its main model during the early development years was Fortran, so much even that for a short time PL/I was expected to be upwards compatible with Fortran. During this phase its name was Fortran-VI, but it later changed to NPL. The first compiler was developed at Hursley, England, where the British National Physical Laboratory (NPL) objected against the name until IBM changed it to PL/I.

Many syntax constructs in PL/I can even be expressed in more than one way, leading to a monstrous language syntax. Because it includes too many concepts in too many ways, PL/I did not live up to its expectations. Despite its Gargantuan size, PL/I has evolved into one of the more rigidly defined languages in use.

During the era of its development, programming language designers still believed that defaults and features such as implicit conversion functions were of great value, since they could save the programmer a few key strokes during data entry. These practices, however, lead to subtle errors that are hard to find. The time gained during program creation was easily lost in long and nerve-racking debugging sessions. In the period of Fortran to PL/I, the writeability of programs was emphasized much more than their readability. Today the language C still hangs on to this principle.

Algol-68

Algol-68 was designed from 1966 to 1968. Its formal definition was published in 1969 in the Algol-68 Report, an almost unreadable document. Algol-68 is not another release of Algol-60, even though the name might suggest this. In fact, Algol-68 has less to do with Algol-60 than Pascal does. It is very complex and very hard to compile, but with the exception of its intricate syntax rules, it is an outstanding language.

One of the many beneficial innovations in Algol-68 is the forced closure, which eliminates such old ambiguity problems as the dangling ELSE and overall enhances the readability of source programs. It is unfortunate that such a great language has not gained much wider acceptance in the programming world.

Pascal

In 1969 Wirth introduced Pascal, a small but well-designed language meant primarily for teaching purposes. Since then Pascal has gained more popularity than anticipated. Its main flaw is that it is too good a language for the modest aim for which it was invented. Thus programmers try to use Pascal for all kinds of tasks, even though it is clearly not an all-purpose language. Standard Pascal does not support physical modularization, and it has only very limited IO capabilities. Also Pascal lacks the forced closure as found in Algol-68 and now Ada.

Nevertheless, Pascal is one of the few very well-designed languages in wide use. Typical for Pascal (and Modula-2, PL/I, and C) is the explicit pointer symbol for the dereferencing of pointer type data. Pointer dereferencing in Ada and Algol-68 is done implicitly by the compiler, based on information derived from context.

C

Around 1972, the programming language C appeared on PDP11 machines. It is a general-purpose, not very high level language, mainly used as the systems language for a well-known operating system named Unix. (Unix is a trademark of AT&T.) In C programmers are aware that the NULL pointer, the boolean FALSE, and the numeric integer value 0 all have the identical, internal machine representation of binary zero. Since it includes a very rich set of intelligently chosen operators, and since it is possible to access words in raw memory, it is suited as a systems language. Also it is possible to view data as it is represented in the physical machine and to set or to read an arbitrary bit substring of a machine word.

C includes a powerful mechanism for declaring structured data, but it lacks the safety of more rigorous, strongly typed languages. One of its major drawbacks, along with the unfortunate lack of nested function scopes, is the absence of the distinction between pointer and array type data. Generally, the type concept of C is fuzzy. For some systems applications this may be perceived as a blessing, since all forms of "cheating" are allowed, no matter how unsafe. But for large-scale programming the lack of type checking is a curse. A "strongly typed" language strongly enforces the type equivalence of operands that enter into a common operation.

The C implementors are clearly aware of the advantages of strong typing, so they usually provide a "Lint" preprocessor. It performs type and consistency checks but emits no code. Lint's type checking is much more rigorous than that of the C compiler. For the sake of reliability, every C program should first be scrutinized by Lint. Then, when Lint finds nothing more to complain about, the C source should be submitted to the C compiler for code generation. C is aimed more toward efficient code generation for the PDP11 family than toward ease of understanding and source program maintenance. It is well-suited for operating systems implementation. And systems written in C are clearly more portable than those written in assembly language. In fact, the Unix operating system has been rehosted on a large variety of machines with only minimal rewriting effort.

Modula-2

In 1980 Niklaus Wirth published another outstanding language, Modula-2, designed at the Eidgenössische Technische Hochschule (ETH) Zürich in Switzerland. Modula-2 is a general-purpose programming language, also designed for systems programming. Understandably it is a very close relative to Pascal with the major Pascal errors corrected. Modula-2's name comes from one of its most important features—a solution to the physical modularization problem.

A cosmetic but nevertheless important improvement over its elder brother, Pascal, is the forced closure of Modula-2 statements. The keyword END uniformly terminates all structured statements. Unfortunately, Modula-2 identifiers are case sensitive and IO is not defined as part of the language proper.

Ada

In 1983, after almost a decade of careful study of previous errors in programming language design, a promising language named Ada was introduced. An ANSI standard language, Ada is expected by some in the computer science field to be the first language with the potential of becoming the universal, almost exclusive language of the future for embedded systems. An "embedded system" is part of a larger system, for which the computer provides a specific function. For example, the auto-pilot of a Jumbo-jet is an embedded system. Whether Ada can meet these high expectations remains to be seen. There is no doubt, however, that it is a good language. It enjoys the unique advantage of having been defined as an American National Standard before any implementation became available, saving it from a proliferation of corrupted language versions. It has incorporated Pascal's best ideas and corrected its errors and omissions. Moreover, its range of applications is much wider than Pascal's. It includes the facility of parallel processing by allowing the definition of TASK objects, and it strongly supports separate compilations. Even more than Pascal, Ada is strongly typed.

Though it is quite a good language, Ada is not without problems. IO, for example, is not defined as part of the language. Instead, predefined Ada

Packages are required for performing the IO functions. Since they are expressed in Ada, it is not possible to reference IO procedures with a varying number of arguments as PL/I or Pascal allow.

Prolog

Lisp's applicability to Artificial Intelligence inspired Philippe Roussel of the Groupe d'Intelligence Artificielle at the University of Marseille to develop another nonprocedural language. Roussel focused on a special application of functional languages, loosely described as "Logic Programming." Thus Prolog was conceived in 1972. The first Prolog interpreter was written in Algol-W, but lately implementations in Pascal have gained considerable use. In a Prolog program it is not only not necessary to express "how" a problem is to be solved, it is not even possible. The programmer specifies only "what" has to be done. Prolog does the rest. A Prolog program requires a data base of facts or knowledge. The programmer can ask questions, and Prolog responds with the list of all possible, correct answers that are inferred from the data base of facts. If there are no answers, Prolog simply says no.

If we compare Prolog with procedural languages, we may find it unusual that the textual order of most clauses in a Prolog program is immaterial. Prolog's clauses for establishing the data base can be executed in any order. From this it follows that they may be run in parallel. Once this concept was clear, Prolog became a natural candidate as the systems language on the Japanese fifth generation supercomputers, named "inference engines" (see Raloff [1984]). These machines have a large number of processors, which can execute many Prolog clauses in parallel, thus achieving considerable speed despite the fact that a typical, single Prolog operation consumes a lot of processor time. But there is still more inherent parallelism than in conventional, procedural, single-processor programming languages, and it is here that Prolog and the fifth generation machines form a perfect match.

Summary

We have barely scratched the surface of the history of computers and programming languages, but we have pointed out some important milestones. In the hardware field these are von Neumann's machine and the inference engines; in the software field, Algol-60, Ada, and Prolog are the major milestones. Even though the last two sections represent only a quick run through history, the reader should have some appreciation for the development of computers and their programming languages. In the next section we acquaint the audience with BNF and Syntax Diagrams, metalanguages that serve as a tool for describing languages.

1.3 Syntax Specifications

In order to describe the syntax and semantics of any language, including a programming language, we need some vehicle of communication. This vehicle is just another language, called the *metalanguage.* English, for example, is a possible tool for this purpose. The disadvantage of using English as a metalanguage is its inherent ambiguity and lack of preciseness. The obvious advantage in using English, however, would be that we know this medium already and therefore do not need to learn yet another language. A further advantage for using English as a metalanguage is its expressive power, but for our purposes the ambiguity offsets all its merits. Rather than English we use BNF, which became popular through the Algol-60 report. Then we present a second metalanguage, syntax diagrams, to express syntax rules.

Syntax Specification Via BNF

One scheme widely used for the representation of artificial languages is the *Backus Naur Form,* usually referred to by the acronym BNF. We define a specific form of BNF in this section, extended BNF, which will be used throughout this text. Also we present sample BNF grammars, give a short, formal definition of context free grammars, and present a sample grammar G4 for expressions that will come up more than once throughout the remainder of this book.

A BNF grammar G is a set of rules or productions of the form

```
left_side ::= right_side
```

where the left side is a nonterminal symbol, and the right side is a string of nonterminals and terminals. A *terminal* represents the value written; 123 for example is a terminal, standing for the decimal value one hundred and twenty three. A *nonterminal* stands symbolically for other symbols, as defined to the right of the ::= operator. We should read the ::= operator as "is defined as," or "produces." With these definitions we understand the preceding rule means: "The nonterminal 'left_side' produces the string 'right_side.'"

We should not feel discouraged by such a dry formalism. After all, it refers to something we know already, only in a different notation. From grammar school we remember the rules for constructing English sentences. A sentence is composed of subject and predicate. In BNF we express this simple fact as follows:

```
english_sentence ::= subject predicate
```

But knowing that a sentence has a subject and a predicate does not help much in mastering the English language. We need to know more than this very abstract definition.

Proceeding to the next lower level in our effort to describe English via BNF, we define the two components that in turn define the "english_sentence." These are "subject" and "predicate."

We know that a subject must have a noun and may have an article. In our terminology we say the article is "optional." To indicate this in BNF, we place *article* in square brackets. Similarly, a predicate is composed of a verb with an optional object. This is expressed in BNF in Example 1-1.

```
subject   ::= [ article ] noun
predicate ::= verb [ object ]
```

Example 1-1 Next Level of Refinement of English Sentence in BNF

Although we have covered one more level in our naive attempt to define the rules for the English language, we still have not constructed a single sentence. We still must define the four symbols "article," "noun," "verb," and "object" before we know what an "english_sentence" could possibly be. But, unfortunately, the number of symbols tends to increase more and more.

The reader might become suspicious and ask, does this substitution ever end? Are we always replacing symbols by new symbols, maybe even by previously used symbols? Before the reader has a chance to get apprehensive, we shall give expansions that complete the process for the four symbols just mentioned. We end the substitution process by defining terminal symbols; these are symbols that stand for themselves and cannot be substituted by anything smaller in the world of BNF. To visually distinguish terminal symbols from other symbols, we capitalize them here. The other symbols we call nonterminal symbols. Some examples of nonterminals already encountered are "verb" and "predicate." Nonterminals are spelled in lowercase letters. This is only a convention. We could reverse it, or not use such notational aids at all. The promised terminal symbols follow in Example 1-2.

```
article ::= THE
noun    ::= WORLD
noun    ::= TIME
verb    ::= WILL WELCOME
          | FLIES
object  ::= LOVERS
```

Example 1-2 Substituting Nonterminals with Strings of Terminals

We see in Example 1-2 that "noun" is defined twice, once as WORLD and once as TIME. This means that we can make a choice when generating English sentences from our short BNF grammar. Another BNF notation for "making a choice" is shown in Example 1-2 for nonterminal "verb." "Verb" also produces two terminals, either WILL WELCOME or FLIES. But rather than specifying the nonterminal "verb" twice on the left-hand side, we use a new metaoperator, the vertical bar. The vertical bar separates the two choices on either side. Naturally we can have more than just two choices.

One last comment is in order before we explain a mechanism for generating the complete list of all English sentences that can be composed from our grammar. The first rule for "verb" produces two symbols, the terminal WILL and the terminal WELCOME. In BNF we simply say that these two terminals are *concatenated.* So "verb" cannot produce WILL alone; it can produce FLIES alone, but if we choose WILL, we must also take the WELCOME right after it. All of this nitty-gritty detail is expressed in a concise fashion in BNF. Now we list our complete grammar for the modest language named "english_sentence."

```
english_sentence ::= subject predicate
subject          ::= [ article ] noun
predicate        ::= verb [ object ]
article          ::= THE
noun             ::= WORLD
                   | TIME
verb             ::= WILL WELCOME
                   | FLIES
object           ::= LOVERS
```

Example 1-3 Summary of BNF Rules for a Small English Language

How Do We Construct a Sentence?

The BNF grammar in Example 1-3 is a recipe that explains in detail how sentences can be constructed. We start with a distinguished nonterminal, called the *start symbol.* Every generation of a sentence must begin with this start symbol, hence it classifies the complete grammar—in our case "english_sentence." Then we substitute this "start symbol" by its right-hand side. If this step produces more nonterminals, we continue to substitute nonterminals by other symbols, until no more nonterminals are left. Sometimes we have a choice, as seen already for "verb" and "object." In such a case we arbitrarily pick. We shall go through the generation of one sentence in detail, and write down its derivation. Another notation for the same derivation is the *parse tree,* which is a graphical representation for replacing left-hand sides of the grammar by their corresponding right-hand sides. But first we present an example for the derivation of a terminal string in the "english_sentence."

```
english_sentence ::= subject predicate
                 ::= article noun predicate
                 ::= article noun verb object
                 ::= THE noun verb object
                 ::= THE WORLD verb object
                 ::= THE WORLD WILL WELCOME object
                 ::= THE WORLD WILL WELCOME LOVERS
```

Example 1-4 Derivation of a Sentence

Finally all symbols are terminals, so no more replacement is possible. We have derived (or generated) the sentence "THE WORLD WILL WELCOME LOVERS," while reusing the metasymbol ::= to indicate each replacement step. The same idea can be expressed pictorially in a parse tree. See Figure 1-1, which represents a "typical" tree, one that grows from the ceiling down to the floor.

```
                       english_sentence
                              |
           .--------------v--------------.
           |                             |
        subject                      predicate
           |                             |
     .-----v-----.                 .-----v-----.
     |           |                 |           |
  article       noun              verb        object
     |           |                 |           |
    THE        WORLD         WILL WELCOME    LOVERS
```

Figure 1-1 Parse Tree for Sentence from Our English Grammar

Instead of continuing to define the English language, which would be a Herculean task, we switch back to the development of our BNF tool. BNF was devised for describing programming languages, a much simpler task than describing the full English language, due to the severe restrictiveness and simplicity of most artificial languages.

We start by defining the terminology. Actually we have already snuck in most of the terminology in our example, so the rest of this section should be easy. Then we will take a closer look at those types of BNF grammars that have left recursive and empty rules. We demonstrate how to transform this kind of grammar into an equivalent one with properties that are more suitable for a compiler.

Metasymbols

Terminal symbols stand for themselves and no other string can be derived from them. Hence terminal symbols can never appear on the left-hand side of a rule. Nonterminals, on the other hand, must derive other strings, including the empty string, terminals, or further nonterminals. The empty string is a terminal named "LAMBDA."

By convention, nonterminal symbols are represented in lowercase letters, terminal symbols in uppercase. In addition to letters and digits, terminals can also be composed of special symbols. The end of a production is indicated by the beginning of a new rule or by the end of the grammar; we use no explicit symbol to mark the end of a rule. The metasymbol ::= serves as the production operator. A choice between alternatives is expressed by the metasymbol vertical bar |, repetition of zero or more times is expressed by paired curly braces { and }, and an optional part is enclosed in square brackets [and]. The metasymbols used here are ::= [ ] { } |.

In the rare but possible case that the terminal symbol of a described language is identical to the metasymbol of our BNF language, we have another conflict that needs resolution. In our form of extended BNF we have only a few cases of this ambiguity. One case comes forward in Ada's multiple "case choices" that are separated from one another by the | special symbol. The actual grammar is listed in Section 7.3. Since this clause is allowed any number of times, expressed by the { metasymbol in BNF, we find the string { | in our grammar. We follow the precedent set in the Ada standard and define that in this context the | is the terminal symbol "vertical bar."

A similar situation arises with PL/I's logical OR operator and the concatenation operator. The former is denoted by the | special symbol in PL/I, and the latter by | |. By convention, in our form of BNF the string { | | will be the metaoperator { followed by the | | terminal symbol.

Another escape mechanism is the embedding of conflicting symbols in double quotes. Such conflicts arise from symbols that are already reserved for metasymbols but are also used as part of the language described by the metalanguage. We use this escape in one case—to classify the square brackets [and] as terminal symbols in Pascal's Set value constructors. So in the grammar for Pascal expressions we shall see "[" and "]" to denote the terminal symbols [and]. To exercise our understanding of BNF as a metalanguage, we analyze the sample grammar G1 in Example 1-5, which has three rules or productions, two nonterminals, and three terminal symbols.

```
s ::= t$
t ::= AtB  | AB
```

Example 1-5 Grammar G1 for Language L1

In G1 “s” is the distinguished nonterminal symbol, called the start symbol, and “t” is the second nonterminal. “A,” “B,” and “$” are the terminals. The language L(G1) defined by grammar G1 is the set of all strings having any number (but at least one) of A symbols to the left, and the same number of B symbols on the right side. This string is followed by one $ token. Note that all A’s and B’s are together in that order. We should have no problem verifying that the length of all strings in L(G1) is odd and that the language is infinite.

A Formalism for Grammars and Languages

Now we have gathered a sufficient body of terms to formalize our intuitive notion of grammar. A *context-free grammar (CFG)* is a quadruple G=(N,T,P,S), where N is a set of nonterminals, and T a set of terminal symbols disjoint from N. P is a set of productions of the form introduced earlier, and S is the distinguished start symbol. The grammar is context-free, if there is only a single nonterminal in each rule, to the left of the ::= operator. The language defined by such a grammar can also be described as a set of strings by enumerating all set elements. For languages with an infinite number of strings this would be a wearisome task if performed literally. Therefore we use shorthand formulas, which are effectively different encodings of the associated BNF productions. With this formalism we can generalize G1 and L(G1) as follows.

```
G1  = ( {s,t}, {A,B,$}, {s::=t$, t::=AB, t::=AtB}, s )
        L(G1) = L1 = { A**n B**n $  | n>0 }
```

Example 1-6 Meta-Meta-Language for Grammers

In these two lines the curly braces { and } are used as set delimiters. They are not the metasymbols used for repetition of our extended BNF. These two lines not only define the productions of grammar G1, but are also yet another metalanguage defining our metalanguage BNF.

Readers interested in the topics of automata theory and formal languages are referred to the excellent book by Hopcroft and Ullman [1979]. We shall abandon the sole, dry formalism here and include a more intuitive style, which will make us more susceptible to misinterpretation, but more at ease with the subject.

Grammar G2

Next we present language L2 = L(G2), already substantially more complex than L1; L2 defined by G2 is the set of all those strings over A and B, whose number of A's equals the number of B's. Different from L1 is the missing $ symbol in L2, and the relaxation that the terminal symbols A and B no longer need to be contiguous. Even though both languages are infinite, L2 contains more strings than L1. First, L2 includes all strings in L1, but without the trailing $. Also L2 contains additional strings not in L1. The grammar G2 is shown in Example 1-7.

```
s ::= Ab  | Ba
a ::= A   | As  | Baa
b ::= B   | Bs  | Abb
```

Example 1-7 Grammar G2 for Language L2

A proof for the preceding claim is given in Hopcroft and Ullman [1979], page 81. Some sample strings in L2 are AABB, ABAB, BAABBA.

Ambiguity

G3, which follows, reveals an interesting problem of BNF grammars—namely language ambiguity. If there are two or more distinct parse trees for the same terminal string in L, then the grammar for L is ambiguous. G3 in Example 1-8 is one such ambiguous grammar.

```
e ::=  n  | (e)  | e + e  | e * e
n ::=  d  | n d
d ::=  0  | 1  | 2  | 3  | 4  | 5  | 6  | 7  | 8  | 9
```

Example 1-8 Grammar G3 for Language L3

Language L3 resembles restricted arithmetic expressions, having only the operators + and * for addition and multiplication, parenthesized expressions, and integer numbers. Expression 1+0*9 has two parse trees, as shown in Figure 1-2.

```
    e                   e
    |                   |
.---.---.           .---.---.
|   |   |           |   |   |
e   +   e           e   *   e
|       |           |       |
n   .---.---.   .---.---.   n
|   |   |   |   |   |   |   |
d   e   *   e   e   +   e   d
|   |       |   |       |   |
1   n       n   n       n   9
    |       |   |       |
    d       d   d       d
    |       |   |       |
    0       9   1       0
```

*Figure 1-2 Two Parse Trees for Terminal String 1+0*9*

Depending on what we use the language for, we may appreciate the ambiguity or we may perceive it as a disaster. If we cannot accept an ambiguous grammar, we should replace it by an equivalent, unambiguous one. If this cannot be done, the language is inherently ambiguous. If we wish to retain the ambiguous grammar, we must spice the language definition with additional conditions, to force a preferred interpretation of a string that could have multiple interpretations. This is a convention outside the expressive power of BNF.

Additional rules that are meant to clarify or complete the pure syntax rules of context-free grammars are called *context conditions.* Programming languages need context conditions for their complete description and semantic rules to associate meaning with strings in the language. BNF alone does not suffice; English is still needed.

Operator Precedence and Associativity

What is wrong with grammar G3? The arithmetic expression "1+0*9" does not strike us as ambiguous; it clearly means "1+(0*9)," since multiplication has a higher precedence than addition. Only G3 has no notion of precedence. To convey the full meaning of operators, including associativity and precedence, we rewrite G3 by applying two more conventions. For each operator precedence level we introduce a separate nonterminal symbol, and the binding strength of associated operators increases with increasing "distance" from the start symbol. This convention is illustrated by transforming two alternatives of the first rule of G3 as shown in Example 1-9.

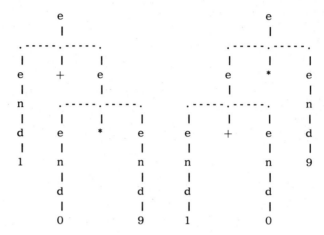

```
e ::= e + t  | t
t ::= t * f  | f
```

Example 1-9   Different Nonterminals for Different Precedence

The multiplication operator * is "further away" from the start symbol "e," so the priority of * is higher than that of the + operator. To complete the grammar we must define "f." G3 , shown in Example 1-10, completes the transformation.

```
e ::= e + t  | t
t ::= t * f  | f
f ::= n  | ( e )
n ::= n d  | d
d ::= 0  | 1  | 2  | 3  | 4  | 5  | 6  | 7  | 8  | 9
```

Example 1-10   Unambiguous Grammar G3 for Language L3

The second convention used here resolves the associativity of multiple occurrences of the same operator. If an operator producing rule is left recursive, such as "e::=e+t," then this operator associates from the left. In G3 the + and * operators are therefore left associative. Using right recursive rules implies right associativity. For example, the production

```
factor ::= primary ^ factor  | primary
```

specifies the ^ operator to associate from the right. This is indeed the usual meaning for the exponentiation operator in many languages. We must remember that the two notational means introduced here are nothing but conventions, like implied rules expressed in English but needing no extra words. If we express multiple operators by means other than recursive rules, as for example by the { and } metaoperators, this convention breaks down. Then we'll have to use English to describe semantics.

Context-Free Versus Context-Sensitive

The grammars we have shown so far are context-free, since all nonterminals are expanded independently of their context. Let us clarify this with an example, using the nonterminals "a" and "b." If "a" appears juxtaposed to "b" in a partial derivation there is nothing "special" about the concatenation "ab." In other words, "a" and "b" concatenated will generate the same set of terminal strings that "a" alone would generate when concatenated with the strings derivable from "b." It is easy to check whether a grammar is context-free: if all rules have only a single nonterminal symbol on the left of the production operator, the grammar is context-free.

Context-free grammars (CFG) are a convenient tool to describe the syntax rules for most real programming languages. But, surprisingly, almost none of typical programming languages are completely context-free. For example, the common rule that names in a program must be declared before referenced cannot generally be expressed by a CFG. As another example, most languages require the number of actual parameters in procedure calls to match exactly the number of formal parameters. This requirement renders a defining grammar to be context-sensitive. For more in-depth reading we refer to chapter 4 in Aho and Ullman [1979].

```
expression           ::= relation { AND relation }
                       | relation { OR  relation }
                       | relation { XOR relation }

relation             ::= simple_expression
                         [ relational_op simple_expression ]

simple_expression    ::= [ unary_add_op ] term
                           { binary_add_op term }

term                 ::= factor { multiply_op factor }

factor               ::= primary [ ^ primary ]

primary              ::= name
                       | ( expression )
                       | NULL
                       | numeric_literal
                       | string_literal

relational_op        ::= = | < | >

unary_add_op         ::= + | -

binary_add_op        ::= + | - | &

multiply_op          ::= * | /

numeric_literal      ::= rules for constructing number

name                 ::= rules for constructing
                         identifiers but AND, OR, XOR,
                         NULL are excluded

string_literal       ::= rules for constructing strings
```

Example 1-11 Grammar G4 for Ada-like Expressions

An Expression Grammar

The fourth grammar, G4, is already of practical interest. G4 resembles a subset of one of the languages treated here, Ada, and we shall stumble over it various times throughout the text. But G4 is not complete. Some nonterminals such as "name" and "numeric_literal" are left undefined in the grammar. We assume for pragmatic reasons that the meaning of these is so obvious that they require no explicit BNF rules. The size of the grammar would grow substantially otherwise. But to make sure the reader does understand, we include a few examples. "Numeric_literal" is a rule generating terminals such as 1943 and 1982.5, while "name" generates identifiers like MIN, MAX, and MAIN_PROGRAM.

If we would try to add semantics or meaning to the expressions generated by G4, we would observe again a clear limitation in the expressive power of BNF grammars. The arguments of boolean operators, for example, must satisfy definite type requirements. These requirements are not missing from grammar G4 due to an oversight, but because they cannot be expressed by grammar rules, except in simple cases. They must therefore be added on by context conditions. The context conditions are spelled out in English. So in reality we use a combination of formalism and natural language to describe the fairly simple artificial language L(G4).

A Simple Language

To round out our understanding, we shall describe a primitive language, called L(G5), that resembles a subset of Ada. The start symbol of the grammar is "simple_language."

```
simple_language ::= PROCEDURE proc_name IS
                      dcl_list
                    BEGIN
                      stmt_list
                    END [ proc_name ] ;

dcl_list        ::= { declaration }

declaration     ::= name : type_mark ;

type_mark       ::= INTEGER | CHARACTER | BOOLEAN
                  | FLOAT

stmt_list       ::= [ stmt_list ] statement

statement       ::= while_stmt | if_stmt | null_stmt
                  | assignment_stmt | io_stmt
```

```
io_stmt          ::= get( variable ) ;
                   | get_line( variable ) ;
                   | put( expression ) ;
                   | put_line( expression ) ;

null_stmt        ::= NULL ;

if_stmt          ::= IF expression THEN stmt_list
                   { ELSIF expression THEN stmt_list }
                   [ ELSE stmt_list ] END IF ;

while_stmt       ::= WHILE expression LOOP stmt_list END LOOP ;

assignment_stmt ::= variable := expression ;

variable         ::= name
```

Example 1-12 Grammar G5 for a Simple Language

In Example 1-12 "simple_language" uses "expression" as defined in grammar G4. The rule for "declaration" allows any name to the left of the terminal symbol colon. Hence a declaration of the form "integer : integer;" is legal in the simple language. Since we know that this is illegal in Ada we understand that L(5) is less related to Ada than it seems at first.

Next we draw a parse tree for a sample expression in L(G4). This will help us to become familiar with grammars and parse trees in general, and it will serve as a preparation for a problem, which we shall encounter in Section 2.7. The parse tree in Figure 1-3 represents the expression "-84+19*100."

```
                         expression
                             |
                          relation
                             |
                      simple_expression
                             |
         .-----------.----v----.-----------.
         |           |         |           |
   unary_minus     term   binary_add_op   term
         |           |         |           |
         -         factor      +     .--------.--------.
                     |               |        |        |
                  primary         factor multiply_op factor
                     |               |        |        |
            numeric_literal       primary     *     primary
                     |               |                 |
                    84       numeric_literal   numeric_literal
                                     |                 |
                                    19                100
```

*Figure 1-3 Parse Tree for String –84+19*100 in L(G4)*

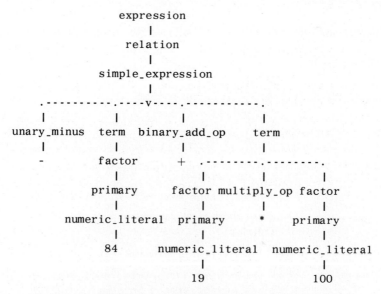

The unary minus and the binary operator for addition have the same priority; the production for "simple_expression" shows this in the grammar, and the parse tree shows this, since both operators are on the same level. The "distance" from the start symbol is the same in either case. Both operators appear on a higher level in the tree than the multiplication operator, which indicates that they do not bind as strongly as the multiplication. In other words, bottommost nodes reflect highest priority, and the nodes higher up in the tree have lower binding strength.

Left Recursion and LAMBDA Rule Elimination

We have seen the advantages of BNF, such as conciseness and clarity, but we have also discovered expressive limitations. Next we explain that there are properties that are sometimes undesirable. These properties are left recursion and lambda-production. A rule is *left recursive,* if it contains at least one alternative that starts with the defined nonterminal. This will be explained further in a moment. A rule has *lambda-productions,* if at least one alternative produces only LAMBDA.

Grammars that derive an infinite number of terminals must use the metaoperators for repetition, or must use at least one nonterminal recursively. This will allow partial derivations of the form "a ::= x a y," where "x" and "y" are strings of terminals and nonterminals not containing "a," and that may not both be empty. If "x" is empty, we have a left recursive rule; if "y" is empty, we speak of a right recursive rule.

Definition of Left-Recursion

The right-hand side of a left recursive rule starts with the very nonterminal symbol that is defined by that production. Production "a ::= a A," for example, is a left recursive rule. The nonterminal "a" is defined in this rule, the right-hand side starts with "a", hence "a" is used left recursively.

For some applications it is necessary to transform left recursive rules into equivalent rules without left recursion; we shall see such a case shortly. This is achieved using the pattern shown in Example 1-13.

```
a   ::= a A | B
L6 = L(G6) = { BA**n | n >= 0 }
```

Example 1-13 Grammar G6 for Language L6

Left Recursion Elimination

Language L6 is the set of all strings that start with one capital B, followed by any number of capital A characters. After a short investigation we find there are many grammars for the same language. One such grammar is G7, shown in Example 1-14.

```
a   ::= B a'
a'  ::= A a'  | LAMBDA

L7 = L(G7) = L6 = { BA**n | n >= 0 }
```

Example 1-14 Grammar G7 for Language L7

LAMBDA stands for the empty string. The empty string is one particular symbol that happens to be invisible; we enforce its visibility by the symbolic name "LAMBDA." We must not confuse LAMBDA with the empty language, which is a language having no strings at all.

Grammar G6 is left recursive, but G7 is not. Both grammars describe the same language. This equivalence provides us with a template for transforming some left recursive rules into nonleft recursive ones. If we cannot deduce grammar G7 from G6 theoretically, then we can pretend that just by chance we have found two equivalent grammars for the same language, one having nicer properties than the other. We must keep in mind that generally there is an infinity of equivalent grammars, all capable of expressing the same language. The number is infinite due to the option of including redundant rules.

Why is it advantageous to rewrite left recursive rules? A certain class of top-down parsers, named *recursive descent parsers,* is written by directly mapping a language grammar into a parsing program. Each nonterminal to the left of a production in the grammar maps into the definition of a recursive procedure in the parser. Each occurrence of a nonterminal to the right of a production maps into a procedure call. If such a nonterminal is used left recursively, this causes a direct recursive procedure call immediately at the beginning of a procedure's body. This is, of course, undesirable, since the sequence of calls would never end. Hence the writer of such a compiler has to transform each left recursive rule into an equivalent one that is not left recursive.

LAMBDA Rule Elimination

It is also sometimes desirable to have no lambda-productions in a grammar. This is achieved by systematically replacing all lambda-productions in each rule (except possibly for the start symbol) by additional alternatives with the lambda-producing nonterminal omitted. Thus G7 transforms into the equivalent grammar G8, shown in Example 1-15.

```
a  ::= B a'  | B
a' ::= A a'  | A
```

Example 1-15 Grammar G8 for Language L8

Syntax Specification Via Syntax Diagrams

Syntax diagrams are yet another form of metalanguage. They are easier to understand than BNF and have been successfully used for describing Pascal. We'll explain here the mapping of BNF grammars into syntax diagrams (or rail road diagrams).

Nonterminal references are represented as rectangular boxes with the name written inside. Terminal symbols are denoted as rounded boxes, again with the terminal included. See Figure 1-4.

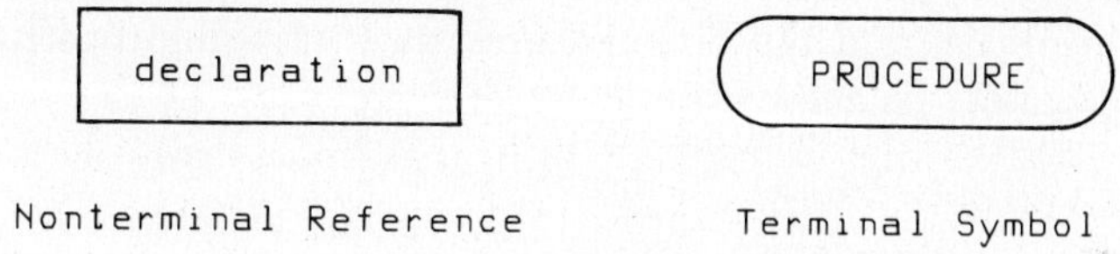

Figure 1-4 Elements of Syntax Diagrams

Concatenation is expressed by a directed line between the connecting elements. The choice is expressed by a forking line. Figure 1-5 shows the choice between the terminal symbols + and -, concatenated with "expression."

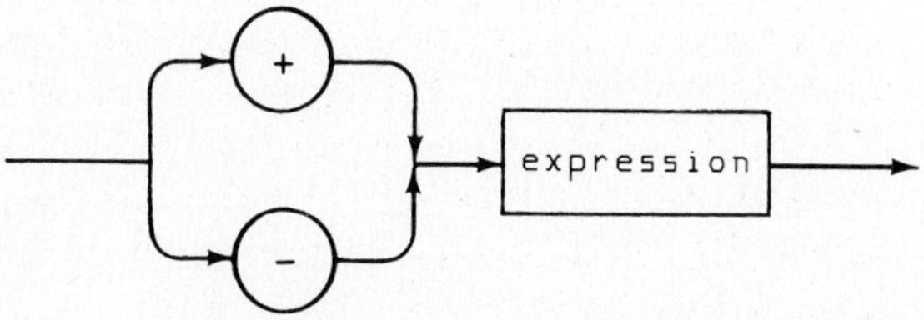

Figure 1-5 Syntax Diagram for Choice and Concatenation

Finally, a complete rule is composed of the nonterminal being defined, which heads an arbitrarily complex network of lines plus connecting terminal and nonterminal symbols. The syntax diagram in Figure 1-6 defines the nonterminal "statement," but it is not complete. To complete the example, we would need further diagrams that define "while_stmt," "call_stmt," "return_stmt," and "assign_stmt."

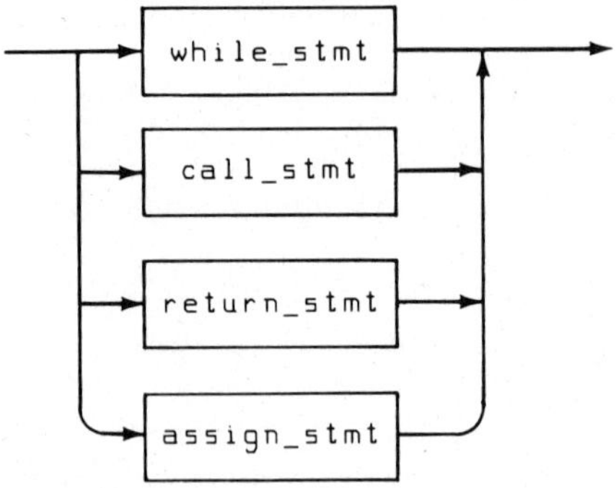

Figure 1-6 Syntax Diagram for "Statement"

Figure 1-7 shows the "simple_language" as syntax diagrams. Rectangular boxes represent nonterminal symbols, defined by other syntax diagrams; rounded boxes are terminals; and the directed arcs tie everything together. Figure 1-7 appears on the next page.

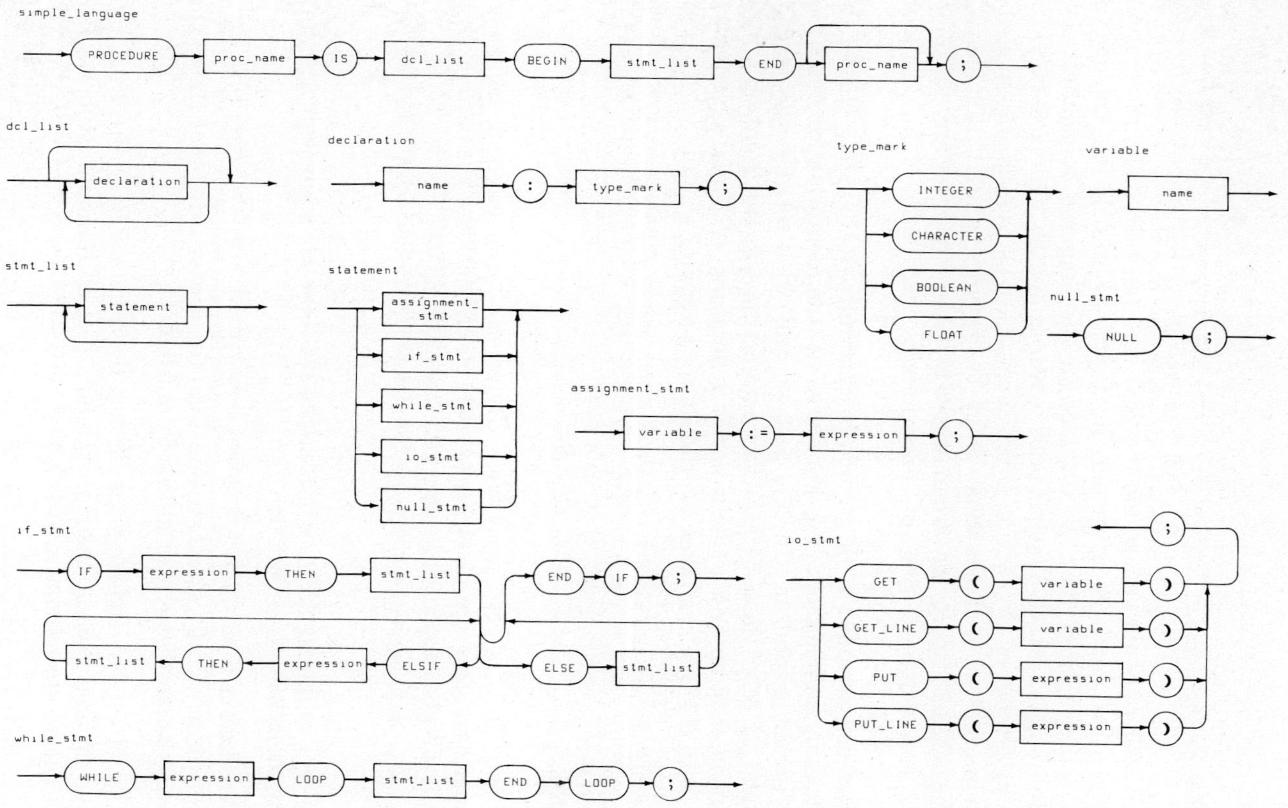

Figure 1-7 Syntax Diagram for Simple Language

1.4 Summary

By now the reader should understand the BNF and rail road diagram notation. When given a context-free grammar in BNF, we should be capable of generating source strings that are included in the language so defined. We should also understand that such skills cover only the syntax aspects of programming languages. Mastering BNF alone makes us experts only in string manipulation, not in understanding what the strings mean. But, having covered the syntax aspect, we are now ready to progress toward the more important, less tangible side of programming languages—that is, their semantics.

We shall use extended BNF grammars constantly in this text. One of the most interesting applications for grammars is the definition of input for automatic parser generators. In this text we only wish to raise the reader's curiosity, and we refer those with further interest to Aho and Johnson [1974], which is an interesting article about parser generators. The next chapter will introduce us to the way compilers see the source program.

1.5 Exercises

1. Grammar EG1 is left recursive. Transform EG1 into an equivalent grammar EG1 that has no left recursive rules. Hint: Use the pattern given in the text to introduce a rule that produces LAMBDA.

   EG1 : s ::= s + E | E

2. Transform grammar EG1 from exercise 1 into an equivalent grammar EG without lambda-productions.

3. The terminal string "WHILE i < max LOOP i := i + 1 END LOOP;" is allegedly generated by grammar G5. Find the syntax error that shows that the string cannot be derived in this form from G5.

4. Describe in English the language defined by grammar EG2. EG2 has only one nonterminal symbol, the start symbol. List all terminal symbols. How long is the shortest string in L(EG2)?

   EG2 : s ::= (s) s | LAMBDA

5. Prove that the language defined by EG2 includes all strings as derived in Exercise 4. Hint: Use induction based on the length of terminal strings.

6. List all terminal, nonterminal, and metasymbols used in the grammar EG3. What causes the ambiguousness of EG3? Propose another grammar, defining the same language as EG3 that is not ambiguous.

```
EG3:     disj ::= conj   | disj AND disj
         conj ::= term   | conj OR  conj
         term ::= FALSE  | TRUE
```

7. Let L1 be the empty language, which is the language without a single string. Let L2 be the language having only the one string LAMBDA. Remember that LAMBDA is the empty string. Are the two languages equivalent? In other words, can we write one and the same grammar for both L1 and L2?

8. Generate all sentences that can be derived from the small grammar Example 1-3, with the start symbol "english_sentence."

9. Draw the syntax diagram that corresponds to the BNF grammar for the following "for_statement:"

```
for_statement ::= FOR name IN expression .. expression LOOP
                     sequence_of_statements
                  END LOOP ;
```

2

Programming Languages and Their Compilers

The nice thing about standards is
that you have so many to choose from;
furthermore, if you do not like any of them,
you can just wait for next year's model.

Andrew S. Tanenbaum
Computer Networks

This chapter begins by describing the standards that govern programming languages. Then we explain why programming languages are needed at all. To start on an equal footing and to prepare the reader for the next two chapters, we also briefly describe what languages have in common, and we list the criteria that constitute a good programming language. Since many of these criteria are contradictory, the reader will develop a sense for the difficulties in programming language design.

An understanding of high level programming languages is dependent on a comprehension of their translators; therefore we include a short section about compilers. This will not only get us accustomed to the compiler terminology, but it may also widen our understanding of machine-independent language design. Ideally, the compiler section will also give the reader a feeling for what is easy and what is hard for a translator to understand. The section on compilers explains how the translator perceives the source program and presents a high level view of compiler organization.

2.1 Standards

The Standard as a Contract

A language standard is intended to define the rules for program composition and to specify the meaning of each construct. In other words, it consists of the syntax rules and outlines the semantics. Ideally, the syntax rules are short and the semantics are unambiguous. A standard also serves as a contract between users and implementors. The implementor takes the standard and creates a program that compiles (or interprets) the language exactly as it is outlined in the standard. This program is called the *language compiler.*

If the implementor changes the syntax rules or the semantics of syntactically correct programs, this represents a breach of contract. Also if the implementor chooses to add facilities not described in the standard, or if only a portion of the whole language is implemented, then the claim of having implemented exactly the standard language is not justified.

Portability

A programmer uses the language standard as a reference document for learning how to program in that language. The user trusts that the implementor has created a compiler that does exactly what the standard defines. It does not matter to the user how the implementor has written the compiler as long as the compilation speed is tolerable and the execution speed of the correctly running object code is satisfactory. All the user cares about is the correctness and completeness of the implementation.

Portability means that source programs running on one machine run equally on all other machines with the same language compiler. As a fringe benefit even programmers become portable. Education in a high level language eliminates the need to be conscious of a particular machine architecture. Retraining is thereby minimized, representing a substantial savings in cost and frustration.

Superset Implementations

Depending on the environment, superset implementations may be quite useful, but any addition over the standard language must be clearly marked as such. Then the trusting user can make a deliberate choice between using such extensions or abstaining from them. If we use a language extension in our program we should visibly mark each occurrence. This makes us and future readers aware that this program will not compile and run on another machine, even if that other system had the "same" standard language compiler. It would be too unlikely that the other implementation would have the identical extension with the same syntax. Such a program is nonportable. If a programmer never uses extensions to the standard language, all source programs remain portable.

Specific Standards

This outline conveys some appreciation for the existence of standards. However, the reader is cautioned to take these goals with a grain of salt. Portability is an ideal. Subtle differences across diverging machine architectures cause different semantics on different machines, even if the language implementor makes no changes to the language. For example, on a small machine the possible value range of "integer" type objects may be much smaller than on a large machine, hence the semantics of the languages differ.

Not all programming languages are defined by standards; also some languages were in wide use before their standards were finally accepted. In just a few cases has the standard been issued before any implementation existed. Of the languages treated in this text, Ada, Fortran, Pascal, and PL/I are ANSI standard languages. Modula-2, and Prolog are defined in the professional computer science literature.

Ada Standard

Users of Ada are lucky in one regard; the standard was issued and widely published long before any implementation was available. Moreover, the holder of the Ada trademark, the U.S. Department of Defense, makes a conscientious effort in validating only compilers that adhere to the standard.

Fortran Standard

Fortran has been in use for so many years that it has a variety of different standards. In this text we shall refer to Fortran-II, Fortran-IV, Fortran-66, and Fortran-77. The standard for Fortran-66 was announced in 1966, while Fortran-77 is defined in ANSI [1978], together with an allowed subset. All program examples refer to Fortran-77.

Pascal Standard

Pascal is another language that had gained wide use long before it became an ANSI standard in 1983. For years the de facto standard was the "User Manual And Report," see Jensen and Wirth [1978]. In addition to this old definition, the standard Pascal language (ANSI [1983b]) has valuable improvements such as conformant (dynamic) arrays, making the task for programmers much easier. In this text we shall cover standard Pascal.

PL/I Standard

PL/I was also a widely used language, mainly on IBM equipment, long before the PL/I standard was issued (ANSI [1976]). Now the two PL/I languages, standard PL/I and IBM PL/I, are different to some degree, which is the typical danger with languages that are implemented *before* their standardization. For example the standard does not include Case Statements, while the IBM implementation does include a Select Statement, which is effectively a Case Statement. Again, in this text we describe the ANSI standard language, but our sample PL/I program listings come from a third source: the PL/I compiler implemented on a CDC Cyber machine, which offers yet another flavour of the language.

As we can observe with Fortran, standardization per se is no safeguard against language incompatibilities, particularly if there are too many standards, and if subset and superset implementations are practiced.

Modula-2

The programming language Modula-2, covered in this text, is described in Wirth [1982]. It is a direct descendant of Pascal and Modula, Wirth [1977]. Modula-2 is very young but is rapidly gaining popularity. At the current time it is not an ANSI or ISO standard, and we can only speculate if it will ever become a standard. Modula-2 is so promising as both a general-purpose and a systems implementation language that we have included various source samples in this text.

Prolog

Prolog is a nonprocedural language used for logic programming. Source programs in Prolog look similar to formal correctness proofs applied to procedural languages. The attribute "procedural" should not be confused with the facility to declare and call procedures. Cobol, for example, is also a procedural language, even though no procedure can be declared. "Procedural" indicates the presence of side effects and the need to specify in full detail each step to be executed. In conjunction with a designed-in termination condition, such procedures become algorithms. "Functional" as an attribute for programming languages means freedom from side effects and a high level of abstraction. Ideally, in a functional language one need say only what is wanted, not how to achieve it.

At the current time Prolog is not an ANSI or ISO language, and we cannot foresee which of the numerous Prolog dialects will prevail. Therefore, when we discuss the Prolog language, we must clearly qualify which of the languages we have in mind. For sample programs, we chose the interpreter from the University of New South Wales, and as a language reference document we used the refreshing text by Clocksin and Mellish [1981].

2.2 Why Have Programming Languages?

Programming languages are the medium through which users communicate with a computer. The forms of communication include a wide spectrum of levels, spanning the "low level" machine and assembly languages to the "high level" machine-independent languages. All of the languages discussed here are higher level procedural languages, with the exception of Prolog, which is a language for logic programming.

A high level programming language allows the programmer to express complex instruction sequences and data structures directly in that language. A low level language requires an additional transformation from the conceptual idea to the actual data structures and instructions. What takes a year of programming effort in machine language may take as little as a few weeks in a high level language. Another measure for the level of a programming language is the extent to which it allows the programmer to ignore machine-specific detail. The more the actual computer can be ignored, the higher is the language level, and the more convenient it becomes to "code" programs.

But we do pay a price for this increased convenience. High level language programs often run slower than assembly language programs, because the high level algorithm must be translated via a compiler into machine language. This induces inefficiencies. Also we lose some control over resource utilization such as data and code space. Most of the time, however, the high level language approach is preferable, since memory space and a few seconds of machine time are less precious than a programmer's time.

2.3 What Programming Languages Have in Common

Before we discuss the advantages and disadvantages of each language individually, we will first mention what they have in common. All these higher level languages assume the source program to be presented as input to the compiler on some physical medium, consisting of text lines. The text is represented in some standard character set such as Ascii, Ebcdic, or an in-house character set. Whatever character set is chosen, it must be guaranteed that the creator of the text file and the compiler both agree about that standard. Problems can occur when a source program is ported from one machine to that of another manufacturer. The two implementations of the same language may agree about syntax rules and semantics, but they may disagree about the character set used. Sometimes this obstacle is overcome by system provided functions, translating text from one character set into another. Otherwise the language compiler will not be able to recognize what is a perfectly good source to another translator.

Individual characters are the smallest, atomic language entities of source programs. From these characters are composed lexical units, often called *lexical tokens* or just *tokens.* These lexical tokens are strung together to form source programs following the rules of the language syntax. Finally, each syntactically correct program has some meaning or performs some action, as defined by the semantics of the language.

Lexical tokens can be grouped into identifiers, keywords, literals, and special symbols. *Identifiers* are names for other entities, while *literals* are values that stand for themselves. This should remind us of nonterminals and terminals, which we have covered earlier. *Keywords* are identifiers with a predefined meaning. Sometimes they are reserved, which means that no user-defined name with another meaning may have the same spelling (Ada, Modula-2, Pascal). Other times they are not reserved, as is the case in PL/I and Fortran. Literals come in various flavours, including numeric integer literals, numeric floating-point or fixed-point literals, string literals, character literals, and boolean literals.

Special symbols are used as operators or separators. Typical operators are the + for addition, * for multiplication, and = or := for assignment. Other operators such as the logical AND function are represented as reserved keywords (Ada, Modula-2, Pascal), special symbols such as & (PL/I), or as composite symbols like .AND. (Fortran). As we know from mathematics, those special operator symbols may be combined with operands to form more and more complex arithmetic expressions. However, the particular rules governing the priority and associativity of operators differ widely from language to language.

Some specific separators are the semicolon, comma, the blank character, and the carriage return. Fortran takes exception to the blank as a separator.

All languages have some form of a comment for documenting the source text without affecting the actual program.

With the exception of Pascal, programs can be composed of more than one physical module or compilation unit, but all languages allow the composition of physical modules from smaller, logical modules, thus greatly reducing the programming effort. These logical modules contain local data and various instructions for assignments, conditional statements, IO statements, iterative statements, and procedure calls.

Also common to all procedural programming languages covered is a small set of primitive, intrinsic data types such as integer, character, and boolean. In addition, the "array" data structure is also included. An array is a collection of primitive elements, all of the same type. Except for Fortran, the languages considered here have a generic structuring mechanism that allows the grouping of elements of different types into one data structure named "record" or "structure." Individual record fields are referenced by their unique field names, yielding "qualified names." Each record field may in turn be a record, thus permitting an unbounded nesting level for data structures.

2.4 What Constitutes a Good Programming Language?

Probably the most controversial issue except for missed deadlines, an issue that heats the minds and hearts of even the calmest and coolest programmers, is the question, "What is a good programming language?" Many of us "know" the answer: our pet language is the best one. In the following paragraph, however, we try to explain a bit more objectively what constitutes a good language, even though some basic principles, considered to be "good" by some, might not be interpreted that way by everybody. Although we do discuss quality criteria, we must be aware that most of the goals are conflicting. A perfect language, therefore, can never be designed; at best only an optimum compromise can be achieved.

Nevertheless, there are certainly some minimal requirements for a good language. A reasonable set of primitive data types and operations, built-in functions, and statements must be included. Practically all procedural languages satisfy this. But more is needed than the predefined data types, no matter how large their number. A useful language needs arrays, pointers, and a data-structuring facility. Depending on the anticipated use, a good language will also include multitasking, a character string data type, and special operators for string concatenation and substring extraction. Since a good language should be easy to learn, it should not express the same idea in multiple ways so that too much time is required to develop a sense of mastery.

We shall see in Chapter 20 that Prolog, since it is not a procedural language, satisfies practically none of these criteria; we shall, however, be surprised about its usefulness.

Consistency

Orthogonality is another quality criterion. This means that once a concept is included in a language, it should be used in the same way, irrespective of context and independent of what else is included. For example, it is not a good idea to permit a general arithmetic expression in some places, but to allow only restricted expressions in other places. This has been done in the older Fortran definitions for array subscripts. The new Fortran-77 standard subset language disallows array subscripts and functions in array subscripts, but in the full Fortran-77 language these in today's terms silly rules have fortunately been eliminated. They violate the orthogonality principle by making the learning process for a language more complex. A programmer must learn two concepts, even though one would be enough. Also the compiler must have two modules—the first for handling full expressions and the second for expressions used in subscripts—even though one would be enough.

Rules like these may sound arbitrary to us today, but they usually have an interesting historical explanation. The Fortran rule for subscripting is a good example. Subscripts, like any other aspect of the language, were designed specifically for an IBM machine, on which code compaction rather than programming ease was the driving design force. This machine provided only a restricted set of operations for its index registers. Also Backus's revolutionary language had to contend with assembly language programmers, so the machine code emitted for subscripts had to be "optimal." Backus was familiar with an optimization technique known as *strength reduction,* which he could conveniently apply as long as only the restricted form of expressions was used. Strength reduction is the replacement of an operator by an equivalent one that executes faster. We shall briefly revisit strength reduction in Section 2.8. Rather than permitting a mediocre code to be generated for some class of expressions, the old Fortran definitions do not permit them in the first place. "Denial of service is better than degradation of performance" was the principle applied here. The restriction was a political move, and we speculate that this political move was one more contributor to Fortran's success.

Explicitness

A good language also should be explicit. Explicitness means that there is no vagueness or ambiguity in the expression. A program is explicit if its intended function is clearly derivable from the source text. Explicitness is greatly enhanced by rigorous syntax rules. Initially this is often perceived as painful, especially by less experienced programmers, since it requires declarations rather than defaults. Actions during execution time should be directly extractable from the source text. This principle is often violated, quite notably by one of PL/I's and Fortran's well-known features, the "automatic" or "implicit" type conversion, which we'll describe next.

Type Conversion Functions

Languages need to offer operations that transform an object of one type into an equivalent object of another type. These are *type conversions.* The two predominant philosophies can be characterized as "implicit" and "explicit" conversion. With explicit conversions it is the user's responsibility to write down the detailed nature of the conversion in the source program, while in languages with implicit type conversions the compiler takes care of this. Which of the two is better?

Explicit conversion encourages the programmer to consider each data alteration carefully during program design and to state which conversions are intended in which order. Thus the writing effort increases, but reading (understanding) becomes easier. With implicit type conversions all detail is hidden. The responsibility is offloaded from the programmer to the compiler. The writing effort decreases, but understanding such programs becomes hard. This is because several steps of data transformations can occur without the programmer's knowledge and cause surprises during execution time.

Implicit type conversions were not introduced by oversight. The language designers believed them to be of great value, since they would save a few key strokes of typing during source program entry. In the "stone ages" of programming, though, key strokes literally meant having to hammer on ugly card punch machines. In those dark days, saving key strokes did make sense. Today, in an era with convenient screen-oriented text editors, this argument should no longer influence programming language design, and saving key strokes should no longer be accepted as an excuse for sacrificing readability.

Ultimately, this issue is only one aspect of "strong" strict versus "weak" loose typing. Ada is a strictly typed language, while PL/I is loosely typed. Pascal and Modula-2 fall in between, but are oriented toward strict typing.

High Level Data Structures

The increasingly abstract interpretation and specification of data remove the programming language from the physical data representation on a particular machine. Thus high level languages are not automatically suited for all applications, specifically not for systems programming, where it may be crucial to have access to a particular bit string in memory. Therefore a good high level language, intended for systems applications, must include a clean, well-controlled loophole for explicit data packing and physical data access. For this reason Pascal is not well-suited as a systems language. All data packing is done under the compiler's control. Ada has the "Representation Specification" for this purpose, and C allows the explicit storage specification of bits in structure declarations. PL/I has provisions for programmer-controlled data packing.

Ideally, a good programming language should lend itself to formal correctness proofs. This way the programmer's initial suspicion or intuition about the program's correctness can be readily automated. Even though much progress has been made in this area of computer science, the current state of the art is far from being practical. The few automated correctness proving systems that are reasonably complete are made impractical by their tremendous compute time. These limitations render this last quality criterion a bit speculative.

2.5 How the Compiler Sees the Source

In this section we place the reader inside of a compiler to provide a close look at how such a complex software system functions. The goal here is not to learn how to write compilers, but to learn about the interaction of programming language and translator.

First, we look at the incoming source, not with the intelligent eyes of a reader, who can quickly glance over a large section of source to get contextual information, but with the simplistic eyes of a compiler, which reads one character or at best a few lines at a time. Then we discuss various internal modules and data structures found in all compilers in some form. Last, we look at the other end, at the output side of a compiler, to familiarize ourselves with the primary objective of compilers, and to understand why certain information is remembered in the compiler's internal data structures.

The Compiler's Task

In its most abstract form, the compiler is a function that transforms an incoming stream of tokens into another, equivalent string of records. The incoming character stream that composes the tokens must adhere to the lexical, syntactic, and semantic rules of the analyzed programming language. The outgoing records are instructions to a computer system that can process these records. The analyzed programs form the *source language;* the compiler is written in a *host language,* runs on a *host machine,* and generates output for a *target machine,* expressed in the *target language.* The emitted output is also called *object.*

Stated a bit more informally, a compiler reads source characters and synthesizes them into lexical tokens. These tokens are composed into syntactic entities, such as declarations, expressions, and statements. If the compiler finds nothing wrong with the incoming source, it applies the semantic rules to transform the syntax units into equivalent target machine instructions. The target can be a fictitious, nonexisting machine, as long as another software system is available to simulate the virtual target machine. But this is transparent to the compiler.

If the compiler does find something wrong with the source, it signals the error condition to the programmer. A very primitive compiler will stop working altogether at the first occurrence of an error, emit a very cryptic message, and leave it up to the programmer to find out exactly what is wrong. A more sophisticated compiler generates on demand a listing that includes a readable error message in a natural language, stating precisely the location and the nature of the error. It will also continue to analyze the source, since the program may contain additional errors that can be detected and flagged in the same run. This will save the programmer time during initial program development, because several errors can be corrected after only one analysis. There are situations, however, where the compiler is so lost that it no longer knows what it is doing. Then it is time to abort the compilation. All further messages and other outputs would be meaningless anyway.

Since a compiler only translates a source program into another, equivalent program expressed in the target language, we might ask, why have a compiler in the first place? Why couldn't the target machine execute the source program directly? The answer is quite clear: computers are too simple-minded to understand high level language programs directly. Therefore, compilers are necessary to span the gap between the low level target language that a computer can understand and execute, and the high level source language in which programmers wish to express their instructions. Compilers are just special-purpose programs that perform this transformation. It remains to be seen whether the fifth generation inference engines will be equally simple-minded, or whether they will be capable of executing logic programs directly.

Interpreters

If the target language were "close" to the source language, the translation process would become simple, in its extreme form even unnecessary. In recognition of this fact another type of translator transforms the source into such *intermediate code.* This intermediate code then is directly executed by an *interpreter.* The disadvantage of interpretation versus compilation is the slow execution; since each intermediate code instruction is executed by a software routine, it runs orders of magnitudes slower than a "hard" machine instruction. On the other hand, it is usually much simpler to write an interpreter than a compiler.

Problems and Limitations

In this section we argue that there exist no perfect compilers; they all have limitations and most even have flaws.

A "correct" compiler is able to translate source programs that conform to the language rules, and will reject incoming source strings that have at least one error. A "complete" compiler can translate *all* correct source programs, and flag *all* source strings with errors. However, no high level programming language imposes a limit on the physical size of source programs, and yet no compiler in the world can handle very large source programs. This is not as bad as it sounds. It is sufficient for a realistic compiler to be correct for most interesting programs. By definition, source programs of infinite size are uninteresting. Since programmers can never construct them, why should anyone bother to build a compiler that could analyze them? The problem is where to draw the line between programs that must still be compilable and those that are too large.

Once we have accepted the fact that there are physical limitations to the analyzed programs, we understand that a compiler designer must make a well-balanced engineering decision as to what the physical limits should be. The best principle is to let the compiler abort due to resource exhaustion only if all available space is consumed for internal data structures, such as the symbol table, which we'll discuss in the next section.

Are we discussing a genuine problem here? This depends on the reader's level of exposure to real-world compilers! We have encountered compilers used for production work that limit the maximum number of source lines to just a few hundred. The true reason for this limit was improper internal space management, but the reason given was that it is better to modularize programs physically.

The bugs and errors even in a good compiler pose a more realistic problem than the size limitation imposed on the incoming source program. Some compilers will occasionally misinterpret correct source programs as incorrect. This certainly causes a nuisance or even confusion, since as conscientious programmers we have to go back and reassess our understanding of the language. It is little consolation when we find that the compiler is wrong and we are right. We still can't succeed without the compiler's cooperation. In such a situation we have to wait until the compiler is corrected or work around the problem by expressing the correct algorithm via another, equivalent algorithm with which the compiler has no problem.

But the most critical problem is of quite the opposite nature. Some compilers are incorrect, because they do not detect all errors in a source program. As programmers we get the impression that our program is acceptable, when in reality we made an error, only because the compiler writer made the same flaw we did. The successful compilation creates an illusion. This illusion will soon be shattered when we try to run the program. It will not work as intended. What is so devious about this class of error is that we have no clue as to what could be wrong; everything looks correct. So we have to suspect everything.

The Symbol Table and Code Buffer

A compiler is not allowed to store the complete source program in its internal data structures, because this would set a too restrictive limit on the maximum size. Similarly, a compiler should not store all generated object in some code buffer, set aside for this purpose, even though it may feel tempted to do so; storing would have the nice benefit that all references could be resolved by the compiler before the end of the translation process. But again, this would limit the maximum size of source programs too drastically.

On the other hand, a program includes references to names throughout the source. Such names are procedure names, function names, compilation units, variables, symbolic constants, type marks, labels, loop parameters, block names, and many more. Since the compiler is better off not to store the complete source, it must have another mechanism for understanding references to such names. This is the purpose of the *symbol table.* The symbol table holds all information provided in the declarations. It does not matter that sometimes the declaration does not show up explicitly in the source, as for example in Fortran's and PL/I's implicit declarations. As long as a name lives, it occupies an entry in the symbol table. Indexed by this name, the compiler then can retrieve all stored information about the name. A very intelligent compiler also accumulates hidden, subtle information. For example, it is valuable for a programmer to know if a symbol has been declared but never used. In such a case we may consider omitting such a declaration altogether.

For languages with separate compilation units such as Ada, Modula-2, or UCSD-Pascal, the symbol table is not only an internal data structure. Since other units may reference names of the current compilation unit, the compiler must write information from the symbol table onto external files. Then, when a reference occurs to a name of a previous compilation, the compiler can read the external symbol table information and extract all pertinent information from there. This helps us understand why the compilation speed for modular languages that perform type checking across separate modules can be very slow.

Output

The compiler generated object program may be in assembler source form, in which case an assembler still has to generate binary object, or it may be in binary form. There are even translators, which translate the incoming source into another, high level target language.

The most critical issue during the code generation phase is the preservation of the source language semantics. Good error messages, fast compilation, good quality code are only of secondary importance.

2.6 Compiler Organization

This section presents a high level overview of the different compilation phases, but does not provide the kind of detail that would explain how these phases accomplish their work. Since they are so crucial and related to the subject of programming languages, parsing and code generation are also discussed separately in more detail in the last two sections of this chapter.

The compilation process is usually too complex to be accomplished in one step. Instead it is broken into multiple phases. A *phase* is a logically closed unit of work, and is sometimes confused with a pass. A *pass* is a full scan over the complete input in original source form or in some intermediate form. For our level of understanding we don't need to care too much what a pass does and what a phase accomplishes. Both are logical functions, implemented as programs that transform their input into equivalent output. Eventually, the composition of all these functions ends up performing the compilation.

We distinguish the following compilation phases: lexical analysis, syntax analysis, semantic analysis, optimization, code generation, and peephole optimization. For simple languages it is possible to combine all phases into one pass, in which case the compilation is fast. For many languages, however, the compiler is organized in multiple passes. Each pass (except the first) receives the output of the previous one as its input, and then performs its own transformation. During this process it emits the new information onto yet another file. The output of the final pass is the desired object code for the target machine.

The block diagram in Figure 2-1 helps us to visualize these individual steps. It does not matter whether we interpret the vertical list of boxes in the center as passes or phases. The box on the left represents the symbol Table information, which is created and used by several steps. In a multipass compiler this information resides on a file, while a one-pass compiler can store the table in its internal data structure. The box on the right represents the listing processor that uses the accumulated error messages.

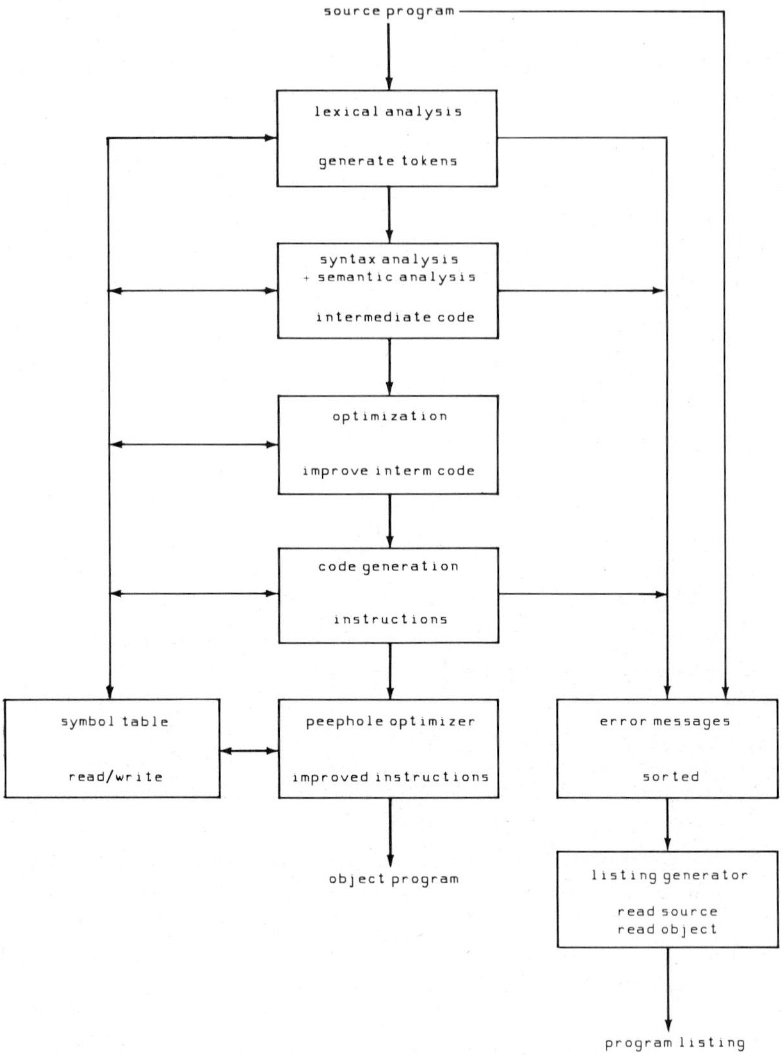

Figure 2-1 Block Diagram of Compiler Phases

Lexical Analysis

The purpose of the *lexical analyzer,* also called *scanner,* is to recognize tokens. In their input form, tokens are of varying length, while the translated output tokens have a uniform format more palatable to the rest of the compiler. During this process the scanner also has to filter out the white space. *White space* consists of comments, blanks, newlines, and tabulation characters. For format-free languages such as Ada, Modula-2, Pascal, and PL/I, the white space carries no explicit information except that it can serve as a delimiter between successive tokens. For format-sensitive languages like Fortran and Cobol the lexical analyzer must store column- and line-specific information.

Source strings of interest to the scanner can be as short as a single character, such as <. Here the transformation is trivial, the token is a "Less Than Operator." But even for such a simple token the scanner's work can be complicated, if the analyzed language allows tokens that start with a common prefix. Ada, for example, includes the tokens <<, <=, and <>, so the scanner must be at least a finite state machine to remember a few adjacent characters.

Other tokens are not easily recognized. For example, when the Fortran compiler reads the first "." character in the following statement

```
IF(4.GT..5)
```

the scanner does not know if the string "4" before the period was an integer number, or if it was the integral portion of a floating point number. One more character look-ahead is needed to resolve this issue. But when the scanner sees the "G" character, it knows that the "4" was an integer literal. Also the scanner must remember that it just skipped the "." character.

In Section 17.1, "Lexical Peculiarities," we shall encounter more complex situations, where the Fortran scanner knows only at the end of a line what the first token on the same line was. Since a logical line can be broken into many physical lines via the continuation mark, this essentially primitive issue becomes quite a challenge for the scanner.

Overall, lexical analysis is still the simplest phase in the compilation process. In fact it is so simple that scanners can be generated automatically. One of the better known scanner generators is LEX, a tool provided under Unix. To produce a lexical analyzer, LEX must only be fed a set of rules that describe the lexical tokens and out comes a scanner, written in C.

Syntax and Semantic Analysis

The purpose of the *syntax analyzer* is to check if the incoming source string is in the language. The module performing syntax analysis is called the *parser.* Pure syntax analysis, however, generates only a boolean value as output to indicate whether the analyzed string was correct or not. Clearly, this is insufficient for a compiler. Syntax analysis in a compiler must be combined with the generation of an object program. Also the syntax analysis phase must be enhanced by the semantic analyzer. During this phase, also, those source strings are flagged as incorrect that adhere to the syntax but violate other rules. An example is the multiple declaration of a variable in the same scope.

In most instances the parser and semantic analyzer emit a tree that exactly represents the source program in a different encoding. This tree may reside on a file or in the compiler's memory. Other kinds for storing intermediate forms of the source program are triples, quadruples, or yet to be completed object code. We shall briefly explain quadruples in the next section.

To perform complete syntax analysis, the parser must know all syntax rules and many semantic rules. A reasonable parser builds tree elements only as long as the incoming source is correct. The whole purpose of the tree is to make it easy for the compiler to manipulate the encoded program. It becomes easier for the compiler to handle a tree, if it can trust that the tree is correct.

The theory of parsing is a solidly researched area for the languages of interest as programming languages. This is the restricted class of context-free languages. The field is so well understood that parser generators have been implemented with success. *Parser generators,* also known by the pretentious misnomer "compiler compilers," read as input the grammar for the analyzed language and emit the source for a parser. One of the currently best-known parser generators is YACC. Together with LEX, YACC provides a nice basis for a compiler; only the crucial and most difficult parts, the semantic analysis and the code generation, are missing.

Code Optimization

The *code optimization* phase is optional. Its purpose is to take some intermediate form of the compiled program and transform it again, so that the new form is better with respect to some resource. If time is the critical resource, then the optimizer creates a new form that runs faster. Usually the total code size increases during this process. If object code space is critical, the optimizer aims at generating a new form that is more compact. This form normally will run slower. In a few lucky situations an optimizer can achieve both. Also, it is not obvious why an optimizer sometimes generates programs with worse behaviour than the original one. In such cases the cause is due to a violation of assumptions. The optimizer "guesses," for example, that a loop is performed many times, so it moves invariant code from the loop into the loop header. But, unfortunately, this loop is executed less than once on the average. The loop header is longer now and executed once every time, while the loop body is run every once in a while.

There is only one thing an optimizer may not do under any circumstances—that is, to change the semantics of the original source program. An optimizer would do better to quit working altogether than to alter the meaning of even one little statement. The phases before the optimizer have already transformed the original source into another, hopefully equivalent form that is easier to manipulate for the rest of the compiler's phases. With the optimization phase, yet another transformation takes place. Again the compiler must ensure that the semantics remains unaltered. We anticipate, of course, the next transformation, which is the actual code generation from the intermediate form. Again, no semantics modification is allowed. By now we should have a feeling for the high delicacy of this affair, always ripping a source program to pieces, and then synthesizing it into another form. Sadly, there is one more thing that an optimizer cannot solve in general—that is, to generate optimum code. The name "optimizer" carries a claim that cannot be verified. A more realistic and modest name would be "improver."

Code Generation

It is the task of the *code generator* to emit object code. For most compilers the code generator's input is the intermediate (tree) representation of the source program. Writing a good code generator is the most difficult part in the design of a compiler. Although there are many reasons for this, we'll list just a few.

The target machine has only a limited set of resources, such as registers. Nevertheless, the programmer is completely shielded from such petty detail. It is the compiler's task to map the multitude of programmer-defined objects onto a restricted, limited machine. Also, some machines can address only segments up to a maximum size that is quite small, certainly too small to let the programming language convey such limitations. Again, the compiler is responsible for mapping the programmer's request for large data objects onto multiple, smaller memory areas. We should learn from this how important it is to separate the programming language design from the anticipated target machines.

Peephole Optimization

Peephole optimization, another optional compilation phase, is concerned with eliminating obvious deficiencies, which have been caused by separate compiler phases that did not perfectly communicate with one another. A peephole optimizer considers only a narrow sequence of instructions for improvement. However, these few instructions can be far apart in some optimizers. Typical cases that need improvement are the addition of 0, or a multiplication by 1. Both may be eliminated without altering the semantics. Under rare circumstances it may be meaningful to add a zero to some object. For example, the status register or machine toggles must be set at a well-defined moment during program execution. For this reason the programmer or compiler might insert such otherwise redundant NOOP instructions. The peephole optimizer has to be informed about this insertion or it will "optimize" things away that were necessary, and create incorrect object code.

Also, branches to branches can be simplified or the sequence of a store instruction followed by a load from the same location is redundant on many machines. Some of these improvements spawn chances for further improvements, so peephole optimizers often work repeatedly until the object does not change anymore. This is how such a simple phase can become quite time consuming. Particularly in simple compilers that have no optimizer, the peephole phase has a valid purpose.

2.7 Parsing

In this section we explain two parsing techniques in just enough detail to help us understand how the syntax analysis phase interacts with the design of a programming language. We cannot expect to be able to write parsers after reading this short sketch. The first technique, known as "recursive descent," describes a top-down, predictive analyzer. The second technique explains a bottom-up parser.

The parser, receiving its input tokens from the scanner, must verify that the tokens occur only in patterns allowed by the language rules. As long as this holds, the parser then generates a tree representation of the legitimate input. To be able to do this, it has to know all syntax rules.

Recursive Descent, Top-Down Analysis

In a *recursive descent parser* the rules of the grammar are encoded in the program itself. One such rule is the production for the start symbol. Therefore the parser will start out with a procedure that represents the start symbol. Initially the parser predicts that it will see a "program," or whatever the name of the start symbol may be. Let us continue this explanation with a practical example. We shall start with grammar G4, which we have seen already in the previous chapter, and explain what a recursive descent parser would look like for the language L(G4).

The parser for L(G4) starts with the procedure "expression." The body of "expression" is written in a form that exactly reflects the rules for G4 expressions. Therefore, this procedure can predict, or even demand that it find a "relation." "Relation" is again just the name for another procedure that handles everything pertinent to relations. Look back at the grammar G4 in the previous chapter so you remember the rules for G4 and understand, why a parser for G4 can demand certain rules. "Demanding" here means to continue to parse as long as the prediction holds and, otherwise, to emit an error message that states exactly what was expected and what was found instead.

If the parser for G4 ever successfully finishes executing the procedure "expression," it will have parsed a complete expression. Along the way it will have performed numerous recursive calls, starting with a call to "relation," and then one to "simple_expression," just as the grammar demands. Any parse tree that we can draw for a string in the analyzed language will be an exact image of the sequence of calls performed by a recursive descent parser. In Figure 2-2 we clarify this principle by the sample string of tokens -84+19*100, to be analyzed by a parser that knows the rules for grammar G4.

```
                   expression
                       |
                    relation
                       |
                simple_expression
                       |
      .--------.----v----.-----------.
      |        |         |           |
unary_minus  term  binary_add_op   term
      |        |         |           |
      -      factor      +    .--------.--------.
               |              |        |        |
            primary        factor multiply_op factor
               |              |        |        |
      numeric_literal    primary       *     primary
               |              |                 |
              84        numeric_literal  numeric_literal
                              |                 |
                             19                100
```

*Figure 2-2 Parse Tree for String –84+19*100*

The recursive descent parser can build this structure directly as a tree or in another intermediate form that is equivalent. Quadruples are commonly used to store the intermediate object. As we find so often during the compilation process, most forms are just equivalent representations of the source program, but the further the compilation proceeds, the less visible this becomes.

Expression "-84+19*100" is represented in Table 2-1 in quadruples. Each quadruple holds one operator field that characterizes its function, and two operands. Unneeded operands are marked by "Nil." If we want to refer to a literal directly, we express this by the built-in function "Lit." The fourth quadruple field defines the destination of the result.

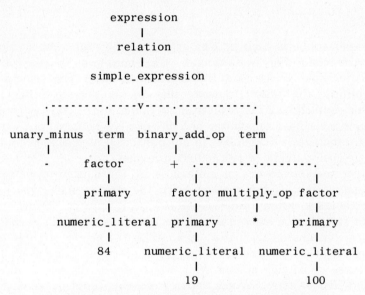

*Table 2-1 Quadruples, Representing Tree for −84+19*100*

	Operator	Operand1	Operand2	Destination
1	Uminus	Lit(84)	Nil	t1
2	Multiply	Lit(19)	Lit(100)	t2
3	Add	t1	t2	t3

Bottom-Up Parsing

Top-down parsers begin their task by expanding the start symbol. Bottom-up parsers work the other way around. The bottom-up parser shifts over contiguous terminals and tries to find a matching rule. When such a rule has been identified, the parser reduces this to its corresponding left-hand nonterminal, until finally the reduced nonterminal is the start symbol. If the whole source input has been shifted and no error has occurred previously, then the parser terminates successfully. In our previously used sample grammar G4 the ultimate goal would be to reduce to "expression."

In order to remember what state it is in, the bottom-up parser uses a compile time stack. Its top element holds the current state, while elements deeper in the stack define formerly seen states. Eventually, former states and the current state can be reduced to one single state, so that in the end only the start symbol remains on the parse stack. With the help of a *parse table,* the bottom-up parser knows what to do next for every incoming symbol. There are four types of parsing actions from which it can choose. Shift, Reduce, Accept, and Report Error. Which action it should take depends on the entry in the parse table. The parse table is indexed by the current state and the input symbol. For more detail, we recommend Aho and Johnson [1974] as an interesting reference.

What makes this family of parsers so fascinating is that they can be generated automatically. This is quite a blessing, because the manual generation of the parse tables, necessary for bottom-up parsers, is terribly tedious and error prone. Computers seem to have no problems with this type of work and never complain about repetition. When the language becomes interestingly complex, the parse table size is quite substantial.

We have mentioned YACC before, one such parser generator available on Unix. The input to YACC is a grammar that defines the syntax rules of the language, for which a parser is needed. Effectively, the generated parser is a large Case Statement whose case choices are the parser states. YACC also produces the parse table. With this table and based on the incoming source program the generated parser can determine exactly which sequence of states it has to go through. YACC is nice enough to add on the necessary flesh to the Case Statement to make it a full C program, and moreover, one that cooperates with the scanner LEX.

Semantic actions or code generation routines must be added by the compiler designer, typically in the form of procedure calls interspersed with the grammar that went into YACC. All the compiler writer has to do is to link the bodies of the semantic routines with the parser, and the compiler is ready. This sounds much easier than it is in reality.

2.8 Code Generation and Optimization

In this section we present a brief impression of those code generation and optimization techniques that do not require any special background in compiler theory. The optimization techniques we cover are common subexpression elimination, strength reduction, and some loop optimizations. In all cases we assume that the critical resource is time, so the goal of all optimizations is to speed up the execution, even if this is at the expense of code space. With the large address spaces of modern machines it always seems possible to buy more memory with dollars, while time cannot be purchased with any currency. So, following the capitalistic principle, we consider time the more valuable commodity.

Common Subexpression Elimination

Programs that handle multidimensional arrays frequently contain statements of the form

```
a[ i + j ] := b[ i + j ] * c[ i + j ];
```

Here it is evident that a simple-minded, not necessarily dumb code generator will emit the same code sequence three times, if the bounds and element types of all three arrays "a," "b," and "c" are identical. Indeed this is quite often the case. If the element types were incompatible, the compiler would have to emit an error message. Since these identical expressions occur in a single statement they are called *common subexpressions.* These expressions all yield the same value, as long as there are no side effects, causing the pertinent variables to assume different values at different evaluation times.

Common subexpressions are of interest in *basic blocks.* For our purpose in the context of programming languages it is sufficient to see basic blocks as instruction sequences without embedded labels and branches. Only the first instruction has a label, and the last instruction is a branch.

Now the "intelligent" code optimizer comes into play. It recognizes that the subexpression "i+j" is computed three times. But, since neither "i" nor "j" change, the optimizer might as well transform the earlier statement into an equivalent statement pair as follows:

```
temp := i + j;
a[ temp ] := b[ temp ] * c[ temp ];
```

In this modified form the generated code will run faster, even though an additional assignment statement has been introduced.

For a moment we need to digress into a discussion of programming style. Seeing the preceding statement pair, one school of thought argues that one should not bother a code optimizer with such mundane transformations. The user should instead have written the same by hand. The counter arguments, however, are convincing. First, the statement sequence is more difficult to read than the original, single statement. Repeated hand optimizations do clutter up the code. Second, and more important, the new statement

```
a[ temp ] := b[ temp ] * c[ temp ];
```

still causes a lot of redundant code to be emitted due to hidden code for subscript computation. Over this code the programmer has no control. This leaves the statement, nevertheless, an excellent candidate for optimization. Now, as far as the detector for common subexpressions is concerned, it does not matter to this module whether the index is a simple "temp" or a more complicated expression "i+j." It will recognize any common subexpression. In the section about loop optimization, we shall see what an optimizer can do with repeated indices.

Strength Reduction

The essence of *strength reduction* is to replace operations by equivalent ones that are cheaper. For example, if the concatenation operation in a PL/I run time system is expensive, as is usually the case, then a statement of the form

```
L = LENGTH( STRING1 || STRING2 );
```

can be replaced by a cheaper statement of the following form:

```
L = LENGTH( STRING1 ) + LENGTH( STRING2 );
```

This assumes that the concatenation is more expensive than one add operation plus an additional invocation of the built-in function LENGTH.

Another typical strength reduction is the replacement of exponentiation by multiplication, or the substitution of multiplication by addition. Also, in many cases, a multiplication by powers of 2 can be replaced by an instruction that performs a left-shift instruction. See the models in Example 2-1.

```
j := k * 2;--same as:
j := k + k;--which is faster

i := j ** 2;--same as:
i := j * j;--which is faster
```

Example 2-1 Strength Reductions

Loop Optimizations

In the common subexpression section we claimed that the code emitted for even the simplest subscripts, when occurring more than once in the same statement, can be improved substantially by an optimizer. We shall demonstrate this claim here. To make this more rewarding, we put this critical code into the body of a For Statement to compound our savings.

There is another reason why we wish to choose a For Statement in this example. Some language designers maintain a critical attitude toward high level languages, and particularly such loop statements, because they supposedly induce excess machine code overhead. And when performance is a critical issue, such objection seems justified. In this short section, we expose exactly the amount of overhead, but at the same time, we will show that an optimizer can eliminate all of this extra cost and generate code sequences that sometimes execute as fast as assembler programs. With an optimizer we can get the best of two worlds at the expense of compilation time. We can use high level languages and get fast performance.

We shall analyze the Ada program fragment "demo_loop_opt" in Example 2-2 and present two translations to quadruples. The first time the quadruple sequence is written as if it had been emitted by a simple-minded code generator. The second time we let an intelligent optimizer perform various improvements on the quadruples and create a new sequence that performs substantially faster.

```
PROCEDURE demo_loop_opt IS
  TYPE array_type IS ARRAY( 6 .. 9 ) OF integer;
  a, b : array_type;
  p, q : integer;
BEGIN--demo_loop_opt
  --other statements
  p := 0;
  q := 17;
  FOR i IN 6 .. 9 LOOP
    p := p + a(i) * b(i) + q * 13;
  END LOOP;
END demo_loop_opt;
```

Example 2-2 Ada Program Fragment, to Be Optimized

In order to develop a feeling for the overhead incurred by the For Statement, we rewrite this procedure in Example 2-3 in a restricted form of Ada that is closer to quadruples. This "broken-down" version of "demo_loop_opt" will have no more complicated expressions except for subscripts. These will be compiled into elementary code sequences, when we show quadruples, yet another step later.

```
PROCEDURE demo_broken_down IS
 TYPE array_type IS ARRAY( 6 .. 9 ) OF integer;
  a, b : array_type;
  p, q : integer;--t0, t1, t2, t3 etc. are temporaries
 BEGIN--demo_broken_down
  --other statements
  p := 0;
  q := 17;
  i := 6;
<<L1>> IF i > 9 THEN GOTO L2; END IF;
  t1 := a(i);
  t3 := b(i);
  t5 := t1 * t3;
  t7 := p + t5;
  t9 := q * 13;
  p := t7 + t9;
  i := i + 1;
  GOTO L1;
<<L2>> NULL;
 END demo_broken_down;
```

Example 2-3 Ada Program Fragment, High Level Constructs Broken Down

The original Ada program "demo_loop_opt" shines through, but the language level is lower in "demo_broken_down." Before we translate the Ada source into quadruples, the compilation of subscript operations will need some explanation.

Subscripting

The subscript itself provides an offset from the start of the accessed array. For a correct computation, the lower bound must be subtracted from the actual index expression, and the difference must be multiplied by the element size of the array. If the lower bound happens to be zero, the compiler does not bother to subtract. Similarly, if the element size of an array is 1, the compiler will not emit a multiply instruction. Here we will assume that the code generator emits instructions for a target machine that has integers of four bytes, so we generate "multiply by 4" instructions. We are for the moment not concerned about strength reduction, and leave the multiplications by 4 in the code sequence.

In Table 2-2, we finally see the sequence of quadruples, compiled from the Ada program "demo_loop_opt." To make the step from the source to quadruples easier to understand, we recommend that the reader study "demo_broken_down" first. Quadruples 6, 7 and 11, 12 perform the necessary, invisible operations for the subscripts.

In the operand fields in Table 2-2 we have conveniently used a few built-in functions that need explanation. The "Addr" function yields the address of the argument. So in quadruple 5, for example, Operand1 yields the address for array "a." This value will be modified, depending on the index expression, the lower bound of the array, and the element size.

Table 2-2 Unoptimized Quadruples, for "demo_loop_opt"

	Operator	Operand1	Operand2	Destination
1	:=	Lit(0)	Nil	p
2	:=	Lit(17)	Nil	q
3	:=	Lit(6)	Nil	i
4	Greater	i	Lit(9)	<<L2>>=21
5	:=	Addr(a)	Nil	t0
6	Subtract	i	Lit(6)	t1
7	Multiply	t1	Lit(4)	t1
8	Add	t0	t1	t1
9	Deref	t1	Nil	t1
10	:=	Addr(b)	Nil	t2
11	Subtract	i	Lit(6)	t3
12	Multiply	t3	Lit(4)	t3
13	Add	t2	t3	t3
14	Deref	t3	Nil	t3
15	Multiply	t1	t3	t5
16	Add	p	t5	t7
17	Multiply	q	Lit(13)	t9
18	Add	t7	t9	p
19	Add	i	Nil	i
20	Goto	Nil	Nil	<<L1>>=4
21	Return	Nil	Nil	Caller

The "Deref" operation used in quadruples 9 and 14 replaces Operand1 with the value found at that address and stores this integer value in Destination. With this we should be able to understand quadruples.

If the code generator had a common subexpression recognizer, it would never have generated the quadruple sequence 6 through 9 several times. We notice that quadruples 11 through 14 perform the identical function. While we present the common subexpression elimination scheme, we also present another convenient loop optimization along the way, known as code motion. We see that the value "q*13" is computed during each iteration. Literal 13 cannot change, and variable "q" just happens to be invariant over the loop execution. So "q*13" is a "loop invariant expression" and can be moved out of the For Statement without changing the meaning.

A much improved sequence of quadruples is shown in Table 2-3. Code motion of the loop invariant expression has taken place, and the common subexpression has been reduced to a single expression. The code motion causes the program to run faster, while the common subexpression elimination has reduced the total number of instructions and improved the run time. So we are lucky. The optimized code here is faster *and* shorter; this is not always achievable.

The reader should carefully compare the "optimized" quadruple sequence in Table 2-3 with the "simple-minded" quadruple sequence shown in Table 2-2.

Table 2-3 Optimized Quadruples,

	Operator	**Operand1**	**Operand2**	**Destination**
1	:=	Lit(0)	Nil	p
2	:=	Lit(17)	Nil	q
3	:=	Lit(6)	Nil	i
4	Multiply	q	Lit(13)	t9
5	Greater	i	Lit(9)	<<L2>>=19
6	:=	Addr(a)	Nil	t0
7	Subtract	i	Lit(6)	t1
8	Multiply	t1	Lit(4)	t1
9	Add	t0	t1	t4
10	Deref	t4	Nil	t0
11	:=	Addr(b)	Nil	t2
12	Add	t2	t1	t3
13	Deref	t3	Nil	t3
14	Multiply	t0	t3	t5
15	Add	p	t5	t7
16	Add	t7	t9	p
17	Add	i	Lit(1)	i
18	Goto	Nil	Nil	<<L1>>=5
19	Return	Nil	Nil	Caller

The optimized version has 14 quadruples in the loop, while the first quadruple sequence includes 17 elements in the loop body. Very roughly speaking, this is a 17% improvement. The actual improvement depends on the real instructions generated from the quadruples.

2.9 Summary

The description of language standards has developed our feeling for the impact of language standardization on source and programmer portability. More subtly even, we have seen how the time, the actual date of issuing a standard affects the compatibility of source programs. The rule to learn is "First publish the standard, then release the compiler."

We justified high level programming languages with increased programmer efficiency. In cooperation with their compilers, high level languages allow us to utilize a scarce resource—the human thinking potential—in a more effective manner than a less precious resource—the computer's processor time. Programs are strings of lexical tokens. The strings are arranged in accordance with the language's syntax rules and incorporate a specific meaning. The prime quality criteria in the design of programming languages are readability, consistency, explicitness, and a convenient method for data abstraction and modularization.

Our discussion of compiler architecture has exposed a few interdependencies between programming language design and the translation process. For example, languages with separate compilation may compile slower than languages with independent compilation units. For separate compilations the translator has to create and retrieve interface information. This information serves for type and consistency checking; both the checks and the retrieval cost compilation time, but it may turn out to be a good investment when contrasted with what can be saved in debugging time. In the next chapter we become familiar with two languages, Ada and Modula-2, that have such a modularization concept. Also we have seen that the computation of subscripts can be costly, if the lower bound is different from 0 and if the element size is different from 1.

2.10 Exercises

1. The original definition of the Fortran language included a special rule for expressions used in subscripts; these expressions were restricted for the sake of efficient code generation. Discuss whether it is a good idea from a language design standpoint to include those special rules.
2. Discuss advantages and disadvantages of Pascal's single compilation units. Are there any benefits at all?
3. Discuss the following claim: "The more features a language has the better it is."
4. What is the advantage of implicit Type Conversion?
5. Describe one disadvantage of implicit Type Conversion.
6. There is an infinite number of source programs that are legal, according to the language definition, but that, nevertheless, cannot be compiled even by very powerful compilers. Give a possible reason for this.

7. Can we write a Pascal or Ada source program of unbounded size—say, 100 billion lines long—that still can be compiled by relatively simple, small compilers? The answer may not assume that these lines contain comments or blank lines.

8. When a Modula-2 compiler has completed the analysis of some local, nested procedure "p," it can discard all names local to "p" from the symbol table space. Why can't the compiler drop the name "p" as well?

9. Which kind of compiler error is worse: not recognizing a source program error and instead pretending that the analyzed program is correct, or flagging as incorrect a source program that is actually correct? Explain why!

10. One advantage of implicit declarations, as found in Fortran and PL/I is that the compiler does not need to fill up symbol table space for such names. Give reasons for and against this claim.

11. When the lexical analyzer of a Pascal compiler sees the character : in the source, can it immediately report that a "colon" is found?

12. A code optimizer finds the following code skeleton in an object program.

```
500: BRANCH 600
     ...
     ...
600: BRANCH 700
```

Can the unconditional branch at location 500 be replaced by a branch to 700? If yes, what impact does this have on the object program? Can the branch at location 600 be eliminated?

3

Language Structure

And the details are the jungle
in which the devil hides.

Niklaus Wirth
Programming in Modula-2

We assume that the reader is not intimately familiar with some of the languages covered in this text. Those readers who are already familiar are advised to skip to Chapter 5. For those who continue with this chapter we include the definition of key terms used throughout this text.

The first two chapters have provided historical and theoretical background information and thus have not directed our attention toward specific languages. Chapters 3 and 4 by contrast are devoted to language-specific detail. With these four chapters we create a common body of knowledge that is a smallest common denominator required for the reader to follow our discussion of language concepts in subsequent chapters. It is not the goal of this text to teach any of the languages in full depth and detail. Nevertheless, we compare important issues across all the languages. In order to establish that common base, even for readers not conversant in some of the languages covered here, we give a short introduction to the overall language. This overview starts at both ends: the microscopic level of lexical rules, and the macroscopic level of compilation units. Blocks and scopes are also covered and fall right in between the top-down and bottom-up method of presentation. But first come the promised definitions of key terms.

Key Definitions

Scope is a domain of source program text, over which a name is defined. *Block* is almost a synonym for scope, but is used with preference for scopes delineated by Begin-End brackets. Such blocks are also called Begin-End-Blocks. *A compilation unit* is an integral unit of source text that a compiler translates as a whole to generate an object module. A complete program can be composed out of one or more compilation units, depending on the language. If multiple compilation units share no common information they are called *independent compilation units;* if information is passed from one to another, they are *separate compilation units. Storage* is a computer resource that holds data. If the data live during the whole lifetime of a program, they are *static;* if they come into existence only when the owning scope becomes active and vanish when the scope is inactive, they are *automatic.*

3.1 Language Overview

This section presents a short summary of each language. It is not meant as a tutorial for beginners of programming; in depth knowledge of at least one language is assumed. Familiarity with the others is certainly helpful.

Overview of Ada

The exact requirements for the language that would become Ada were first outlined in 1974 in a series of documents and were later refined in the "Steelman Requirements," June 1978. The driving force behind this language definition was the U.S. Department of Defense (DoD) in conjunction with other government agencies in a fierce effort to reduce its multibillion dollar programming expense. Their excessively high programming expenses were caused in part by the large number of standard languages they were using, and in part by the poor quality of the languages.

Various companies submitted proposals for language definitions fulfilling the Steelman Requirements. The winner in this open bidding process was the French company Honeywell-Bull. All competitors were colour coded to keep the company name behind the language proposal secret in an effort to minimize nepotism and prejudice. Honeywell-Bull's submittal was coded the "Green Language." Even after their proposal was accepted, the language required three more years of rigorous refinement and correction before it became a standard, ANSI [1983a].

Ada's ambitious goal is to reduce the number of military standard languages. Ideally, there would only be one military standard language: Ada. Consequently, it has to be quite complex and complete. The more direct goal, however, is to reduce the mental effort and time necessary for software development, and, at the same time, increase the reliability, security, and maintainability of Ada-based software. To improve the credibility of Ada compilers, the Softech Corporation in Waltham has been contracted to produce an Ada Compiler Validation Capability (ACVC), meant to detect compiler errors, incomplete implementations, and outlawed supersets. The DoD has trademarked the name Ada and requires any Ada compiler to be validated by the ACVC.

It is unique to the Ada language definition that subset and superset implementations are not allowed. This requirement has been heavily criticized, notably by Toni Hoare in his Turing Award Lecture, see Hoare [1981]. He observes: "If you want a language with no subsets, you must make it small." Clearly, he criticizes the size of Ada. He does not observe, which he should have done for the sake of fairness, "If you want a language with no supersets, you must make it big." Ada's size remains an issue of vigorous debate.

Currently, at the end of 1984, there are only four full, validated Ada compilers. One of these has been implemented at New York University. It was written in the very high level interpretive language, SETL, is hosted on a VAX, and compiles only a few lines per minute. The others have been developed in California—one at record speed by Rolm Corporation in conjunction with Data General. This second compiler was funded privately and is hosted on and targeted for Data General's 32 Bit Eclipse system. The third validated compiler was developed by Western Digital. A fourth Ada compiler is being marketed by a small San Diego Software company, Telesoft. Telesoft achieved completion of a full compiler in the middle of 1984. At about the same time the Rolm and NYU Ada compilers were revalidated, as is required annually for each compiler to maintain its validity. The annual revalidation is a necessary guarantor of conformance.

Ada is a statement-oriented rather than an expression language; it is of very high level and strongly typed. The type equivalence rule states simply that two objects are type equivalent if they are defined by the same type mark. *Type mark* is the Ada term for type identifier. Statements are terminated by a required semicolon. Despite much justified condemnation of Goto Statement abuse, the Ada language designers were not so frivolous to omit the Goto Statement from the language definition. They apparently believed that the absence of a potentially dangerous construct does not guarantee safe programs. However, the use of GOTO is restricted and labels are marked quite visibly.

Multiprocessing or multitasking is included in Ada, as are separate compilation and information hiding via PRIVATE and LIMITED PRIVATE names. Data abstraction, enumeration types, and data structuring are all included in a clean and complete form. Ada is a block-structured language, and all subprograms, which are FUNCTION and PROCEDURE blocks, are inherently recursive. The package concept allows the hiding of irrelevant information and permits a well-controlled way of encapsulating data. Packages represent one of Ada's most useful innovations.

Some of these terms used to characterize Ada may be new to the reader. However, most of them will be treated in the remainder of the text. Multitasking will be covered in the chapter on "Concurrent Programming," data abstraction in the chapter on "Operands" and "Data Structures," so that after study of the text we completely understand the characterization. At the current stage most of these terms are not essential for understanding the "Language Overview."

Ada has a tolerably large set of reserved keywords. The source text layout is format-free, so there is no special meaning associated with special columns. Newlines and blanks function as delimiters between lexical tokens; comments are introduced by a double hyphen and terminated at the end of the same line. Ada includes both the type character and the type string, which is a natural extension of the Array of Character.

Overview of Fortran

The first version of Fortran was developed and implemented from 1954 to 1957 in a project led by John Backus at IBM. Fortran was intended primarily for numeric computation and has gained extremely wide popularity. Since the language is fairly simple, compilers have been available on virtually all manufacturers' machines, in many cases long before any standard definition had been published. This led to the practice that most implementors offered *their* modified Fortran superset. Without fail users found applications for the extensions, defeating one of the original goals—that of easy portability. It is almost true to claim that the only features common to all the different Fortran versions are the END and CONTINUE Statements.

At the time of Fortran's development it was not known that language implementors have an instinctive desire to add embellishments to the language, when they are cheap to add and the benefits high. Programming Language Design was not considered a difficult problem in the early days; the problem was implementing them. Anybody smart enough to successfully implement a higher level language had no lack of confidence of also being a good language designer.

Another goal of Fortran was to ease the pain of writing in assembly language. Fortran is not a very high level language and does not have many types. Thus the issue of strong versus weak typing does not seriously come up. Compared with assembly or machine language programming, however, Fortran is effortless.

Even though Fortran is statement-oriented, it has no notion of an explicit statement terminator or separator. The end of a line (newline) functions as the implicit statement terminator. Excessive use of Goto Statements has been practiced and criticized in Fortran. GOTO and CONTINUE are some of the most frequently used statements. Neither intercompilation type checks nor data structuring beyond arrays are available. Two of the least safe Fortran features, the multiple entry points into subroutines and multiple return points from subroutines, are explained in more detail in Section 3.3. Note the caveats given there!

A Fortran program is composed of one or more independent compilation units. We use the term independent compilation unit rather than separate compilation unit, since there is no enforceable connection between any of the compilation units of a program. There exists a scope attribute COMMON, through which separate compilation units may communicate. But the language and, hence the compilers, enforce no intercompilation unit checking. This is in contrast to Ada and Modula-2, for example.

Fortran keywords are not reserved. Thus, it is perfectly legal to give a subroutine the name END, GOTO, or FORMAT, but we cannot give a subroutine the name "subroutine," because that name would be longer than six characters and would therefore violate another rule. Blanks are insignificant except inside character string literals (formerly also called Hollerith literals). This "insignificant blank rule" poses an interesting problem to the compiler. Variables of type character string, in older Fortran terminology called A-format, are available on most implementations. Only Fortran-77 (ANSI [1978]) has special operators for concatenation and substrings. The layout of the source text is column dependent, reflecting how old the language is.

Unique to Fortran are the multiple Return (point) Statements, while Fortran and PL/I both allow the declaration of multiple ENTRY points in a Function or Procedure body. It will become clearer in Section 3.3 that Fortran's multiple Return Statements are not a mechanism for multiple points *from* which to return, but provide multiple targets for each Return Statement where to return *to*.

Overview of Pascal

Pascal was designed between 1968 and 1970 by Niklaus Wirth at the ETH Züerich. The language was strongly influenced by Algol-W, a close relative of Algol-60. The first implementation was available in 1970 on a CDC-6000 series machine. Until 1983, when Pascal became a standard language, ANSI [1983b], the de facto standard was the concise but incomplete monograph Jensen and Wirth [1978].

Pascal was intended as a teaching tool for illustrating the proper design of data structures and structured statements, a goal for which it is ideally suited. A simple, sequential IO scheme is included, but separate compilations are not.

Initially, it was Wirth's intention to write the Pascal compiler in Fortran. This was the obvious strategy to achieve widespread use of the compiler, since Fortran was so universally available. As we have mentioned, Fortran's inherent lack of portability made Wirth change his mind. He found it easier to start with a small subset in assembly language, and then bootstrap the compiler as a self-compiler. The first implementation was a top-down, recursive descent, single-pass compiler, entirely written in Pascal.

Pascal proved to be so well-suited for compiler writing, that the phenomenally fast CDC-6000 compiler could translate the whole compiler in just a few seconds. This led Wirth to the unfortunate decision to design Pascal as a monolithic language. He argued that since the total recompilation cost on a CDC is only a few seconds of time, there is no need to bother with separate compilations. If one wishes to modify a program, the time for the required recompilation is short. Unfortunately, this is true only for machines as powerful as a multimillion dollar CDC machine—and still today there are some people who don't own one!

Like Modula-2, Pascal is statement-oriented. The semicolon is used to separate statements from one another—in contrast to Ada and PL/I, where it terminates statements. An additional semicolon does no harm except in a few contexts, since the language includes the Empty Statement. The language is block-structured and has two types of blocks the PROGRAM and the inherently recursive subprograms (FUNCTION and PROCEDURE).

The set of reserved keywords in Pascal is quite small, 35 to be exact. Many implementations add a few names to this list; in particular EXTERN, FORWARD, MODULE, and VAL are good candidates. The source text in Pascal is format-free and line-oriented. Blanks, newlines, and comments function as separators between adjacent tokens.

For the type character all needed operations such as assignment and relational operators are included, but the type character string is only an add-on. Strings exist only in the form of string literals, which are assignment compatible with packed arrays of characters of identical length. Substrings and concatenation are unknown in Pascal.

The University of California at San Diego undertook the challenging project of implementing Pascal on microcomputers at a time when memory space was limited and expensive. The successful project is known now under the name UCSD-Pascal, marketed by Softech Microsystems. This Pascal implementation includes extensions that correct the obvious shortcomings of Pascal, so string handling and separate compilation units are a matter of course in UCSD-Pascal.

Equally interesting in UCSD-Pascal's approach is the close integration of the text editor, the compiler, and other utilities. For example, when the compiler detects a syntax error, it can immediately switch back to the editor, point to the critical text, and give the programmer the opportunity to correct on the spot and continue the compilation. Other integrated utilities like the file manager, however, are ridiculously inefficient by today's standards. The user has to manage the physical file space on secondary storage devices by an act known as *crunching.*

Overview of PL/I

PL/I was IBM's answer to the software crisis during the third computer generation. It was designed by a joint IBM and IBM user committee, apparently a very large one. The committee's ambitious goal of defining an appropriate language for scientific, business and systems programming was hard enough. Very rigid scheduling constraints imposed by IBM and the need to interact smoothly with IBM's coming OS-360 did not help to make it easier. A very educational summary of this development effort is Radin [1978].

Intended as a replacement for Algol, Cobol, and Fortran, it had to include a large variety of data structures and statements. The first compilers were available on IBM equipment, either as subsets (PL/I D-Compiler) or as full implementations (PL/I F- and H-Compiler) on machines with vast resources.

The language is statement-oriented, with a semicolon as the mandatory statement terminator. Like in Pascal, an additional semicolon does not hurt; it simply demarks the Empty Statement. PL/I has multiprocessing and data structuring modeled after Cobol. PL/I's data structuring mechanism is as convenient as Pascal's, but more general even by allowing explicit packing and alignment instructions. PL/I is not strongly typed, has a very general IO definition, and does allow independent compilation units.

During PL/I's definition phase, Cobol, a language with hundreds of reserved keywords, was already widely known. Since so many programmers had such traumatic experiences with the large list of Cobol reserved keywords, PL/I went to the other extreme: it has *no* reserved keywords! The compilers and readers have to determine from the context whether a name is a keyword or a user-defined identifier. Another motivation of the language designers for having no reserved keywords was to allow language extensions without invalidating old programs. We strongly encourage the reader to contemplate about the validity of this argument. An extreme but correct source string using this capability is shown in Example 3-1.

```
IF if = then THEN
  then = else;
ELSE
  else = if;
```

Example 3-1 Reserved Keywords or Not?

Using lower- and uppercase letters makes this intentionally confusing source more readable. Also the indentation structure provides hints to the reader. But Example 3-1 is the same to the compiler as the string: "IF IF=THEN THEN THEN=ELSE;ELSE ELSE=IF;."

Blanks, comments, and newlines are only significant in PL/I inside string literals or when they function as separators. The source text is usually format free. However, some PL/I implementations do not allow characters in column one.

The character string type is a true, general extension of the predefined type character. PL/I has a rich set of operators and functions that operate on string objects. It even has very convenient VARYING strings, the actual length of which may vary between zero and some maximum defined value. A fuzzy version of the type boolean exists in the form of bit strings, with a bit string of length one being equivalent to a boolean value. Bit string literals are denoted like character strings but have a letter B appended to the right. So '1'B is the PL/I equivalent for boolean "true" and '0'B for "false."

In the area of labels and Goto Statements, PL/I has quite unique features; some however, are of questionable value. Labels can be passed as parameters, assigned, declared as arrays, and reached from virtually anywhere. The language is block-structured. There are PROCEDURE and BEGIN blocks in PL/I. Procedures are not inherently recursive, but the RECURSIVE attribute can be explicitly given to procedures. Similar to Ada's Declare Statement, PL/I has BEGIN blocks that allow the creation of very local environments.

PL/I does not cleanly distinguish in syntax or in its terminology between functions and procedures, nor between declarations and statements. Functions are just procedures, returning a value, the type of which is fixed by the Returns Phrase. Declarations are simply named "Declaration Statements." PL/I even tries to be consistent there and syntactically permits a declaration to occur wherever another statement is allowed. Real use of this liberty leads to programs, in which the compiler has to virtually relocate such declarations by moving them to the header of the enclosing block. Without this extra work on the part of the compiler, the initialization clauses for example would be executed each time a "Declaration Statement" is reached in a loop, which could be quite undesirable.

Similar to Fortran, PL/I allows multiple entry points to a subprogram. Also since parameters can be of type "label," and global *Gotos* out of a subprogram scope are permitted, PL/I has the same unsafe effect as Fortran with its multiple Return Statements. Despite a number of very valuable facilities offered by PL/I, it failed to replace Fortran and Cobol. Surely one of the reasons for failing is its complexity. Even in the early days of PL/I's development, when it still had the name NPL, one committee member compared it to 100-blade swiss army knife, while another wondered "why the kitchen sink had been omitted from the language," documented in Wexelblat [1978]. Twenty years later, Niklaus Wirth argues in his Turing award lecture that the "Swiss army knife idea has its merits, but if driven to excess, the knife becomes a millstone."

Overview of Modula-2

Modula-2 is clearly a brain-child of Niklaus Wirth, and therefore a descendant of Pascal. It was first defined and implemented in 1975, then under the name Modula, but underwent various refinements. In 1977 the Institut für Informatik at the ETH Zürich launched a research project with the goal of designing an integrated software-hardware system, entirely written in a single, high level language. This system later became known as the "Lilith Machine," and the language that emerged from this effort was Modula-2.

Lilith was designed to support multiprogramming, which is to say that the operating system was far from trivial. Consequently, Modula-2 supports concurrent processes and coroutines. In these areas many ideas were borrowed from "Concurrent Pascal" and the predecessor language Modula. Also, since all device drivers and other low level systems software were to be written in Modula-2, the language had to include the capability for direct machine access.

While Pascal's weakest point for use as a general-purpose language (for which it was not designed) is the lack of physical modularization, Modula-2 offers a clean, safe, and convenient device for separate compilation. Modula-2 demonstrates how a young prodigy—in this case Pascal—develops the maturity of a rich genius. While the two languages share a considerable body of syntax and semantics, Modula-2 excels in numerous areas.

Names across separate compilation units can be shared only if they have been declared in a Definition Module, and then imported into the using module. Importing modules have to add an explicit IMPORT list that states in turn, which of the exportable names are in fact needed. A name is sharable across two separate modules only if it is declared in the defining module and imported in the referencing one. IO routines for example are not known automatically, but must instead be selectively imported, like any other external resource. There does exist, however, a small set of predefined identifiers such as "TRUE" and "FALSE" that need no explicit importing. We shall see an IMPORT example in the "Gcd" program below.

Modula-2 has an incomplete form of conformant arrays named “open array parameters.” Also the language includes “based” numeric literals, forced closure for every statement that starts with a keyword, and an optional “By Clause” in For Statements—just to list a few extensions over Pascal. Compared to Pascal, the “procedure type” has been generalized. Modula-2 allows objects of type procedure; so this class is not restricted to parameters and calls as we know from Pascal, but is widened to include variables and other operations permissible on variables.

To familiarize the Modula-2 novice with the general flavour of the language, we include a short source program in Example 3-2. This module is a full, main procedure that reads two positive integers and prints their greatest, common divisor. For simple programs the similarity between Modula-2 and Pascal is striking.

```
MODULE Gcd;
  FROM InOut
    IMPORT ReadCard, WriteString, WriteLn, WriteCard;
  VAR
    a, b : CARDINAL;
  BEGIN (* Gcd *)
    WriteString( " Enter a: " );
    ReadCard( a );
    WriteLn;
    WriteString( " Enter b: " );
    ReadCard( b );
    WriteLn;
    WHILE a <> b DO
     IF a > b THEN
      a := a - b
     ELSE (* a < b *)
      b := b - a
     END;
    END;
    (* a = b *)
    WriteString( " GCD = " );
    WriteCard( a, 6 );
    WriteLn;
  END Gcd.
```

Example 3-2 Gcd Program in Modula-2

The Gcd program uses and therefore must import a good number of IO routines. Example 3-2 shows that an exact spelling of their names is crucial. Since lower- and uppercase are distinct, an inadvertent call to procedure “Readcard” would have caused an error message by the compiler.

The semicolon serves as separator between statements. Due to the forced closure, any number of statements is permitted in the body of structured statements without having to create artificial BEGIN END Statements. Comments may be nested in Modula-2, which is helpful, though quite unusual.

3.2 Lexical Rules

Lexical rules define tokens. A *token* is composed of characters, the smallest atomic units of source programs. In this section we learn the rules for creating lexical tokens in the different languages.

Tokens are classified as identifiers, literals, keywords, and special symbols. For example, when the three characters E, N, and D are concatenated, they form the lexical token END, a reserved keyword in Ada and Pascal. The Fortran lexical rules, on the other hand, define that END can be either a user-defined identifier or a keyword.

Lexical Rules For Ada

The Ada character set consists of the upper- and lowercase letters, the ten digits, the blank, and the following special characters:

! % " # & ' ( ) * + , - . / : ; < = > |

Since the source is line-oriented, the special characters line feed, form feed, carriage return, horizontal and vertical tab are also included. The following characters can be used interchangeably.

! replaces | % replaces "   : replaces #

Identifiers are composed of letters, digits, and underline characters but must start with a letter. Underlines are significant; they may not be consecutive or terminate an identifier. An identifier's maximum length is limited to the number of characters per source line. Every character of an identifier is significant, but the case does not matter. Thus A_B is equivalent to a_b, A_b, or any other permutation of lower- and uppercase letters.

The complete list of reserved Ada keywords is as follows.

ABORT	DELAY	GOTO	OUT	SEPARATE
ABS	DELTA	IF	PACKAGE	SUBTYPE
ACCEPT	DIGITS	IN	PRAGMA	TASK
ACCESS	DO	IS	PRIVATE	TERMINATE
ALL	ELSE	LIMITED	PROCEDURE	THEN
AND	ELSIF	LOOP	RAISE	TYPE
ARRAY	END	MOD	RANGE	USE
AT	ENTRY	NEW	RECORD	WHEN
BEGIN	EXCEPTION	NOT	REM	WHILE
BODY	EXIT	NULL	RENAMES	WITH
CASE	FOR	OF	RETURN	XOR
CONSTANT	FUNCTION	OR	REVERSE	
DECLARE	GENERIC	OTHERS	SELECT	

The complete list of Ada special symbols is as follows.

&	ampersand	=	equal
'	apostrophe	>	greater than
(	left parenthesis	|	vertical bar
)	right parenthesis	=>	arrow
*	star, multiply	..	double dot
+	plus	**	double star, exponentiate
,	comma	:=	becomes
-	hyphen, minus	/=	not equal
.	dot, period	>=	greater than or equal
/	slash, divide	<=	less than or equal
:	colon	<<	left label bracket
;	semicolon	>>	right label bracket
<	less than	<>	box

Numeric literals have either the implicit base 10, or any of the explicitly given bases 2 through 16. Isolated underlines are allowed in numbers just as in identifiers, but they are not significant. Thus, 12 000, 1 2 0 0 0, and 12000 all stand for decimal twelve thousand. The rules for decimal literals and based literals are given in Figure 3-1.

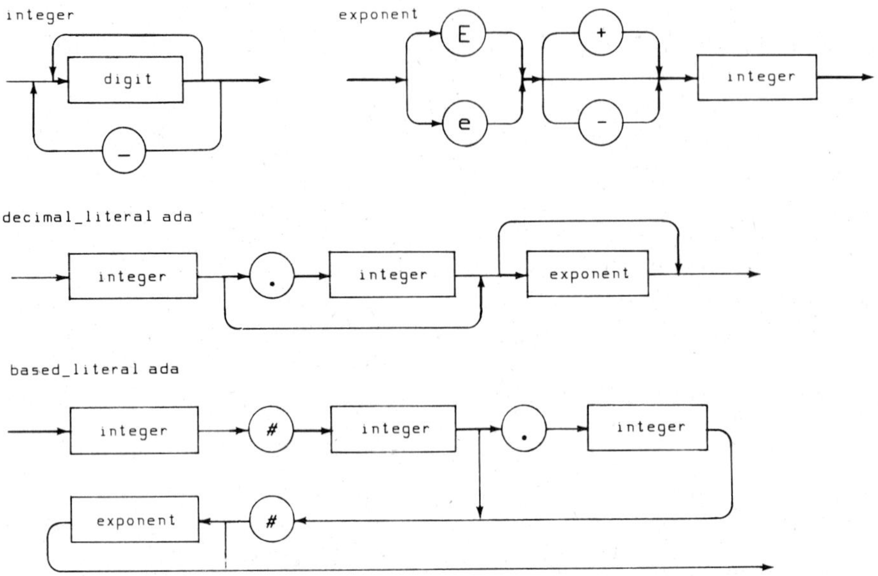

Figure 3-1 Syntax Diagram for Ada Numeric Literals

Ada distinguishes between character and string literals. Note also that in Ada the apostrophe by itself forms a complete, lexical token. Character literals are single characters embedded between two single quotes. This includes the single quote itself. Examples are 'A', 'Z', and '''. A string literal is embedded between double quotes and may be empty. The maximum length of a string literal is limited by the line length holding the source text. If longer string literals are desired, they must be concatenated via the string concatenation operator &. The double quote character, if part of a string, must be represented twice. Some sample string literals are shown in Example 3-3.

```
"Hey You"       is the string:       Hey You
""              is the empty string
""""            is the string:       "
"PA" & "+MA"    is the string:       PA+MA
"PA" & " MA"    is the string:       PA MA
""""""""        is the string:       """
```

Example 3-3 Sample Ada String Literals

Lexical Rules for Fortran

The source text in Fortran is column-oriented. Columns 1 through 5 are reserved for numeric statement labels and column 6 is reserved for the continuation character (any legal character except the blank). The actual program resides in columns 7 to 72. There are a couple of exceptions to these strict column designations. A line with the character C in column 1 is a comment line; a line with a 0 in column 6 defines in some implementations the first executable statement. A blank line is a special comment line. Fortran allows lines to be continued 9 times; Fortran-77 extends this to 19 times.

The Fortran character set consists of the uppercase letters, the ten digits, the blank, and the following special characters:

```
= + - * / ( ) , .  $ ' :
```

Some implementations—for example, Fortran-77 on Unix—also allow the lowercase letters in identifiers. Identifiers are composed of letters and digits, but must start with a letter. The maximum length is six. Note that blanks are insignificant in Fortran; thus the identifier MAX may also be spelled M AX or M A X. Again some implementations extend these rules by allowing the $ character to be used as a letter. This is true, for example, for the Fortran-IV compiler on IBM systems.

Fortran keywords are not reserved, so there is no point in distinguishing between predefined names such as READ, WRITE, and keywords such as END or CONTINUE. The following list contains only the major Fortran keywords.

```
COMMON     DIMENSION   EQUIVALENCE   FUNCTION    LOGICAL
COMPLEX    DO          EXIT          GOTO        RETURN
CONTINUE   END         EXTERNAL      IF          STOP
DATA       ENTRY       FORMAT        IMPLICIT    CALL
```

There are special keywords, marked by a period character on either side. Due to this unique spelling, they might also be called special symbols. The complete list of these special tokens, which function as operators, is as follows.

```
.AND.   .OR.     .LT.      .LE.    .GT.    .GE.      .EQ.
.NE.    .TRUE.   .FALSE.   .NOT.   .EQV.   .NEQV.
```

The complete list of special Fortran symbols is as follows:

=	equals	)	right parenthesis
+	plus	,	comma
-	minus	.	decimal point
*	multiply	$	currency symbol
/	slash, divide	'	apostrophe, single quote, quote
(	left parenthesis	:	colon
**	exponentiate	//	concatenate

The rules for numeric literals are given in Figure 3-2.

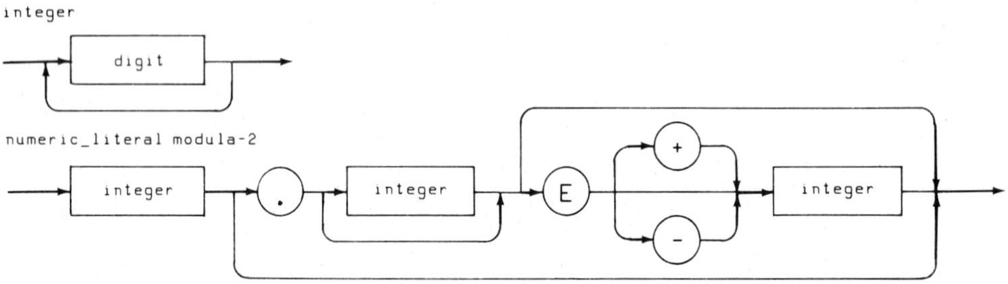

Figure 3-2 Syntax Diagram for Fortran Numeric Literals

Character literals are strings of characters delimited by single or double quotes; the starting and ending delimiter must be the same. Blanks and quotes are significant inside character literals; therefore, each quote that is part of the literal must be doubled. Thus 'SDSU' is the character literal SDSU, while literal '''' is the single quote. It can also be expressed as "'".

Lexical Rules for Pascal

The character set from which Pascal lexical tokens are composed consists of the upper- and lowercase letters, the ten digits, the blank, and the following special characters:

( ) ' * + , - . / : ; < = > ^ [ ] { } @

The special characters line feed and carriage return are also included. The case and font representation of letters occurring anywhere outside of a character string literal is insignificant to the semantics of a Pascal program.

Identifiers are composed of letters and digits but must start with a letter. The maximum length as defined by the ANSI and ISO standard is limited by the number of characters that will fit on a source line. The complete list of reserved Pascal keywords is as follows:

AND	DOWNTO	IF	OR	THEN
ARRAY	ELSE	IN	PACKED	TO
BEGIN	END	LABEL	PROCEDURE	TYPE
CASE	FILE	MOD	PROGRAM	UNTIL
CONST	FOR	NIL	RECORD	VAR
DIV	FUNCTION	NOT	REPEAT	WHILE
DO	GOTO	OF	SET	WITH

The complete list of special symbols in Pascal includes the following:

+	plus	<	less than
-	minus	<=	less than or equal
*	times	>=	greater than or equal
/	real divide, slash	>	greater than
:=	becomes	(	left parenthesis
.	dot, period	)	right parenthesis
,	comma	[	left bracket
;	semicolon	]	right bracket
:	colon	{	left curly brace, start comment
'	not a symbol	}	right curly brace, end comment
=	equal	^	pointer to, pointed to
<>	not equal	..	double dot
(*	substitute for {	*)	substitute for }
(.	substitute for [	.)	substitute for]
@	substitute for ^		

Note that the single quote is not a symbol by itself. It is used as a legal character in a more complex symbol, the literal of type character string.

The syntax rules for integer and real literals are shown in Figure 3-3.

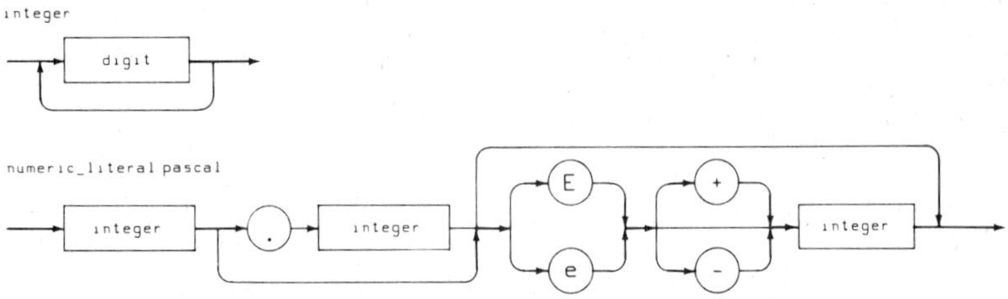

Figure 3-3 Syntax Diagram for Pascal Numeric Literals

A character string literal is embedded between single quotes and must be at least one character long. The maximum length of a string literal is not defined by the ISO and ANSI standard, but implementations will usually impose limits, often 255 or more. The single quote character, if part of a string, must be represented twice. Some instances are shown in Example 3-4.

```
''''       is the character:  '
'A'        is the character:  A
'Pascal'   is the string:     Pascal
'"'''      is the string:     "'
```

Example 3-4 Sample Pascal String Literals

Standard Pascal has two forms of comment delimiters, the pairs { } and (* *), which are equivalent. Thus a comment may start with { and end with a *), or may start with (* and end with }. A logical nesting of comments is not allowed. While this rule applies to standard Pascal, many popular Pascal compilers do not conform to it and hence are superset implementations. Either way, comments may span any amount of source text, from a fraction of a line to any number of lines. The same rule holds for PL/I and Modula-2.

Lexical Rules for PL/I

PL/I is defined for two kinds of character sets, one more restricted than the other, with certain character combinations being substitutes for unavailable characters. One such unavailable character is the Ebcdic character used for negation, also named "hook," represented here by the ¬ character. Note that the hook, and the tilde ~, are alternative graphics for the same character in Ascii. In the restricted character set this symbol is replaced by the keyword

NOT. We concentrate on the lexical rules for the full character set.

The PL/I character set consists of the uppercase letters, the ten digits, the blank and the following special characters:

$ @ # & ' ( ) * + , - . / : ; < = > | ¬

It is important to learn that in PL/I the three characters # $ @ count as letters. Since the format-free source is line-oriented, the special characters line feed and carriage return are also included. Identifiers are composed of letters, digits, and the underline character but must start with a letter. The underline is not a letter. Given these rules, all of the following are legal identifiers:

PL_I   #   PLI   MIN_VALUE   ##$$@@

The maximum length for identifiers is 32 characters. Multiple underlines and the trailing underline are allowed in PL/I. Every character is significant. PL/I keywords are not reserved, so there is no point in distinguishing between predefined names such as MIN and MAX and keywords such as PROC or MAIN. The following list shows those keywords that have alternate, abbreviated spellings in PL/I. First we list the keyword, then its allowed abbreviation. The full list of predefined names and keywords is quite large and therefore is not included here.

ALLOCATE	CTL	INITIAL	PROC	UNDERFLOW
ALLOC	CONVERSION	INIT	SEQUENTIAL	UFL
BINARY	CONV	OVERFLOW	SEQL	VARYING
BIN	DECIMAL	OFL	STRINGRANGE	VAR
CHARACTER	DEC	PICTURE	STRG	ZERODIVIDE
CHAR	DECLARE	PIC	STRINGSIZE	ZDIV
COLUMN	DCL	POINTER	STRZ	
COL	FIXEDOVERFLOW	PTR	SUBSCRIPTRANGE	
CONTROLLED	FOFL	PROCEDURE	SUBRQ	

The complete list of special symbols in PL/I for the 60-character set is as follows:

- = equal, assign
- + plus
- - minus
- * multiply
- / slash, divide
- (left parenthesis
- ** exponentiate
- || concatenate
- <= less than or equal
- >= greater than or equal
- ¬< not less than
- /* start comment
- -> dereference, qualify
-) right parenthesis
- , comma
- . decimal point, qualification
- ¬ negation, replaced by NOT
- ' apostrophe, not a symbol by itself
- & and
- | or
- < less than
- > greater than
- ¬= not equal
- ¬ > not greater than
- */ end comment

The rules for numeric integer, floating point, and fixed point literals are shown in Figure 3-4.

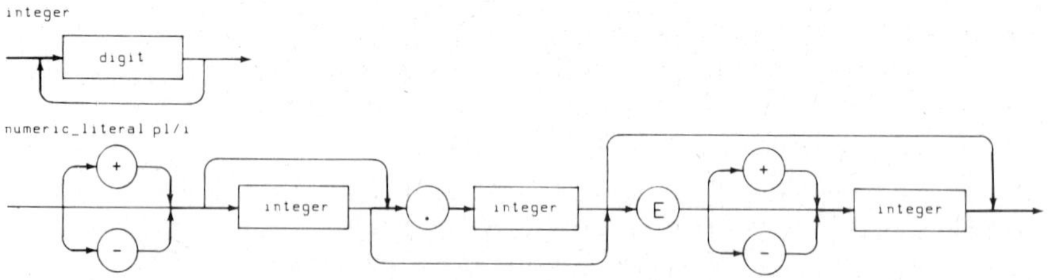

Figure 3-4 Syntax Diagram for PL/I Numeric Literals

Character string literals are delimited by apostrophes. Blanks and quotes are significant inside character literals, but each single quote that is part of the literal must be denoted twice. The empty character string is defined by only two single quotes. Thus 'DORIAN' is the character string literal DORIAN, '' is the empty string, and literal '''' is the single quote.

Depending on the system on which a PL/I compiler is hosted, some characters may not be available due to character set incompatibilities. For these implementations an alternate spelling of special symbols is also defined in PL/I. A full PL/I compiler is not required to understand the alternate character set. Table 3-1 lists the characters that have alternate spellings.

Table 3-1 Alternate Special Symbols in PL/I

60-char	48-char
;	.,
:	..
%	//

Table 3-2 lists alphabetic spellings for special PL/I symbols. These identifiers are RESERVED keywords, even though the full 60-character PL/I language permits the redefinition of keywords. An Assignment Statement of the form

```
BIT_VAR = OR OR AND;
```

is not allowed in the 48-character implementation.

Table 3-2 Alternate Identifiers in PL/I

<table>
<tr><th>60-char</th><th>48-char</th></tr>
<tr><td>¬</td><td>NOT</td></tr>
<tr><td>&</td><td>AND</td></tr>
<tr><td>|</td><td>OR</td></tr>
<tr><td><</td><td>LT</td></tr>
<tr><td>></td><td>GT</td></tr>
<tr><td><=</td><td>LE</td></tr>
<tr><td>>=</td><td>GE</td></tr>
<tr><td>¬<</td><td>NL</td></tr>
<tr><td>¬></td><td>NG</td></tr>
<tr><td>||</td><td>CAT</td></tr>
<tr><td>-></td><td>PT</td></tr>
</table>

Lexical Rules for Modula-2

Modula-2 distinguishes between the string of symbols that creates a program and the sequences of characters that create these symbols. The former can be expressed by machine-independent rules, while the latter certainly depend on the hardware used, because different computers incorporate different character sets. All lexical rules for Modula-2 described here refer to the ISO character set; implementations for other character sets should approximate these rules.

The Modula-2 character set consists of the lower- and uppercase letters, the ten digits, and the following special characters. The invisible characters carriage return, line feed, and the blank are also included as separators.

+ - * / : = & # < > ( ) [ ] { } ^ , . ; |

Identifiers start with a letter and are composed of any number of letters and digits that fit on one line. It is important to see that no additional character is permitted to support ease of reading; in particular the underline character is excluded. Equally important is the rule that lower- and uppercase letters are distinct. Therefore, the following four identifiers are all different.

```
Marianne   MARIANNE   MariAnne   marianne
```

The complete and relatively short list of reserved keywords follows. All Modula-2 keywords are spelled in uppercase.

AND	ELSIF	LOOP	REPEAT
ARRAY	END	MOD	RETURN
BEGIN	EXIT	MODULE	SET
BY	EXPORT	NOT	THEN
CASE	FOR	OF	TO
CONST	FROM	OR	TYPE
DEFINITION	IS	POINTER	UNTIL
DIV	IMPLEMENTATION	PROCEDURE	VAR
DO	IMPORT	QUALIFIED	WHILE
ELSE	IN	RECORD	WITH

The following complete list of Modula-2 special symbols includes a brief explanation of their use.

```
+   plus, set union                 -   minus, set difference
*   multiply, set intersect         /   divide, symmetric set difference
:=  becomes                         &   logical AND
=   equal                           ^   pointed to, dereference
#   not equal                       <>  not equal
<   less than                       >   greater than
<=  less than or equal              >=  greater than or equal
(   left parenthesis                )   right parenthesis
[   left square bracket             ]   right square bracket
(*  start comment, nested           *)  end comment, nested
,   comma                           .   dot, period
;   semicolon                       :   colon
..  double dot, range               |   variant separator
'   start string (ended by ')       "   start string (ended by ")
```

Numeric literals can be of type INTEGER or REAL. The uppercase spelling here emphasizes the Modula-2 convention for those predefined type identifiers. If literals include a decimal point, an integral and fractional part, or if they include a scale factor, then they are of type REAL; otherwise they are of type

INTEGER or CARDINAL. CARDINAL is simply the unsigned interpretation of an INTEGER value. The letter E in the scale factor must be in uppercase.

If an integer literal is followed by the letter capital C, then it represents a character literal with the value, corresponding to the ordinal number.

Numeric literals without explicit base are decimal numbers. If an integral number is followed by the letter B, then it is interpreted as an octal number. Naturally, no octal digit may be greater than '7'. Integers followed by the letter H are hexadecimal numbers. Hexadecimal digits include the conventional, extended letters A..F, only in uppercase. Is the string "FFH" a hexadecimal number or is it the identifier FFH in capital letters? To avoid confusion between identifiers and such hexadecimal numbers that consist exclusively of extended digits the hexadecimal numbers need a redundant, leading zero digit. A few correct samples are shown in Table 3-3.

Table 3-3 Sample Modula-2 Numeric Literals

Decimal	Hexadecimal	Octal	Real Number
32767	7FFFH	77777B	32767.0
0	0H	0B	0.0
1984	0AAAH	120B	19.84E+2

Again, the lexical rules for integer and real literals are expressed in Figure 3-5.

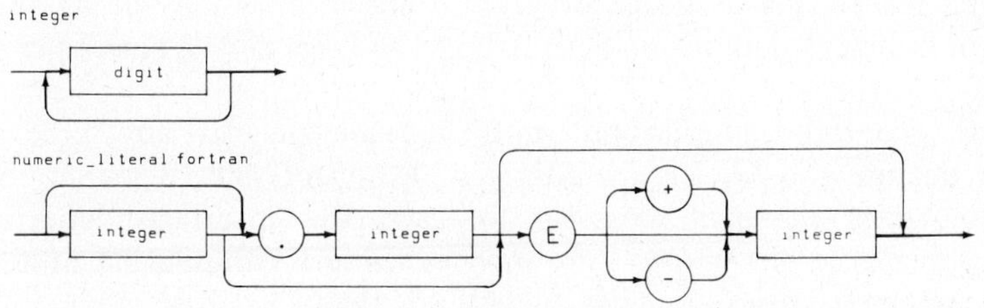

Figure 3-5 Syntax Diagram for Modula-2 Numeric Literals

Character strings may be of any length. They start either with the single or double quote character. If a character literal starts with the single quote, it is terminated at the first occurrence of another single quote. From this follows that such a string may not contain a single quote. This same holds for the double quote. Otherwise, all printable characters are allowed inside strings. There is no way provided in Modula-2 for string literals to contain both single and double quotes. See Table 3-4.

Table 3-4 Sample Modula-2 String Literals

Modula-2 String	Value
'MODULA-2'	MODULA-2
''	Empty String
""	Another Empty String
'Pereat Mundus, Fiat Iustitia'	wishful Romans
"Caesar's 'De Bello Gallico'"	Caesar's 'De Bello Gallico'
'He said: "Hands Up!"'	He said: "Hands Up!"
Impossible in Modula-2	Caesar's "De Bello Gallico"

Comments may be nested. This allows the textual inclusion of Modula-2 program text in a comment, even if that text in turn contains comments. Thus, the logical end of the modified comment is not altered.

3.3 Compilation Units

A *compilation unit* is the smallest syntactical unit a language compiler expects to see when translating a source program. These units may be as small as a subprogram interface definition, as in Ada, or as large as the entire program, as in Pascal.

Having separate compilation units is essential to any programming enterprise outside the toy programming or semiprofessional world. Separate compilation units make it possible to keep the interface definition and implementation portions apart. Any module using a compilation unit need be aware only of the interface, not the algorithmic detail.

There are other advantages to separate compilation units. A minor change in a source program requires only the recompilation of one physical module. Large projects can easily be split into subprojects, which can be designed, coded, and tested (via stubs) before integrating the overall program. A considerable degree of parallelism can be achieved that is hard to reach when using a monolithic language.

Ada Compilation Units

An Ada program is composed of one or more compilation units. It does not matter whether multiple compilation units are physically represented on a single source file, or if there exists a separate source file for each unit. After the last successful compilation and before run time, all compilation units are linked together to form an executable program.

The compilation units can be either subprograms or packages and are optionally preceded by so-called context clauses. Specifying a context clause for example of the form

```
WITH text_io; USE text_io;
```

informs the compiler that it must include the predefined package "text_io" with the current compilation unit and that all "text_io" names are directly imported and need not be qualified. Ada has numerous forms of compilation units, but in this text we shall concentrate on only the simplest form of Ada compilation units, which are subprogram and package bodies.

Ada Subprograms

When subprograms are defined on the outermost lexicographical level, they are compilation units. It is also legal to nest subprograms within other subprograms or packages, which makes them local. The visibility of local subprograms is restricted to the embedding scope. The rules for subprogram declarations and subprogram bodies are expressed in Example 3-5.

```
subprogram_declaration    ::= subprogram_spec ;
subprogram_spec           ::= PROCEDURE identifier [ formal_part ]
                            | FUNCTION designator  [ formal_part ]
                              RETURN type_mark
designator                ::= identifier | operator_symbol
operator_symbol           ::= string_literal
formal_part               ::= ( parameter_spec { ; parameter_spec } )
parameter_spec            ::= identifier_list : mode type_mark
                            [ := expression ]
mode                      ::= [ IN ] | OUT | IN OUT
subprogram_body           ::= subprogram_spec IS
                            [ declarative_part ]
                              BEGIN
                                sequence_of_statements
                            [ EXCEPTION
                                exception_handler
                                { exception_handler } ]
                              END [ designator ] ;
```

Example 3-5 Grammar Fragment for Ada Subprograms

There are two kinds of subprogram specifications, those for procedures and those for functions. Procedures are invoked by a Procedure Call Statement; functions are activated when used as expressions. Consequently, functions must return a value. Note that a subprogram specification is only a type declaration for the subprogram name. It does not constitute any action. Actions are defined via the sequence of statements in the body of the subprogram.

The body is identical for functions and procedures. It is introduced by the keyword IS, replacing the semicolon in the declaration, and followed by a possibly empty list of declarations. Then comes the required keyword BEGIN and a nonempty sequence of statements. An exception handler, introduced by EXCEPTION is optional before the required END keyword. The subprogram name may be repeated at the close of the subprogram block.

A subprogram declaration can be abbreviated to specify only the type of the subprogram name, in which case the declaration has no body and is terminated by a semicolon. This is useful when declaring two mutually recursive procedures. Since a name in Ada may not be referenced textually before its declaration, there might arise a deadlock situation, but the forward announcement via the declaration offers a loophole, similar to Pascal's FORWARD declaration. The name of a subprogram is specified and the associated body can be resolved later.

In the declaration of a subprogram body with parameters it is necessary to repeat all parameters, even if these have already been specified in a forward subprogram declaration. The language definition is so rigorous to require that this repetition be lexically identical; it is not sufficient to give a functionally equivalent repetition. The type and mode of formal parameters, and in the case of functions the type of the return value, contribute to the type of a subprogram name. A formal parameter specification with several identifiers is equivalent to a repetition of single parameter specifications with the same type mark.

```
PROCEDURE x( a, b, c : IN my_type ); -- is equivalent to:

PROCEDURE x( a   : IN my_type;
  b    : IN my_type;
  c    : IN my_type );
```

Example 3-6 Equivalent Subprogram Declarations

When the parameter mode is not given, the mode IN is assumed. Formal IN parameters are comparable to "value parameters" of other languages, but in Ada they may not be used as variables. Thus it is not legal to use an IN parameter on the left-hand side of an Assignment Statement, or as an actual parameter for a formal OUT or IN OUT parameter.

Formal OUT parameters may be substituted by uninitialized actual parameters, but they must receive a value in the subprogram called. If this does not happen, then the actual parameter is undefined upon PROCEDURE return. It would be nice, therefore, if an implementation could explicitly initialize all OUT parameters to a distinguishable UNDEFINED value and test for that value after the return. If the actual parameter is still UNDEFINED, a trap can be activated. Formal IN OUT parameters generally hold a valid value upon entry and receive a new value during execution of the activated subprogram.

Ada is very careful about the requirements concerning the implementation of the parameter passing mechanism. For formal OUT and IN OUT parameters the compiler may choose passing by address or passing by value-result for structured type data. For primitive data types an implementation must choose value-result passing to OUT and IN OUT parameters. Any program, however, that relies on the one or the other is by definition erroneous. Unfortunately, there exists no general, computable function that can indicate whether such reliance is embedded in a source program. Thus a compiler cannot provide any dependable help.

Ada is unique in allowing an optional initialization clause for formal parameters. Since Ada also allows a partial actual parameter list in subprogram calls, the initialization is a handy and necessary way of providing a value for those formal parameters that were not substituted. Ada has positional and named parameter substitutions. An actual parameter list may start out with positional substitution, and then switch over to named substitution. From then on, though, it is no longer possible to use positional substitution.

Example 3-7 lists an Ada program fragment, using positional, default, and named parameter substitution.

```
PROCEDURE do_this(
  p1 : IN integer   := 140;
  p2 : IN character := 'X';
  p3 : IN boolean   := true ) IS
BEGIN--do_this
  --sequence of statements
END do_this;

PROCEDURE call_do_this IS
  i  : integer    := 150;
  c  : character  := 'Y';
  b  : boolean    := false;
BEGIN--call_do_this
  do_this( i, c, b );     --substitution by position
  do_this;       --takes on default values
  do_this( 140, 'X', true );  --as above, with parameters
  do_this( p3=>b, p1=>i, p2=>c ); --named substitution
END call_do_this;
```

Example 3-7 Ada Parameter Substitutions

Procedure "do_this" in Example 3-7 is called four times. The first call substitutes all formal parameters by primitive expressions. The association of actual to formal parameter is by position. The second call uses only default values, indicated in the initialization clause of the formal declaration. Call three supplies the actual parameters by using literals, while the fourth Call Statement demonstrates named parameter association.

The optional assignment to formal IN parameters should not be confused with an initialization that takes place during each call. It provides a default value only in the case that no actual parameter is provided for that formal parameter.

Recall that two objects are compatible only if their types are defined by the same type mark. From this follows the Ada rule that parameters and the return type of a FUNCTION must be defined by a type mark rather than by an anonymous type definition. This type compatibility rule, applied to parameter passing and assignment, is illustrated in Example 3-8. Some parameter substitutions are illegal, due to incompatible types, or types that have been declared incorrectly.

```
PROCEDURE good_ada_1 IS
  TYPE my_type IS NEW integer RANGE 0 ..15;
  x, y : my_type;
BEGIN--good_ada_1
  x := 4;
  y := x; -- good assignment, x and y are type compatible
END good_ada_1;

PROCEDURE illegal_ada_1 IS
  TYPE caps_1 IS NEW character RANGE 'A' .. 'X';
  TYPE caps_2 IS NEW character RANGE 'A' .. 'X';
  -- CAPS 1 and CAPS 2 define DIFFERENT type marks
  letter1 : caps_1 := 'B';
  letter2 : caps_2;
BEGIN -- illegal_ada_1
  letter2 := letter1;
  -- I L L E G A L .  Different types
END illegal_ada_1;

PROCEDURE good_ada_2 IS
  min : CONSTANT integer := 0;
  max : CONSTANT integer := 1024;
  TYPE b_type IS NEW integer RANGE min ..  max;
  x : b_type := min;
 PROCEDURE b_test( bounds : IN b_type ); -- body later
 BEGIN -- good_ada_2 -- executable statements
  b_test( x ); -- good parameter substitution
END good_ada_2;
```

Example 3-8 Demonstration of Type Compatibility Rules

Name Overloading

Another Ada rule that might delight programmers accustomed to more conventional programming languages concerns *name overloading.* Subprogram names and the names of enumeration literals may be overloaded. This allows the same name to be defined more than once in the same scope. In order to distinguish overloaded subprogram names from one another, they must differ in their parameter types, number, order, or in their return types. At the place of call, the types of the formal parameters yield the information necessary to make a clear distinction. The program in Example 3-9 demonstrates name overloading.

```
PROCEDURE overload_demo IS
  c : character := '7';
  i : integer   :=  70;
PROCEDURE my_print( arg : character ) IS...END my_print;
PROCEDURE my_print( arg : integer ) IS...END my_print;
BEGIN--overload_demo
  my_print( c );--which of the two is invoked? the first!
  my_print( i );--which of the two is invoked? the second!
  my_print( '6' );--which of the two is invoked? the first!
  my_print( 123 );--which of the two is invoked? the second!
  my_print(false);--error; no my_print subprogram for booleans
END overload_demo;
```

Example 3-9 Overloaded Ada Procedure Name

Subprogram Names

Usually the name of an Ada subprogram will be a regular identifier. This is familiar from other programming languages. In addition to this, Ada allows a new construct: the name of a subprogram may be a character string. This new construct allows the overloaded definition of conventional operators like “+” or “>=” for other than their predefined purposes. Since the language syntax requires these names to be string literals, they are embedded in double quotes. When the function is actually invoked, its name is spelled without the double quotes. A sample definition is shown in Example 3-10.

```
FUNCTION "+" (
  arg1 : IN nibble_type;
  arg2 : IN nibble_type ) RETURN nibble_type IS
BEGIN -- "+
" --  sequence of statements
RETURN arg1'last;
END "+";
```

Example 3-10 Character String as Function Name

All predefined operators such as “+,” “>,” are already overloaded and may be redefined and further overloaded. However, the “/=” is an exception, since redefinitions of the “=” operator implicitly define its inverse function as well.

This is a good moment to pause and analyze the new Ada rules, which at first glance strike the reader as unusual or tricky. Overloading and character strings as subprogram names seem amazing at first. But are these rules really something new? Isn't the Pascal “write” procedure also overloaded? In fact, many Pascal or PL/I IO routines accept a variety of different arguments. And this is exactly what Ada allows; except Ada spells out this mechanism, gives it a name.

The same is true for strings as function names. We are quite familiar from procedural programming languages with the mathematical functions "+" for addition, "-" for subtraction, and so on. Moreover, these functions are overloaded. The arguments can be integer or real, and in Fortran even complex types. The distinction between the mathematical modulus operation, for example, spelled "a MOD b" as in Pascal, or spelled "MOD(a,b)" as in PL/I, is purely syntactical. Either way, MOD is a dyadic operator. So are "+," "-," and all other string names that Ada permits. Again, Ada only observes these conventions, and allows them in a generalized fashion. There is, after all, very little new about the tricky overloading and string name concept.

Packages

So far, we have mainly been concerned with the structure of subprograms as Ada compilation units. In the next paragraphs we shall encounter another higher level of abstraction that permits the physical and logical modularization of complex problems into smaller units. This is the Ada package mechanism, a scheme that closely resembles the Modula-2 solution for compilation units.

In contrast to what happens in packages, the storage attribute of variables in PROCEDURE and FUNCTION compilation units is still automatic, not static. Both terms will be explained in detail in the chapter on "Storage Classes." Even if a PROCEDURE is a main procedure, then it just so happens that its variables last for the complete program execution and are indistinguishable from static data. Here we have a rare case where the boundary line between automatic and static lifetime fades.

Ada's *packages* are the key structure for creating modular, maintainable software "in the large." They provide an understandable, formal mechanism for encapsulation and information hiding. Similar to the way known from subprograms, Ada defines a package declaration and a package body. But in contrast to subprograms, package bodies require the reserved word BODY. In Example 3-11 we list the BNF grammar rules for Ada packages.

```
package_declaration    ::= package_spec ;
package_spec           ::= PACKAGE identifier IS
                              { basic_declarative_item }
                           [ PRIVATE
                             { basic_declarative_item } ]
                             END [ identifier ]
package_body           ::= PACKAGE BODY identifier IS
                               [ declarative_part ]
                           [ BEGIN
                               sequence_of_statements
                           [ EXCEPTION
                               exception_handler
                               { exception_handler } ] ]
                             END [ identifier ] ;
```

Example 3-11 Grammar Fragment for Ada Packages

Note that the "basic declarative item" in the package specification may only contain objects, types, and subprogram declarations. Bodies of any form that would include executable statements are illegal in a package declaration. How then can package declarations be used?

First, every package has a declaration, but not necessarily a body. Packages without a body form encapsulated modules that hold variables, constants, type names, and any kind of compilation unit without a body. Such package declarations can function as global names to any other module that chooses to include them via a context clause. When such a package is used as a compilation unit, the lifetime of all included objects is static. Various other compilation units may use these global objects, declared in the so-called visible part, as a means of communicating with one another.

Ada also permits the nesting of package specifications and bodies just as subprograms do. In this case, the lifetime of included objects is no longer static. The lifetime of automatic variables is determined by that of the block containing the package.

In addition to its implicitly visible part, a package may have an explicit private part, introduced by the keyword PRIVATE. Any name defined there is invisible to other packages. This is meaningful when used in conjunction with a package body: only the body has control over, and access to, names in the private section.

The visible part of a package body declaration may hold subprogram declarations. This way it releases only the interface specification of a subprogram to other modules, but keeps the implementation of the subprogram body secret to the package body. The similarity here between Ada and Modula-2 is quite striking.

This solves a classical problem encountered in large software projects: when an implementor finds a better, more correct, or faster solution to a subprogram, then as long as the logical function and hence the interface is preserved, the person in charge may "secretly" go and modify the body of that subprogram. The users of that module do not need to be informed about the recent change, and normally they do not want to know! They are busy solving another problem. All they need to know about is the interface, and that remains unchanged.

In Example 3-12 we show a package sample. This package has been modularized into two parts. The first is the interface module, and the second the implementation module.

```
PACKAGE rational_number_package IS
 TYPE rational IS
  RECORD
   num, denom : integer;
  END RECORD;
 FUNCTION "=" ( arg1, arg2 : IN rational ) RETURN boolean;
 --  similarly for "<," ">," "+," "-," "*," and "/"
END rational_number_package;

PACKAGE BODY rational_number_package IS
 PROCEDURE normalize( arg1, arg2 : IN OUT rational ) IS
 BEGIN--normalize --
 -- outside need not know inside of this subprogram
 END normalize;
FUNCTION "="( arg1, arg2 : IN rational ) RETURN boolean IS
  a, b : rational;
 BEGIN-- "="
   a := arg1;
   b := arg2;
   normalize( a, b );
 RETURN a.num = b.num; -- denominators are equal
 END "=";
FUNCTION "<"( arg1, arg2 : IN rational ) RETURN boolean IS ..  END;
FUNCTION ">"( arg1, arg2 : IN rational ) RETURN boolean IS ..  END;
FUNCTION "+"( arg1, arg2 : IN rational ) RETURN rational IS
BEGIN-- "+"
 normalize( arg1, arg2 );
 return ( arg1.num + arg2.num, arg1.denom );--integer "+"
END "+";
FUNCTION "-"( arg1, arg2 : IN rational ) RETURN rational IS ..  END;
FUNCTION "*"( arg1, arg2 : IN rational ) RETURN rational IS ..  END;
FUNCTION "/"( arg1, arg2 : IN rational ) RETURN rational IS ..  END;
END rational_number_package;
```

Example 3-12 Package, Interface, and Implementation Part

Fortran Compilation Units

There are three kinds of compilation units in Fortran: main procedures, subroutines, and functions. For each running Fortran program there may only be a single main procedure, but any number of subroutines and functions is legal. These subroutines or functions may reside in the same source file together with the main procedure. The main procedure may be listed anywhere in the sequence of compilation units. Also subroutines and functions may reside in different, independent files and be compiled independently. In that case the generated objects are saved and added to a private object library. A skeleton grammar for Fortran compilation units is shown in Example 3-13.

```
fortran_compilation    ::= main_program
                         | fortran_function
                         | fortran_subroutine

main_program           ::= [ PROGRAM program_name ]
                             main_body
                           END

fortran_subroutine     ::= SUBROUTINE subroutine_name [ formals ]
                             subroutine_body
                           END

formals                ::= ( [ parameter { , parameter } ] )

parameter              ::= identifier | *

fortran_function       ::= [ type ] FUNCTION function_name [ formals ]
                             function_body
                           END

subroutine_body        ::= statement { statement }

function_body          ::= { { statement } function_assignment
                           { statement } }

main_body              ::= non_entry_statement {non_entry_statement}

statement              ::= non_entry_statement
                         | entry_statement

entry_statement        ::= ENTRY [([ parameter { , parameter } ])]

program_name           ::= name

subroutine_name        ::= name

function_name          ::= name
```

Example 3-13 Grammar Fragment for Fortran Compilation Units

Fortran Main Program

Fortran main procedures may not even have a header. In such a case the main procedure is identified by its source file name. Like all other compilation units, the main procedure must be terminated by an END Statement. Fortran-77, however, does allow a special header in the form of a PROGRAM Statement at the beginning of the main procedure. The name following the keyword PROGRAM identifies the main procedure. This name is external and may not match any other external name nor any other name local to the main procedure.

The body of the main procedure contains TYPE, EXTERNAL, DIMENSION, COMMON, EQUIVALENCE, and DATA Statements, statement functions, and the actual executable statements in that order. Except for executable statements, all other statement parts may be empty. Like PL/I, Fortran does not make a clean distinction between statements and declarations. A declaration is named rather awkwardly a "Declaration Statement." A primitive sample Fortran program is shown in two versions in Example 3-14. The commentary line starting with a C in column one separates the two.

```
   10  FORMAT( ' '/, 5X, ' YOUR FIRST PROGRAM SAYS HELLO'/ )
       WRITE( 6, 10 )
       END
C----  In Fortran-77 this could also be written as follows:
       PROGRAM FIRST
   10  FORMAT( ' '/, 5X, ' YOUR FIRST PROGRAM SAYS HELLO'/ )
       WRITE( 6, 10 )
       END
```

Example 3-14 Sample Fortran Main Programs

In Example 3-14 the Format Statements contain two slashes. These instruct the IO system to emit carriage returns; the "5X" causes five blanks to be printed. Formats and other "magic" symbols will be explained in the chapter on "Input Output." Notice that the Format Statement is marked by the label 10. IO Statements may reference these labels to generate layout information for the IO arguments. See the two Write Statements above.

The second line, a WRITE Statement, contains two instructions, the numbers 6 and 10. In most Fortran implementations these are standard "magic" numbers used to identify files or format specifications. The 6, for example, identifies the output device. In some systems, this may be the line printer, but nowadays it is more often a CRT screen. If the program contained a READ Statement, the corresponding input file identifier would be the number 5. Other numbers are allowed and depend on the implementation, but 5 and 6 refer to "standard input" and "standard output."

Fortran Function

A function is introduced by the function header, starting with a type specification, followed by the keyword FUNCTION, the name of the function, and the parenthesized list of "dummy" parameters. The term *dummy* is Fortran's word for formal parameter. The only function types allowed are INTEGER, REAL, COMPLEX, and LOGICAL. If the function's type can be derived from its name, it need not be stated explicitly.

Fortran's rules for implicit type determination are as follows. Any name starting with a letter I through N has, by default, the type INTEGER, unless explicitly overruled. Any other first letter implies the type REAL. See the sample function "ADDS" in Example 3-15.

```
   PROGRAM FUDEMO
10    FORMAT( /, ' THE SUM IS:', I10, / )
      INTEGER A, B, C  INTEGER ADDS
      A = 3
      B = 4
      C = ADDS( A, B )
      WRITE( 6, 10 ) C
   END
C-----
   INTEGER FUNCTION ADDS( A, B )
    INTEGER A, B
    ADDS = A + B
   END
```

Example 3-15 Fortran Function Return Type

Just like the main procedure, a function must be terminated by an END Statement, and the body may contain TYPE, EXTERNAL, DIMENSION, COMMON, EQUIVALENCE, DATA Statements, and statement functions, all optional, in that order. Since a function must return a value to the location of its name reference, there must be at least one Assignment Statement providing a value of compatible type.

A function is a separate compilation unit. Hence there can arise no confusion between names in the main procedure and the names declared in the function (or a subroutine). In particular the dummy parameter names may be, but need not be, identical to the actual parameters. Also statement numbers in functions, subprograms, and the Main Program are independent and may be repeated without chance of mixup.

Be careful about what the textbook by Kaufman [1978] says on page 144 concerning function parameters. Kaufman claims function parameters are all passed by value, which would mean an assignment to a dummy parameter in the activated function has no effect on the actual parameter after the function return. This is a good recommendation but is not a language requirement. The Fortran standard defines that parameters are passed by reference; a specific implementation is not dictated. Since literals are permissible as actual parameters, a likely implementation technique is by value-result. On the other hand, since assignments to dummy parameters that correspond to literals used as actual parameters are illegal, an implementation by address passing would work as well. This is discussed in much detail in the chapter on "Parameters."

It is, however, good programming practice to minimize the assignments of values to dummy function parameters. Such assignments would have a permanent effect on the corresponding actual parameters.

The correspondence between actual and dummy parameters is by position. There is no way in Fortran to alter this correspondence—as it is possible, for example, in Ada, using named association. Also it is not legal to omit some parameters. The number and type of all dummy parameters must be compatible with the actual ones.

Fortran Subroutine

A subroutine starts with a Subroutine Statement, similar to the declaration of a function, but there is no need to indicate a type, since subroutines return no value. Instead they communicate with the outside world or the callers via reference parameters and common variables.

Names declared as COMMON can be referenced in all blocks that choose to declare the same names with the attribute COMMON. The scope attribute of common names is external and the storage attribute is static. After the Subroutine Statement come again the TYPE, EXTERNAL, DIMENSION, COMMON, EQUIVALENCE, DATA Statements in that order. These are followed by optional statement functions and the subroutine's statement body. As expected, an END Statement must come last.

Parameter passing to subroutines is done by reference. Some Fortran-66 compilers implement this by value-result. Either way, parameters in Fortran work like a two-way street. Upon call, the dummy parameters already have an initial value, which is the last value of the actual parameter before the call. They may also, as a side effect, return a value to the caller. Some Fortran implementations—the one on Burroughs 6700, for example—allow the value parameter passing in the same way as PL/I allows.

Fortran ENTRY Declaration

Both Fortran and PL/I allow multiple entry points to subroutines and functions. An Entry Statement permits a procedure to begin execution with any statement in the function or subroutine marked by the Entry Statement.

This entry declaration may be used anywhere except between a Block If Statement and its corresponding END IF, or between a Do Statement and the terminal statement of its do loop.

If the Entry Statement appears in a subroutine, the defined name is also a subroutine name. If it is used in a function, then the defined name is an external function name. If there are no dummy arguments, either an empty pair of parentheses or no parentheses at all may be given in the formal declaration. A reference to such a function, however, still requires the empty list of parentheses. For the parameterless entry subroutine call, this is again optional.

Asterisk dummy parameters are allowed only for entry subroutines, not for entry functions. The declaration of dummy parameters for the entry name is independent of the dummy parameters for the heading subroutine or function. Care must be taken at the place of call to have the actual list correspond in number and type with the formal list. Even more care must be taken in the subroutine body to avoid referencing any of the other dummy parameters, since they will be undefined. The Fortran program fragment in Example 3-16 shows multiple entry points with distinct dummy parameters declared at each entry point. The comments give clues about where the different dummy parameters can be referenced.

```
      SUBROUTINE HEAD( A, B )
C----- HERE A, B ARE WELL DEFINED
C----- USE A, B
      ENTRY FIRST( C, D )
C----- C, D DEFINED, BUT UPON "CALL FIRST" A, B UNDEFINED
C----- USE C, D IF "FIRST" WAS CALLED
C----- USE A, B IF "HEAD" WAS CALLED
      ENTRY SECOND( E, F )
C----- E, F DEFINED.  "CALL SECOND" A, B, C, D UNDEFINED
C----- USE E, F
      END
```

Example 3-16 Multiple Entry Points with Dummy Parameters

Fortran RETURN and Multiple Return Statement

Fortran allows a special type of dummy parameter that is syntactically denoted by an asterisk. The asterisk indicates that the parameter takes on the value of a statement label. An index is associated with these dummy parameters, enumerated from left to right in the dummy list, starting with index 1. See the sample program in Example 3-17.

```
      SUBROUTINE OBSCURE( A, *, B, *, * )
        INTEGER A, B
        IF ( A .EQ.  12345 ) RETURN 2
        IF ( A .EQ.  666 ) RETURN 1
      END
```

Example 3-17 Asterisk Parameters and Multiple Return Statement

In the "OBSCURE" subroutine in Example 3-17 there are three asterisk parameters. The one between dummy parameters "A" and "B" has index 1; the next one, index 2; and the last one before the right parenthesis has index 3. Suppose a Return Statement in the subroutine body of Example 3-17 contains an integer type expression with value bounded by 1..3, and say the value is 2. Then the return activity not only terminates execution of the subroutine, but also causes execution to continue at the place defined by the actual label, passed as the second asterisk parameter. Under no circumstances should this Return Statement be mistaken for a PL/I or Ada statement of the form "RETURN e," where the value of expression "e" is returned by a function. For clarification of Fortran's multiple Return Statement a program fragment is shown in Example 3-18, containing a call to "OBSCURE" and actual label parameters.

```
      A = 12345
      CALL OBSCURE( A, *100, B, *300, *200 )
C---- NOTE ASTERISK IN THE ACTUAL LIST PRECEDING LABELS
 50   D = 44
      GOTO 900
 100  D = 55
      GOTO 900
 200  D = 66
      GOTO 900
 300  D = 77
C---- OTHER EXECUTABLE STATEMENTS
 900  ...
```

Example 3-18 Passing Label Parameters

Let us assume the subroutine body of "OBSCURE" is active due to the call, and in the body of "OBSCURE" a "return 2" statement is executed. Then after termination of "OBSCURE" the next active statement is not the one labeled 50, as it would normally be. Instead, statement 300 is the next one executed because it is labeled by the the second actual argument of the three asterisk parameters in the parameter list of "OBSCURE."

If the integer expression of the Return Statement falls outside the bounds of the star indices, then a regular RETURN is executed. Again this out-of-bounds value is *not* returned. The out-of-bounds condition will always hold for negative values and for 0, since index counting starts at 1 and can only be higher than 0, never negative. The statements in Example 3-19 are trivially equivalent.

```
RETURN -100
RETURN -1
RETURN 0
RETURN
```

Example 3-19 Equivalent Fortran Return Statements

Serious programmers should forget immediately everything that has been said about multiple Return Statements! Such obscure language facilities should be abandoned altogether, since they make programming in the large extremely difficult.

Fortran Subroutine Call and Function Invocation

Subroutines are invoked by Call Statements. The keyword CALL introduces the activity, while the subroutine name specifies which one of a pool of subroutines is to be activated by the call. If the formal specification of the subroutine has dummy parameters, then a parenthesized list of actual parameters must be given in the Call Statement after the subroutine name. Actual and formal parameters must match in number, are associated by position, and must be pairwise type compatible. Syntactically, subroutine calls and entry calls are identical. The same holds for functions as well. Some sample Call Statements are given in Example 3-20.

```
C----- SRO has no parameters
       CALL SRO
C----- pass one-dimensional array, and two integers to SR3
       CALL SR3( ARR1, B, ARR1( 12 ) )
```

Example 3-20 Sample Fortran Call Statements

A function is invoked by being referenced in an expression, where the keyword CALL may not be used. The function return type must be compatible with the type of the expression at the place of invocation. If there are dummy parameters in the formal function declaration, then the same number of type compatible actual parameters must be given at the place of invocation. The whole list is enclosed within parentheses. If, on the other hand, the function has no dummy parameters, then the empty pair of parentheses must still be given in the expression. This clearly informs the Fortran compiler that here is a function reference, not just some yet undeclared variable reference. See

Example 3-21.

```
X = F0()
Y = F1( 19 )
Z = F2( F1( 18 ), F0() )
```

Example 3-21 Sample Fortran Function Calls

If the actual parameter list contains nested function invocations, then successively the innermost functions are activated first. For example, in "A=F3(F2(F1(ARG)))" the function "F1" is active first, returning a value of some type compatible with "F2's" dummy parameter. Then "F2" will be active, returning a properly typed value as an actual parameter for "F3." Finally "F3" yields the result that is assigned to variable "A."

Before a function can correctly terminate, it must receive an appropriate value via a regular Assignment Statement. Function assignment and Return are separate activities. The actual return step may be stated explicitly by a RETURN Statement or implicitly when the execution reaches the function's End Statement. See Example 3-22.

```
      INTEGER FUNCTION MAX( A, B )
       INTEGER A, B
       IF ( A .GE.  B ) GOTO 100
       MAX = B
       RETURN
100    MAX = A
      END
```

Example 3-22 Fortran Function Assignment

Fortran Array Parameter Substitution

It has been pointed out that actual and dummy parameters must be type compatible with one another in Fortran. This does not mean the language is strongly typed. There is a certain laxness, especially for array parameters. The number and size of the actual and dummy array parameters may differ radically, provided that the actual array supplies sufficient space for the corresponding dummy declaration. This is explained by the arrays shown in Example 3-23.

```
      PROGRAM ADEMO
       DIMENSION A( 1 : 20 )
       DIMENSION B( 1 : 20 )
       DIMENSION C( 1 : 8 )
 10    CALL ARRAYS( A )
C----- IS LEGAL, 20 REALS PROVIDED, ONLY 10 NEEDED
 20    CALL ARRAYS( B( 5 ) )
C----- IS LEGAL, 16 REALS PROVIDED, B(5..20), ONLY 10 NEEDED
 30    CALL ARRAYS( C )
C----- IS ILLEGAL, 8 REALS PROVIDED, BUT 10 NEEDED
      END
      SUBROUTINE ARRAYS( A )
       DIMENSION A( 1 : 10 )
C----- USE ANY 10 ELEMENTS OF ARRAY "A"
      END
```

Example 3-23 Fortran Array Parameters

Calling program "ADEMO" issues two legal calls and one illegal call to subroutine "ARRAYS." Statement 10 supplies sufficient space for the subroutine called. Statement 20 passes the array element "B(5)" as an actual parameter, so one might suspect this is also an illegal call, since only one element is provided. Not so in Fortran! Fortran passes only the array address as a parameter, in this case the address of "B(5)." Upon call, the subroutine "ARRAYS" believes that the actual parameter is an array with 10 elements, and since truly 10 or even more are provided, no catastrophe can happen.

A reference to "A(3)" in "arrays" results in referencing "B(5+3-1)," which is "B(7)." All other uses of "A" with proper indices in the range 1..10 will result in valid references to "B." Statement 30 is erroneous, since the actual parameter provided supplies only 8 of the necessary 10 locations. So a reference to "A(9)" or "A(10)" would access invalid locations, certainly not part of actual parameter "B."

The array dimensions in subroutines or functions do not need to be fixed by literals. It is also possible to create adjustable dimensions by passing the actual bounds as parameters. This is demonstrated in Example 3-24.

```
      PROGRAM ADJUST
      DIMENSION A( 1 : 20 )
      DIMENSION B( 1 : 20 )
   10 CALL ARRAYS( A, 10 )
C-----  OTHER EXECUTABLE STATEMENTS
   20 CALL ARRAYS( B, 20 )
C-----  OTHER EXECUTABLE STATEMENTS
      END

      SUBROUTINE ARRAYS( A, N )
      INTEGER N
      DIMENSION A( 1 : N )
C-----  REFS OF "A" LIKE "A(8) = A(I) * A(7)" POSSIBLE
      END
```

Example 3-24 Fortran Array Parameters Need Not Match

It is easy to misinterpret this facility as dynamic array parameters, which it is not. The truth is that Fortran arrays are still statically allocated, regardless of what is passed to a subroutine. So the adjustable facility does not save any data space, nor does the fixed bound array parameter waste any data space. All Fortran arrays and other data live during the full program execution.

Pascal Compilation Units

Pascal programs are monolithic, single compilation units. Therefore, if a program is logically complex, a physically large source file is created. Hence the sinister attribute "monolithic." A compilation unit is introduced by the reserved keyword PROGRAM and followed by the program name. Then comes a list of external file names, enclosed in parentheses and terminated by a semicolon. A Pascal block follows, and the whole program is terminated by a period.

A block in Pascal is a sequence of LABEL, CONST, TYPE, and VAR declarations in that order, each of which may be empty. After these come the optional PROCEDURE and FUNCTION declarations, including the FORWARD announcements, and one Compound Statement. This scheme is consistent in Pascal with the other two contexts where blocks are allowed, the PROCEDURE and FUNCTION scopes.

```
pascal_program   ::= PROGRAM identifier ( identifier_list ) ;
                     block .
identifier_list ::= identifier { , identifier }
block            ::= [ label_dcl ]
                     [ const_dcl ]
                     [ type_dcl ]
```

```
                  [ var_dcl ]
                  { subprogram }
                  BEGIN
                    statement_list
                  END
subprogram     ::= PROCEDURE identifier [ parameter_list ]
                    tail
                 | FUNCTION  identifier [ parameter_list ] :
                    type_identifier tail
tail           ::= ; block ;
                 | ; FORWARD ;
parameter_list ::= ( parameter { ; parameter } )
parameter      ::= parameter_spec
                 | VAR parameter_spec
                 | FUNCTION parameter_spec
                 | PROCEDURE identifier_list
parameter_spec ::= identifier_list : type_identifier
```

Example 3-25 Grammar Fragment for Pascal PROGRAM

All names declared in the program scope are global, thus any procedure or function scope may also reference these names, unless they have been redeclared with a different meaning locally or in some intermediate level. Note that global does not mean external. In fact, none of these names except perhaps the program name, is external. But there is no need for external names in Pascal since programs are single compilation units.

In addition every procedure and function scope may declare its own local names. Some of these may again be procedure or function names with a deeper nested scope. More detail is given in Section 3.4.

Parameters are passed by reference or by value. Reference parameters are explicitly marked by the reserved keyword VAR, while all unmarked parameters are value parameters. Certain restrictions apply: files can only be passed as reference parameters, while procedure and function parameters must be value parameters. Program "params" in Example 3-26 shows one reference and one value parameter example.

```
PROGRAM params( input, output );
 VAR
   c : char;
 PROCEDURE refs( VAR c : char );
   BEGIN { refs }
     c := '7'; { actual parameter will be '7' }
   END; { refs }
 PROCEDURE vals( c : char );
   BEGIN { vals }
     c := 'Y'; { actual parameter unmodified }
   END; { vals }
 BEGIN { params }
   c := 'A';
   refs( c ); { c = '7' }
   vals( c ); { c will still be '7' }
END.  { params }
```

Example 3-26   Reference and Value Parameters in Pascal

PL/I Compilation Units

A PL/I program comprises a list of external procedures and must include one main procedure. The MAIN attribute must be explicitly specified for one of the external procedures of the program. Similar to Fortran, any external procedure can call any other external procedure, irrespective of whether the procedure resides on the same source file as the caller, or on a separate file. The only PL/I requirement is that the called external procedure must be announced in the one issuing the call via an ENTRY declaration.

An incomplete grammar for PL/I compilation units, after some translation from the standard ANSI [1976] p. 33, is given in Example 3-27.

```
pl1_compilation      ::= proc_declaration

proc_declaration     ::= prefix_list procedure_statement
                           [ unit_list ] ending

unit_list            ::= unit { unit }

unit                 ::= [ statement_name_list ]
                       { declare_statement  | default_statement }
                       | statement_name_list entry_statement
                       | prefix_list format_statement
                       | proc_declaration
                       | executable_unit

ending               ::= [ statement_name_list ] END
                         [ statement_name ] ;

prefix_list          ::= prefix { prefix }
```

```
prefix               ::= ( condition_prefix { condition_prefix } ) :
                       | statement_name :
procedure_statement ::= PROCEDURE { entry_information } ;
entry_information   ::= [ ( identifier { , identifier } ) ]
                        [ returns_descriptor ] [ options ] [ RECURSIVE ]
executable_unit     ::= [ prefix_list ] { executable_unit_rest }
executable_unit_rest::= group | begin_block | on_statement
                      | if_statement | executable_single_statement
```

Example 3-27 Grammar Fragment for PL/I Procedures

The four PL/I procedures in Example 3-28 are sketches only, but they provide sufficient information for how to construct compilation units.

```
P1: PROCEDURE;
 DECLARE ( P3, P4 ) ENTRY;
 /* OTHER EXECUTABLE STATEMENTS */
 CALL P3;
 /* OTHER EXECUTABLE STATEMENTS */
 CALL P4;
 /* OTHER EXECUTABLE STATEMENTS */
END P1;

P2: PROCEDURE OPTIONS( MAIN ); /* IS THE MAIN PROGRAM */
 DECLARE ( P1, P4 ) ENTRY;
 /* OTHER EXECUTABLE STATEMENTS */
 CALL P1;
 /* OTHER EXECUTABLE STATEMENTS */
 CALL P4;
 /* OTHER EXECUTABLE STATEMENTS */
END P2;

P3: PROCEDURE;
 DECLARE P4 ENTRY;
 /* OTHER EXECUTABLE STATEMENTS */
 CALL P4;
 /* OTHER EXECUTABLE STATEMENTS */
END P3;

P4: PROCEDURE;
 /* EXECUTABLE STATEMENTS */
END P4;
```

Example 3-28 PL/I Procedure Skeleton

PL/I procedures may also return values, and thus be used as functions. For this purpose the type of the returned value must be declared by the Returns Clause. Also if any of the external procedures have parameters, the types of these must be specified in the ENTRY declaration; names need not be given. If an external procedure is used as a function, its return type must also be indicated. See Example 3-29.

```
P1: PROCEDURE( A );
 DCL A BIN FIXED;
 DCL B CHAR(1);
 /* EXECUTABLE STATEMENTS */
END P1;

ANDRE: PROCEDURE OPTIONS( MAIN );
 DCL P1 ENTRY( BIN FIXED );
 DCL MY MIN ENTRY( BIN FIXED, BIN FIXED )
  RETURNS( BIN FIXED );
 DCL ( A, B ) BIN FIXED;
 /* EXECUTABLE STATEMENTS */
END ANDRE;

MY_MIN: PROCEDURE ( A, B ) RETURNS( BIN FIXED );
 DCL ( A, B ) BIN FIXED;
 /* EXECUTABLE STATEMENTS */
END MY_MIN;
```

Example 3-29 PL/I Parameter and Function Type Declarations

PL/I has the concept of reference and value parameters, but it is not at all visible from the declaration of the formal parameter which of the two forms will be used. The problem with PL/I is that either of the two can happen for the same parameter. Only at the place of call, where an actual parameter is substituted for the formal one, can the parameter form be distinguished.

If the actual parameter is a variable, it is passed by reference. If it is an expression, then passing by value takes place. A problem can arise, however, when a variable is used as an expression, even if a very primitive expression. How, given the preceding rules, can a variable be enforced to become an expression? The answer is simple: syntax tricks. If the parameter type is integer (BIN FIXED in PL/I), then adding a redundant zero to the variable reference will clearly mark it as an expression. Or, redundant parentheses will do the trick as well. Redundant parentheses work with all types of variables, not just with integers.

The sample PL/I program Example 3-30 shows two calls to procedure "VAL_OR_REF." In either case variable "X" is passed. The first time redundant parentheses mark the reference to "X" as a value parameter; in the second case "X" is passed by reference.

```
VAL_OR_REF: PROCEDURE( A );
 DCL A BIN FIXED;
 PUT LIST( ' PARAMETER A = ', A );
 A = 9999;
END VAL_OR_REF;

P2: PROCEDURE;
 DCL VAL_OR_REF ENTRY( BIN FIXED );
 DCL X BIN FIXED INIT 555;
 CALL VAL_OR_REF( ( X ) ); /* X IS EXPRESSION */
 PUT LIST( ' X AFTER BY VALUE PASSING:', X ); /* 555 */
 CALL VAL_OR_REF( X ); /* X IS VARIABLE REF */
 PUT LIST( ' X AFTER BY REF PASSING:', X ); /* 9999 */
END P2;
```

Example 3-30 PL/I Parameter Passing by Value and by Reference

Passing Array Parameters

When a formal parameter is an array, then each dimension of the array is simply indicated by an asterisk, while the element type must be spelled out. Notice that this implies the index to be of type integer. Nothing else is possible in PL/I anyway, but not all languages suffer from such a deliberate restriction.

If the formal parameter is a structure, then the hierarchy of the structure must be given by the level numbers, and the elementary field type must be spelled out explicitly.

```
DCL ARRAYS ENTRY( ( *, * ) BIN FIXED, ( * ) CHAR( 1 ) );
DCL STRUCT ENTRY( 1,2 FLOAT, 2,3 BIN FIXED, 3 BIN FIXED, FLOAT );
```

Example 3-31 PL/I Array and Structure Parameters

The external procedure “ARRAYS” has two parameters; a two-dimensional array of integers, and one single-dimensional array of characters. The second external procedure, named “STRUCT” also has two parameters; one structure and one floating point parameter of default precision. The structure layout is illustrated in the PL/I structure declaration in Example 3-32.

```
1 A,
 2 B FLOAT,
 2 C,
  3 D BIN FIXED,
  3 E BIN FIXED;
```

Example 3-32 Sample PL/I Structure Declaration

Most older implementations will have restrictions about the maximum length of external names. On IBM equipment this is normally 7 characters due to extra-linguistic constraints.

Modula-2 Compilation Units

Throughout this text we use the term *module* to describe any logically enclosed domain that can hide information from the outside and provide a specific function. This hidden information is defined by local objects, which are known only inside the "module," while the module's functionality is available to the outside world through an interface. This interface is a contract the module promises to keep. Given this broad definition, a module can be a full, physical compilation unit, a single subprogram, or one package that is a logical portion of a larger unit. Generally, the term module has a range of related interpretations.

Modula-2 has both kinds of modules, but we shall focus on those modules that are compilation units. If we use the other meaning of module in this section, then we shall use the qualified term *logical module.* Modula-2's "local modules," which are similar to nested packages in Ada, will not be discussed here. Modules gave Modula-2 its name. Modules are the key feature distinguishing Modula-2 from its ancestor Pascal. Modula-2 has three types of physical modules: program modules, implementation modules, and definition modules. We describe these modules together with their required modes of interaction, in this section.

Modula-2 is a "fairly strictly" typed language. It is not as rigorous as Ada, but much more selective than PL/I. Consistent with this idea, Modula-2 extends the need for type checking to modules. When two compilation units agree about a common interface, a Modula-2 compiler will have to ascertain the type compatibility of each common object. This led Modula-2 to adopt the philosophy of separate compilations, instead of independent compilation units. *Independent compilation units* are, as the name implies, units that can be compiled independently from one another. If, for example, one module interprets a common object as an "integer" object, but another module understands the same object as a "real" object, no conflict will arise in independent compilation units. On the other hand, *separate compilation units* provide the safety of type checking even across compilations. Separate compilation units agree about a common set of conventions. These conventions have to be verified by the translator. If any module violates such conventions, the compiler will flag this as an error. The essence of separate compilations is the physical distribution of one common contract over multiple, physical compilation units. This philosophy suggests library units.

In a nutshell, Modula-2 provides separate compilation, distinguishes between the definition part and the implementation part, and requires all names that are shared across compilation units to be explicitly listed on "export" and "import" lists. The defining module may export any of its names if it so chooses, while the referencing module must import any exportable name that it wishes to use. A name that has not been marked explicitly for EXPORT cannot be imported by another module. See the grammar fragment in Example 3-33.

```
compilation_unit        ::= program_module
                          | implementation_module
                          | definition_module

implementation_module ::= IMPLEMENTATION program_module

program_module          ::= MODULE module_name [ priority ] ;
                            { import } block module_name .

priority                ::= '['integer_literal']'

block                   ::= { declaration }
                            BEGIN
                             statement_list
                            END

declaration             ::= constant_definition
                          | type_definition
                          | variable_definition
                          | procedure_declaration
                          | module_declaration

procedure_declaration ::= see later section

procedure_heading       ::= see later section

module_name             ::= identifier

definition_module       ::= DEFINITION MODULE module_name ;
                            { import } [ export ] { definition }
                            END module_name .

definition              ::= constant_definition
                          | type_definition
                          | variable_definition
                          | procedure_heading ;

constant_definition     ::= CONST constant_declaration
```

```
                          { constant_declaration }
constant_declaration   ::= identifier = constant_expression ;
type_definition        ::= TYPE type_declaration { type_declaration }
type_declaration       ::= identifier = modula2_type ;
variable_definition    ::= VAR variable_declaration { variable_declaration }
variable_declaration   ::= identifier_list : modula2_type ;
import                 ::= [ FROM module_name ] IMPORT identifier_list ;
export                 ::= EXPORT [ QUALIFIED ] identifier_list ;
```

Example 3-33 Grammar Fragment for Modula-2 Compilation Units

Program Module

A Modula-2 *program module* roughly corresponds to a Pascal "PROGRAM." In Modula-2, program modules take over the role of main procedures, whether other modules are involved or not. We have encountered a sample already in the section entitled "Overview Of Modula-2" earlier in Section 3.2. The program "Gcd" is a complete program, consisting of a single compilation unit, hence it is a program module. But it also makes assumptions about another module, in this case "InOut." Therefore "Gcd" must explicitly import every name it intends to use from "InOut." The programmer of "Gcd," however, does not have to program "InOut." Nobody except the compiler implementor even knows the internals of this IO module, and nobody should be required to know. All a user should be concerned with is the functionality of individual IO routines.

Like a Pascal program, a Modula-2 program module is a block of declarations and statements. In the simplest case the list of declarations may be empty. In a more complex program the declarations include full procedure declarations, functioning as logical modules. Execution starts with the first statement of a block's list of statements, again just as in Pascal.

There are some minor differences, though. Labels don't exist, the module name must be repeated at the end, IO routines must be explicitly imported, and external file names need no mention in the header line of the module definition. Except for these improvements, Modula-2 program modules look pretty much like Pascal programs, at least at first glance.

In Example 3-34 we have used Modula-2 to demonstrate how a buffer manager can be implemented using a program module. Following sections will show the same task can be accomplished with a definition module, and an implementation module.

In this first sample much of the details of object space acquisition and of processing start and termination are omitted. Only the logic effecting insertions into and deletions from the buffer are included. We can see that every logical module has full visibility and hence total control over the main data structure. Using this knowledge could cause problems. For example, since the main data structure is implemented as a stack, something that could easily be done otherwise, programmers might be tempted to bias the logic of their algorithm with this knowledge. What looks like an advantage today could easily become a disadvantage tomorrow if the main data structure suddenly changed. It is always cleaner and safer to separate a program's logic from the particular detail how to achieve the logic.

Both the definition and implementation modules are designed to withhold such knowledge from the user of the buffer manager.

```
MODULE BufferManager;

 (* Program Module Skeleton for LIFO Buffer Management *)

 FROM InOut
  IMPORT (* Whatever is needed to perform Text IO *)

 CONST
  MinIndex     =  0;
  MaxIndex     =  200;

 TYPE
  CodeType     = ( Cars,Lollipops,AirPlanes,Candy,Computers,Others );
  ItemType     =
   RECORD
    ItemCode    : CodeType;
    Quantity    : CARDINAL;
    OrderNum    : INTEGER;
   END;
  BufferRange   = [ MinIndex ..  MaxIndex ];
  BufferType    = ARRAY BufferRange OF ItemType;

 VAR
  Buffer          : BufferType;
  NonEmpty,
  NonFull,
  MoreWork        : BOOLEAN;
  Top             : INTEGER; (* values IN [ MinIndex ..  MaxIndex ] *)

 PROCEDURE init;
  BEGIN (* init *)
   Top   := MinIndex - 1;
```

```
  MoreWork := TRUE;
  NonEmpty := FALSE;
  NonFull := TRUE;
 END init;

PROCEDURE Put( Item : ItemType );
 BEGIN (* Put *)
  NonEmpty := TRUE;
  IF Top < MaxIndex THEN
   Top := Top + 1;
   Buffer[ Top ] := Item;
  ELSE
   NonFull := FALSE;
  END;
 END Put;

PROCEDURE Get( VAR Item : ItemType );
 BEGIN (* Get *)
  NonFull := TRUE;
  IF Top >= MinIndex THEN
   Item := Buffer[ Top ];
   Top := Top - 1;
  ELSE
   NonEmpty := FALSE;
  END;
 END Get;

BEGIN
 init;
 WHILE MoreWork DO
  (* Get Items *)
  (* Put Items *)
  (* Get Items *)
 END;
END BufferManager.
```

Example 3-34 LIFO Buffer Manager in Modula-2, as Program Module

Definition Module

Definition modules work together with implementation modules. The definition module communicates only a selected amount of information about the implementation module to the outside world. For example, the outside world may know nothing about its algorithmic detail, and this deliberate hiding of detail is the whole purpose of these two modules.

Definition modules do two things: they export a list of names, and they define the nature of these names. The names may be any kind of Modula-2 objects, including variables, constants, and type identifiers. Variables defined in a module exist during the entire lifetime of the program, so they are static, although they are visible only in those modules that explicitly import them. In other modules they are not visible.

Procedures defined in a definition module consist of a header only. All parameters, including names and types, must be repeated as specified in the associated implementation module. Only the procedure's body is missing.

We should draw attention to the way Modula-2 functions are declared. Since the FUNCTION keyword does not exist, the function declaration starts out just like a procedure declaration, but after the optional parameter list there must follow a colon and a type indication. In Example 3-35 we have reimplemented the buffer manager, but this time using two modules to separate the definition and implementation tasks from one another. In the definition part of the solution that follows here, it is not visible that in fact the access policy has been changed to a first-in-first-out policy.

```
DEFINITION MODULE BufferManager;

(* Assumes IMPLEMENTATION Module *)

EXPORT QUALIFIED Get, Put, NonEmpty, NonFull;

TYPE
 CodeType  = ( Cars,Lollipops,AirPlanes,Candy,Computers,Others );
 ItemType  =
 RECORD
 ItemCode  : CodeType;
 Quantity  : CARDINAL;
 OrderNum  : INTEGER;
 END;

VAR
 NonEmpty,
 NonFull    : BOOLEAN;

PROCEDURE Put( Item : ItemType );

PROCEDURE Get( VAR Item : ItemType );

END BufferManager.
```

Example 3-35 FIFO Buffer Manager in Modula-2, Definition Module

Implementation Module

While definition modules hold only declarations of the names to be exported, their associated *implementation modules* contain a statement list in the main block. Also, each procedure or function that is announced as exportable in the definition module must be fully defined in the implementation module and must have a body. In addition to the exported subprogram names, the implementation module may have any number of further subprograms, for example, to initialize shared data. Except for the leading keyword IMPLEMENTATION, an implementation module looks just like a program module. Note that neither may contain export lists. The explicit exporting is the responsibility of definition modules.

In Example 3-36 we show the implementation module that is associated with the definition module shown earlier. We have intentionally replaced the LIFO policy by a FIFO policy. This can be observed only by studying the implementation, not by reading the definition module.

```
IMPLEMENTATION MODULE BufferManager;

(* Program Module Skeleton for FIFO Buffer Management *)

CONST
 MinIndex     =  0;
 MaxIndex     =  200;

TYPE
 CodeType     = ( Cars,Lollipops,AirPlanes,Candy,Computers,Others );
 ItemType     =
 RECORD
  ItemCode    : CodeType;
  Quantity    : CARDINAL;
  OrderNum    : INTEGER;
 END;
 BufferRange = [ MinIndex ..  MaxIndex - 1 ];
 BufferType  = ARRAY BufferRange OF ItemType;

VAR
 Buffer       : BufferType;
 NonEmpty,
 NonFull,
 MoreWork     : BOOLEAN;
 Count,       (* Number of elements in FIFO Q *)
 Head,        (* head of Q, newest element *)
 Tail         (* Tail of Q, oldest element *)
              : INTEGER;

```

```
PROCEDURE init;
 BEGIN (* init *)
  Head := MinIndex - 1;
  Tail := MinIndex;
  Count := 0;
  MoreWork := TRUE;
  NonEmpty := FALSE;
  NonFull := TRUE;
 END init;

PROCEDURE Put( Item : ItemType );
 BEGIN (* Put *)
  NonEmpty := TRUE;
  IF Count < MaxIndex THEN
   Count := Count + 1;
   Head := ( Head + 1 ) MOD  MaxIndex;
   Buffer[ Head ] := Item;
  ELSE
   NonFull := FALSE;
  END;
 END Put;

PROCEDURE Get( VAR Item : ItemType );
 BEGIN (* Get *)
  NonFull := TRUE;
  IF Count > 0 THEN
   Count := Count - 1;
   Item := Buffer[ Tail ];
   Tail := ( Tail + 1 ) MOD MaxIndex;
  ELSE
   NonEmpty := FALSE;
  END;
 END Get;

BEGIN
 init;
 WHILE MoreWork DO
  (* Get Items *)
  (* Put Items *)
  (* Get Items *)
 END;
END BufferManager.
```

Example 3-36 FIFO Buffer Manager in Modula-2, as Implementation Module

3.4 Scopes and Blocks

Scopes and blocks are closely related with one another. Every block forms also a new scope, but not every scope is a block. The term *scope* addresses compilation time considerations, while *block* is of interest also at execution time. This section explains both terms, and provides samples to further an in-depth understanding.

Scopes

Scope is a domain of source text over which a name is uniquely defined. The widest scope attribute is external, close to the Fortran attribute "common." An external name is not only known in the defining scope, but available systemwide.

The next smallest scope attribute is *global,* a term, having two different though related meanings. First of all, global means "defined in the outermost block." For example, the CONST, TYPE, VAR, PROCEDURE, and FUNCTION declarations in Pascal programs on the PROGRAM level have the global scope attribute. This means all names defined on this level may be referenced or used anywhere in the program as long as it is after the definition.

Notice the distinction between scope and storage attributes: all variables with scope attribute global implicitly have the storage attribute static, since their lifetime is that of the main procedure. Other global names such as TYPE or FUNCTION names have no storage attribute whatsoever, which gives evidence that these two concepts are distinct. The Ada program Example 3-37 shows the declaration of names, and the scope over which these names are valid.

```
-- some Ada scopes
PROCEDURE outside IS          -- outside is EXTERNAL name
 max  : CONSTANT integer := 32767; -- max is GLOBAL
 min  : CONSTANT integer := - max; -- min is GLOBAL
 TYPE int_type IS RANGE mi ..  max; -- int_type is GLOBAL
 a, b : int_type;             -- a, b are GLOBAL, STATIC

 PROCEDURE assign IS          -- assign is GLOBAL name
  x, y, z : int_type;         -- x, y, z LOCAL, AUTOMATIC
  BEGIN -- assign
   x := a;
   y := b;
   -- other executable statements
 END assign;

BEGIN -- outside
 a := 16;
 b := a ** 2;
 assign;
 -- other executable statements
END outside;
```

Example 3-37 Ada Scopes

The other, related meaning of global (or nonlocal, for short) is that of a name that may be referenced in a scope without having been declared there. Thus the same local name in one scope can be global in another, nested scope. This arises only in block structured languages such as Ada, Pascal, Modula-2, or PL/I that allow blocks and hence scopes to be embedded in one another. See also the Pascal scopes in Example 3-38. Example 3-38 also introduces the *local* scope attribute. Local names and their associated automatic storage live only as long as the defining block is active. Upon termination of that block, all local names and their storage disappear. Space acquisition and reclamation is under system control, hence the storage attribute "automatic."

```
1  1  0  0   PROGRAM level0( output ); { external }
2  2  0  0    CONST
                max    = 32767;          { max global }
3  4  0  0      min    = - max;          { min global }
4  5  0  0    TYPE
                inttype = min ..  max;   { global }
5  7  0  0    VAR
                g      : inttype;        { g global }

6  10 0  0      PROCEDURE dothis;        { dothis global }
7  11 1  0       VAR
                   i, j  : inttype;      { i,j automatic }
```

```
 8  14  1  0     PROCEDURE init;             { local to "do_this" }
 9  15  2  0      VAR
                   x, y   : inttype;         { x, y automatic }
10  17  2  0      BEGIN { init }
10  18  2  1       x := i;                   { i global to init }
11  19  2  1       { statements }
                  END { init };

12  22  1  0      BEGIN { dothis }
12  23  1  1       i := g;
13  24  1  1       init;
14  25  1  1       { executable statements }
                 END { dothis };

15  28  0  0    BEGIN { level0 }
15  29  0  1     g := min;
16  30  0  1     dothis;
17  31  0  1      { executable statements }
                END { level0 }.
```

Example 3-38 Pascal Scopes

Things are not always as simple and clear as the preceding model seems to suggest. There are two major exceptions to the simple model. Some languages allow the explicit storage attribute *static,* even for names with the scope attribute local. These names will be inaccessible whenever the defining block is inactive, but the storage associated with the vanished locals continues to exist, even though nobody can use it for a while. If that block becomes active again at some later time, the same storage is still reserved for the reincarnated local name, thus also making the previous, last value available again. The NCR internal systems language L, PL/I, and the language C allow this meaningful explicit storage attribute.

The second exception to the simplified model of Example 3-38 is the storage class (or attribute) *controlled,* also named *heap space* in Modula-2, Pascal, and Ada. Heap space can be requested at any time during program execution and accessed via pointer variables. As long as the pointers are available, the space pointed at is also available, even if the actual acquisition of space took place in a long vanished local block. It is crucial to preserve the value of the pointer to that heap space. Should this pointer become unavailable, so will the addressed space, even if the data inside are still perfectly valid. So the program designer must carefully synchronize the freeing of heap space with the disappearance of associated pointer variables. Naturally it would be much more desirable to have the run time system automatically release this space.

Blocks

Blocks are integral syntactic program units that acquire and release storage during execution. Every block also introduces a new scope. In the languages treated here there are two kinds of blocks; *declare blocks* and *subprogram blocks.* Fortran only uses the latter, which includes functions and the main procedure.

In Ada, the For Statement creates a third kind of very special and restricted block. The control variable or "loop parameter" of a For Statement is created on the fly, and its scope is restricted to the text of that For Statement. This automatic creation of a local control variable that cannot be altered adds safety, but it can make programming marginally more awkward. This is particularly the case when the last value of the control variable must be preserved until after the loop. The same concept is already known from Algol-W and is also used in Algol-68. The Ada program Example 3-39 demonstrates that the value of the For Statement loop parameter is inaccessible outside the For Statement.

```
PROCEDURE for_demo IS
  i, j : integer := 0;
 BEGIN -- for_demo
  i := 88;
  FOR i IN 1 ..  100 LOOP
   -- other executable statements
   j := i * i; -- assign 10000 in last iteration
  END LOOP;
  IF i /= 88 THEN
   put_line( " THIS IS A WRONG COMPILER" );
  ELSIF j /= 10000 THEN
   put_line( " THIS IS A WRONG COMPILER" );
  ELSE
   put_line( " loop parameter handled o.k." );
  END IF;
 END for_demo;
```

Example 3-39 Ada for Statement

Subprogram blocks must have a name and are called by referencing that name. They may have parameters, be recursive, and, upon termination, return to the position following the call, except in the case of Fortran's multiple RETURN Statements. Declare blocks, on the other hand, need not have a name. They cannot be called, can have no parameters, and cannot be recursive. And after termination the execution continues with the statement immediately following the declare block, unless some other instruction such as a GOTO explicitly changes the regular flow of control. The Ada program fragment Example 3-40 shows a Declare Block.

```
-- Ada declare block
i := 3;
WHILE i < 7 LOOP
 j := i ** 2; -- other executable statements
 ada_declare_block:
 DECLARE
  TYPE letter_type IS NEW character RANGE 'A' ..  'Z';
  letter : letter_type;
 BEGIN -- ada_declare_block
  letter := letter_type'first;
  -- other executable statements
 END ada_declare_block;
 k := j;
END LOOP;
```

Example 3-40 Ada Declare Block

The declare block in Example 3-40 works just like any other statement. Each time control reaches the top of that block, however, new storage is allocated for the local, automatic variables. When control reaches the End Statement, the allocated space is automatically freed. Pascal has no such declare blocks. The Pascal Compound Statement, even though similar in appearance to PL/I's Begin Statement, allows no local declarations. The PL/I BEGIN block does allow these, and they may in fact be arbitrarily interspersed with the statements inside the BEGIN END brackets.

The PL/I liberty of allowing the mix of declarations and statements opens the door to another touchy problem. Can a name be used before it is defined? "Before" here refers to textual order, not to execution time. The PL/I and Modula-2 answer to this question is "yes"; the other languages say "no." A PL/I begin block as shown in Example 3-41 is legal.

```
  /* PL/I BEGIN BLOCK */
1 PLI:
2  BEGIN
3   X = MAX_VAL + 12;
4   DCL X BIN FIXED INIT 77;
5   IF X = LIMIT THEN
6   /* OTHER EXECUTABLE STATEMENT */
7 END PLI;
```

Example 3-41 Declarations Intermixed with Statements in PL/I Begin Block

The local variable "x" is already used on line 3, though it is not declared until line 4. Some PL/I aficionados imagine this to be of great value, but its usefulness has yet to be demonstrated. This liberty is a forward reference.

Pascal is quite rigorous in its rules about the order of block components. LABEL declarations must come first. CONST declarations must come before the TYPE declarations, and so on. Due to this restriction alone, Pascal makes programs like Example 3-41 impossible. But Ada allows a higher degree of freedom in ordering declarations. As long as no bodies are involved, declarations may come in any order. However, these are strictly separated from the statements, which come after the BEGIN keyword. The Ada programmer must take care that situations like the one above in the PL/I example do not occur. Otherwise the compiler will complain bitterly. The Example 3-42 of Ada is wrong: constant "last_dec" is referenced before the declaration.

```
1 wrong_ada_program_segment: -- an erroneous Ada DECLARE block
2  DECLARE
3   first_dec : CONSTANT character := '0';
4   TYPE digit_type IS NEW character RANGE first_dec ..  last_dec;
5   last_dec  : CONSTANT character := '9';
6   digit    : digit_type := first_dec;
7   BEGIN
8   -- executable statements
9  END wrong_ada_program_segment;
```

Example 3-42 Illegal Reference Before Declaration in Ada

The Ada compiler will emit an error message for line 4 in Example 3-42, since "last_dec" is undefined when first referenced. It is not precise to say the name "last_dec" is accessible in the whole declare block named "wrong_ada_program_segment". "Last_dec" is known only in that portion of the block that comes textually after the declaration.

3.5 Summary

In this chapter we have looked at high level, procedural languages from different angles. We have listed the lexical rules, which present the languages at a low level of detail. Then we discussed compilation units, thus presenting the languages at a high level. In the next chapter we shall write complete though simple programs and apply our knowledge acquired so far.

By now we should be able to distinguish between separate and independent compilation, and know the difference between scope and storage attributes. We must remember that independent compilation units make no assumptions about each other during the compilation process. From this follows that the compiler needs to generate only a minimum amount of information in addition to the emitted object code. Also we should be aware that separate compilation units typically enhance safer programming. We are now familiar with key terms such as local, global, automatic, and static.

3.6 Exercises

1. How can we identify the main procedure in a sequence of Fortran compilation units, all physically on one single file?
2. How is the main procedure of a PL/I program identified?
3. Given two mutually recursive procedures, A and B. Write a correct program skeleton in Ada that defines procedures A and B and that calls A and B in either body. Do the same for Pascal and PL/I.
4. How can a recursive algorithm be solved programmatically using the language Fortran?
5. The symbol <> is a complete lexical token in some of the languages treated here. List the languages and the meanings of the <> symbol.
6. Given a PL/I source program with the lexical token END followed by the = symbol, with no explicit declaration of END anywhere in the correct program. How can a compiler or reader know whether the symbol END is a keyword or a user-defined identifier?
7. How many characters long is the shortest possible Ada string literal? Count every character involved. How many characters does the shortest possible Ada character literal have? Write down the Ada character literal denoting the single quote.
8. How many functionally distinct relational operators are defined in PL/I? How many nonredundant ways of writing these are there in the full language PL/I? Write all of them down. Consecutive use of the negation operator as in $\neg\ \neg=$ is considered a redundancy.
9. Which Ada syntax construct corresponds directly to the Pascal FORWARD announcement for procedures and functions?
10. Is it legal in Ada to assign a character literal to a variable of type "array of character" with length one?
11. What determines whether an actual parameter is passed by reference or by value in PL/I?

12. A Fortran function without explicit type has the name INCR. What is the type of the returned value?

13. Inspect the grammar for Ada Declare and PL/I Begin Statements. Except for the different syntax, is there an essential difference between the two?

14. Inspect the syntax for Pascal Begin and PL/I Begin Statements. Despite both having a similar syntax there is one important construct allowed in PL/I that is not permitted in Pascal. What is it?

15. What is the storage attribute for a variable declared in a nested Pascal procedure?

16. What is the storage attribute for a type mark declared in a nested Ada procedure? (Careful)

17. Ada only allows a string literal to span one source line. When we need to initialize an array of characters in an Ada program with a character string literal that is several lines long, how can we achieve this directly in the source, without having to write a loop that reads strings from a file?

18. How many kinds of scopes are defined in Fortran? Give all of them meaningful names.

19. Discuss the advantages and disadvantages of Fortran's syntax rule that allows a line to be continued at most 19 times. Extend this discussion to the more general case where a language requires some construct an "odd" number of times. With odd we mean here any number different from zero, one, or infinity.

20. Is global a scope or a storage attribute?

21. Is automatic a scope or a storage attribute?

4

Becoming Familiar Via Sample Programs

The readability of programs is immeasurably more important than their writeability.

C. A. R. Hoare
Hints on Programming Language Design

The best way to develop familiarity with a programming language and its translator is by writing programs. While the previous chapter covered broad subjects like compilation units and scopes, the current chapter defines various small programming projects that the reader is encouraged to solve. For reference and for completeness, a sample solution in each of the treated languages is included. After the sample solutions we explain the key language constructs contained in each, so that the readers gradually acquire sufficient working knowledge to write programs of their own.

In most cases the sample solutions are compiler listings to minimize the chances for syntax errors and to have the convenience of line number references.

Primitive Prime Number Test

Problem Definition

We write a program that reads integer numbers and tests them for primality as long as the numbers are greater than zero. For inputs of zero or less the program should terminate. At the start of execution we print a message that explains the termination condition. Each time a test number has been analyzed, we output whether the analyzed number is prime or not. The algorithm used should be very primitive in order to minimize the physical program size and complexity.

Sample Solution Shown

Algorithms for prime number generation are growing in importance for data encryption algorithms. It is not our goal in this text to demonstrate one of these better schemes, useful for the tests of very large numbers. We only explain simple, obvious solutions for the sake of "programmability." Our primary goal at this time is to familiarize the reader with various programming languages, not with efficient prime number generators. First we list a solution in Ada. The same approach is carried through for Fortran, Pascal, PL/I, and Modula-2.

In our sample solutions we let variable "test" be successively divided by a candidate number "cand," the "max" value of which is test/2. If any of the divisions yield a remainder of zero, then "test" is known to be nonprime. Otherwise "test" is prime. An obvious, better bound for "max" is the square root of "test," but in this first primitive solution we are not yet concerned with minimization of run time.

Another Solution Proposal, Sieve of Eratosthenes

For later reference in one of the exercises we outline a prime number computation algorithm known as the Sieve of Eratosthenes. Given the infinite array of all positive integers in ascending order, the procedure explains how to eliminate the nonprimes. Starting with 2, we go sequentially through the array and eliminate all multiples of 2, since by definition these cannot be primes. Then we search for the next highest number that is still in the array; we find 3. Again all multiples of 3 are eliminated for the same reason. Note that the 2 and the 3 stay.

The next number included in the array is not the 4, since it was eliminated in a previous step. The next number is 5. Again all multiples are eliminated, but the 5 itself remains. This process continues until only primes are left. We start with a solution in Ada.

```
 1                     |-- Perform simple prime number test. TEST is
 2                     |-- divided by candidates. If remainder is 0, TEST
 3                     |-- can't be prime. Otherwise check all the way to MAX.
 4                     |-- MAX := TEST / 2. Better MAX values are possible.
 5                     | WITH text_io; USE text_io;
 6                     | PROCEDURE prime_test IS
 7           1         | TYPE my_int IS RANGE -32767 .. +32767;
 8           1         | test,           --number to be tested
 9        4  1         | cand,           --divide test by 3, 5, ...
10        4  1         | max             --max value of cand
11        4  1         |                 : my_int;
12        7  1         | is_prime        : boolean;
13        8  1         |
14        8  1         | PROCEDURE get_number IS
15           2         | BEGIN--get_number
16           2         |  put_line( " next test number" );
17     3     2  1      |  get( test );
18     7     2  1      |  new_line;
19     8     2  1      | END get_number;
20     8     1         |
21     8     1         | PROCEDURE start IS
22     9     2         | BEGIN--start
23     9     2         |  put_line( " End when test <= 0" );
24    12     2  1      |  get_number;
25    16     2  1      | END start;
26    16     1         |
27    16     1         | BEGIN--prime_test
28    17     1         |  start;
29    20     1  1      | WHILE test > 0 LOOP
30    24     1  1      |  is_prime := test REM 2 /= 0 OR ELSE test < 4;
31    36     1  2      |  max := test / 2;
32    43     1  2      |  cand := 3;
33    48     1  2      |  WHILE is_prime  AND  cand <= max LOOP
34    54     1  2      |   is_prime := test REM cand /= 0;
35    61     1  3      |   --yields false if EVEN division
36    61     1  3      |   cand := cand + 2;
37    68     1  3      |  END LOOP;
38    69     1  2      |  IF is_prime THEN
39    71     1  2      |   put_line( " is prime" );
40    74     1  3      |  ELSE
41    74     1  2      |   put_line( " NOT A PRIME" );
42    78     1  3      |  END IF;
```

```
43    78       1  2 |    get_number;
44    81       1  2 |  END LOOP;
45    82       1  1 | END prime_test;
```

Example 4-1 Primitive Prime Number Test in Ada

Annotation

In this section we explain very briefly the Ada context clause introduced by WITH, the compilation unit, the type and object declarations, and various statements. We also comment about the boolean type expressions used.

The Context Clause

The With Clause on line 5 in Example 4-1 tells the Ada compiler to include the predefined package "text_io." This package defines text IO library routines such as "text_io.put" or "text_io.put_line." In order to avoid the rewriting of "text_io," the Use Clause is also given on line 5, to allow an abbreviated reference of the names available in the package "text_io." That way, any reference to "put_line" after line 5 is complete and stands for the longer form "text_io.put_line."

Line 6 introduces an Ada compilation unit, in this case a nonnested procedure named "prime_test"; nonnested packages form another kind of compilation unit. Declarations local to "prime_test" are enclosed between the procedure name specification and the associated keyword BEGIN on line 27, while the BEGIN and its related END on line 45 embrace the statement list of procedure "prime_test."

On line 7 we see the declaration of Type Identifier "my_int." Such Type Identifiers are called *type marks* in Ada terminology. My_int is the type mark for a constrained integer range from -32767 to 32767. The following four lines, 8 through 11, declare the variables "test," "cand," and "max," all of type "my_int." Observe that variable declarations may define a list of names, separated from one another by a comma, while type declarations can only define one single type mark.

Ada uses no special keyword for a variable declaration, in Ada terminology called object declaration. As long as no other conflicts such as forward references arise, multiple object and type declarations are allowed in any order. Line 12 declares variable "is_prime," using the predefined type mark "boolean" from package "standard."

The statement body of "prime_test" contains two While Statements, one If Statement, and various procedure calls and assignments. The most interesting Assignment Statement is the one on line 30, which sets "is_prime" to true, if the variable "test" is odd or less than four. But note that the or condition is written as OR ELSE. That way the second condition is evaluated only if the first one yields false. Consequently, no superfluous tests are performed.

It is interesting to contrast the way Ada and Pascal handle this same statement. In Ada the priority of relational test operators is higher than that of the OR operator. Pascal, however, does not have such a fine granularity of operator levels and forces the programmer to add parentheses in compound conditions. See the Pascal sample further in Example 4-3. For an explanation of the REM operator on lines 30 and 34 see Section 6.5.

This concludes our informal introduction to Ada syntax. The next program is a listing of the Fortran solution to the same problem. The line numbers have been added for reference; they are not part of the language.

```
C-----  Fortran-77 Prime Number tester
        PROGRAM PRMTST
         INTEGER TEST, CAND, MAX
         LOGICAL PRIME
C-----   PRINT THE RULES
         CALL START( TEST )
 30      IF ( TEST .GT. 0 ) THEN
          PRIME = ( MOD( TEST, 2 ) .NE. 0 ) .OR. ( TEST .LT. 4 )
          MAX = TEST / 2
          CAND = 3
 40       IF ( PRIME .AND. ( CAND .LE. MAX ) ) THEN
           PRIME = MOD( TEST, CAND ) .NE. 0
           CAND = CAND + 2
           GOTO 40
          END IF
          IF ( PRIME ) THEN
           WRITE( 6, * ) " IS PRIME"
          ELSE
           WRITE( 6, * ) " NOT A PRIME"
          END IF
          CALL GETNUM( TEST )
          GOTO 30
         END IF
        END

        SUBROUTINE GETNUM( TEST )
         INTEGER TEST
 10      FORMAT( I10 )
         WRITE ( 6, * ) " ENTER NEXT TEST NUMBER"
         READ( 5, 10 ) TEST
        END

       SUBROUTINE START( TEST )
```

```
34            INTEGER TEST
35            WRITE( 6, * ) " PROGRAM TERMINATES WHEN TEST <= 0"
36            CALL GETNUM( TEST )
37           END
```

Example 4-2 Primitive Prime Number Test in Fortran

Annotation

This section explains some of Fortran's lexical rules, the handmade While Loop structure, and the If and Format Statements. The Fortran solution has some features that will immediately strike the reader's attention. First, identifiers are short and cryptic. Picking the program name "PRMTST" is not by choice alone. The language restricts a name to at most six characters. Also the convenient underline character is not legal even for the short names.

Second, the numeric labels on the left-hand column of the listing are striking. Fortran labels must be numeric; a more mnemonic form is not provided. Third, a sequential scan of the listing does not reveal the program's intent as easily as in the other sample solutions. This is partly caused by the short names, the many labels, and the numerous Gotos. The above Fortran-77 solution reads easier than an equivalent implementation in Fortran-66, which has no Block If Statements. Also note the cumbersome lexical spelling of relational operators. Even though we are accustomed to operators like > for "greater than" and < for "less than," Fortran forces us to spell these as .GT. and .LT..

The numerous labels are necessary, since so many structured statements, conveniently available in more modern languages, must be custom designed by the programmer. Label 30 and the statement GOTO 30 delineate the outer WHILE loop, and label 40 with its associated GOTO 40 form the inner WHILE. At least Fortran-77 has a convenient form of If Statement, allowing the THEN and closing END IF keywords. This way the If Statement is as simple and general as in Ada, and less ambiguous than in Pascal and PL/I.

Striking is the Format Statement on line 28 with its cryptic argument. Format Statements give precise instructions about the physical layout of input and output data. The slash we have seen in previous programs causes a carriage return and line feed for text output files; upon input the slash skips the remainder of the current text line and starts with the following line.

The argument I10 in the Format Statement on line 28 specifies that an integer number of at most 10 decimal positions will be read or written. Both Fortran and PL/I allow the format to be totally separated from the referencing IO Statement. This has the advantage that the same Format Statement, which must be labeled for reference, can be used in numerous IO Statements. It has the disadvantage that the effort for analysis and understanding increases when the format is remote from the referring IO Statement. Again, here we find the old tradeoff between readability and number of key strokes.

"PRMTST" has been modularized into three logical modules, following the Ada pattern. The Fortran solution differs from Ada in the fact that all logical modules are also physical modules or compilation units. This renders "START" and "GETNUM" external names, just as the program name "PRMTST" is.

Note that MOD is an intrinsic function in Fortran, not an operator as in Ada, Modula-2, and Pascal. Next we show the same solution implemented in Pascal.

```
 1    1  0  0   { Primitive prime number test. TEST is }
                { divided by cand. If remainder is 0, TEST }
                { can't be prime. Otherwise check up to MAX, }
                { MAX := TEST DIV 2. Better bounds possible }
               PROGRAM primetest( input, output );
 2    7  0  0   TYPE
                 myint = -32767 .. +32767;
 3    9  0  0   VAR
                 test, max, cand : myint;
 4   11  0  0     isprime        : boolean;

 5   13  0  0    PROCEDURE getnumber;
 6   14  1  0     BEGIN { getnumber }
 6   15  1  1      writeln( output, ' Next test number' );
 7   16  1  1      readln( input, test );
 8   17  1  1     END; { getnumber }

 9   19  0  0     PROCEDURE start;
10   20  1  0     BEGIN { start }
10   21  1  1      writeln( output, ' End when test <= 0' );
11   22  1  1      getnumber;
12   23  1  1     END; { start }

13   25  0  0     BEGIN { primetest }
13   26  0  1      start;
14   27  0  1      WHILE test > 0 DO
15   28  0  1       BEGIN
15   29  0  2        isprime := ( test MOD 2 <> 0 ) OR ( test < 4 );
16   30  0  2        max := test DIV 2;
17   31  0  2        cand := 3;
18   32  0  2        WHILE ( isprime ) AND ( cand <= max ) DO
19   33  0  2         BEGIN
19   34  0  3          isprime := test MOD cand <> 0;
20   35  0  3          { yields false if EVEN division }
                       cand := cand + 2;
21   37  0  3         END;
```

```
23    38  0  2      {END WHILE}
                    IF isprime THEN
24    40  0  2       writeln( output, ' is prime' )
                    ELSE
25    42  0  2       writeln( output, ' NOT A PRIME' );
26    43  0  2      {END IF}
                    getnumber;
27    45  0  2     END;
29    46  0  1    {END WHILE}
                 END. { primetest }
```

Example 4-3 Primitive Prime Number Test in Pascal

Annotation

This section explains the Pascal TYPE and VAR declarations, the "semicolon-as-separator" rule, forced closure, some arithmetic operators, and complex boolean expressions.

After the program header on line 6 the Pascal "primetest" solution starts out with a TYPE and VAR declaration in that order. This is not by coincidence: Pascal enforces that order. All type declarations are grouped together and introduced by the reserved keyword TYPE. Similarly, all variable declarations are grouped and introduced by the VAR keyword. In Pascal type declarations the special symbol '=' equates the defined type identifier on the one side with the type definition on the other. Ada uses the keyword IS for that purpose.

Note the subtle but important difference in lexical rules for string literals in Ada and Pascal. Pascal requires a string and char literal to be embedded in a pair of single quotes, as shown on lines 15 and 21. Ada requires double quotes for string literals and single quote pairs for character type literals.

Programmers seem sometimes willing to fight violent, religious wars about the next issue: should the semicolon be used as a separator or as a terminator? We attempt to clarify this controversy by means of a Pascal If Statement, starting on line 39. At the end of the Then Clause on line 40 the Write Statement may not be followed by a semicolon, since an Else Clause follows. If we would write a semicolon, then the If Statement would be complete and no Else Clause could follow. But we need the If Statement complete, with an Else Clause. As long as such a complete If Statement has been designed in from the beginning of a program's development, no trouble lurks behind the ELSE. But if an Else Clause is added on to a syntactically correct program during the maintenance phase, the compiler's legitimate error message near the ELSE keyword usually surprises the novice programmer. It takes a lot of experience, until one automatically deletes the previously required semicolon. Ada and PL/I both avoid this problem by requiring that a semicolon terminate each statement.

"Primetest" is a very primitive program, hence the nesting structure of statements is simple as well. In more complex problems the nesting level increases. In such situations Pascal's and PL/I's lack of forced closure becomes a nuisance, since numerous nested Compound Statements must be written using BEGIN END. See the simple structure on line pairs 33, 37 and 28, 45 in Pascal program "primetest." The "forced closure," a mandatory ending keyword at the end of a structured statement, eliminates the need for this artificial syntax trick. What is the nature of the trick? Let us demonstrate this with the Pascal While Statement. After the WHILE header, following the keyword DO, Pascal requires exactly one statement. If, on the other hand, we want two or more statements to be dependent on the same WHILE condition, we must group them into a BEGIN END block, which syntactically forms one single Compound Statement.

Balanced parentheses, as used in the two relations on line 29, are necessary in Pascal, when the OR or AND operator combines these relations to a single condition. The priority of relational test operators is the lowest of all in Pascal expressions. Hence without parentheses on line 29 the compiler would attempt to logically OR the literal 0 with the variable "test" and, of course, complain bitterly, since neither the 0 nor "test" are boolean type operands as required. Parentheses, on the other hand, direct the compiler to evaluate the embedded subexpressions first, as intended by the programmer.

The harmless-looking MOD operator on lines 29 and 34 is not as simple as it appears. For arguments with different signs, some Pascal compilers generate code to yield the remainder; others compute the true Modulo Function. The language standard specifies clearly that MOD is only defined for the right operand being positive. As long as both arguments have the positive sign, there is no problem. For opposite signs, however, many compilers work incorrectly. See Table 6-2 with REM and MOD operator examples in Chapter 6.

This concludes our brief familiarization with Pascal. In the next section we show the PL/I solution.

```
0        PRIME: PROC OPTIONS(MAIN);
1         DCL ( TEST, CAND, MAX ) BIN FIXED;
1         DCL IS_PRIME BIT(1);

1         GETNUM: PROC;
2          PUT SKIP LIST( ' ENTER NEXT TEST NUMBER:' );
2          GET LIST( TEST );
2         END GETNUM;

1         START: PROC;
2          PUT SKIP LIST( ' PROGRAM ENDS, WHEN TEST <= 0' );
2          CALL GETNUM;
2         END START;
```

```
12    1          CALL START;
13    1          DO WHILE ( TEST > 0 );
14    1    1       IS_PRIME = MOD( TEST, 2 ) ^= 0 ! TEST < 4;
15    1    1       MAX = TEST / 2;
16    1    1       CAND = 3;
17    1    1       DO WHILE ( IS_PRIME & CAND <= MAX );
18    1    2         IS_PRIME = MOD( TEST, CAND ) ^= 0;
19    1    2         CAND = CAND + 2;
20    1    2       END;
21    1    1       IF IS_PRIME THEN
22    1    1         PUT SKIP LIST( ' IS PRIME' );
                   ELSE
23    1    1         PUT SKIP LIST( ' NOT A PRIME' );
                   /*END IF*/
24    1    1       CALL GETNUM;
25    1    1     END; /*DO*/
26    1        END PRIME;
```

Example 4-4 Primitive Prime Number Test in PL/I

Annotation

The PL/I compiler used for the examples here is hosted on a CDC system, whose native character set is neither Ascii nor Ebcdic. As a consequence, neither the special PL/I character ¬ for "negation" nor the special PL/I character | for "logical or" are available. The CDC replacement for negation is the ^ character, and the substitute for logical or is the ! mark. Here we see an instance of the existing incompatibility of character sets; all these are standard character sets, but all different standards.

Since PL/I makes no formal distinction between statements and declarations, there is no need for a BEGIN keyword to separate the scope brackets PROC and END into two disjoint sections, one for declarations only and the other for statements only. Declarations may be intermixed with statements, but we strongly discourage this practice.

PL/I uses the equals sign as assignment operator, which is also used as the equality test operator. In expressions of type boolean, called BIT(1) in PL/I terminology, this can cause confusion. For example, the PL/I statement

```
a = b = 144;
```

is not a multiple assignment as known from Algol; it is a single Assignment Statement. In Algol x:=y:=555; would cause both "x" and "y" to receive the value 555. In PL/I, on the other hand, "b" is tested for equality with 144. If equal, "a" is set to '1'B or logical true, otherwise to '0'B or logical false. The multiple Assignment Statement in PL/I is expressed as

```
a, b = 144;
```

As already seen in Ada, PL/I requires a semicolon as statement terminator. Contrary to Ada, procedure calls are identified by the keyword CALL, which precedes the procedure name; see lines 10, 12, and 24 above.

The sample program "PRIME" uses so-called list-directed IO, which will be explained in more detail in Chapter 15. Here it is sufficient to know that PL/I's list-directed IO separates a page of text into six logical columns. Each output statement places the next string into the next available logical column, and if six strings have been written on a line, an implicit newline is emitted.

Example 4-5 shows our last variation on prime number generators implemented in Modula-2. The line numbers in the left column are merely added for reference.

```
1        MODULE PrimeTest;
2         FROM InOut
3          IMPORT WriteLn, WriteString, ReadCard;
4         TYPE
5          myint = [ -32767 .. +32767 ];
6         VAR
7          test, max, cand : myint;
8          isprime         : BOOLEAN;
9
10       PROCEDURE getnumber;
11        BEGIN (* getnumber *)
12         WriteString( ' Next test number' );
13         ReadCard( test );
14        END getnumber;
15
16       PROCEDURE start;
17        BEGIN (* start *)
18         WriteString( ' End when test <= 0' );
19         WriteLn;
20         getnumber;
21        END start;
22
23       BEGIN (* PrimeTest *)
24        start;
25        WHILE test > 0 DO
26         isprime := ( test MOD 2 <> 0 ) OR ( test < 4 );
27         max := test DIV 2;
28         cand := 3;
29         WHILE ( isprime ) AND ( cand <= max ) DO
30          isprime := test MOD cand <> 0;
31          (* yields false if EVEN division *)
32          cand := cand + 2;
```

```
33        END;
34        IF isprime THEN
35         WriteString( ' is prime' );
36        ELSE
37         WriteString( " Not a Prime" );
38        END;
39        WriteLn;
40        getnumber;
41       END;
42      END PrimeTest.
```

Example 4-5 Primitive Prime Number Test in Modula-2

Annotation

Modula-2 programs that consist of a single program module have a great similarity with Pascal programs. For this reason we relate our observations about Modula-2 syntax to Pascal's syntax rules. We know a good part of these already.

First, we observe that the routines for IO are explicitly imported. *Importing* is the Modula-2 term for the process of making names visible that are defined in other modules. These modules are either programmer-defined or supplied by the compiler. In this case the Modula-2 compiler supplies a predefined module named "InOut," from which sample program "PrimeTest" imports the predefined IO procedures "WriteLn," "WriteString," and "ReadCard." "WriteLn" is equivalent to Pascal's "writeln" without arguments, and "ReadCard" reads a cardinal type argument from standard input as a string of digits. Assembly language programmers will recognize the well-known data type "unsigned" in the Modula-2 type "CARDINAL." All IO routines with the "Card" postfix interpret their data as being unsigned integers.

We also observe the TYPE keyword on line 4, introducing a type declaration followed by VAR declarations. This order looks familiar because we know it from Pascal. Different from Pascal, and not shown in Example 4-5, Modula-2 allows any number of CONST, TYPE, and VAR declarations in the declarative portion of a block.

All structured Modula-2 statements are closed by the END keyword. We see While- and If Statements. The required ender, also-called "forced closure," eliminates the need for nested BEGIN END Statements. This renders the source a bit more readable than the equivalent Pascal source, and reduces the number of source lines marginally.

The last line closes the module. We see here that the module name "PrimeTest," introduced on the first line, is repeated in the closing End Statement. This is necessary in Modula-2. Pascal, in contrast, does not allow this nice documentation aid, while Ada leaves it optional. It is a recommended programming practice, and Modula-2 goes so far as demanding this valuable convention.

4.2 Towers of Hanoi (Co Loa)

The second programming problem, the well-known Towers of Hanoi puzzle, is quite an amusing game, and will help readers to think recursively and will serve as an introduction to several new syntax constructs in each language. Recursion and all syntax rules will be discussed in more detail in later chapters. The saga and the puzzle actually originated in the small Vietnamese town Co Loa, but it has become known by the catchy name of the more familiar, modern town, Hanoi.

Our task is to write a program that solves the fascinating puzzle. Here are the rules of the game:

A tower is composed of n individual disks, one residing on top of another. All disks are of different sizes, stacked so that the largest disk is in the bottommost position and the smallest disk is on top. Initially, the tower is sorted in strictly descending order, going from the bottom to the top. Throughout the game, a larger disk may never sit on a smaller one. Figure 4-1 shows the start configuration.

```
                        |             |             |
disk 1                 -|-            |             |
disk 2                --|--           |             |
disk 3               ---|---          |             |
disk 4              ----|----         |             |
...                     .             .             .
disk n            ------|------       |             |
                        +             +             +
                      Start         Final         Buffer
```

Figure 4-1 Start Position of "Towers of Hanoi"

The problem is to move the whole tower, one disk at a time, to a "final" location. However, there are only three positions in which a disk may be at any time during the game: in the "start" position, in one "buffer" position, or in the "final" new position. We can see that it would not be an exciting game if the whole tower could be moved in one single step. So, to add a little thrill, we must observe the rule of moving only one disk at a time. Also, if the game would allow a large number of positions for placing disks, it would be easy to solve the puzzle. All we would need to do is to disassemble the tower and place the disks individually onto the numerous places. A reassembly onto the final destination then could be done without much thought. Therefore, again, to add excitement and encourage thinking, only the three locations mentioned are permitted. In the following solutions we shall always obey the rules.

The best way to visualize this problem is by actually playing the game: we can stack a quarter, a nickel, and a dime in that order at the "start" location. Then we try to move all three coins to some "final" location, by using at most one additional "buffer." But we must remember never to move more than one coin at a time and never to let a larger coin rest on a smaller one.

When readers feel comfortable with the game, we suggest adding a half dollar coin and a full silver dollar to increase the size of the tower. Again, starting with the smallest coin on the top, we need to relocate the entire tower, according to the preceding rules. Once the solution is understood this way, it is time to write the program solution.

Programming the Solution

The program should first read the number of disks as an integer number, and then print one sentence for each move, stating exactly which disk is moved where. We choose to name the number of disks "disks". The solution is quite simple once our minds are accustomed to thinking recursively. In this section we only outline some particular recursive solution; a general treatment follows in Chapter 11.

First Step of Solution

It would be easy to move the whole tower of n disks from "start" to "final," if somehow we could move the first n-1 disks from "start" to "buffer." Then we would have to move the single remaining disk "n" from "start" to "final." At the end we move the subtower of n-1 disks still sitting on "buffer" to "final," and we would be done.

Unfortunately we don't know yet how to move n-1 disks so swiftly around without violation of rules, unless n-1 had the value 1 just by chance. However, we have made some progress: we reduced an n bounded problem to a simpler problem, bounded by n-1. So now we can concentrate our attention on solving a simpler problem.

The simpler problem is to move n-1 disks from "start" to "buffer." But we have just given the solution for a tower of "n" disks already. At the risk of boring the reader with repetition, we shall express the solution one more time for the n-1 bounded problem.

Second Step of Solution

It would be easy to move the n-1 disks from "start" to "buffer" if somehow we could move the first n-2 disks from "start" to "final" this time using "final" as the "buffer" for an intermediate step. Then we would have to move the sole remaining disk n-1 from "start" to "buffer." After this we would still have to move the subtower of n-2 disks sitting on "final" to "buffer," and we would be done with this subtask.

Now the overall problem has been reduced to an n-2 bounded problem, and if we only apply the same principle often enough, then the n-m tower will be a tower of a single disk, which we know is easy to move. A programming language with recursive procedures often allows us to implement the solution in terms of the logical solution, and it should come as no surprise to see how simple the Ada, Modula-2, Pascal, and PL/I programs are, and how closely they resemble the abstract solution.

```
 1                    | WITH text_io; USE text_io;
 2                    |
 3                    | PROCEDURE towers_of_hanoi IS
 4              1      |  SUBTYPE short_string IS string( 1 .. 5 );
 5              1      |  disks : integer;
 6         5    1      |  PACKAGE int_io IS NEW integer_io(integer); USE int_io;
 7         5    1      |  PROCEDURE tower(
 8              2      |   disks    : integer;
 9         5    2      |   start,
10         5    2      |   final,
11         5    2      |   buffer   : short_string ) IS
12        20    2      |  BEGIN--tower
13              2      |   IF disks > 0 THEN
14     4        2   1  |    tower( disks - 1, start, buffer, final );
15    20        2   2  |    put( " move disk: " );
16    22        2   2  |    put( integer'image( disks ) );
17    24        2   2  |    put( " from " );
18    26        2   2  |    put( start );
19    29        2   2  |    put( " to " );
20    31        2   2  |    put_line( final );
21    35        2   2  |    tower( disks - 1, buffer, final, start );
22    51        2   2  |   END IF;
23    51        2   1  |  END tower;
24    51        1      |
25    51        1      | BEGIN--towers_of_hanoi
26    52        1      |  put_line( " enter number of disks: " );
27    55        1   1  |  get( disks );
28    57        1   1  |  tower( disks, "start," "final," "buffr" );
29    67        1   1  | END towers_of_hanoi;
```

Example 4-6 Towers of Hanoi in Ada

Annotation

In this section we discuss recursion, IO Statements, and the syntax for array declarations in Ada. The "towers_of_hanoi" solution includes the recursive procedure "tower." On line 14, inside the body of "tower," we find a reference to the same procedure name. From the procedure name declaration on line 7 alone, we cannot derive whether "tower" is ever used recursively. To find out, visual inspection of the statement list is necessary. Ada, Pascal, and Modula-2 define subprograms to be inherently recursive, they require no explicit attribute.

In "tower" we observe two kinds of Output Statements, several Put Statements and a Putline Statement. These are similar to Pascal's Write and Writeln Statements, the only difference being that the Ada version must have exactly one output argument, while the Pascal form may have more. Since a line of program output is composed of six substrings, the Ada program requires a total of six Output Statements. This rule can make the coding effort quite cumbersome. Even in the primitive program of Example 4-6, more than half the statements are for output. Compare this with the brief Pascal or PL/I solution.

Line 27 is an example of how Ada handles Input Statements; in this case, the statement reads an integer value into variable "disks" of type integer. Just like Pascal's Read Statement, "get" skips all leading carriage returns, blanks, and zero digits, before the actual integer is scanned. No specific length is given for the integer, so the input routine reads until all digits are exhausted or until an error occurs.

Ada's syntax rules for array declarations, just like PL/I's, require a pair of parentheses around the array bounds. Languages of the Algol family such as Pascal and Modula-2 use square brackets. One such declaration is shown on line 4. "String," a predefined type mark, is an array of characters with lower bound 1 and an open ended upper bound; this upper bound must be set in the actual object declaration. "Short_string" of line 4 above does just that by setting the upper array bound to 5. Formal parameters "start," "final," and "buffer" are initialized to string values via string literals on line 28 above.

The Ada implementation explained uses a recursive algorithm; we shall see the same algorithm in Pascal, PL/I, and Modula-2. Since Fortran is nonrecursive, we shall demonstrate a different solution in the next section below.

```
      PROGRAM HANOI
       INTEGER DISKS
10     FORMAT( ' ENTER NUMBER OF DISKS WANTED' )
20     FORMAT( I10 )
30     WRITE( 6, 10 )
       READ( 5, 20 ) DISKS
       IF ( DISKS .GT. 0 ) CALL TOWER( DISKS )
       IF ( DISKS .GT. 0 ) GOTO 30
      END

      SUBROUTINE TOWER( TOTAL )
       INTEGER TOTAL
       INTEGER FROM, TO, DISK, TEMP, I
       INTEGER BITSTR( 10 ), HOLD( 10 )
       CHARACTER * 6 PLACE( 3 )
       DATA PLACE /'START ', 'BUFFER', 'FINISH'/
       DO 10 I = 1, 10
        BITSTR( I ) = 0
10      HOLD( I ) = 1
       TEMP = 3 - MOD( TOTAL, 2 )
       DO 20 I = 1, 2**TOTAL - 1
        DISK = INCR( BITSTR )
        IF ( DISK .EQ. 1 ) THEN
         FROM = HOLD( 1 )
         TO = 6 - FROM - TEMP
         TEMP = FROM
        ELSE
         FROM = HOLD( DISK )
         TO = 6 - HOLD( 1 ) - HOLD( DISK )
        END IF
        WRITE(6,*) ' MOVE DISK ',DISK,' FROM ',PLACE(FROM),
     *               ' TO ', PLACE( TO )
        HOLD( DISK ) = TO
20     CONTINUE
      END

      INTEGER FUNCTION INCR( BITSTR )
       INTEGER BITSTR( 10 )
       INTEGER I
       I = 1
10     IF ( BITSTR( I ) .EQ. 0 ) THEN
        BITSTR( I ) = 1
        INCR = I
        RETURN
       ELSE
        BITSTR( I ) = 0
        I = I + 1
        GOTO 10
```

```
            END IF
          END
```

Example 4-7 Towers of Hanoi in Fortran

Annotation

In Fortran the Towers of Hanoi problem is solved nonrecursively. Here we will explain this very special solution and clarify the Fortran syntax elements introduced, such as the Array Declaration, the Write Statement, and the Block If Statement.

The Towers of Hanoi algorithm as shown in the Ada solution is inherently recursive. We might, therefore, be tempted to conclude that the problem is not solvable in Fortran. In one sense this is correct, since we cannot directly translate the Ada solution into Fortran source. However, as programmers, we can apply the same mental process that a compiler goes through when generating code from a recursive source program for a general-purpose register machine instruction set. In other words, if recursion is not part of the source language, we can explicitly simulate recursive properties via a run time stack with the necessary return addresses, and parameters. Such a solution to the Towers of Hanoi puzzle is given in Chapter 11.

A simpler way of solving a recursive problem using a nonrecursive language is applying an equivalent, but nonrecursive algorithm. Finding such an algorithm, however, may represent the major problem.

There are many nonrecursive Towers of Hanoi solutions, but the one presented here is new, beautiful, very simple, and efficient. It was discovered by a San Diego State University student, Donald J. Perkins, when he was a youngster in the fourth grade. Both the explanation and the program are based on Perkins' scheme, which he dubbed the Fourth Grade Solution. For more detail see also Mayer and Perkins [1984].

Fourth Grade Solution

The locations that can hold the disks are numbered 1, 2, and 3, respectively, with 1 arbitrarily being the start location and 3 the final destination. During final output these numbers will be used as indices in an array of character strings, producing nicely readable output. The disks are numbered 1 through n, with 1 being the smallest disk.

The first decision is where to move the first disk, which is, of course, always disk number 1. We find by induction that for the optimum solution, requiring exactly 2**n-1 moves, disk 1 is moved to the "final" location when n is odd, and to "buffer" when n is even. As an example, and as base for the induction, this can be verified by simple towers. If n = 1, then disk 1 moves to "final" and we are finished. If n = 2, then disk 1 moves to "buffer," disk 2 to "final," and then disk 1 from "buffer" to "final." But note that the first move is to "buffer."

Now we are ready to solve the puzzle from within a loop. The kernel of the idea is based on the observation by Perkins that the index of the disk to be moved is identical to the index of the bit in a binary number that changes from '0' to '1' when counting from 0 to 2**n-1. Given a binary number with n bits, there are 2**n different representable values and 2**n-1 transitions. Let the rightmost or lowest order bit have index 1 and the leftmost or highest order bit have index n. We know that in a binary count sequence from 0 to 2**n-1, only one single bit changes from '0' to '1' during each increment. There are exactly 2**n-1 increments. Here are two short examples.

The fifth step of the count sequence changes a decimal 4 or binary '00000100' to a decimal 5 or binary '000000101', hence the bit that flips from '0' to '1' is bit 1. This means that for every tower the fifth move is a relocation of disk number 1. Notice that disk 1 is moved on every odd-numbered iteration, so this may not be very surprising. Let us analyze iteration number 8. The binary sequence '00000111' changes to '00001000', indicating that disk number 4 has to be moved, since the bit indexed 4 flips from '0' to '1'.

Once we identify which disk to move, we still must determine where to move it. Given that we must move disk 1, we can move it to one of two places; we never violate the rule to always put a smaller on a larger disk, since 1 is the smallest. Since we remember where 1 was in the previous move, and given that we know where 1 is now, there is only one possibility left.

If we must move a disk different from 1, then we must realize that all disks' moves are dictated by the position of disk 1, since we cannot move on top of it. Because of this restriction and since we cannot leave a disk at the old place, there is again only one choice left.

Using the knowledge where disk 1 is and where the disk to be transferred resides, we can use the following formula, to calculate where to move that disk.

```
to_position := 6 - where_1_is - where_i_am;
```

INCR of the Fortran solution has a double function. First, it is called 2**n-1 times. Each time it is called, it increments the bit string. This string was initially zero. The increment operation terminates as soon as a zero bit changes to a one. Otherwise the bit string would grow by more than 1 during each step. The second function of INCR is to return the index of the bit that changes from '0' to '1'.

A Newly Used Fortran Constructs

In Fortran program "PRMTST" in Example 4-2 we have already seen a few important language constructs. Here we explain new language elements. On line 14 of the Fortran program "HANOI," we see for the first time in this text the declaration of a one-dimensional array of characters. It is three elements long, and each element holds six characters. Also novel is the initialization of this array in the next statement, a so-called Data Statement. This initialization represents the only value assignment to the declared variable "place," which is only used as an indexable constant to output proper names for the three locations.

The WRITE Statement on line 31 contains no format specifier; an asterisk is given in its place. Fortran-77 defines that if the format specifier is an asterisk, the statement is a list-directed Output Statement and a record specifier may not be present. Record specifiers are used for direct access IO, which is covered briefly in Chapter 15.

Program "HANOI" contains the third form of Fortran's If Statement, the Block If Statement. This offers programmers a scaffold for structuring source text. Exponentiation, which is used on line 21, can be applied to integer, real, and double type operands. For integer type expressions a negative exponent is meaningless. Next we present the recursive solution in Pascal.

```
 1    1  0  0       PROGRAM towersofhanoi( input, output );
 2    2  0  0        TYPE
                      shortstring = PACKED ARRAY[ 1 .. 5 ] OF char;
 3    4  0  0        VAR
                      disks : integer;

 4    7  0  0        PROCEDURE tower(
 4    8  1  0         disks   : integer;
                      start,
                      final,
                      buffer  : shortstring );
 5   12  1  0        BEGIN { tower }
 5   13  1  1         IF disks > 0 THEN
 6   14  1  1          BEGIN
 6   15  1  2           tower( disks - 1, start, buffer, final );
 7   16  1  2           writeln( output, ' move disk: ', disks, ' from ',
                          start, ' to ', final );
 8   17  1  2           tower( disks - 1, buffer, final, start );
 9   18  1  2          END;
11   19  1  1         {END IF}
                     END; { tower }

12   22  0  0       BEGIN { towersofhanoi }
12   23  0  1        writeln( output, ' enter number of disks: ' );
```

```
13   24  0  1           readln( input, disks );
14   25  0  1           tower( disks, 'start', 'final', 'buffr' );
15   26  0  1          END. { towersofhanoi }
```

Example 4-8 Towers of Hanoi in Pascal

Annotation

This section comments briefly on Pascal's use of IO Statements, recursion, and the End Statement at the closing of procedure and program definitions.

Again, a recursive program solution is presented, and as discussed in the Ada program earlier, recursion is an inherent attribute of Pascal procedures and functions. Thus it is not visible at the place of definition, whether recursion will be used or not. Consequently, a compiler cannot simply generate two sequences of instructions, one more efficient for nonrecursive subprograms, and another more complex for recursive calls. Even though an optimizing compiler can construct an explicit call graph, this requires considerable compile time overhead. In general, such information is not available to the programmer and the compiler.

In contrast to the wordy solution in Ada, Pascal has only a single Output Statement in the body of "tower." See line 16. The "readln" on line 24 is almost identical to the PL/I and Ada versions.

Pascal does not allow the repetition of the procedure or function name for documentary purposes at the end of a subprogram declaration. A conscientious programmer may still wish to simulate this effect by using a comment after the END keyword. As a case in point see the end of procedure "tower" on line 20 and the program end on line 26. Note the square brackets on line 3 for the declaration of array bounds in Pascal. A solution in PL/I follows below.

```
 1    0          HANOI: PROC OPTIONS(MAIN);
 2    1           DCL ( START, FINAL, INTER ) CHAR(5);
 3    1           DCL DISKS BIN FIXED;

 4    1           TOWER: PROC( DISKS, START, FINAL, INTER ) RECURSIVE;
 5    2            DCL ( START, FINAL, INTER ) CHAR(5);
 6    2            DCL DISKS BIN FIXED;
 7    2            IF DISKS > 0 THEN
 8    2             DO;
 9    2     1        CALL TOWER( DISKS-1, START, INTER, FINAL );
10    2     1        PUT LIST( ' MOVE ',DISKS,' FROM ',START,' TO ',FINAL );
11    2     1        PUT SKIP;
12    2     1        CALL TOWER( DISKS-1, INTER, FINAL, START );
13    2     1       END;
                   ELSE
14    2             /*NULL*/;
```

```
                       /*END IF*/
15     2             END TOWER;

16     1             DISKS = 1;
17     1             DO WHILE ( DISKS > 0 );
18     1     1         PUT LIST( ' ENTER NUMBER OF DISKS' );
19     1     1         PUT SKIP;
20     1     1         GET LIST( DISKS );
21     1     1         CALL TOWER( DISKS, 'START', 'FINAL', 'INTER' );
22     1     1         PUT SKIP;
23     1     1       END;
24     1           END HANOI;
```

Example 4-9 Towers of Hanoi in PL/I

Annotation

The nested procedure "tower" has one integer and three string type parameters. Formal parameter types are declared at the same place where other variables are declared in PL/I. They are not specified inside the parentheses of the formal parameter list, as we have seen in Ada, Modula-2, and Pascal. Also note the explicit attribute RECURSIVE for procedure "tower" in statement 4.

"Tower" is called three times, twice recursively from inside the body of "tower" itself, and once from the main procedure in statement 21. The actual string parameters of statement 21 are expressions; see the pairs of single quotes. Hence, in this call, parameter passing by value takes place for the string arguments. In the two other calls, the actual parameters are variables. See statements 9 and 12. Here the string parameter passing mechanism is by reference. This could have been overruled by embedding the three variables "start," "inter," and "final" in redundant parentheses, or by concatenating them with empty strings. Two instances are shown in Example 4-10.

```
CALL TOWER( DISKS, ( START ), ( INTER ), ( FINAL ) );
CALL TOWER( DISKS, START || '', INTER || '', FINAL || '' );
```

Example 4-10 Value Parameter Passing

Both times the first parameter is passed by reference, since variable "DISKS" rather than an expression substitutes the formal parameter. More detail is presented in the chapter on "Parameters."

When a PL/I Output Statement references no explicit file, then the standard output file is assumed implicitly. In PL/I terminology, the name for this file is "sysprint." We know the same concept already from Pascal, where standard output is named more modestly "output." For Input Statements this works analogously, and the name of the standard input file in PL/I is "sysin."

Now we leave the PL/I implementation, and inspect the Modula-2 solution. As mentioned before, the line numbers are not part of the Modula-2 language. They have been added as a convenience for referencing source lines.

```
MODULE TowersOfHanoi;
 FROM InOut
  IMPORT WriteString, WriteLn, ReadCard;
 TYPE
  ShortString = ARRAY[ 1 .. 5 ] OF CHAR;
 VAR
  Disks         : CARDINAL;

 PROCEDURE Tower(
  Disks         : CARDINAL;
  Start,
  Final,
  Buffer        : ShortString );
 BEGIN (* Tower *)
  IF Disks > 0 THEN
   Tower( Disks - 1, Start, Buffer, Final );
   WriteString( " move disk: " );
   WriteString( Disks );
   WriteString( " from " );
   WriteString( Start );
   WriteString( " to " );
   WriteString( Final );
   WriteLn;
   Tower( Disks - 1, Buffer, Final, Start );
  END;
 END Tower;

BEGIN (* TowersOfHanoi *)
 WriteString( " enter number of Disks: " );
 ReadCard( Disks );
 Tower( Disks, "Start", "Final", "Buffr" );
END TowersOfHanoi.
```

Example 4-11 Towers of Hanoi in Modula-2

Annotation

The Modula-2 implementation of the Towers of Hanoi problem looks suspiciously like the Pascal solution, but there are important differences. One thing that strikes the eye is the repetitious use of the "WriteString" IO procedure. It is here that Modula-2 becomes more type conscious than its predecessor, Pascal.

Modula-2 demands a special procedure for text IO for each type of argument. "WriteCard," for example, accepts only CARDINAL type arguments, and converts the expression into its corresponding string representation before printing. "Write," on the other hand, assumes a CHAR type argument, while "WriteString" requires a character string. Exactly one single argument is accepted. So if a complete line of text is composed of multiple substrings, then "WriteString" is called once for each component. This explains the funny-looking sequence of WriteString Statements.

In Modula-2 IO statements we rediscover a clumsiness of text format, already mentioned for Ada. Each substring of a long line of text has to be written with one complete IO statement at a time. This can cause the source to degenerate into long vertical text, while Pascal and PL/I need only one single statement. Artificial concatenation eliminates this problem somewhat, but the programmer looses control over the length specification of individual substrings.

4.3 Summary

This concludes our discussion of programming languages on a broad level. In chapter 3 we have discussed compilation units and scopes, in chapter 4 we analyzed complete sample programs. We have seen Ada's Context Clause, required to access IO routines; later we have encountered the same idea in Modula-2. We have seen samples of Fortran's Do Statement, its cryptic identifiers, and the numerous Goto Statements and Labels. In Pascal we learned that each kind of declaration is introduced by a special keyword, we have shown TYPE and VAR. PL/I has special operators, with = assuming the double role of equality test and assignment operator. With Modula-2 we closed the cycle of sample programs by showing that many ideas of Modula-2 are replicated in Ada.

The following chapters go into detailed analysis of individual syntax constructs such as operators, operands, If Statements, parameters, recursion, and the like.

4.4 Exercises

1. A variation of the previous problem is the "Towers of Annoy" puzzle. Consider the n disks on the start position to be alternately coloured black and white. Let the largest disk be arbitrarily black. The goal is to move the disks in accordance with the Towers of Hanoi rules, so that the black disks make one tower on the start position, and the white disks make

another on the final position. Write a program "annoy" that prints a message for every disk moved.

2. How many steps or moves "a(n)" does the Towers of Annoy problem require? Express the number of steps as a function of n, n being the number of disks. Prove "a(n)" by induction.

3. Explain why it takes less moves for the Towers of Annoy than for the original Towers of Hanoi problem.

4. In the prime number solutions earlier, numbers are divided successively by candidate numbers to see whether the remainder is zero. The maximum value for these candidate denominators is test/2. Give a much better bound.

5. What is the main disadvantage in using the Sieve of Eratosthenes for prime number computations?

6. Write a "good" prime number generator that prints out the first 250,000 primes. Use an improved version of the algorithm applied in Exercise 4, by dividing "test" only by primes. For this purpose, an array of primes must be available. Recomputation of all primes up to max=sqrt(test) each time would be unacceptably inefficient. Before starting, we estimate the value of the largest prime, the one having index 250,000. This will give a clue about the largest divisor "max_div," by which all "test" numbers will be divided. Also estimate conservatively how many primes must be stored. Print 10 primes per line, 50 lines per page.

7. Find a "better" prime number algorithm. Before including improvements in the algorithm, prove that it represents a saving in execution time.

8. In many respects Modula-2 programs look almost identical to Pascal programs. Analyze the Modula-2 listings presented so far and observe the differences with Pascal.

5

Operands and Data Structures

How complex or simple a data structure is
depends critically upon the way in which we describe it.
Most of the complex structures found in the world
are enormously redundant,
and we can use this redundancy
to simplify their description.
But to use it, to achieve the simplification,
we must find the right representation.

Herbert A. Simon
The Sciences of the Artificial

Operands are the programming elements that provide values. These values may be of *scalar* or of *composite* type. Scalar operands are the value-generating "atoms," while the composites are the "molecules" that can become arbitrarily complex. When multiple objects are ordered in a linear or hierarchical fashion to create new entities, we call them composite or *structured* types. In this discussion we use composite and structured synonymously. We start out with the scalar types, which include numeric, character, boolean, and enumeration types. We do not cover the type "complex," available in Fortran and PL/I. Numeric types are subdivided into integer, floating point, and fixed point. "Real" is frequently used as a synonym for floating point. Integer, boolean, character, and enumeration type operands are grouped together as "discrete" types and can be used for subscripting. We cover these in detail; reals will not be covered.

After covering the scalars, we discuss operands of the structured types Array, Record, and Pointer in that order. Sets are not covered. Structured type operands promise to become quite interesting because their treatment is tied together by an attractive programming project, in which we shall implement a general cross reference generator for each class of composite type. Since all languages offer the Array data structure, we could implement the first solution in any of them. We chose Ada for this purpose since the program is relatively easy to follow. When we cover Records, we use Ada again and discover that the differences of the Arrays-only solution with the solution employing Records are minimal. Due to the similarity we show only the differing listing portions. Our final, third generation cross reference generator uses Pointers to Records and is implemented in Pascal.

This chapter is complementary to Chapter 6 and should be studied in conjunction with it. Together they explain the way values are generated. Values (or more generally expressions) will be used as building blocks in the various statements addressed in subsequent chapters.

5.1 Scalar Types

In mathematics we are accustomed to distinguishing between integer, real, complex, and logical operands. This classification into types is equally crucial for programming languages, which in addition provide enumeration types (Ada, Pascal, and Modula-2) and character types for text processing. Different from mathematics, where we can distinguish operand types from the context or even from the typeface of the printed text, in the programming languages treated here, we have to declare the type of each object. Standard, predefined type names (type marks) are "integer," "real," "char," or "boolean" and vary from one language to another.

Integer Operands

Integers form a contiguous, small subrange of the whole numbers. *Integer operands* are attractive because of their exact machine representation and the high speed with which most machines can process them. One inherent limitation in the use of integers, however, is their different interpretation on different machines. On a typical microcomputer the Pascal type "integer" may be restricted to the range -32768 .. +32767, while on a large computer operands of this type can span a much wider range—for example, -281474976710656 .. +281474976710656. The numbers themselves are not very important, but they clearly demonstrate the point that "integer" is not always the same! The sequence of statements in Example 5-1 is probably correct in all Ada implementations. But their execution on a microcomputer could cause an abnormal program termination.

```
i := 30000;--Ada assignment
j := 25000;
k := i + j;--is 55000 representable??
```

Example 5-1 Integer Operands

Because of the limitation of the integer range, the associative and distributive laws do not always apply in computer programs. We shall see a detailed example of this in Chapter 6. In recognition of this inherent danger, Pascal and Ada permit some degree of parameterization and checking via a symbolic constant. In Pascal it is spelled "maxint," in Ada "max_int." With this constant a programmer has the option of checking the meaning of "integer" and of detecting extensions. Compilers for limited targets tend to add multiple precision integer types. See the Pascal sample in Example 5-2.

```
CONST
 mymaxint          = 200000; { could be integer or long integer }
...
BEGIN
 IF mymaxint > maxint THEN
  writeln( ' Native integer type too small' );
```

Example 5-2 Symbolic Maximum Integer

PL/I allows a similar, meaningful parameterization of its integers in a more machine-specific way, by setting the exact number of bits needed for (the absolute value of) integers. The PL/I declaration is as follows:

DCL A BIN FIXED(23); /* 1 sign bit, 23 value bits */

Integer literals are spelled as in conventional arithmetic, though Ada also allows a scaled and based form as follows:

```
7E9    --scaled, meaning 7000000000 in Ada
16#FF# --base 16, equals 255 in Ada
```

Symbolic literals (constants) as available in Ada, Fortran, Modula-2, and Pascal can significantly enhance the readability and maintainability of programs. In Fortran the same can be expressed via the Parameter Statement; see 8-8 in the Fortran-77 standard. Equivalent samples are shown in Example 5-3 for the different languages.

```
i_value : CONSTANT integer := -5;--Ada
CONST ivalue = -5; { Pascal }
C------ FORTRAN
PARAMETER ( IVALUE = -5 )
CONST Ivalue = -5; (* Modula-2 *)
```

Example 5-3 Symbolic Constant Declarations

Operations on Integers

The standard arithmetic operations of addition, subtraction, multiplication, and division, as well as all relational tests, are legal on integer type operands. Equally important, though less frequently used, are the modulus and (in Ada) the remainder operator. All languages provide the function of absolute value via a monadic operator (Ada) or a built-in function. Ada, Fortran, and PL/I also provide the exponentiation operator for integers. In addition, all languages have a varying number of built-in functions, the list of which is substantial in PL/I. The more typical ones are the successor, predecessor, round, trunc, and odd functions.

Character Operands

The primary purpose of *character operands* is for text manipulation. Characters form an ordered, contiguous range of values hence the relational operators and the predecessor and successor function are meaningful. Typical predefined type marks are "char" or "character." The literals are enclosed in paired single quotes; Fortran and Modula-2 also permit double quotes.

The problem with characters is the existence and widely scattered use of a variety of different standards. Two of the better known ones are Ascii (American Standard Code for Information Interchange) and Ebcdic (Extended Binary Coded Decimal Interchange Code). The former has 128, the latter 256 possible values. Another widely used "standard" character set is the CDC 6-bit set with only 64 different values. Since any character set has to provide a number of special characters, we can easily see that the CDC set has no room for lowercase and uppercase letters, which makes it particularly difficult to port source text to CDC systems.

Letters

In the Ascii character set it is relatively easy to check if a character type operand is a lowercase or uppercase letter. If "c" is a character variable, then the Ada expression

```
c IN 'A' .. 'Z'  --Ascii uppercase in Ada
```

will yield true, if "c" is indeed an uppercase letter. Similarly, the following Pascal expression yields true if "c" is a lowercase letter.

```
c IN [ 'a' .. 'z' ]     { Ascii lowercase in Pascal }
```

In the Ebcdic character set the letters are not contiguous, which renders the same test more awkward. The programmer must know where the "holes" are and code correspondingly. See the following Pascal example:

```
c IN [ 'a' .. 'i', 'j' .. 'r', 's' .. 'z' ] { Ebcdic, Pascal test }
```

At least the holes in the uppercase letter sequence appear in positions that match the holes for lowercase letters.

Digits

The ordering of the character values allows a one-to-one mapping onto an integer subrange. The first character is mapped onto zero, the second to one, and so on. Since the digit '0' is not the first character in any of the widely used character sets, its corresponding positional number is greater than zero. The positional number of any character operand can be found by the built-in function "ord" in Modula-2 and Pascal, or by the attribute "pos" in Ada. For example "i:=ord('4')" assigns "i" the value 52 in Pascal if Ascii is used, or 244 in Ebcdic. But to convert '4' into the numeric value 4, it is, therefore, necessary to subtract the value of literal '0'. This will be demonstrated in Example 5-4.

Next we design a Pascal program that reads a sequence of digits from standard input and constructs the integer value expressed by the digit string. Leading blanks are skipped without action, and leading zero characters do not contribute to the final, integer value. Our program will be very simple because we trust that the incoming string of digits will never represent an integer value that could cause overflow. If no more digits are found, the program prints the resulting integer value and terminates. The key action is the conversion of a digit to its numeric value by subtracting the offset of '0'. Subtraction of character operands is not possible in Pascal. Therefore the characters must be converted to integers. We show only the significant program portion; the declarations are omitted.

```
begin { atoi }
 result := 0;
 c := ' ';
 writeln( ' enter digits, but not too many.' );
 skipblanks;
 while c in [ '0' .. '9' ] do
  begin
   result := 10 * result + ( ord( c ) - ord( '0' ) ); { no check }
   read( c );
  end;
 {end while}
 writeln( ' the number was = ', result );
end { atoi }
```

Example 5-4 String of Digits Converted to Integer (Without Checks)

Operations on Characters

Besides being assigned and passed as parameters, character type operands can be tested for all relations. Typical built-in functions that manipulate characters are the successor and predecessor functions, and the conversion to their integer value. In PL/I and Fortran such conversions are implicit. Modula-2 and Pascal must spell them out as "ord." Ada mystifies this simple operation behind the "pos" attribute.

Boolean Operands

The boolean operand defines the range of truth values. In Ada, Modula-2, and Pascal this range includes "false" and "true" in that order. The equivalent Fortran term is "logical" with the literals .FALSE. and .TRUE.. In PL/I bit strings of length 1 provide the same function. The bit string values '0'B and '1'B stand for "false" and "true" respectively. Ada's predefined package "standard" defines the type mark "boolean" as follows:

```
TYPE boolean IS ( false, true );
-- Ada Type declaration
```

The ordering of "false" and "true" implies that the relation "false<true" holds. Even though Ada so carefully defines even this type mark in terms of Ada, there is still "magic" applied to "boolean," because expressions that appear in If

and While Statements must be of precisely boolean type. No other bivalued type would be legal in such contexts. Pascal and Modula-2 do the same, except they do not attempt to define boolean in terms of the language. "Boolean" is simply one of several predefined type marks.

Operations on Booleans

The predecessor and successor functions can be applied to boolean operands, but they are not very helpful because of the restricted number of boolean values. Other valid operations are assignment, the relational tests, and logical Not, And, and Or.

Enumeration Operands

Some problems involve operands that are not numeric, boolean, or character. In these cases only the enumeration of all distinct values would be meaningful. For example, when we record the sex of a person in a data base, it is quite expressive to refer to attributes like "male" or "female." Numbers like 1 and 2 might be equivalent encodings of the same information, but are of less documentary value. Even the inventor of such a remote encoding could just once mix up the convention and might sometimes map the women, other times the men onto 1, causing a bug that is hard to track. Here an enumeration operand is in order.

Of the languages covered here, only Ada, Modula-2, and Pascal provide enumeration types. The kernel of the syntax for the type specification itself is identical in all three languages, except that Ada offers two additional features. In Example 5-5 we show the same enumeration type example in the three languages.

```
TYPE destination_type IS ( Heaven, Purgatory, Hell );--Ada
TYPE DestinationType   = ( Heaven, Purgatory, Hell ); (* Modula-2 *)
TYPE destinationtype   = ( Heaven, Purgatory, Hell ); { Pascal }
```

Example 5–5—Enumeration Types

The parenthetical identifiers are the enumeration literals; at least one is required. They form the new type mark. Objects of this new type may have any of the enumeration literals as values, and no other value. Ada's rules for enumeration type operands are more liberal.

In Ada enumerative type identifiers and character literals may be mixed. This makes it possible to define the predefined type "character" fully in terms of Ada. The fragmentary type declaration in Example 5-6 has been taken from the predefined Ada package "standard."

```
TYPE character IS
( nul,    soh,    stx,    etx,       eot,    enq,    ack,    bel,
  bs, ...
  '@',    'A',    'B',    'C',       'D',    'E',    'F',    'G',
  'H', ...
  'x',    'y',    'z',    '{',       '|',    '}',    '~',    del );
```

Example 5-6 Enumeration Literals

The second convenience available in Ada is the overloading of enumeration literals. In the other languages the identifiers must be unique not only in the parenthesized list of the type specification, but also in the whole scope that encloses that type. Ada, on the other hand, permits enumeration names to be reused in other enumeration type declarations. In case of possible ambiguity the "qualified expressions" discussed in Chapter 6 serve to resolve any type problem. In Example 5-7 we show two Ada enumeration types that cannot be literally translated into Modula-2 or Pascal. Note that the literals "red," "yellow," and "green" are overloaded; they have more than one meaning in the same scope.

```
TYPE light_type  = ( red, yellow, green );
TYPE colour_type = ( red, orange, yellow, green, blue, indigo, violet );
```

Example 5-7 Overloaded Ada Enumeration Literals

Each enumeration literal has an associated position number, which we have already observed for boolean and character type operands. This ordinal number can be acquired via built-in functions in Pascal and Modula-2, and via attributes in Ada. The Pascal expression "ord(Hell)" when referring to the "destinationtype" in Example 5-5 will return the integer value 2. Next, in Example 5-8 we show a Pascal program that reconverts integer values in the correct subrange back to enumerative types. Since no built-in function is provided for this inverse conversion, tricks can be used. But here we prefer to present a clean and portable way of converting Pascal integers to enumeration types.

The first 11 lines of the program in Example 5-8 contain declarations and perform initialization. From then on it will always be possible to convert an integer expression in the range 0 .. 6 to the enumeration type "colourtype." We apply such a conversion on line 13.

```
program i2enum( output );
 type
  colourtype = ( red, orange, yellow, green, blue, indigo, violet );
 var
  i           : integer;
  colour      : colourtype;
  i2colour    : array[ 0 .. 6 ] of colourtype;
 begin { i2enum }
  for colour := red to violet do
   i2colour[ ord( colour ) ] := colour;
  {end for}
  i := 4; { arbitrarily }
  colour := i2colour[ i ];
  writeln( ord( colour ) );
 end { i2enum }.
```

Example 5-8 Clean Conversion from Integer to Enumeration

Operations on Enumeration Type Operands

Enumeration type operands can be assigned, passed as parameters, and tested for all relations. The successor and predecessor function, and conversion to integer can be applied as well. It is important to know that Array indices may be of enumeration type, which in some applications is very appropriate.

After this introduction into the scalar types we shall explain the structured types. Composite types normally consist of a number of scalars and other, simpler composite type operands. But, ultimately, every structured type is composed of scalars.

5.2 Composite Operands

In this section we present, in order, Arrays, Records, and Pointers. As the data structures become more and more sophisticated, the programming solutions in the new structures become increasingly simple and comprehensible. It may look like we demonstrate the complicated problems first and the simpler ones last, thus violating an elementary didactic principle. The reason behind this apparent lack of pedagogy is an attempt to have the reader learn to appreciate firsthand how important it is to select the appropriate data structure for a given problem. When we pick one that is overly simplistic, it is only natural that the programming solution is more complicated than it should be. When we choose the right data structure, the program becomes simpler. Therefore, in our discussion of structured data, we progress from simple to complex, but our associated programs become simpler.

When a language offers no variety in data structures, the selection of the right one is always easy; we pick the only one available. This is why in Fortran the Array is always the right data structure. When the language does provide a generic mechanism for building any kind of data structure, we have a chance of constructing one that is optimal for the problem at hand. With Records, whose fields can be Records again, Arrays, Pointers, Files, or any other legal type, we have the option and the challenge of composing a type that is a direct reflection of the underlying logical data structure. Naturally we can also make errors and select one that is inadequate; we pay for this later in the statement section. During the design phase we should allocate an appropriate amount of time for the data structure layout. In complex problems this can consume half of the design effort.

Maybe this is an appropriate place to pay our respects to Cobol. Clumsy as the language may now appear, Cobol was the pioneer in offering users a scheme for defining data structures that reflect the problem rather than the limitations of the host machine. PL/I benefitted from this farsighted design early on, and in more recent programming languages, structured data types have become a matter of course.

Arrays

We start this section by explaining those facets of the Array data structure that are common to all languages. Then we cover rules that are specific to each language and explain how Arrays are stored. Finally we present our first "crossref" solution, implemented exclusively using Arrays.

Sometimes, when we process many operands of the same type in the same way, we prefer to treat the distinct objects as one homogeneous structure. Then it is opportune to use the Array data structure. An Array is an ordered, linear sequence of elements, all randomly accessible under the same name. If the elements in turn are Arrays, then the structure is multidimensional. To select one specific element, the Array name must be *subscripted;* we also call this operation *indexing.*

For each dimension the type of the subscript expression must be compatible with the type of the declared bounds. The smallest possible index value is called the lower bound, the largest one, the upper bound.

In this section we learn the specific rules about Arrays and their use in the various languages. We mention the related type "string" briefly, but we skip Arrays with flexible bounds. During the discussion of Fortran Arrays we shall explain the term *column major order,* while in the Modula-2 section we present an example of *Row Major Order.*

Arrays in Ada

Because of Ada's strict type rule that states that two objects are type compatible only if they are defined by the same type mark, operations on Array types are not as liberal as in the other languages. Let us start with a definition of what constitutes an Array type in Ada. The type of an Array is characterized by the number of indices (dimensions) the type and position of each index, the lower bound and upper bound of each index, and the type of the Array components (elements). There is no limit on the number of dimensions. Subscripts may be of any discrete type. Unique in Ada are the Null Arrays. A Null Array is an Array in which at least one dimension is defined as a Null Range. Such Arrays have no elements and consume no memory space. In Example 5-9 we show sample array type and object declarations.

```
TYPE line_type  IS ARRAY( 1 .. 132 ) OF character;
 line1, line2      : line_type := blank_line;
 line3             : ARRAY( 1 .. 132 ) OF character;
BEGIN--subprogram body
 line2( 5 ) := 'X';
 line1 := line2;--legal Ada assignment
 line3 := line1;--illegal; types are distinct
```

Example 5-9 Ada Arrays

Array Indexing

The number of indices given for an indexed component must be identical to the number of dimensions specified in the Array declaration. This requirement is carried through in Ada with utmost accuracy, as we shall see in Examples 5-10. While Modula-2 and Pascal allow equivalent "full" and "abbreviated" forms of subscripting, there is no choice in Ada. The Array type exactly dictates the indexing choice. To clarify this we resort to examples.

```
TYPE page_range  IS RANGE 1 .. 50;
 page1             : ARRAY( page_range ) OF line_type;--defined above
 page2             : ARRAY( page_range, 1 .. 132 ) OF character;
BEGIN--subprogram body
 c := page1( i )( j );--correct, "page1" is one-dimensional
                       --elements happen to be Arrays again
 page2( i, j ) := c;o --also correct, "page2" is two-dimensional
```

Example 5-10 Indexing

Even though the indexing methods in Example 5-10 look different, they in fact adhere to the same language rule. The number of specified subscripts must match the number of dimensions given in the declaration. "Page1" is a one-dimensional Array, hence we see a singly-indexed parenthetical expression following the Array name. Since the element is in turn an Array as well, a second, single subscript must be specified to reference its component. "Page2," on the other hand, is a two-dimensional Array. Hence the parentheses must contain two expressions, separated from one another by a comma. No other combinations are legal.

Arrays can be tested for equality and unequality. If the elements of two type compatible Arrays are discrete, then such Arrays can be tested for all relations applicable to the discrete type. If the component type is boolean, then the permissible operations on Arrays include the unary NOT and all binary, logical operators. See Example 5-11.

```
 s1, s2, s3 : ARRAY( work_days ) OF boolean;
BEGIN
 s3 := s1 AND s2;
```

Example 5-11 Ada Boolean Arrays

String Types

One-dimensional Arrays of characters that have positive, integer subscripts are defined to be "strings." The predefined Package "standard" includes the following type declarations. In order to declare a particular string type object, the type mark must be constrained with a definite upper bound.

```
SUBTYPE positive IS integer RANGE 1 .. integer'last;
TYPE string IS ARRAY( positive RANGE <> ) OF character;
...
digits     : string( 1 .. 10 ) := "0123456789";
ten_stars  : string( 1 .. 10 ) := ( 1 .. 10 => '*' );--"**********"
line       : string( 1 .. 132 );
```

Example 5-12 Ada Strings

Ada offers one more convenience that is known in other languages as the substring operation. This is the slicing of one-dimensional Arrays. A *slice* is a sequence of consecutive elements, specified as a range. We can extract a slice from the variable "digits" in Example 5-12 as shown in Example 5-13. The second line uses a slice that spans the complete range of "digits."

```
digits( 6 .. 10 ) := digits( 1 .. 5 );--digits = "0123401234"
pagel( 17 )( 1 .. 10 ) := ( 1 .. 10 => '0' );--slice of 10 '0's
```

Example 5-13 Ada Slices

Arrays in Fortran

Arrays in Fortran are simpler but also more restricted than in Ada. The elements may be of any scalar type, but the index type can only be integer. The maximum number of dimensions is 7 for Fortran-77. If the lower bound is not explicitly specified, it is assumed to be 1, and the upper bound cannot be less than 1. When both bounds are given, they are separated from one another by a colon, and the upper bound must be at least as great as the lower bound. We show some sample Array declarations in Example 5-14.

```
C------- FORTRAN ARRAY DECLARATIONS
INTEGER AMOUNT( 10 )
LOGICAL SCHED ( -2 : 2, 0 : 4 )
INTEGER TWODIM( 1 : 4, 1 : 2 )
```

Example 5-14 Fortran Arrays

Array "AMOUNT" in Example 5-14 has 10 elements, indexed from 1 to 10. "SCHED" is a two-dimensional Array. Its first dimension has 5 elements, indexed from -2 to +2, and the second dimension has 5 elements indexed from 0 to 4. Hence the total is 25 elements. "TWODIM" has 8 integer elements; we shall investigate this Array in detail shortly.

A very unusual Fortran rule affects the way multidimensional Arrays are stored and addressed. The standard ANSI [1978] defines in detail (page 5-6) how to compute an element's position by effectively providing a mapping from multidimensions into one dimension. The elements in the equivalent, one-dimensional Array are numbered from 1 to n. We explain how this mapping works for two dimensions.

Given a declaration of bounds (l1:u1,l2:u2) for a two-dimensional Array, and a pair of indices (s1,s2) for this Array, then the element indexed by (s1,s2) has a positional number in the one-dimensional equivalent, as shown in the following formula:

```
position( element(s1,s2) ) = 1+( s1-l1 )+( s2-l2 )*( u1-l1+1 )
```

The mapping formula shows that an element indexed with all lower bounds has the positional number 1. We show this for TWODIM as follows.

```
position( TWODIM(1,1) ) = 1 + (1-1) + (1-1)*(2-1+1) = 1
```

The last element has a position number that is equal to the number of elements in the Array.

```
position( TWODIM(4,2) ) = 1 + (4-1) + (2-1)*(4-1+1) = 8
```

The element TWODIM(3,2), for example, has the positional number 7 in Fortran. Again we apply the formula provided in the standard.

```
position( TWODIM(3,2) ) = 1 + (3-1) + (2-1)*4 = 7
```

When we apply the formula to all elements, we can create an exact map of all locations in the Array relative to one another. This is shown in Figure 5-1 and is known as *column major order.* The term is based on the observation that, if one reads from left to right, the column index (right) varies only after the row-selecting index has progressed through its full range.

```
Element    1     2     3     4     5     6     7     8
         +-----+-----+-----+-----+-----+-----+-----+-----+
         | 1,1 | 2,1 | 3,1 | 4,1 | 1,2 | 2,2 | 3,2 | 4,2 |
         +-----+-----+-----+-----+-----+-----+-----+-----+
                                                ^
                                   TWODIM(3,2)  |
```

Figure 5-1 Ordering of Indices in Column Major Order

In other languages the rightmost index varies most rapidly when we do a linear scan through all Array elements. This is called "row major order" and will be demonstrated in the "Arrays in Modula-2" section, which follows.

Fortran requires that the number of subscripts be equal to the number of dimensions defined. This is natural and easy for a compiler to verify. In an attempt to promote program safety, Fortran has more subtle, quite interesting rules, which cannot in general be verified by a compiler. One such rule (page 5-6 ANSI [1978]) states that it is illegal for functions, used as expressions in subscripts, to have side effects on variables used in the same subscript.

```
K = A( F(I), I )
```

If the function "F" used in the subscripts has a side effect on "I," this example is no longer a legal Fortran statement.

Fortran is quite forgiving in treating invalid Array indices. Even though the number of subscripts must match the number of dimensions, the individual indices do not need to reside inside the specified range, as long as the resulting position number falls inside the Array. See Example 5-15.

```
INTEGER WILD( 1 : 5, 1 : 5 )
WILD( 20, 1 ) = -99
```

Example 5-15 No Bounds Check in Fortran

Chances are good that the outrageous assignment statement will execute in most implementations without causing problems. The Fortran compiler we used to test it caused element WILD(4,5) to be set to -99. This element has the positional number 24, which cannot be derived by using the mapping formula shown earlier. It is, therefore, good advice to abstain from using such dangerous subscript values. Other languages, including Modula-2, which is covered next, will cause a run time error with an Array bounds violation.

Arrays in Modula-2

Like in Ada, Modula-2 Arrays may have one or more dimensions; the language specifies no upper limit. Multidimensional Arrays are specified either by multiple index ranges, by the fact that the element is an Array type, or by a combination of both. Unlike Ada, it is insignificant in Modula-2 how the multiple dimensions are defined. For clarification we show a two-dimensional declaration in the full form in Example 5-16, with indentation highlighting the hierarchical structure.

```
Sample : ARRAY[ 1 .. Dim1 ] OF
    ARRAY[ 1 .. Dim2 ] OF
     REAL;
```

Example 5-16 Multi-Dimensional Ada Array

This declaration is equivalent to the abbreviated form coming next, except that the full form is a bit longer to write.

```
Sample : ARRAY[ 1 .. Dim1 ], [ 1 .. Dim2 ] OF REAL;
```

The syntax for Array subscripts allows the same degree of freedom: the abbreviated form "Sample[i,j]" can be used interchangeably with the full form "Sample[i][j]." We have observed that programmers use the convention of reflecting the declaration by the mode of subscripting. If "Sample" had been declared in the full form, then those programmers would use the full form in subscripts as well. The multiple bracket pairs in the declaration, separated from one another by commas, strike us as unusual. They are explained in the following section in terms of Modula-2 subranges.

If a variable is known to assume only a small, contiguous range of values of some scalar type, it is appropriate to reflect this in its type so that the compiler and the run time system can perform checks. Ada and Pascal allow a similar construct. In Modula-2 the syntax varies a bit from Pascal by using explicit brackets. See Example 5-17.

```
TYPE
 SmallT     = [ 1 .. 10 ];
 LetterT    = [ 'A' .. 'Z' ];
VAR
 Small      : SmallT;
 Letter     : LetterT;
 Digit      : [ '0' .. '9' ];
BEGIN (* Procedure body *)
 Letter := '0'; (* <<<<---- Illegal *)
 Letter := 'M';
 Small  :=   5;
 Digit  := '5';
```

Example 5-17 Modula-2 Ranges

If the lower bound of a subrange is a negative integer, then the resulting type is integer; otherwise it is cardinal.

```
TYPE
 SmallCardT = [ 0 .. 100 ];
 SmallIntT  = [ -100 .. +100 ];
VAR
 SmallCard  : SmallCardT;
 SmallInt   : SmallIntT;
BEGIN
 WriteCard( SmallCard, NumOfDigits );
 WriteInt( SmallInt, NumOfDigits );
```

Example 5-18 Integer or Cardinal

Once we know that the bracket pairs in Array type declarations are part of the subrange, we understand the surprising syntax. If we define Array indices by type marks, then no brackets are required at all. For multiple dimensions the comma must still separate one bounds specification from another.

```
VAR
 SmallIntBuff : ARRAY SmallInt OF INTEGER; (* no brackets *)
 CharBits     : ARRAY CHAR, BOOLEAN OF CHAR; (* separated by , *)
```

Example 5-19 Array Bound Without Brackets

Subranges and hence Array bounds must include at least one element in Modula-2. Also, Array elements are stored in row major order, which is explained in the following section.

Elements of multidimensional Arrays in Modula-2 are stored in a way that seems intuitive and is consistent with the mapping of one-dimensional Arrays. After all, a multidimensional Array is nothing but an Array of Arrays. If the elements are Arrays, then it seems natural to store them the same way. Virtually all languages with the prominent exception of Fortran conform to this practice.

We explain the row major order way of storing and accessing Array elements by the sample Array "TwoDim," familiar from the Fortran section. In Figure 5-2 we see a Modula-2 declaration of "TwoDim" together with a memory map that shows the order of the elements relative to one another.

```
VAR
TwoDim  : ARRAY[ 1 .. 4 ], [ 1 .. 2 ] OF INTEGER;
        +-----+-----+-----+-----+-----+-----+-----+-----+
        | 1,1 | 1,2 | 2,1 | 2,2 | 3,1 | 3,2 | 4,1 | 4,2 |
        +-----+-----+-----+-----+-----+-----+-----+-----+
                                          ^
                              TwoDim[3,2] |

        | TwoDim[1] | TwoDim[2] | TwoDim[3] | TwoDim[4] |
```

Figure 5-2 Ordering of Indices in Row Major Order

Again we have put the index pair of an Array element into its associated rectangle. The left index defines the "row," the right index the "column." When we scan the elements from left to right, we observe that the right index varies more frequently. This ordering allows us to interpret, say, TwoDim[1,1] and TwoDim[1,2] as a small subarray, and the entire subarray as the element TwoDim[1]. In a nutshell this is what distinguishes row major order from column major order.

Arrays in Pascal

Having covered Modula-2, we do not need to go into the details of Pascal Arrays, since the two are very close. We'll simply highlight the differences and main points.

Pascal Arrays cannot be empty. The abbreviated and full forms are equivalent for both the declaration and the indexing operation. Arrays can be specified as packed by the reserved keyword PACKED. This is primarily meant as a clue to the translator to economize space at the expense of time. An implementation is not required to treat packed structured data in any way different from unpacked ones. PACKED is only a recommendation. Not only Arrays, but all structured data, including Sets, may be packed. Packed Array elements and the fields of packed Records may not be passed as actual parameters to formal reference parameters.

A packed, one-dimensional Array of characters with lower bound 1 is called a "string" in Pascal. Strings can be assigned character string literals of the same length and can be compared with one another. Pascal provides no substring operation or an automatic adjustment if the lengths are not identical. Before we discuss substrings and automatic length adjustments in PL/I, where they are a matter of course, we present in Example 5-20 Pascal examples of Array declarations and subscript operations.

```
type
 linetype  = array[ 1 .. 132 ] of char;
 pagerange = 1 .. 50;
 pagetype  = array[ 1 .. 50, 1 .. 132 ] of char;
var
 page1     : pagetype;
 page2     : array[ pagerange ] of linetype;
 page3     : array[ pagerange, 1 .. 132 ] of char;
begin
 page1[ i, j ] := ' ';
 page1[ i ][ j ] := ' ';
 page2[ i, j ] := ' ';
 page2[ i ][ j ] := ' ';
 page3[ i, j ] := ' ';
 page3[ i ][ j ] := ' ';
```

Example 5-20 Equivalent Pascal Arrays

All three variables "page1" through "page3" are of the same type, which is a similarity we shall rediscover later in PL/I. All six Assignment Statements are correct; the full and abbreviated forms of indexing are equivalent. Since many Pascal compilers have been written at a time before the standard ANSI [1983b] was issued, most programs that use the liberty of Example 5-20 will be flagged as wrong. In practice this means that we would have to modify the source and come to an agreement with a particular translator; but per language definition the above declarations and statements of Example 5-20 are all correct, and any compiler in disagreement should be revised.

Arrays in PL/I

Being an older language, PL/I still requires all dimensions to be defined as integer ranges. The range may not be empty and its lower bound is optional. If only the upper bound is given, it must be at least 1 and the lower bound is assumed to be 1. See Example 5-21.

```
DCL A1( 1 : 10, 1 : 10 ) BIN FIXED;
DCL A2( 1 : 10, 10 ) BIN FIXED;
DCL A3( 10, 10 ) BIN FIXED;
```

Example 5-21 Equivalent PL/I Arrays

"A1" through "A3" have the same types, or in PL/I terminology the same attributes. Multiple declarations can be lumped into one. An equivalent of Example 5-21 is as follows.

```
DCL ( A1(10,10), A2(10,10), A3(10,10) ) BIN FIXED;
```

A Pascal programmer migrating to PL/I might feel tempted to declare an Array with an index type "char." We show one such declaration, which is indeed legal, but its meaning in PL/I is not the same as in Pascal. PL/I defines that the index type is integer. Therefore, a declaration of the form

```
DCL MYSTERY( CHAR ) CHAR; /* LEGAL PL/I */
```

implicitly defines the parenthetical "CHAR" to be an integer variable that has no initial value. The loader or run time system does not have sufficient information to allocate an array and will most likely cause an abort. Notice that the "CHAR" attribute after the parentheses is a totally different entity from the "CHAR" variable that defines the upper bound.

PL/I variables can be initialized, and Arrays are no exception. Initial values are listed in parentheses following the INIT keyword. Should a value be assigned repeatedly, then a handy abbreviation can be used, as shown in Example 5-22.

```
DCL SALES( 1970 : 1990 ) DECIMAL FIXED INIT( (16)0, (5)-999.00 );
DCL TABLE( 2, 3 ) BIN FIXED INIT( 11, 12, 13, 14, 15, 16 );
```

Example 5-22 PL/I Array Initialization

In the second initialization in Example 5-22 we observe again an implied mapping of a multidimensional Array into a one-dimensional. Hence it is necessary to know the relative order of the elements. PL/I specifies that Arrays are stored in row major order. This is sufficient information to know the positions of all elements of "TABLE," listed in Example 5-23.

```
TABLE( 1, 1 ) = 11;
TABLE( 1, 2 ) = 12;
TABLE( 1, 3 ) = 13;
TABLE( 2, 1 ) = 14;
TABLE( 2, 2 ) = 15;
TABLE( 2, 3 ) = 16;
```

Example 5-23 PL/I Row Major Order

PL/I tries to consider variables, whether scalar or composite, in a consistent light. In this strive for consistency it is not only allowed to compare Arrays (and, as we shall see later, Records) for all relations, but arithmetic and IO operations are permitted as well on full Arrays. This can mean quite a convenience in programming for some applications. See Example 5-24.

```
DCL ( TAB1( 4, 5 ), TAB2( 4, 5 ) ) BIN FIXED;
DCL TAB3( 4, 5 ) BIN FIXED INIT( (5)1, (5)4, (5)9, (5)16 );

TAB1 = TAB3; /* ALL ELEMENTS OF TAB1 ARE ASSIGNED */
GET LIST( TAB2 ); /* 20 ELEMENTS READ */
IF TAB1 = TAB2 THEN
 TAB3 = TAB3 ** 2;
```

Example 5-24 PL/I Array Operations

Array elements with one exception, must be scalars. The scalar type CHAR may have an explicit length attribute. If that attribute is not specified, the length 1 is assumed; otherwise we specify a character string of the given length. This length must be at least 1 and at most 32767. As long as the string variable exists, its length remains invariant. Despite this, PL/I allows operations on different length strings. Implicit truncation or padding with blanks of a shorter string to the right is provided by the system.

```
1        DCL S1 CHAR( 12 );
2        DCL S2 CHAR( 6 ) INIT ( 'STEIN' );
3        DCL S3 CHAR( 6 );
4        S1 = 'FALKEN'; /* S1 = 'FALKEN      ' */
5        SUBSTR( S1, 8, 6 ) = S2;
6        S3 = S1;
```

Example 5-25 PL/I String Operations

The assignment on line 4 provides automatic padding of S1 with blanks, because the sending string is too short. After the assignment, "S1" equals "FALKEN." The built-in function "SUBSTR" on line 5 allows part of "S1" to receive the value of the sending string "S2," so the new value of "S1" is "FALKEN STEIN." Line 6 causes again a truncation, since the receiving string is shorter than the sending one. In Ada, Modula-2, and Pascal such strings are incompatible, and the compiler would have flagged the assignment statement on line 6.

Despite the convenience of truncation and padding, the PL/I strings in Example 5-25 are fixed in length, as specified in the declaration. For strings that change their actual length, PL/I provides the attribute VARYING. Such varying strings are declared with a maximum length, but the actual length may vary between 0 and that defined maximum. The run time system keeps track of the actual length.

The Cross Reference Generator

Now that we have introduced the Array data structure, we are ready to write the crossref program. The first generation of our solution uses Arrays exclusively. To symbolize this we modify the program name to "crossref_arrays." We write the same program two more times, once with Arrays of Records, and the third time using Pointers to Records.

Let's start with a problem statement. Crossref reads a text file and sorts all unique lowercase identifiers (names) in lexicographical order. These names are stored in a binary tree. For each occurrence of an identifier, crossref stores the linenumber. When the whole file has been read, crossref prints all names in alphabetical order and emits the linenumbers where they occur.

Only the first 16 significant characters of each identifier are considered; the rest is simply skipped. Each node of the binary tree has five elements called "name," "first," "last," "smaller" and "bigger." "Name" holds the up to 16 characters of the identifier, "smaller" defines the subtree with all names that come before, and "bigger" describes the subtree with names coming after the current identifier. "First" and "last" delineate a linked list of linenumbers for each name. If an identifier appears just once in a text file, then "first" and "last" hold identical information. Otherwise, "first" points to the head and "last" identifies the tail of the linked list. This way an insertion can be accomplished in one step rather than running through all elements of a chain.

The binary tree is not guaranteed to be balanced. Therefore, if the incoming identifiers are not equally distributed, the tree can develop anomalous growth. In the worst case (there are, unfortunately, many of them) the tree can deteriorate into a linked list. But this should not disturb us here. Our goal is to learn about structured data types, not about tree balancing, so we choose to live with that danger.

Logically, all information is stored in a tree. Each node contains the previously mentioned five fields, two of which describe a linked list of linenumber items. Since we choose to restrict the solution to Arrays, we cannot group the five fields into a Record; this will be done in the second generation of our "crossref" program. Also the linked list of linenumber items and the two subtrees of each node cannot be implemented via Pointers because of our voluntary restriction. Instead we must express this via Array indices. To help us understand the solution, we draw a sample node in Figure 5-3.

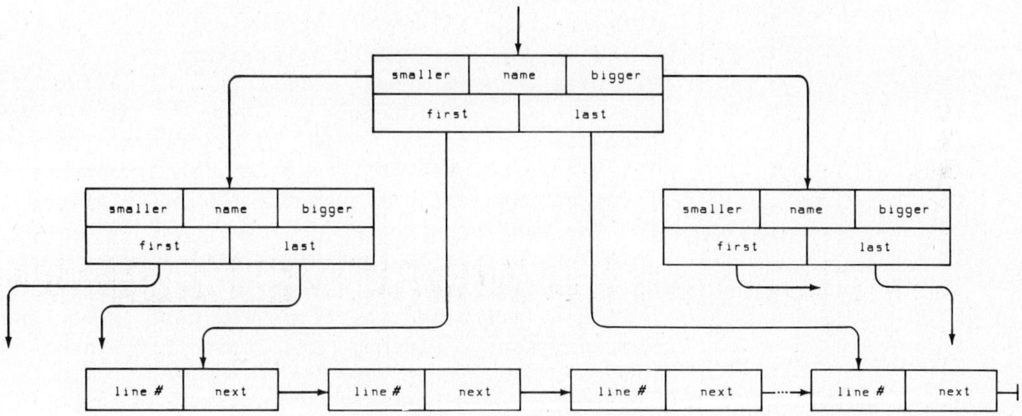

Figure 5-3 Graph of Nodes

The Ada program in Example 5-26 declares 5 one-dimensional Arrays with identical bounds in order to represent a collection of the five data items "name," "first," "last," "smaller," and "bigger." The items pointed at by "first" and "last" are also described via Arrays, both with the same bounds. The latter is larger than the five other Arrays, since we expect that the total number of identifier occurrences will be larger than the number of unique identifiers.

Initially, the tree is empty, hence "root" is set to "nil." In the Arrays-only solution "nil" is an integer constant that signifies this special meaning. Then, as long as the end of the source file has not been reached, the program processes one line after another and builds the tree. Finally, the tree is printed. For interested readers we recommend studying the listing in Example 5-26 from the bottom up; start with lines 157 to 167. Then understand "processline" and "printtree."

```
                 | WITH text_io; USE text_io;
                 | PROCEDURE crossref_arrays IS
           1     |  signifchars      : CONSTANT integer :=  16;
      10   1     |  numsperline      : CONSTANT integer :=   8;
      10   1     |  digitspernum     : CONSTANT integer :=   6;
      10   1     |  maxnode          : CONSTANT integer := 250;
      10   1     |  maxitem          : CONSTANT integer := 500;
      10   1     |  nil              : CONSTANT integer :=  -1;
      10   1     |  TYPE alfarange IS RANGE 1 .. signifchars;
           1     |  TYPE noderange IS RANGE 0 .. maxnode;
           1     |  TYPE itemrange IS RANGE 0 .. maxitem;
           1     |  TYPE alfa      IS ARRAY( alfarange ) of character;
           1     |  root             : integer;
      11   1     |-- node has 5 elements. "Name" is the stored identifier.
      11   1     |-- "First" is pointer to item-node with linenumber of
      11   1     |-- first occurrence in the source. "Last" similar
      11   1     |-- for the last occurrence.
      11   1     |-- "Smaller" points to subtree with all idents lexi-
      11   1     |-- cally smaller than the current. "Bigger" again
      11   1     |-- points to all names that come lexically after the
      11   1     |-- current ident. "Linenum" and "next" for linked list.
      11   1     |  nextnode         : integer;
      12   1     |  nextitem         : integer;
      13   1     |  curchar          : character;
      14   1     |  sourcelinenum    : integer;
      15   1     |  buff             : alfa;
      31   1     |  linelength,
      10   1     |  curcharindex     : integer;
      33   1     |  line             : ARRAY( 0 .. 132 ) OF character;
     166   1     |  name             : ARRAY( noderange ) OF alfa;
    4182   1     |  first,
      10   1     |  last,
      10   1     |  smaller,
      10   1     |  bigger           : ARRAY( noderange ) OF integer;
    5186   1     |  linenum,
      10   1     |  next             : ARRAY( itemrange ) OF integer;
    6188   1     |
    6188   1     | FUNCTION getnextnode RETURN noderange IS
           2     |  BEGIN--getnextnode
           2     |   nextnode := nextnode + 1;--no check for overflow
 6         2  1  |   RETURN nextnode;
11         2  1  |  END getnextnode;
11         1     |
11         1     | FUNCTION getnextitem RETURN Itemrange IS
13         2     |  BEGIN--getnextitem
13         2     |   nextitem := nextitem + 1;--no check for overflow
19         2  1  |   RETURN nextitem;
24         2  1  |  END getnextitem;
```

```
49   24         1    |
50   24         1    | PROCEDURE search(
51   26         2    |   root          : IN OUT integer ) IS
52   26   11    2    |   item          : integer;
53   26   12    2    | BEGIN--search
54   26         2    |   IF root = nil THEN
55   31         2  1 |     root := getnextnode;
56   37         2  2 |     item := getnextitem;
57   43         2  2 |     name( root ) := buff;
58   50         2  2 |     smaller( root ) := nil;
59   56         2  2 |     bigger( root ) := nil;
60   62         2  2 |     first( root ) := item;
61   68         2  2 |     last( root ) := item;
62   74         2  2 |     linenum( item ) := sourcelinenum;
63   80         2  2 |     next( item ) := nil;
64   86         2  2 |   ELSIF buff < name( root ) THEN
65   96         2  1 |     search( smaller( root ) );
66  104         2  2 |   ELSIF buff > name( root ) THEN
67  114         2  1 |     search( bigger( root ) );
68  122         2  2 |   ELSE--equal
69  122         2  1 |     item := getnextitem;
70  129         2  2 |     linenum( item ) := sourcelinenum;
71  135         2  2 |     next( item ) := nil;
72  141         2  2 |     next( last( root ) ) := item;
73  151         2  2 |     last( root ) := item;
74  157         2  2 |   END IF;
75  157         2  1 | END search;
76  157         1    |
77  157         1    | PROCEDURE printtree(
78  159         2    |   root          : integer ) IS
79  159   11    2    |
80  159   11    2    |   PROCEDURE printnode(
81  159         3    |   node      : integer ) IS
82  159   11    3    |   nums      : integer;
83  159   12    3    |   item      : integer;
84  159   13    3    |   BEGIN--printnode
85  159         3    |   put( name( node ) );
86  167         3  1 |   item := first( node );
87  174         3  1 |   nums := 0;
88  177         3  1 |   WHILE item /= nil LOOP
89  181         3  1 |    IF nums = numsperline THEN
90  185         3  2 |     new_line( output );
91  186         3  3 |     nums := 0;
92  189         3  3 |      put( "               " );
93  191         3  3 |    END IF;
94  191         3  2 |    nums := nums + 1;
95  196         3  2 |    put( linenum( item ), digitspernum );
96  203         3  2 |    item := next( item );
```

```
 97  210        3  2  |   END LOOP;
 98  211        3  1  |   new_line( output );
 99  212        3  1  |   END printnode;
100  212        2     |
101  212        2     | BEGIN--printtree
102  214        2     |  IF root /= nil THEN
103  219        2  1  |   printtree( smaller( root ) );
104  228        2  2  |   printnode( root );
105  232        2  2  |   printtree( bigger( root ) );
106  241        2  2  |  END IF;
107  241        2  1  | END printtree;
108  241        1     |
109  241        1     | PROCEDURE getcurchar(
110  243        2     |  curchar      : IN OUT character ) IS
111  243    11  2     | BEGIN--getcurchar
112  243        2     |  IF curcharindex = linelength THEN
113  248        2  1  |   sourcelinenum := sourcelinenum + 1;
114  253        2  2  |   linelength := 0;
115  256        2  2  |   curcharindex := 0;
116  259        2  2  |   WHILE NOT end_of_line( input ) LOOP
117  262        2  2  |    linelength := linelength + 1;
118  267        2  3  |    IF NOT end_of_file( input ) THEN
119  270        2  3  |     get( input, line( linelength ) );
120  275        2  4  |    END IF;
121  275        2  3  |   END LOOP;
122  276        2  2  |   linelength := linelength + 1;
123  281        2  2  |   IF NOT end_of_file( input ) THEN
124  284        2  2  |    line( linelength ) := ' ';
125  290        2  3  |    skip_line( input );
126  291        2  3  |   ELSE
127  291        2  2  |    curcharindex := linelength;
128  295        2  3  |   END IF;
129  295        2  2  |  END IF;
130  295        2  1  |  curcharindex := curcharindex + 1;
131  300        2  1  |  curchar := line( curcharindex );
132  307        2  1  | END getcurchar;
133  307        1     |
134  307        1     | PROCEDURE processline IS
135  309        2     |  length       : integer;
136  309    11  2     | BEGIN--processline
137  309        2     |  getcurchar( curchar );
138  315        2  1  |  WHILE curcharindex < linelength LOOP
139  319        2  1  |   IF curchar IN 'a' .. 'z' THEN
140  324        2  2  |    length := 0;
141  327        2  3  |    buff := "        ";
142  330        2  3  |    WHILE curchar IN 'a' .. 'z' OR
                              curchar IN '0' .. '9' LOOP
143  340        2  3  |     IF length < signifchars THEN
```

```
344      2  4  |       length := length + 1;
349      2  5  |       buff( length ) := curchar;
355      2  5  |      END IF;
355      2  4  |      getcurchar( curchar );
360      2  4  |     END LOOP;
361      2  3  |     search( root );
366      2  3  |    ELSE
366      2  2  |     getcurchar( curchar );
372      2  3  |    END IF;
372      2  2  |   END LOOP;
373      2  1  |  END processline;
373      1     |
373      1     | BEGIN--crossref_arrays
375      1     |  root := nil;
379      1  1  |  nextnode := nil;
382      1  1  |  nextitem := nil;
385      1  1  |  sourcelinenum := 0;
388      1  1  |  curcharindex := 0;
391      1  1  |  linelength := 0;
394      1  1  |  WHILE NOT end_of_file( input ) LOOP
397      1  1  |   processline;
400      1  2  |  END LOOP;
401      1  1  |  printtree( root );
405      1  1  | END crossref_arrays;
```

Example 5-26 Cross Reference Generator in Ada, Using Arrays

Records

An Array is a linear collection of distinct objects with identical type, randomly accessible under one name. A *Record* is a collection of individually named objects with possibly different types. The names are known as *Record Fields* and serve to qualify the Record name. In PL/I (Algol-68 and C) the term *Structure* is used in place of Record. Records provide a mechanism for physically grouping objects together under one name that logically should belong together despite permissible differences in type. For example, we can express complex numbers as Records. These may consist of an ordered pair of real numbers, one known as "ImaginaryPart" and the other as "RealPart." A Modula-2 declaration that does this and related qualified references are shown in Example 5-27.

```
TYPE
 ComplexType      =
  RECORD
   RealPart       : REAL;
   ImaginaryPart  : REAL;
  END;
VAR
 C1, C2, ComplexSum : ComplexType;
BEGIN
 C1.RealPart := 12.0;
 C1.ImaginaryPart := 12.0;
 C2.RealPart := C1.RealPart + 5.54;
 C2.ImaginaryPart := C1.ImaginaryPart + 5.54;
 ComplexSum := C2;
```

Example 5-27 Qualified Modula-2 Names

A data base that stores all pertinent information about employees of a company may represent the people as a collection of Records, as expressed in Pascal in Example 5-28.

```
TYPE
 sextype        = ( male, female );
 yearrange      = 1800 .. 2100;
 datetype       =
  RECORD
   day          : 1 .. 31;
   month        : 1 .. 12;
   year         : yearrange;
  END;
 persontype     =
  RECORD
   name,
   firstname    : alfa;
   middle       : char;
   birthdate,
   hiredate     : datetype;
   sex          : sextype;
   salary       : real;
  END;
VAR
  president      : persontype;
BEGIN
  president.name := 'EINSTEIN  ';
  president.first := 'ALBERT    ';
  president.hiredate.day := 1;
  president.hiredate.month := 7;
```

Example 5-28 Qualified Pascal Names

Example 5-28 demonstrates another point regarding qualified Record names. Quite frequently a large number of statements use the same prefix to access a Record field. In Example 5-28 we see the prefix "president" and "president.hiredate" used repeatedly. If the structures become more complex, such common prefixes also become more complicated and involve Pointer dereferences and Array indices as well. To abbreviate the writing effort somehow and to allow the translator to emit efficient code without having to invoke an optimization phase, Pascal and Modula-2 provide the With Statement. However, we decided not to cover the With Statement here because of its built-in disadvantage: it renders the source less readable and can become a dangerous construct. Readers who are interested in finding out more detail about the mentioned danger are referred to a short treatise written by a promoter of the With Statement, Wirth [1982], pages 68 and 69.

Figure 5-4 represents the "persontype" Record structure in a pictorial way. For readers with little prior understanding of Records, the picture may be of help to interpret the Record declarations of Example 5-28. As is visible from Figure 5-4, the fields of a Record can themselves be Records. Any depth of nesting is possible. To reference a field, a fully qualified name must be given in Ada, Modula-2, and Pascal. In PL/I (and Cobol) an abbreviated form is legal by specifying only part of the qualified name, as long as that portion is unambiguous. Fortran has no Records, so the issue does not come up.

Mapping Records onto Storage

How does a compiler map Record fields into addressable units of physical memory? It maps them the same way it maps a sequence of scalar variables into memory. We list only a few ground rules here. Sometimes the operand types involved and the addressability of the target machine go hand in hand. In that case the mapping, also inappropriately known as storage allocation, is simple. For example, on a word-addressable target machine where each integer consumes a full 60-bit word, the mapping of an integer variable is one-to-one. But typically source programs contain a mix of boolean, character, and integer type variables. This is true for individual scalars as well as Records. We know that a boolean operand could be packed into less than a full word; indeed one single bit would be sufficient to store all of its possible values. Or a character type operand would need only 7 bits in Ascii (8 bits in Ebcdic), not a full word. How does a compiler react when faced with the challenge to pack? What are its choices?

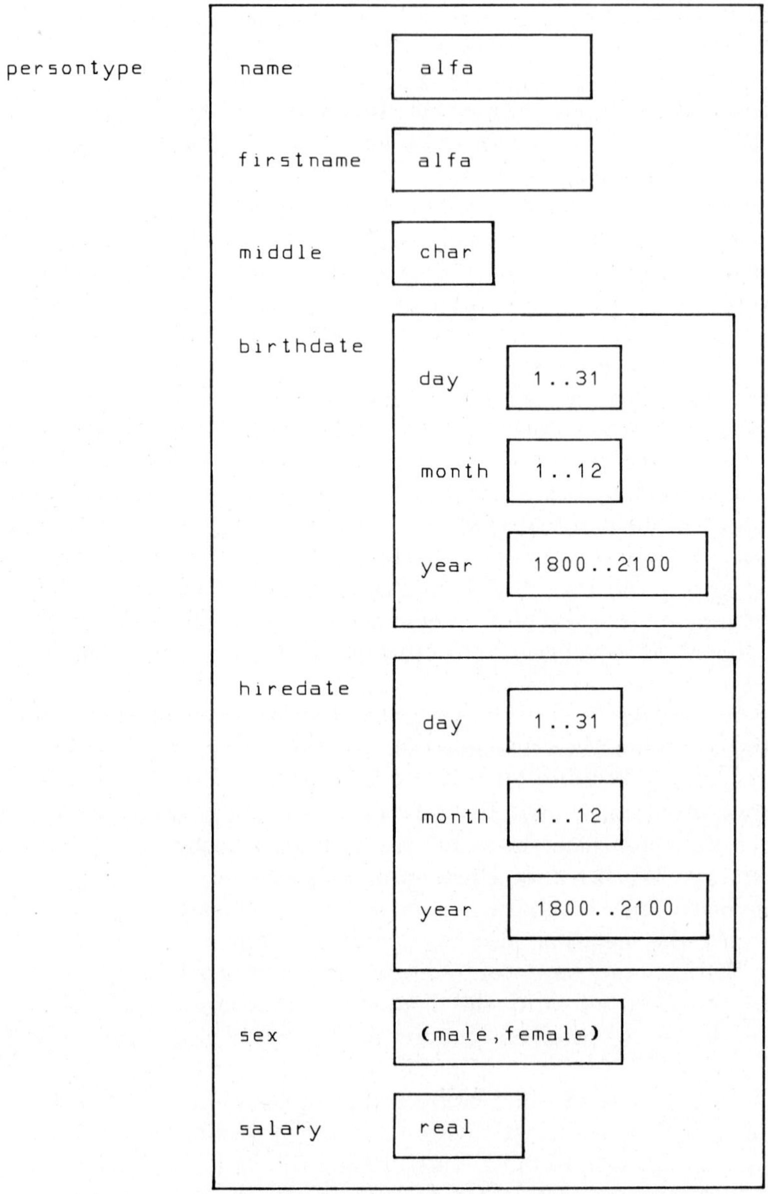

Figure 5-4 Pictorial Representation of Persontype

Packed or Unpacked?

If we continue with our initial assumption of a word-addressable target, where each unit is 60 bits wide, the compiler could pack quite a number of booleans and characters into one word. But there is a price to be paid if the 60-bit machine word can be addressed only as a whole. In order to extract the value of a single bit it would be necessary to generate careful shift and mask instructions, to preserve the values of other objects that reside in the same addressable unit. Clearly this increases the object code size and slows down execution. On the other hand, the compiler could map storage in a nonconservative way and provide a full 60-bit word for each boolean, character, and enumeration type variable. Many currently used compilers use this simplistic approach. Either approach has its advantage. Users don't always like the choice taken by the compiler. Therefore ADA provides the representation specification, and Pascal the PACKED attribute. The purpose of the *representation Specification* is to give the programmer full control over the number of smallest storage units (bits) and positions for each operand. The Pascal PACKED attribute indicates to the compiler which of the storage mapping strategies, the space-conserving or the time-conserving one, is preferred by the user. Specifying a PACKED Array or Record does not guarantee that the compiler will really pack data more densely than in the unpacked form.

The whole issue becomes more complex on machines that have alignment requirements. On IBM (360-family) machines, for example, individual bytes are addressable, but an integer operand must still start on a word boundary. If our source program declares a Record with one integer, a character, and another integer type field, then the mapping algorithm can easily create "holes." For a demonstration see Example 5-29.

```
VAR
 tricky  =
  RECORD
   i1    : integer;
   c1    : char;
   i2    : integer;
   c2,
   c3,
   c4    : char;
  END;
```

Example 5-29 Data Mapping

```
  0   1   2   3   4   5   6   7   8   9   10  11  12  13  14  15
+---+---+---+---+---+---+---+---+---+---+---+---+---+---+---+---+
|               |   | ??  ??  ?? |              |   |   |   | ?? |
+---+---+---+---+---+---+---+---+---+---+---+---+---+---+---+---+
|<----- i1 ----->|<c1>|<-- hole -->|<----- i2 ----->|<c2>|<c3>|<c4>|hole|
```

Figure 5-5 Order Preserving Mapping of Declarations onto Storage

If the compiler maps data in the order of occurrence in the source, which is indeed a simple and very often used policy, then there are suddenly three holes in memory. Three bytes of storage between "c1" and "i2" are associated with no object. Chances are that the byte with address 15 will also become a "hole." Another policy that is slightly more complicated looks ahead and attempts to group together multiple short fields that have no alignment requirements. See Figure 5-6.

```
  0   1   2   3   4   5   6   7   8   9   10  11
+---+---+---+---+---+---+---+---+---+---+---+---+
|               |   |   |   |   |               |
+---+---+---+---+---+---+---+---+---+---+---+---+
|<----- i1 ----->|<c1>|<c2>|<c3>|<c4>|<----- i2 ----->|
```

Figure 5-6 Mapping of Rearranged Declarations onto Storage

The advantage of the second method is obvious. All data are equally accessible, but less storage is required. A "real life" compiler has a much harder task. Many target machines have multiple annoying restrictions, such as the previously cited alignment requirement. These samples have been listed here only to provide a flavour of the problem. A full discussion of this belongs in the related topics of compiler construction, not programming languages.

Variant Records

Quite commonly we wish to interpret the same data structure by more than one type. The stricter the type checking policy of a language, the less possible becomes such a wish. Still, there are situations where we can "guarantee" that one object at one moment of time has exactly one of several interpretations. It seems plausible to use the same storage area instead of a separate area for each distinct type. Later on we shall see that the violation of this guarantee is a typical source of a severe programming error. Modula-2 and Pascal provide *Variant Records* to accommodate our wish for type reinterpretation. Type reinterpretation in Ada's Variant Records is possible only under special conditions—the Pragma that suppresses discriminant checks must be used. PL/I's DEFINES declarations and Fortran's EQUIVALENCE Statement provide a similar service.

Variant Records allow us to define as part of a Record a variety of types, only one of which will be effective at any one time. Which of the type cases applies is controlled by a "tag variable" in Modula-2 and Pascal, and a "discriminant" in Ada. Modula-2 and Pascal also offer tagless Variant Records. Before we confuse the issue for readers who are unfamiliar with the subject, let us present an example.

Suppose a data base for medical applications stores vital data for each person. Since the data base "knows" that a person can only be male or female, it stores some information separately for men and women. For women the number of children born and children alive is stored, for men the length of their beard. Facts common to both are also stored. All of this is shown expressed in Pascal in Example 5-30.

```
TYPE
 medicalpersontype =
  RECORD
   name              : alfa;
   birthyear         : 1800 .. 2100;
   CASE sex          : ( sextype ) OF
    male             : (
     beardlength     : integer );
    female           : (
    childrenborn     : integer;
    childrenalive    : integer );
   {END CASE}
  END;
```

Example 5-30 Variant Record Mapping

The common part precedes the variant part (in Ada and Pascal). The variant part starts with the reserved keyword CASE and ends at the end of the Record. Tag variable "sex" has two possible values, for each of which we list one case variant enclosed in parentheses. Inside the parentheses may come any number of Record fields, all mutually exclusive from the common part and from other case variants. The exact syntax rules are expressed in the following language-specific sections.

Let a "medicalperson" of the type in Example 5-30 have the attributes assigned by the following statements in Example 5-31.

```
medicalperson.name := 'Mary      ';
medicalperson.birthyear := 1946;
medicalperson.sex := female;
medicalperson.childrenborn := 3;
medicalperson.childrenalive := 3;
```

Example 5-31   Variant Record Fields

If we access the field "beardlength" for Mary defined in this example, we would violate our promise to interpret the variant part consistently. Whatever the "beardlength" turns out to be, it would be invalid and we cause a severe programming error. Notice that a compiler cannot generally check if the reference to a field in a case variant is legal.

This introduction into Records and Variant Records has covered much of the commonalities in the various languages. The next sections discuss particular rules for the respective languages.

Records in Ada

For an empty Ada statement we must explicitly write NULL, and such a Null Statement, like any statement, must be terminated by a semicolon. Ada treats Records analogously; the empty (or null) Record is allowed, but must be expressed by the explicit NULL field. Each record component is explicitly terminated by a semicolon, again in analogy with the rules for statements.

It is important to realize that Ada Record fields may be initialized. Each Record object whose type mark includes such an initialization value will receive that value at the time it comes to life, but the default initialization can be explicitly overwritten.

```
TYPE complex_type IS
 RECORD
  real_part       : real := 0.0;
  imaginary_part  : real := 0.0;
 END RECORD;
  a, field_vector : complex_type;--initialized to ( 0.0, 0.0 )
  b, c            : complex_type := ( 5.0, 3.3 );--initialization
```

Example 5-32   Ada Record Initialization

Record variables "b" and "c" are not initialized to the default but are assigned the explicit Record type aggregate (5.0, 3.3). "A" and "field_vector," on the other hand, receive the default initial value.

Next comes the grammar for Ada Records (see Example 5-33); the tie-in of the discriminant part will be explained verbally. Overall Ada Records have the largest number of rules, only very few of which are explained in this text. We refer the interested reader to Chapter 3.7 in the Ada LRM (Language Reference Manual) ANSI [1983a].

```
ada_record_type        ::= RECORD component_list END RECORD
component_list         ::= component_declaration { component_declaration }
                         | { component_declaration } variant_part
                         | NULL ;
component_declaration ::= identifier_list : subtype_indication
                          [ := expression ] ;
variant_part           ::= CASE discriminant_name IS
                            variant { variant }
                           END CASE ;
variant                ::= WHEN choice { | choice } => component_list
choice                 ::= simple_expression
                         | discrete_range
                         | OTHERS
discriminant_part      ::= ( discriminant_spec { ; discriminant_spec } )
discriminant_spec      ::= identifier_list : type_mark [ := expression ]
```

Example 5-33 Grammar Fragment for Ada Records

The grammar for Ada Records does not show how the variant part ties in with the discriminant. This is because the specification of discriminants is separated from the Record proper and is part of the type mark. We shall give an example for the discriminants in a moment, but first let us explain the purpose of discriminants.

Discriminants

Discriminants have two distinct functions. First, a Record field like any other object may be constrained. The discriminant, which must be type compatible with such a constrained range, defines the lower or upper bound. Second, the discriminant serves to select one from a set of Variants in a Variant Record, based on the value of a choice. If no choice matches the value of a discriminant, then the OTHERS choice is required and becomes effective. See Examples 5-34 and 5-35.

```
TYPE buffer_type( size : size_type := 100 ) IS
 RECORD
  value  : string( 1 .. size );--discriminant sets upper bound
  length : buffer_length_type;
 END RECORD;
small_buff : buffer_type( 200 );--overwrite discriminant's default
message    : buffer_type;       --use discriminant's default
```

Example 5-34 Discriminant Used to Fix Constraint

```
TYPE device IS ( printer, disc, streamer );
TYPE state  IS ( open, closed );
TYPE peripheral( unit : device := disc ) IS
 RECORD
  status     : state;
  CASE unit IS
  WHEN printer =>
   line_count : integer RANGE 0 .. page_size;
   page_count : integer RANGE 0 .. max_page;
  WHEN streamer =>
   byte_count : integer RANGE 0 .. max_int;
   block_count : integer;
  WHEN OTHERS =>
   cylinder     : cylinder_index_type;
   track        : track_range;
  END CASE;
 END RECORD;
SUBTYPE streaming_tape IS peripheral( streamer );
SUBTYPE main_disc      IS peripheral( disc );
```

Example 5-35 Discriminant Used to Select Choice from Variants

Ada is quite safe in treating Variant Records. Changing the value of a discriminant alone via an Assignment Statement or by using the discriminant as an OUT or IN OUT parameter in procedure calls is not allowed. Instead the value of the complete Record must be changed, thus possibly also changing the discriminant. The compiler (or run time system) can then perform type checks and detect any possible, dangerous abuse of Variant Records.

Records in Modula-2

Similar to Ada, Modula-2 Variant Records include a catchall case in the form of the Else Clause. With the Else Clause it is not necessary to enumerate all possible values of the tag field. If given, the Else Clause must come last. Different Variant cases are separated from one another by a vertical bar. We should realize that this presents a particular notational problem for the

Modula-2 grammar in Example 5-36, because the | symbol is also used as a metasymbol. We have explained the escape mechanism in Chapter 1, but we repeat again: if the { metasymbol is immediately followed by a vertical bar |, then the | is interpreted as a terminals symbol. We have adopted this not very elegant escape hatch from ANSI [1983a], the Ada standard.

The most unusual side of Modula-2's Records is the liberty of having any number of variant parts in one Record. The variant part does not need to be the last Record component. See Example 5-36.

```
SexType     = ( Male, Female );
PersonType =
 RECORD
  LastName,
  FirstName        : NameType;
  MiddleInitial : CHAR;
  CASE sex : SexType OF
   male: MilitaryService : BOOLEAN |
   female: MaidenName      : NameType;
  END;
  SocialSecurityNumber    : SSNType;
  BirthDate               : DateType;
  CASE MaritalStatus      : StatusType OF
   married: SpouseName    : NameType;
   ChildrenBorn : CARDINAL;
   WeddingDate   : DateType |
   single:   |
   widowed: Since          : DateType
 END
END
```

Example 5-36   Multiple Variants in Modula-2 Records

Modula-2 Variant Records are not as safe as Ada's. Since it is legal (though not advisable) to modify the tag field without setting the Record fields of the associated variant,

```
modula2_record_type ::= RECORD component_list END
component_list      ::= field_list { ; field_list }
field_list          ::= identifier_list : type_mark
                      | LAMBDA
                      | variant_field_list
variant_field_list  ::= CASE [ identifier : ] type_mark OF
                        variant { | variant }
                        [ ELSE component_list ]
                        END
variant             ::= case_label_list : component_list
case_label_list     ::= case_labels { , case_labels }
case_labels         ::= constant_expression [ .. constant_expression ]
```

Example 5-37 Grammar Fragment For Modula-2 Records

the tag field provides the illusion of correct data. This would make it possible, for example, to change a variant from "Male" to "Female," but maintain the "MilitaryService" and leave "MaidenName" uninitialized. The programming error will be devious and is in general not detectable by the compiler.

The vocabulary in the Modula-2 world uses *tag field* and *discriminator* interchangeably, one term displaying the close Pascal relationship, the other reminding us of Ada's terminology.

Records in Pascal

Records in Pascal are very similar to those in Modula-2, but are more restrictive. We list the predominant restrictions. Variant Records have no Else Clause; therefore all values of the tag field must be enumerated. If a number of choices forms a close range, it is still required in Pascal to enumerate them all individually, separated from one another by commas. We shall encounter the same programming nuisance later in Pascal's Case Statement. Modula-2 and Ada allow a range specification as a convenient shorthand.

Even though Pascal Variant Records may be nested arbitrarily deep, any Record level can have only one variant. The variant must be listed last in the Record. A complete BNF grammar is shown in Example 5-38.

```
pascal_record_type      ::= [ PACKED ] RECORD component_list END
component_list          ::= component_declaration { ; component_declaration }
                           [ ; variant_part ] [ ; ]
                           | variant_part [ ; ]
component_declaration   ::= identifier_list : type_mark
                           |
variant_part            ::= CASE [ identifier : ] type_mark OF
                            variant { ; variant }
variant                 ::= case_label_list : ( component_list )
case_label_list         ::= case_label { , case_label }
case_label              ::= constant
```

Example 5-38 Grammar Fragment for Pascal Records

The BNF grammar for Pascal Records shows us that Records and variants may be empty. Moreover, any variant of the variant part may have an empty component declaration.

Structures in PL/I

By convention, the PL/I term for Record is *structure.* A structure is identified by a level number that precedes the structure name being declared. All fields or substructures underneath are also marked by level numbers. The absolute value of these level numbers is not significant; in particular, the level of nesting does not equal the level number. It is the relative ordering of these level numbers that determines which field and which substructure are embedded in another structure. See Example 5-39.

```
DECLARE
 1 BOOK,
    4 TITLE CHAR( 25 ),
    3 NUMPAGES BIN FIXED( 15 ),
    3 CHAPTERS,
       4 TITLE1 CHAR( 25 ),
       4 TITLE2 CHAR( 25 );
```

Example 5-39 PL/I Structure

"BOOK" is the major structure, because it is not embedded in any other structure. "TITLE" and "NUMPAGES" have type attributes, hence they are not structures but elementary fields. These can be treated like any other variable. "CHAPTERS," however, is a minor structure. We identify it as a structure because it has no type attributes; it is not a major structure, so it must be a minor one. The level number 4 for "TITLE" is greater than 1, which makes this field a subordinate to "BOOK."

Next comes a more tricky situation. Level number 3 for "NUMPAGES" is not greater than the previous level number 4, hence it cannot be a subordinate of "TITLE." Also 3 is not equal to any other minor structure level, since there are none so far. Therefore, the 3 defines "NUMPAGES" to be on the same level as the 4 does for "TITLE." The same holds for the next level number 3 of "CHAPTERS."

The next two level numbers 4 are both subordinates of "CHAPTERS," so we see that two identical level numbers can define different levels in the same structure. The 4 for "TITLE1" is nested one level deeper than the 4 for "TITLE." In Example 5-40 we list a very abbreviated grammar for PL/I structures.

```
pl1_structure_type ::= structure_field { , structure_field } ;

structure_field    ::= high_level
                     | low_level
                     | group

high_level         ::= level_number field_name

low_level          ::= level_number field_name type_specification

group              ::= ( high_level { , high_level } ) type_specification

level_number       ::= integer_constant

field_name         ::= identifier
```

Example 5-40 Shortened Grammar Fragment for PL/I Structures

PL/I has no equivalent of Variant Records in the structure declaration. We shall not cover the DEFINED declaration that can accomplish a similar service.

PL/I offers an abbreviation in qualifying structure fields directly inherited from Cobol. The general rule for qualifying names is "a name needs to be qualified only to the extent to yield an unambiguous path." Since all structure names on the same level (not level number!) need to be unique, a fully qualified name is always unique and hence causes no ambiguity. Any subpart thereof may be omitted, as long as the remaining name cannot be mistaken for another. See Example 5-41.

```
DECLARE
 1 STUDENT,
 2 CAMPUS,
    3 ADDRESS CHAR( 30 ),
    3 TEL     CHAR( 10 ),
 2 HOME,
    3 ADDRESS CHAR( 30 ),
    3 PHONE   CHAR( 10 ),
 2 REGISTRATION,
    5 CLASS( 10 ) CHAR( 5 ),
    5 GRADES( 10 ) FIXED,
    5 GPA DEC FLOAT;
```

Example 5-41 PL/I Structure Levels

The PL/I names STUDENT.CAMPUS.TEL, STUDENT.TEL, CAMPUS.TEL, and even TEL alone are all unambiguous and refer to the same object. ADDRESS alone is not sufficient, because we have two of them—one in the minor structure CAMPUS, the other in HOME. Similarly STUDENT.ADDRESS is ambiguous. We have to add either CAMPUS or HOME.

Another "interesting" abbreviation is the liberty of placing Array subscripts anywhere inside a qualified name, as long as the relative order of multiple subscripts remains invariant. In the structure in Example 5-41 we have only two single-subscripted variables. But even here the Assignment Statements in Example 5-42 with the index in different positions all mean the same thing.

```
STUDENT.REGISTRATION(1).GRADES = 4.0;
STUDENT(1).REGISTRATION.GRADES = 4.0;
STUDENT.REGISTRATION.GRADES(1) = 4.0;
```

Example 5-42 PL/I Name Qualification

Neither REGISTRATION nor STUDENT are Arrays, but the first two Assignment Statements imply that they are. Only after checking the declaration do we see that both are structures. We leave it as a challenging exercise for the reader to find out what this facility in PL/I is good for.

The Cross Reference Generator Using Records

We have sufficiently covered Records to present a "crossref" implementation that uses this data structure. The main differences between the program in Example 5-43 and the previous solution are consequential to the differences of parallel Arrays and Arrays of Records. We need two Record types, both presented in the "Graph of Nodes" in Figure 5-3: one Record for the node of five fields, the other for a linenumber item. Our Records types have the names "nodetype" and "itemtype."

As a consequence of the new structure, the operands are referenced differently. While in the previous solution five distinct Arrays are accessed individually, always with the same index for the same logical node, here we access only one Array element, which is a Record. We then qualify the Record to find any of the five fields.

In Example 5-43 we show only sections of the solution to highlight the differences with the Arrays-only implementation.

```
                       |  ...
13              1      |  TYPE nodetype   IS
14              1      |  RECORD
15              1      |    name              : alfa;
16              1      |    first,
17              1      |    last              : integer;
18              1      |    smaller,
19              1      |    bigger            : integer;
20              1      |  END RECORD;
21              1      |  TYPE itemtype   IS
22              1      |  RECORD
23              1      |    linenum     : integer;
24              1      |    next        : integer;
25              1      |  END RECORD;
                       |  ...
35       166    1      |  nodes        : ARRAY( noderange ) OF nodetype;
36      5186    1      |  items        : ARRAY( itemrange ) OF itemtype;
                       |  ...
50       24     1      | PROCEDURE search(
51       26     2      |   root       : IN OUT integer ) IS
52       26  11 2      |   item       : integer;
53       26  12 2      | BEGIN--search
54       26     2      |   IF root = nil THEN
55       31     2  1   |     root := getnextnode;
56       37     2  2   |     item := getnextitem;
57       43     2  2   |     nodes( root ).name := buff;
58       50     2  2   |     nodes( root ).smaller := nil;
59       58     2  2   |     nodes( root ).bigger := nil;
60       66     2  2   |     nodes( root ).first := item;
61       74     2  2   |     nodes( root ).last := item;
62       82     2  2   |     items( item ).linenum := linenum;
63       89     2  2   |     items( item ).next := nil;
64       97     2  2   |   ELSIF buff < nodes( root ).name THEN
65      107     2  1   |     search( nodes( root ).smaller );
66      117     2  2   |   ELSIF buff > nodes( root ).name THEN
67      127     2  1   |     search( nodes( root ).bigger );
```

```
 68  137          2  2 |   ELSE--equal
 69  137          2  1 |    item := getnextitem;
 70  144          2  2 |    items( item ).linenum := linenum;
 71  151          2  2 |    items( item ).next := nil;
 72  159          2  2 |    items( nodes( root ).last ).next := item;
 73  173          2  2 |    nodes( root ).last := item;
 74  181          2  2 |   END IF;
 75  181          2  1 |  END search;
 76  181          1    |
 77  181          1    | PROCEDURE printtree(
 78  183          2    |  root         : integer ) IS
 79  183     11   2    |
 80  183     11   2    |  PROCEDURE printnode(
 81  183          3    |   node       : integer ) IS
 82  183     11   3    |   nums       : integer;
 83  183     12   3    |   item       : integer;
 84  183     13   3    |  BEGIN--printnode
 85  183          3    |   put( nodes( node ).name );
 86  191          3  1 |   item := nodes( node ).first;
                       |   ...
 99  241          3  1 |  END printnode;
100  241          2    |
101  241          2    | BEGIN--printtree
102  243          2    |  IF root /= nil THEN
103  248          2  1 |   printtree( nodes( root ).smaller );
104  259          2  2 |   printnode( root );
105  263          2  2 |   printtree( nodes( root ).bigger );
106  274          2  2 |  END IF;
107  274          2  1 | END printtree;
                       | ...
```

Example 5-43   Cross Reference Generator in Ada, Using Arrays of Records

Pointers

Why are Pointers treated in this section at all? A *Pointer* by itself does not represent a structured data type. On a physical level we can interpret Pointers as addresses, not as structures. But Pointers allow us to create the most general data structures, those with inherently recursive properties and those with dynamic space requirements.

Pointers to the Heap or Anywhere?

The world of "pointer users" is split into two camps. One expresses the philosophy that Pointers should be able to point to anything, code and data. PL/I (and C) follow this direction. The other side promotes the more restricted view that pointers are tied to a specific type and can only reference data objects allocated from a special data pool called the system "heap." Ada, Modula-2, and Pascal represent this school of thought. The name "heap" indicates that its storage will be managed in a wild, unpredictable fashion.

The size of storage requested is implied by the type of the operand for which space is to be allocated. An extra operand is not necessary when the Pointer is tied to that type. Pieces of the heap are allocated upon request in the size requested, but while allocation continues, older pieces no longer used are being returned to the heap manager for recycling. Since the allocation scheme cannot be implemented by a stack or a queue, it ended up with the less graceful name "heap." In our subsequent discussion we shall concentrate on the second philosophy and mention PL/I Pointers only briefly.

Dynamic Structures

The structured data types discussed so far, Arrays and Records, have one severe limitation: once they are allocated, their size remains fixed. Even if the bounds of Arrays can be defined as late as execution time, once set, they remain locked. Unfortunately, a program's need for storing data may suddenly grow beyond the fixed bounds. Pointers are one handy way to solve this restriction. With Pointers we can build lists, trees, and general graphs, the size and shape (structure) of which can become arbitrarily complex and limited only by the finite heap size.

Elements (also called *nodes)* of such data structures are linked together by Pointers and the nodes in turn contain Pointers to other nodes. Usually nodes are of type Record, with some fields being Pointers to other Records. It is perfectly legal to have the Record containing the Pointer and the Record at which it points be of the same type. Here we are reminded of recursion in procedure calls. Just as recursive procedures must eventually stop calling each other (or themselves), so Pointers at some time must stop establishing further relationships (links) amongst nodes. The nodes that do this are called *end-nodes* or *leafs,* and they hold a special value. This value, called NIL, must be different from every possible legal value. It must express "I point nowhere!"

The NIL value in Ada is expressed by the reserved word NULL. Pointer types are not referred to as Pointers but are called Access Types. Thus we observe in programming languages the same tricks used in the world of fashion: inventing a new name for an old idea makes the old idea seem new.

Dereference Operator in Modula-2 and Pascal

Let "r" be a Record type mark, and "pr" be a Pointer variable tied to such Records. Then the operand "pr" alone designates only the address of some anonymous Record variable, *not* the variable itself. If we wish to designate the variable, we must explicitly dereference its address, spelled "pr^" in Modula-2 and Pascal. In Ada this dereference is implied by name qualification.

New and Dispose

In order to acquire a node from the heap, we must ask a special system function to perform this service for us. In Ada this is accomplished via the allocator NEW, which is used as part of an expression. In Modula-2 the built-in procedure "NEW," also called "Allocate," performs this function. Consistent with Modula-2's policy of requiring the explicit IMPORT of system functions actually used, Modula-2 programs must import Allocate and Deallocate from "Storage." Pascal provides the intrinsic function "NEW" for this purpose. Its single argument is a Pointer type variable that addresses the anonymous, allocated variable, or returns NIL if there is insufficient space.

In order to free previously acquired space, the program must explicitly call the dispose function, and pass the Pointer to the node to be freed as an actual parameter. It is up to the heap manager to recycle the returned space. In either case, it will set the passed Pointer variable to NIL. After "new" returns, we must carefully check whether the passed Pointer is valid. Otherwise it will be NIL.

We need to draw attention to a typical programming error. When we dispose of a storage area, we must ensure that no Pointer other than the one passed as a parameter addresses the freed variable. We cannot expect the runtime system to keep track of multiple Pointers addressing the same heap space, and resetting them all to NIL when one of them disposes that space. Instead we have to set them to NIL via explicit Assignment Statements. Notice that it is always a programming error to dereference a NIL Pointer. NIL is the only value that is compatible with all possible Pointer types.

It is the recursive nature of their type that makes Pointers such a powerful tool for data structuring. During compile time the program contains only very few, in many instances just one single, Pointer type variable. Only during execution time does the data structure come to life, accessible via the Pointer variable.

```
   { Pascal }
1  TYPE
2   nodepintype    = ^ nodetype;
3   nodetype       =
4    RECORD
5     key          : integer;
6     left,
7     right        : nodepintype;
8    END;
9  VAR
10  temppin,
11  nodepin        : nodepintype;
12  node           : nodetype;
13 BEGIN { subprogram body }
14  new( nodepin );         { nodepin points to RECORD in heap }
15  nodepin^.key := somedata;
16  nodepin^.left := NIL;
17  nodepin^.right := NIL;
18  temppin := nodepin;     { temppin points to same RECORD }
19  node := temppin^;       { the whole RECORD is moved }
```

Example 5-44 Sample Pascal Pointers

The Pointer itself does not own the data structure at which it points, and the Pascal (and Modula-2) syntax makes a clear distinction between a reference to a Pointer variable and the dynamic variable at which it points. In Ada this visibility is somewhat obscured by the absence of an explicit dereference operator. See Examples 5-44 and 5-45. We observe something very surprising on line 2 of the Pascal source text in Example 5-44. The type declaration references an undeclared name. This is in complete contrast to Pascal's philosophy that a name must be declared before it can be used. There is one exception to this, and that is in the declaration of recursive Pointer types. The identifier referenced forward must, however, be defined later on in the same type declaration. Ada solves this problem of mutual dependency differently, as we shall see in Example 5-45. Modula-2 is very similar to Pascal with the exception of the reserved words OF POINTER instead of the ^ symbol in a Pointer type declaration. To dereference a Pointer, Modula-2 also uses the ^ symbol. In Example 5-45 we show how Ada solves the issue of recursive Pointer types.

```
        --Ada
 1      TYPE node_type;
 2      TYPE node_pin_type IS ACCESS node_type;
 3      TYPE node_type IS
 4       RECORD
 5        key           : integer;
 6        left,
 7        right         : node_pin_type;
 8       END RECORD;
 9      temp_pin,
10      node_pin        : node_pin_type;
11      node            : node_type;
12     BEGIN--subprogram body
13      node_pin := NEW node_type;--node_pin points to heap
14      node_pin.key := 12345;
15       -- node_pin.left := NULL;    --initialize to NOWHERE, done by default
16       -- node_pin.right := NULL;   --initialize to NOWHERE, done by default
17      temp_pin := node_pin;     --points to same object
18      node := node_pin.ALL;     --move the whole object
```

Example 5-45 Sample Ada Pointers (Access Types)

How does Ada solve the problem of forward reference for the recursive type mark "node_pin_type"? On line 1 we see an incomplete type declaration. It has the sole purpose of announcing the type mark. Even though the reader and the compiler do not know at that moment what the exact type will be, we know that it exists and that it is a type mark: it has been declared and can be referenced. Naturally, a complete declaration of the incomplete type mark must follow. The introduction of an incomplete Ada type mark solves the problem of forward reference for recursive Pointer types in the same way that Ada solves mutually recursive Procedure Calls. We shall rediscover this in Chapters 9 and 11.

On line 18 we see a striking difference from the earlier Pascal solution. Since Ada has no explicit dereference operator, the language must have some means of expressing that we wish to reference the whole dynamic object, accessed by "node_pin." This is accomplished with the pseudo Record field ALL, expressed by the reserved keyword. The name alludes to our wish to reference *all* of the fields. This solution presents an interesting programming language design problem: which solution is more readable, the one taken by Ada (and Algol-68) or the one of Modula-2 and Pascal?

Linked List Manager in Ada

In the next section we demonstrate the use of Pointers in the different languages by actual program examples. We start out with a linked list manager in Ada. The list will be augmented at its "head," hence all data are accessible in the reversed order of their occurrence. Later we show a solution in Modula-2, where a list element is added at the "tail."

```
 4     TYPE node_type;
 5     TYPE node_pin_type IS ACCESS node_type;
 6     TYPE node_type IS
 7      RECORD
 8       data : integer;
 9       next : node_pin_type;
10      END RECORD;
11     first,
12     node_pin : node_pin_type;--automatically NULL
13     data     : integer;
14    BEGIN--linked_list_handler
15     put_line( " Enter list of integers. Last one must be 0." );
16     -- initializations and bookkeeping
17     LOOP
18      read( data );
19      node_pin := NEW node_type;--if heap empty, Raise STORAGE_ERROR
20      node_pin.next := first;
21      node_pin.data := data;
22      first := node_pin;
23      EXIT WHEN data = 0;
24     END LOOP;
25     WHILE node_pin /= NULL LOOP
26      put( " next data element: " );
27      put_line( integer'image( node_pin.data ) );
28      node_pin := node_pin.next;
29     END LOOP;
```

Example 5-46 Linked List Handler Using Ada Access Types

Line 4 announces "node_type" as a type mark, which can henceforth be used in other type declarations. Line 5 declares "node_pin_type" to be an Access type (Pointer) to "node_type" just announced, and line 6 already resolves the incomplete type mark. In Ada one must write one line more of type declarations for recursive Pointer types than in Pascal or Modula-2, but the issue of forward references is solved in a clean manner. On Line 19 we see the allocator "NEW." Syntactically the Ada solution is different from Pascal and Modula-2, but at least the name of the allocator "NEW" contains a strong hint about the semantic commonality with Pascal's built-in function "new."

Linked List Manager in Modula-2

The Modula-2 program fragment in Example 5-47 allocates Records of "ItemType" from the system heap and builds a linked list by adding new elements at the list's tail. In this implementation, elements (nodes) can be accessed in the order of their appearance. The same method will be used in the "crossref" project later in this chapter.

```
 0    FROM Storage IMPORT ALLOCATE, DEALLOCATE;
 1    TYPE
 2     ItemPtrType = POINTER TO ItemType;
 3     ItemType    =
 4      RECORD
 5       Data       : CARDINAL;
 6       Next       : ItemPtrType;
 7      END;
 8    VAR
 9     ItemPtr,
10     FirstPtr,
11     LastPtr      : ItemPtrType;
12   BEGIN  (* Modula-2 Procedure *)
13    LastPtr := NIL;
14    REPEAT
...
15     NEW( ItemPtr );
16     ItemPtr^.Data := OtherData;
17     ItemPtr^.Next := NIL;
18     IF LastPtr = NIL THEN
19      FirstPtr := ItemPtr;
20     ELSE
21      LastPtr^.Next := ItemPtr;
22     END;
23     LastPtr := ItemPtr;
24    UNTIL OtherData = 0;
25    WHILE FirstPtr # NIL DO
26     WriteCard( FirstPtr^.Data, 10 );
27     FirstPtr := FirstPtr^.Next;
28    END;
```

Example 5-47 Linked List Handler Using Modula-2 Pointer Types

Line 0 shows that the predefined procedure "ALLOCATE" must be explicitly imported. The system module "Storage" provides all heap management functions. Line 2 shows the same exceptional forward reference of a name that we have already seen in Pascal. "ItemType" is yet undefined, but since it occurs in the context of a POINTER type declaration, the compiler expects a resolution later. This happens already on the next line.

Since the Modula-2 solution adds new nodes at the end of the linked list, and since the list is expected to be processed from its head, an additional local variable is required. Therefore we see two declarations on lines 10 and 11.

Tree Traversal in Pascal

The program "pascalsearch" in Example 5-48 builds a binary tree of nodes. Each node has one character type data field, and two Pointers to subtrees. The subtree named "left" holds all characters that are smaller than the one in the current node, and "right" holds all larger ones. The global variable "root" points to the root node of the complete tree at all times, and can be used to search for elements in the tree. We shall encounter similar examples in Chapter 11.

```
program pascalsearch( output );
 type
  nodepintype = ^ nodetype;
  nodetype    =
   record
    data       : char;
    left,
    right      : nodepintype;
   end;
  var
   root        : nodepintype;

 procedure enter(
  var
   root        : nodepintype;
   data        : char );
  begin { enter }
   if root = nil then
    begin
     new( root );
     root^.data := data;
     root^.left := nil;
     root^.right := nil;
    end
   else if root^.data > data then
    enter( root^.left, data )
   else if root^.data < data then
    enter( root^.right, data )
   else
    writeln( data, ' already in tree.' );
   {end if}
```

```
32      end { enter };
33
34    procedure search(
35      root        : nodepintype;
36      data        : char );
37     begin { search }
38      if root = nil then
39       writeln( data, ' not found.' )
40      else if root^.data > data then
41        search( root^.left, data )
42      else if root^.data < data then
43       search( root^.right, data )
44      else
45       writeln( data, ' found in tree.' );
46      {end if}
47     end { search };
48    begin { pascalsearch }
49     root := nil;
50     enter( root, '5' );
```

Example 5-48 Tree-Build and Search Algorithm Using Pascal Pointer Types

On line 3 we see again the familiar forward reference, which is again resolved on the next line. In this sample program, each Pointer is associated with a Record that has two Pointer fields to Records of the same type. These are "left" and "right." Line 20 shows a call to the predefined allocation procedure "new." Its sole argument must be a Pointer variable, but it may be a Pointer to any type. On lines 26 and 28 we see recursive invocations of the procedure "enter." It is very interesting here to notice the similarity between the recursive procedure that traverses tree nodes and the Record data structure that describes the nodes. Whenever algorithm and data structure are so similar, we can suspect that we have done something right! Notice also the similarity of procedure "enter" with the data structure; "search" calls itself recursively twice, on lines 41 and 43. The only differences in "enter" and "search" are the semantic actions taken in the case that the tree is NIL.

The Cross Reference Generator Using Pointers

Our introduction to Pointers has covered sufficient material to discuss the next "crossref" solution. In this third version of our cross reference generator we have used Records, but we have enhanced the tree representation. Each valid node now has the actual data and Pointers to its "smaller" and "greater" successor. Nodes are allocated from the system heap only in the quantities actually needed. For the interested reader a complete listing is included in Example 5-49.

```
program crossrefpointers( source, output );
 const
  signifchars  =  10;  { only <signifchars> count }
  numsperline  =   8;  { number per line }
  digitspernum =   6;  { print 6 chars per digit }
 type
  alfarange    = 1 .. signifchars;
  alfa         = packed array[ alfarange ] of char;
  nodepin      = ^ nodetype;
  itempin      = ^ itemtype;
  nodetype     =
   record
    name       : alfa;
    first,
    last       : itempin;
    smaller,
    greater    : nodepin;
   end;
  itemtype     =
   record
    linenum    : integer;
    next       : itempin;
   end;
 var
  root         : nodepin;
  linenum      : integer;
  buff         : alfa;
  source       : text;

 procedure search(
  var
   root        : nodepin );
  var
   temp        : nodepin;
   item        : itempin;
  begin { search }
   temp := root;
   if temp = nil then
    begin
     new( temp ); { trust we found space }
     new( item ); { trust we found space }
     temp^.name := buff; { no check for heap exhaustion }
     temp^.smaller := nil;
     temp^.greater := nil;
     temp^.first := item;
     temp^.last := item;
     item^.linenum := linenum; { no check for heap exhaustion }
     item^.next := nil;
     root := temp;
```

```
   end
  else if buff < temp^.name then
   search( temp^.smaller )
  else if buff > temp^.name then
   search( temp^.greater )
  else { equal }
   begin
    new( item );
    item^.linenum := linenum;
    item^.next := nil;
    temp^.last^.next := item;
    temp^.last := item;
   end;
  {end if}
 end { search };

procedure printtree(
  root          : nodepin );

 procedure printnode(
    node        : nodetype );
   var
    nums        : integer;
    item        : itempin;
  begin { printnode }
   write( ' ', node.name );
   item := node.first;
   nums := 0;
   while item <> nil do
    begin
     if nums = numsperline then
      begin
       writeln;
       nums := 0;
       write( ' ' : signifchars + 1 );
      end;
     {end if}
     nums := nums + 1;
     write( item^.linenum : digitspernum );
     item := item^.next;
    end;
   {end while}
   writeln;
  end { printnode };

 begin { printtree }
  if root <> nil then
   begin
    printtree( root^.smaller );
```

```
      printnode( root^ );
       printtree( root^.greater );
      end;
     {end if}
    end { printtree };

   procedure processline;
    var
     length      : integer;
    begin { processline }
     linenum := succ( linenum );
     while not eoln( source ) do
      begin
      if source^ in [ 'a' .. 'z' ] then
       begin
        length := 0;
        buff := '          ';
        while ( source^ in [ 'a' .. 'z', '0' .. '9' ] ) do
         begin
          if length < signifchars then
           begin
            length := length + 1;
            buff[ length ] := source^;
           end;
          {end if}
          get( source );
         end;
        {end while}
        search( root );
       end
      else
       get( source );
      {end if}
      end;
     {end while}
     get( source );
    end { processline };

   begin { crossrefpointers }
    reset( source );
    root := nil;
    linenum := 0;
    while not eof( source ) do
     processline;
    {end while}
    printtree( root );
   end { crossrefpointers }.
```

Example 5-49 Cross Reference Generator in Pascal, Using Pointers to Records

5.3 Summary

The third "crossref" program is slightly shorter and therefore more readable than the earlier two. The brevity is only incidental and is not the true reason why indeed that third solution is of superior quality. The brevity is caused by our choice of Pascal's IO Statements. We chose the Get Statement that allows us to inspect the next element in a file without actually reading it, or more precisely, without advancing the file Pointer. The Ada solutions use sequential text IO, comparable to Pascal's. This causes us to write a small procedure for lexical analysis in Ada. This procedure, "getcurchar," manages a full line of text.

Pascal program "crossrefpointers" is superior since it allocates nodes and builds the corresponding tree only as needed. For very short input the storage consumption is moderate; for large input the program requests more and more nodes from the system heap, and never consumes more than required.

This project has provided a realistic exercise for generating operands. We have used elementary operands, but have also learned how to create composite structures from more elementary objects. The simple lead us to the more complex form of operand, but we closed the cycle by learning how to reference an elementary item from a complex structure.

In the next chapter we shall study how to combine multiple operands via operators to form single values again. Even such combined values may be elementary or structured.

5.4 Exercises

1. Type identifiers such as "integer" are predefined in Modula-2 and Pascal. Thus it is possible to redefine such types explicitly. Explain if there is any value to this; or would it be better language design if "integer" were expressed by a reserved keyword?

2. What is the merit in defining symbolic constants? This question addresses programming language complexity. If it were an equally sound programming practice to use literals instead of the symbolic constants (parameters in Fortran), then a language without this facility would be better, since it would be simpler. Simplicity is certainly a value in language design.

3. In the Ebcdic character set the letters 'A' through 'Z' (and 'a' through 'z') are not contiguous. The characters between 'I'..'J' and 'R'..'S' are, however,

non-alphabetic and occur rarely in practice. Analyze the Pascal test for "c" being a "letter" in the following:

```
c IN [ 'A' .. 'Z' ]
```

Is this a correct test for all standard character sets? If not, which program quality is sacrificed?

4. To convert an Ascii character "c" in the range '0'..'9' to the numeric value 0 through 9, it is possible to write the conversion expression "ord(c)-ord('0')" in Pascal. It is known that in Ascii the integer value of '0' is 48. Is the expression "ord(c)-48" therefore an equivalent substitute for the previous expression? If not, which quality in program design is jeopardized?

5. Fortran Arrays have up to seven dimensions, identifiers up to six characters. A Fortran statement may be continued over no more than 19 additional lines. All of these are magic numbers for the user and must be remembered. Is the use of magic numbers good programming language design?

6. A two-dimensional Fortran Array named "X" is declared as shown in the following statement. Find the position number of element "X(3,5)."

```
INTEGER X( 2 : 4, 3 : 6 )
```

Notice that the position number of the first element in a Fortran Array is 1 by convention.

7. Find the offset of the Modula-2 Array element "x [3,5]" if "x" is declared as follows.

```
VAR x : ARRAY [ 2 .. 4 ], [ 3 .. 6 ] OF INTEGER;
```

Notice that the offset of the first element from the origin of an Array is 0 in Modula-2.

8. Fortran requires that a function used in Array subscripts have no side effect on any of the variables in the same subscript sequence. What are the reasons for this rule?

9. Let us assume that a Pascal compiler for an IBM-360-family target machine maps Pascal variable declarations onto storage in the order of occurrence in the source. On such a machine each individual byte is addressable, but integers have to be aligned on word addresses. These are addresses that divide evenly by 4. Design a memory chart that shows how the compiler maps the following Pascal declarations. Start with address 0.

```
VAR
b1     : boolean;
i1     : integer;
b2     : boolean;
i2     : integer;
```

10. Assume another Pascal compiler for the same target rearranges declarations so that the variables are equally accessible as in the first case, but storage consumption is minimized. How does the memory chart look in this case?

11. A linked list of nodes is represented via Pointers to Records in some Modula-2 program. Let the Records have tow fields, named "data" to store integer type data, and "next," to point to the next Record if there is one. The variable "head" points to the first element of the linked list. At some time the list has three elements as shown in the following figure, with the value in the data fields as indicated.

```
head          data   next           data   next           data   next
+-----+       +------+------+       +------+------+       +------+------+
| o-->---->| 1230 | o--->---->| 2340 | o--->---->| 3450 |o-->-- |.
+-----+       +------+------+       +------+------+       +------+------+
                   First                 Second                Third
```

Write a single Modula-2 operand that references the data field in the third (last) Record. Notice that there is no other explicit Pointer variable except "head."

12. Write a sample program that creates a circular list of Records of the type shown in the previous exercise. How can we detect programmatically if the same circular structure is processed again? In other words, which mechanism must we employ to guarantee that an algorithm will terminate?

6

Operators and Expressions

In fact, a programmer's need
for an understanding of his language is so great,
that it is almost impossible
to persuade him to change to a new one.

C. A. R. Hoare
Hints on Programming Language Design

Chapter 5 is a natural introduction for this chapter. We have learned so far how to generate operands and how to specify their allowable range of values and their type. In this chapter we learn how to combine multiple elementary operands and mold them into a new, single value. This is what we usually call an *expression;* in a more formal sense, a simple operand is also an expression. To create more complex ones we need operators, which form the topic of the current chapter. We use extended BNF to articulate the syntax rules for expressions and to manifest the relation of multiple operators with one another. We emphasize various important but subtle points about expressions and clarify these points by means of sample programs.

One such subtle subject is the analysis of two source strings that look textually identical in Ada and Pascal but have different meanings. Other, quite tricky issues are operator associativity in the different languages, short circuit expression evaluation, the modulus operator, and unary operators.

Associativity plays a key role in various sample programs of this chapter, so we start out with a clarification of this crucial term. Associativity is a characteristic specific to operators that occur more than once in a single expression. From elementary school we still remember that the meaning of the expression 2+3+4 is either (2+3)+4 or 2+(3+4) equivalently. If we evaluate 2+3+4, we add 2 and 3 first, and then add 4 to the sum. We are accustomed to this from our convention of reading from left to right. There is nothing magic behind this rule. Here we say, the + operator "associates left to right," or + is "left associative." We would not make a big issue out of such a natural rule in programming languages, if computers would agree to this convention. Computers, however, are strange animals and do not agree that in general (a+b)+c is the same as a+(b+c). We shall understand why after having studied the current chapter.

Precedence, the second key term used in this chapter, defines the relative strength of binding of different operators. For example, the expression 2+3*4 yields 14, because the * operator binds stronger than the + operator. Hence 3*4 is computed first, yielding 12, and a 2 will be added later on. It does not matter that textually the + occurs before (to the left of) the *. We say that * has a higher precedence than the + operator. If this were not the case, the result of 2+3*4 would be 9.

In this chapter we discuss the rules concerning the precedence and associativity of various operators. Subsequent chapters will cover statements that use operands and expressions explained so far.

.1 Syntax for Expressions

First we'll give the BNF grammar for expressions and then we'll interpret the finer points. In most cases we do not attempt to present the complete syntax; for example, nonterminals such as "literal" and "variable" are left undefined. Since they are intuitively clear to the reader, they would not contribute to the subject of dissecting expressions, and would overload the grammar with a multitude of rules.

We have intentionally used different writing styles for the expression grammars of the various languages in order to demonstrate that the order of grammar rules is insignificant. Sometimes the rules are textually written top-down, with the start symbol appearing as one of the first rules. Other times we use bottom-up notation, in which case the start symbol comes last. For a full understanding the reader need only be aware of which symbol is the start symbol. To make this easy we use the following naming convention: the start symbol for Pascal expressions is "pascal_expression," for Ada expressions it is "ada_expression," and analogously for the other languages.

Also, our form of extended BNF allows two equivalent but textually different ways of denoting repeated clauses. One form uses nonterminals recursively, the other form applies the metasymbols { and } for repetition. Recursive rules have the advantage of being concise and of conveying associativity information. When the explicit repetitive form is used, associativity principles must be stated in extra context conditions. We use either style at least once for the sake of demonstration.

```
ada_expression     ::= relation { AND      relation }
                     | relation { AND THEN relation }
                     | relation { OR       relation }
                     | relation { OR ELSE  relation }
                     | relation { XOR      relation }
relation           ::= simple_expression
                     [ relational_op simple_expression ]
                     | simple_expression [ NOT ] IN range
                     | simple_expression [ NOT ] IN type_mark
range              ::= simple_expression .. simple_expression
simple_expression  ::= [ unary_add_op ] term
                     { binary_add_op term}
term               ::= factor { multiply_op factor }
factor             ::= primary [ ** primary ]
                     | ABS primary
                     | NOT primary
primary            ::= name
                     | ( ada_expression )
                     | NULL
                     | function_call
                     | numeric_literal
                     | string_literal
                     | type_conversion
                     | qualified_expression
                     | allocator
relational_op      ::= = | /= | < | > | <= | >=
unary_add_op       ::= + | -
binary_add_op      ::= + | - | &
multiply_op        ::= * | / | MOD | REM
name               ::= see Ada syntax rules
numeric_literal    ::= see Ada lexical rules
```

Example 6-1 Grammar Fragment for Ada Expressions

Operator Associativity

Since the BNF grammar for Ada expressions does not use nonterminals recursively, the grammar alone does not convey the associativity of operators. Ada's operator associativity is determined by the following two principles:

When an expression contains no short circuit control form, then the order of evaluation of OPERANDS is not defined. For a sequence of OPERATORS of the same priority, the operators are associated in textual order from left to right. Only explicit parentheses can overrule this association.

The principle of leaving the operand evaluation order undefined, which seems to purposely render the language more vague than necessary, is specifically included to discourage programmers from relying on side effects in their programs. Thus, the stated principle is just another way of postulating that programs are erroneous if they assume a specific order of operand evaluation. Unfortunately, language compilers cannot in general detect whether a program makes any such assumptions. A little error message to that effect would certainly come as a surprise, since this would virtually require mind reading on the part of the compiler.

Ada is unique in separating between the evaluation order of operators and operands. This distinction makes the language more complex, since there are more rules to remember, but it decreases the degree of ambiguity. Such rules narrow down that class of programs that are correct according to the language definition, but that would execute differently on different computers. Ideally there would be no programs that execute correctly on one machine but cause a run time exception on another system. Realistically the world is full of such programs. In Chapter 5 we learned how a good language definition increases safety and portability by using symbolic literals such as "maxint." One of the goals of this text is to introduce the reader to the world of subtle difficulties and ambiguities that arise from omitted rules, rules that should have been defined but weren't.

Nonassociativity of Exponentiation

An interesting restriction in the grammar for Ada expressions is the single occurrence of the exponentiation operator. For example a**b**c, perfectly legal in Fortran and PL/I, is not permitted in Ada. Hence the reader of Ada source does not need to worry whether association is from left to right or right to left. Except for overflow conditions, this is not a real issue anyway for most arithmetic operators, since the result is independent of the evaluation order. For the computation of a+b+c it is irrelevant whether the meaning is (a+b)+c or a+(b+c), not considering overflow. The result will be the same with either associativity.

Exponentiation is the only operation where it does make a difference. A quick arithmetic check will verify that 2**3**2 yields either 512, when interpreted as 2**(3**2), or 64, when interpreted as (2**3)**2. This may look like Ada is denying a useful service—being deliberately restrictive where expressive power matters.

Luckily, this is not the case. Instead Ada only forces the writer to be more explicit, thus making the source text more readable. This turns out to be an effort-sparing and a cost-saving blessing, which shows up during the program maintenance phase. Multiple ** operators are clearly possible in Ada, but explicit parentheses are required. Then it will become obvious to the reader of source programs, without having to ponder the language rules and reading the thick manual, whether left to right or right to left association applies. So a:=b**(c**d); and a:=(b**c)**d; are both good Ada statements, and in either case it is evident what is meant.

Multiple Boolean Operators

Ada's boolean operators offer yet another related instance where language restrictiveness promotes program safety by forcing readability. This is concisely expressed in Example 6-1. We see that boolean operators like AND and OR can occur any number of times in an expression. But it requires a careful look at the grammar to understand that these operators cannot be mixed. If we wish to construct a complex boolean expression in Ada, including the AND and OR operator, then the different operators have to be separated from one another by parentheses. Multiple occurrences of the same boolean operator don't need to be decorated with parentheses. Isn't it remarkable how the BNF rules can express so many subtle language requirements so tersely?

What has been gained by such restrictive rules? Let us analyze this situation by a practical example. We wish to express a complex boolean expression of the form

```
a OR b AND c
```

For simplicity we assume that "a," "b", and "c" are boolean type variables. This expression cannot be incorporated literally in an Ada source program. At compilation time we would get an error message, informing us that the operators AND and OR may not be mixed. So we are forced to rewrite the expression in either of the following forms by adding parentheses.

```
( a OR b ) AND c
a OR ( b AND c )
```

In two of the possible eight combinations the boolean results are different, hence the expressions are not equivalent. The language, therefore, forces us to state explicitly which of the two forms we intend. The reader of our source program will be very grateful for having such obvious hints. The same principle applies to the XOR, AND THEN, and OR ELSE operators.

Concatenation Operator

It is easy to overlook the & operator, listed among the binary add operators in the grammar in Example 6-1. This operator performs the Ada string concatenation function, so its two operands must be one-dimensional arrays of characters. "String" is the convenient abbreviation for the more verbose type "ARRAY(low .. high) OF character." Like all operators that can be repeated any number of times, multiple concatenation operators associate from left to right.

Use of OUT Parameters in Expressions

There is a delicate exception to the general use of formal parameters. A formal parameter of mode OUT may not be referenced in expressions; it may only be used as a variable. The reason for this becomes clear once the parameter modes are understood. OUT implies that upon call the corresponding actual parameter may be uninitialized, and it is mandatory for a safe language to strongly discourage references of undefined data. The Ada restriction is one step in that direction.

Slices

The syntax for Ada expressions in Example 6-1 defines the nonterminal "primary." *Primaries* provide a means of producing elementary values, as already known from Pascal's "factors." Primaries, therefore, include indexed array components. Ada's slices are an unusual and very convenient extension of this concept. A *slice* is a sequence of consecutive components of a one-dimensional array; we can view it as a contiguous range of expressions. The type of a slice is the base type of the array, and the type of the discrete slice range must equal the type of the array bounds. Moreover, the range values must be within the array's index bounds. The only exception is the "null slice," which has no component at all. All values yielding a null slice are legal, even if individually the low or high bounds would fall outside of the array bounds.

For a one-dimensional array "a," the primary a(n) yields a single array component, provided "n" is within proper limits, but a(n..n) is a slice of "a" with one component. Hence the type of a(n..n) is "array of component type," while the type of a(n) is "component type" of "a." A(m..m−1) is a null slice, irrespective of whether "m" and "m−1" are within proper array bounds.

Slices of variables are variables, and slices of constants are still constants. See the use of a sample Ada slice in Example 6-2.

```
PROCEDURE slices IS
   TYPE lilli_range IS RANGE 5 .. 10;
   TYPE biggi_range IS RANGE 1 .. 35;
   lilli : ARRAY( lilli_range ) OF integer;
   biggi : ARRAY( biggi_range ) OF integer;
BEGIN--slices
   FOR i IN biggi_range LOOP
      biggi( i ) := integer( i ) ** 2;
   END LOOP;
   lilli := biggi(5..10);--one full array, one slice
   IF lilli(8) /= 64 THEN
      put_line( "Wrong slice implementation." );
   END IF;
END slices;
```

Example 6-2 Ada Program Demonstrating Slices

Type Conversion, Qualified Expression, Attribute in Ada

Operands are the means by which values are generated. In the Ada syntax these operands are called primaries, and as the expression grammar in Example 6-3 shows, there is a rich variety of these. Such primaries can be combined via operators to yield new values, as defined by the semantics of the individual operator. Usually programming languages choose infix notation for binary operators, but this is equivalent to the mathematical function notation with two arguments. One area causing a great deal of confusion is the distinction between type conversions, qualified expressions, and attributes. Common to all of these is that they are providers of values; they are primaries.

```
type_conversion       ::= type_mark ( expression )

qualified_expression  ::= type_mark ' ( expression )
                        | type_mark ' aggregate

attribute             ::= prefix ' attribute_designator

attribute_designator  ::= simple_name [ ( static_expression ) ]
```

Example 6-3 Grammar for Special Ada Expressions

From Example 6-3 we see that the syntax for qualified expressions, attributes, and type conversions is quite similar. Probably this closeness in syntax has contributed to the confusion. The goal of this short section is to clear up all mystery in the delicate expression area. We'll present enough material about type conversion, qualified expressions, and attributes to make it clear just how they differ.

Type Conversion

A type conversion transforms the expression, given in parentheses, into an expression of another but closely related type. This related type is specified by the type mark. The two types may be identical. The target type is specified by the type mark, while the source type of the operand must be determinable independently of the target type. If a type conversion is used in an Assignment Statement, then the type information of the left-hand side variable cannot be used to decide what the target type will be. Also the expression may not be the NULL literal, a string literal, an allocator, or an aggregate. Some samples of legitimate type conversions for Ada are given in Example 6-4.

```
   i, j, z : integer;
   TYPE sequence IS ARRAY( integer RANGE <> ) OF integer;
   SUBTYPE dozen_type IS sequence( 1 .. 12 );
   dozen : dozen_type;
   ledger : ARRAY( 1 .. 100 ) OF integer;
   sl : sequence(1..100);
   r : float;
BEGIN
   r := float( j );--explicit integer -> float
   z := integer( -0.4 );--explicit float -> integer
   sl := sequence( ledger );--bounds 1 .. 100
   dozen := dozen_type(sl(50..61));--bounds are 1..12
```

Example 6-4 Ada Type Conversion Samples

Qualified Expressions

Qualified expressions are used to resolve type specifications that would otherwise remain unresolved due to overloading. As is the case with type conversions, the expression type and final type may be identical, but the parenthesized operand must have the same base type as the type mark.

Again, this is clarified by examples. The two output statements in Example 6-5 show a typical, correctly qualified expression. A reference to "dec" alone would have been ambiguous, since "put_line" is overloaded. Also the first three For Statements use qualified expressions correctly to define the type of the loop parameter. The last For Statement creates a type clash. The loop parameter "m" could either be of type "opcodes" or of type "mask." It is exactly this class of ambiguities that is solvable via qualified expressions.

```
TYPE
    opcodes IS ( fix, inc, dec, float, add, bin );
TYPE
    mask    IS ( fix, dec, bin );
BEGIN--body
    put_line( mask'( dec ) );--"dec" alone would be ambiguous
    put_line( opcodes'( dec ) );--"dec" alone would be ambiguous
    FOR j IN fix .. mask'( dec ) LOOP ... END LOOP;
    FOR k IN mask'( fix ) .. bin LOOP ... END LOOP;
    FOR l IN opcodes'( fix ) .. opcodes'( bin ) LOOP ... END LOOP;
    FOR m IN fix .. dec LOOP ... END LOOP;--ambiguous, error
```

Example 6-5 Sample Qualified Expressions in Ada

Attributes

Attributes specify a predefined operation performed on the operand. When the operation is simple, like generating the first value from a static range of values, no explicit operand needs to be specified. Otherwise an explicit parenthesized operand has to be given. The operation is identified by the predefined simple name. The easiest way to understand attributes in Ada is to view them as built-in functions with a slightly unconventional syntax. In Example 6-6 we list a few attribute examples of the simple kind; then follow attributes that need an explicit operand.

```
    TYPE letter_type IS RANGE 'A' .. 'Z';
    TYPE digit_type  IS RANGE '0' .. '9';
    letter : letter_type;
    digit  : digit_type;
    i      : integer;
    addr   : system.address;
BEGIN
    digit  := digit_type'first;--digit = '0'
    letter := letter_type'last;--letter = 'Z'
    addr   := i'address; --addr holds address of i
```

Example 6-6 Simple Attributes in Ada

We have used three attributes in this example, "first," "last," and "address." When the prefix of "first" is a scalar type—in Example 6-6 it is a constrained character range—then "first" yields the lower bound of that scalar type.

Similarly, the "last" attribute yields the upper bound of the scalar type prefix. In either case the type of the attribute is the same as the type of the prefix. The "address" attribute yields the machine address of its prefix. This value is of type "address," as defined in a predefined package named "systems."

```
    next_char : character;
    c : character;
    i : integer;
    digit_val : integer;
BEGIN
    next_char := character'succ( next_char );--next in sequence
    i := integer'pred( i ); i := i + 1;
    digit_val := character'pos( '0' );--integer value of '0'
    c := character'val( digit_val + 1 );--c = '1'
```

Example 6-7 Ada Attributes with Explicit Operand

In Example 6-7 we have used the "succ," "pred," "pos," and "val" attributes. "Succ" and "pred" work just like the built-in functions with the same name in Pascal, except that Ada requires a bit of redundant type information. While the result type could be derived from the parenthesized argument, an explicit prefix of discrete type is required.

The "pos" attribute yields the integer value of the position number of the parenthesized argument. The prefix, in this case "character," must be a base type of the operand type. "Val" is the inverse function of "pos"; the result type is the type of the prefix, and the result is the value whose position number is the integer value corresponding to the parenthesized argument.

Syntax for Fortran Expressions

```
primary             ::= literal
                      | variable
                      | ( fortran_expression )
factor              ::= primary [ ** factor ]

term                ::= [ term * ] factor
                      |  [ term / ] factor

arith_expression    ::= + term
                      | - term
                      | [ arith_expression +  ] term
                      |  [ arith_expression -  ] term
                      | [ arith_expression // ] term

condition           ::= [ arith_expression  relational_op ]
                        arith_expression

relational_op       ::= .LT. | .LE. | .EQ. | .NE. | .GT. | .GE.

logical_factor      ::= [ .NOT. ] condition
```

```
logical_term         ::= [ logical_term .AND. ] logical_factor

logical_disjunctive ::= [ logical_disjunctive .OR. ] logical_term

fortran_expression  ::= [ fortran_expression  .EQV. ]
                              logical_disjunctive
                       | [ fortran_expression .NEQV. ]
                              logical_disjunctive

literal              ::= see lexical rules for Fortran

variable             ::= see syntax rules for Fortran
```

Example 6-8 Grammar Fragment for Fortran Expressions

Recursive Rules

In contrast to the BNF grammar for Ada expressions, which uses the metasymbols { and } for repeated operators, the grammar for Fortran expressions in Example 6-8 uses recursion. This will be the only time we use the recursive notation.

"Factor" is defined as a "primary," optionally followed by the exponentiation operator ** and another factor. Hence we see a right recursive rule, in which the metasymbols [and] are sufficient to express arbitrary repetition of the ** operator. But this is the only right recursive rule in the grammar, and ** is the sole binary operator, which associates from right to left when used repeatedly without intervening parentheses or other operators. As in high school arithmetic, in Fortran the meaning of a**b**c is a**(b**c). It does not matter that in high school we were used to stacking operands vertically to represent the exponentiation operation. The two notations are equivalent.

Associativity

"Term" is defined left recursively as "term" followed by either of the multiplication operators, unconditionally followed by "factor." So the multiplication operators * and / have lower precedence than ** and associate from left to right. Therefore a*b*c is interpreted as (a*b)*c in Fortran, again a familiar rule from conventional arithmetic. The remaining lower priority operators are all associated from left to right.

Fortran has a more complex hierarchy of logical operators than Ada. While AND and OR have identical binding strength in Ada, the Fortran .AND. has higher precedence than .OR., which in turn binds stronger than .EQV. and the converse .NEQV. operator. Note that due to the left recursive rule for

Fortran expressions multiple .EQV. and .NEQV. operators are allowed.

String Concatenation

The relative priority of the concatenation operator //, which has the same level as the adding operators, is not critical, since both arguments must be of type string. Unless parentheses are used to overrule the left to right association, no other binary string operator is available. The substring operation, also known in Fortran-77, has the same priority as a string "primary."

As in Ada, the logical .NOT. operator may be used only once. For redundant repeated negation, explicit parentheses must be used—as, for example, in .NOT.(.NOT.(min.GT.average)), which is equivalent to min.GT.average.

Syntax for Pascal Expressions

```
factor              ::= literal
                      | variable
                      | ( pascal_expression )
                      | NOT factor
                      | "[" set_value_list "]"
                      | function_identifier [ ( parameter_list ) ]
set_value_list      ::= set_values [ , set_value_list ]
                      | LAMBDA

parameter_list      ::= parameter { , parameter }

parameter           ::= expression | variable

set_values          ::= expression [ .. expression ]

term                ::= factor { multiply_op factor }

multiply_op         ::= * | / | DIV | MOD | AND

simple_expression   ::= [ + | - ] term { adding_op term }

adding_op           ::= + | - | OR

pascal_expression   ::= simple_expression
                            [ relational_op simple_expression ]

relational_op       ::= = | > | < | >= | <= | <> | IN

literal             ::= NIL
                      | numeric_literal
                      | string_literal

string_literal      ::= see lexical rules for Pascal strings

numeric_literal     ::= see lexical rules for Pascal numbers
```

```
variable            ::= see syntax rules for Pascal
```

Example 6-9 Grammar Fragment for Pascal Expressions

Coarse Granularity of Operator Priority

Pascal offers undoubtedly the simplest precedence hierarchy of the languages discussed. With the logical NOT having the highest priority, there are only four distinct levels in the language. Unique to Pascal and Modula-2 is the treatment of the logical AND and OR. Even though the two are on different levels, with AND binding stronger than OR, they are grouped together with the multiplication operators and adding operators, respectively. In conjunction with the complete lack of the ** operator, this reflects the initial intent of Pascal's inventor to keep the language simple.

Nevertheless, there are two distinct operators for division: one for integer type operands, denoted DIV, yielding an integer type result, and the other for floating point type operands, denoted by the conventional slash.

The logical NOT operator may be used repeatedly without parentheses. Naturally, for unary operators, only right to left association is meaningful. So NOT NOT NOT (a>b) means NOT(NOT(NOT(a>b))) and is equivalent to NOT(a>b) or (a<=b).

We remind the reader again of the escape mechanism used in Example 6-9. The string "[" distinguishes the metasymbol [from the literal symbol [, used in Pascal for Set value constructors. Why haven't we used this same escape mechanism in the other languages? Simply because we have left most grammars incomplete. We have not specified the rules for primaries (or operands); hence there was no need to specify the syntax for subscripting.

Syntax for PL/I Expressions

```
pl1_expression      ::= expression_7 { | expression_7 }
expression_7        ::= expression_6 { & expression_6 }

expression_6        ::= expression_5
                          { comparison_op expression_5 }

comparison_op       ::= > | >= | = | < | <= | ¬> | ¬= | ¬<

expression_5        ::= expression_4 { || expression_4 }

expression_4        ::= expression_3 { adding_op expression_3 }

adding_op           ::= + | -

expression_3        ::= expression_2 { multiply_op expression_2 }

multiply_op         ::= * | /

expression_2        ::= expression_1
```

```
                          | prefix_expression
                          | ( pll_expression )
                          | primitive_expression

expression_1          ::= primitive_expression ** expression_2
                          | ( expression ) ** expression_2

prefix_expression     ::= prefix_op expression_2

prefix_op             ::= + | - | ~

primitive_expression::= reference | constant | isub

constant              ::= see lexical rules for PL/I

isub                  ::= see rules for subscripted expressions

reference             ::= see syntax rules for variable references
```

Example 6-10 Grammar Fragment for PL/I Expressions

Granularity of Precedences

Of the procedural languages discussed here, PL/I has the most complex operator hierarchy, even slightly more detailed than Fortran. There are eight distinct levels, with the signs and the exponentiation operator at the top level. For a full understanding of this grammar for PL/I expressions we remind the reader that the strings { | and { | | consist of the metasymbol { followed by the terminal symbols | and | |, respectively.

Analyzing the PL/I grammar closely, we see that the unary operators, named "prefix operators" in PL/I jargon, occur at two different levels for expressions. This complex scheme is meant to resolve the ambiguity when analyzing expressions like -a**b and a**-b. The former could be interpreted as -(a**b) or as (-a)**b. The latter means a**(-b), indicating that the unary minus here binds stronger than the exponentiation. If we used the binding strength of the latter sample as the general principle, the former expression should be interpreted as (-a)**b, but this is exactly what PL/I does not define. Instead the PL/I meaning is -(a**b), again following mathematical convention, hence the complicated grammar.

To prove our point in Example 6-11 we shall list the leftmost derivation for the expression under discussion. Since no low precedence operators are present in -a**b, we may safely start the derivation sequence with the grammar rule for "expression_2."

```
expression_2 ::= prefix_expression
             ::= prefix_op expression_2
             ::= -expression_2
             ::= -expression_1
             ::= -primitive_expression ** expression_2
             ::= -a ** expression_2
             ::= -a ** primitive_expression
             ::= -a ** b
```

*Example 6-11 Leftmost Derivation, Generating –a**b from the Start Symbol*

This type of language complexity can be defended as user friendly, since it makes extreme efforts to have the programming language approach the natural language. But it causes a considerable amount of work for the language implementors and the users.

In another case we argued that Ada's very delicate rule of leaving the operand associativity explicitly undefined is good, sound language design. Can we argue the same way here? Is the intricate hierarchy of PL/I expressions in the interest of the programmer? Or does the simple, "golden rule" of writing expressions still apply: "When in doubt, parenthesize!"? These are questions the programming language designer has to address. Both design approaches can be correct. We have pointed out the advantage of a complex precedence hierarchy. Now we'll present the advantages of a language that has only one single precedence level.

APL for Contrast

APL is an interesting programming language of the opposite extreme, opposite to any of the languages treated here, including PL/I. All APL operators have identical priority. Thus, if "reasonable" precedences are desired for complex expressions, explicit parentheses are required. We should notice a similarity in APL's policy with Ada's rules for complex boolean expressions. Another, equally unusual rule of APL is that all operators associate from right to left.

C has yet a more complex hierarchy structure for expressions than PL/I. C offers a total of 14 different precedence levels. However, once a programming language becomes so complex, memorizing this amount of information becomes a problem. But again the "golden rule of expressions" can bail us out here.

Syntax for Modula-2 Expressions

```
modula2_expression    ::= simple_expression
                          [ relational_operator simple_expression ]

simple_expression     ::= [ + | - ] term { add_operator term }

term                  ::= factor { multiply_op factor }

factor                ::= numeric_literal
                          | string_literal
                          | set
                          | function_designator [ ( parameter_list ) ]
                          | ( modula2_expression )
                          | NIL
                          | variable
                          | NOT factor

parameter_list        ::= parameter { , parameter }

parameter             ::= modula2_expression
                          | variable

relational_operator   ::= = | <> | # | < | <= | > | >= | IN

add_operator          ::= + | - | OR

multiply_op           ::= * | / | DIV | MOD | AND | &
```

Example 6-12   Grammar Fragment for Modula-2 Expressions

Modula-2 Expressions Are Nothing New

There are only minor differences between the rules for Pascal and Modula-2 expressions. Both hierarchies are identical, the exponentiation operator is missing, and the logical operators AND and OR are interspersed on the same levels with arithmetic operators. Operators associate from left to right, and there are two operators for division: one for integer, the other for real type arguments. Only simple expressions may be signed, and there can be at most one sign. These rules keep the language definition and implementation simple.

New in Modula-2 are only a few additional operators. The operator for testing inequality in Modula-2 can be spelled either <> or # with the same meaning. The logical AND operator may be expressed as the & special symbol.

6.2 Testing Operator Associativity

The various precedence levels of different operators and the associativities of repeated, identical operators have been treated thus far. In practically all cases the association of binary operators is from left to right. The main exception to this is exponentiation in Fortran and PL/I, where evaluation proceeds from right to left. Also in all languages except PL/I the relational operators do not associate. Note that for unary operators, single or multiple, association is no issue; only right to left binding is meaningful.

Ada, Pascal, and to some degree Fortran mention explicitly the evaluation order of operands. Less thoroughly designed languages normally imply that operand evaluation proceeds in the same way that operators are processed, and in all cases the left one of a pair first. So in the PL/I expression a**b**c, "b" is computed first, "c" next, and then "a." Ada and Pascal address the issue by stating explicitly that a program's logic may not rely on any assumptions of this kind.

Paragraph 6.7.2.1 in the Fortran Standard ANSI [1978] states that "the order of evaluation of the operands of a dyadic operator shall be implementation-dependent." Implementation-dependent means "that the operands may be evaluated in textual order, or in reverse order, or in parallel or they may not be evaluated." The Fortran-77 standard does mention that commutative, binary operators may be evaluated in implementor-defined order. From this follows the same restriction as mentioned for Ada. Stated more directly, programmers are discouraged from playing with explosive material, such as expressions with side effects.

Once the operator and operand associativity of a language are understood, it is an interesting experiment to write programs that check how particular compilers go about fulfilling the language specifications. Examples 6-13 and 6-14 include such program listings; Example 6-13 will test the operand evaluation order, Example 6-14 tests operator evaluation. These sample programs are meant as a stimulus for the readers to write test programs in their preferred programming languages. The output will indicate how much confidence we should put into particular compilers. Compilers treat such tricky issues incorrectly more often than is "healthy" for safe software.

Operand Experiment

Program "operand_order" in Example 6-13 contains expressions with multiple occurrences of the same arithmetic operators. The only type of operand used in each case is the integer function "five." "Five" is called with a character type argument whose purpose is to distinguish the various invocations from one another. It then prints a trace of this identity before returning the integer value 5.

On line 12 of the Ada listing we see the use of two plus operators that connect the three operands "five." The first is marked with the character literal '1', the second with '2,' and so on. Four lines of execution time output follow the compiler source listing, giving a clear trace of the order in which the different incarnations of the function have been activated. Since Ada postulates that the order for operands is arbitrary, any permutation of '1,' '2,' and '3' must be acceptable. The final and not surprising permutation is consistent for all four arithmetic operators used.

```
 1                 |  WITH text_io; USE text_io;
 2                 |  FUNCTION five( name : character ) RETURN integer IS
 3         5   1   |   BEGIN--five
 4             1   |    put( name );
 5    2        1 1 |    put( " " );
 6    4        1 1 |    RETURN 5;
 7    8        1 1 |   END five;
 8    8            |
 9    8            |  PROCEDURE operand_order IS
10    9        1   |   BEGIN--operand_order
11    9        1   |    put( " Ada +  arg sequence: " );
12   11        1 1 |    IF five('1')+five('2')+five('3') /= 15 THEN
13   31        1 1 |     put_line( " wrong compiler " );
14   34        1 2 |    ELSE
15   34        1 1 |     put_line( " any order o.k." );
16   38        1 2 |    END IF;
17   38        1 1 |    put( " Ada -  arg sequence is: " );
18   40        1 1 |    IF five('1')-five('2')-five('3') /= -5 THEN
19   61        1 1 |     put_line( " wrong compiler " );
20   64        1 2 |    ELSE
21   64        1 1 |     put_line( " any order o.k." );
22   68        1 2 |    END IF;
23   68        1 1 |    put( " Ada *  arg sequence: " );
24   70        1 1 |    IF five('1')*five('2')*five('3') /= 125 THEN
25   90        1 1 |     put_line( " wrong compiler " );
26   93        1 2 |    ELSE
27   93        1 1 |     put_line( " any order o.k." );
28   97        1 2 |    END IF;
29   97        1 1 |    put( " Ada /  arg sequence: " );
30   99        1 1 |    IF five('1')/five('2')/five('3') /= 0 THEN
31  119        1 1 |     put_line( " wrong compiler " );
32  122        1 2 |    ELSE
33  122        1 1 |     put_line( " this order o.k." );
34  126        1 2 |    END IF;
35  126        1 1 |   END operand_order;
```

```
Ada +  arg sequence: 1, 2, 3,  any order o.k.
Ada -  arg sequence: 1, 2, 3,  any order o.k.
```

```
Ada *  arg sequence: 1, 2, 3,  any order o.k.
Ada /  arg sequence: 1, 2, 3,  this order o.k.
```

Example 6-13 Order of Evaluation of Operands in Ada

Operator Experiment

The previous test provides an exact trace for the order, in which the various OPERANDS of an expression are evaluated. Now we perform the same kind of test for OPERATORS. We are interested in the exact sequence in which operators are executed. This is not as easy to solve as the previous experiment, since predefined operators such as * cannot be biased with parameters of any kind. Hence, they cannot readily produce any visible, order-dependent trace information. But with subtle tools we can nevertheless learn something about operator evaluation order.

Use of Subtle Clues

We claimed previously that "except for overflow conditions" the operator associativity has no impact on the resulting value. So these same overflow conditions are a good tool for producing clues about operator evaluation order. Pascal program "overflow" in Example 6-14 performs this test.

The expression we put under the microscope has the form a+b+c. By definition, in Ada and Pascal the meaning of this expression is (a+b)+c, not a+(b+c). Mathematically, there is no difference, since mathematics knows of no largest number, and therefore has no overflow. Computers are limited and do have largest, representable numbers, hence overflow does occur. On some systems this condition is simply ignored, but on the systems used here this condition raises "run time exceptions," causing the software to abort. The knowledge that overflow can abort the software is utilized in Example 6-14, to provide clues about operator evaluation order. This sounds very subtle and mysterious, but as we shall see, we merely follow language rules exactly.

The essence of the idea is to assign "a," "b," and "c" values at the machine-representable positive or negative limit. Then, if "b" and "c" are both largest numbers, subexpressions like "b+c" definitely cause an overflow. If, on the other hand, "a" is the smallest machine-representable number, then adding "a" to this critical value may just compensate enough to avoid the overflow. But this rescue action happens only if the addition of a negative number is executed *before* the addition of the two large, positive numbers. And this is just what we are after: clues about which operator is executed first.

Line 12 in the Pascal "overflow" program contains an expression that could cause "Integer Overflow," depending on the operator evaluation order. The variables "biggest" and "temp" both hold maximum integer values that are added up, but the operation is preceded by the addition of the negative integer variable "smallest," which may compensate for the overflowing value.

From the run time outputs we see that Pascal implements the plus operator associativity correctly, since only the fourth expression "biggest+temp+smallest" causes an overflow. Three lines of run time output are produced, showing that so far no overflow condition has occurred. But the expression on line 31 does cause overflow and the program aborts. Our primary learning experience here is that OPERAND and OPERATOR evaluation order are in no way correlated.

```
 1    1  0  0        PROGRAM overflow( output );
 3    3  1  0          VAR
                       biggest,      { close to largest,  positive integer }
                       temp,         { also a value close to maxint }
                       smallest      : integer;
 4    7  1  0          BEGIN { overflow }
 4    8  1  1            biggest := 32767;
 5    9  1  1            temp := biggest;
 6   10  1  1            smallest := -biggest;
 7   11  1  1            writeln( ' Pascal + associativity test' );
 8   12  1  1            writeln( output );
 9   13  1  1            writeln( ' biggest   = ', biggest );
10   14  1  1            writeln( ' temp      = ', temp );
11   15  1  1            writeln( ' smallest = ', smallest );
12   16  1  1            IF smallest + biggest + temp = biggest THEN
13   17  1  1              writeln( ' Code sequence 1 o.k.' )
                         ELSE
14   19  1  1              writeln( ' Error in sequence 1.' );
15   20  1  1            {END IF}
                         IF ( smallest + biggest ) + temp = biggest THEN
16   22  1  1              writeln( ' Code sequence 2 o.k.' )
                         ELSE
17   24  1  1              writeln( ' Error in sequence 2.' );
18   25  1  1            {END IF}
                         IF biggest + ( temp + smallest ) = biggest THEN
19   27  1  1              writeln( ' Code sequence 3 o.k.' )
                         ELSE
20   29  1  1              writeln( ' Error in sequence 3.' );
21   30  1  1            {END IF}
                         IF biggest + temp + smallest > 0 THEN
22   32  1  1              writeln( ' Code sequence 4 is illegal.' )
                         ELSE
23   34  1  1              writeln( ' Message 4 should not come out.' );
```

```
24    35  1  1              {END IF}
                          END. { overflow }

Pascal + associativity test
biggest  = 32767
temp     = 32767
smallest = -32767

Code sequence 1 o.k.
Code sequence 2 o.k.
Code sequence 3 o.k.
```

Example 6-14   Order of Evaluation of Operators in Pascal

6.3 Why Parenthesize Expressions?

We mentioned earlier in the section entitled "APL for Contrast" that in APL there are no priority levels for different operators. Multiple operators, different and identical ones alike, are evaluated from right to left. Except for the most primitive expressions, this rule forces the programmer to explicitly parenthesize to avoid unwanted results. This may require a few more key strokes than in other languages, but these expressions are easily readable and can be readily hand-translated into other languages without modifications.

Programmers frequently believe that the process of hand-translating source from one language to another does not occur. They assume that automatic translators exclusively perform such tedious tasks. In reality this translation process can happen when a programmer reads source listings in an unfamiliar language. While glancing over the source, we compare the unfamiliar strings with what we believe to be equivalent expressions in a familiar language. Due to the mandatory parentheses, understanding a complicated APL expression becomes easy for anybody knowing arithmetic. Reading a complicated Ada or C expression without explicit parentheses can be misleading for a Pascal expert.

Even if source-to-source translation is automatic, which is currently in vogue for Ada-to-Pascal translation, parentheses in the original expression remove all possible ambiguity. Without these parentheses, a careful analysis must take place to the effect of adding parentheses at certain places in the new expression. Omission of these additional parentheses can cause very surprising results. We analyze some sample expressions in this section, to demonstrate just how helpful and time-saving it can be to use parenthetical expressions.

Same Expression in Ada and Fortran

A boolean expression, involving the operators NOT and >, is assigned to variable "a." This statement is implemented in both Ada and Fortran. There are necessarily some differences in the notation of the two programs due to different lexical rules for assignment, relational, and logical operators. Despite differences in notation, however, one might expect the same logic to be performed. The allegedly identical statements are shown in Example 6-15.

```
a := NOT b > c;                  --in Ada
A = .NOT. B .GT. C               C- in Fortran
```

Example 6-15 Operator Priorities Ada and Fortran

All variables involved are of type boolean and are properly initialized. The source listings follow.

```
                |WITH text_io; USE text_io;
                |PROCEDURE bools IS
            1   | a, b, c : boolean;
       13   1   |BEGIN--bools
            1   | b := false;
  4         1 1 | c := true;
  7         1 1 | a := NOT b > c;
 13         1 1 | IF a THEN
 15         1 1 |  put_line( "NOT false > true = true in Ada." );
 18         1 2 | ELSE
 18         1 1 |  put_line( "NOT false > true = false in Ada." );
 22         1 2 | END IF;
 22         1 1 |END bools;
```

```
NOT false > true = false in Ada.
```

```
C----- Fortran expression .NOT. b .GT. c
      PROGRAM BOOLS
        LOGICAL A, B, C
        B = .FALSE.
        C = .TRUE.
        A = .NOT. B .GT. C
        IF ( A ) THEN
          WRITE( 6, * ) 'NOT FALSE > TRUE = TRUE IN FORTRAN.'
        ELSE
          WRITE( 6, * ) 'NOT FALSE > TRUE = FALSE IN FORTRAN.'
        END IF
      END
```

```
NOT FALSE > TRUE = TRUE IN FORTRAN.
```

Example 6-16 Ada Versus Fortran

We have intentionally mislead the reader. It looks plausible that the two statements in Example 6-16 would perform the same function, but they do *not!* Where and why they differ is explained in the remainder of this section.

The Fortran execution yields ".TRUE.," while the Ada program computes "false." This happens in two out of the four combinations for the variables involved. Why is there a difference?

Justification of Result

In Ada, the Not operator binds stronger than all relational operators; in fact, NOT is on the highest precedence level of all operators. Therefore, the value of the boolean variable "b," initialized to "false," is negated, yielding "true." Then it is tested whether this subexpression "NOT b" is greated than "c." Since "c" is initialized to "true," the relation does not hold, yielding the final result "false." We need to bring to mind here that "false" and "true" are just two enumerative type literals, predefined in the Standard Package. For all enumerative literals the position number of the first is zero; the position number for each other enumeration literal is one more than for its predecessor. Therefore, only the relation "false<true" holds, not the inverse.

In Fortran, the priority of .NOT. is below that of the .GT. operator. Consequently, the relation "B .GT. C" is evaluated first, yielding .FALSE. As the final step, this subexpression is negated, producing the value .TRUE. in the Fortran program.

This explains why two expressions that logically seem identical can produce different results. The truth is that the two statements are semantically different. To make them identical in functionality there are two choices, depending on which of the two possible meanings we want. If stronger binding for > is preferred, the Ada expression must be parenthesized. Naturally the Fortran statement may be parenthesized as well without harm. If we wish the NOT operation to be performed first in both programs, the Fortran subexpression "NOT B" has to be parenthesized (see Example 6-17).

```
a := NOT ( b > c );          --mandatory in Ada
A  = .NOT. B .GT. C
A  = .NOT. ( B .GT. C )       C- redundant parentheses in Fortran
```

Example 6-17 Relation Binds Stronger

Conversely, if we want NOT to bind stronger, the Fortran expression must have parentheses (see Example 6-18). Again the Ada expression may be parenthesized as well.

```
a := NOT b > c;
a := ( NOT b ) > c;        --redundant parentheses in Ada
A  = ( .NOT. B ) .GT. C     C- mandatory in Fortran
```

Example 6-18 "Not" Binds Stronger

Same Expression in Ada and Pascal

Things can be even more devious. This time we compare two expressions, one in Ada the other one in Pascal, where even the lexical disparity has vanished, and still the computed results differ. But by now the reader is surely alert enough not to believe that two programs in different languages will perform the same function only because their source text is identical.

The relevant expression has the form (a = b OR c) with all three variables having boolean type. The following listings show that again two value combinations out of eight have different results. What is the explanation here?

The problem is essentially the same as in Example 6-18. In Ada the logical OR operator has the lowest priority; the relational test operator binds stronger. Hence in Ada the meaning of the expression is

```
( ( a = b ) OR c ).
```

In Pascal the equality test has the lowest priority, while OR belongs to the next higher level. Therefore, in Pascal the meaning of the same string is, again expressed via explicit parentheses,

```
( a = ( b OR c ) ).
```

In order to force both expressions to adopt equal meaning, parentheses are required in at least one of the source strings. They would not hurt in the other. See Example 6-19.

```
writeln(  output, a =   b OR c    ); {  Pascal default }
writeln(  output, a = ( b OR c ) ); {  parens don't hurt }
put_line( a = ( b OR c ) );--Ada requires parens
```

Example 6-19 Operator Priorities Ada and Pascal

If the other meaning is desired, the Pascal expression's default binding must be overruled by explicit parentheses. See Example 6-20.

```
writeln(  output, ( a = b ) OR c ); { Pascal needs parens }
put_line(    a = b    OR c );--Ada default
put_line( ( a = b ) OR c );--parens don't hurt
```

Example 6-20 Ada Versus Pascal

These examples were meant to demonstrate that the use of parentheses has nice portability and maintenance benefits, without incurring any cost, except for the initial investment of two more key strokes per pair. In particular it should be clear that parenthesized expressions do not generate one more bit of object code, hence they cost nothing more in terms of execution time or code space. Examples 6-21 and 6-22 are Ada and Pascal program listings that create all eight value combinations of the boolean variables "a," "b," and "c" for the expression discussed. We see that the emitted run-time output differs for two expressions.

```
                      | PROCEDURE boolean_op_precedence IS
                1     |  count : integer;
          11    1     |  BEGIN--boolean_op_precedence
                1     |   count := 0;
     4          1  1  |   FOR a IN false .. true LOOP
     8          1  1  |    FOR b IN false .. true LOOP
    12          1  2  |     FOR c IN false .. true LOOP
    16          1  3  |      count := count + 1;
    21          1  4  |      put( integer'image( count ) );
    23          1  4  |      put( "    a: " );
    25          1  4  |      put( boolean'image( a ) );
    27          1  4  |      put( " b: " );
    29          1  4  |      put( boolean'image( b ) );
    31          1  4  |      put( " c: " );
    33          1  4  |      put( boolean'image( c ) );
    35          1  4  |      put( "    (a = b OR c):    " );
    37          1  4  |      put_line( boolean'image( a = b OR c ) );
    44          1  4  |     END LOOP;
    45          1  3  |    END LOOP;
    46          1  2  |   END LOOP;
    47          1  1  |  END boolean_op_precedence;

1   a: FALSE b: FALSE c: FALSE   (a = b OR c):   TRUE
2   a: FALSE b: FALSE c: TRUE    (a = b OR c):   TRUE
3   a: FALSE b: TRUE  c: FALSE   (a = b OR c):   FALSE
4   a: FALSE b: TRUE  c: TRUE    (a = b OR c):   TRUE
5   a: TRUE  b: FALSE c: FALSE   (a = b OR c):   FALSE
6   a: TRUE  b: FALSE c: TRUE    (a = b OR c):   TRUE
7   a: TRUE  b: TRUE  c: FALSE   (a = b OR c):   TRUE
8   a: TRUE  b: TRUE  c: TRUE    (a = b OR c):   TRUE
```

Example 6-21 Eight Value Combinations of Three Boolean Variables in Ada

```
 1    1  0  0          PROGRAM boolops( output );
 2    2  0  0           PROCEDURE booleanopprecedence;
 3    3  1  0            VAR
                          count : integer;
 4    5  1  0             a,
                          b,
                          c      : boolean;
 5    8  1  0            BEGIN { booleanopprecedence }
 5    9  1  1             count := 0;
 6   10  1  1             FOR a := false TO true DO
 7   11  1  1              FOR b := false TO true DO
 8   12  1  1               FOR c := false TO true DO
 9   13  1  1                BEGIN
 9   14  1  2                 count := succ( count );
10   15  1  2                 writeln( count, '  a:', a, ' b:', b, ' c:', c,
                              '   (a = b OR c):   ', a = b OR c ); { <<< }
11   17  1  2                END;
13   18  1  1               {END FOR}
                           {END FOR}
                          {END FOR}
                         END; { booleanopprecedence }
14   22  0  0           BEGIN { boolops }
14   23  0  1            booleanopprecedence;
15   24  0  1           END. { boolops }
1  a:F b:F c:F  (a = b OR c):  T
2  a:F b:F c:T  (a = b OR c):  F
3  a:F b:T c:F  (a = b OR c):  F
4  a:F b:T c:T  (a = b OR c):  F
5  a:T b:F c:F  (a = b OR c):  F
6  a:T b:F c:T  (a = b OR c):  T
7  a:T b:T c:F  (a = b OR c):  T
8  a:T b:T c:T  (a = b OR c):  T
```

Example 6-22   Eight Values of Three Boolean Variables in Pascal

.4 Short Circuit Evaluation

Definition

Multiple conditional expressions can be combined via AND and OR operators. When the first expression of such an AND condition is false, then it is known that the resulting AND condition will also yield false, irrespective of the truth value of the second expression. In most run time systems, the code for the second condition and for the AND operation is still executed.

If, on the contrary, the a priori knowledge of the result is used to prevent the second operand from being evaluated, then we refer to this abbreviation as *short circuiting.* Similarly, if the first operand of an OR condition is true, the resulting condition will yield true, even if the second operand is false. If in such a situation the second boolean expression is not executed and the OR operation is not performed, then the overall expression is said to be "short circuited."

Short Circuit Operators in Ada

Only Ada provides explicit "short circuit" evaluation operators. This section will first explain how short circuit operators work and then show just how useful they can be by comparing an Ada and a Pascal program. Fortran and Pascal leave short circuit evaluation up to the implementor, while even less completely designed languages leave this tricky issue completely open.

The Ada short circuit operators, AND THEN and OR ELSE, are defined for two operands of boolean type and produce a boolean result. The left operand is always evaluated first. If the left operand of the AND THEN operator evaluates to false, the right operand is not processed at all and the result is false. Skipping the second operand evaluation is safe, since for the "and" condition it is known that the result yields false if the first operand is false.

If the left operand of the OR ELSE operator is true the right operand is not evaluated and the result is true. Saving the evaluation of the second operand is safe again, since the result of the boolean "or" condition is true, if the first operand yields true. If both operands are evaluated, AND THEN will deliver the same result as AND, while OR ELSE will produce the same value as OR.

Inclusion of these operators elegantly resolves an old programming language designer and implementor question. Should short circuit evaluation be applicable to the AND and OR operators? One school of thought argues that short circuit evaluation must be disallowed altogether so that side effects that have been mysteriously built into the second operand will be generated. This is the argument of the purists in programming language design and it is in some sense correct and logical. But it also tends to produce unintelligible and unmaintainable programs. As a general rule it is good practice to abstain from side effects!

The argument of the opposition is not much better. It claims that short circuit evaluation should be mandatory in order to save an occasional microsecond due to unexecuted portions of a condition. From a pragmatic point of view this argument makes sense as well.

Ada solves the problem in a clean way. Where short circuit evaluation is needed, the proper operator is provided; otherwise AND and OR can be used. So Ada offers "everything to everybody," but the price to be paid here is increased language complexity. Therefore the short circuit operator discussion is a paradigm for tradeoffs in programming language design.

The intent of these novel operators is not only to save execution time, but to give programmers explicit control over exception conditions. The Ada program in Example 6-23 illustrates this with an explicit check for an illegal zero valued denominator. The same logic implemented in Pascal requires one additional, nested If Statement, thus rendering the source program slightly less readable and less maintainable.

```
 1              |PROCEDURE short_circuit IS
 2         1    | numerator,
 3      4  1    | denominator   : integer;
 4      6  1    |BEGIN--short_circuit
 5         1    | numerator := 17;
 6   3     1  1 | denominator := 0;
 7   6     1  1 | put_line( " Before 1 zerodivide test in Ada." );
 8   9     1  1 | IF denominator /= 0  AND THEN
                   numerator / denominator > 0 THEN
 9  20     1  1 |  put_line( "Good positive quotient." );
10  23     1  2 | END IF;
11  23     1  1 | put_line( " After test. Now cause zerodivide." );
12  26     1  1 | IF denominator /= 0 AND
                   numerator / denominator > 0 THEN
13  36     1  1 |  put_line( "Good positive quotient." );
14  39     1  2 | END IF;
15  39     1  1 | put_line( " This is impossible to reach." );
16  42     1  1 |END short_circuit;
```

Example 6-23 Short Circuit Operator AND THEN

```
IF denominator <> 0 THEN
  IF numerator DIV denominator > 0 THEN
    writeln( 'Good positive quotient.' );
  {END IF}
{END IF}
```

Example 6-24 Simulating AND THEN in Pascal by Nesting If Statements

The nested Pascal If Statements in Example 6-24 perform the same function as the Ada If Statement on lines 8 through 10 in Example 6-24.

Short Circuit Operators Reduce Source

Two sections of Ada source in Example 6-25 demonstrate that the intelligent use of short circuit operators can reduce the total code size. The physically larger Pascal version is contrasted with the terse Ada form. We need to state clearly that the intent in the translation from Ada to Pascal is to produce a logically "identical" program, not a program that is only close in logic. A less stringent "closeness" in logic would permit different run time conduct of one form versus the other.

```
-- Ada Source
IF cond_1 AND THEN cond_2 THEN
  v;
ELSE
  w;
  x;
  y;
END IF;
```

```
{ Pascal Source }
IF cond_1 THEN
  IF cond_2 THEN
    v
  ELSE
    BEGIN
      w; x; y;
    END
  {END IF}
ELSE
  BEGIN
    w; x; y;
  END;
{END IF}
```

Example 6-25   Short Ada Versus Long Pascal Equivalent

Pascal, Fortran, and PL/I have to duplicate the sequence of statements in Example 6-25, if the program logic is to be translated exactly. Naturally a simple logical "and" condition is a close, though not exact, translation.

```
-- Ada Source
IF cond_3 OR ELSE cond_4 THEN
  m;
  n;
  o;
ELSE
  p;
END IF;
```

```
{ Pascal Source }
IF cond_3 THEN
  BEGIN
    m; n; o;
  END
ELSE IF cond_4 THEN
  BEGIN
    m; n; o;
  END
ELSE
  p;
{END IF}
```

Example 6-26   Short-Circuit OR ELSE

6.5 MOD and REM Operators

Among the various programming languages there is a wide functional commonality for arithmetic operations, even though the lexical and syntactic methods of expressing these vary widely. Hardly any function, however, is interpreted so differently in the various languages as the harmless-looking modulus (and remainder) operator. In fact most languages do not even differentiate between them. There is agreement in a few languages, however, that the second operand may not be zero. This section lists the modulus and remainder definitions and summarizes sample results in tabular form.

Ada Modulus and Remainder Definition

Ada distinguishes between the modulus and the remainder function. They are distinct binary operators, denoted by the reserved keywords MOD and REM, respectively. Both operands must be of type integer, and the returned result is also of integer type. On pages 4-17 and 4-19 of the Ada standard ANSI [1983a] the definition reads as follows:

"Integer division and remainder are defined by the relation

```
A = (A/B)*B + (A REM B)
```

where (A REM B) has the sign of A and an absolute value less than the absolute value of B. Integer division satisfies the identity

```
(-A)/B = -(A/B) = A/(-B)
```

The result of the modulus operation is such that (A MOD B) has the sign of B and an absolute value less than the absolute value of B; in addition, for some integer value N, this result must satisfy the relation

```
A = B*N + (A MOD B)
```

For positive A and B, A/B is the quotient and A REM B is the remainder when A is divided by B. The following relations are satisfied by the REM operator:

```
A  REM (-B) =   A REM B
(-A) REM   B  = -(A REM B)
```

For any integer K, the following identity holds:

A MOD B = (A + K*B) MOD B "

In case the verbal definition of the MOD operator is insufficient, the standard includes a table of sample operand values and MOD and REM results to demonstrate what is meant. The Ada program in Example 6-27 produces this table of values.

```
                 |WITH text_io; USE text_io;
                 |PROCEDURE main IS
            1    |
            1    | PROCEDURE modulus( b : integer ) IS
        11  2    |  BEGIN--modulus
            2    |   new_line( 1 );
  2         2  1 |   FOR a IN 10 .. 14 LOOP
  6         2  1 |    put( integer'image( a ) );
  8         2  2 |    put( integer'image( b ) );
 10         2  2 |    put( integer'image( a / b ) );
 14         2  2 |    put( integer'image( a MOD b ) );
 18         2  2 |    put_line(integer'image( a REM b ) );
 23         2  2 |   END LOOP;
 24         2  1 |
 24         2  1 |   new_line( 1 );
 25         2  1 |   FOR a IN REVERSE -14 .. -10 LOOP
 31         2  1 |    put( integer'image( a ) );
 33         2  2 |    put( integer'image( b ) );
 35         2  2 |    put( integer'image( a / b ) );
 39         2  2 |    put( integer'image( a MOD b ) );
 43         2  2 |    put_line(integer'image( a REM b ) );
 48         2  2 |   END LOOP;
 49         2  1 |  END modulus;
 49         1    |
 49         1    | BEGIN--main
 51         1    |  modulus( +5 );
 56         1  1 |  modulus( -5 );
 61         1  1 | END main;
```

Example 6-27 Ada Test for MOD and Rem

Other Modulus Definitions

Fortran Modulus Definition

Fortran has only the mod operation, which is not a modulus, but is functionally equivalent to the Ada REM operator. Syntactically, it is not a predefined operator, as it is in Ada and Pascal, but a built-in function. For this reason two actual parameters or arguments in parentheses are required instead of an operand on either side. The name of the integer type function is "mod." For real and double precision types there are two more built-in functions named "amod" and "dmod." The "mod" function is defined by the identity mod(a1,a2) = a1-int(a1/a2)*a2. "Int" is a function that returns the integral portion of its argument.

Pascal Modulus Definition

In Pascal the modulus operator is handled just as it is in Ada. MOD is a predefined binary operator, taking two integer type operands and yielding an integer result. The standard definition reads as follows:

"A term of the form i MOD j shall be an error if j is zero or negative, otherwise the value of i MOD j shall be that value of (i-(k*j)) for integral k such that 0 <= i MOD j < j. Note: Only for i >= 0 and j > 0 does the relation (i DIV j)*j + i MOD j = i hold."

This definition is a bit difficult to understand, so we shall present some examples for clarification. First, we should be aware that the mysterious factor "k" in the definition, in (i-(k*j)), may certainly be negative, just as long as the condition for i MOD j—that it be greater or equal to zero and less than the positive j—is fulfilled. If, for example, i is -11 and j is 5. Then after trying several values for k, we find one integer such that both conditions are satisfied. By trial and error, varying k from 3 to -3, we find the value k=-3 for the combination i=-11 and j=5.

Table 6-1 Trial and Error Search for "–11 MOD 5"

i	j	k	i-(k*j)	0<=i MOD j<j
-11	5	3	−26	NO
-11	5	2	−21	NO
-11	5	1	−16	NO
-11	5	0	−11	NO
-11	5	-1	−6	NO
-11	5	-2	−1	NO
-11	5	-3	4	Yes, finally -11 MOD 5 = 4

PL/I Modulus Definition

The PL/I standard follows the example of the Algol-68 report in being very unreadable, probably for the benefit of increased correctness. Correctness, however, is hard to verify in a document which is that hard to read! Nevertheless we managed to extract a definition of the built-in function "mod" from the document.

In functionality the PL/I modulus definition follows its predecessor Fortran. The "mod" built-in function for integer type results is defined by the identity mod(u,v) = u - w*floor(u/w). Floor is an intrinsic function, returning the integral part of its argument. The results indicate that the PL/I compiler that was used computes the modulus function just as it is defined in Ada.

Modula-2 Modulus Definition
As in Pascal, the Modula-2 MOD operator is only defined for the second operand being positive. The results of all tests are summarized in Table 6-2. Whenever a language specifies a value as being "undefined," this is marked by a "u".

Table 6-2 Divide, Mod, Rem Results

		Ada			Fortran		Modula-2		Pascal		PL/I	
a	**b**	/	**MOD**	**REM**	/	**MOD**	/	**MOD**	/	**MOD**	/	**MOD**
10	5	2	0	0	2	0	2	0	2	0	2	0
11	5	2	1	1	2	1	2	1	2	1	2	1
12	5	2	2	2	2	2	2	2	2	2	2	2
13	5	2	3	3	2	3	2	3	2	3	2	3
14	5	2	4	4	2	4	2	4	2	4	2	4
-10	5	-2	0	0	-2	0	-2	0	-2	0	-2	0
-11	5	-2	4	-1	-2	-1	-2	4	-2	4	-2	4
-12	5	-2	3	-2	-2	-2	-2	3	-2	3	-2	3
-13	5	-2	2	-3	-2	-3	-2	2	-2	2	-2	2
-14	5	-2	1	-4	-2	-4	-2	1	-2	1	-2	1
10	-5	-2	0	0	-2	0	u	u	u	u	-2	0
11	-5	-2	-4	1	-2	1	u	u	u	u	-2	-4
12	-5	-2	-3	2	-2	2	u	u	u	u	-2	-3
13	-5	-2	-2	3	-2	3	u	u	u	u	-2	-2
14	-5	-2	-1	4	-2	4	u	u	u	u	-2	-1
-10	-5	2	0	0	2	0	u	u	u	u	2	0
-11	-5	2	-1	-1	2	-1	u	u	u	u	2	-1
-12	-5	2	-2	-2	2	-2	u	u	u	u	2	-2
-13	-5	2	-3	-3	2	-3	u	u	u	u	2	-3
-14	-5	2	-4	-4	2	-4	u	u	u	u	2	-4

6.6 Unary Operators

Arithmetic and logical unary operators are provided in all of the languages treated here. We'll explain the arithmetic first and then the logical unary operators. A frequently encountered synonym for unary operator is *monadic,* and for binary operator is *dyadic.*

Arithmetic Unary Operators

The Ada unary operator ABS is interesting because the language chooses to identify this operator via the reserved keyword ABS, rather than by the predefined built-in function "abs," as the other languages do. This is, however, consistent in Ada and we observed the same already for NOT, MOD, and REM.

The more knotty unary arithmetic operators are the unary plus and minus. Ada, Fortran, Modula-2, and Pascal restrict the signs by dedicating low priorities to them. Next to the relational and logical operators, the signs have the lowest binding strength, are nonassociative, and can appear only at the beginning of a full numeric expression. Consequently, expressions like 3+-4, equivalent to 3-4 in conventional arithmetic, are not possible in these four languages. There is only one context in which a sign is permitted, and that is at the beginning of a complete, arithmetic expression. Some examples of correct expressions are given in Example 6-28.

```
-2**3       --legal in Ada, Fortran, PL/I          =  -8
            --Pascal, Modula-2 have no **
-2*3        --legal in all                         =  -6
-2+3        --legal in all                         =   1
-2**(+3)    --legal in Ada, Fortran, PL/I          =  -8
            --Pascal, Modula-2 have no **
-2*(-(-3))--legal in all                           =  -6
-2+(+(3))   --legal in all                         =   1

IF ( -2*3 > +a*b ) THEN--legal in Ada, Pascal, Modula-2, PL/I
IF ( -2*3 .GT. +A*B ) THEN
C---- equivalent in Fortran
```

Example 6-28 Legal Ada Expressions

Even though the following expressions look quite inconspicuous, they are not permitted in any of the languages covered here except PL/I.

```
--2**3    --illegal in Ada, Fortran, Modula-2, Pascal
          --no ** in Pascal and Modula-2, one sign in Ada, Fortran
-2*+3     --illegal in Ada, Fortran, Modula-2, Pascal
          --only complete numeric expression may be signed
          --not a subexpression
-2+-3     --illegal in Ada, Fortran, Modula-2, Pascal
          --only complete arithmetic expression may be signed
          --not a subexpression
```

Example 6-29 Illegal Ada Expressions

Unary Operators in PL/I

PL/I sticks to its goal of permitting everything; consequently, such a familiar use of the sign is permissible. The grammar for PL/I expressions given in Example 6-10 shows that the signs have highest priority. Hence formulas like -2*-3 are legal and are functionally equivalent to (-2)*(-3). The indirect recursion between the nonterminals expression_2, prefix_expression, and back to expression_2 in the PL/I grammar shows that unary operators or prefixes are associative. Therefore, --2*--3 is permitted, and means simply (-(-2))*(-(-3)). Also note in the PL/I grammar that the priority for the exponentiation operator equals that of unary operators.

Logical Unary Operators

NOT is the only logical unary operator. In Ada, NOT has the highest precedence (with ABS) and is not associative; hence "NOT NOT false" is not a legal Ada source string. The Fortran .NOT. operator adheres to the same rules as found in Ada.

The logical "not," denoted NOT in Pascal and ¬ in PL/I, shows one of the few similarities between these two languages. NOT can only be right associative to be meaningful and has the highest binding strength. Thus a Pascal condition like

```
((a > b) AND NOT NOT (c < d))
```

can be expressed equivalently in PL/I by

```
((a > b) & ¬ ¬ (c < d)).
```

Abs Unary Operator in Ada

Ada is unique in defining the ABS operator consistently with the other operators. If it is a good idea to specify the predefined operator NOT by a reserved keyword, why shouldn't the same be good for ABS as well? Consequently, in Ada ABS is reserved and defines the unary operator that returns the absolute value of the same type as its following operand. It took the Ada language designers quite a number of review iterations before ABS was finally defined in this way. For us, describing an existing language after its definition, it is always easy in retrospect to invent the "obvious" rationalizations behind syntax rules. The fact remains that language design is a difficult art, and sound principles such as consistency and simplicity are only road signs that can point us in the right direction; they cannot guarantee a good quality, final product.

Note that while parentheses are permitted, they are by no means necessary. ABS behaves like any other unary operator. The argument of the ABS operator is an Ada primary. From this follows something quite subtle, of which programmers should be aware. Again, parentheses are not necessary because ABS is a unary operator. No other operator in Ada has a higher priority. Now we challenge the reader to find the value that is printed by the Put_line Statement in Example 6-30.

```
i := -3;--Ada source
j := +7;--Ada source
k := ABS i - j;
put_line( integer'image( k ) );
```

Example 6-30 Tricky Use of ABS in Ada

It is not uncommon to believe that "10" will be printed, which is quite incorrect. ABS only applies to argument "i," yielding 3. Deduct 7 from this, and the result is -4. Here we discover another example where the inclusion of redundant parentheses would improve the readability of the source. All three Ada statements in Example 6-31 are equivalent, but the latter two express more directly the meaning.

```
k := ABS i - j;
k := ( ABS i ) - j;
k := ABS( i ) - j;
```

Example 6-31 ABS Operator in Ada

The different Pascal expression "ABS(i-j)" that would yield 10 has to be rewritten in Ada identically as "ABS(i-j)."

.7 Summary

In the previous chapter we have discussed various types of operands and data structures. The introduction to structured data types was not intended to demonstrate their appropriateness in the design of structured programs, but to show how their referencing yields operands. In this chapter we have learned how to combine multiple operands via operators to form more complex expressions. Since each language has quite a variety of different operators, and since many of these may occur repeatedly in the same expression, we had to explain the precedence and associativity rules that govern their sequential evaluation. The extended BNF notation plays a key role here by expressing these rules in a concise fashion. We have also presented the advantage of parenthesizing expressions and some limitations in porting arithmetic expressions from one system to another.

Also we have analyzed expressions in different languages that seemed very similar, in one case identical, but still had a language-dependent meaning. The knowledge acquired so far will be applied in the subsequent chapters, where we discuss statements that use operands and expressions. Our next subject will be "Conditional Statements," execution of which depends on the value of a particular expression.

6.8 Exercises

1. Mathematically, the two expressions "a+(b+c)" and "(a+b)+c" are equivalent. Despite the + operator's commutativity, which also holds in most programming languages, why are the two expressions not always equivalent in the world of programming?

2. Add redundant parentheses to the Ada expression in the following Assignment Statement in order to highlight explicitly the evaluation order as defined by the language.

```
x := a=b OR c>d OR c<=e;
```

3. Can the original expression of the Assignment Statement in Exercise 2 be interpreted as a correct Pascal expression? If not, what has to be added to make it semantically equivalent to the Ada expression?

4. Use the grammars for expressions of the languages treated here to determine whether multiple unary minus operators are allowed. Assuming a and b are properly declared variables, in which languages is the expression (a + + b) legal?

5. Program "overflow" was run on a 16-bit machine with a maximum integer value of 32767. During the addition of two operands, both initialized to this maximum value, an overflow exception condition did occur. Will this exception condition also happen if the identical program text is moved to a 32-bit computer, recompiled, and executed there?

6. Ada defines that the evaluation order of the operands in expression "a*b*c" is not defined. Evaluation of operators with same priority, on the other hand, proceeds textually from left to right. Does the second requirement dictate the order of operand evaluation? Clarify the answer by hypothetical sequences of equivalent object code.

7. Rewrite the PL/I expression (a<=b) using the > test operator and any other operator needed.

8. Rewrite the PL/I expression MOD(MOD(71,20),7) in Ada. Which value is generated?

9. Use the grammar for Fortran expressions to determine the number of different levels of operators. Do not count parentheses as operators.

10. Let "i" and "j" be integer type variables, and "a" and "b" be floating point type variables. Rewrite the PL/I expressions i/j and a/b in Pascal.

11. Write the parse tree for the PL/I expression -a**-b or use a leftmost derivation as shown in the text.

12. Ada expressions with short circuit operators appear in the following If Statements. Rewrite the logical equivalent of the Ada source in Pascal.

```
IF a /= 0 AND THEN b / a > max THEN
    c := max;
END IF;
IF pin = NULL OR ELSE pin.value = 0.0 THEN
    invalid_data;
END IF;
```

13. Writing redundant parentheses represents an effort. Explain any potential benefit that could make this effort worthwhile.

14. Can the Ada source string "integer(next_char)," assumed to be correct and not part of a string literal, be a qualified expression?

15. Pascal converts enumerative type constants or variables into integers via the built-in function ORD. The following source program fragment illustrates this operation. What can be done to convert integers of the proper range to enumerative types? Add all necessary Pascal declarations and statements to allow this inverse conversion. Do you detect any shortcoming of Pascal here?

```
TYPE
 workdaytype = ( monday, tuesday, wednesday, thursday, friday );
VAR
 workday       : workdaytype;
 i             : integer;
BEGIN
 workday := monday;
 i := ord( workday ); { conversion is no problem }
 i := ord( monday );  { also o.k. to convert literal }
 i := succ( i );
 workday := ??; { how can we assign "i" to "workday" ?? }
```

The goal is to assign the current value of "i" to "workday" via legal Pascal means so that the compiler will not flag any type incompatibility. The issue here is a conversion of an integer type value to a variable of type "workdaytype"; the issue is *not* to assign "tuesday" to "workday." But hopefully, after the Pascal statement shown here, the value of "workday" would be "tuesday."

16. We have presented extended BNF grammars for expressions in two styles, one using the metaoperator pair { and } for iteration, the other using the metaoperator pair [and] for an optional phrase. The optional phrase sometimes uses the defined nonterminal recursively. See the following samples.

```
a.)    expr1    ::= expr2 { OP1 expr2 }
b.)    expr2    ::= [ expr2 OP2 ] expr3
c.)    expr3    ::= { expr4 OP3 } expr4
d.)    expr4    ::= expr5 [ OP4 expr4 ]
```

List the associativity of the operators OP1 .. OP4, as defined by the grammar rules.

17. Rewrite the Ada program "operand_order" in another language, execute it, and analyze the generated output.

18. Assume that "operand_order" is rewritten in Pascal and creates the output "Pascal + arg sequence 3, 2, 1," for the plus operator test. Design a possible code sequence for a hypothetical machine that preserves the left associativity of the plus operator, even though in this case the operands are generated from right to left.

7

Conditional Statements

Votre dernière lettre m'a fait parfâitement satisfait.
J'admire votre méthode pour les parties,
d'autant mieux que je l'entends fort bien;
ella est entièrement vôtre,
et n'a rien de commun avec la mienne,
et arrive au même but facilement.
Voilà notre intelligence retablie.

Blaise Pascal
Lettres de Pascal à Fermat, 1654

Older programming languages have only one kind of conditional statement known as the *If Statement.* We'll cover this first in the current chapter. Newer languages include a clean way of selecting one statement list from a series of statement lists, based on the value of some expression. These are the *Case Statements.* Both If and Case Statements are *conditional statements* (also called selective statements). Conditions are special-purpose operands or expressions, which have been explained already in the previous two chapters. For If Statements the condition is a boolean type expression, for Case Statements any scalar expression is permitted. The Computed Goto Statement of Fortran is related to Case Statements but is covered in more detail in Chapter 12.

We take a glance back in history to show the development of the If Statement from more primitive instructions before we present the BNF syntax of If Statements. All explanations are spiced with practical examples. Then we show the Case Statement, again after a short historic retrospective, and demonstrate an interesting equivalence between the two forms of conditional statements. The main lesson for the design of programming languages will be our understanding the advantages of forced closure, of the Elsif Clause in If Statements, and of the range of Choices and the Others Clause in Case Statements.

7.1 If Statement Overview

First Stage

During the early years of programming in machine (and assembly) language the If Statement did not exist; the idea of structured statements had yet to be developed. Nevertheless, programmers needed the effect of If Statements. How did they accomplish this?

One of the simplest machine instructions that could serve as a building block for If Statements was the SKIP instruction. Assembly language programs assumed an Instruction Register IR, which indexes the next instruction to be executed, and an Accumulator, which holds the result of the last computation. The meaning of the SKIP instruction is to skip the following instruction if the accumulator contains nonzero. For example, the If Statement header

```
IF a = b THEN
```

could be expressed as shown in Example 7-1.

```
LD      A   --Load A into Accumulator
SUB     B   --A-B in Accumulator
SKIP        --IF A-B /= zero, then
GOTO    L   --don't GO TO Label L
<then>
L:    <else>
```

Example 7-1 An Old-Fashioned If

With the SKIP instruction it is possible to simulate even the most complicated If Statement structure. But it is awkward to do so. Conditional branches represented the next level of "sophistication" in the If Statement development.

Effectively, a conditional branch combines the SKIP and the GOTO in one instruction. On the machine model in Example 7-1 a branch-if-not-zero (BRNZ) instruction could make coding a bit easier, as shown in Example 7-2.

```
LD      A    --Load A into Accumulator
SUB     B    --A-B in Accumulator
BRNZ    L
<then>
L:    <else>
```

Example 7-2 The Next Generation If

Second Stage

Fortran's Arithmetic If Statement is a generalization of this idea. It provides a three-way branch for the choices of an expression yielding a value of less than, equal to, or greater than zero. This has been further generalized in the Computed Goto Statement, explained in detail in Section 12-4. The following is a sample Arithmetic If with explanations.

```
IF (A-B) 100, 200, 300
```

Should A-B be less than zero, the next instruction is the one labeled 100; if A-B yields zero, statement 200 is executed next, otherwise statement 300. This retrospective, presented in two development stages, may serve as a motivation for the development of the contemporary If Statement.

If Statements in Higher Level Languages

The meaning of a contemporary If Statement is evident from the syntax; we use almost the same syntax in our daily conversation in English. One aspect that needs explanation is the type of If Statement with a large number of sequential conditions and hence statements to choose from. Such If Statements can be constructed in Pascal and PL/I by nesting simple If Statements; in Ada, Fortran, and Modula-2 they can be constructed by using the Elsif Clause. Even in a complex If Statement the conditions are evaluated in strictly sequential order. As soon as one yields true, the associated statement (list) is executed, and the If Statement terminates. When used in a nested fashion, different from the sequential order mentioned earlier, If Statements can provide a binary tree of decision paths, which itself can become quite complex. This forces the programmer to make a nontrivial design tradeoff between other means of modularization and conditional statements.

The body of an If Statement embeds another statement, the execution of which depends on the if-condition. It is essential to the If Statement that this condition can be a general run time expression: any of its constituent operands may be variable, hence of unknown value at the time of compilation. Naturally a trivial anomaly such as the one in Example 7-3 is also permitted.

```
IF false THEN
 perform_one;
ELSE
 perform_two;
END IF;
```

Example 7-3 Anomalous If Statement

At compile time it is already known that "perform_two" will be executed. Even a simple optimizing compiler will recognize this fact and reduce the If to the Call Statement "perform_two" used in the Else Clause. But the statement in Example 7-3 is atypical; "if conditions" generally contain variables.

In some languages the nested statement may itself be an If Statement. This is used quite frequently in real life programs. Nesting is in fact so common that Ada, Algol-68, and Modula-2 provide a special syntax that reduces the logical complexity of certain decision trees into linear sequences of decisions, which are much easier to comprehend. This special form is known as the Elsif Clause in Ada and Modula-2, and "elif" clause in Algol-68. ELSIF and ELIF are the keywords used in the respective languages.

7.2 If Statement Syntax

We present the syntax for If Statements via BNF grammar rules and highlight their meaning by using identical sample source fragments for all languages covered. Two interesting problems are illustrated. One is known as the "Dangling Else" problem, and shows up in languages having an optional Else Clause but no forced closure. The second problem addresses branches into an If Statement from the outside.

If Statement Syntax in Ada

Ada If Statements must have at least one condition and one sequence of statements, but they may also include any number of Elsif Clauses and one optional Else Clause. The various conditions are processed in strict sequence until one yields true or until all conditions have been exhausted. If one condition is true, the associated sequence of statements is executed and the If

Statement terminates. Otherwise, if an Else Clause is included, its statement list is executed. Should no condition result in true and no Else Clause be present, the If Statement will terminate without any of the statement lists ever executing.

This idea is common to If Statements in practically all languages. If we design our own procedural language, chances are we shall provide an If Statement. We should take a close look then at how Ada and Modula-2 define syntax and semantics; there is not much room for improvement. See Example 7-4.

```
ada_if_statement     ::= IF condition THEN
                            sequence_of_statements
                         { ELSIF condition THEN
                            sequence_of_statements }
                         [ ELSE
                            sequence_of_statements ]
                           END IF ;

Example:

   --day_update, all months have 31 days

       IF day = 31 THEN
        IF month = december THEN
         day := 1;
         month := january;
         year := year + 1;
        ELSE
         month := month_type'succ( month );
         day := 1;
        END IF;
       ELSE
        day := day + 1;
       END IF;
```

Example 7-4 Day Update Program in Ada

Like other languages with forced closure, Ada's syntax is well designed by allowing a sequence of statements after the Else, Elsif, and Then Clauses. This forced closure END IF, terminated by a required semicolon, eliminates the "Dangling Else" problem.

Definition of "Dangling Else Problem"

The problem of the *Dangling Else* has been well known since the definition of Algol-60. When two (or more) If Statements are nested and only one Else Clause is given, it is not clear from the BNF syntax rules for Algol-60, Pascal, or PL/I which If Statement the Else Clause belongs to. The fragments for "pascal_if_statement" and "pl1_if_statement" cause the overall grammar to be ambiguous. The problem is not inherently ambiguous, hence we can construct an unambiguous BNF grammar for the If Statement, but this grammar is relatively complicated. To solve this issue anyway even with the short grammar, the following context condition is typically added: "an Else Clause is always associated with the nearest If Statement that does not already have an Else Clause." For more information about the unambiguous grammar for If Statements see Exercise 6 at the end of this chapter. We shall also present a Dangling Else example in the section entitled "If Statement Syntax in Pascal" later in this chapter. In Ada it is always clear to which If Statement an Else Clause belongs. There is no choice: it is the deepest nested If Statement not yet closed by an END IF closure.

Branches via Goto Statements from the outside into an If Statement are not allowed due to a restriction on the Goto Statement itself. Goto Statements originating in If Statements are clearly permitted, whether they lead outside or into the same section of the same, originating If Statement. Labels, however, may freely be defined for any of the statements nested inside an If Statement.

Elsif Clauses transform a certain class of nested If Statements into a linearized sequence, which is slightly easier to understand than the strictly nested equivalent. See the lexical scanner fragment using Ada If Statements in Example 7-5.

```
-- Nested If Statements
IF cur_char = '=' THEN
 get_next_character;
 token := eq_token;
ELSE
 IF cur_char = '>' THEN
  get_next_character;
  IF cur_char = '=' THEN
   get_next_character;
   token := ge_token;
  ELSE
   token := gt_token;
  END IF;
 ELSE
  IF cur_char = '<' THEN
   get_next_character;
  IF cur_char = '=' THEN
   get_next_character;
   token := le_token;
   ELSE
    token := lt_token;
   END IF;
```

```
--Series of Elsif Clauses
IF cur_char = '=' THEN
 get_next_character;
 token := eq_token;
ELSIF cur_char = '>' THEN
 get_next_character;
 IF cur_char = '=' THEN
  get_next_character;
  token := ge_token;
 ELSE
  token := gt_token;
 END IF;
ELSIF cur_char = '<' THEN
 get_next_character;
 IF cur_char = '=' THEN
  get_next_character;
 token := le_token;
ELSE
 token := lt_token;
 END IF;
ELSE
 error;
```

```
    ELSE                                  END IF;
      error;
    END IF; --cur_char = '<'
  END IF; --cur_char = '>'
END IF; --cur_char = '='
```

Example 7-5 Lexical Scanner Fragment Via Ada If Statements

Analyzing the lexical scanner fragment, we note that the conditions of all If Statements depend on a single variable, named "cur_char," which is compared with various character constants. This unique combination allows an If Statement to be replaced in a natural way by an equivalent Case Statement. We shall revisit the same problem in our treatment of Case Statements in the section entitled "Case Statement Syntax in Ada" later in this chapter.

Comparing the two different implementations of nested If Statements in Example 7-5, we see that the left version implies a deeper nesting structure than the right solution. Note the plethora of END IF closures in the left solution. The right implementation is a closer reflection of the true logic: the conditions are not nested, hence not getting more and more complicated. Instead there is simply a variety of conditions, which are to be checked in a sequential fashion, only if previous conditions have not yet produced a "true" result. A Case Statement would have been the appropriate control structure in the first place.

Had we used at least one variable instead of only character constants, it would be difficult to replace the If Statement by a Case Statement. Later in this chapter and in the Exercises we will show that the mapping of If and Case Statements is, however, one-to-one and complete. But there are cases where this mapping is not meaningful, since the resulting source is illegible and hence unintelligible.

If Statement Syntax in Fortran

Fortran-66 provides two versions of If Statements, both of which are somewhat restricted in use and not overly convenient. They are known as the Arithmetic and Logical If Statements. Neither of these has an Else Clause, an Elsif Clause, or an explicit closure. They may not be nested.

With the definition of Fortran-77, however, a third kind was introduced: the Block If Statement that is much more general and useful than the older two. See Example 7-6.

```
f77_if_statement    ::= arithmetic_if
                      | logical_if
                      | block_if

arithmetic_if       ::= IF ( expression ) s1, s2, s3

logical_if          ::= IF ( condition ) restricted_statement

block_if            ::= IF ( condition ) THEN
                          sequence_of_statements
                      { ELSE IF ( condition ) THEN
                          sequence_of_statements }
                      [ ELSE
                          sequence_of_statements ]
                        END IF
```

Example 7-6 Fortran If Statement Grammar

Arithmetic If

The Arithmetic If Statement starts with the keyword IF, followed by a parenthesized arithmetic expression. If the expression yields less than zero, the statement labeled "s1" is executed; if it results in zero, execution is transferred to statement "s2"; otherwise, statement "s3" is executed. All three may be, but need not be, distinct Fortran statement labels. See Example 7-7.

```
         I = -12
         IF ( I ) 10, 20, 30
10        WRITE(6,*)"o.k."
20        WRITE(6,*)"here too"
30        WRITE(6,*)"here too"
```

Example 7-7 Fortran Arithmetic If

The Arithmetic If Statement in Example 7-7 will cause execution of the statement labeled 10. But, since the other two statements follow directly in sequence, the generated output consists of one message "o.k." and two messages "here too."

This form of conditional statement is quite rigid, very typical for older Fortrans, and of limited value. The reader is invited to translate the sample If Statement named "day_update" in Example 7-4 into Fortran's Arithmetic If. Certainly this is possible, but the final source looks less readable than in Ada or in Fortran-77's Block If Statements.

Logical If

The Logical If Statement also starts with the keyword IF and has a parenthetical condition. If this condition is true, the associated restricted statement is executed; otherwise, the successor of the Logical If Statement is executed. Logical If Statements may not be nested; the restricted statement may not be a DO, block IF, ELSE IF, ELSE, END IF, or END statement.

Should the logical expression yield false, then the effect of that If Statement is null except for possible side effects caused by function calls included in the evaluation of the expression. The "day_update" program is implemented in Example 7-8 via Logical If.

```
C---- DAY UPDATE
C---- Assume all Months have 31 days
      SUBROUTINE UPDATE( DAY, MONTH, YEAR )
       INTEGER DAY, MONTH, YEAR
       IF ( DAY .LT. 31 ) GOTO 10
        IF ( MONTH .LT. 12 ) GOTO 20
         DAY = 1
         MONTH = 1
         YEAR = YEAR + 1
         GOTO 50
20      DAY = 1
        MONTH = MONTH + 1
        GOTO 50
10      DAY = DAY + 1
50      WRITE( 6, * ) DAY, MONTH, YEAR
      END
```

Example 7-8 Fortran Logical If

Block If

Whereas the ANSI standard invents a special-purpose If-level counting scheme to define the Block If Statement, we use a simpler description via extended BNF and English, already familiar to the reader from other sections. The Block If Statement looks almost identical to the Ada If Statement, except for a very subtle difference in the ELSE IF Clause and END IF closure. Remember that each Fortran source line may hold at most one statement. In order to provide a visually descriptive layout of keywords and embedded statements, the Fortran standard simply defines the END IF and ELSE keywords as statements. Thus the keywords appear on different lines than the included statements and the resulting Fortran source can turn quite readable. Analogously, the ELSE IF Clause is defined as a statement, with the subsequent condition and THEN being part of it. Our lexical scanner fragment rewritten in Fortran Block If Statements is given in Example 7-9.

```
IF ( CURCHR .EQ. '=' ) THEN
 CALL GETCHR
 TOKEN = 1
ELSE IF ( CURCHR .EQ. '>' ) THEN
 CALL GETCHR
 IF ( CURCHR .EQ. '=' ) THEN
  CALL GETCHR
  TOKEN = 2
 ELSE
  TOKEN = 3
 END IF
ELSE IF ( CURCHR .EQ. '<' ) THEN
 CALL GETCHR
 IF ( CURCHR .EQ. '=' ) THEN
  CALL GETCHR
  TOKEN = 4
 ELSE
  TOKEN = 5
 END IF
ELSE
 CALL ERROR
END IF
```

Example 7-9 Lexical Scanner Fragment Via Fortran Block If

We have emphasized already that Fortran statements are line-oriented. Another rule specific to Fortran, which says that blanks are insignificant except inside character strings, seems at first glance to cause ambiguity and trouble in certain programs. One such program, Example 7-10, is listed here to prepare the reader for the coming demonstration in Example 7-11. Line numbers have been added for the sake of reference and are not part of the source.

```
      PROGRAM IF2
      INTEGER I, J, IENDIF, JENDIF
10    FORMAT( ' SOMETHING WRONG' )
20    FORMAT( ' EVERYTHING O.K.' )
      I = 12
      J = I ** 2
      I END IF = 99
      J END IF = 88
      IF ( I .EQ. 12 ) THEN
       I = I END IF
       IF ( J .EQ. 144 ) THEN
        J = J END IF
        WRITE( 6, 20 )
       ELSE
        WRITE( 6, 10 )
       END IF
      ELSE
       WRITE( 6, 10 )
      END IF
      END
```

Example 7-10   Fortran Program IF2

Source program “IF2” in Example 7-10 defines two integer variables, “IENDIF” and “JENDIF,” which the reader should find suspicious. At first glance there may be nothing strange about these, but if we keep in mind that blanks are insignificant, we see that the variables may be spelled as “I END IF” or “J END IF.” The question now arises, how can a human reader or a Fortran compiler distinguish when variable “I” followed by the END IF keywords is meant, and when the variable “IENDIF” is intended? Remember that the compiler and the human reader have the identical set of language rules available—those listed in the standard. If a compiler can keep track, so can we. So the reader should carefully read “IF2,” always bearing in mind that blanks are insignificant, even if they might suggest something.

The next source program “IF3” in Example 7-11 is a variation of “IF2” and is written to confuse and delight the reader. We invite you to detect the syntax error in the source before continuing to read. Line numbers are again included for reference.

```
 1           PROGRAM IF3
 2           INTEGER I, J, IENDIF, JENDIF
 3   10      FORMAT( ' SOMETHING WRONG' )
 4   20      FORMAT( ' EVERYTHING O.K.' )
 5           I = 12
 6           J = I ** 2
 7           I END IF = 99
 8           J END IF = 88
 9           IF ( I .EQ. 12 ) THEN
10            I = I
11                  END IF
12            IF ( J .EQ. 144 ) THEN
13             J = J END IF
14             WRITE( 6, 20 )
15            ELSE
16             WRITE( 6, 10 )
17            END IF
18           ELSE
19            WRITE( 6, 10 )
20           END IF
21           END
```

Example 7-11 Fortran Program IF3

In the previous program, "IF2," line 10 contained the source "I = I END IF," identical to "I = IENDIF." The faulty program "IF3" splits this into two lines. See lines 10 and 11 in "IF3." The program's error results from the following.

Fortran demands "one complete statement per line." Line 10 in "IF3" holds only a partial statement. By coincidence this partial statement happens to be a correct Fortran statement too, but one with a different meaning. To make things worse, line 11, also only a half statement, happens to be yet another complete Fortran statement, namely the END IF Statement. Hence the compiler cannot issue an error message on either line. As soon as lines 18 and 20 are parsed, however, the spurious ELSE and END IF keywords will be detected. These are definitely out of place, since the previous program fragment is interpreted as correct Fortran. And, in fact, a Fortran compiler will issue error messages, saying that ELSE and END IF are unrecognizable statements.

In order to reintroduce the original semantics without giving up the split line, a continuation mark may be used on line 11, indicating that this line is part of the Assignment Statement. These examples are meant to have the reader appreciate the interplay of three Fortran rules: first, the rule that blanks are insignificant; second, that each line must hold a complete statement, and third, that END IF (and similarly ELSE) is a complete, legal statement.

Once more we should point out that in Ada a separator is mandatory between END and IF for the statement terminator. In Fortran it does not matter. For Fortran ENDIF and END IF are identical, while an Ada compiler would interpret ENDIF as an identifier, most likely undeclared.

If Fortran did not have the rule "one complete statement per line," the insignificant blank rule would suddenly render Fortran-77 an ambiguous language. So, in combination, two clumsy rules can make good sense in an outdated language.

No Dangling Else in Fortran

Since both the Arithmetic If and the logical If allow no Else Clause, the Dangling Else problem is nonexistent for these statements. Also remember that nesting is impossible for the Arithmetic If Statement and disallowed for the Logical If Statement. Block If Statements have the END IF forced closure, which alleviates the problem. We will have to wait for the Pascal treatment to see a classical Dangling Else demonstrated.

Branch into If Statement

Again Fortran is safe here. Since the Arithmetic and Logical If must be written on a single line, a label cannot be defined that will permit a branch into the middle. The Fortran-77 standard ANSI [1978] clearly states (11-4, line 25 f.) that the transfer of control into an if block from the outside is prohibited. Hence a Fortran compiler is expected to perform some kind of flow analysis in order to enforce this rule.

If Statement Syntax in Pascal

Pascal's If Statement is very similar to that of Algol-60. An optional Else Clause is provided, but a terminating closure is not permitted. Conditions need not be parenthesized, since the reserved keywords IF and THEN provide sufficient clues on how to parse the source. Also, since If Statements may be nested, we can finally demonstrate the Dangling Else problem in its purest form, equaled only by PL/I and Algol-60. See Example 7-12.

```
pascal_if_statement ::= IF condition THEN
                          statement
                        [ ELSE
                          statement ]
```

Example 7-12 Grammar for Pascal If

Before we list sample programs, we need to emphasize two key issues that can cause confusion. As shown by the grammar in Example 7-12, only one single statement may follow the Then Clause and the Else Clause. Remember also that in Pascal statements are not terminated by a semicolon. A semicolon can only separate two contiguous statements from one another. This leads many beginning programmers to commit the classical programming error shown in Example 7-13.

```
IF number MOD 2 = 1 THEN { Pascal source }
 nexteven := succ( number );
ELSE
 nexteven := number;
{ For non-negative <number>, the same as: }
nexteven := number + number MOD 2;
```

Example 7-13 Classical Semicolon Error

Dangerous Semicolon

Upon first inspection the If Statement in Example 7-13 does not appear erroneous at all, but most compilers will complain about the ELSE keyword and lament that an unrecognizable statement has been found. Very friendly compilers will complain about the semicolon after the right parenthesis, issue a warning, and inform us that the semicolon has been generously swallowed.

Either way, the cause of the error is the same. Only the error recovery varies slightly. The Pascal grammar for the If Statement says clearly that only one statement is allowed after THEN, before the ELSE. Our If Statement in Example 7-13, however, has two statements at that place, one Assignment Statement and one empty statement, and both are separated from one another by the semicolon. To correct the error the semicolon must be removed.

The second semicolon after the Else Clause in this context is not necessarily wrong. However, should this If Statement be embedded in another If Statement's Then Clause, then we repeat the same error in a nested fashion.

The semicolon problem can become even more devious. In conjunction with the empty statement there is a place in the If Statement where the semicolon is permitted but where its occurrence will annihilate the effect of the If Statement. When used this way without the Else Clause, no error message can be emitted. The reader is invited to determine under which conditions the Compound Statement in Example 7-14 will be executed.

```
IF day IN workdays THEN; { Pascal source }
 BEGIN
  finaltransactions;
  computebalance;
  printreport;
 END;
{END IF}
```

Example 7-14 Devious Error in Pascal If Statement

We have tried to create the false impression that in the If Statement final transactions will be made, balances computed, and reports printed only on workdays, but this is wrong! The semicolon after the THEN, although allowed, terminates the If Statement altogether. The most devious effect of this kind of subtle error is that the presumed single If Statement is transformed into two syntactically correct statements: one void If Statement, followed by a Compound Statement. Compilers cannot report anything wrong here.

Dangling Else

Since the Else Clause is optional and If Statements can be nested inside one another, the statement in Example 7-15 has two possible interpretations:

```
IF sickdays = 0 THEN { Pascal source }
  IF vacationdays < maxvacation THEN
    vacationdays := succ( vacationdays )
  ELSE
    payment := payment + payperday
```

Example 7-15 Closer to the Dangling Else Problem

The interpretations depend on which If Statement the Else Clause belongs to. One might argue that the textual indentation clearly shows the ELSE to belong to the nested, inner if. But Pascal is format-free, and hence, the same source, with the identical ambiguity, could be rewritten as shown in Example 7-16.

```
IF sickdays = 0 THEN { Pascal source }
  IF vacationdays < maxvacation THEN
    vacationdays := succ( vacationdays )
ELSE
  payment := payment + payperday
```

Example 7-16 Which IF Does the ELSE Belong to?

This example is meant only to prove that the textual layout bears no meaning. It may include hints to the reader, but they are just that. A compiler will ignore layout, and the human reader might be misled if a programmer has accidentally mixed up the indentation structure.

Back to the two interpretations. We see that payment could be increased if vacation days are greater or equal to max vacation, or payment could be adjusted when sick days are unequal to zero. Usually languages avoid ambiguity by defining that any ELSE belongs to the innermost If Statement not yet matched up with an Else Clause. Pascal follows this convention. Therefore, the meaning of both If Statements, in Example 7-15 and 7-16 is to increase payment when sick days equals zero and the number of vacation days is already max vacation or greater.

If the payment should really be increased for the case of sick days not equal to zero, then an empty Else Clause must be added. This is expressed in Example 7-17:

```
IF sickdays = 0 THEN { Pascal source }
 IF vacationdays < maxvacation THEN
  vacationdays := succ( vacationdays )
 ELSE
  { nothing }
 {END IF}
ELSE
 payment := payment + payperday
{END IF}
```

Example 7-17 Increase Payment, If Sickdays Not Equal Zero

If Statement Abuse

Given a boolean type variable named "found," it would be abusive to compute its value as in the program in Example 7-18.

```
IF wanted = table[ i ] THEN { Pascal source }
 found := true
ELSE
 found := false;
{END IF}
```

Example 7-18 Abused If Statement

A shorter, faster, and equally readable and correct solution is the direct assignment of the expression as follows:

```
found := wanted = table[ i ];
```

But we must be careful. If the original statement is an If Statement without an Else Clause, then the Assignment Statement is no longer equivalent and therefore cannot replace the longer if construct. See Example 7-19.

```
IF condition THEN { Pascal source }
 marked := true
{END IF}
{is NOT the same as}
marked := condition;
```

Example 7-19 Assignment Versus If

The reason is simply that "marked" may be true already, and if ever true, we may want to preserve that fact. So it should not be overwritten with false, just because some time "condition" yields false. The original meaning is to preserve true, hence "marked := condition" has a different meaning.

Branch into If Statement
Pascal does not permit a Goto Statement to lead into a structured statement from the outside. This restriction applies to If Statements as well. It is, however, perfectly legal to originate a Goto Statement from the level that the target label is defined on. Also, it is legal to branch out of an If Statement. See Example 7-20.

```
        IF condition1 then
         BEGIN
200:        process1;
          IF condition2 THEN
           GOTO 300; { branch out, 2 levels, legal }
          {END IF}
          process2;
          IF condition 3 THEN
           GOTO 200; { legal, is branch OUT, not INTO If Statement }
          {END IF}
         END
        ELSE
         GOTO 400;  { branch out, 1 level, legal }
        {END IF}
300:     process3;
        ...
400:     process4;
        ..
        GOTO 200; { ---> ILLEGAL <--- }
```

Example 7-20 Legal and Illegal Gotos into If Statements

Begin End Nuisance
The Pascal rule allowing just one statement after the Then Clause and the Else Clause causes a minor nuisance. If the program logic forces two or more statements to depend on the same If Statement condition, then the language forces the programmer to embrace these multiple statements in a Compound Statement. This is shown in Example 7-21, which uses the familiar "day_update" fragment.

```
{ dayupdate }
 if day = 31 then
  if month = december then
   begin
    day := 1;
    month := january;
    year := year + 1;
   end
  else
   begin
    month := succ( month );
    day := 1;
   end
  {end if}
 else
  day := day + 1;
{end if}
```

Example 7-21 More Than One Statement Depending on Same Condition

If Statement Syntax in PL/I

PL/I If Statements are very similar to those of Pascal, the only difference being that in PL/I statements must be terminated by a semicolon. It is, therefore, not surprising that we find the Dangling Else problem and the Begin End nuisance just as we do in Pascal. Even the "dangerous semicolon" problem has not vanished completely; it reappears under a different sign. As we see in Example 7-22, the grammar is almost identical to the Pascal grammar.

```
pl1_if_statement    ::= IF condition THEN
                          statement
                        [ ELSE
                          statement ]
```

Example 7-22 PL/I If Statement Syntax

Knowing that PL/I statements must be terminated by a semicolon, we might conclude that the grammar in Example 7-22 should require such a semicolon after the nonterminal "statement." However, this grammar fragment fits into an overall PL/I grammar, which has already placed a semicolon after each individual statement, including the If Statement. Another semicolon in this grammar would produce wrong source strings with two semicolons required after If Statements. This should serve as a clarification or stimulus for readers who are not confident about the grammatical differences between "terminator" and "separator" semicolons.

PL/I has the analogue to the "dangerous semicolon" of Pascal shown in Example 7-14. But it develops in the reverse logic. When an empty Else Clause is inserted to clarify the "Dangling Else" problem, exactly as done in Pascal, then the additional ELSE keyword *must* be terminated by a semicolon. This is to make sure that the empty statement, following the ELSE keyword, is properly terminated. Beginning PL/I programmers frequently forget this, but the compiler will usually point out the omitted semicolon. The PL/I version of the "Increase Payment" program of Example 7-17 follows in Example 7-23. To demonstrate the empty Else Clause, we chose to increase the "payment," if "sick_days" is unequal to zero.

```
IF sick_days = 0 THEN
 IF vacation_days < max_vacation THEN
  vacation_days = vacation_days + 1;
 ELSE; /* semicolon required */
  /* empty */
ELSE
 payment = payment + pay_per_day;
```

Example 7-23 Empty Else Clause in PL/I

The previous discussion of If Statement abuse in Pascal applies to PL/I in the same way. PL/I also permits the assignment of a boolean expression, called Bit(1) expression in PL/I language, to a variable of corresponding type. Also the devious semicolon problem after the THEN keyword exists in PL/I. See Exercise 3 at the end of this chapter.

If Statement Syntax in Modula-2

In many respects Modula-2 is a simple language, strongly modeled after its ancestor Pascal. The If Statement, however, looks almost identical to that of Ada. Multiple Elsif Clauses are permitted, each introduced by the ELSIF keyword, and an optional Else Clause is included. Due to the forced closure, no Dangling Else ambiguity can arise. The syntax rules expressed in extended BNF are given in Example 7-24.

```
modula2_if_statement  ::= IF condition THEN
                            sequence_of_statements
                        { ELSIF condition THEN
                            sequence_of_statements }
                        [ ELSE
                            sequence_of_statements ]
                          END
```

Example 7-24 Modula-2 If Statement Syntax

An If Statement with multiple Elsif Clauses has a variety of conditions. Each of these conditions is evaluated, in turn, until one yields true. Then the associated sequence of statements is executed, and the If Statement terminates. Should other Elsif Clauses follow, their conditions will not be evaluated.

7.3 Case Statement Overview

Case Statements, the second form of conditionals, are more complex than their If Statement counterpart. A single, general expression of primitive type controls the logic of the Case Statement. This is the Case Expression, to be tested for equality with one of the possible choices. Each choice has a sequence of statements associated with it. If one of the choices equals the Case Expression, then the associated statement list is executed. Usually exactly one of the choices must match, but this may vary from language to language.

Note the difference between If and Case conditionals. If Statement conditions must be of boolean type and may include variables. Case Statements include one general Case Expression, but all Case Choices are restricted to expressions, consisting exclusively of literals. The type of all choices must be compatible with the Case Expressions.

Case Statements are, therefore, more restrictive. As a nice consequence of this higher restriction, it is possible for compilers to translate Case Statements into code that executes faster than the equivalent nest (or sequence) of If Statements. The reader should realize that all Case Statements can be expressed by equivalent If Statements, but only some If Statements can be easily mapped into equivalent Case Statements. For more detail see the exercises.

Fortran and PL/I have no Case Statement. The Fortran Computed Goto Statement has some similarity with a Case Statement, as will be seen in the treatment of the historical background. One PL/I implementation has a nonstandard extension, the so-called Switch Statement, which has some similarity with Case Statements. Also the PL/I data type Array of Label can be used like unrestricted Case Statements.

Development of the Case Statement, Historical Background

As already observed with the If Statement, it is quite common to break a programming problem into numerous subproblems, from which exactly one is picked for execution. The selection is controlled by an expression. This can be expressed by nested If Statements. Example 7-25 shows this in Pascal.

```
IF x = 1 THEN
 action1
ELSE IF x = 2 THEN
 action2
ELSE IF x = 3 THEN
 action3
 ...
{END IF}
```

Example 7-25 Need for Case Statement

This is a correct but bothersome way of expressing selection. It is time consuming for the programmer and the computer; the former writes too much, the latter executes too much. Fortran's Computed Goto Statement offers a more convenient shorthand, as shown in Example 7-26.

```
GOTO ( 100, 200, 300 ... ) X
...
100      <action1>
...
200      <action2>
...
300      <action3>
...
```

Example 7-26 Almost a Case Statement

If x=1, then execution continues at label 100; if x=2 statement 200 is executed; and so on. Here the compiler can generate efficient code by using a branch table, and the user does not need to write so many If Statement conditions. The problem with this is that the statement labels (100, 200, etc.) can be anywhere in the program—before, after, close to, and far away from the actual Goto Statement. It would require voluntary discipline from the programmer to develop a coding style that reflects the logic of a Case Statement. This is possible, but the Fortran compiler cannot enforce it.

Algol-68 provides a more advanced version of Case Statement via its "Case Clause." The Case Expression (called Enquiry Clause) of type integer selects one of the subsequent actions. If the Case Expression yields 1, the first action is executed—if it yields 2, the second is selected; and so on. See Example 7-27.

```
CASE i IN
 action1,
 action2,
 action3,
 action4,
 ...
ESAC
```

Example 7-27 Algol-68 Case Statement

This "second generation" Case Statement enforces structure upon source programs through syntax, which the "first generation" solution of Fortran's Computed Goto is unable to guarantee. Clearly, the Algol-68 solution is superior, but it still has three critical flaws.

Restricting the type of the Case Expression to integer is a minor nuisance. More seriously, if we wish to select the same action for various values of the Case Expression, we must list the action repeatedly in the source program. In Example 7-28, which is still in Algol-68, we assume that "action1" is called if the Case Expression yields 1, 4, or 5.

```
CASE i IN
 action1,
 action2,
 action3,
 action1,
 action1,
 ...
ESAC
```

Example 7-28 First Generation Case Statement in Algol-68

This blows up the source code and thus makes it less readable. Even this is not the most serious drawback.

What happens if we have one action too many or if we delete one accidentally? This may sound contrived to a programming novice, but it easily happens during program maintenance. The problem is that the resulting program would still be syntactically correct, but the implied association of integer values and actions would be lost. This requirement for positional correspondence is the most critical flaw, since it causes subtle errors that cannot be caught by the translator.

The Pascal style Case Statement, modeled after a proposal by Toni Hoare, solves the preceding problems by requiring explicit Case Labels. These explicitly associate the value of the Case Expression with a selected action. All order dependence vanishes and multiple labels are allowed per action. It took Toni Hoare more than one try to propose a safe Case Statement syntax a la Pascal; for reference, see Hoare's earlier proposal Hoare [1964], published in the Algol Bulletin. Ada, Modula-2, and Pascal provide "safe" Case Statements. Moreover, Ada and Modula-2 allow an optional catchall phrase for the situation that there is no match between Case Expression and choice. See the Pascal sample in Example 7-29.

```
CASE i-2 OF
 1, 4, 5:
  action1;
 2: action2;
 3: action3;
END;
```

Example 7-29 A Safer Case Statement in Pascal

Case Statement Syntax in Ada

Ada's Case Statement selects for execution one of a possibly large number of alternative sequences of statements. The alternative chosen is determined by the Case Expression and the matching choice. All choices must be of the same type and must be compatible with the type of the Case Expression. Permitted are the discrete types, which are any types that could also serve as array indices. Therefore, choices of floating point type are not possible.

All possible cases must be covered. If the Others Choice is specified, it must be the last choice and cannot be combined with further values. The Case Statement syntax is shown in Example 7-30.

```
ada_case_statement          ::= CASE expression IS
                                      case_alternative
                                    { case_alternative }
                                  END CASE ;
case_alternative            ::= WHEN choice { | choice } =>
                                  sequence_of_statements
choice                      ::= static_simple_expression
                                  | static_discrete_range
                                  | OTHERS
static_simple_expression    ::= expression
                                --whose operands are all literals
```

Example 7-30 Grammar for Case Statements

The program in Example 7-31 is a variation of the lexical scanner fragment, encountered in Example 7-5. Here we added a few modifications to demonstrate the multiple choice and the range of choices that are so convenient in Ada.

```
CASE cur_char IS--Ada source
 WHEN '=' =>
  get_next_token;
  token := eq_token;--scan =
 WHEN '>' =>
  get_next_token;
  IF cur_char = '=' THEN
   get_next_token;
   token := ge_token;--scan >=
  ELSE
   token := gt_token;--scan >
  END IF;
 WHEN '<' =>
  get_next_token;
  IF cur_char = '=' THEN
   get_next_token;
   token := le_token;--scan <=
  ELSE
   token := lt_token;--scan <
  END IF;
 WHEN '/' | '#' =>
  not_yet_completed;
 WHEN '(' .. ')' | '[' .. ']' =>
  special_consideration;
 WHEN OTHERS =>
  error;
END CASE;
```

Example 7-31 Sample Ada Case Statement

It is mandatory during program execution that one of the choices matches the Case Expression. It follows from this requirement that all possible cases must be enumerated. If the match between choice and case expression cannot be established during execution, then the Others Clause must be provided in the Case Statement; otherwise, the program is in error. When OTHERS is given, it must be the last choice. From this it follows that there may be only one single Others Clause.

The simple expression and the discrete ranges must be static. Notice that static is more restricted than constant. A *static* value is known at the time of compilation and consists of literals exclusively. *Constants* are just not allowed to change their value during execution, but their initial value may well be taken from a variable.

Using a discrete range is more concise than, but functionally equivalent to, listing all choices of that range in any order. Also note that the null range is permitted, in which situation the case alternative will never be executed. Every choice must be included exactly once.

Unless one choice matches the Case Expression, the Others Clause, included as the last one, will be selected for execution. All choices must have the same type as the Case Expression. In Example 7-32 we list a rudimentary "Five Function Calculator" that is neither safe nor convenient to use, but correct and highlights the Ada Case Statement.

```
                 |PROCEDURE calc IS--assume integer_io PACKAGE
        5   1    | result, number : integer;
        7   1    | operator       : character;
            1    |BEGIN--calc
            1    | result := 0;
  4         1  1 | operator := '+';
  7         1  1 | LOOP
  7         1  1 |  get( number );
  9         1  2 |  CASE operator IS
 11         1  2 |   WHEN '+' => result := result  +  number;
 16         1  3 |   WHEN '-' => result := result  -  number;
 22         1  3 |   WHEN '*' => result := result  *  number;
 28         1  3 |   WHEN '/' => result := result  /  number;
 34         1  3 |   WHEN ' |' => result := result MOD number;
 40         1  3 |   WHEN OTHERS =>  RAISE constraint_error;
 42         1  3 |  END CASE;
 51         1  2 |  get( operator );
 53         1  2 |  EXIT WHEN operator = '=';
 58         1  2 | END LOOP;
 59         1  1 | put( " result = " );
 61         1  1 | put_line( integer'image( result ) );
 64         1  1 |END calc;
```

Example 7-32 Five Function Calculator in Ada

Case Statement Syntax in Pascal

Pascal's Case Statement is not as comfortable to use as Ada's. First, all choices must be listed individually; if by chance some choices are contiguous, they still must be listed one-by-one in Pascal. Second, Pascal has no equivalent of Ada's Others Clause. A Pascal program is in error if none of the choices matches the Case Expression. This error state must be detected by the run time system. It is unfortunate (but understandable from an implementation standpoint) that the type of the Case Expression may not be string. Hence it is not possible to make a case selection based on different string literals. This feature is frequently desired by programmers but not even offered in Ada or Modula-2. Example 7-33 shows the BNF skeleton for Pascal's Case Statements.

```
pascal_case_statement ::= CASE expression OF
                            case_alternative
                           { ; case_alternative } [ ; ]
                          END

case_alternative      ::= constant { , constant } : statement
```

Example 7-33 Pascal Case Statement Syntax Rules

If the Case Expression is of type integer, then the case alternatives start with an integer number followed by a colon. This looks suspiciously like a label, but is something quite different. Case labels cannot be referenced in a Goto Statement. If a correct label and a Case Label happen to hold the same numeric value, no misinterpretation is possible; the Case Labels come first, the labeled statement is nested inside. See Example 7-34.

```
PROCEDURE caselabel; { Pascal source }
 LABEL 1, 2, 3;
 TYPE shorttype = 1 .. 4;
 VAR short : shorttype;
 BEGIN { caselabel }
  { other statements }
  CASE short OF
   1: action1;
   2: 3: BEGIN
          { some action }
          IF condition THEN GOTO 3; { above }
          { other actions }
         END;
   3: ; 4 : action3; { confusing?? }
  END;
  IF condition THEN
   GOTO 2;
  {END IF};
  { other statements }
  2: short := 2;
  { other statements }
 END; { caselabel }
```

Example 7-34 Pascal Program, Showing Labels and Case Labels

The program skeleton in Example 7-34 not only shows case labels, it also includes regular statement labels, and in one situation even a combination of the two. On the line starting out with "2:3:," we have a Case Label, followed by a statement label. Label 3 can be reached only from within the Case Statement itself; a branch from the outside would be illegal. Then comes Case Label 3, with an empty statement to its right. Next follows the Case Label 4.

It has been written onto the same source line to confuse the reader. But the program skeleton is perfectly legal, provided that all sketchy segments like "condition" contain legal Pascal text.

Example 7-35 shows a solution of the five function pocket calculator using Pascal Case Statements. Since the logic and source are so close to the Ada solution shown in Example 7-32, this example needs no further comment.

```
 1    1  0  0      PROGRAM calc( input, output );
 2    2  0  0       VAR
                     result, number : integer;
 3    4  0  0        operator       : char;
 4    5  0  0       BEGIN { calc }
 4    6  0  1        result := 0;
 5    7  0  1        operator := '+';
 6    8  0  1        REPEAT
 6    9  0  2         readln( input, number );
 7   10  0  2         CASE operator OF
 8   11  0  3          '+' : result := result  +  number;
 9   12  0  3          '-' : result := result  -  number;
10   13  0  3          '*' : result := result  *  number;
11   14  0  3          '/' : result := result DIV number;
12   15  0  3          '|' : result := result MOD number;
13   16  0  3         END; {CASE}
15   17  0  2         readln( input, operator );
16   18  0  2        UNTIL operator = '=';
18   19  0  1        writeln( output, ' result = ', result );
19   20  0  1       END. { calc }
```

Example 7-35 Desk Calculator, Demonstrating Pascal Case Statement

Case Statement Syntax in Modula-2

The Case Statement takes Modula-2 out of the class of simple languages. Everything a programmer ever needed but didn't get when programming in Pascal is available in Modula-2's Case Statement. An optional Else Clause is provided for the situation where none of the Case Labels matches the Case Expression. Also, the Case Labels allow the specification of ranges, and no longer require the tedious listing of all individual values. Again, the Modula-2 language definition resembles Ada more than Pascal. Examle 7-36 contains the syntax rules.

```
modula2_case_statement ::= CASE expression OF
                             case { | case }
                             [ ELSE sequence_of_statements ]
                           END
case                   ::= case_label_list : sequence_of_statements
case_label_list        ::= case_label { , case_label }
case_label             ::= constant_expression [ .. constant_expression ]
```

Example 7-36   Modula-2 Case Statement Syntax

Consistency
Like Pascal, Modula-2 uses the semicolon to separate statements from one another rather than terminating them. In the definition of the Case Statement, the Modula-2 language designers tried to be consistent and applied the same principle to the different "cases." Hence, one "case" is separated from the next one by a special symbol, the | token. It would have been inconsistent if the different cases of a Case Statement had a terminator, while general statements have a separator from one another. We list a sample Modula-2 Case Statement in Example 7-37.

```
CASE NextChar OF
'a' .. 'z':
  ScanIdentifier  |
'0' .. '9':
  ScanNumber      |
'"':
  NextChar;
  ScanString;
  NextChar        |
'>', '<', '=', '#':
  RelationalOps
ELSE
  SpecialSymbols;
END;
```

Example 7-37   Modula-2 Case Statement

7.4 Summary

Conditional statements select one (or none) of a set of statement lists, depending on a condition. For If Statements this is a boolean type expression of the most general form. Case Statements select an action if the Case Expression matches one of the constant Case Choices. We have presented the

Dangling Else problem and have shown that the problem does not surface in languages with forced closure. As far as expressive power is concerned, all If Statements are equal. The Elsif Clause and forced closure provide nothing that could not also be expressed via more primitive If Statements; but programs with Elsif Clauses and forced closure are more readable, hence become more reliable, and ultimately decrease the cost of software maintenance. Also, we have presented the advantage of the Elsif Clause in If Statements and the benefits of the range of Case Choices and of the Others (or Else) Clause in Case Statements. Readers who design their own programming languages should be aware of the advantages of such constructs. The next chapter will cover Iterative Statements, again using operands and expressions, but this time to control iteration rather than selection.

.5 Exercises

1. Why is it a bad idea to use a Pascal Case Statement with an integer type Case Expression?

2. Is Fortran limited since it has no Case Statement? The question does not address writing comfort, but asks if there are any programs using Case Statements that cannot be rewritten in Fortran.

3. How many times will the message HELLO be printed by the following PL/I program fragment? Pay attention to semicolons.

```
DO I = 1 TO 10 BY 1;
 IF MOD( I, 2 ) = 0 THEN;
  PUT SKIP LIST( ' HELLO ' );
END;
```

4. Detect the syntax error in the following Pascal program segment:

```
IF ( day = Saturday ) OR ( day = Sunday ) THEN
 rest;
ELSE
 work;
```

5. Detect the error in the following Fortran function FU.

```
      INTEGER FUNCTION FU( A, B )
       INTEGER A, B
       IF ( A .GT. B ) THEN
        FU = A
        GOTO 10
       END IF
       IF ( B .GT. A ) THEN
        FU = B
10      RETURN
       END IF
       FU = A
      END
```

6. The context-free grammar for the Pascal If Statement is ambiguous; see the Dangling Else problem. Write another BNF grammar for the If Statement that resolves the problem. The new grammar must be unambiguous. Hint: literature reference Aho and Johnson [1974].

7. Prove or disprove the claim: "All Case Statements can be expressed by equivalent If Statements!"

8. Translate the following Case Statement into an equivalent If Statement.

```
CASE next_char IS
 WHEN 'a' .. 'z' => scan_ident;
 WHEN '0' .. '9' => get_base;
                   scan_number( base );
 WHEN '''         => scan_char_literal;
 WHEN '"'         => scan_string_literal;
 WHEN OTHERS       => scan_special_symbol;
END CASE;
```

9. Prove or disprove the claim: "All If Statements can be expressed by equivalent Case Statements!"

10. Translate the following Ada If Statement into an equivalent Ada Case Statement. Hint: It is possible to satisfy this challenge, but the resulting program may look much less readable than the version with If Statements.

```
IF a > b AND c /= d THEN
 do_action_1;
ELSIF e < f THEN
 do_action_2;
ELSIF func( a, g ) THEN
 do_action_3;
ELSE
 do_action_4;
END IF;
```

8

Iterative Statements

Hofstadter's LAW: It always takes longer than you expect,
even when you take into account Hofstadter's Law.

Douglas R. Hofstadter
Gödel, Escher, Bach: An Eternal Golden Braid

Iterative Statements are necessary for a wide range of applications, including sorting, searching, file processing, and approximation computations. *Loop* is a popular synonym for Iterative Statement. Our study of Iterative Statements in this chapter is partly based on knowledge that we have acquired already: all loops except the "pure" or "bare" loop are controlled by one or more expressions (conditions) to determine the next step. What exactly this next step is depends on the personality of the loop. This chapter deals with the various loop constructs.

Loops are the one syntax construct that warrant the conscientious programmer to consider performance improvements, also more commonly known by the misnomer "optimization." When we are dealing with loops, it is not unusual to find that 90% of a program's execution time is spent in less than 10% of the total code space. And these 10% will usually contain loop statements, especially inner loops.

But conscientious programmers, be cautioned! Rather than relying on our intuition to detect which loops are the critical ones, we should use execution timing meters. Ideally, a run time system provides software tools that emit histograms or tables of time units consumed as a function of subprograms or even of basic blocks. More often than not we will find that it is an inconspicuous looking little loop that is creating the bottleneck. All other code sequences should be left intact, not corrupted with "optimizations," since such "improvements" usually require a price in decreased readability.

This chapter is dedicated to loops in general and to the investigation of a simple search algorithm. We shall look at the run time improvements that can be achieved with this algorithm, and we shall see how the speed improvements affect program readability. By the end of this chapter the reader will have learned to choose the right loop construct for a particular application, and, more importantly, to design a suited loop construct for a new programming language.

.1 Simple Linear Search and Variations

One algorithm known to all programmers and shunned by many is the *linear search,* also known as *sequential search.* We analyze a sample implementation in Ada and explain various ad hoc improvements, as suggested in Knuth [1974]. We discuss linear search here not because we recommend it as an adequate searching strategy, but because of its simplicity and its reliance on iteration, which is this section's subject.

After using a straightforward form of linear search that introduces Ada's While and For Statements, we show how the search time can be improved by an additional guard element, known as the sentinel. Further speed improvements such as doubling-up follow. Along the way we become intimately familiar with the bare Loop Statement.

We have a one-dimensional array "a" of 1000 elements, initialized with integer values, for which we write a search function. This search function has one input parameter, the value we are seeking. We call this value "wanted." If "wanted" is found, the array index of that integer is returned. Otherwise zero is returned to indicate that "wanted" is not included in "a." The search begins at one of the array's bounds, and terminates either when "wanted" has been found or the array has been completely searched without success.

When writing our program, we must rule out the array index 0, since 0 is the signal "not found." The value 1000 for the number of elements is by no means sacred. We choose it arbitrarily but make it large enough to demonstrate the loop behaviour in contrast to other necessary program sections. In the samples on the following pages, the search function will be called 50 times with an argument that we know does not reside in array "a." This is done so that, at least logically, the complete array must be inspected and will decrease our relative error in measuring the execution time with a stopwatch.

Simple Linear Search

The first linear search implementation in Example 8-1 inspects array elements as long as the index variable "i" holds values in the index range of array "a," and as long as "wanted" has not been found. This is conveniently accomplished with a While Statement. At completion of the While Loop we know that either the index is 0 and the wanted element is not in the array, or that "i" points to the proper index.

```
                 |WITH text_io; USE text_io;
                 |PROCEDURE linear_search_1 IS
            1    | first    : CONSTANT integer := 1;
       10   1    | last     : CONSTANT integer := 1000;
       10   1    | a        : ARRAY( first .. last ) OF integer;
     1010   1    | index    : integer;
     1011   1    |
     1011   1    | FUNCTION search(
            2    |  wanted : IN integer ) RETURN integer IS
       11   2    |  i       : integer;
       12   2    | BEGIN--search
            2    |  i := last;
  4         2  1 |  WHILE i >= first AND THEN a( i ) /= wanted LOOP
 17         2  1 |   i := i - 1;
 22         2  2 |  END LOOP;
 23         2  1 |--either i < first OR a(i) = wanted
 23         2  1 |  RETURN i;--found at index i
 28         2  1 | END search;
 28         1    |
 28         1    |BEGIN--linear_search_1
 30         1    | FOR i IN first .. last LOOP
 35         1  1 |  a( i ) := -2*last + 4*i;--arbitrary
 48         1  2 | END LOOP;
 49         1  1 |--array initialized
 49         1  1 | put_line( " 50 unsuccessful searches" );
 52         1  1 | FOR i IN 1 .. 50 LOOP
 56         1  1 |  index := search( -12434 );
 63         1  2 | END LOOP;
 64         1  1 |END linear_search_1;

914264 STEPS   TIME 6:21
```

Example 8-1 Simple Linear Search

We also perform an old-fashioned time measurement. As soon as the initialization is complete, a message appears on the system console, and the operator presses the stopwatch. The execution time starts running.

In this particular case we use a single-user microcomputer, based on the Intel 8086 processor. The algorithm is compute bound; in fact no IO at all is performed during the loop operation. The compiler used emits hypothetical Acode object, which is then interpreted. Consequently, the measured time units are quite long. But this is helpful in reducing the relative measuring error.

Fortunately, the measuring errors at start and completion offset each other to some degree. When the start message appears on the screen, there is some delay between registering the order visually and pressing the stopwatch manually. When the completion message appears, there will be a second delay. As long as these delays are similar in size, the relative error is small. In addition, all samples have been run numerous times. This not only yields an acceptable average, but it also strongly biases the controller of the stopwatch to know when to pay attention; after the first run of each experiment we know what time to expect, so there is no need to raise the attention level all the time. The average time for experiment "linear_search_1" is 381 seconds. Note that this time is consumed exclusively by two nested loops, primarily the For Statement on line 26, which includes a call to "search" with argument -12434. Function "search", in turn, contains a While Statement, which cycles 1000 times, since the wanted element is never found.

Linear Search Sentinel

We are all familiar with the linear search and know its inherent drawback, but not all programmers know the variant with a *sentinel.* In the sentinel implementation we use a phantom array element, guaranteed to hold the "wanted" element. The phantom element sits at the index right adjacent to the limits of the array. In our case, since we are counting downward, the "wanted" element resides at the next lower value, which is 0. We enforce inclusion of the phantom element via an explicit assignment statement before the loop body. The additional array element in "a" must therefore be provided. See line 12 in Example 8-2 for setting the sentinel.

The additional insertion must be counted as overhead. But here is the key: the time-consuming task needs to be performed only once, regardless of the array size. Hence for large arrays, say 50 elements or more, the dominant time element is consumed in the loop, while the additional prelude becomes negligible.

What has been gained is a simpler loop condition. In the first solution, "linear_search_1," the While Statement was controlled by an AND condition. The sentinel solution needs to check only one of the two operands since the second condition is known to yield true eventually. The body of the critical loop remains invariant.

```
      1012   1      | FUNCTION quick_search(
             2      |  wanted : IN integer ) RETURN integer IS
        11   2      |  i      : integer;
        12   2      | BEGIN--quick_search
             2      |  a( first ) := wanted;--the Sentinel
  7          2   1  |  i := last;
 10          2   1  |  WHILE a( i ) /= wanted LOOP
 18          2   1  |   i := i - 1;
 23          2   2  |  END LOOP;
 24          2   1  |--a(i) = wanted
 24          2   1  |  RETURN i;--found at index i
 29          2   1  | END quick_search;

664614 STEPS   TIME 4:46
```

Example 8-2 Fragment of Linear Search Program with Sentinel

The average time for experiment "linear_search_2" is 286 seconds, already representing a decrease of 26% in execution time. What makes this improvement even more rewarding is that readability has not been compromised. Either solution is equally readable; the second is just faster.

Doubling Up of Loops

Without adding any assumption or restriction to our algorithm, it is still possible to further improve the execution time of the linear search by "doubling-up" loops. *Doubling-up* cuts the number of times the loop is executed in half but increases the overhead for each iteration. This is done by duplicating the text of the loop body. Rather than waiting for the next iteration to compare the next value, we can test the current and the next value already during the current iteration. Then we increment the control variable by two. During the next iteration, we again investigate two array elements. For arrays with an odd number of elements we must take care that during the last iteration there will indeed be two elements left to look at.

Naturally, if we need more speed, this principle can be applied to a "doubled-up" loop as well, so that we quadruple loops. Optimizing compilers use this technique quite well, particularly when the bounds of the control variables are known at compile time. This is called *loop unrolling.* Unfortunately, the doubled-up source program is less readable due to the introduction of additional statements. But it is still the right thing to do if execution speed is at a premium. See more explanations in Knuth [1974].

Note that we need an additional element for the doubling-up implementation and an extra array element for the sentinel. Does this mean two additional indices are necessary? Luckily the one extra location can serve either purpose; "linear_search_3" in Example 8-3 is correct with respect to array bounds.

```
                 |WITH text_io; USE text_io;
                 |PROCEDURE linear_search_3 IS--called 50 times
            1    | first   : CONSTANT integer := 0;
        10  1    | last    : CONSTANT integer := 1000;
        10  1    | a       : ARRAY( first .. last ) OF integer;
      1011  1    | index   : integer;
      1012  1    |
      1012  1    | FUNCTION doubled_up(
            2    |  wanted : IN integer ) RETURN integer IS
        11  2    |  i      : integer;
        12  2    | BEGIN--doubled_up
            2    |  a( first ) := wanted;
   7        2  1 |  i := last;
  10        2  1 |  LOOP
  10        2  1 |   IF a( i ) = wanted THEN
  18        2  2 |    RETURN i;
  23        2  3 |   ELSIF a( i - 1 ) = wanted THEN
  34        2  2 |    RETURN i - 1;
  41        2  3 |   ELSE
  41        2  2 |    i := i - 2;
  47        2  3 |   END IF;
  47        2  2 |  END LOOP;
  48        2  1 | END doubled_up;

564414 STEPS   TIME 4:08
```

Example 8-3 Doubled-Up Linear Search with Sentinel

.2 Systematic Characterization of Loops

This chapter started out with the analysis of simple loops that displayed radically different behaviour after seemingly minor changes. Familiarity with the While and For Statements was gradually acquired. Now we take a much more scrutinizing look at other forms of Iterative Statements.

Most languages contain various of the following loop constructs, which we shall investigate: Hand-Manufactured Loops, Bare Loops, While Loops, Repeat Loops, and For Loops. None of the discussed languages has the form of Iterative Statement that provides an exit from the middle of the loop body as part of the loop syntax proper, sometimes referred to as "loop and a half" construct. In Ada and Modula-2 it is, however, quite straightforward to simulate this effect with the Exit Statement embedded inside a Bare Loop. A justification for the "loop and a half" construct can be found in Knuth [1974], together with various proposals for an integrated syntax.

Hand-Manufactured Loops

The *Hand-Manufactured Loops,* long known from assembly language programming, are composed of If Statements and Goto Statements in higher level languages. The IF condition checks for some termination criterion, while the one or two Goto Statements provide a branch back to the loop head and eventually a branch out of the loop. As the name implies, Hand-Manufactured loops can be custom-tailored for all purposes. Hence, they are most general and invincible in terms of execution time.

Since the If Statement controlling the termination condition may be placed anywhere—at the loop head, the end, or any place in the middle—this loop construct is the most flexible, general, and powerful one. But we should not be surprised to observe a penalty of decreased readability. Consequently, this class of loops lends itself toward less reliable programs, since the programmer has a hard time understanding and thus maintaining programs that include these constructs. Precisely this construct is what caused the rage against Goto Statements in the 1970s in the field of programming languages.

All procedural languages discussed here allow this form of loop with only minor differences of cosmetic nature: the syntax for a label definition varies from language to language, and in Modula-2 the Goto Statement is reduced to the Exit Statement, as already mentioned for the "loop and a half" construct.

Bare Loops

Some languages provide *Bare Loops* (or Pure Loops) as an easy way to construct infinite loops. Haven't we learned in our programming classes to avoid infinite loops? So why would a language even propose a construct that makes it easy to write just that? Obviously, only some infinite loops should be avoided—those whose perpetual iteration is unintended. But there are definitely some algorithms, typically found in operating systems software and real time control functions, that assume continuous execution. Of the languages discussed here, only Ada and Modula-2 supply an explicit construct for the Bare Loop.

Ada's Bare Loop

The syntax for Ada's endless loop requires the reserved keyword LOOP at the beginning, the keywords END LOOP at the end, with the semantics that the enclosed sequence of statements is executed indefinitely. The Modula-2 syntax is similar except for the simpler closure END. An Ada sample is given in Example 8-4.

```
LOOP
 IF empty( process_q ) THEN
  execute( idle_task );
  check_requests( process_q );
 ELSE
  serve( process_q );
 END IF;
END LOOP;
```

Example 8-4 Infinite Loop in Ada

An infinite loop with the same meaning can be written in the other languages, but the required syntax looks more awkward. PL/I, for example, will need a while condition that is always true; Pascal will need a repeat termination criterion that is never true. See Example 8-5.

```
 DO WHILE ( '1'B );
  IF EMPTY( PROCESS_Q ) THEN
   DO
    CALL SERVE( IDLE_TASK );
    CALL CHECK_REQUESTS( PROCESS_Q );
   END;
 ELSE
  CALL SERVE( PROCESS_Q );
END;
```

Infinite Loop in PL/I

```
 REPEAT
  IF empty( process_q ) THEN
   BEGIN
    serve( idle_task );
    check_requests( process_q );
   END
 ELSE
  serve( process_q );
UNTIL false;
```

Infinite Loop in Pascal

Example 8-5 Infinite Loop

While Loops

While Loops control the repetitive execution of a list of statements depending on a boolean condition. This condition is checked before each iteration. Because this test occurs at the head of the While Loop, it can happen that the dependent statement (list) is never executed. The boolean expression may yield "false" right from the start.

When writing a While Loop, we must be aware that the termination condition has to be satisfied eventually. To avoid an unintended infinite loop, we have to ensure that during execution something will change so that the boolean condition will eventually yield "false." As we shall see shortly, a minor typographical error can turn a syntactically correct program into another correct one with a never-ending loop.

Each of the procedural languages discussed have While Statements with the exception of Fortran. Fortran can simulate a While Statement with a labeled Block If Statement and a Goto Statement at the end of the Then

Clause. See the sample Fortran program ECONST later in Example 8-13.

```
ada_while_statement       ::= [ loop_name : ] WHILE condition LOOP
                                 sequence_of_statements
                              END LOOP [ loop_name ] ;
fortran_whilesimulation ::= label IF ( condition ) THEN
                                    sequence_of_statements
                                    GOTO label
                                  END IF
pascal_while_statement   ::= WHILE condition DO
                                statement

pl1_while_statement       ::= DO WHILE ( condition );
                                 { statement }
                              END ;
modula2_while_statement ::= WHILE condition DO
                               sequence_of_statements
                              END
```

Example 8-6 Grammar of While Statements

Context Conditions

Ada's While Statement may be "named," but we must be careful not to mistake a "name" for a "label"! It is easy to become confused, since both are statement markers. A label may be used as the destination of Goto Statements and is set off by the distinctive << and >> symbols in Ada. Statement names, on the other hand, look more like labels in other languages—introduced by an identifier and followed by a colon. Their sole purpose in Ada is the identification of Iterative (and Declare) Statements with the name serving for reference in Exit Statements.

Once a loop has a name, the same name must be repeated at the end of the loop, before the semicolon. This helps the reader to visualize that an Exit Statement of the form "EXIT loop_name;" does not transfer control to the head of the loop, but instead exits the loop. We show equivalent While and Loop-plus-Exit Statements in Example 8-7.

```
main_loop:                          main_loop:
 WHILE NOT end_of_file LOOP          LOOP
  more_source;                        EXIT main_loop WHEN end_of_file;
  process_source;                     more_source;
 END LOOP main_loop;                  process_source;
                                     END LOOP main_loop;
```

Example 8-7 Loop Names

In Ada, Modula-2, and PL/I the While Statement is terminated by a forced closure keyword. Since Pascal knows no such safeguard, it is easy to run into trouble. The While Statement in Example 8-8 is written correctly according to Pascal's rules, but it causes an inadvertent, infinite loop, performs an act quite different from the one intended.

```
{ Pascal Source }
a := 5; b := 6;
WHILE a < b DO;
 BEGIN
  process( a ); { no side effect }
  a := a + 1;
 END;
{END WHILE}
```

Example 8-8 A Delicate Infinite While Loop

As demonstrated in previous Pascal examples, the problem is the excess semicolon after the keyword DO. This semicolon causes the Empty Statement to be executed ad infinitum to no avail. Programmers most likely to write this syntax, quite in accordance with the rules, are PL/I programmers switching over to Pascal. PL/I forms the habit of always appending the semicolon.

All languages, even PL/I with its generous misconception of a programmer's freedom, disallow the branching into the body of a While Statement body from the outside. Fortran's simulated While Statement with the Block If also forbids a brute force branch into its body, since branches from the outside into Block If Statements are illegal.

In the remainder of this chapter we apply our knowledge about Iterative Statements. First, we shall compute the value of the natural constant "e." It will be most interesting to learn that loops permit us to compute this value up to an arbitrary level of precision. Then we shall write a function that computes the square root of the passed argument. Such a function can be incorporated into the standard library of a run time system. We cover Repeat Statements, and lastly, we shall discuss the For Statement.

Computation of "e"

We know the constant "e" from dealing with natural logarithms. In the current section we present a formula that computes the value of "e**x." Then we shall use a simplified version of this formula in iterative programs to actually compute the value of "e."

Starting with the power series for the function e**x, we have a simple way of computing the value for "e" itself by setting x equal to one.

$$e^{x} = x^{0} / 0! + x^{1} / 1! + x^{2} / 2! + x^{3} / 3! + x^{4} / 4! + \ldots + x^{n} / n!$$

*Example 8-9 Power Series for e**x*

A While Loop is an appropriate control structure to compute "e" up to a desired precision. To illustrate the computation of "e," we use program samples in Pascal and Fortran. The former runs on a 16-bit microcomputer with an inherent limitation on the maximum natural integer; the latter runs on a 32-bit computer, permitting a much higher precision without having to apply a more complex algorithm. In both cases we use a simplified form of the preceding formula to compute "e". See Example 8-10.

$$e = 1/0! + 1/1! + 1/2! + 1/3! + 1/4! + \ldots + 1/n!$$

Example 8-10 Power Series for "e"

The algorithm "computee" in Example 8-11 relies on a strongly limited tool—a machine with limited precision for numeric values. Therefore, at least two things can go wrong here. Either the denominator, which is the factorial value of some integer, may grow too large, thus causing integer overflow, or the difference between two adjacent approximations of "e" may become so small that it is no longer representable on the machine. It is a good policy to stop computing before either exception occurs.

As another alternative, we could choose to represent the integer type denominator by a floating point number. This would make each summand potentially less precise, since not all large integral values are representable in floating point, but it would allow more summands of the series to be computed. A wise numerical analysis decision should be made here when high precision is crucial.

For our purposes, however, we are concerned only about the While Statement, which is used in the following examples. If precision were crucial, we could abandon the native integer type altogether and simulate the numeric computations by string manipulations. Then the true power of the Iterative Statements would show, permitting us any degree of precision. We will be limited only by the amount of available storage on the computer, or by the time we are willing to wait for the result.

```
 1    1  0  0        PROGRAM computee( input, output );
 2    2  0  0          { use expansion for e** x to compute e, set x=1 }
                       { e**x = 1+x**1/1!+x**2/2!+x**3/3! + ...+x**n/n! }
                      VAR
                       olde,
                       e      : real;
 3    7  0  0          n,
                       fact   : integer;
 4    9  0  0         BEGIN { computee }
 4   10  0  1          olde := 0.0;
 5   11  0  1          e := 1.0;
 6   12  0  1          n := 1;
 7   13  0  1          fact := 1;
 8   14  0  1          WHILE ( abs( olde - e ) > 0.00001 ) AND
                        ( fact < 5000 ) DO
 9   16  0  1           BEGIN
 9   17  0  2            olde := e;
10   18  0  2            e := e + 1/fact;
11   19  0  2            n := n + 1;
12   20  0  2            fact := fact * n;
13   21  0  2           END;
15   22  0  1          {END WHILE}
                       IF fact >= 5000 THEN { no fact = 5000 exists }
16   24  0  1           writeln( output, ' fact too big' )
                       ELSE
17   26  0  1           writeln( output, ' sufficient precision ' );
18   27  0  1          {END IF}
                       writeln( output, ' n = ', n, ' fact = ', fact );
19   29  0  1          writeln( output, ' e = ', e : 14 : 12 );
20   30  0  1         END. { computee }

fact too big
n = 7 fact = 5040
e = 2.718055725098
```

Example 8-11 Computation of "e" Via Pascal While Statement

Analysis of Pascal Result

"Computee" terminates because the factorial value is getting dangerously large. The next value for "fact" would be 40320, which can no longer be stored on the 16-bit microcomputer in integer type objects. Unfortunately, we don't know how many of the desired digits to the right of the decimal point have actually been computed. The result is not even nearly as accurate as the printed image suggests, since the termination is caused by "fact" growing so large that the desired delta value 0.00001 is never reached. From the iteration count "n = 7" we only know that the first six summands of the infinite series have been considered.

Fortran Solution

The following implementation in Fortran is interesting because the actual result is more precise than the Pascal solution. From the standpoint of the While Statement alone, the solutions are, of course, identical. Delta here is one millionth, and the Fortran program named "ECONST" terminates because two adjacent approximations differ by less than one millionth.

First, we list the values for "e" here with 31 positions of precision, taken from a mathematical handbook. The arrow under the digit "8" indicates, where the Fortran results start being imprecise. Then we list the values for "e" as output by the two Fortran programs:

```
e = 2.718,281,828,459,045,235,360,287,471,352+
              ^
e = 2.718,281,984,329   --ECONST
```

Example 8-12 Values of "e" with Various Precisions

```
       PROGRAM ECONST
        REAL OLDE, E
        INTEGER FACT, N
        OLDE = 0.0
        E = 1.0
        N = 1
        FACT = 1
10      IF ( ABS( OLDE - E ) .GT. 0.000001 .AND.
-           FACT .LT. 100000000 ) THEN
         OLDE = E
         E = E + 1.0 / FACT
         N = N + 1
         FACT = FACT * N
         GOTO 10
        END IF
        IF ( FACT .GT. 100000000 ) THEN
         WRITE( 6, * ) " FACT TOO BIG = "
        ELSE
         WRITE( 6, * ) " SUFFICIENT PRECISION "
        END IF
        WRITE( 6, * ) " N = ," N, " FACT = ," FACT
        WRITE( 6, 20 ) E
        20      FORMAT( F15.12 )
```

```
END

SUFFICIENT PRECISION
N =  11  FACT =  39916800
2.718281984329
```

Example 8-13 Successful Computation of "e"

Newton's "Sqrt" Approximation

To compute the square root of an argument "arg," we use Newton's recurrence relation. We express the recurrence iteratively via a While Loop. As in Example 8-13, the iteration terminates when the result is sufficiently precise.

Let the argument and the result be named "arg" and "root," respectively, and let "root" have the initial value of "arg." Then Newton's approximation formula is

```
root := ( root + ( arg / root ) ) / 2 .
```

In contrast to Example 8-13, the condition in Newton's algorithm is simple; it is not a logical And of two conditions. To assess the running time of a While Loop, it is necessary to consider the time for the condition as well as for the body. Either is executed for each iteration, with the exception of the loop body after the last test. Also two invisible branches, automatically generated by the compiler, contribute to the total execution time. One unconditional branch transfers control back to the loop header after each iteration, while the conditional branch at the loop head is executed just once—when the loop terminates.

Newton's formula assumes an initial solution estimate; if this estimate happens to be exact, then the precision is as desired and the algorithm terminates. Otherwise, the algorithm converges toward the correct solution, irrespective of the absolute value of the solution estimate.

One programming danger, however, lurks behind this convenient and elegant algorithm: if the difference of two adjacent solutions is always greater than the specified delta, the While Loop never ends. This happens when this delta is chosen too ambitiously, and the machine cannot generate two distinct floating point values of so small a difference.

The implementation written in Pascal in Example 8-14 requires one tenth of a million of precision, which is achievable even on the typical 16-bit microcomputer with floating point data.

```
 1    1  0  0        PROGRAM newtonsapproximation( input, output );
 2    2  0  0         VAR
                        i      : integer;

 3    5  0  0         FUNCTION sqrt( arg : real ) : real;
 4    6  1  0          VAR
                         oldroot,
                         newroot : real;
 5    9  1  0          BEGIN { sqrt }
 5   10  1  1           oldroot := arg;
 6   11  1  1           newroot := 1.0;
 7   12  1  1           WHILE abs( newroot - oldroot ) > 0.0000001 DO
 8   13  1  1            BEGIN
 8   14  1  2             oldroot := newroot;
 9   15  1  2             newroot := ( oldroot + ( arg / oldroot ) ) / 2;
10   16  1  2            END;
12   17  1  1           {END WHILE}
                        sqrt := newroot;
13   19  1  1          END; { sqrt }

14   21  0  0         BEGIN { newtonsapproximation }
14   22  0  1          FOR i := 1 TO 10 DO
15   23  0  1           writeln( output, ' sqrt(', i : 5 : 2, ') = ',
                          sqrt( i ) : 14 : 8 );
16   24  0  1          {END FOR}
                      END. { newtonsapproximation }
sqrt( 1.00) =      1.00000000
sqrt( 2.00) =      1.41421354
sqrt( 3.00) =      1.73205078
sqrt( 4.00) =      2.00000000
sqrt( 5.00) =      2.23606801
sqrt( 6.00) =      2.44948983
sqrt( 7.00) =      2.64575124
sqrt( 8.00) =      2.82842708
sqrt( 9.00) =      3.00000000
sqrt(10.00) =      3.16227770
```

Example 8-14 Newton's Square Root Approximation in Pascal

Repeat Loops

Pascal and Modula-2 have a proper Repeat Loop. Introduced by the reserved keyword REPEAT, the contained statement list is executed at least once. If the final condition following the keyword UNTIL yields true, the loop body is no longer executed; otherwise, execution continues at the loop header. PL/I allows an optional Repeat Clause, following the start expression in the For

Statement. With the intent to add power and the possible effect to confuse, this PL/I Repeat Clause may also be combined with a While Condition, but we prefer not to treat this hybrid construct here.

Repeat Statements are the easiest of all loops, both from the user's view, and from the standpoint of the compiler that must generate code. In Example 8-15 we give the grammar for the Pascal Repeat Loop and a software simulation that indicates the kind of code to be emitted by a code generator. The syntax for Modula-2's Repeat Statement is identical to Pascal's, an indication that the language designer (Niklaus Wirth) must have felt content with its specification.

```
repeat_statement        ::= REPEAT
                              statement
                              { ; statement }
                            UNTIL condition
```

Example 8-15 Grammar for Pascal (and Modula-2) Repeat Statement

The following example illustrates how easy it is to generate code for a Repeat Statement. The Pascal Repeat Statement on the left is translated into equivalent pseudo-code on the right. See Example 8-16.

```
REPEAT                        rep:  (* Pseudo Label *)
 stmt1;                        stmt1;
 stmt2;                        stmt2;
UNTIL condition;              IF NOT condition THEN
                               GOTO rep;
```

Example 8-16 Repeat Statement Translated into Pseudo-Code

The sample Pascal program "roman" in Example 8-17 demonstrates one Repeat Statement. From the loop body a procedure call is issued and an Assignment Statement is executed. The called procedure contains a loop as well, but it is a While Statement. Since While Statements are not always executed, they cannot be rewritten by Repeat Statements, unless an extra enclosing If Statement is added.

```
1    1  0  0        PROGRAM roman( output );
2    2  0  0         VAR
                      power2 : integer;

3    5  0  0         PROCEDURE printroman( power2 : integer );

4    7  1  0          PROCEDURE next(
4    8  2  0           VAR
                       value    : integer;
```

```
                        step   : integer;
                        digit  : char );
 5  12  2  0           BEGIN { next }
 5  13  2  1            WHILE value >= step DO
 6  14  2  1             BEGIN
 6  15  2  2              write( output, digit );
 7  16  2  2              value := value - step;
 8  17  2  2             END;
10  18  2  1            {END WHILE}
                        END { next };

11  21  1  0          BEGIN { printroman }
11  22  1  1           write( output, power2 : 8, ' ' );
12  23  1  1           next( power2, 1000, 'M' );
13  24  1  1           next( power2, 500,  'L' );
14  25  1  1           next( power2, 100,  'C' );
15  26  1  1           next( power2, 50,   'L' );
16  27  1  1           next( power2, 10,   'X' );
17  28  1  1           next( power2, 5,    'V' );
18  29  1  1           next( power2, 1,    'I' );
19  30  1  1           writeln( output );
20  31  1  1          END { printroman };
21  32  0  0         BEGIN { roman }
21  33  0  1          power2 := 1;
22  34  0  1          REPEAT
22  35  0  2           printroman( power2 );
23  36  0  2           power2 := power2 * 2;
24  37  0  2          UNTIL power2 = 2048;
26  38  0  1         END { roman }.

1 I
2 II
4 IIII
8 VIII
16 XVI
32 XXXII
64 LXIIII
128 CXXVIII
256 CCLVI
512 DXII
1024 MXXIIII
```

Example 8-17 Pascal Program "Roman," Demonstrating Repeat Statement

For Loops

For Statements are Iterative Statements, whose maximum number of iterations (and hence termination condition) can be computed before the first execution of the loop body. Algol-60's For Statement is more general and does not fit this definition, but for the languages we describe, including PL/I, this definition applies. Three parameters characterize the For Loop behaviour: the "start value," "the final value," and the "step size." A *control variable,* also named *loop parameter,* steps through a progression of values from the start to the final value in increments of the step size. When the step size is not specified explicitly, it is 1 by default. The control variable can also step through the range in decreasing sequence.

Loop Control Variable

During each step the particular iteration value is accessible by referencing the control variable. We use the terms "loop parameter" and "loop control variable" interchangeably. Algol-68 turns out to be most general by allowing one kind of For Loop without loop parameter. This can be useful when the program only executes the defined iterations, but does not need to reference any of the particular stepping values. Usually, though, a control variable is involved.

The loop parameter comes in various incarnations in the different languages. Either it is defined "on the fly" at the loop header and then ceases to exist after completion of the loop, or it must be declared like other names. Another variant in loop parameter use is the permission to assign values to it. Some languages allow this, others don't. Ada, Fortran, and Pascal do not permit this, while PL/I knows no such restraint. Modula-2 only includes a recommendation that such crimes "should not" be committed. Assigning values to the control variable is, in most cases, an aberration with surprising effects, and if we design our own programming language, we should follow the example set by Ada, Fortran, and Pascal to forbid this.

The designation "For Loop" does not imply that the keyword FOR is used. In fact Fortran and PL/I use the keyword DO. What is essential to a For Statement is the discrete stepping and the computation of the step bounds before execution of the For Loop starts.

Since the For Statement is the most rigid of all Iterative Statements, the associated syntax rules are the most complex. Consequently, the amount of work for a compiler in terms of checks and emitted code is also quite high. In Example 8-18 we give the grammar for the syntax rules of For Statements in each language. Then come numerous explanations and context conditions.

```
ada_for_statement       ::= [ loop_name : ]
                            FOR loop_parameter IN [ REVERSE ] range LOOP
                               sequence_of_statements
                            END LOOP [ loop_name ] ;

range                   ::= e1 .. e2 | range_type_mark

fortran_for_statement   ::= DO label [,] do_variable = e1, e2 [,e3 ]
                               { statement }
                            label

pascal_for_statement    ::= FOR control_variable := e1 up_down e2 DO
                               statement

up_down                 ::= TO | DOWNTO

pl1_for_statement       ::= DO control_variable = spec_comma_list
                               { statement }
                            END [ label ] ;

spec_comma_list         ::= spec { , spec }

spec                    ::= e1 [ to_by ]

to_by                   ::= TO e2 [ BY e3 ] | BY e3 [ TO e2 ]

modula2_for_statement   ::= FOR control_variable := e1 TO e2 [ BY e3 ] DO
                               sequence_of_statements
                            END
```

Example 8-18 Grammar for Various For Statements

For Statement Rules in Ada

Starting and final values are specified by a discrete range in Ada. From this it follows that the types of the two expressions involved must be identical. To familiarize the Ada novice immediately with the For Statement syntax, we offer the following sample header:

```
FOR next_char IN 'a' .. 'z' LOOP
```

Here the starting value is 'a,' and the final value is 'z,' which are clearly compatible with one another. Whether the REVERSE keyword is included or not, the upper bound of the range must be greater than or equal to the lower bound, if the loop body is to be executed at all. The so-called null range is legal, in which case the For Statement will not iterate. If REVERSE is given, the individual step values are elaborated in descending order; otherwise they are in ascending order.

The loop parameter is implicitly declared for the scope of the For Loop only. Thus another name with the same spelling can be redefined without overloading it. In order to access the redefined identifier, a qualified name is required. Note that the redefined name could even be another loop parameter.

In this short section we choose the term *loop parameter* for *loop control variable,* since this is the term exclusively used in the Ada standard. This may bewilder the reader seeking consistency in terms, but it offers exposure to the dispersed vocabulary found in the literature.

```
PROCEDURE for_demo1 IS
 i : integer;
BEGIN--for_demo1
 i := 5;
 FOR i IN 1 .. 3 LOOP NULL; END LOOP;
 IF i /= 5 THEN
  put_line( " should be 5" );
 END IF;
 FOR i IN 0 .. 10 LOOP
  for_demo1.i := i;
 END LOOP;
 IF i /= 10 THEN
  put_line( " should be 10" );
 END IF;
END for_demo1;
```

Example 8-19 Redefinition of "I" by Loop Parameter

Ada does not treat loop parameters as variables, hence they cannot be passed as actual parameters to formal OUT or IN OUT parameters, and may not be used on the left-hand side of an Assignment Statement. We know this characteristic behaviour already from formal IN parameters. So the easiest way to remember the rules for loop parameters is to pretend that they are the same as IN parameters. See the illegal code sequence in Example 8-20.

```
PROCEDURE double( a : IN OUT integer ) IS
 BEGIN--double, this is an order!!
  a := a * 2;
 END double;

PROCEDURE illegal_loop IS
 BEGIN--illegal
 FOR i IN 1 .. 2 LOOP
  i := 3;--illegal, don't use i on l.h.s. of :=
  double( i );--illegal for formal IN OUT, OUT
  get( i );--as above
 END LOOP;
END illegal_loop;
```

Example 8-20 Illegal Uses of Ada Loop Parameter

Discrete Ranges

Ada's For Statement syntax requires a *discrete range,* and we have seen a good number of examples already. Discrete ranges are also required for the bounds specification of arrays, and are allowed for the choices in Case Statements. The discrete ranges we have used so far in our examples consisted of one expression for the lower value, the double period symbol (..), and an expression for the upper bound. Ada also allows a type mark in this place, as long as the specified type defines a range. See Example 8-21.

```
min : CONSTANT integer := 0;
max : CONSTANT integer := 55;
TYPE bounds IS RANGE min .. max;
TYPE square IS ARRAY( bounds, bounds ) OF integer;
matrix  : square;

PROCEDURE initialize_matrix IS
 BEGIN--initialize_matrix
  FOR i IN bounds LOOP
   FOR j IN bounds LOOP
    matrix( i, j ) := 0;
   END LOOP;
  END LOOP;
 END initialize_matrix;
```

Example 8-21 Ada Program Showing "Discrete Ranges"

For Statement Rules in Fortran

The Fortran subculture calls its For Loops "DO Statements," and PL/I has picked up the same terminology. This is to emphasize the importance of the starting keyword DO.

The required label after DO must mark another Fortran statement in the same compilation unit that comes textually after the referencing line. This labeled statement is known as the terminal statement of the Do Loop. All statements between the loop header up to and including the terminal statement are executed with each iteration, if any. Unfortunately, Fortran has a whole list of exceptions for the terminal statement.

We copy paragraph 20 page 11-6 from the standard ANSI [1978], in order to give the reader some flavour of the Fortran terminology. "The terminal statement of a DO-loop must not be an unconditional GO TO, assigned GO TO, arithmetic IF, block IF, ELSE IF, ELSE, END IF, RETURN, STOP, END, or DO Statement. If the terminal statement of a DO-loop is a logical IF statement, it may contain any executable statement except a DO, block IF, ELSE IF, ELSE, END IF, END, or another logical IF Statement."

Such a plethora of special cases increases the language complexity and is evidence for inconsistent language design. We must be aware that these funny exceptions all make sense in the complete framework of Fortran. They are indicative of a language that has gradually developed over a long period of time. In retrospect Fortran appears to be poorly designed, but we should not judge here without considering the historical context. It is, however, a good policy in programming language design to abstain from exceptions.

A Fortran Do Variable must be of type integer, real, or double precision. It is not declared and therefore does not vanish after loop completion. Its last value may be interrogated freely without the extra cost of having to remember it in a temporary variable. The value of the Do Variable after loop completion is the value it had during the last iteration. Like all other variables, the Do Variable may be declared implicitly in Fortran.

Different Meanings of "Implicit"

We must be careful not to confuse the "implicit" loop parameter declaration of Ada (and Algol-68) with the "implicit" variable declaration in Fortran and PL/I. A Fortran compiler will add an implicit declaration of a Do Variable behind the scenes so to speak, if an explicit declaration is not provided by the programmer. The type of an implicitly declared variable is derived from the first letter.

"Implicit" or "on the fly" declarations for loop parameters in Ada derive their type from the starting and final expressions. Their lifetime is limited to the scope of the For Statement, and hence they vanish as soon as the loop is completed.

The starting value of a Fortran Do Variable, the final value, and the increment are evaluated only once—that is, at loop entry. Should any of the variables involved in these expressions change during loop execution, then this change has no effect on the subsequent loop behaviour. When the step size is omitted, 1 is assumed. Note that the step size of 0 is not allowed in Fortran, since a progression of values would become impossible; the starting value could never change.

Fortran-77 also disallows assignments to the Do Variable in the loop body. This constitutes a second context condition, defining the semantics of Fortran's Do Statements. Since they are quite delicate and important, we summarize the rules once more:

1. The value of the step size, named "e3" in the Fortran grammar in Example 8-18, may not be zero.

2. Assignments to the Do Variable inside the body of the Do Statement are illegal.

We have contrived two programs in Examples 8-22 and 8-23 that deliberately violate these rules. Such counter-educational practice is applied here to let the reader appreciate one rule in programming language design. This rule concerns the detection of illegal constructs:

"If a construct is outlawed, it should be detectable by the translator. If it cannot be detected, maybe it shouldn't be outlawed."

The illegal programs in Examples 8-22 and 8-23 demonstrate the response of a typical Fortran-77 compiler. The names of these wrong programs are "BADDO1" and "BADDO2." A compiler could easily flag the illegal assignments to the do variable inside the loop. This is not done in the source program "BADDO1."

```
      PROGRAM BADDO1
       INTEGER I
       DO 100 I = 4, 50, 1
        WRITE( 6, * ) " I = ," I
        IF ( I .EQ. 6 ) THEN
         I = 133
        END IF
100    CONTINUE
      END
```

Example 8-22 Illegal Assignment to DO Variable in Fortran

Also, a good compiler can detect a step size of zero at run time, but clearly this requires the emission of some code to perform these tests. We see from the output of program "BADDO2" that the Do Loop that references label 200 is executed just once. When the step size is fetched, its zero value causes the loop to terminate. The run time system was correct enough to cause termination, but not complete enough to emit a clearly visible message that spells out the reason for this abort.

```
      PROGRAM BADDO2
       INTEGER I, J
       I = 0
       DO 200 J = 6, 8, I
        WRITE( 6, * ) " J = ," J
200    CONTINUE
      END
```

Example 8-23 Illegal Step Size of 0 in Fortran

Empty Fortran Do Loop

What happens if the start value and final value are set such that the iteration count is zero? This question is particularly relevant, since its answer varied with different Fortran standards. Older Fortrans required even an empty loop to be executed at least once. In Fortran-77 this is no longer necessary. If the iteration count yields zero at the time of loop entry, then program execution continues after the Do Loop, without executing the body.

Implied Do Loops for IO of Arrays

A convenient, special-purpose form of Do Loop is provided in the argument list of IO Statements. This form can be used favourably for reading and writing arrays and matrices, as shown in program "IMPLDO" in Example 8-24. For multidimensional arrays these implied Do Loops may even be nested. We remember from Chapter 5 that Fortran stores arrays in column major order. To demonstrate that consistent use of nesting of loop variables causes no problem in Fortran despite the column major order, we give four permutations of an Output Statement with nested implied Do Loops. We see in the first solution that the output can be generated as expected if we imagine two-dimensional arrays to be conventional tables of information. In most cases we don't need to be concerned about how Fortran compilers store arrays.

```
      PROGRAM IMPLDO
100   FORMAT( 5 ( I2, I2, I4, '   ' ) )
50    FORMAT( / )
      INTEGER A( 1 : 5, 1 : 5 )
      INTEGER I, J
      DO 10 I = 1, 5
       DO 10 J = 1, 5
        A( I, J ) = I * I + J - 1
10     CONTINUE
      WRITE( 6, 50 )
      WRITE( 6, 100 ) ( ( I, J, A( I, J ), I=1, 5 ), J=1, 5 )
      WRITE( 6, 50 )
      WRITE( 6, 100 ) ( ( I, J, A( J, I ), I=1, 5 ), J=1, 5 )
      WRITE( 6, 50 )
      WRITE( 6, 100 ) ( ( I, J, A( I, J ), J=1, 5 ), I=1, 5 )
      WRITE( 6, 50 )
      WRITE( 6, 100 ) ( ( I, J, A( J, I ), J=1, 5 ), I=1, 5 )
      END
```

Example 8-24 Program Listing, Implied Do Loops

1	1	1	2	1	4	3	1	9	4	1	16	5	1	25
1	2	2	2	2	5	3	2	10	4	2	17	5	2	26
1	3	3	2	3	6	3	3	11	4	3	18	5	3	27
1	4	4	2	4	7	3	4	12	4	4	19	5	4	28
1	5	5	2	5	8	3	5	13	4	5	20	5	5	29

1	1	1	2	1	2	3	1	3	4	1	4	5	1	5
1	2	4	2	2	5	3	2	6	4	2	7	5	2	8
1	3	9	2	3	10	3	3	11	4	3	12	5	3	13
1	4	16	2	4	17	3	4	18	4	4	19	5	4	20
1	5	25	2	5	26	3	5	27	4	5	28	5	5	29

1	1	1	1	2	2	1	3	3	1	4	4	1	5	5
2	1	4	2	2	5	2	3	6	2	4	7	2	5	8
3	1	9	3	2	10	3	3	11	3	4	12	3	5	13
4	1	16	4	2	17	4	3	18	4	4	19	4	5	20
5	1	25	5	2	26	5	3	27	5	4	28	5	5	29

1	1	1	1	2	4	1	3	9	1	4	16	1	5	25
2	1	2	2	2	5	2	3	10	2	4	17	2	5	26
3	1	3	3	2	6	3	3	11	3	4	18	3	5	27
4	1	4	4	2	7	4	3	12	4	4	19	4	5	28
5	1	5	5	2	8	5	3	13	5	4	20	5	5	29

Example 8-25 Output of Implied Do Loops

For Statement Rules in Pascal

The Pascal control variable must be declared explicitly in the closest subprogram scope that contains the For Statement. Its type must be compatible with the types of the start and final values. These, in turn, may be of any primitive (scalar) types except real and must be compatible as well. If the DOWNTO form of For Statement is chosen, then the final value must be less than or equal to the start value; otherwise, the loop body is not executed.

The language rules prohibit any assignment to the loop control variable in the loop body. Since the expressions for start and final value are evaluated once at the time of loop entry, a change in value of any variable involved in start and final value will have no effect on the subsequent iterative conduct.

Pascal does not permit explicit control over the step size; it is always 1, whether the progression of value is upward or downward. Notice in particular the contrast to Fortran and PL/I, which permit step sizes of type real.

Pascal also requires that the value of the control variable be undefined after normal completion of the loop. This sounds surprising at first, since the declaration rules keep the control variable happily alive after loop termination. Not only does this language restriction have an educational effect on the language users, but it is also intended to support efficient implementations. Many systems have a fast instruction to increment and test. Compilers can utilize this instruction in cases where no overflow can occur. Making the control variable undefined allows an implementation to use the best code sequence, even if this would violate type constraints.

Let us demonstrate this point by an example. If we assume, contrary to Pascal's definition, that the value of the control variable is the successor of the highest value, then the following program fragment would be legal and still cause a runtime type constraint error. Variable "b" would have to assume the successor value of "true"; unfortunately, no such value exists. See Example 8-26.

```
PROGRAM outofrange( output );
 VAR
  b    : boolean;
 BEGIN { outofrange }
  FOR b := false TO true DO
   writeln( ord( b ) );
  {END FOR}
  writeln( ord( b ) );
 END. { outofrange }
```

Example 8-26 Illegal Use of Control Variable after For Statement

Newcomers to Ada, Modula-2, and Pascal often do not realize that the control variable may be of any scalar type, including the enumeration type. Some suggestive, abbreviated examples are given in Example 8-27.

```
BEGIN
 FOR c := 'A' TO 'Z' DO
  table[ c ] := somevalue;
 {END FOR}
 FOR workday := monday TO friday DO
  laborcost( workday );
 {END FOR}
END;
```

Example 8-27 Control Variable of Char and Enumeration Type in Pascal

The sample Pascal program "harmonic" in Example 8-28 prints the first 15 harmonic values with up to eight digits of precision after the decimal point. Whether these digits are really significant digits of the actual result depends on the machine's floating point precision and the algorithm used. But again this discussion belongs into the field of numerical analysis, not programming languages. The program uses a For Statement, the bounds of which are of type integer and specified explicitly by a low value and a high value.

```
 1    1  0  0     PROGRAM harmonic( input, output );
 2    2  0  0      CONST
                    limit = 15;
 3    4  0  0     VAR
                    n      : integer;
 4    6  0  0       harm   : real;
 5    7  0  0     BEGIN { harmonic }
 5    8  0  1       harm := 0.0;
 6    9  0  1       FOR n := 1 TO limit DO
 7   10  0  1         BEGIN
 7   11  0  2           harm := harm + 1.0 / n;
 8   12  0  2           writeln( ' Harmonic (', n:2 , ') = ', harm:14:8 );
 9   13  0  2         END;
11   14  0  1       {END FOR}
                  END. { harmonic }
```

Example 8-28 Computation of Harmonic Via Pascal For Statement

For Statement Rules in PL/I

PL/I has it all! Whatever is allowed in any of the languages discussed so far, PL/I allows the same, and much more. This holds equally for the For Statement in PL/I, but two extensions stand out. In this section we investigate these two special constructs.

First the loop parameter specification may be repeated any number of times, each time separated from the previous specification by a comma. For reference see the extended BNF grammar in the "For Statement" section earlier in this chapter. This same For Loop structure has been known since Algol-60, from which PL/I probably adopted it.

It is also legal in the loop parameter specification to include a By Clause for the step size, a To Clause for the final value, or both clauses, or neither. If neither is given, then the loop is only executed once with the start value. A REPEAT option may substitute the To or By Clause, in which case the PL/I DO Statement becomes a close relative to the (Pascal and Modula-2) Repeat Statement.

The second extension in PL/I allows the while condition to be "slapped on" to the proper For Loop. Even though this creates a crossbreed between For and While Statement, it allows the writing of less Goto-prone programs when there are multiple termination conditions in a loop. We shall encounter one such situation shortly in the next section, "A Post Rationalization."

Start value, final value, and step size are evaluated once in PL/I at the time of loop entry. Subsequent assignments to variables that take part in these three values therefore have no effect. But PL/I is unclean in permitting assignments to the loop control variable, which of course may cause obscure program execution, and programs that are hard to trace and difficult to debug. The PL/I principle of "everything goes" seems to be the prevailing theme.

Like Fortran, PL/I also provides the implied Do Loop in the argument list of IO Statements. Syntax and semantics are almost identical to those of Fortran. An instance of this has been shown in the Fortran program "IMPLDO" in Example 8-24.

One syntax rule that causes confusion for programmers who migrate from Fortran to PL/I is the multiple For Loop specification, which separates each specification from the next with a comma. Fortran's way of defining start and final value looks identical to PL/I's multiple loop specification. The Fortran Do Loop in Example 8-29 progresses through the range 1..25.

```
C----- F O R T R A N
       DO 500 I = 1, 25
```

Example 8-29 Fortran DO

The correct PL/I statement in Example 8-30

```
/* PL/I */
DO I = 1, 25;
```

Example 8-30 Different PL/I DO

does *not* perform the same function, even though the text resembles that of Fortran. The PL/I statement only executes the loop body twice—once with I=1, and the second time with I=25. To achieve the same semantics as the Fortran statement, we have to write

```
/* PL/I */
DO I = 1 TO 25;
```

Example 8-31 Same PL/I DO

Various Ways to Do the Same

The program sections in Example 8-32 illustrate several Do Statements, which have one thing in common: they all compute values for the ten indices 1 .. 10 of array "X." The order and the syntactic way of defining that order varies in each example. We have also included one illustration of the PL/I crossbreed Do Statement with While Clause.

```
A:  DO I = 1, 2, 3, 4, 5, 6, 7, 8, 9, 10;
      X(I) = I**2;
    END;
B:  DO I = 1 TO 10;
      X(I) = I**2;
    END;
C: DO I = 10 TO 1 BY -1;
     X(I) = I**2;
   END;
D: DO I = 1 TO 5, 6 TO 10;
     X(I) = I**2;
   END;
E: DO I = 1, 2, 3 TO 4, 5 TO 9 BY 2, 6 TO 10 BY 2;
     X(I) = I**2;
   END;
F: DO I = 1, 10, 2, 9, 3, 8, 4, 7, 5, 6;
     X(I) = I**2;
   END;
G: DO I = 1 TO 10 WHILE ( TABLE( I ) <= CRITICAL );
     X(I) = I**2;
   END;
```

Example 8-32 Equivalent Variations of the Same PL/I For Statement

For Statement Rules in Modula-2

The Modula-2 For Statement is again a luxury edition of the simpler Pascal version. The two enhancements that make the For Statement so much more convenient are the mandatory END keyword and the optional By Clause. The Modula-2 For Statement is designed to have a sequence of statements be executed repeatedly, while a progression of values is assigned to the loop control variable. This control variable cannot be the field of a record, an imported variable, or a parameter. The Modula-2 manual, Wirth [1982], recommends that the control variable "should not be changed by the statement sequence."

This is the disadvantage of working with a nonstandardized language. A recommendation as the one just mentioned does not help much. It is like making a law: "You should not steal." Such a law is well intended, but not sufficient. What is missing is the clear specification about what happens when such a rule is violated. Also, the manual defines that the start and final values should not be altered during the For Statement execution. What we need to know is whether assigning values to the control variable, the start value, or the final value is an error.

In Example 8-33 we give a sample Modula-2 For Statement, which copies all elements of array "a" into another array "b." This is correct, but such an assignment can be expressed more conveniently in Modula-2 by "b := a."

```
VAR
 a, b : ARRAY[ MinIndex .. MaxIndex ] OF SomeType;
 i    : CARDINAL;
BEGIN
 FOR i := MinIndex TO MaxIndex BY 1 DO
  b[ i ] := a[ i ];
 END;
(* same as *)
 b := a;
```

Example 8-33 Sample Modula-2 For Statement

A Post Rationalization

The issue of implicit or explicit declaration of the loop parameter has almost a religious side to it. One camp of programming language designers strongly defends explicit loop parameters, since this allows the inspection of the last step value after the completion of a loop. Sometimes the loop may terminate after complete exhaustion of all possible values of the range. Other times a special event causes premature termination. When it is necessary to determine whether complete exhaustion or the special case has caused termination, then Ada's For Loop comes up short. With its implicitly declared loop parameter the last value is unavailable, unless we add an action, such as the one shown in Example 8-34. Procedure "remember_last" remembers the value of the loop parameter "i" during each iteration in the local variable "last." When the For Statement terminates, the last value of "i" can, therefore, be interrogated.

```
PACKAGE io IS NEW integer_io( integer ); USE io;
PROCEDURE remember_last IS
 last,  --last value of loop parameter
 num    --causing special case
          : integer
BEGIN--remember_last
 FOR i IN min .. max LOOP--max >= min
  get( num );
  process( num, i );
  last := i;--ref of "i" is o.k.
  EXIT WHEN num = 0;
 END LOOP;
--use "last"
END remember_last;
```

Example 8-34 Remember Last Value of Loop Parameter in Ada

Truly the mechanism of "last" in Example 8-34 is clumsy, but we don't really have a For Loop here. The statement instead characterizes a While Loop. Example 8-35 shows the program rewritten properly.

```
PROCEDURE proper_loop IS
 last  : integer := min;--use global min <= max
 num   : integer;
BEGIN--proper_loop
 WHILE last <= max LOOP
  get( num );
  process( num, last );
  EXIT WHEN num = 0;
  last := last + 1;
 END LOOP;
--condition num=0 gives termination reason
END proper_loop;
```

Example 8-35 No Need to Remember Last Value of Loop Parameter

Undoubtedly, there will be cases where it is desirable to remember the last value of the control variable. But there are many features for which it would be convenient to have a new construct. No language can have them all and nobody would be able to remember them all.

An ideal programming language includes any imaginable feature, including safe For Statements, and a mechanism to remember the last value of the loop parameter. An ideal programming language is also simple, so it can be learned and mastered quickly and verifiable compilers can be written. These two obvious goals are already in conflict. A programming language designer must make an conscientious decision about which "feature" to eliminate for the sake of simplicity and which one to include to be useful.

We must keep in mind that programming language design is a nontrivial activity. Trading off between completeness and simplicity, while difficult by itself, is only part of the problem. The greatest obstacle in programming language design is the filtering out of capabilities that are not worth being included.

.3 Summary

In the previous chapter we learned about selective program execution; in this chapter we covered iteration. We started with variations on the "linear search" problem. The first solution was simple but slow; the second was more complex, but executes faster. During the presentation of these sample programs we also slipped-in Ada For and While Statements. Then we presented yet a faster linear search by *doubling up,* and thus introduced a sample Bare Loop in Ada.

After these practical examples we characterized loops systematically and showed the Repeat Statement, available only in Modula-2 and Pascal. It is crucial for a programmer to be able to distinguish, when a loop should be expressed as a While, and when as a For Statement. We have presented the same concept from different angles, showing how different languages define the same type of Iterative Statement. In particular the For Statement leaves many design variations. We are now not only in the position to express all programming problems, but also to design our own solution to programming constructs.

Selection and iteration together with Assignment Statements, suffice to write all programs, but it may not always be convenient to do so. The next three chapters present the main tool that renders programming convenient and pleasant: modularization into subprograms. As we'll see, procedure calls are necessarily associated with subprograms, and in some languages such calls may even be recursive.

4 Exercises

1. After execution of the following Fortran program "FIRST", the values for I, J, K, and N are well defined. What are these values when the END Statement is executed?

```
        PROGRAM FIRST
         INTEGER I, J, K, L, N
         N = 0
         DO 100 I = 1, 10
          J = I
          DO 100 K = 1, 5
           L = K
100      N = N + 1
101      CONTINUE
        END
```

2. Given the following Fortran program "SECOND", what values do N, I, J, K, and L have upon termination when the END Statement is executed?

```
        PROGRAM SECOND
         INTEGER I, J, K, L, N
         N = 0
         DO 200 I = 1, 10
          J = I
          DO 200 K = 5, 1
           L = K
200       N = N + 1
201      CONTINUE
        END
```

3. To implement the "sine(x)" function with parameter x, we use the infinite series (-1)**n*x**(2*n+1)/(2*n+1)!, where n runs from 0 to infinity, and x is the argument. Don't write the program, just think about the nature of the main loop. Should the kernel of the function have a While or a For Statement? Give your reason.
   Assume we compute the sine function up to a precision of Delta, some very small number. Are we guaranteed that this Delta can be achieved on all implementations?

4. Process all elements of an array with indices from 1 to 10000. Again, don't implement the function in this exercise, just characterize the main loop. Should the main loop be a While or a For Statement? Include reasons.

5. Write an Ada function named "bin_search" that performs a binary search on the global array "key." The integer type array bounds are known to be "min" and "max," and the elements are of type "integer." Function "bin_search" assumes that all elements in "key" are sorted, and that the "wanted" symbol, which is passed as an IN parameter, will be in the one-dimensional table. All "bin_search" has to do is to return the index of "wanted" in "key."

6. The sample program "linear_search_3" in Example 8-3 uses the "doubling-up" technique to reduce the number of loop iterations. Apply the technique again so that the loop is executed only once for every four array elements. Let the name of the search function be "quadrupled."

7. Rewrite Newton's approximation algorithm for the square root computation in Fortran. Let the main program "ROOT" call a real type function "SQROOT."

9

Subprogram Calls

It would be very nice to know
whether those procedures are actually going to be called,
because if not, we need not bother compiling them.
Unfortunately, not only can such a check not be made quickly,
it cannot be made at all.

Michael Machtey, Paul Young
An Introduction to the General Theory of Algorithms

In this chapter we justify subprogram calls, and explain two syntactic forms of calling procedures and two different ways of returning function results. Related details of parameter passing, recursion, and side effects are mentioned in this chapter, but a more thorough and detailed elaboration on these follows in subsequent chapters.

Subprograms calls, being the least elaborate concept, are treated first. Parameter passing is a more complex subject and is covered next, while recursion is the most difficult topic of these related constructs. We shall discuss these themes in the order of increasing degree of difficulty over the next few chapters.

We start out by contrasting macros with subprograms. Then we argue that the concept of defining and calling subprograms raises the language effectively to a higher level than assembler code or Turing Machine code. The Turing Machine discussion is primarily of interest for readers who have some acquaintance with the model.

1 Why Have Subprograms?

In the process of developing large programs it happens regularly that some operation or function is performed repeatedly at more than one place. We are not referring to the situation where such an operation is embedded in a loop. We refer to physically distinct portions of a program, each of which requires the same function, iteratively or as straight-line code. How do we implement multiple occurrences of the same code sequence? We shall argue that this problem can be handled conveniently with subprograms. But this is not the only purpose of their existence. Another major reason for subprograms is the notion of "divide and conquer" applied to complex problems. Difficult problems map into long programs that can be made manageable only if broken up into smaller sections. It is not necessary for these smaller sections (or logical modules) to be called more than once.

Two Approaches

There are two approaches to solving this problem. One way is to literally duplicate the same statements over and over each time that function is needed; we shall call this method *macro expansion.* The second method sets aside the statement sequence that performs this function. Each time the function must be performed, a "call" to this set-aside code sequence is executed. Consequently, this set-aside statement list must be informed where to return to once the function has been completed. We refer to this method as the *subprogram call.* The mechanism of breaking complex problems into smaller, manageable sections can be referred to as *logical modularization.* If modules become separate compilation units, this can be called *physical modularization.*

Macro Expansion

The macro expansion method is simple and quite old. It was commonplace in second-generation computer systems, when assembly language was still widely used and macro assemblers supported the tedious work of the programmer. The advantage of this method is obvious: it is the fastest possible way the function can execute. There is no overhead due to calls and no cost for the return step. The disadvantages are equally obvious: the source program becomes very large, and the amount of code grows directly proportional with the number of times the function is needed. If the function is complex and used often, the generated code size can exceed the total code space. The recursive invocation of macros created a special problem that was solved via conditional macro expansion. However, since this topic is related to assembly language programming we shall not cover it here further.

Macro assemblers do provide at least a cure for the readability problem in the following way. They allow the critical function to be defined as a macro, identified by a name. Each time the function is needed, the programmer only refers to the macro name in the assembler source program. The assembler fills in the rest. This way the source listing remains readable, but the necessary code expansion is performed by a machine, an automaton quite suited to perform such a boring, tedious task.

Subprogram Call

The *subprogram call* method forces the program designer to modularize the overall program. All operations that can be identified as subprograms are logically extracted and physically set aside. Subprograms are smaller submodules, which in conjunction with the calling environment form an overall program.

The disadvantage of this method is clear: each time a function is called, it is necessary to set aside a return address, to branch to the subprogram, and finally to branch back to the saved return address, which costs execution time. The advantage is equally obvious. The amount of code space for this method is dependent not on the function's size, but on the code required for performing a call and return. Usually this latter operation takes a few assembler instructions. The called function itself may be thousands of instructions long. In such a situation, just two calls are substantially more economical than two macro expansions. If, as programmers, have a choice as to which method to choose, we just need to weigh our driving constraint. Is it time or space?

Turing Machine Program or High Level Language?

Two main arguments, one less tangible than the other, are involved in the defense of subprogram calls. The less tangible one really boils down to the argument for and against the use of high level languages. Every high level source program can be translated into an equivalent Turing Machine program that uses only a very primitive set of instructions. Even though we can model any number of levels of Turing Machines, in its most primitive setting the Turing Machine has no subprogram call operation. Calls would be accomplished by Goto Statements, and parameter passing would be expressed by communicating via global Turing Machine variables.

Such an "equivalent" Turing Machine program, however, will be more difficult to write, less readable, and substantially longer in terms of source lines. The advantage of higher level programs here is really software reliability. Though Turing Machine code is not inherently unreliable compared to high level program code, logical errors are more likely to occur in a low level language because of the human factor, assuming that the error rate of programmers is constant over time. A very fascinating, but not yet scientifically supported theory about language level and error rate measurement has been developed by Maurice Halstead [1979] Halstead provides formulae for the computation of "language level" and estimated errors in a source program purely on the basis of the number of operators and operands. If his theory can be proven to be correct, we can build tools that perform a static analysis of source programs. The tools would indicate the language level of each analyzed program.

A more tangible (but less critical) advantage of high level languages is the higher code compaction through the use of subprogram calls. Here the relationship of high level language versus Turing Machine is identical to the relation of high level language versus assembler language. The latter we have discussed already briefly. If a subprogram is called more than once, the total code size is generally small compared to the alternative, "inline expansion."

However, having recognized the speed advantage of inline code over called subprograms, the new language Ada, for example, gives programmers explicit control over the tradeoff with the predefined Inline Pragma. In other words, with Ada a programmer has the choice between macro expansion and subprogram call.

Even if code size is no issue, it may still be advisable to break an algorithm into multiple logical modules, in the form of subprograms, just to make the problem more manageable for the designer and programmer. The cost of introducing procedure calls is the call and return overhead; the gain is improved understanding of the problem logic.

.2 Procedure Call versus Function Invocation

In most languages there are two kinds of subprogram calls, named *procedure call* and *function invocation.* Both change the flow of control to a named environment different from the place of call. Procedure calls return control to the place after the Call Statement, while function invocations also deliver a value of agreed type to the referencing expression, from whence the function has been invoked.

In expression languages such as Algol-60, Algol-68, or C this distinction between subprogram calls and function invocation fades away. C, for example, does not differentiate at all between functions and procedures. There are only functions, all of which must return a value. One may, however, have a function deliver a void value. Thus the effect is identical to that of a procedure call, as soon as the returned result is thrown away upon completion of the Call Statement.

Algol-68 draws a delicate line between functions and procedures by requiring procedures to return a value of type Void, while functions return a genuine value of some defined type.

9.3 Two Forms of Calls and Returns

Procedure calls are either expressed by the explicit keyword CALL, as in Fortran and PL/I, or implicitly denoted by referencing the respective procedure name, together with the appropriate list of actual parameters. The latter form is used in Modula-2, Pascal, Ada, and most higher level languages. Note that the first approach, requiring the CALL keyword, nicely enhances readability, while the latter keeps the source program terse and concise by omitting the semantically redundant keyword. See Examples 9-1 and 9-2.

```
CALL FACTOR( LEFT_TREE );
IF OP = '+'  | OP = '-' THEN
 BEGIN
  CALL SCAN; /* Throw away + or -, available in op */
  CALL FACTOR( RIGHT_TREE ); /* build another tree */
  CALL TIE( LEFT_TREE. RIGHT_TREE. LEFT_TREE );
 END;
/*FI*/
```

Example 9-1 PL/I Call Statements

```
CALL FACTOR( LEFT )
IF ( OP .EQ. '+' .OR. OP .EQ. '-' ) THEN
 CALL SCAN
 CALL FACTOR( RIGHT )
 CALL TIE( LEFT, RIGHT, LEFT )
END IF
```

Example 9-2 Fortran Call Statements

The advantage of Fortran's and PL/I's calling convention is clearly visible. The keyword CALL identifies the Call Statement and eliminates any misinterpretation. We don't need to have a preconception of "FACTOR," "SCAN," and "TIE." The source text shows us they are procedures, and the parenthetical list indicates the number and types of parameters. The advantage here is readability due to self-documentation.

In Examples 9-3, 9-4, and 9-5 we list the same statements in Ada, Modula-2, and Pascal. Overall we notice slight variations in syntax, but common to all three versions is the missing CALL keyword. This renders the source marginally less explicit but shorter and thus more readable. Ultimately, it is a matter of personal taste whether the self-documenting CALL keyword brings a greater advantage than the more concise alternative.

```
factor( left_tree );
IF op = '+' OR op = '-' THEN
 scan;
 factor( right_tree );
 tie( left_tree, right_tree, left_tree );
END IF;
```

Example 9-3 Ada Call Statements

```
Factor( LeftTree );
IF ( op = '+' ) OR ( op = '-' ) THEN
 Scan;
 Factor( RightTree );
 Tie( LeftTree, RightTree, LeftTree );
END;
```

Example 9-4 Modula-2 Call Statements

```
factor( left_tree );
IF ( op = '+' ) OR ( op = '-' ) THEN
 BEGIN
  scan;
  factor( right_tree );
  tie( left_tree, right_tree, left_tree );
 END;
(*END IF*)
```

Example 9-5 Pascal Call Statements

Function Return Values

We have seen two principle ways of procedure calls; one requires the reserved keyword CALL, the other references only the procedure name. There are also two principle ways of providing function return values. One form references the function name like a (pseudo) variable that receives a value via a conventional Assignment Statement. Fortran and Pascal use this alternative. These special Assignment Statements only supply the function return value; they *do not* cause the function to terminate. In the general case, the function continues to execute happily, and may even receive further return results, thus making the previous assignments obsolete. Pascal functions return when execution reaches the End Clause. Fortran also has an explicit Return Statement.

The other form of providing a function return value requires an expression as argument for a Return Statement; Ada, Modula-2, and PL/I take this second approach. In addition to supplying the function return value, these statements also cause the function to terminate immediately. We must be aware that this is not the case with the other form.

By now the reader should be familiar with both forms of procedure calls and both methods of providing function return results. But Example 9-6 and the following explanations probably shed more light on the subject by demonstrating a legal construct that seems almost impossible. This strange construct is the redefinition of a function in a function that has the identical name. Is this possible, what does it mean, and which languages allow this? Explaining these issues should make the proper subject, "function return values," more clear.

We implement a hand-manufactured function with four arguments named "min." The body of "min" contains another function, also called "min," with only two parameters. It is possible in Ada to reuse a subprogram name locally without loss of functionality. Certainly such a naming convention does not elucidate the program, but it shows what impact the design of the syntax for the function return value has on other sides of the programming language. It is not possible to do the same in Pascal.

```
                  |WITH text_io; USE text_io;
                  |PROCEDURE function_return_demo IS
             1    |
             1    | FUNCTION min( a, b, c, d : integer ) RETURN integer IS
        14   2    |
        14   2    |  FUNCTION min( a, b : integer ) RETURN integer IS
        12   3    |  BEGIN--min
             3    |   IF a < b THEN
 5           3  1 |    RETURN a;--a clearly smaller
10           3  2 |   ELSE
10           3  1 |    RETURN b;--b <= a
16           3  2 |   END IF;
16           3  1 |  END min;
16           2    |
16           2    | BEGIN
18           2    |--RETURN min( min( a, b ), min( c, d ) );
18           2    |  IF min( a, b ) < min( c, d ) THEN
31           2  1 |   RETURN min( a, b );
40           2  2 |  ELSE
40           2  1 |   RETURN min( c, d );
50           2  2 |  END IF;
50           2  1 | END min;
50           1    |
50           1    |BEGIN--function_return_demo
52           1    | put_line( integer'image( min( 2**1,2**2,2**3,2**4 )));
```

```
26   70        1  1  | put_line( integer'image( min( 3**4,3**3,3**2,3**1 )));
27   87        1  1  | put_line( integer'image( min( 4**2,4**1,4**4,4**3 )));
28  104        1  1  |END function_return_demo;
  2
  3
  4
```

Example 9-6 Ada Min Function, Has Nested Min Function

We remember from previous discussions of Pascal functions that the language requires an Assignment Statement to be executed that provides the function return value. Based on this rule it follows that there may be no redefinition of a local name in the function with the same name as the function name. A very complete compiler must check for this.

.4 Parameter Passing in Subprogram Calls

When we design a parameter passing method, we should keep four generally applicable guidelines in mind. First, the Procedure Call Statement must somehow provide an actual parameter for each formal parameter. Second, the types of all pairs of actual and formal parameters must be compatible. Third, the order of elaboration of actual parameters must be determined by language rules. Fourth, not specific to parameters, but applicable to expressions in general, the order of evaluation of nested expressions must be defined.

Incomplete Parameter List

We have seen in several languages that the number of actual parameters must match the number of formal parameters. What happens if the actual parameter list contains fewer arguments than required by the formal specification? The answer varies with the language. Ada, for example, includes a novel concept of default IN parameters. When a formal parameter of mode IN has an initial value and no actual parameter is supplied at the place of call, then the compiler provides the default value in place of the missing actual parameter. Notice that this is not the same as an initialization. An initial value would be supplied each time; the default, however, is provided only if no actual parameter is provided.

C, on the other hand, does not care; the language not only puts the responsibility for a complete parameter list into the hands of the programmer, but it also puts the blame on the programmer if the number of actual arguments does not agree with the formal specification. If, for any reason, some actual parameters have been omitted, the compiler does not offer any support by flagging such an obvious error. During execution the program will most likely abort or behave strangely. The compiler writer can plead "not guilty" by claiming: "The language told you to supply the right number of parameters." A more colloquial response that can be heard in "red neck" programming shops for such situations is the somber "You got what you deserved!" As programming language designers we must weigh the advantage of making life easy for the compiler writer versus the advantage of making programming easy for the user. Also, keep in mind that the compiler is written only once, programs will be written all the time.

Parameter Association and Evaluation Order

Most languages specify that actual parameters are evaluated in order from left-to-right. Actual parameters correspond with their associated formal ones by position. In addition to allowing such positional parameter association, Ada also permits named parameter association. Both can be mixed in the same call, but once named association is used, we cannot revert to positional association. In Example 9-7 we show instances of parameter passing in Ada. Two of the statements use the "named parameter association."

```
PROCEDURE exch( left, right : IN OUT integer );--following some calls to exch
exch( a, b );
exch( left => a, right => b );--same as above
exch( right => b, left => a );--same as above
```

Example 9-7 Positional and Named Parameter Substitution in Ada

Another rule typical for Ada governs the order of evaluation of actual parameters. The standard ANSI [1983a] defines in 6.4 that the parameter associations of a subprogram call are evaluated in some order not defined by the language. Hence, any program that relies on a particular order is by definition erroneous. Unfortunately, it will only "by definition" remain erroneous, since it is generally impossible for a compiler to detect and flag such errors.

Tracing the Order of Parameter Evaluation

Ada program "parameter_order" in Example 9-8 uses three procedure calls to trace the order in which actual parameters are evaluated. First, the procedure "three_params" is called with three actual parameters; for this experiment any order must be acceptable, since the language leaves the evaluation sequence intentionally open. In the next experiment the single parameter procedure "nested_params" is called, but the actual parameter is a triply nested function call. Here the order of evaluation is well defined by the rules for expressions. The third call is a combination of the previous two extreme cases.

The run time output of the Ada program "parameter_order" is unpredictable. Ada specifies that the order of evaluation of actual parameters in a Procedure Call Statement is undefined. We recommend the reader run the following program on some available Ada run time system. There is a good chance that the actual parameters are evaluated left-to-right, but any other order is acceptable as well.

```
                |PROCEDURE parameter_order IS
          1     |
          1     | FUNCTION f1( arg : integer ) RETURN integer IS
       5  2     |  BEGIN--f1
          2     |   put_line( "      in f1." );
  3       2  1  |   return arg + 1;
  9       2  1  |  END f1;
  9       1     |
  9       1     | FUNCTION f2( arg : integer ) RETURN integer IS
 10    5  2     |  BEGIN--f2
 10       2     |   put_line( "      in f2." );
 13       2  1  |   return arg + 1;
 19       2  1  |  END f2;
 19       1     |
 19       1     | FUNCTION f3( arg : integer ) RETURN integer IS
 20    5  2     |  BEGIN--f3
 20       2     |   put_line( "      in f3." );
 23       2  1  |   return arg + 1;
 29       2  1  |  END f3;
 29       1     |
 29       1     | PROCEDURE three_params( a1, a2, a3 : integer ) IS
 30    7  2     |  BEGIN--three_params
 30       2     |   put_line( " Now in three_params." );
 33       2  1  |  END three_params;
 33       1     |
 33       1     | PROCEDURE nested_params( a1 : integer ) IS
 34    5  2     |  BEGIN--nested_params
 34       2     |   put_line( " Now in nested_params." );
 37       2  1  |  END nested_params;
 37       1     |
 37       1     | BEGIN--parameter_order
 38       1     |  put_line( " calling three params" );
 41       1  1  |  three_params( f1( 1 ), f2( 2 ), f3( 3 ) );
 56       1  1  |  new_line( output );
 57       1  1  |  put_line( " calling nested params" );
 60       1  1  |  nested_params( f1( f2( f3( 99 ) ) ) );
```

```
37   73       1  1 |  new_line( output );
38   74       1  1 |  put_line( " calling three params" );
39   77       1  1 |  three_params(f1(1), f2(f3(2)), f3(f2(f1(3))));
40  101       1  1 | END parameter_order;
```

Example 9-8 Tracing the Order of Actual Parameter Evaluation

9.5 Side Effects

Definition of Side Effect

Side effects are changes in program state caused by assignments to reference parameters or by changes of global variables. The term *global variable* is to be taken quite general here and must refer to any global objects, including files. If a function performs a read/write operation during its invocation, and the file is accessible to other subprograms, then this operation must be classified as a side effect.

We expect procedures to change the state of the program. Therefore, side effects should not cause any surprise. Such changes are the very purpose of procedures. It is in functions where side effects surprise us. Functions are invoked as part of an expression, and it strikes the eye as unbelievable that in an expression like "f(a)+g(a)+a" the variable "a" could have different values each time used. It is hard to believe because at that source line we don't see why the value of "a" would change. But it surely can be changed as a side effect in any of the functions involved in the expression.

In Chapter 6 we very carefully outlined the rules for operand evaluation order and the associativity of operators. We raised the question whether evaluation order matters at all, and demonstrated that for some extreme cases these seemingly picky language rules are crucial.

Again we can ask, does it matter in which order actual parameters are evaluated? Again we shall be surprised. In Example 9-9 we show a sample Pascal program, named "sneak," illustrating different effects based on different parameter evaluation orders. The first time the two actual parameters are evaluated from left-to-right, and the second time we simulate a behaviour, as if the same actual parameters were processed from right to left.

The trick used to achieve this is quite simple. Procedure "sufferfrom," so named since it suffers from a side effect, has two value parameters of identical type. We write two calls, and in the second call simply reverse the order of the actual parameters. Since the state of the program and the values of all variables are identical before either call, and since the evaluation imposed by the same compiler clearly remains invariant, the second call behaves like the first one with actual parameters evaluated from right to left. The outputs are demonstrably different.

```
 1    1  0  0    PROGRAM sneak( output );
 2    2  0  0     VAR
                   a      : integer; { used as global }

 3    5  0  0     FUNCTION sideeffect : integer;
 4    6  1  0      BEGIN { sideeffect }
 4    7  1  1       sideeffect := a;
 5    8  1  1       a := a + 1;
 6    9  1  1      END; { sideeffect }

 7   11  0  0     PROCEDURE sufferfrom( a, b : integer );
 8   12  1  0      BEGIN { sufferfrom }
 8   13  1  1       IF a <> b THEN
 9   14  1  1        writeln( output, ' Different. a=', a, ' b=', b )
                    ELSE
10   16  1  1        writeln( output, ' Identical. a=', a, ' b=', b );
11   17  1  1      END; { sufferfrom }

12   19  0  0     BEGIN { sneak }
12   20  0  1      a := 10;
13   21  0  1      sufferfrom( a, sideeffect );
14   22  0  1      a := 10; { recreate old state, a=10 }
15   23  0  1      sufferfrom( sideeffect, a ); { right to left }
16   24  0  1     END. { sneak }

Identical. a=10 b=10
Different. a=10 b=11
```

Example 9-9 Side Effect in Pascal Program

Annotation of "Sneak"

The purpose of Pascal program "sneak" is to demonstrate side effects that alter actual parameters in a procedure call. "Sneak" consists of two subprograms: function "sideeffect" and procedure "sufferfrom." The critical and only common data structure is the integer variable "a." As we shall see, this is an extremely simple program, but it demonstrates succinctly what side effects are.

The function "sideeffect" does two things: it fetches the current value of global variable "a" and assigns it to the function for later return. Then, before the actual return, it increments the value of the global "a." See lines 7 and 8. Such a change of global variables is generally called a side effect.

Procedure "sufferfrom" does not access global data. It only compares the values of its two formal parameters, "a" and "b," and prints them. See the If Statement on lines 13 through 16. Notice that the name of formal parameter "a" has no association with the global variable "a." The same name was chosen arbitrarily, just to alert the reader and encourage very careful study.

The program body, lines 21 to 23, contains two calls to "sufferfrom." In either case the actual parameters are "a" and the value returned from "sideeffect." Since "sideeffect" returns nothing but the current value of "a," a superficial reader might suspect the values must be identical. This is where we have to be careful! We remember that "sideeffect" increments "a" just before returning. Thus, after its return, "a" has changed.

If we assume that actual parameters are evaluated from left-to-right, then the call on line 21 will pass two actual parameters of identical value. Only after the call is complete, the value of "a" will have changed. On line 23 we have reversed the order of the actual parameters. If again we assume left-to-right evaluation, then the first actual parameter passes the current value of "a." But, since the value is provided by "sideeffect," "a" has changed. Now the second parameter, which fetches the value of "a," will fetch the new value, one higher than before. Therefore the outputs of "sufferfrom" are different.

9.6 Mutually Recursive Subprogram Calls

A subprogram is recursive if it can call itself either directly or indirectly from its own body of statements. Indirect recursive calls involve at least one other, intermediate subprogram call before the recursive invocation. In this section we address the problem of "mutually recursive" subprogram calls and comment on its effect on programming language design.

Problem Definition

Two subprograms "a" and "b" are mutually recursive if "a" issues calls to "a" and "b," and if "b" also calls both "a" and "b." This mutual recursion is complete if "a" and "b" can in addition also be called from outside. This simply implies that "a" or "b" cannot be nested in one another. Most recursive programming languages permit this calling pattern. Ada and Pascal impose the restriction that a name cannot be referenced in a source program unless its formal declaration has been processed. This rule has an impact on the design of the language, and we shall clarify this interrelationship here largely by source examples.

How can subprogram "a" call both "a" and "b" in light of the "declaration before reference" rule? This causes no problem; the call to "a" is a directly recursive call, clearly permitted in both Ada and Pascal, and "b" has to be defined textually before "a." On the other hand, how can "b" call both "a" and "b"? Again a solution seems to be at hand; the call of "b" from "b" is a directly recursive call and is permitted. "A" can be called if it is textually defined before "b" in the source program. But now there exists a contradiction: only one of the two subprograms under discussions can be the one declared first. Here the need for mutual recursion impacts language design or restricts programming practice if forward references are not permitted. Modula-2 and PL/I by contrast do permit forward references, hence the problem does not exist there. For Ada and Pascal it is a real language design issue. The program skeleton in Example 9-10 demonstrates mutual recursion in Modula-2.

```
PROCEDURE a;
 BEGIN (* a *)
  ...
  a; (* directly recursive call *)
  ...
  b; (* forward reference to b is legal *)
  ...
 END a;
PROCEDURE b;
 BEGIN (* b *)
  ...
  a; (* is by now well defined *)
   ...
  b; (* directly recursive call *)
  ...
 END b;
```

Example 9-10 Mutual Recursion in Modula-2

If we design programming languages without allowing forward references and provide no special device for the problem of mutual recursion, then general mutual recursion would not be trivial. Partial mutual recursion, however, still could be implemented. Subprogram "a" could be nested inside "b" or vice versa. This would restrict the programming style! The nested subprogram is a local object and can therefore not be called from outside the embedding scope. One of the two names, "a" or "b," would effectively be lost for the rest of the program. A sample Ada skeleton demonstrates this in Example 9-11.

```
PROCEDURE a IS
 PROCEDURE b IS
  BEGIN--b
    a;--is known, global name
    ...
    b;--directly recursive call
    ...
  END b;
 BEGIN--a
  ...
  a;--directly recursive call
  b;--call local procedure
  ...
 END a;
--Now b is not available anymore
```

Example 9-11 Partial, Mutual Recursion in Ada Without Forward

Therefore language designers must provide a device to announce subprogram names. In Pascal this is achieved by the keyword FORWARD. Despite its "key" function, FORWARD is not reserved. Ada accomplishes the announcement of a subprogram name with the "subprogram_declaration." The declaration consists of the header and a semicolon. It includes no body. The body is defined later.

So far there is no difference, except for the syntax, in the way Ada and Pascal handle the explicit forward announcement. But there is one more rule we must be aware of. While in Pascal the parameters and the return type for functions are defined only once—that is in the announcement—in Ada it is necessary to repeat the formal definitions in the same way at the later declaration. The Pascal sample skeleton in Example 9-12 demonstrates unrestricted use of mutual recursion with the FORWARD announcement.

```
PROCEDURE b; FORWARD; { abbreviated form for b }
PROCEDURE a; { complete form for a }
 BEGIN { a }
  ...
  a; { direct recursion }
  b; { "b" is known via FORWARD announcement }
  ...
 END { a };
PROCEDURE b; { complete form for b }
 BEGIN { b }
  a; { a is completely defined }
  ...
  b; { directly recursive call }
  ...
 END { b };
```

Example 9-12 Unrestricted Mutual Recursion in Pascal

External Subprograms

Outermost level PL/I procedures are implicitly external, which makes such names available to all PLI procedures in all scopes. Hence, mutually recursive calls do not impose any problem. The same holds for functions in C. PL/I resolves the issue of complete mutual recursion via two devices. Since all names can be referenced forward, procedures "A" and "B" can be mutually recursive even if they are local to another procedure. Second, PL/I permits programs to be composed of multiple compilation units; each outermost level procedure is external, and external names break all textual scope restrictions. A possible call scheme is outlined in Example 9-13.

```
A: PROC( ARG ); RECURSIVE;
 DCL ARG BIN FIXED( 31 );
 /* STATEMENTS */
 CALL A( ARG - 1 );  /* DIRECTLY RECURSIVE */
 ...
 CALL B( ARG - 2 );  /* INDIRECTLY RECURSIVE */
END A;
B: PROC( ARG ); RECURSIVE;
 DCL ARG BIN FIXED( 31 );
 CALL B( ARG - 1 );  /* DIRECTLY RECURSIVE */
 ...
 CALL A( ARG - 2 );  /* INDIRECTLY RECURSIVE */
END B;
C: PROC OPTIONS( MAIN );
 DCL ( A, B ) ENTRY( BIN FIXED );
 DCL ( X, Y ) BIN FIXED( 31 );
 CALL A( X );
 ...
 CALL B( Y );
END C;
/* A AND B EXTERNAL. EVERYTHING POSSIBLE */
```

Example 9-13 Unrestricted Mutual Recursion of External PL/I Procedures

Mutual Recursion with Restricted Algol-60 Compilers

In the early years of Algol-60 implementations, programmers frequently were stuck with incomplete compilers. Quite often the restrictions were caused by machine limitations. For the sake of speed, Algol-60 was implemented as a single-pass compiler. Programmers were, nevertheless, faced with solving mutually recursive problems. In particular the compiler, when implemented in recursive descent architecture, had to use mutual recursion. A well-known technique, published in Atkins [1973] that would overcome the limitation was based on the following idea. We need to keep in mind that Algol-60 has no forward directive, and a one-pass compiler therefore strictly enforces the "declaration before reference" rule.

Let the two mutually recursive procedures be named "a" and "b." Introduce the artificial procedure "switch" with a single parameter and declare "a" and "b" local to "switch." This nesting hides the names "a" and "b" outside the scope of "switch." However, in the statement list of "switch" both "a" and "b" are accessible. The outside scope now can treat "switch" as a path that leads to either "a" or "b," and the single parameter takes over the function of selecting one of the two. We present a Pascal program skeleton with this technique in Example 9-14.

```
PROGRAM restrictedcompiler( input, output );
...
PROCEDURE switch( awanted : boolean );
  PROCEDURE a;
   BEGIN { a }
    ...
    a; { directly recursive call }
    switch( false ); { call to b }
    ...
   END { a };
  PROCEDURE b;
   BEGIN { b }
    a; { a is well defined by now }
    ...
    b; { directly recursive call }
    ...
   END { b };
  BEGIN { switch }
   IF awanted THEN
    a
   ELSE
    b;
   {END IF}
  END { switch };
  BEGIN { restrictedcompiler }
    switch( true ); { call a }
    switch( false ); { call b }
  END { restrictedcompiler }.
```

Example 9-14 General, Mutual Recursion Without Forward Directive

9.7 Summary

We started out by presenting the advantages and disadvantages of procedure calls versus macros. The primary idea of either is the aim to increase readability by logical modularization. We showed two principle forms of calls and two forms of generating function return values. In the section on procedure Call Statements we defined side effects and provided a sample to show its hidden dangers. Finally we presented a short introduction to parameter passing and mutually recursive calls. A sample program was included to trace the order of evaluation of actual parameters during runtime.

9.8 Exercises

1a. Which programming language is used for the following correct procedure call statement?

```
CALL SETMAX( RESULT, A, B )
```

1b. In which source language is this correct procedure Call Statement expressed?

```
CALL COMPUTE MAX( RESULT, A, B );
```

1c. Once more, in which source language is the following correct procedure Call Statement expressed?

```
computemin( result, a, b )
```

1d. Determine which programming language is used in this fourth correct Call Statement.

```
compute_min( result, second => a, third => b );
```

2. Are the following two Assignment Statements, which use nested invocations of function "min," equivalent?

```
result := min( min( a, b ), min( c, d ) );
result := min( min( min( a, b ), c ), d );
```

3. The following Ada procedure "named_parameters" prints only the values of its formal parameters. Which output is generated if "named_parameters" is initiated by the procedure Call Statement listed underneath the declared procedure?

```
PROCEDURE named_parameters(
 c1 : IN character := 'A';
 c2 : IN character;
 c3 : character := 'a';
 c4 : character;
 c5 : IN character := 'M';
 c6 : character := '.' ) IS
BEGIN--named_parameters
 put_line( c1 & c2 & c3 & c4 & c5 & c6 );
END named_parameters;--other declarations

BEGIN--enclosing scope
 named_parameters( 'P', 'e', c5 => 'e', c4 => 'c' );
 --other statements
END;
```

4. Procedure "nested2refs" in the following Pascal program "indirect" prints the values of all six accessible variables. Which values are printed?

```
program indirect( output );
 var
  a, b  : integer;

 procedure pass2refs(
  var
   x, y : integer );

  procedure nested2refs(
   var
    i, j : integer );
   begin { nested2refs }
    b := j;
    writeln( ' a = ', a );
    writeln( ' b = ', b );
    writeln( ' i = ', i );
    writeln( ' j = ', j );
    writeln( ' x = ', x );
    writeln( ' y = ', y );
   end; { nested2refs }

  begin { pass2refs }
   nested2refs( x, a );
  end; { pass2refs }

 begin { indirect }
  a := -1;
  b := +555;
  pass2refs( a, b );
```

```
30   end. { indirect }
```

5. Procedure Call Statements in Fortran and PL/I are identified by the keyword CALL. List an advantage for this syntax. Calls in Ada, Modula-2, and Pascal are identified by merely referencing the procedure name. What is the advantage here?

10

Parameters

What a shame
that the name parameter
is the default.

C. A. R. Hoare
Hints On Programming Language Design

Not only do programming languages have different concepts of parameter passing, but different implementations of the same language invent various ways of solving the same concept. We must learn to distinguish clearly between the logical parameter passing concept, defined by the language, and the physical parameter passing method, as implemented by the compiler.

This chapter explains why we need parameters at all. It introduces most conventional parameter passing methods while shedding some light on their different implementations, and shows how to choose the best parameter passing method for a specific task. Along the way to this goal, however, we will take a look at numerous parameter-related terms and group them under the more general terms "in-parameters" and "out-parameters." This should help guide the student through a jungle of terms that are often really synonyms.

10.1 Why Have Parameters?

Parameters make programming easier and more fun, and they make our programs more reliable. Subprogram calls covered in the previous chapter represent a considerable convenience for the craft of writing programs, but without parameter passing, this tool is not nearly as useful. For example, let's take a simple trigonometric function such as "sine." If it could not be parameterized—that is, if we could not specify the argument for which we need the "sine" computed—the function would be useless. If we accomplish this by the alternate method of biasing functions via global variables, we immediately decrease our software reliability. A set of parameters creates a new personality for a called subprogram, thus increasing the convenience of writing software and effectively raising the programming language level.

10.2 Terminology

The overall terminology accompanying parameter passing is a small Tower of Babel in its own right, reminding us of the hopeless proliferation of programming languages. And this should not come as a surprise, since each language definition reserves the privilege of creating its own vocabulary. But once we become familiar with the major methods of parameter passing, we find that there are really only two different concepts expressed in a variety of terms and defined with slight variations in semantics. These two concepts are best described by the terms *in-parameter* and *out-parameters,* both of which we have pirated from Ada. To avoid any confusion, we will capitalize the terms when they refer specifically to Ada's own version of these concepts.

In-Parameters

In-parameters must have an initial value, which is maintained for the actual parameter across the call. This value preservation is guaranteed whether or not the language allows assignments to the corresponding formal in-parameters. As we shall see in Exercise 4 at the end of this chapter, this decision has an impact on the chosen implementation technique. Substituting an uninitialized variable as an actual parameter for a formal in-parameter is a programming error.

Students will encounter the following terms that are essentially the same thing as in-parameters: value parameters, call by value parameters, parameters passed by copy-in, and constant parameters. *Value parameter* is the preferred term in various Algol-like languages and usually implies that assignments to the formal are permitted; *call by value* is simply a more baroque synonym. *Copy-in* alludes to the implementation method of creating a copy of the actual for the formal parameter. *Constant parameter* implies the language restriction that assignments to the formal parameter are illegal. Such is the case with Ada; an older version of Pascal had the same facility on top of its current two parameter types. More detail about in-parameters follows in Section 10.4.

Out-Parameters

Out-parameters return new values computed in the called environment and bring them to the place of call. In order to hold the newly assigned value, the actual parameter must be a variable; an expression in its place is illegal. If the called subprogram fails to set the formal out-parameter, this is a programming error.

We frequently see the following synonyms for out-parameter: reference parameter, call by reference, value result parameter, call by value result, and address parameter. The terms prefixed with *call by* are simply archaic, though popular, forms that we shall avoid. *Reference parameters* leave it open whether the associated formal parameter is used in the called environment or not. If it is, our preferred term is *in-out-parameter,* again pirated from Ada. *Address parameter* alludes to the implementation of passing the address of the actual; this way actual and formal parameters become aliases. *Value result parameters* are implemented by copy-in at the place of call, and copy-out at the place of return. Hence actual and formal are distinct entities across the call. We shall make use of this knowledge in a sample program in which we trace down the implementation method for out-parameters. Out-parameters are treated in more detail in Section 10.5.

10.3 Selecting a Parameter Passing Concept

In this section we describe how a programming language lets a user specify the selection of a parameter passing concept. We are not addressing why a programmer would select in-parameters over out-parameters or vice-versa. But we do describe a programming language designer's choices that give the programmer control over the selection. Principally there are three choices: (a) selection through the formal parameter declaration, (b) selection at the place of call, and (c) selection by language default.

Selection Via the Formal Parameter Declaration

The first principle requires that the chosen parameter passing method be spelled out explicitly at the place of the formal parameter declaration. This concept emphasizes modular programming by giving the called environment preferential treatment regarding program readability. Ada, Algol-60, Modula-2, and Pascal apply this first principle.

Selection at the Place of Call

The second principle also allows a choice of method, but in this case the programmer must define the method at the place of call. It will not be visible at the place of the formal declaration. PL/I is the only language we know of that applies this second principle. Since it resolves the parameter passing method by the call, the expressions "call by value" and "call by reference," which indicate the the methods used, are meaningful in PL/I. In languages using other ways of specifying the parameter passing method, the "call by" prefix is nonsense, since by definition the call has no impact on the passing method nor is the call itself impacted.

Selection by Language Default

The third and most restrictive principle gives the programmer no selection at all. Parameters are all treated alike and the passing method is defined by default. Algol-68, C, and Fortran have only this default concept; however, Algol-68 and C know in-parameters exclusively, while Fortran uses only out-parameters. Since in Fortran it is also legal to pass general expressions such as literals as actual parameters, and since literals may not assume new values, the semantics are a bit conflicting. Fortran resolves the issue by language restrictions. In older Fortran implementations it was possible to assign the literal "2" a new value in a called subroutine, and henceforth use the "2" as an alias for "7." This naturally created ridiculous programs. Fortran-77 has solved this problem by disallowing assignments to formals if the actual is a literal.

The use of a default parameter passing method causes less of a limitation than one might suspect. We shall come back to this interesting constraint with a program called "inpointers" in Example 10-3, but first we refine the definitions of in- and out-parameters and explain them in more detail via sample programs.

10.4 In-Parameters

Two properties are essential for in-parameters. First, the actual parameter supplies the corresponding formal parameter with an initial value. Second, in-parameters guarantee that the actual parameter will not change as a result of having been used as a parameter, even if the language permits assignments to the formals. Intentionally we phrase this second condition with great care. It may be so that after completion of a subprogram call a variable used as an actual for a formal in-parameter does hold a new value. But then this will be due to a side effect, not to its use as a parameter. In other words, the side effect would have taken place even if the variable had never been substituted for a parameter. To illustrate this point we give a sample Pascal program in Example 10-1, but we re-iterate: actual parameters that replace formal in-parameters are unmodified after the call.

On line 13 in program "inparam" in Example 10-1 we see a call to "nosideeffect." Global variable "a" is associated with the formal parameter, also named "a," and receives a new value in the subprogram. But, since the formal declaration specifies "a" as an in-parameter, this assignment has no permanent effect on the actual parameter "a."

Line 15 calls a similar subprogram named "sideeffect." Here the formal parameter "a" is still passed by value, but in the body, on line 9, global variable "a" is changed. Therefore it is modified after the call, but the modification has nothing to do with the use of "a" as an actual parameter.

```
1    program inparam( input, output );
2     var a : integer;
3     procedure nosideeffect( a : integer );
4      begin { nosideeffect }
5       a := a + 1;
6      end { nosideeffect };
7     procedure sideeffect( b : integer );
8      begin { sideeffect }
9       a := a + 1; { side effect, reference of global }
10      end { sideeffect };
11     begin { inparam }
12      a := 10;
13      nosideeffect( a );
14      writeln( ' a = ', a );
15      sideeffect( a );
16      writeln( ' a = ', a );
17     end { inparam }.
```

Example 10-1 Pascal Program "Inparam"

Actuals that replace in-parameters retain their initial values. Again, this is a firm commitment that must be guaranteed even if the corresponding formal parameter receives new values during execution of the call. To satisfy this commitment, some implementations generate a copy of the actual parameter in place of the formal parameter. This implementation method is also known as "copy-in" parameter.

Ada does not allow the use of formal in-parameters as variables. Hence, they cannot be used on the left side of the assignment operator, and cannot be substituted for formal out-parameters. This includes system routines for input. Ada in-parameters are only useful as operands in expressions, just like constants. For this reason, they are also known as constant parameters. A formal constant parameter is a restricted class of in-parameter that is not assignable. For instance, see the Ada procedure "in_param" in the compilation unit in Example 10-2. We shall observe some parallelism here between For Statement "loop parameters" and procedure "in-parameters." When we are aware of this identity in concept, the Ada term “loop parameter” becomes more sensible.

The inability to assign in-parameters can impact the implementation technique used for the translator. Since an assignment is not possible, the actual parameter may, but need not, be passed by copying. Passing an address is legal as well, and the commitment to remain invariant after the call is still guaranteed. Example 10-2 demonstrates that any attempt to misuse an in-parameter as a variable is flagged by the compiler.

```
 1                  | WITH text_io; USE text_io;
 2                  | PROCEDURE in_out_param( i : IN OUT integer ) IS
 3        11   1    | BEGIN--in_out_param
 4             1    |  i := i + 1;
 5    6        1  1 | END in_out_param;
 6    6             |
 7    6             | PROCEDURE in_param( i : IN integer ) IS
 8    8   11   1    | BEGIN--in_param
 9    8        1    |  get( i ); --should be flagged
===== ERROR =====>  |        ^ Variable or OUT-param exp
10    9        1  1 |  i := i + 1;        --also not legal
===== ERROR =====>  |  ^ cannot be used as variable. =>   9
11   14        1  1 |  in_out_param( i );--yet another error
===== ERROR =====>  |                   ^ Variable or OUT-param exp =>   10
12   19        1  1 | END in_param;
```

Example 10-2 Ada IN-, IN-OUT-Parameters with Illegal Use

We need to dwell a bit more on the exact rules for parameter passing in Ada. The language defines that the implementation method for scalar parameters is by copying. Formal scalar parameters of mode IN or IN OUT are copied in during subprogram call, while scalar parameters of mode OUT and IN OUT are copied back upon return. This is also known as passing by “value result.” For nonscalar parameters such as arrays or records, the language gives the implementor the choice to pick any method that works correctly.

If the language specifies the parameter passing method in the formal declaration, as do Ada, Algol-60, Modula-2, and Pascal, then the actual parameter may be an expression or a variable. In PL/I cause and effect are reversed. If the actual parameter is an expression, it is intended as an in-parameter. Otherwise, the actual parameter is a variable and is used as an out-parameter.

The formal declaration in PL/I contains no clue about the passing method. The obvious disadvantage of this reversed thinking creeps up during the program maintenance phase. During this phase reading, not writing, is emphasized. When analyzing a PL/I procedure, we cannot conclude from the assignment to a formal parameter anything about the effect on its actual substitute. Instead we must search in other places of the source program for "this" call; only from the combination of both call and declaration can we tell whether a side effect will take place. This makes software maintenance difficult. A language designer who considers such a concept valuable must be aware of the tradeoff between increased convenience in writing and decreased readability.

We should understand now that in-parameters represent a fairly safe but restrictive mechanism. In our immodest desire for more we may feel handicapped, especially when using languages like C or Algol-68 that have in-parameters exclusively. The situation in Fortran, which also provides only one default parameter concept, does not seem so bad, since the one mechanism provided is the more general out-parameter concept. But even in Algol-68 and C things are not so bleak; both languages have pointers. Thus we can work around the restriction and maintain the safeness as well by using value parameters of type pointer.

Consistent with the value parameter concept and commitment, the passed actual pointer cannot be modified in the called subprogram, but the objects being pointed at can easily be altered. See Example 10-3.

```
program inpointers( output );
 type pintype       = ^ integer;
 var  pin           : pintype;

 procedure indirectinparam( pin : pintype );
  begin { indirectinparam }
   pin^ := 999;
  end { indirectinparam };

 begin { inpointers }
  new( pin );
  pin^ := 100;
  indirectinparam( pin );
  writeln( pin^ );
 end { inpointers }.
```

Example 10-3   Pascal Program "Inpointers," Using Pointers as In-Parameters

In summary, in-parameter passing is a concept that is typically implemented by "copy-in." If the language is more restrictive about formal in-parameters, passing can also be implemented by other techniques. The actual parameter passed in can be a simple expression or an arbitrarily complex data structure, depending on the type of the formal. Even if the actual is just a pure variable, it will be unaltered after the call.

10.5 Out-Parameters

Out-parameters are the exact opposite of in-parameters. While in-parameters have an initial value guaranteed by the actual expression and maintained across the called environment, out-parameters must be variables whose values are generally altered after the call. For out-parameters it is not clear whether they provide an initial value. In fact either outcome is possible: they only return a value, or they supply an initial value and return a result. The first we call out-parameter, the latter in-out-parameter. Most languages make no distinction between the two, and it is here that Ada excels. Ada knows two kinds of reference parameters: one of mode OUT, the other of mode IN OUT. The former are by definition uninitialized and are only required to return a value. Consequently, out-parameters may not be used in expressions. Other terms for this mechanism are *return parameter, transient parameter,* or *result parameter.* Ada implementors can even go so far as to explicitly assign the value "Undefined" to any variable used as an actual parameter for a formal out-parameter. A test for "Undefined" after the return would reveal a language violation.

Out-Parameters Implemented by Value Result

Value result passing creates a local copy of the actual parameter, just like in-parameter passing by "copy-in" does, but immediately before the return of the called subprogram the local copies are moved into the actual parameters. During execution there is some period of time where the values of the formal and actual parameter can be different: the actual is still holding its old value, while the formal contains a new value. At only two well-defined moments are both guaranteed to be in synchrony. One is at procedure entry time, when the actual initializes the formal; the other is at procedure exit time, when the current value of the formal is copied back into the actual parameter. This is not the case for out-parameters implemented by address passing. Here formal and actual always represent the same object. Accessing the formal out-parameter is synonymous with accessing the actual variable except that its name may be spelled differently.

The Ada program "in_and_out_demo" in Example 10-4 shows the different effects of in- and out-parameters. Note that an assignment to local variable "x," defined in procedure "in_and_out" on line 5, would be illegal. An erroneous attempt to do this was properly flagged by the Ada compiler for a similar case in Example 10.2. Also notice that for scalars, the in-out-parameter implementation in Ada is by copy-in and copy-out, better known as passing by "value result."

Ada does not prescribe the implementation technique for parameters of type Record or Array. Instead implementors may choose any method they desire. But remember the parameter passing method for in- and in-out-parameters of scalar types is by "copy-in, copy-out." This latter rule adds one iota more security in programs that go awry during execution. If an "Exception" occurs in a called subprogram after assignments to formal out- or in-out-parameters, then the corresponding scalar type actual is unmodified after continuing at the exception handler. For the majority of all cases the exception handler can rely on a well-defined situation and attempt a reasonable recovery from the exception. This well-defined situation is based on the old values of all parameters before the call.

Pascal explicitly demands that reference parameters, which in the Pascal subculture are named VAR parameters, must be implemented by address. See 6.6.3.3 in ANSI [1983b]. The program in Example 10-4 tests the semantics of in- and out-parameters.

```
 1                    |WITH text_io; USE text_io;
 2                    |PROCEDURE in_and_out_demo IS
 3              1     | a, b : integer;
 4         12   1     | PROCEDURE in_and_out(
 5              2     |  x : IN integer; y : OUT integer ) IS
 6         12   2     | BEGIN--in_and_out
 7              2     |  y := x;
 8    4         2  1  | END in_and_out;
 9    4         1     |BEGIN--in_and_out_demo
10    6         1     | a := 5555; b := 6666;
11   13         1  1  | in_and_out( a, b );
12   18         1  1  | IF a /= 5555 THEN
13   22         1  1  |  put_line( " in-parameter error." );
14   25         1  2  | ELSIF b /= 666 THEN
15   30         1  1  |  put_line( " out-parameter error." );
16   33         1  2  | END IF;
17   33         1  1  |END in_and_out_demo;
```

Example 10-4 Ada Program, Testing Correct In- and Out-Parameter Passing

Variables "a" and "b" are used as actual parameters on line 11. "A" substitutes an in-parameter; "b" replaces a formal out-parameter. If the value of "a" were altered after the call, the message of line 13 will be printed. Should "b" not return the required value 666, then the message on line 15 would appear.

Tracing the Out-Parameter Implementation

Since we are curious, we might want to find out which technique our particular compiler uses to implement out-parameters. Or, in our search for a software error, we might wish to verify that the compiler lives up to the language postulate. The Modula-2 Example 10-5 shows how we can track down the implementation method. To this end we make use of the fact that passing by address makes the actual and formal out-parameters aliases, while the value result implementation temporarily creates a new entity. The use of aliases is a potential for subtle errors, and is particularly easy in block-structured languages. Block-structured languages allow the nesting of scopes inside one another and the use of global variables in inner blocks, unless the local block redeclares these names. We use this facility to our advantage by accessing actual parameters via two naming conventions: once through the formal parameter name and once directly as global variable. Thus, tracing down a *by address* or a *value result* implementation is simple. Having the same object accessible under more than one name is called *aliasing.* Aliasing is one of the most dangerous devices in the art of programming. It can make complex problems impossible to comprehend.

Fortran is not block-structured, so this kind of aliasing is not possible. But in Fortran we still have two scopes: a local scope for all subprograms and an external scope, called *Common.* We can use common variables as actual parameters in subroutine calls and then use both, the formal (dummy) parameter alias and the common name. This way there is still an aliasing mechanism and we can trace down the physical implementation method for out-parameters.

The Modula-2 program in Example 10-5 determines whether the run time system implements out-parameter passing by address or by value result. Ada is required to pass scalar out-parameters by value result, while Pascal requires passing by address.

```
MODULE AddressOrValueResult;
 FROM InOut IMPORT WriteString, WriteLn;
 VAR a : CARDINAL;

PROCEDURE Determine( VAR x : CARDINAL );
 BEGIN (* Determine *)
  x := 200;
  IF ( x = 200 ) AND ( a = 200 ) THEN
   WriteString( " Out-parameters by address" );
  ELSIF ( x = 200 ) AND ( a = 100 ) THEN
   WriteString( " Out-parameters by value/result" );
  ELSE
   WriteString( " Magic way to pass out-parameters" );
  END;
  WriteLn;
 END Determine;

BEGIN (* AddressOrValueResult *)
 a := 100;
 Determine( a );
END AddressOrValueResult.
```

Example 10-5 Modula-2 Program, Tracing Out-Parameter Implementation

0.6 Algol-60 Parameters

Parameter passing in Algol-60 is quite unique. First, there is only minimal type checking between actual and formal parameters. Algol-60 is "generous" and unsafe by permitting objects of almost any type to be used for actual parameters. Second, name parameters behave different from other kinds described so far and are rarely found outside of Algol-60. The only other language that always applies the name parameter concept is Simula. Some implementations of Logo, particularly the interpretive ones, use name parameters.

Name Parameters

Parameter passing *by name* is the default in Algol-60. We do not cover Algol-60 in detail in this text, but its important role in the history of programming language design and the uniqueness of the defining report warrant a detailed treatment of the parameter passing mechanism. According to the revised Algol-60 report Naur [1963] the language has two parameter passing methods, passing by value and passing by name. Since the reader is already familiar with in-parameter passing, a synonym for value parameter, we will only treat name parameters in this section. *Name parameters* are actual parameters that textually substitute each occurrence of the formal parameter at the moment of evaluation.

Let "f" be a formal name parameter in procedure "p." Then every reference to "f" in the body of "p" behaves as if "f" were replaced by the text of the corresponding actual parameter. Actual parameter evaluation is not initiated at the moment of call. Instead the formal parameter is replaced by the text of the actual at each instance, not earlier. We don't need to take this textual substitution rule literally; practically all implementations only simulate such textual replacement by other, more efficient means. To explain the mechanism from another angle we can say that the binding of actual to formal parameter is delayed until the last possible moment—that is, when the formal parameter is referenced in the called environment. Each reference creates a new binding. By contrast the binding for most in- and out-parameters occurs earlier, at the moment of call.

Name parameters are the dinosaurs among the parameter species. They are powerful and unwieldy, and will likely become extinct, just as their terrestrial counterparts have long ago. The concept is quite important, though, and must be standard knowledge when we evaluate programming languages or when we design new ones. The definition of name parameters certainly gives no hint as to just how enormously powerful these can become. We will illustrate this mechanism in Example 10-6.

```
PROCEDURE byname( a, b );
 INTEGER a, b;
 BEGIN
  b := 4;
  a := 5;
 END;
```

Example 10-6 Algol-60 Procedure "byname" with Name Parameter

Now let us assume that we have an enclosing block with an array variable "x[1:50]," all elements initialized to 10, and an integer variable i set to 33. Let us analyze what happens when the Procedure Call Statement "byname(x[i], i);" is executed. If out-parameters were used, then x[33] would be 5 and i would be 4 after the call. But Algol-60 defines name parameters with a different semantics. Hence the program state after the call is i=4 and x[4]=5. X[33] remains unaffected.

```
PROCEDURE byname( x[i], i );
 integer x[i], i;
 BEGIN
  i := 4;              COMMENT i=4;
  x[4] := 5;           COMMENT x[4]=5;
 END;
```

Example 10-7 Formal Name Parameters Replaced by Text of Actuals

If an implementation would really substitute the text of the actual for the formal parameter, we can imagine that the execution time overhead would be tremendous. Nobody would really want to implement name parameters this way. Compiler implementors, therefore, have to invent other techniques that reduce the cost of the name parameter passing mechanism while granting the same semantics.

In Algol-60 compilers the effect of passing parameters by name is simulated instead via *thunks,* which do what the Algol-60 report demands for name parameters, but without incurring the high associated cost. Thunks were first implemented by Peter Ingerman, as documented in Ingerman [1961]. They are parameterless execution time routines, one per formal name parameter, that run each time a formal parameter is evaluated in the called procedure. The Algol-60 call overhead grows substantially with the number of formal parameter references when compared to other, more simplistic parameter passing methods. We should understand this clearly: thunks only simulate the "text substitution" of actual for formal parameter. In reality they represent a different, faster method for name parameter passing. Macrolike textual substitution is, however, a convenient tool for the reader of Algol-60 programs to verify the effect of name parameters. Thunk is a technical colloquialism that cannot be found in Webster [1981]; it also cannot and should not be eradicated from the compiler writer's vocabulary. Probably it is a word created in Ingerman's laboratory.

It is astonishing that one of the inherent limitations of the name parameter passing mechanism is its very power. Certain simple effects that are no problem for regular out-parameters cannot, in general, be implemented with name parameters. To explain this point we implement the sample procedure "swap" with two arguments in Example 10-9. The intent of "swap" is to exchange the values of its two actual parameters, and we implement "swap" with reference and name parameters. We shall be surprised. A direct implementation in PL/I follows in Example 10-8.

```
SWAP: PROCEDURE( A, B );      /* PL/I */
         DCL ( A, B, TEMP ) BIN FIXED( 31 );
         TEMP = A;
         A = B;
         B = TEMP;
      END SWAP;
```

Example 10-8 PL/I Procedure "Swap"

A PL/I statement of the form "CALL SWAP(I,J);" exchanges the values of "I" and "J." Also "CALL SWAP(I,A(I));" exchanges the values of "A(I)" and "I." If "I" is 7 and A(7) is 99, then after statement "CALL SWAP(I,A(I));" "I" equals 99 and "A(7)" holds the value 7. The other array elements are unaffected. The corresponding implementation of "swap" in Algol-60 looks almost identical. See Example 10-8. Even the calls are similar, except that Algol-60 needs no CALL keyword. Surprisingly, the effect is quite different.

```
PROCEDURE swap( a, b );    COMMENT Algol-60;
 INTEGER a, b;
 BEGIN
  INTEGER temp;
  temp := a;
  a := b;
  b := temp;
 END;
```

Example 10-9 Algol-60 Procedure "Swap"

We rewrite the preceding two PL/I calls in Algol-60 and pretend for the sake of demonstration that textual substitution does take place. Since both "a" and "b" are declared as integers without the qualifier VALUE, they are name parameters. With the qualifier VALUE the program would, of course, never work properly, since value parameters (in-parameters) do not return results from the called environment. See Example 10-10.

```
swap( i, j );          temp := i;
                       i := j;
                       j := temp;

swap( i, a[i] );       temp := i;
                       i := a[i];
                       a[i] := temp;
```

Example 10-10 Algol-60 Calls to "swap," and Procedure Body Expansion

Contrary to what we might expect after reading the PL/I procedure in Example 10-8, it is not the array element a[7] that changes, but element a[99]. Should no such element exist, we are in the unfortunate situation of causing an array bounds violation and are likely to experience a program abort. We have shown one instance where the swap operation does not function with name parameters; we know it will never work with value parameters. This astonishing limitation of the most powerful parameter passing scheme has already been mentioned in Gries [1971], by now a classic in compiler construction.

Hidden Power of Algol-60 Parameters

This section will be a joy for aficionados of Algol-60; we shall look very carefully at the name parameter mechanism. Without knowing it we will also acquire a good body of general Algol-60 knowledge along the way. To accomplish all this, we analyze sample programs that perform the summation of one-, two-, and three-dimensional vectors.

We introduce a sample solution in Ada for the one-dimensional case, which is trivial and will affirm our confidence. We contrast the Ada solution with its functional equivalent in Algol-60, though the body of procedure "algolsum1" is quite different. We don't use the structured For Statement but replace it by a hand-coded version. But, as we will gradually discover, the look-alike solution is radically different, though functionally equivalent. This will lower our confidence by just one notch, which is good; otherwise, we might not dedicate enough attention to understanding the solution for the multidimensional case.

We must instead dedicate our full attention to the two-dimensional case. From then on we shall have a grasp for the general n-dimensional solution. Once the reader understands how the simple, old language Algol-60 can solve the summation of arbitrary-dimensional arrays with the mere power of its name parameter, something our modern and sleek Ada cannot accomplish, then this unique parameter mechanism will finally and fully be understood.

We treat name parameters in such detail not only to explain the concept itself, but also to make programming language designers aware of its associated cost, limitations, and power. It is safe to conclude that the power is not needed and the run-time cost unproportionally high. But first we'll demonstrate its unusual capability.

Problem Definition

Let's start by describing the problem and its solution in Ada. Function "sum1" is expected to add all elements of a one-dimensional array and return the sum to the calling expression. The actual parameter is an array, named "a1," with the bounds in the range 3 to 5. Its elements have been initialized in the body of the main program, and the whole array is passed to function "sum1" by value. See line 6 in the Ada program in Example 10-11, which defines the formal parameter "a1" to be an in-parameter. The kernel of the solution is simple. A For Statement steps through all elements, and adds their values to the current "result," initially zero. Finally, "result" is returned.

```
 6         13  1    | FUNCTION sum1( a1 : IN a1 type ) RETURN integer IS
 7         13  2    |  result : integer;
 8         14  2    | BEGIN--sum1
 9             2    |  result := 0;
10    4        2  1 |  FOR i IN a1'first .. a1'last LOOP
11    8        2  1 |   result := result + a1( i );
12   17        2  2 |  END LOOP;
13   18        2  1 |  RETURN result;
14   23        2  1 | END sum1;
```

Example 10-11 One-Dimensional Vector Summation in Ada

Function "sum1" in Example 10-11 has only one single parameter. This parameter is a one-dimensional array, each element of which is referenced and added up to yield the total vector sum. We need to keep the parameter type in mind for the comparison later with the Algol-60 solution.

In Example 10-12 we show just such a solution, inspired by Randell and Russell [1971]. We recommend the reader study the following Algol-60 program carefully to absorb "via osmosis" some of the Algol-60 syntax. The line numbers in the leftmost column have been included for ease of reference.

```
1    BEGIN
2     integer ARRAY a1[ 3 : 5 ];
3     integer summation, i;
4     integer PROCEDURE algolsum1( a, k );
5      integer a, k;
6      BEGIN
7       integer sum;
8       sum := 0;
9       k := 3;
10     loop:
11      sum := sum + a;
12      IF k = 5 THEN GOTO finish;
13      k := k + 1;
14      GOTO loop;
15     finish:
16      algolsum1 := sum;
17     END;
18    COMMENT initialize array "a1," but not i;
19    summation := algolsum1( a1[ i ], i );
20   END;
```

Example 10-12 One-Dimensional Vector Summation in Algol-60

Hand-Manufactured Loops like the one in the Algol-60 program in Example 10-12 should by now be familiar. That portion of the Algol-60 solution does correspond to the Ada program, where we have used the more structured For Statement. But what a difference in formal parameters!

The Algol-60 function has two parameters of type integer; neither is an array. Since the qualifier VALUE is missing in the formal type specification of the parameters, both "a" and "k" are name parameters. See lines 4 and 5 in Example 10-12.

How can the Algol-60 function "algolsum1" perform the summation of a vector that is neither passed as a parameter nor referenced globally? Quite simply! In the first actual parameter the calling expression provides the first of the array elements, indexed by "i." The second parameter passes "i" itself. By modifying the index in the body of the called function, other elements of that same array will become accessible, provided the index remains within legal bounds. By using pointers and performing pointer arithmetic, some other languages permit the same functionality. For example, in C, arrays are always passed to a function by providing the address of the first element. Inside the function, the pointer variable can then be dereferenced to provide access to the object pointed at. Modifying the pointer provides access to all other elements of the array. It is critical, however, for such a solution, to have the pointer be properly initialized, and to modify the pointer in increments identical to the element size of the array. Too often this deteriorates into machine-dependent programming, for which reason we wisely abstain from more detail and warn language designers from including such opaque constructs.

This brings us to the second, though very subtle difference from the original Ada solution. When the two actual parameters "a[i]" and "i" are passed, "i" is still uninitialized. Notice that the Algol-60 program in Example 10-12 starts execution with the Assignment Statement on line 19. At that time "i" has no value. Consequently "a[i]" references no legal array element. Why then doesn't the Algol-60 program abort? The answer lies in the definition of the name parameter. If passing is by name, it is not necessary, and in fact in this case not possible, to fetch any of the values or addresses of the actual parameters at the time of call. "A[i]" has no address, because of the illegal index "i." Instead the name parameter definition implies that both actuals are quasi passed as textual strings. So inside the body of "algolsum1" every occurrence of the formal "a" is virtually replaced by the string "a1[i]," and formal "k" is replaced by "i." Luckily, just before the first reference to "i," this variable is assigned the initial value 3 on line 9. Remember that the formal "k" on this line is to be replaced by the actual "i." From then on, only legal references to "a1[i]" are performed, since "i" steps from 3 through 5, just as allowed.

Some Algol-60 Syntax Rules

Along the way we have also picked up some Algol-60 syntax. We know how arrays are declared. The extension to multidimensional arrays is achieved by a comma list of indices. We have also seen where formal parameters and local variables must be declared. And we have seen a sample definition of a function. For a procedure we simply omit the leading type identifier. This knowledge makes it easy to understand the syntax of the next Algol-60 program in Example 10-13. But here we have to focus on very subtle semantics. Algol-60 name parameters allow for the recursive activation of a function (or procedure) by means of an actual parameter.

The effect of the Assignment Statement on line 19 in Example 10-13 is to perform a double summation of the two-dimensional array "a2." Integer variable "summation" will hold the sum of all integer elements in "a2." Try to do this in Ada! In Pascal or Modula-2 we may be able to accomplish this with the use of function parameters.

```
1         BEGIN
2          integer ARRAY a2[ 3 : 5, 3 : 5 ];
3          integer summation, i, j;
4          integer PROCEDURE algolsum2( a, k );
5           integer a, k;
6           BEGIN
7            integer sum;
8            sum := 0;
9            k := 3;
10          loop:
11           sum := sum + a;
12           IF k = 5 THEN GOTO finish;
13           k := k + 1;
14           GOTO loop;
15          finish:
16           algolsum2 := sum;
17          END;
18         COMMENT initialize array "a2," not i, j;
19         summation := algolsum2( algolsum2( a2[ i, j ], i ), j );
20        END;
```

Example 10-13 Two-Dimensional Vector Summation in Algol-60

The Algol-60 program in Example 10-13, containing the function "algolsum2," provides only few syntactic novelties. Global array "a2" has two dimensions, and the Assignment Statement that calls "algolsum2" is a bit more complicated. At this point we are not concerned about syntax rules. We must try to understand the expressions on lines 11 and 19.

How can this single expression perform the summation of a two-dimensional array? Function "algolsum2" is invoked recursively. We see that inside the actual parameter list of the called function "algolsum2" the first parameter is also a call to the same function. As in the one-dimensional case, the corresponding formal parameter is *not* an array, but just a single, simple integer name parameter. Since name parameters require a (quasi) string substitution of the formal by the actual parameter, the body of "algolsum2" for the first call looks like Example 10-14.

```
8            sum := 0;
9            j := 3;      COMMENT k replaced by j;
10          loop:
11           sum := sum + algolsum2( a2[ i, 3 ], i );
12           IF j = 5 THEN GOTO finish;
```

Example 10-14 String Substitution for Formal Name Parameter

The interesting and difficult portion here is line 11. We see that the formal integer parameter "a" has been replaced by a more complex string. This string is "algolsum2(a2[i,j],i)." By the time execution reaches line 11, the second parameter "j" has received its initial value 3. Notice that "i" is still uninitialized at this point. But this should not concern us anymore. A few moments earlier we just covered the problem of a one-dimensional vector summation via Algol-60 name parameters. So before line 11 can complete, it must issue a recursive call to "algolsum2," which delivers the sum of all "i" elements for the slice "a2[i,3]" upon returning. This is performed three times—once for j=3, for j=4, and for j=5. And each time "algolsum2" is called recursively, during which activation it initializes "i" to 3 and iterates up to i=5.

We learn from this that integer name parameters can be substituted by any actuals that yield integers. This can be integer variables, integer array elements, or functions returning integer results. The extension to the summation of n-dimensional arrays is straightforward.

10.7 Procedure and Function Parameters

Algol-60 based languages, including Pascal and Modula-2, have a very convenient but difficult to implement parameter type named procedure or function parameter. Fortran also has a restricted form of subprogram parameters. *Procedure parameters* are not what the name seems to imply—that is, just parameters to procedures. That would be redundant. We know that all parameters are associated with a procedure or function. Instead procedure parameters are parameters of type procedure. This makes it possible for a procedure name to be passed as an actual parameter. The use of formal procedure parameters is usually restricted to calls only. It is not possible to reference the formal names in expressions, nor to assign them values. *Function parameters* are invoked like user-defined functions and they return results. It is certainly not obvious what this parameter concept could possibly be good for. But Example 10-15 shows a nice application of this rare construct.

In brief, we have written a "software plotter" that prints sample values of a function within a given range. The graphical results are represented as offsets from the x-axis and are marked by an asterisk character. See Figure 10-1. Note that the x-axis is aligned vertically on the printer paper to allow for an arbitrarily long output. The exact function chosen is the product of two functions to give us more flexibility.

It would be a pity if for every function to be plotted we would have to write another program. Wouldn't it be much more convenient to just have one single plot subprogram and pass the name of the function to be plotted as an argument? To truly appreciate the beauty of the procedure parameter concept in Pascal, it may be necessary to try doing this in Ada. The "plot" procedure in Example 10-15 is actually quite general. Even though the product of two functions is being plotted, it is possible to replace one of the function parameters by the identity function and thus have the effect of a single function.

Notice that several names defined in program “funcparams” are never referenced. These are the names for the formal parameters of function parameters. Both formal parameters “d” on lines 5 and 6 are not used, because they cannot be referenced. We stress this point to expose a minor flaw in the Pascal language design: Pascal requires the programmer to define a name for something that can never be used. The language designers should have followed the sample set by Algol-68 and adopted in Modula-2. These languages do not require the formal parameters of function and procedure parameters to have names. Since it is known a priori that such names can never be referenced, why clutter up programs with them? The types of these parameters must naturally be defined in a strongly typed language. Note that in the original Pascal definition Jensen and Wirth [1978] the parameters of formal procedure and function parameters needed no specification at all. This left a type loophole in the language, which the standard language ANSI [1983b] attempts to rectify. Unfortunately, this correction introduces the inconsistency just exposed.

```
1   program funcparams( input, output );
2    function sine( arg : real ) : real; begin sine := sin( arg )end;
3    function expo( arg : real ) : real; begin expo := exp( arg )end;
4    procedure plot( phases, probes, amplitude : integer;
5     function func1( d : real ) : real;
6     function func2( d : real ) : real );
7     const pi      = 3.1415926535; { old friend }
8     var x, y      : real;
9      i            : integer;
10    begin { plot }
11     for i := 0 to phases * probes do
12      begin
13       x := i / probes;
14       y := func1( -x ) * func2( 2 * pi * x );
15       writeln( ' ' : round( amplitude*y) + amplitude + 1, '*' );
16      end;
17     {end for}
18    end { plot };
19   begin { funcparams }
20    plot( 2, 24, 50, expo, sine );
21   end { funcparams }.
```

Example 10-15 Pascal Program with Function Parameters

Figure 10-1 Output of Pascal Procedure "Plot"

10.8 Summary

In this chapter we have explained the major parameter passing methods. We have also pointed out execution time and readability costs that should give a programming language designer reasons for or against inclusion of some parameter passing methods. The large number of parameter-related terms and the fading line between logical concept and implementation method makes the topic appear more obscure than it really is. Hopefully we have succeeded in convincing the reader that there are just two major concepts, known as in-parameter and out-parameter, plus a few exotic concepts that programming languages can easily live without. Parameters are inseparably tied to procedure calls, which were covered in the previous chapter, and with recursion, which will be treated next.

10.9 Exercises

1. The Algol-60 procedure "swap," as defined in the text, is called three times. Which ones of the three calls have the desired effect of exchanging the values of the two actual parameters?

```
a.)     SWAP( I, J );
b.)     SWAP( TABLE( K ), K );
c.)     SWAP( L, TABLE( L ) );
```

2. Identify the errors in the following Ada program.

```
PROCEDURE bad_mistakes( a : IN integer; b : OUT integer ) IS
BEGIN--bad_mistakes
  a := b * -1.5;
END bad_mistakes;
```

3. Explain the difference between Ada in-parameters and Pascal in-parameters.

4. Assume that we have the following two procedures, "value_ada" and "value_pascal," both of which have one in-parameter "a" of type array. Both procedures only use the passed array elements; they do not assign new values to "a." Explain an implementation method for Ada that is substantially faster than the implementation in Pascal.

```
 -- Ada sample
PROCEDURE including IS
 SUBTYPE many_data IS string( 1 .. 30000 );
 many : many_data;
 PROCEDURE value_ada( a : IN many_data ) IS
 BEGIN--value_ada
  --uses of a(i), no assignments
 END value_ada;
BEGIN--including scope
 value_ada( many );
END including;
```

```
 (* Pascal sample *)
PROCEDURE including;
 TYPE many_data = ARRAY[ 1 .. 30000 ] OF char;
 VAR many : many_data;
PROCEDURE value_pascal( a : many_data );
 BEGIN (* value_pascal *)
  (* uses of a(i), no assignments *)
 END; (* value_pascal *)
BEGIN (* including *)
 value_pascal( many );
END including;
```

5. Let us pretend for a moment that Pascal subprograms do not have parameters. This exercise translates the recursive algorithm for the following "fact" function into such a restricted Pascal.

```
FUNCTION fact( arg : integer ) : integer;
BEGIN { fact }
 IF arg = 0 THEN
  fact := 1
 ELSE
  fact := fact( arg - 1 ) * arg;
 {END IF}
END { fact };
```

   Hint: Use the global variable "arg" and initialize it to the value of which we wish to compute the factorial. Inside of function "fact" this global has to be modified appropriately.

6. The function "algolsum1," discussed in the text in Example 10-12, is invoked with two actual parameters on line 19. The parameters are "a[i]" and "i," and they are passed by name. At the place of call "i" has not been initialized, hence "a[i]" does not designate a legal array element. If parameters were passed by value or by reference the program would abort. Why does this not cause a problem in this Algol-60 program?

7. Write a Pascal program that traces down whether out-parameters are implemented on your system by address passing or by value result.

11

Recursion

of course, the example discussed
can be quite easily adapted to show
that the general question of whether a particular procedure
is recursive in an Algol-60 program is undecidable.

Michael Machtey, Paul Young
An Introduction to the General Theory of Algorithms

Sometimes recursion seems to brush paradox very closely.
For example, there are recursive definitions.
Such a definition may give the casual viewer the impression
that something is being defined in terms of itself.
That would be circular and would lead to infinite regress,
if not to paradox proper.
Actually, a recursive definition (when properly formulated)
never leads to infinite regress or paradox.
This is because a recursive definition
never defines something in terms of itself,
but always in terms of simpler versions of itself.

Douglas R. Hofstadter
Gödel, Escher, Bach: An Eternal Golden Braid

Let's start with the definition of a simplified form of *recursion.* In the course of the current section the full meaning of recursion will gradually become clear.

An algorithm is formulated recursively if it is partly expressed by simpler versions of itself. A subprogram is directly recursive if its body contains a call to itself. It is recursive if it can issue a call to itself directly or indirectly before its termination.

Assuming that the preceding definitions of recursion are meaningful, we must postulate that such a directly recursive call be conditional. In other words, the call must be embedded in some form of conditional statement. Along the chain of calls this condition must change so that eventually the sequence will terminate. Otherwise, we would have an infinite chain of calls, a very unfortunate program behaviour.

Recursion is one of the more controversial and valuable programming tools, comparable in merit to other high level constructs, such as modularization or the declaration of abstract data structures. In fact, rules for data structure declarations are inherently recursive themselves. As a case in point, not only can record declarations contain further records, in which case the structure is nested, but record types may also reference the very record under definition, in which case we have a recursive dependency. To avoid infinite types, an intermediate pointer (or in Ada access) type is required.

Recursion is occasionally frowned upon by those who rarely have to solve truly recursive problems. After all, some execution time overhead is associated with recursion that does not surface in subroutine calls of the Fortran style. Yet other programmers are skeptical about recursion, because their pet language does not provide this device; therefore, so they speculate, such a capability cannot be worthwhile! But genuinely recursive problems do exist, and for these a recursive programming language is the appropriate tool.

This chapter will give the reader a full appreciation for recursion. First, we shall learn to simulate recursion via nonrecursive techniques. The goal here is to bring us to the same level of understanding of recursion that a compiler designer must have when writing semantic routines for recursive programs that run on general-purpose target computers.

Our second goal is to implement a highly recursive algorithm using a recursive programming language. For the first goal we need an understanding of how recursion is implemented. In the second approach we let the recursive programming language solve the recursive portion of the problem for us. A third aspect of recursion, known as "mutual recursion," also fits nicely into the current frame of problems. One strategy for solving this interesting problem has already been shown in Section 9.6. In the current chapter we explain a more general solution.

To gain appreciation for recursion, we go back into "ancient" computer science history, about 20 years ago, and review a recursive function, published by Donald Knuth in the *Algol Bulletin* in 1964. This recursive function was invented for the sole purpose of separating the Algol-60 "man compilers" from the "boy compilers." We should be relieved to find that today such tests are no longer a challenge for languages and their translators. Even microcomputers pass them as a matter of course.

In Section 11.3 we shall demonstrate the implementation of recursion by using the factorial function. In Section 11.4 we crack a harder nut. Our definition of Fibonacci numbers uses the Fibonacci function twice in a recursive fashion. We shall simulate this more complex problem by using nonrecursive means and come one step closer to our first goal.

In antithesis to our familiarization with recursion we get acquainted with a function that is so highly recursive that it should scare or at least caution us. This is the mysterious Ackermann function. Ackermann recurses so strongly that even for small arguments the largest machine resources are quickly exhausted. This experience is intended to make us aware of the cost associated with recursion.

Section 11.6 revisits an old friend, the Towers of Hanoi. Here we find our ultimate challenge: if we can simulate recursion via iterative means for the Towers, we have mastered our first goal and can simulate any other recursive problem as well!

Section 11.7 presents a technique known as *recursive descent,* frequently used in compilers for designing parsers and for the processing of expressions. We shall use grammar G4 from Chapter 1 and write a full compiler for this small language. This technique is applicable a large class of recursively defined problems, and can be used advantageously for tree and graph processing. Designing the parser will conclude our second goal.

1.1 Recursion Versus Iteration

For certain problems recursion offers a concise and elegant solution, usually minimizing the time required to write programs. But we must be aware that there is an execution time cost associated with recursive calls. Stack space must be acquired and at some later time be freed, return addresses must be saved, and more hidden bookkeeping must take place. In contrast to a subroutine jump that merely saves a return address, this cost can be substantial. Compared to iteration, which requires a test and a conditional branch, the cost of recursion is high.

When run time is crucial, we must carefully weigh the pros and cons of recursion. If we choose against recursion, there are still several ways to solve the same problem. The first and obvious method is to find a nonrecursive algorithm that is equivalent to the recursive one. We have shown one such instance in the discussion "Towers of Hanoi in Fortran" in Section 4.2; the so-called "Fourth Grade Solution" in the same section is an iterative algorithm equivalent to the recursive one. The unfortunate shortcoming with searching for a nonrecursive "substitute" is that one might not be ready at hand. We emphasize substitute here. While it is always possible to simulate recursion via iteration, it is not always possible to find a different, nonrecursive solution for a recursive one. Also, the iterative substitute may be unattractive for other reasons.

But we may still use a second recourse, explained in much detail in the current section. After all, most high level language compilers implement recursion by generating code for target machines that have no notion of recursion. If a compiler can do this, we can certainly achieve the same!

Recursive calls do incur some execution time overhead. We might feel that this cost can be saved by abstaining from using recursion and simulating recursion via iterative means. In most higher level languages this would lead matters from bad to worse, since the explicit stack management with numerous index operations probably creates much more overhead than the recursive call that is to be saved. For example, in Table 11-1 we shall give execution time measurements for recursive Fibonacci implementations. Our motivation is to help programmers to know when to use and when to abstain from recursion. If the problem is recursive and the host language allows recursion, we should use what is natural. When the problem is recursive but the language permits no such comfort, then we can simulate recursion in the way suggested in this chapter.

It is so trivial to rewrite the factorial function iteratively that it can serve as a paradigm of recursion misuse. The game of the Towers of Hanoi, on the other hand, proves the opposite; the recursive solution is simple to comprehend and easy to implement. Both the iterative solution and an iterative approximation are substantially more complex than the recursive counterpart. However, recently a number of interesting publications have shown simple iterative solutions to the Towers of Hanoi; see Birtwistle [1984], Franklin [1984], Meyer [1984], and Stadel [1984].

The factorial function and the Towers of Hanoi are extreme cases. The algorithm for finding Fibonacci numbers is in the middle. We can easily write an iterative program for Fibonacci numbers, but the conceptual solution is quite naturally expressed recursively.

Recursion is a programming tool like others. In some situations it will be the appropriate construct to use. Recursive programs have the tendency to be concise, to be readable for a mathematically oriented mind, and to express beauty and elegance. There will be other situations, in which recursion should not be used, either because the problem is nonrecursive, or because outside constraints make it impossible.

Man Or Boy, A Recursive Challenge

In the early 1960s the implementation of a full Algol-60 compiler presented quite a challenge. Some compilers ran on very limited machines, while others were restricted due to their ad hoc methods. In order to measure and test the recursion aspect of compilers, Donald Knuth invented the Algol-60 function "a." Function "a" is highly recursive, uses procedure parameters, passes parameters by name except for one integer argument, and employs multiple Assignment Statements. Even though "a" is just a few lines long, and even though Knuth claims that "this uses nothing known to be tricky or ambiguous," his hand-calculated and guessed results were wrong, as he had already suspected. Playfully and tongue-in-cheek, Knuth uses "a" as a milestone for separating the "man compilers" from the "boy compilers;" see Knuth [1964]. The Algol-60 version of "a" is shown in Example 11-1.

```
BEGIN      COMMENT an Algol-60 Source program;
  real PROCEDURE a( k, x1, x2, x3, x4, x5 );
  VALUE k; integer k;
  BEGIN
    real PROCEDURE b;
    BEGIN
      k := k-1;
      b := a := a( k, b, x1, x2, x3, x4 );
    END;
    IF k <= 0 THEN
      a := x4 + x5
    ELSE
      b
  END;
  outreal( a( 10, 1, -1, -1, 1, 0 ) )
END;
```

Example 11-1   Knuths Algol-60 Program to Separate Boy from Man Compilers

At that time Knuth had no man compiler available. But a few weeks after Knuth's publication, the industrious Algol-60 programmer J. A. Zonneveld at the Mathematisch Centrum in Amsterdam published the results for "a" with arguments k=1..10. Zonneveld encountered some problems of his own, since the first machine he used ran out of memory space when computing "a" for k=10. Another of his computers, called the Kiel Machine, that had a larger memory finally delivered the correct result.

In Example 11-2 we give a Pascal approximation of function "a," but we should note some differences between the Algol-60 version and the Pascal substitute. Most notably, the Algol-60 multiple Assignment Statement "b:=a:=a(..);" cannot be translated directly into Pascal; Pascal has no multiple assignment. It could be simulated by using a temporary variable. In this particular case the effect of the multiple assignment is achieved by substituting the call to "b" in the Else Clause with an assignment of function "b" to "a"; see line 26.

One more difference is caused by Pascal's tighter type checking rules. Algol-60 is much more permissive, and in fact the formal parameters "x1" through "x5" are substituted by actual integer literals and real functions. This adaptability of parameter types must be simulated in Pascal via dummy real functions "x1" through "x5," trivially returning the values of hard coded literals.

The reader is encouraged to compare the Algol-60 version in Example 11-1 with the Pascal solution in Example 11-2. At least for the tested values of "k" the Pascal run time system yields the same results as Zonneveld's Kiel Machine.

```
 1  program manorboy( input, output );
 2   var i : integer;
 3   function x1 : real; begin {x1} x1 :=  1; end {x1};
 4   function x2 : real; begin {x2} x2 := -1; end {x2};
 5   function x3 : real; begin {x3} x3 := -1; end {x3};
 6   function x4 : real; begin {x4} x4 :=  1; end {x4};
 7   function x5 : real; begin {x5} x5 :=  0; end {x5};
 8   function a(
 9     k : integer;
10     function x1 : real;
11     function x2 : real;
12     function x3 : real;
13     function x4 : real;
14     function x5 : real ) : real;
15
16    function b : real;
17     begin { b }
18      k := k - 1;
19      b := a( k, b, x1, x2, x3, x4 );
20     end { b };
21
22    begin { a }
23     if k <= 0 then
24      a := x4 + x5
25     else
26      a := b;
27     {end if}
28    end { a };
29
30   begin { manorboy }
31    for i := 0 to 10 do
32     writeln( ' i = ', i, round( a( i, x1, x2, x3, x4, x5 ) ) );
```

```
    {end for}
  end { manorboy }.
i =         0       1
i =         1       0
i =         2      -2
i =         3       0
i =         4       1
i =         5       0
i =         6       1
i =         7      -1
i =         8     -10
i =         9     -30
i =        10     -67
```

Example 11-2 "Man or Boy" Program Rewritten in Pascal

11.3 The Factorial Function

In this section we take a very close look at the well-known factorial function, or more precisely, at the recursive formulation of that function. It is not our goal to demonstrate what a wonderful and elegant tool recursion can be by virtue of solving the factorial function. We are well aware that recursion is too powerful a tool to crack such a small nut. The power and elegance of recursion are shown later, when we present a compact compiler for expressions. In this demonstration we will use the factorial function for illustrating how a recursive problem can be implemented by keeping the recursive solution but using nonrecursive tools. We start with this example, because we have found no simpler recursive function.

We develop four ground rules for transforming recursive algorithms into iterative programs expressed in a low level assemblylike language. Then we present Pascal program "factorial1," which applies these four rules literally to the recursive factorial problem. We abuse Pascal somewhat by writing a low level program. "Factorial1" will contain a critical compile time error, which is why we have to develop solution "factorial2."

Formulated recursively, the factorial function is defined as follows: the argument "arg" must be a nonnegative integer. Then "factorial(0)" yields 1, while "factorial(arg)" for arg>0 yields factorial(arg-1)*arg. To understand the mechanisms of recursive calls, let us first analyze the problem a bit closer. See Example 11-3.

```
1   FUNCTION factorial( arg : integer ) : integer;
2    BEGIN { factorial }
3     IF arg = 0 THEN
4      factorial := 1
5     ELSE
6      factorial := factorial( arg - 1 ) * arg;
7     {end if}
8    END { factorial };
```

Example 11-3 Factorial in Pascal, Revisited

On line 6 in Example 11-3 we see a directly recursive call. Once function "factorial" returns from that recursive call, it does two things: first, it yields a value, which is the factorial of the next smaller argument, and, second, it guarantees that execution continues after the function invocation. In this case this is the middle of an expression and a multiplication has yet to take place. After the multiplication is complete, the product is assigned to "factorial," so that this invocation of "factorial" in turn yields a proper value. Then the next statement, if any, can be executed. Incidentally, there is no further statement, neither in the Then Clause of the If Statement nor afterwards, so the current invocation of the function can terminate. These observations lead us to the following rules for simulating recursion in a low level language.

Four Rules for Simulating Recursion by Iteration

1. Provide a stack of record elements for each recursive function or procedure. An element must be able to hold all parameters, local variables, the return address, and the function return value. The associated variable "top" indexes the next usable stack element.

2. For each recursive call, increase the stack by one element. The return address must be saved, and the values of the actual parameters copied into the corresponding record fields that hold the formal parameters. Finally branch to the head of the statement list of the recursive subprogram to be simulated.

   In our examples we shall not use local variables to reduce the amount of work. Conceptually, local variables must be handled like parameters, but we shall not mention them anymore in our simulations.

3. During the actual call we must guarantee that the function return value is generated. For the translation of a correct recursive Pascal program this means that the function Assignment Statement is translated into an assignment to the top record field, which holds the function return value.

4. For each return decrement the stack by one element. The popped-off return address must be used to determine where execution will continue.

Whether the function return value belongs to the caller or callee, is only a matter of convention. The schemes are equivalent and both work. In our factorial sample the function result word belongs to the caller. The stack elements used in the solution in Example 11-4 have three fields, named "fact," "arg," and "ret." Field "ret" holds an integer value that determines the return address. "Fact" is the result returned by the function, and "arg" is the function argument.

Solution "factorial1" in Example 11-4 applies the preceding four rules literally, and we encourage the reader to study the solution carefully. Unfortunately, such a blind translation of the original recursive solution into the corresponding iterative one can lead to programming errors if we are not really using assembly language. See the Goto Statement on line 37, which jumps into the middle of an If Statement -- a cardinal sin in Pascal. Therefore the compiler emits an error message.

```
 1  program factorial1( output );
 2   var
 3    i : integer;
 4
 5   function fact( arg : integer ) : integer;
 6    label 1, 2, 3;
 7    const
 8     maxstack    = 10;
 9    type
10     stackrange = 0 .. maxstack;
11     stacktype  =
12      record
13       arg,
14       fact,
15       ret        : integer;
16      end;
17     var
18      stack      : array[ stackrange ] of stacktype;
19      top        : stackrange;
20     begin { fact }
21      top := 0;
22      stack[ top ].arg := arg;
23      stack[ top ].ret := 3;
24   1: if stack[ top ].arg = 0 then
25       stack[ top ].fact := 1
26      else
27       begin
28        top := top + 1;
29        stack[ top ].arg := stack[ top - 1 ].arg - 1;
```

```
30         stack[ top ].ret := 2;
31         goto 1;
32   2:    top := top - 1;
33         stack[ top ].fact := stack[ top + 1 ].fact * stack[ top ].arg;
34        end;
35       {end if}
36       if stack[ top ].ret = 2 then
37        goto 2;
38       {end if}
39   3: fact := stack[ top ].fact;
40     end { fact };
e 37 - Goto 2 is into a structured statement
```

Example 11-4 Simulation of Recursive Factorial with Syntax Error

Notice the If Statements needed for selecting branch destinations in Pascal. This is caused by Pascal's lack of an explicit data type Label, which we do know from PL/I. The stylized program in Example 11-5 shows the kind of programming we are forced to use in most higher level languages.

```
IF return_address = 1 THEN
  GOTO 1
ELSE IF return_address = 2 THEN
  GOTO 2
ELSE IF return_address = 3 THEN
  GOTO 3
ELSE ... etc.
```

Example 11-5 Determination of Branch Destination in Pascal

With an explicit type Label as we find in PL/I, this can be expressed more concisely by "GOTO label_var(i)" after proper initialization of "label_var." But we do not lament the absence of such low level data types from Ada, Modula-2, or Pascal. Its availability encourages low level programming, which is exactly what we do when we break down recursion into explicit stack handling and iteration. We employ such low level constructs merely for the sake of demonstration.

How Return Addresses Are Saved

The factorial function "factorial" earlier expressed in Pascal in Example 11-3, shows that there are two different places of return. One goes back to the outside caller that initiated the function for the first time; the other returns to the place after the recursive invocation. The first return address, therefore, needs to be saved just once, while the second one must be stored once for each recursive call. Exactly that happens on lines 23 and 30 in "factorial1" in Example 11-4. The statement "stack[top].ret:=3" ensures that upon complete processing of the stack the function can return, but not without assigning the final result to the function; see line 39 in Example 11-4. On the other hand, the statement "stack[top].ret:=2" guarantees that after each recursive step, processing continues at label 2. Label 1 never needs to be saved. This label takes over the role of the function entry by serving as the destination of a Goto Statement. It simulates the recursive call.

The next solution, designated "factorial2" in Example 11-6, avoids the problem of branching into the middle of an If Statement by relocating the portion of code that contains the target label. That portion is part of an Else Clause and is moved outside of the If Statement. To prevent the program from executing this relocated Else Clause after the Then Clause, another unconditional branch, and a new label are required. See Label 4 and "Goto 4" in Example 11-6.

We emphasize again that the reader should study "factorial1" most carefully, even though it does not compile correctly. "Factorial2" is a complete solution, emerging from the first one after correcting the obvious syntax error. The four rules listed earlier do not consider this class of errors. Such errors are likely to occur when using a language like Ada or Pascal. But they will not surface if we use nonrecursive assembly language.

```
program factorial2( output );
 var
  i : integer;

 function fact( arg : integer ) : integer;
  label 1, 2, 3, 4;
  const
   maxstack   = 10;
  type
   stackrange = 0 .. maxstack;
   stacktype  =
    record
     arg,
     fact,
     ret       : integer;
    end;
   var
    stack      : array[ stackrange ] of stacktype;
    top        : stackrange;
   begin { fact }
    top := 0;
    stack[ top ].arg := arg;
    stack[ top ].ret := 3;
 1: if stack[ top ].arg = 0 then
```

```
      begin
        stack[ top ].fact := 1;
        goto 4;
      end;
     {end if}
     {stack[ top ].arg > 0 }
     top := top + 1;
     stack[ top ].arg := stack[ top - 1 ].arg - 1;
     stack[ top ].ret := 2;
     goto 1;
  2: top := top - 1;
     stack[ top ].fact := stack[ top + 1 ].fact * stack[ top ].arg;
  4: if stack[ top ].ret = 2 then
      goto 2;
     {end if}
  3: fact := stack[ top ].fact;
   end { fact };
```

Example 11-6 Simulation of Recursive Factorial, Syntax Error Eliminated

11.4 Fibonacci Numbers

We use Fibonacci numbers as a second and more interesting example to demonstrate how recursion can be simulated by iteration. First, we list program "fibonacci1" in Example 11-7, which is a direct, programmatic solution of the recursive definition for Fibonacci numbers. Then we apply our four rules for translating recursion into iteration, resulting in program "fibonacci2" in Example 11-8. Since we perform this translation literally, the outcoming program "fibonacci2" again branches into the body of If Statements. Finally, program "fibonacci3" in Example 11-7 eliminates these syntax errors. Again we use Pascal as the simulation language. To be more accurate, we should say that we use a subset of Pascal. We are free to use every construct in Pascal except recursion, since it is recursion we want to express by something else. So we pretend that Pascal does not offer this tool. Since Fibonacci numbers can easily be computed by iteration, we close this section with an iterative solution named "fibonacci4" in Example 11-10.

Definition of Fibonacci Numbers

Fibonacci numbers form a sequence of values, the next of which is found by adding up the previous two. This is an intuitive and incomplete definition, but the following sample sequence will make it clear. A partial Fibonacci sequence is 0, 1, 1, 2, 3, 5, 8, 13, 21, 34, .. and so on; just add the last two numbers to find the next.

A more complete definition can be given using a recurrence relation. We let each Fibonacci number be associated with an index, the first being index zero. Negative indices are invalid. Then we define: Fibo(n) = Fibo(n-1) + Fibo(n-2). The sample program "fibonacci1" in Example 11-7 demonstrates this recursive definition in Pascal. The index range from 0 through 23 is limited by our 16-bit host machine. A call to "fibo(24)" would raise the integer overflow exception. "Fibonacci1" is included here to give us a starting position when we sharpen our skills of transforming recursion into iteration.

```
1   program fibonacci1( output );
2    function fibo( index : integer ) : integer;
3     begin { fibo } { assume index = 0 }
4      if ( index = 0 ) or ( index = 1 ) then
5       fibo := index
6      else
7       fibo := fibo( index - 1 ) + fibo( index - 2 );
8      {end if}
9     end { fibo };
```

Example 11-7 Recursive Solution of Fibonacci

We focus our attention on program "fibonacci1" for a moment. If we wish to replace recursion by iteration, then line 7 contains a critical statement. Here, in the body of function "fibo," we find two directly recursive calls to "fibo." The two returned function values are added to yield the next higher function return value. Our task is to simulate these two function calls via iteration. To simulate a recursive call iteratively, we simply need to apply with brute force the four rules stated earlier. Remember that we used these rules in the factorial solution and we will just repeat them here to create "fibonacci2." In "fibonacci2" in Example 11-8 the field "return" holds the return address in a numeric encoding, field "index" is the index of the desired Fibonacci number, and "fibo" contains the function result. Field name "return" would be illegal in Ada, since it is already reserved as a keyword.

The first recursive call is simulated by incrementing the stack for the first time. The function argument is found at the next lower stack index and must be decremented by one. See line 26 in "fibonacci2." The associated return address is given by label 2 and stored in field "return." Then follows the unconditional branch to label 1 on line 28. This is the first simulated recursive call.

At label 2, line 29, we have completed the simulation of the first call; but a second recursive call must still be transformed. So the stack must be increased again by one, and the same action is performed. Line 30 in "fibonacci2" constructs the function argument by subtracting only 1 from the previous argument. Didn't our recursive solution demand that the second call use index minus 2? We are doing nothing wrong here. If we recall that the function argument in the next lower stack element is already reduced by one, subtracting another 1 from it does exactly what is required. The statement on line 30 could also have been written

```
stack[ top ].index := stack[ top-2 ].index-2;
```

To simulate the second recursive call we must save label 3 as the return address, but again branch to label 1. The same function is simulated, so we must branch to the same location as in the previous simulation; only the function argument is now one smaller. The dilemma with this solution is that it doesn't compile! Again, just as in our translation of the factorial example, we have two branches into an If Statement — a cardinal sin!

```
 1  program fibonacci2( output );
 2   function fibo( index : integer ) : integer;
 3    label 1, 2, 3, 4;
 4    const
 5     maxstack    = 10;
 6    type
 7     stackrange = 0 .. maxstack;
 8     stacktype  =
 9      record
10       index,
11       fibo,
12       return    : integer;
13      end;
14    var
15     stack       : array[ stackrange ] of stacktype;
16     top         : stackrange;
17    begin { fibo }
18     top := 0;
19     stack[ top ].index := index;
20     stack[ top ].return := 4;
21  1: if ( stack[ top ].index = 0 ) or ( stack[ top ].index = 1 ) then
22      stack[ top ].fibo := stack[ top ].index
23     else
24      begin
25       top := top + 1;
26       stack[ top ].index := stack[ top - 1 ].index - 1;
27       stack[ top ].return := 2;
28       goto 1;
29    2: top := top + 1;
30       stack[ top ].index := stack[ top - 1 ].index - 1;
31       stack[ top ].return := 3;
32       goto 1;
```

```
33      3: top := top - 2;
34         stack[ top ].fibo := stack[ top + 1 ].fibo + stack[ top + 2 ].fibo;
35        end;
36       {end if}
37    4: if stack[ top ].return = 2 then
38        goto 2
39       else if stack[ top ].return = 3 then
40        goto 3;
41       {end if}
42       fibo := stack[ top ].fibo;
43      end { fibo };
e 38 - Goto 2 is into a structured statement
e 40 - Goto 3 is into a structured statement
```

Example 11-8 Simulation of Recursive Fibonacci with Syntax Error

For dogmatic Software Engineers the source listings "fibonacci2" and "fibonacci3" must stir some agitation. The few lines of Pascal are full of Goto Statements! Who would dare to write such code? But not all is bad that has a GOTO. We should keep in mind that we pretend our host language has no facility for recursive calls. And we should remember that we are familiarizing ourselves with a general algorithm that permits us to translate recursive calls into iterative equivalents. We are virtually writing in assembly language, or at least in low level language. If the solution is expressed in Pascal, this is purely incidental and merely a convenience. We are resorting to more primitive tools, so we should not be surprised to find a lower language level. It is not hard to write low level programs in a high level language. Some people do it all the time!

In "fibonacci3" in Example 11-9 we demonstrate how to get around the problem of creating the illegal Goto Statements that we have seen in "fibonacci2." We use a simple escape by relocating the complete Else Clause onto the outermost statement level. This way, a branch to labels 2 or 3 is legal from anywhere. An additional Goto Statement is required (see line 24) in order to branch over the relocated Else Clause. Again, to understand this example, the reader should first study "fibonacci2" most carefully, even though it is a wrong program. "Fibonacci3" is a translation of the erroneous, low level Pascal program into a correct low level Pascal program.

```
 1    program fibonacci3( output );
 2     function fibo( index : integer ) : integer;
       ...
20       stack[ top ].return := 4;
21    1: if ( stack[ top ].index = 0 ) or ( stack[ top ].index = 1 ) then
22        begin
23         stack[ top ].fibo := stack[ top ].index;
24         goto 4;
```

```
       end;
      {end if}
      top := top + 1;
      stack[ top ].index := stack[ top - 1 ].index - 1;
      stack[ top ].return := 2;
      goto 1;
   2: top := top + 1;
      stack[ top ].index := stack[ top - 1 ].index - 1;
      stack[ top ].return := 3;
      goto 1;
   3: top := top - 2;
      stack[ top ].fibo := stack[ top + 1 ].fibo + stack[ top + 2 ].fibo;
   4: if stack[ top ].return = 2 then
       goto 2
      else if stack[ top ].return = 3 then
       goto 3;
      {end if}
      fibo := stack[ top ].fibo;
    end { fibo };
```

Example 11-9 Correct Simulation of Recursive Fibonacci

Our final example for this section, "fibonacci4," has little in common with the recursive solutions in the previous three examples. Instead of using a recursive algorithm, it uses direct iteration to compute Fibonacci numbers. We include it here for two reasons. As a conclusion to this section we will analyze our different solutions by comparing their run times. We will also look at the number of calls each solution requires to generate the Fibonacci Numbers. And, second, it will give us a chance to become acquainted with an iterative solution.

```
program fibonacci4( output );
 ...
 function fibo( index : integer ) : integer;
  var old1, old2, i, temp : integer;
  begin { fibo } { assume index >= 0 }
   if ( index = 0 ) or ( index = 1 ) then
    fibo := index
   else
     begin
      temp := 0;
      old1 := 1;
      old2 := 0;
      for i := 2 to index do
       begin
        temp := old1 + old2;
        old2 := old1;
        old1 := temp;
       end;
      {end for}
      fibo := temp;
     end;
    {end if}
   end { fibo };
```

Example 11-10 Iterative Solution of Fibonacci

Table 11-1 shows time measurements for all three executable Fibonacci programs. It is interesting to see that the most costly of our running solutions is "fibonacci3," where we simulate recursion via iteration. The fastest performer, as we shall find frequently with nonrecursive algorithms, is the last solution, "fibonacci4."

Table 11-1 Run Times for Fibonacci Solutions

Fibonacci1	27.70 sec.
Fibonacci3	111.40 sec
Fibonacci4	7.10 sec

We should be curious to find out why the clean recursive solution "fibonacci1" is so slow compared to the iterative solution "fibonacci4." Since the code of function "fibo" in "fibonacci1" is even smaller than in "fibonacci4," and since it contains no loop whatsoever, there is only one possible explanation. The recursive calls must consume the time. But how can a call with just one actual parameter be so costly in itself? To answer this question we need to investigate just how many recursive calls are performed. If we let "n" be the cost function, expressing the number of recursive calls, we can compute "n" as a function of "index," which we abbreviate to "i."

If "fibo" is called with i=0, no recursive call is issued and the total number of calls is just one. We say the cost function "n" with argument 0 is one, or n(0)=1. Similarly, if index=1, again no recursion occurs and the total number of calls is one. If index=2, there will be two recursive calls, one costing the same as fibo(1), the second costing the same as fibo(0). There is still an outside call, which initiates the first execution. So the total cost "n" for index=2 is n(2)=n(1)+n(0)+1. We will generalize this simple formula in Table 11-2 and prove that for i>0, n(i) = f(i)+f(i+1)+f(i-1)-1 and for i>=0, n(i) = 2*f(i+1)-1, where f(i) is the Fibonacci number itself with index i.

Table 11-2 Total Number of Calls for Recursive Fibonacci

i	f(i)	n(i)=n(i-1)+n(i-2)+1,i>1			
0	0			1	
1	1			1	
2	1	n(2)=n(1)+n(0)+1	=	3	
3	2	n(3)=n(2)+n(1)+1	=	5	
4	3	n(4)=f(3)+f(4)+f(5)-1	=	9	Formula F
5	5	n(5)=2*f(6)-1	=	15	
6	8	n(6)=2*f(7)-1	=	25	
7	13	n(7)=n(6)+n(5)+1	=	41	
8	21			67	
9	34			109	
10	55			177	

After analyzing the source of "fibo" in program "fibonacci1," we should see that n(i)=n(i-1)+n(i-2)+1 holds for i>1. In Table 11-2 we also use formula F, saying that n(i)=f(i)+f(i+1)+f(i-1)-1 for i>0. Equivalently, formula F defines that n(i)=2*f(i+1)-1. We have shown the values for the cost function "n" only for index values up to i=9, so we still have to prove its generality. This proof will be done by induction.

The base case for i=0, actually for up to 9, has been established. Hence we can assume inductively that F holds for i+1 as well. It follows that

```
n(i+1) = n(i)+n(i-1)+1 = f(i)+f(i+1)+f(i-1)-1 +
              f(i-1)+f(i)+f(i-2)-1 + 1
       = f(i+2)+f(i)+f(i+1)-1    concluding the proof
```

Example 11-11 Number of Calls

We have shown that F holds for all i>0. Note that in Example 11-11 the two summands -1 stem from applying formula F twice, once for n(i) and another time for n(i-1). The single summand +1, on the other hand, is part of the trivial formula n(i)=n(i-1)+n(i-2)+1.

We can now appreciate why the execution of "fibonacci1" takes so long -- 27.0 seconds contrasted with only 7.10 seconds for its purely iterative cousin. The computation of f(23) alone requires more than 50,000 recursive procedure calls. The next section demonstrates a recursive formula, the cost function of which goes beyond all imagination.

1.5 The Ackermann Function: a Top Recurser

With some functions it may not be clear why they ever were invented. But the "reason to live" for the Ackermann function, even if we could discover no other one, is based on its highly recursive behaviour. This makes it the perfect tool for testing whether a particular system can handle recursion and, if so, just how well it handles it. We can also measure precisely how long it takes to execute a recursive program as another test of a particular computer's capacity. All the Ackermann function seems to do is to recurse, so here we have *the* recursion test candidate.

In this section we demonstrate just how to apply this kind of test. First, we'll use Ada to write a program that will solve the Ackermann function. Then we'll run it on different machines. We adopt the following definition of Ackermann's Function from Aho and Ullman [1979]. Both arguments are nonnegative integers.

```
a(0,y) = 1
a(1,0) = 2
a(x,0) = x+2 for x>1
a(x,y) = a(a(x-1,y),y-1) for x>0,y>0
```

Example 11-12 Definition of Ackermann's Function

Admittedly, Ackermann's function is more knotty than the factorial or Fibonacci function, both of which have only one argument; but, at first glance, nothing strikes us as overly complex with the definition in Example 11-12. The Ada function "ackermann" in Example 11-13 can be derived immediately from the definition. For interesting applications of the Ackermann function see the "Berkeley Benchmarks," mentioned in Bailey [1983].

```
 4              1    | FUNCTION ackermann( x, y : integer ) RETURN integer IS
 5         12   2    | BEGIN -- ackermann,  assume x >= 0, y >= 0
 6              2    |  IF x = 0 THEN
 7    5         2  1 |   RETURN 1;
 8   10         2  2 |  ELSIF y = 0 THEN -- x > 0
 9   15         2  1 |   IF x = 1 THEN
10   19         2  2 |    RETURN 2;
11   24         2  3 |   ELSE
12   24         2  2 |    RETURN x + 2;
13   32         2  3 |   END IF;
14   32         2  2 |  ELSE -- x > 0, y > 0
15   32         2  1 |   RETURN ackermann( ackermann( x - 1, y ), y - 1 );
16   52         2  2 |  END IF;
17   52         2  1 | END ackermann;
```

Example 11-13 Recursive Solution of Ackermann in Ada

The surprise comes when we try to execute our correctly compiled "ackermann" function with the embedding main program on a 16-bit target system. The program fails early, at the computation of function value ackermann(3,4), but our Ada run time system is friendly. It emits a tough but clear message, "Halt at instruction 35 due to lack of stack space for the next procedure call" just before it aborts! The instruction so flagged is part of the expression for the last Return Statement; see line 15 in "ackermann."

Why would such a simple function, with only two scalar parameters and no other local variables, need excessive stack space? Our last section alluded to the answer: The Ackermann function must have an inordinate number of recursive calls, which consume all available stack space. Before we go on, we give the reader a clue to one of the exercises. Exercise 6 asks the reader to analyze the function "a(x,2)," abbreviated to "b(x)," where the first argument of "a" is a variable, and the second is the literal 2. Its equivalent "b" is a single-variable function. A look at the run time output provides a hint.

Now assume that we want to know precisely how many recursive calls are issued. This would tell us the capacity of our machine for dealing with recursion. We can trace this by augmenting "ackermann" with routines that will emit one -> symbol for each entry, and one <- symbol for each exit. The routine can also print the current relative recursion level and the maximum level reached at each entry and exit point.

"Ackermanntraced" in Example 11-14 is a Pascal program that performs this duty. To get more relevant data, we implement the program on a Vax, a machine with a virtual address space of several million bytes. And since we know we have substantially more memory available than we had on our 16-bit system, we make our arguments larger. In "ackermanntraced" we let "a" be computed for a(0,0) to a(5,5). For each function entry and exit one line of text is printed. The program starts executing fine, but aborts again. This time the

Pascal program exceeds the maximum disk space for the trace file.

The tail end of this file is given after the listing of program "ackermanntraced." We see that the deepest level of recursion almost reaches 10,000. This happens after emitting more than 75,000 lines of trace text, during calculation of a(3,5). Are we keeping in mind that the output number 9252 is *not* the total number of calls? That number would be much larger. It only means that 9252 calls are still open and active, having not yet performed a return, because they issued a directly recursive call.

Even though merely 36 different function values are computed, in this test run the number of output lines exceeds the default capacity of a large minicomputer. When one resource limit does not hit us, so will another one! This should give us a picture of the tremendously recursive nature of the Ackermann function. Who would have believed that it recurses so deeply? Because of this peculiarity, it is ideally suited to test and benchmark recursive calls, as described in Bailey [1983].

```
PROGRAM ackermanntraced( output );
 VAR
  i, j, linenum, temp, nest, maxnest : integer;
  ...
 FUNCTION a( x, y : integer ) : integer;
  BEGIN { a }
   trace( +1 );
   IF x = 0 THEN
    a := 1
   ELSE IF y = 0 THEN
    IF x = 1 THEN
     a := 2
    ELSE
     a := x + 2
    {end if}
   ELSE
    a := a( a( x - 1, y ), y - 1 );
   {end if}
   trace( -1 );
  END { a };

 BEGIN { ackermanntraced }
  nest := 0;
  linenum := 0;
  FOR i := 0 to 5 DO
   FOR j := 0 to 5 DO
    BEGIN
     maxnest := 0;
     temp := a( i, j );
     writeln( output,' a(',i:1,',',j:1,') = ',temp );
    END;
```

```
    {END FOR}
  {END FOR}
END { ackermanntraced }.
```

Example 11-14 Recursive Ackermann Solution with Traces, Pascal

```
75489     .     .     .     .     .  ->9251 9251
75490     .     .     .     .     .  ->9252 9252
```

Example 11-15 Run Time Traces of Ackermann, Pascal

11.6 Recursive Towers of Hanoi Iteratively

So far we have solved two recursive algorithms iteratively by explicitly simulating a stack. These examples, the factorial and fibonacci functions, are quite primitive. This time we'll choose a more difficult one—our old friend the Towers of Hanoi—to test how well we have understood the simulation process. Let's start out with a listing of the recursive problem. See Example 11-16.

```
1  IF disks > 0 THEN
2   BEGIN
3    tower( disks-1, start, buffer, final );
4    writeln( 'move disk ', disks, ' from ', start, ' to ', final );
5    tower( disks-1, buffer, final, start );
6   END;
7  {END IF}
```

Example 11-16 Recursive Formulation of Towers of Hanoi in Pascal

Lines 3 and 5 of the Pascal implementation contain the recursive calls, which we have to simulate. We see that both recursive calls are in fact embedded in a condition. This is required, in order to guarantee that eventually the sequence of recursive calls will terminate. Parameter "disks" decreases by one with each call, and therefore condition "disks > 0" will eventually fail.

We start out by defining a stack of records. Each element will hold the number of "disks;" the actual names of "start," "final," and "buffer;" and the integer encoded "return" address. A stack of such records is used in procedure "tower," in the Pascal program "nrtowersofhanoi" in Example 11-17. The type and variable declarations are arbitrarily made local to "tower." As a consequence the initialization code, lines 19 through 24, must also be embedded in the same subprogram body. Had we relocated the variable declarations into a global scope, which would have been misleading for a different reason, then we could initialize the "stack" outside of "tower" and start its statement body with label 1.

Lines 25 to 34 follow rule two of our four rules for transformation. The stack grows by one element, all actual parameters are moved into their reserved places, and the recursive call is simulated by branching to the head of the procedure. We repeat the same with the second recursive call. Once more, due to the initialization code, the HEAD of procedure "tower" is label 1, not the first statement after the BEGIN keyword.

When it is time for the "tower" to return, which is right before the final End Statement, we must inspect the stack to determine the destination. Label 1 should never be a candidate for the branch destination. It only serves as destination for the unconditional Gotos when simulating recursive calls. Label 4 will pop up exactly once when the stack is completely processed. However, a branch would be redundant, since label 4 directly follows. So we only need to consider labels 2 and 3.

To avoid illegal branches into an If Statement, we slightly modify the initial test condition. As a consequence, the critical label 2 is no longer located inside an an If Statement, and can, therefore, serve as the destination of all Gotos. See lines 47 and 52 in Example 11-17.

```
 1    program nrtowersofhanoi( output );
 2     type
 3      message       = packed array[ 1 .. 5 ] of char;
 4     procedure tower(
 5      disks          : integer;
 6      start, final, buffer : message );
 7     label 1, 2, 3, 4;
 8     type
 9      stackelem     =
10       record
11        disks        : integer;
12        start, final, buffer : message;
13        return      : integer;
14       end; {record}
15     var
16      top            : integer;
17      stack          : array[ 0 .. 10 ] of stackelem;
18     begin { tower } { assume disks >= 0 }
19      top := 0;
20      stack[ top ].disks  := disks;
21      stack[ top ].start  := start;
22      stack[ top ].final  := final;
23      stack[ top ].buffer := buffer;
24      stack[ top ].return := 4;
25  1: if stack[ top ].disks = 0 then
26       goto 3;
27      {end if} { stack[ top ].disks > 0 }
28      top := succ( top );
```

```
   stack[ top ].disks  := stack[ top - 1 ].disks - 1;
   stack[ top ].start  := stack[ top - 1 ].start;
   stack[ top ].final  := stack[ top - 1 ].buffer;
   stack[ top ].buffer := stack[ top - 1 ].final;
   stack[ top ].return := 2;
   goto 1; { recursive <CALL> }
2: writeln( ' move disk ', stack[ top ].disks, ' from ',
     stack[ top ].start, ' to ', stack[ top ].final );
   top := succ( top );
   stack[ top ].disks  := stack[ top - 1 ].disks - 1;
   stack[ top ].start  := stack[ top - 1 ].buffer;
   stack[ top ].final  := stack[ top - 1 ].final;
   stack[ top ].buffer := stack[ top - 1 ].start;
   stack[ top ].return := 3;
   goto 1; { recursive <CALL> }
3: if stack[ top ].return = 2 then
    begin
     top := pred( top );
     goto 2;
    end
   else if stack[ top ].return = 3 then
    begin
     top := pred( top );
     goto 3;
    end;
   {end if}
4:end { tower };
```

Example 11-17 Simulation of Recursive Towers of Hanoi

11.7 A Recursive Descent Compiler

Now we are sufficiently prepared to grasp one of the most beautiful techniques that uses recursion. The name of this technique is *recursive descent.* Understanding this method is our second major goal in this chapter. The technique is simple, effective, and has been in use ever since recursion was available in programming languages. Whenever the programming problem is expressed as a BNF grammar, the recursive descent technique is a suitable approach to the solution.

Expressed in one sentence, the core of the technique consists of transliterating the grammar of a language into a recursive program so that this program becomes a recognizer or parser for the language. Before we expand this vague and general definition into more complete and precise rules, we shall demonstrate its usefulness with an example. This sample is a grammar, which we first introduced in Section 1.3 and repeat it here for quick reference. See Example 11-18.

```
s  ::= t$
t  ::= AtB  | AB
```

Example 11-18 Grammar G1 for Language L1

We shall use Ada to write a recognizer for this very primitive language by applying the recursive descent technique. Recall that there is a distinguished nonterminal symbol, the start symbol, in this grammar called "s." The other nonterminal symbol is "t." The three terminal symbols are "A," "B," and "$," and the shortest string in L1 is "AB$." We can interpret the $ token as a string terminator, but this means already adding semantics to the language L1. Since this could confuse our issue at hand, we shall not dwell on this point any longer. We just consider the $ symbol a nice terminator, required for all incoming strings.

There are three possible errors. Either the number of consecutive "B" tokens at the string tail is shorter than the leading prefix of "A"s, or the correct number of "B" tokens is yet followed by some garbage text, different from the $ token. The third error is the absence of the leading, required "A" symbol. A message must be emitted in all three cases. Example 11-19 is the Ada source listing of a recognizer for L1. Does the reader spot grammar G1 in the procedures "s" and "t" of program "l1 recognizer?" As soon as we realize this correspondence, we have grasped the essence of Recursive Descent Parsing.

```
                   | WITH text_io; USE text_io;
                   | PROCEDURE l1 recognizer IS
             1     |  found    : character;
       11    1     |
       11    1     |  PROCEDURE scan( wanted : character ) IS
       11    2     |   BEGIN -- scan
             2     |    IF wanted /= found THEN
  5          2  1  |     put( " wanted: " );
  7          2  2  |     put_line( wanted );
 10          2  2  |    END IF;
 10          2  1  |    get( found );
 12          2  1  |   END scan;
 12          1     |
 12          1     |  PROCEDURE t IS
 14          2     |   BEGIN -- t
 14          2     |    scan( 'A' );
 20          2  1  |    IF found = 'A' THEN
 24          2  1  |     t;
 28          2  2  |    END IF;
```

```
28      2 1 |     scan( 'B' );
33      2 1 |   END t;
33      1   |
33      1   | PROCEDURE s IS
35      2   |   BEGIN -- s
35      2   |     get( found );
38      2 1 |     t;
42      2 1 |     IF found /= '$' THEN
46      2 1 |       put_line( " garbage after input" );
49      2 2 |     END IF;
49      2 1 |   END s;
49      1   |
49      1   | BEGIN -- l1 recognizer
51      1   |   s;
55      1 1 | END l1 recognizer;
```

Example 11-19 Parser for Language L1

The "l1 recognizer" includes a procedure named "s" that simulates the rule for nonterminal "s" of language L1. Additionally, there is a simple lexical analyzer, called "scan," that performs all input operations and two of the three types of error checking. Except for one initialization statement and the last error check, this comprises the whole program. Now, using this simple example as a guideline, we are ready to formulate the general rules for transliterating BNF grammars into recursive programs in more detail.

Rules for BNF Transliteration

1. Write a lexical analyzer that is sufficiently powerful to scan all terminal symbols. Typically a finite state automaton is sufficient.
2. For each nonterminal symbol defined in the BNF grammar write a recursive procedure. It is a beneficial convention to give the procedure the name of the nonterminal.
3. For each nonterminal referenced on the right-hand side of a production, call the corresponding procedure.
4. If a terminal symbol is required, call "scan" and verify that the currently scanned token is truly the expected one; if not, emit an error message.
5. If a rule indicates that a terminal symbol is allowed (but not required), then test whether the current token is this terminal. If so, scan the symbol and start this alternative; otherwise, try the next alternative. If no alternative can be found, this is an error.

6. We must be aware that the context-free grammars, serving as templates for top-down parsers, must adhere to certain restrictions. For example, left recursive productions cannot be used to construct such a recognizer directly. The reason is clear; transliteration of a left recursive rule would create a program that recurses infinitely. In section 1.3 we have shown how such productions are transformed into equivalent productions, being no longer left recursive.

We define only loosely the allowable form suited for recursive descent and for the sake of simplicity assume that our BNF grammars fit appropriately. The interested reader is referred to Hopcraft [1979], describing the Greibach Normal Form GNF. GNF is one form of grammar perfectly suited for the transliteration as explained above. Luckily, automata theory has shown us methods of how to transform any context-free BNF grammer into an equivalent one with more restrictive properties that renders the grammar more suitable for automatic processing.

Now let's focus our attention on grammar G4 from Section 1.3. In Example 11-20 we show a compiler for this grammar. A compiler is a parser augmented by semantic routines. The parser, in turn, can draw on the support of a lexical analyzer. All three form an integrated unit, shown in Example 11-20, that is easily comprehensible because the analyzed language L(G4) is so simple. The name of this compiler is "expressiong4." It reads input strings that adhere to the rules of grammar G4. The generated object is Polish Postfix. Note that terminal symbols "name" and "numericliteral" are represented on the output side only in the stylized forms of "I" and "N."

```
program expressiong4( input, output );
 var next : char;
 procedure getnext( var c : char );
  begin { getnext }
   repeat read( input, c ) until ( c <> ' ' ) or eoln( input );
  end { getnext };

 procedure emitobject( c : char );
  begin { emitobject }
   write( output, c, ' ' );
  end { emitobject };

 procedure mustbe( c : char );
  begin { mustbe }
   if next <> c then
    writeln( output, ' expected: ', c );
   {end if}
   getnext( next );
  end { mustbe };

{-------- L E X I C A L   R O U T I N E S ---------}
```

```
function isdigit( c : char ) : boolean;
 begin { isdigit }
  isdigit := c in [ '0' .. '9' ];
 end { isdigit };

function isletter( c : char ) : boolean;
 begin { isletter }
  isletter := c in [ 'a' .. 'z' ];
 end { isletter };

procedure numericliteral;
 begin { numericliteral }
  if isdigit( next ) then
   while isdigit( next ) do
    getnext( next )
   {end while}
  else
   begin
    writeln( output, 'digit expected' );
    getnext( next );
   end;
  {end if}
  emitobject( 'N' ); { <<semantics>> }
 end { numericliteral };

procedure stringliteral;
 begin { stringliteral } { next = "; may not contain " }
  getnext( next ); { skip '"' }
  while ( next <> '"' ) and not eoln( input ) do
   getnext( next );
  {end while} { next = '"' or eoln }
  if not eoln( input ) then
   getnext( next );
  {end if}
  emitobject( 'S' ); { <<semantics>> }
 end { stringliteral };

procedure name;
 begin { name }
  { assume next is letter }
  while isdigit( next ) or isletter( next ) do
   getnext( next ); { skip letter or digit }
  {end while}
  emitobject( 'I' ); { <<semantics>> }
 end { name };

{------- P A R S I N G   R O U T I N E S --------}
```

```

    procedure expression; forward;

    procedure primary;
     begin { primary }
      if next = '(' then
       begin
        getnext( next );
        expression;
        mustbe( ')' );
       end
      else if isdigit( next ) then
       numericliteral
      else if isletter( next ) then
       name
      else if next = '"' then
       stringliteral
      else
       begin
        writeln( output, ' operand expected' );
        getnext( next );
       end;
      {end if}
     end { primary };

    procedure factor;
     begin { factor }
      primary;
      if next = '^' then
       begin
         getnext( next ); { skip '^' }
         primary;
         emitobject( '^' ); { <<semantics>> }
        end;
      {end if} { next <> ^ }
     end { factor };

     procedure term;
      var operator : char;
      begin { term }
       factor;
       while ( next = '*' ) or ( next = '/' ) do
        begin
         operator := next;
         getnext( next ); { skip '*' or '/' }
         factor;
         emitobject( operator ); { <<semantics>> }
        end;
```

```
     {end while} { next <> '*' and next <> '/' }
    end { term };

   procedure simpleexpression;
    var
     unaryop,
     operator : char;
    begin { simpleexpression }
     if ( next = '+' ) or ( next = '-' ) then
      begin
       unaryop := next;
       getnext( next ); { skip '+' or '-' }
      end
     else
      unaryop := ' ';
     {end if}
     term;
     if unaryop = '-' then
      emitobject( '%' ); { <<semantics>> }
     {end if}
     while ( next = '+' ) or ( next = '-' ) or ( next = '&' ) do
      begin
       operator := next;
       getnext( next ); { skip '+' or '-' or '&' }
       term;
       emitobject( operator ); { <<semantics>> }
      end;
     {end while} { next <> '+' and next <> '-' and next <> '&' }
    end { simpleexpression };

   procedure relation;
    var operator    : char;
    begin { relation }
     simpleexpression;
     if ( next = '<' ) or ( next = '=' ) or ( next = '>' ) then
      begin
       operator := next;
       getnext( next ); { skip '>' or '=' or '<' }
       simpleexpression;
       emitobject( operator ); { <<semantics>> }
      end;
     {end if} { next <> '<' and next <> '=' and next <> '>' }
    end { relation };

   procedure expression; { announced forward }
    var operator : char;
    begin { expression }
     relation;
```

```
    while ( next = 'A' ) or ( next = 'O' ) or ( next = 'X' ) do
     begin { 'A' for and, 'O' for or, 'X' for XOR }
      operator := next; { operator 'A', 'O', or 'X' }
      getnext( next ); { skip 'AND' or 'OR' or 'XOR' }
      relation;
      emitobject( operator ); { <<semantics>> }
     end;
    {end while} { next <> 'A' and next <> 'O' and next <> 'X' }
   end { expression };

  begin { expressiong4 }
   getnext( next );
   expression;
  end { expressiong4 }.
```

Example 11-20 Compiler for Expression E4

Pascal program "expressiong4" in Example 11-20 defines one recursive procedure for each nonterminal symbol of grammar g4 as required by our "Rules for BNF Transliteration." Since these procedures are called from only one single procedure body, it is possible to relocate the definition of the called subprograms from the outermost level into the calling scope. This comment is meant as a constructive suggestion for readers who wish to modify this compiler. We turn our attention next to mutual recursion, a topic for which we had presented a simplistic solution earlier.

1.8 Mutual Recursion, A General Solution

Chapter 9 has shown a special method for mutual recursion via the explicit forward declaration. This method is convenient, clean, and leaves the source quite readable. There exists, however, a more general solution to the mutual recursion problem that is applicable for use even with restricted compilers. A compiler is classified as restricted in this context if it does not offer an explicit Forward declaration. Some Algol-60 and Pascal compilers do, in fact, suffer from this restriction. Flanders [1984] published a sketchy, but quite interesting outline of a solution, which is quite related to one described much earlier by Atkins [1973]. (See also Chapter 9.) In the following we show Flander's solution and complement the theory by a practical example using Ada.

We assume that two procedures "a" and "b" are mutually recursive. Furthermore, we assume both procedures must be declared in the same lexical level, since the enclosing scope wishes to call either of the two procedures as well. First, in Example 11-21, we sketch a solution in Pascal, using forward procedure declarations. Then we present the skeleton of a general solution.

```
PROCEDURE b; FORWARD;
PROCEDURE a;
  <declarations_a>
 BEGIN { a }
  <slist_a1>
  a;
  <slist_a2>
  b;
  <slist_a3>
 END { a };
PROCEDURE b;
  <declarations_b>
 BEGIN { b }
  <slist_b1>
  a;
  <slist_b2>
  b;
  <slist_b3>
 END { b };

  BEGIN { enclosing scope }
  a;
  b;
 END;
```

Example 11-21 Mutually Recursive Procedure Calls Using Forward

Procedure "ab" in Example 11-22 performs the same function as "a" and "b" in Example 11-21 do jointly, but "ab" must be set up appropriately via the global variable "control." Also "ab" includes the union of the declarations found in "a" and "b." Hopefully, all names local to "a" and "b" are unique; if not, the duplicate must be renamed and all references in the associated statement section must be changed.

```
TYPE control_type = ( do_a, do_b );
VAR  control      : control_type;
PROCEDURE ab;
  <declarations_a>
  <declarations_b>
  BEGIN { ab }
   CASE control OF
    do_a:
     BEGIN
      <slist_a1>
      control := do_a; ab;
      <slist_a2>
      control := do_b; ab;
```

```
      <slist_a3>
    END;
  do_b:
    BEGIN
      <slist_b1>
      control := do_a; ab;
      <slist_b2>
      control := do_b; ab;
      <slist_b3>
    END;
  END; {CASE}
END; { ab }
  BEGIN { enclosing scope }
    control := do_a; ab;
    control := do_b; ab;
END;
```

Example 11-22 Mutually Recursive Procedures, Using "Super Procedure"

The idea in Flanders's solution is to group all mutual recursors together; all functions of the same return type that are mutually recursive will be mapped into one superfunction. Similarly, all parameter-compatible procedures that are mutually recursive are grouped into one superprocedure. Such superprocedures contain the union of all declarations and all statement lists of the effected procedures. The key idea here is to group the statement lists into a selective statement, conveniently a Case Statement, and to add a control variable. It is the purpose of the control variable to determine which of a variety of selections will be taken. Before each Call Statement, therefore, we must add an Assignment Statement that biases the control variable correctly. The disadvantage of the general scheme is obvious: the source becomes less readable, since all declarations, statements, and additional control are lumped into one subprogram.

1.9 Summary

With this chapter we conclude the important subject of procedure calls. Recursion is only one aspect of procedure calls, which we have presented here in sufficient detail that the reader should have a feeling for its implementation on a general-purpose computer. Our second goal was to show how recursive descent can be used to produce a parser for a context-free language.

After covering such a high level construct, we might have the necessary tolerance to analyze the low level Goto Statement next. Indeed, the Goto Statement covered in Chapter 12 presents a mechanism that is as low level as machine language programming.

11.10 Exercises

1. Write a recursive descent parser for the language EL1, defined by the following grammar EG1.

```
s ::= AsB | AB
```

2. Why is it more difficult to write a recognizer for EL1 than for L1, as shown in the text?

3. Write a recursive definition for the function "power2." Power2 has one nonnegative argument of type integer, which is interpreted as the exponent. The base is 2. Power2(x) equals 2**x.

4. Write a program "recursive_power2" that implements "power2" in Exercise 3. Ensure that integer overflow exceptions are caught gracefully by the program. The type of the function value returned by "recursive_power2" is integer.

5. Write a program "non_recursive_power2" that implements function "power2" without using recursion of the host language. Simulate recursion via an explicitly managed stack.

6. What single-variable function is the simplified Ackermann function "a(x,2)?"

7. In the Ada and Pascal programs "expression_g4," the emitted object contains a letter "I" for every numeric integer in the source, and the letter "N" for every source identifier. Modify the Pascal program "expression_g4" so that terminals are output in the full form. The modified program should emit the name and the numeric integer literally.

8. In both the Ada and the Pascal versions of "expression_g4," there is a procedure called "simple_expression," which permits multiple binary operators "+" in the analyzed source program. Are these adding operators left associative or right associative?

9. Change the Pascal procedure "simple_expression" in "expression_g4" so that the associativity of the binary adding operator is reversed.

10. The Flanders solution increases the size of the superprocedure. This defeats one of the purposes of having separate logical modules: the source program becomes less readable. Propose a "second-generation" variation of the original mutually recursive problem that does not suffer from this quality degradation.

11. The goal of this exercise is to write an Ada program that plots Hilbert Curves. Before we explain Hilbert Curves, we address a possible solution to the mechanics of line drawing even when we have no plotter available.

Plotting on a Line Printer

The "hilbert" program should be written in such a way that it does not matter whether the output goes to a pen plotter or to another hardware device, such as a line printer. A line printer can, of course, only approximate the fine granularity of output that a plotter or laser printer can offer. The program should call "plot" with arguments that identify the new target position of the pen. "Plot" is then expected to draw a straight line from the current pen position, identified by "oldx" and "oldy," to the new position, identified by "newx" and "newy."

In this exercise we simulate a sheet of paper by a square matrix of 33 by 33 characters, named "screen." Once the matrix is filled with valid, printable characters, we output the complete data structure on the line printer. Consequently, the paper consists of only 33**2=1089 distinguishable dots, which in the graphics world are called *pixels*. This is a very coarse granularity when compared with a dot matrix printer or with a graphics terminal. Such terminals can have over a million pixels per screen.

Plotting Horizontal and Vertical Lines

Fascinating and confusing as they may look, Hilbert Curves consist only of horizontal and vertical line segments of the same unit length. Sometimes two or more line segments follow one another in the same direction, thus creating the impression of a longer line. We can still consider this a concatenation of several unit length segments. What simplifies matters is that there are no diagonals. So simulating a plot via a square matrix is particularly easy. A horizontal line is simulated by asterisks in a row of the matrix, while a vertical line is approximated by asterisks in the same column. Assuming that the "start" and "final" indices are known, a For Statement can accomplish this, as the following shows in Ada.

```
-- to draw a horizontal line
 FOR column IN start .. final LOOP
  screen( fixed_line, column ) := '*';
 END LOOP;

-- to draw a vertical line
 FOR line IN start .. final LOOP
  screen( line, fixed_column ) := '*';
 END LOOP;
```

Hilbert Curves

Hilbert Curves are aesthetic graphic patterns that can become incredibly complicated. They come in different degrees of complexity, but common to all is that they are formed by bending a straight line in right angles. The simplest, degenerate form of Hilbert Curve consists of one single dot, which can be viewed as a line of zero length. There is not much bending we can do with this. This is called a Hilbert Curve of degree 0, or H(0) more shortly. The next, more complicated Hilbert Curve, is a square with one side removed. We call this a Hilbert Curve of first degree or an H(1) curve.

In their most general form, Hilbert Curves of degree (n+1) are formed from H(n) curves by adding three unit length line segments to three H(n) curves of the fitting rotation. We don't need to worry about the complexity of higher degree Hilbert Curves; we just need to figure out a systematic way of generating them, and then express this algorithm in a program. Before we clarify how this is done, we need to emphasize that it is our goal to have these single-line curves be drawn by a plotter. So we must keep the sense of direction for the pen movement when composing complex Hilbert Curves.

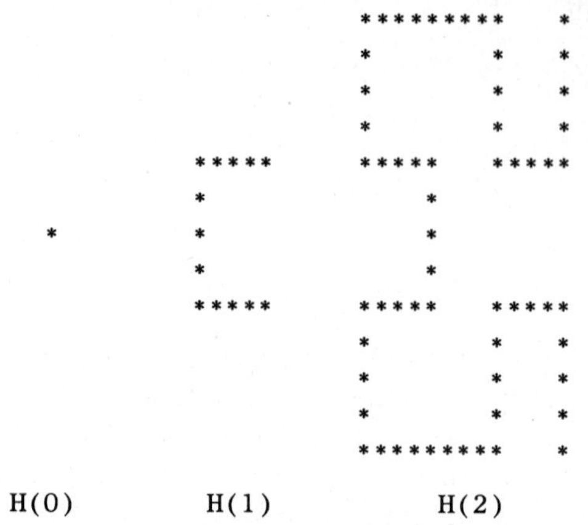

Figure 11-1 Hilbert Curves of Degree 0..2

All nontrivial Hilbert Curves come in four different orientations. The curve proper is the same, but there are four choices in a rectangular coordinate system for the direction of the curve's opening. This is shown in Figure 11-2 with H(1) curves. Also we have given each of the curves a convenient name.

```
*****    *****    *****    *   *
*        *   *        *    *   *
*        *   *        *    *   *
*        *   *        *    *   *
*****    *   *    *****    *****

  A        B        C        D
```

Figure 11-2   Four Basic Patterns of Hilbert Curves

Algorithm for Hilbert Curve Generation

Let us call Hilbert Curves that open to the right, like curve "A" in Figure 11-2, curves of type "a." All Hilbert Curves of degree (n+1) with n>0 can be constructed from simpler ones of degree (n). Then we can compose curve "a" as follows: get one building block "d" of the next lower degree, move the pen one unit length to the left, attach one "a" building block of the next lower degree, and move the pen one unit down. Now attach one more basic building block of type "a," move the pen one unit to the right, and finally append one "b" type curve. In our program we replace left and right movements by +x and -x, while up and down movements are expressed in +y and -y changes. An Ada procedure for H(n) of type "a" is listed as follows.

```
PROCEDURE a( degree : integer ) IS
  BEGIN -- a
  IF degree > 0 THEN
    d( degree - 1 ); newx := newx - unit; plot;
    a( degree - 1 ); newy := newy - unit; plot;
    a( degree - 1 ); newx := newx + unit; plot;
    b( degree - 1 );
  END IF;
  END a;
```

The other three types of curves are constructed analogously. Now we have sufficient material to write a program that prints Hilbert curves of any degree. We need to keep a pragmatic consideration in mind. Since we wish to plot more and more complex curves, we run out of space in our matrix to accommodate larger curves with the same unit length. To avoid this problem, we can keep the same matrix of pixels, and for each increased degree, we can cut the unit length in half. This approach should be used in the Hilbert plot exercise.

Now we are prepared to write an Ada program that plots Hilbert Curves of degrees up to three. A short, interesting treatment of Hilbert Curves can also be found in Wirth [1976].

12. The goal of this exercise is to draw *Sierpinski Curves,* and the program is to be written in Ada or Pascal. Sierpinski Curves are slightly more complex and interesting than Hilbert Curves, as shown in Figure 11-3 for the simplest kind. When we compare the S(1) curve with the next more complicated Sierpinski curve S(2), shown in Figure 11-4, we might feel tempted to single out S(1) as the basic building block for the recursive pattern. After all, don't we recognize the same pattern repeatedly?

    Unfortunately, this will not lead us to an algorithm for the construction of Sierpinski Curves of all degrees. We have to realize that Sierpinski Curves are closed. So the recursive pattern we are after must consist of only part of S(1), with explicit instructions for connecting the partial curve to form a closed one. Since S(1) is symmetrical in two dimensions, a good starting point for finding the recursive pattern is to take part of one-fourth of the curve. Indeed this leads to a correct solution, if we start with the three-line parts, named A, B, C, and D.

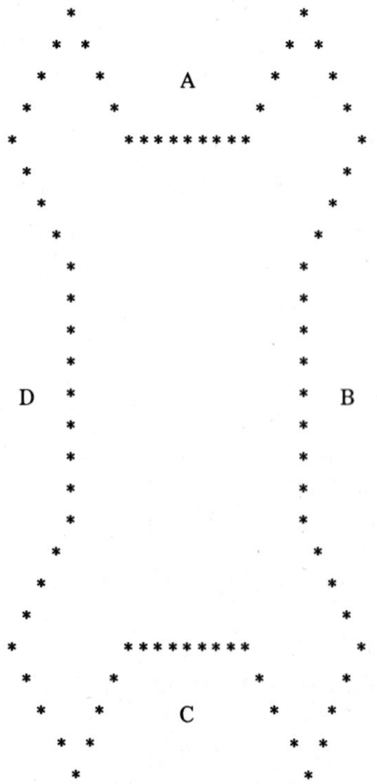

Figure 11-3 Sierpinski Curve of Degree 1,S(1)

To construct a general curve S(n) of degree n, we call the recursive procedures for "a," "b," "c," and "d." After each call, we connect the partial curve with the diagonal line in the extreme corner, so that in the end S(n) is closed.

Each of the recursive procedures "a" through "d," in turn, must also plot the connections of partial curves. From the top portion of S(2), constructed by a call to "a," we see that "a" starts out by calling itself recursively with the next lower degree, and then draws a diagonal line to the lower right. Then "b" is called, a horizontal line is plotted to the right, and "d" is called. The output of "d" is connected with a diagonal line segment, going to the top right, and finally "a" is called again.

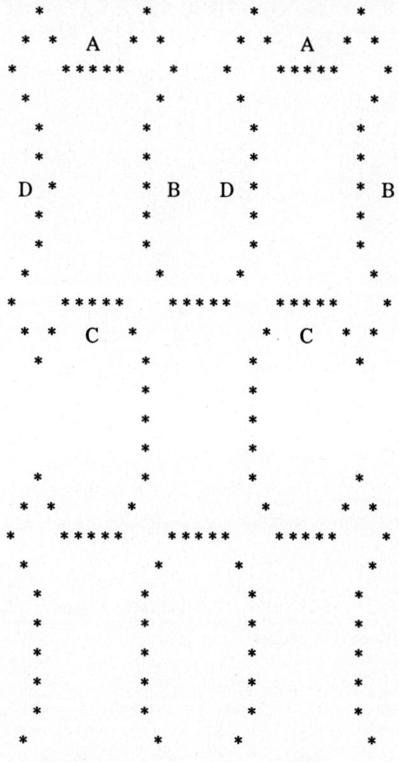

Figure 11-4 Sierpinski Curve of Degree 2,S(2)

The skeleton for procedure "a" is listed as follows. Except for three 90-degree rotations, the other procedures work identically.

```
PROCEDURE a( degree : integer ) IS
 BEGIN -- a
  IF degree > 0 THEN
    a( degree - 1 ); newx := newx + unit; newy := newy - unit; plot;
    b( degree - 1 ); newx := newx + 2*unit; plot;
    d( degree - 1 ); newx := newx + unit; newy := newx + unit; plot;
    a( degree - 1 );
  END IF;
 END a;
```

13. Write the function "add" that returns the sum of its two arguments. "Add" uses only the predecessor and successor functions, relational tests, and, since it is recursive, "add" itself. Hint: The constraints are a strong hint regarding the solution.

12

Goto Statements

There are doubtless some readers who are convinced
that abolition of GO TO statements is merely a fad,
and they may see this title and think,
"Aha! Knuth is rehabilitating the GO TO statement,
and we can go back to our old ways of programming again."

Donald E. Knuth
Structured Programming with GO TO Statements

At first glance Goto Statements seem to have survived without a scratch the long and bitter war they once inflamed. They are definitely still with us and their syntax remains essentially unaltered. A more careful second look at trends in software engineering and methodology will show us, however, that this controversy literally changed the world of programming. It has served as a catalyst in purifying programmers from a shady writing style known as "Spaghetti code."

In this chapter we'd like to present a short recount of this evolution, which can be partly credited to Goto Statements. We will also explain their (with the exception of Fortran) relatively simple syntax. The Exit Statement and the Fortran Computed Goto Statement are also covered.

12.1 The Goto Evolution

In the beginning Goto Statements were used uninhibitedly. Labels and their associated Gotos abounded, creating unreadable code that only sometimes did what it was intended to do. Spaghetti code is the unflattering term used for this style of code. Programs of this era were still relatively small due to restricted computer memories and address ranges, so the software was not overly complex.

With the advent of larger computers, the demand for more complex software made the Goto Statement as it was being used look like the culprit in the crime of unreadable, unmaintainable programs. Thus the pendulum swung and we experienced the antithesis in the form of a "software crisis." A demand for reducing the use of, or even abolishing the Goto Statement was strongly voiced in the vain hope of thereby solving the crisis.

Programming languages such as Modula-2 were proposed that did not even provide a Goto Statement. Goto-free programs, it was hoped, would be the answer. Naturally, the elimination of Goto Statements alone could not solve the crisis anymore than a sickness can be cured by merely eradicating its symptoms. But the occasionally hefty debate created a healthy stimulus. Dijkstra is rumored to have received quite a stack of hate mail, Knuth [1974], after publishing his well-known, though not original, complaint about Goto Statements, Dijkstra [1968]. And it was this atmosphere of debate that finally brought us to the synthesis, nicely epitomized by Knuth's lengthy article about Goto Statements and structured programming. With this succinct description of the problem, it was finally documented that the harmless little Goto never was the culprit. And it was understood that what was really needed was a new way of designing programs.

This new way of designing programs brought about a new technique, all too often named by the catchy phrase "structured programming," which eliminates the need for most Goto Statements. In this text we avoid the term *structured programming,* which should not be misconstrued to mean that we believe the subject warrants no mention. Quite the contrary, the subject is of extreme importance in the context of programming languages, but the phrase has been overused so much that it no longer carries the same meaning. We substitute the term *readable programs* in its stead and will probably thereby involuntarily contribute to the overuse of this phrase.

12.2 Goto Statement Syntax

During program execution the Goto Statement transfers control to the label that follows the GOTO keyword. This argument labels one of the statements in the reach of the Goto Statement, and represents a simple way of altering the straight execution sequence. The syntax usually looks somewhat like this:

```
GOTO argument
```

One might wonder how there can be any discussion about so simple a statement. We would be surprised, however, if we were to list all the possible variations! For example, is the keyword reserved? Can it be spelled GO TO? Is the label argument numeric, or must it be an identifier? Does the scope of the label argument span surrounding blocks; in other words, can the Goto Statement branch to outside scopes? Is the transfer of control permitted into structured statements such as If or Case Statements?

As we shall see, each language has its own unique combination of answers to these questions. We consider it worthwhile therefore to discuss the Goto Statement at length.

Ada Goto Statements

In Ada GOTO is a reserved keyword; only one spelling is permitted. The referenced label must be declared in the same scope as the Goto Statement, but it may be forward referenced. Contrary to Pascal or PL/I, as we shall see, Ada does not allow branching outside of a subprogram with a Goto Statement.

Labels are defined implicitly in Ada by appearing in matching pairs of << and >> symbols. These symbols embrace an identifier, which is the label name. Such a label name can be "gone to" via a Goto Statement but subject to some restrictions. The applicable restrictions effectively disallow two kinds of control transfer: branching into a structured statement from the outside, and branching outside of the current subprogram scope. We must be careful in Ada not to confuse a label identifier with a Loop Statement name, the syntax for which is identical to the label syntax in other languages. A statement name is only the name of some Ada Loop (or Declare) Statement, and it may not be referenced in a Goto Statement. It may be used advantageously in an Exit Statement to terminate the named loop.

Since there is no explicit type attribute for labels or Loop Statement names, it is not possible to declare an object of any such type. Hence a label cannot be passed as a parameter. The Ada source programs in Examples 12-1, 12-2, and 12-3 show correct and erroneous Goto and related statements.

```
1                  |WITH text_io; USE text_io;
2                  |PROCEDURE good_gotos IS
3           1      | i : integer;
4       11  1      |BEGIN--good_gotos
5           1      | i := 12;
6    4      1   1  | GOTO outside1;
7    5      1   1  | i := i + 1;
8   10      1   1  |<<outside1>>
9   10      1   1  | IF i = 12 THEN
10  14      1   1  |  put_line( " Good Branch over increment" );
11  17      1   2  |  loop_name:
12  17      1   2  |  LOOP
13  17      1   2  |   EXIT loop_name;
14  18      1   3  |  END LOOP loop_name;
15  19      1   2  | ELSE
16  19      1   1  |  put_line( " Bad. Branch not taken." );
17  23      1   2  |  GOTO outside2;
18  24      1   2  | END IF;
19  24      1   1  |<<outside2>>
20  24      1   1  | NULL;--needed here, END is no statement
21  24      1   1  |END good_gotos;
```

Example 12-1 Good Ada Goto Statements

The Ada sample program "good_gotos" in Example 12-1 demonstrates two correct label declarations, one good loop name, and two legal Goto Statements. Note that both Goto Statements are forward branches, thus exposing one of the few instances in Ada where a name may be referenced textually before its declaration has been encountered.

The Null Statement labeled by "<<outside2>>" is necessary, because the END alone would not represent an Ada statement, and hence cannot be labeled. In contrast, see the "bad_gotos" in Example 12-2. Also, see line 55 in the Pascal program "nrtowersofhanoi" in Example 11-17.

Exit Statements as exhibited on line 13 in Example 12-1 are a hidden form of Goto Statement, and in languages that do not provide this facility the same idea must be expressed by an explicit Goto Statement. The semantics of an Ada Exit Statement is to terminate the embedding loop. A named Exit Statement terminates the identified loop, including all loops nested therein.

```
                  |WITH text_io; USE text_io;
                  |PROCEDURE bad_gotos IS
           1      | i : integer;
      11   1      |BEGIN--bad_gotos
           1      | GOTO inside1;
===== ERROR =====> |      ^ Illegal Branch Destination
   2       1   1  | i := 12;
```

```
 7    5         1  1 | IF i = 12 THEN
 8    9         1  1 |  <<inside1>>
 9    9         1  2 |  i := 144;
10   12         1  2 | loop_name:
11   12         1  2 |  LOOP
12   12         1  2 |   EXIT loop_name;
13   13         1  3 |  END LOOP;
===== ERROR =====> |              ^ Exp ending name: LOOP_NAME.  => 5
14   14         1  2 |  GOTO loop_name;
===== ERROR =====> |           ^ Illegal Branch Destination  => 13
15   15         1  2 | ELSE
16   15         1  1 |  <<inside2>>
17   16         1  2 |  i := i ** 3;
18   21         1  2 | END IF;
19   21         1  1 | GOTO inside2;
===== ERROR =====> |         ^ Illegal Branch Destination  => 15
20   21         1  1 | <<outside>>
===== ERROR =====> |              ^ Statement expected.  => 19
21   22         1  1 |END bad_gotos;
```

Example 12-2 Erroneous Ada Goto Statements

All three Goto Statements are wrong in the above Ada procedure "bad_gotos" in Example 12-2. The ones on lines 5 and 19 reference labels that are defined inside a structured statement, which has a different nesting level than the referencing Goto. The third Goto Statement does not even reference a label in the first place; it misinterprets a loop name as a label, which is clearly illegal.

Observe also that the last label "<<outside>>" identifies no Ada statement. The procedure tail "END bad_gotos;" does not manifest a statement, hence the last error message.

```
                      |WITH text_io; USE text_io;
                      |PROCEDURE goto_demo IS
              1       | recursion_level : integer;
       11     1       |
       11     1       | PROCEDURE rec IS
              2       | BEGIN--rec
              2       |  IF recursion_level = 0 THEN
  5           2   1   |   GOTO escape;
=====================> |        ^ Illegal branch out of Subprogram
  6           2   2   |  ELSE
  6           2   1   |   recursion_level := recursion_level - 1;
 12           2   2   |   rec;
 16           2   2   |  END IF;
 16           2   1   | END rec;
 16           1       |
 16           1       |BEGIN--goto_demo
 18           1       | recursion_level := 12;
 22           1   1   | rec;
 25           1   1   | put_line( " This should never come out" );
 28           1   1   |<<escape>>
 28           1   1   | put_line( " This is the right place." );
 31           1   1   |END goto_demo;
```

Example 12-3 More Erroneous Ada Goto Statements

The Goto Statement in procedure "rec" in Example 12-3 is illegal since the destination label "<<escape>>" is defined in a surrounding scope. Ada disallows such long distance branches, since they make the reading of programs more difficult. As we shall see in Example 12-8, such Gotos are perfectly legal in Pascal.

If the facility is still needed for handling certain error conditions, Ada provides exceptions. When exceptions are declared and raised, they cause the user-defined exception handlers to take over, even if these are defined within enclosing scopes. We observe here some commonality between exception handlers and Goto Statements.

Fortran Goto Statements

Fortran has three related kinds of Goto Statements: the *unconditional,* the *computed,* and the *assigned Goto.* All labels are numeric in Fortran. Statement labels are defined in columns one through six. They do not need to be in any particular order, but for the sake of tracing or "reading" it is, of course, helpful to follow some kind of strategy, such as an increasing sequence of label numbers.

The syntax for Fortran Gotos is given in Example 12-4.

```
fortran_goto          ::= unconditional_goto
                        | computed_goto
                        | assigned_goto

unconditional_goto    ::= GO TO label

computed_goto         ::= GO TO ( label { , label } ) [,] expression

assigned_goto         ::= GO TO name [ [,] ( label { , label } ) ]

label                 ::= nonzero_numeric_literal
```

Example 12-4 Fortran Goto Statement Grammar

Fortran's Unconditional Goto

In Fortran, blanks are always insignificant except inside character string literals, so the question of the spelling for GOTO really does not come up. Phrased positively, the GOTO keyword may be spelled GO TO or by any other permutation of blanks and the four letters GOTO. A label must identify a statement in the same compilation unit. Since there is no nesting of subprograms, this rule implies that jumps into other compilation units are not allowed.

Fortran's Computed Goto

The Computed Goto is perhaps Fortran's closest analogue to a proper Case Statement, as we shall see in Section 12.4. The integer type expression after the parenthesized list of statement labels selects one of the labels as the target for subsequent execution. At least one label must be given in parentheses. The enclosed labels are numbered from 1 to n, n>=1, and quasi indexed 1..n from left to right. If the integer expression yields a value in that range, the label so selected defines the statement that is to be executed next. Note that the labels in the list need not be distinct.

In Example 12-5 we list the sample Fortran program "COMPTD" to demonstrate the correct use of a Computed Goto Statement. Its closeness with the Case Statement is shown in Section 12.4.

```
      PROGRAM COMPTD
       INTEGER I
       I = 3
       GO TO ( 10, 20, 30, 40 ) i
10     WRITE( 6, * ) " wrong label reached"
20     WRITE( 6, * ) " wrong label reached"
30     WRITE( 6, * ) " Lucky, it worked"
       GO TO 50
40     WRITE( 6, * ) " wrong label reached"
50    END
```

Example 12-5 Sample Fortran Computed Goto Statement

Should the integer expression after the label list generate a value outside the range 1..n, then the effect of the Computed Goto will be that of a Continue Statement.

Fortran's Assigned Goto

The purpose of the Assigned Goto Statement is a bit opaque. It requires an integer type variable to be set via an Assign Statement. This statement assigns an ADDRESS to the integer variable by using a numeric Fortran statement label. This effect is quite different from assigning an integer VALUE to a variable. The notion of "code address" must be conveyed to the language compiler, hence the Assign Statement. The parenthesized list of labels is optional. All included labels must refer to statements in that compilation unit. The labels need not be unique. If a list of labels is given, then the integer variable must be associated with one of the listed labels at the time the Goto Statement is executed.

In Examples 12-6 and 12-7 we show one correct and one erroneous use of Assigned Goto Statements. The second program is wrong, even though the spelling of the Assigned Goto Statement has not changed at all. The only change is the (now illegal) value of the integer variable LAB. In fact this wrong program executed an infinite loop on the host hardware used.

```
      PROGRAM ASSGND
       INTEGER LAB
       GOTO 20
10     WRITE( 6, * ) ' Wrong. At label 10 '
20     ASSIGN 40 TO LAB
30     GOTO LAB, ( 10, 20, 30, 40 )
40     WRITE( 6, * ) " Lucky, it worked"
50    END
```

Example 12-6 Good Assigned Goto Statement

```
      PROGRAM WRONG
       INTEGER LAB
       GOTO 20
10     WRITE( 6, * ) ' Wrong. At label 10 '
20     LAB = 40
C----- ERROR to assign 40, This is no label
30     GOTO LAB, ( 10, 20, 30, 40 )
40     WRITE( 6, * ) " Lucky, it worked"
50    END
```

Example 12-7 Wrong Assigned Goto Statement

The Fortran program “WRONG” in Example 12-7 produces no compile time error message. This should not lead the reader to conclude that “WRONG” is therefore a correct program. When the Assigned Goto Statement is executed, the integer variable “LAB” is expected to hold the value of one of the labels 10, 20, 30, or 40. We know that such an association can be accomplished in Fortran via the Assign Statement. No such statement has been executed, however, at the moment of reaching the Goto Statement.

To fool the reader and maybe the Fortran compiler, the variable “LAB” has been assigned an integer constant; to make the deceit even more devious, the value of this constant is identical to that of one of the statement labels. But, as announced already, at execution time the error surfaces.

Pascal Goto Statements

Pascal's labels are numeric and may be at most four digits long. These numeric values must be announced or declared formally via a label declaration. GOTO is a reserved keyword in Pascal with only one spelling. A Goto Statement may reference labels in surrounding lexical levels, but the target of a Goto may not be nested in a structured statement at a level different from the one of the Goto Statement. This rule is comparable to the Ada restriction.

“A Goto Statement is a simple statement indicating that further processing should continue at another part of the program text.“ So starts the description of the Goto Statement in Jensen and Wirth [1978] on page 31. But what an understatement! Pascal's rules are much more permissive than Ada's. While the Ada compiler has to reject the nonlocal branch “GOTO escape” in the erroneous Ada program “goto_demo” in Example 12-3, the Pascal compiler must grant permission. See the Pascal program “gotodemo” in Example 12-8, line 10.

We have chosen this example to show that a simple Goto Statement may in fact be quite complex as far as code generation is concerned. The Pascal compiler must emit skillful instructions to clear the run time stack of all recursive invocations of the directly recursive procedure “rec.” Only then can the branch to “1” be taken. Also note the numeric labels in Pascal, which must be awkwardly declared. Malicious souls have spread the rumor that Niklaus Wirth intentionally created numeric labels in such an ugly way to discourage programmers from overusing them. More likely this is only programmers' folklore, but it makes the point that the numeric label possesses no documentary value that a label identifier could convey.

In addition to being targets of Gotos, the labels can and should be valuable tools for documenting the meaning of logical paragraphs in a program. Pascal has in this case not made use of this aid to readability. However, as Conway, Gries, and Zimmerman [1976] have pointed out, programmers can still get some documentary use even from numeric labels. They have chosen, for example, to identify loop exits with numeric labels greater than 9000, two-digit labels for another purpose, and so on. This scheme, of course, poses the problems that the reader and the writer of the program must agree about the policy of identifying the labels and that the compiler cannot verify such private policies. But with the use of this scheme we can restore some documentary value to numeric labels. Also some ordering of labels by numeric value can be beneficial in quickly finding referenced pieces of source in a large source listing.

Gotos for loop exits are quite normal, particularly for so-called “n and a half” loops, or loops that terminate based on some criterion in the loop middle. Ada and Modula-2 supply a special-purpose statement for Gotos that branch out of the loop to the statement immediately following. This is the Exit Statement we saw earlier in Example 12-2.

```
 1   1  0  0         PROGRAM gotodemo( output );
 2   2  0  0          LABEL
                       1;
 3   4  0  0          VAR
                       recursionlevel : integer;

 4   7  0  0          PROCEDURE rec;
 5   8  1  0           BEGIN { rec }
 5   9  1  1            IF recursionlevel = 0 THEN
 6  10  1  1             GOTO 1
                        ELSE
 7  12  1  1             BEGIN
 7  13  1  2              recursionlevel := pred( recursionlevel );
 8  14  1  2              rec;
 9  15  1  2             END;
11  16  1  1            {END IF}
                       END; { rec }

12  19  0  0          BEGIN { gotodemo }
12  20  0  1           recursionlevel := 12;
13  21  0  1           rec;
```

```
14   22  0  1          writeln( output, ' This should never come out' );
15   23  0  1        1:writeln( output, ' This is the right place.' );
16   24  0  1          END { gotodemo }.
```

Example 12-8 Good Pascal Goto Statements

PL/I Goto Statement

The PL/I keyword GOTO is not reserved and may be spelled as GOTO or GO TO. Labels are alphanumeric identifiers. In particular the identifier GOTO itself is also legal in PL/I. So the statement "GOTO GOTO" is a correct PL/I phrase, provided the label constant GOTO, followed by the colon, is defined properly.

Measured by today's quality criteria for programming language design, PL/I is quite a poor language, but for Goto Statements, or more precisely, their related label declaration, PL/I displays consistent design. Labels are objects of the language, just like any other. Also, since labels can be passed as parameters, as they can in Fortran, why not permit label variables? PL/I does exactly this. And since it is legal to formally declare variables of attribute label, it only follows that Arrays of labels are permitted as well.

How is a PL/I label Array declared, and what can it be used for? We offer a sample here. The individual label elements may be indexed just like other Arrays, and once so selected, the label elements can be referenced in Goto Statements. The usefulness of this facility is not discussed here. And, since we consider the whole construct to be superfluous, we would at best be willing to assume the role of a devil's advocate.

```
DCL MAGIC( 12 ) LABEL;
```

Variable "magic" is a label Array with 12 elements, each of which may be assigned the value of other label variables or label constants.

Even in PL/I, a language permitting everything syntactically expressible, branching into the middle of another structured statement is not allowed. But the nonlocal or "long distance" branch out of local procedure scopes is permitted, just as it is in Pascal. The PL/I program "GODEMO" in Example 12-9 demonstrates such a use.

```
 1   0          GODEMO: PROC OPTIONS( MAIN );
 2   1                    DCL GLOBAL BIN FIXED;
 3   1           REC:     PROCEDURE RECURSIVE;
 4   2                      IF GLOBAL = 0 THEN
 5   2                        GOTO ESCAPE;
                            ELSE
 6   2                        DO;
 7   2     1                    GLOBAL = GLOBAL - 1;
 8   2     1                    CALL REC;
 9   2     1                  END;
10   2                    END REC;
                        /* MAIN PROGRAM */
11   1                    GLOBAL = 12;
12   1                    CALL REC; /* NON RECURSIVE CALL */
13   1                    PUT LIST( ' IMPOSSIBLE TO REACH.' );
14   1                ESCAPE:
                          PUT LIST( ' BACK FROM REC.' );
17   1                  END GODEMO;
```

Example 12-9 Good PL/I Goto Statement

"GODEMO" performs just like the Pascal program "gotodemo" in Example 12-8. So the PL/I compiler does in fact emit the correct code sequence to void all recursive invocations of "REC" and transfer control to the label "ESCAPE."

12.3 Exit Statements

When the reaction against the software crisis was furiously attempting to eliminate the Goto Statement, it became more and more apparent that certain, restricted labels and branches could not be abolished for real-life programs. The dominating solution then was, still assuming that the Goto Statement would vanish, to invent special-purpose branch statements. These special Goto Statements in disguise were designed to restrict the expressive power of the GOTO. Thus the Exit Statement was born.

The Exit Statement was not the only one introduced in this context, but it is certainly one of the better designed commands. It will be treated here as a representative of a family of new statements, all with the same purpose of promoting safer programming.

Exit Statements are embedded in a loop body and, when executed, cause the termination of that loop. It would be principally correct to replace an Exit Statement with a Goto Statement to the successor of the embedding loop. The advantage of the Exit over the Goto Statement is twofold. First, and not very seriously, the dogmatics in the Goto elimination camp would be pacified, since the string "GOTO" no longer shows up in source programs. More importantly, an Exit Statement carries documentary information with it. When scanning an Exit Statement in a program, the reader knows instantly that there is only a very limited, controlled domain of text this hidden Goto Statement can span. This text is the embedding loop.

Exit Statements come in various styles and sizes. Ada permits the combination of a statement name with the EXIT, in which case the loop identified by that name is terminated. The idea here is to permit the termination of several, nested loops. Modula-2 does not have this additional luxury.

Usually the Exit Statement is executed conditionally. The condition is controlled by an If Statement, holding the Exit Statement. For cosmetic reasons some languages allow an abbreviation of this construct in the form of a When Clause. Ada, for example, includes such an optional When Clause, while Modula-2 is more limited by demanding a full If Statement. The rationale for this clause is to prevent the impression of excessively deep If Statement nesting. Therefore, when we used the attribute "cosmetic" a moment ago, it should not have been misinterpreted pejoratively. Anything that supports program readability should be appreciated. For this construct the cost is again clear: increased programming language complexity. Ada, for example, is more complex than Modula-2, but it allows certain Exit Statements to be written in a way that is clearer and more readable than the equivalent Modula-2 text.

We demonstrate the use of the Exit Statement in the following sections by a sample program—implemented once in Ada, the second time coded in Modula-2. This program sets the lower triangle of a square matrix and prints these values. All matrix elements in the upper triangle are uninitialized and should, therefore, not be printed.

Ada Exit Statement

After a summary of the rules for Ada's Exit Statement, we present the extended BNF grammar and the sample program, printing the lower triangle of a square matrix. Exit Statements must be embedded in some form of explicit Loop Statement. It is not sufficient to write a Hand-Manufactured Loop via If and Goto Statement, or just via a Goto Statement alone, and embed an Exit Statement therein.

The "loop name" is permitted with the Exit Statement, if one of the enclosing loops, in fact, carries such a name. If the Exit Statement with loop name is executed, then the loop so identified is terminated and execution continues after that loop. If the When Clause is present, this is equivalent to nesting the Exit Statement inside an If Statement.

```
ada_exit_statement    ::= EXIT [ loop_name ] [ WHEN condition ] ;
```

Example 12-10 Grammar Fragment for Ada Exit Statement

```
 1                         |WITH text_io; USE text_io;
 2                         |PROCEDURE exit_demo IS
 3                1        | min : CONSTANT integer := 1;
 4         10     1        | max : CONSTANT integer := 10;
 5         10     1        | TYPE matrix IS ARRAY( min..max, min..max ) OF integer;
 6                1        | table   : matrix;
 7        110     1        |
 8        110     1        | PROCEDURE initialize_table IS
 9                2        | BEGIN--initialize_table
10                2        |  FOR i IN min .. max LOOP
11         5      2  1     |   FOR j IN min .. max LOOP
12         9      2  2     |    IF j > i THEN
13        13      2  3     |      EXIT;
14        14      2  4     |    ELSE
15        14      2  3     |      table( i, j ) := i * j;
16        27      2  4     |    END IF;
17        27      2  3     |   END LOOP;
18        28      2  2     |  END LOOP;
19        29      2  1     | END initialize_table;
20        29      1        |
21        29      1        | PROCEDURE print_table IS
22        31      2        | BEGIN--print_table
23        31      2        |  FOR i IN min .. max LOOP
24        36      2  1     |   put( i, 3 ); put( .")" );
25        41      2  2     |   FOR j IN min .. max LOOP
26        45      2  2     |    IF j > i THEN
27        49      2  3     |      EXIT;
28        50      2  4     |    ELSE
29        50      2  3     |      put( table( i, j ), 3 );
30        62      2  4     |    END IF;
31        62      2  3     |   END LOOP;
32        63      2  2     |   put_line(  "  " );
33        66      2  2     |  END LOOP;
34        67      2  1     |  put_line(  "  " );
35        70      2  1     | END print_table;
                              ...
40        79      1  1     |END exit_demo;
```

Example 12-11 Ada Program "exit_demo" Using EXIT Statement

The Ada program "exit_demo" in Example 12-11 initializes a square matrix and prints it. Since we are really only interested in the lower left triangle of the matrix, we don't bother to initialize the other half and also don't print it.

To escape from the For Statements, we use Exits. See lines 13 and 27. In Example 12-13 we shall demonstrate the same program in Modula-2.

Modula-2 Exit Statement

Modula-2 has no Goto Statement. The only statement in Modula-2 that resembles a Goto Statement is the Exit Statement. EXIT must be embedded in a Loop Statement. When executed, the Exit Statement causes transfer of control to the statement after the Loop Statement.

We see from the grammar in Example 12-12 that the syntax for the Exit Statement is close to the Ada syntax. Note that Ada allows an additional When Clause after the EXIT keyword with a special semantics. This is not offered in Modula-2. The BNF grammar for the Exit and Loop Statements is listed in Example 12-12, followed by a sample program segment in Example 12-13, showing the use of Exit and Loop Statements in Modula-2.

```
modula2_loop_statement ::= LOOP
                             sequence_of_statements
                           END

exit_statement         ::= EXIT
```

Example 12-12 Grammar Fragment for Modula-2 Loop and Exit Statements

```
1   MODULE ExitDemo;
2    FROM InOut
3     IMPORT WriteString, WriteCard, WriteLn;
4    TYPE Matrix = ARRAY[ 1 .. 10 ] OF CARDINAL;
5    VAR Table   : Matrix;
6
7    PROCEDURE InitializeTable;
8     VAR i, j : CARDINAL;
9    BEGIN  (* InitializeTable *)
10    FOR i := 1 TO 10 DO
11     FOR j := 1 TO 10 DO
12      IF j > i THEN
13       EXIT
14      ELSE
15       Table[ i, j ] := i * j;
16      END;
17     END;
18    END;
19   END InitializeTable;
20
21   PROCEDURE PrintTable;
22    VAR i, j : CARDINAL;
```

```
BEGIN (* PrintTable *)
 FOR i := 1 TO 10 DO
  WriteCard( i, 3 );
  WriteString( ".)" );
  FOR j := 1 TO 10 DO
   IF j > i THEN
    EXIT
   ELSE
    WriteCard( Table[ i, j ], 6 );
   END;
  END;
  WriteLn;
 END;
 WriteLn;
END PrintTable;

BEGIN (* ExitDemo *)
 InitializeTable;
 PrintTable;
END ExitDemo.
```

Example 12-13 Modula-2 Program "ExitDemo" Using EXIT Statement

12.4 Fortran Computed Goto Statement

This section demonstrates how the Computed Goto Statement can be used as a restricted form of Case Statement. We repeat briefly the syntax rules and explain the typical use of Case Statements. Then we integrate the two concepts into the sample Fortran program "COMPGO," which simulates our well-known Five Function Calculator, presented in Section 7.3. First, we list a sample Computed Goto Statement.

```
GO TO ( 100, 250, 600, 770 ) MIN - 3*K
```

After the GOTO keyword there follows a parenthetical list of labels, indexed from 1 through "n," with "n" being the number of labels. There must be at least one label. An integer type expression on the same line closes the Computed Goto. This integer expression is evaluated to select one of the labels. If the expression is one, execution continues at the statement marked by the first label; if 2, at the second label; and so on. Should the integer expression yield a value outside the range 1..n, then the Computed Goto Statement functions like a Continue Statement.

The Case Expression of a Case Statement is used to select one of a list of choices. There must be at least one choice. If the Case Expression matches one of the choices, the statement sequence identified by that choice is executed. After this selection, the program execution continues with the statement following the Case Statement.

Close inspection of the rules for Computed Goto and Case Statements reveals three differences: first, the labels in a Computed Goto need not be unique, while with Case Statements the duplication of choices is not permitted. Second, the labels in the Computed Goto Statement are indexed and thus selected in a strict arithmetic sequence, starting with one. Case Statements allow a higher degree of freedom that renders source program sections position independent. Only the value of the choice matters, not the position where it is listed. Third, the Computed Goto Statement has no notion of an End Statement. After execution of the statement, indexed by the Computed Goto expression, control continues with the subsequent statement. This will, in most situations, be a fall-through into the next case, unless an unconditional Goto Statement transfers control to the end. A Case Statement, by contrast, will cause an invisible branch to the end. The compiler (for Ada, Pascal, Modula-2) inserts the Goto automatically; the reader knows this from the semantics of the Case Statement. Notice that there exist language dependent variations. The language C, for example, does not provide this function, even though its Case Statement is well designed in all other regards. In C the programmer must add a "break statement" manually, if control is to be transferred to the end.

This short analysis gives us sufficient ammunition to rewrite our old friend, the Five Function Calculator in Fortran using the Computed Goto Statement. To do so, we must ensure that the Goto Expression maps into the integer range 1..n. Also, we must add explicit unconditional Goto Statements after each selectable case so that only one of the selected choices will be executed. A listing of "COMPGO" follows in Example 12-14.

```
      PROGRAM COMPGO
       CHARACTER OPERAT
       INTEGER RESULT, NUMBER, NEWOP
       OPERAT = '+'
       RESULT = 0
10     READ( 5, 20 ) NUMBER
20     FORMAT( I10 )
30     FORMAT( A )
C------ MAP ALL CHARACTERS INTO RANGE 1..5
       IF ( OPERAT .EQ. '+' ) THEN
        NEWOP = 1
       ELSE IF ( OPERAT .EQ. '-' ) THEN
        NEWOP = 2
       ELSE IF ( OPERAT .EQ. '*' ) THEN
```

```
             NEWOP = 3
            ELSE IF ( OPERAT .EQ. '/' ) THEN
             NEWOP = 4
            ELSE IF ( OPERAT .EQ. '|' ) THEN
             NEWOP = 5
            ELSE
             NEWOP = 6
            END IF
C------     NEWOP IN [ 1..6 ]
            GO TO ( 100, 200, 300, 400, 500 ) NEWOP
100          RESULT = RESULT + NUMBER
             GO TO 600
200          RESULT = RESULT - NUMBER
             GO TO 600
300          RESULT = RESULT * NUMBER
             GO TO 600
400          RESULT = RESULT / NUMBER
             GO TO 600
500          RESULT = MOD( RESULT, NUMBER )
600          READ( 5, 30 ) OPERAT
             IF ( OPERAT .NE. '=' ) THEN
              GOTO 10
             END IF
            WRITE( 6, * ) ' RESULT = ', RESULT
          END
```

Example 12-14 Use of Computed Goto, to Simulate a Case Statement

The Fortran program "COMPGO" executes correctly, but not in a very friendly way. It suffers from several flaws. Its most striking programming construct is the complicated Block If Statement. This is required in some form or another, because the Computed Goto Expression, here realized by the integer variable "NEWOP" must map exactly into the restricted range 1..5. Another striking, but not pleasant, feature is the repetition of four Goto Statements, transferring control to label 600. At least for the fifth case it was not necessary to write a Goto Statement, because the target label 600 follows immediately after the fifth case. As in our previous programming solutions of the Five Function Calculator in Ada, Modula-2, and Pascal, error handling is not very friendly.

We learn from this example that the true power of Fortran's Computed Goto can best be exploited when we are processing objects with a continuous value range. This was not the case in Example 12-14 for variable "NEWOP." Its five legal values '+', '-', '*', '/', and '|' are somehow scattered through the character set. Forcing the scattered values into a small, contiguous range makes our program look almost silly.

12.5 Summary

In spite of being a low level construct, the Goto Statement comes in many shapes and colours. Ada's Goto is simple and reasonably restrictive; out-of-scope branches are illegal as are branches into structured statements. Pascal and PL/I are more permissive, and PL/I even provides a very general data type "Label" that can be referenced by Goto Statements. In Modula-2 the Goto Statement only comes in the disguise of the Exit Statement, allowing a branch to the successor of a Loop Statement.

Fortran, on the other hand, has so much relied on Goto Statements over its relatively long history that it has developed a range of different levels. With wise, voluntary restrictions, the Computed Goto Statement can be used to construct the high level Case Statement.

Even though reliance on Gotos tends to make software hard to read and maintain, it is probably not a good idea to exclude it from a general-purpose language. We have, therefore, covered the controversial construct in detail so that programming language designers can make a conscientious decision which semantics to include and which to omit. Such decisions should be based on the anticipated use of the language and the benefits and costs of the features.

The next chapter will cover storage classes. Our main focus will be the logical aspect of scope and storage attributes, but we will also discuss the more physical aspects and how logical storage is arranged in a machine.

12.6 Exercises

1. What is your response to the following claim: "The absence of Goto Statements ensures that the software is well structured."?

2. What is your opinion of the claim: "Software that contains Goto Statements is by definition unstructured."?

3. Can an unconditional Goto to another unconditional branch always be replaced by a simpler construct? If yes, what is the replacement? See the following sample PL/I code sequence for clarification.

```
GOTO START;
/* OTHER STATEMENTS */
START:     GOTO FINISH;
/* OTHER STATEMENTS */
FINISH:    GET LIST( I );
PUT LIST( ' I**2=', I**2 );
```

4. Can an unconditional branch (Goto Statement) to a conditional Goto Statement (i.e., a Goto Statement solely enclosed in an If Statement) always be replaced by a simpler construct? If yes, what is the replacement?

5. Can a conditional Goto to another conditional Goto always be replaced by a simpler construct? If yes, what is the construct?

6. What is suspicious, though not syntactically incorrect, about the following statement sequence? Assume all statements starting with the "do_" prefix to be legal Ada Procedure Call Statements.

```
do_this; GOTO far_away; do_this_next;
```

```
GOTO START;                    /* OTHER STATEMENTS */
START:     GOTO FINISH;
/* OTHER STATEMENTS */
FINISH:    GET LIST( I );
PUT LIST( ' I**2=', I**2 );
```

13

Storage Classes

Class cannot be bought or acquired.
It is an inner quality
found without regard to financial status or family background.
Its essential quality is
integrity, intelligence and lack of pretension.
Education can expand the horizon of a person with class,
but it will not give class to someone without it.
Class is a state of grace that few people have.

Dorothy Cullman
Quoted in New Woman, June 1984, by Mortimer Levitt

The major part of the preceding chapters has covered rules and finer points of algorithmic actions, collectively known as statements. Language compilers translate statements and declarations. Statements are mapped into executable code, declarations into data space. During run time statements are meant to compute results in the data area. In the current chapter we focus on the physical aspects of storage and the lifetime attributes of data; the logical aspect has been treated in Chapters 5 and 6.

We choose the term *storage* rather than *data,* because our primary attention is not directed toward the abstract view of data in high level programming languages. *Storage* refers to the memory space of *real* computers, while *data* is their logical interpretation in a programming language. We concentrate on the interaction between abstract data and their lifetime, and their representation on a physical machine.

We choose the term *class* rather than *type,* because type is a technical term already used in higher level languages to specify an allowable set of values and operations. We shall clarify how long objects exist, and from which program sections (scopes) operations are permitted. Just because an operation is permitted does not always imply that it can be performed from anywhere in the program. And, even more subtly, just because program section X has the right to perform an operation on object Y does not always imply that object Y really exists; X may have to verify this first.

The following kinds of questions will be addressed in this chapter: How is storage allocated (data mapping)? Which classes of storage exist? How long does storage exist or live once it has been allocated (storage attribute)? Which program sections can reference storage that is alive (scope attribute)? How are these storage and scope attributes expressed in programming languages? The storage attributes that will be discussed here are static, automatic, and controlled. Scope attributes examined are external, global, and local. When we discuss the allocation of storage, our model of physical machine memory is a one dimensional list of identical elements that can be addressed by indexing.

13.1 Static Storage

Data that live from a program's inception to the end of its activity are *static.* This by no means implies that such static data are, therefore, accessible from everywhere in this same program. Accessibility depends on the particular programming language, and we shall look at various alternatives.

The policies that govern static storage are so old, simple, and well known that there seems to be no need to explain them at any great length. But readers who grew up with modern languages such as Modula-2 or Ada will be surprised about some properties of static data. C and PL/I, for example, allow the explicit static attribute for variables that otherwise would be automatic. Those objects disappear and are reincarnated later with the last value they had before they vanished. In the following sections we explain just what static data is and how to declare it.

Declaration of Static Storage

Data that are in existence for the whole life of a program are static. Such static data are not necessarily always accessible to the associated name. They are also not always available to other environments that spring to life during the program's activity. Static is a storage attribute, not a scope attribute. Some static data are made accessible to any environment that wishes to access them, in which case they have the scope attribute external. All external data are static, but many static data are not external.

Ada

In Ada, static storage is allocated for those data that are declared in the main program, and for all data declared in outermost level PACKAGEs. Ada does not specify how the main program is selected from a multitude of compilation units, but some of the existing implementations have used an Ada PRAGMA for this purpose. The identifier MAIN, following the keyword PRAGMA, selects one procedure for this task. There is no other, explicit way of telling an Ada compiler that certain data must have a static lifetime. In other words, in Ada the static storage attribute is implicitly granted only to data within certain scopes.

Fortran

Being an older language, Fortran has no other storage attribute but static: all data are static. But this does not tell the whole story. It is also possible to define some data as Common. The attribute Common does not affect the lifetime of data, because it is not a storage attribute. It is a scope attribute that qualifies the data as external. Since it is allowed in Fortran to EQUIVALENCE all data, including common data, this aliasing mechanism can introduce the external attribute to data that don't seem to be external at first glance.

A Fortran program consists of a main program and zero or more functions and subroutines. The latter may have local variables, but all these local variables are static. So when a subroutine is called for, say, the second time, then all its local variables still retain the values previously assigned. This is shown in Example 13-1.

When programmers grow up with Fortran, these rules pose no problem, particularly since they are so simple and clear-cut. There just isn't much to worry about with respect to scope and storage attributes. But when our educational background is based on high level languages like Ada or Pascal and we don't know Fortran thoroughly, we may not be able to predict the output of program "STATIC" in Example 13-1 correctly. The apparent similarity of local data in Fortran subroutines with local data in Pascal procedures might lead us to guess that the storage attribute in Fortran would be automatic. Readers who are not Fortran experts are advised to study Example 13-1 to completely abandon the idea of automatic data in Fortran.

```
      PROGRAM STATIC
       INTEGER CALLS
       DO 10 CALLS = 1, 5
        CALL SUB1( CALLS )
        CALL SUB2( CALLS )
10     CONTINUE
      END

      SUBROUTINE SUB1( NCALLS )
       INTEGER NCALLS, OLD
       IF ( NCALLS .EQ. 1 ) THEN
        OLD = 1
       ELSE
        IF ( OLD .EQ. ( NCALLS-1)**2 ) THEN
         WRITE( 6, * ) 'old is allocated static storage'
         OLD = NCALLS ** 2
        ELSE
         WRITE( 6, * ) ' old is not static'
        END IF
       END IF
      END

      SUBROUTINE SUB2( ARG )
       INTEGER ARG, OLDEST
       IF ( ARG .EQ. 1 ) THEN
        OLDEST = 1
       ELSE
        IF ( OLDEST .NE. 1 ) THEN
         WRITE( 6, * ) ' oldest is not static'
        END IF
       END IF
      END
```

Example 13-1 Fortran Locals Are Static

Example 13-1 demonstrates that local data are static. If the local variables "old" and "oldest" do not retain their values assigned in previous calls, then the message "oldest is not static" would be written. The correct output is the repeated message "old is allocated static storage."

Pascal

Pascal variables declared in the outermost scope are static. Since this outermost scope is "global," meaning that all other, nested scopes have access to names in that scope unless they are redefined, the scope attribute "global" is often confused with the storage attribute static. This confusion occurs most often with Pascal, because there is only one single compilation unit. In Pascal it just so happens that all "global" data (scope attribute) are also the ones that live during the whole program execution, hence are static (storage attribute).

In other words, the confusion of terms causes no conflict in the Pascal world due to another language shortcoming: Pascal lacks multiple compilation units.

In Ada and Modula-2 it is easier to see that "global" and static are two different concepts. For example, we may write an Ada program consisting of two subprograms, the main program "main_procedure" and the subprogram "log2." It is legal to let both be separate compilation units, declared on the outermost level. Data declared inside either subprogram are global to their respective scope, and therefore accessible also in scopes nested therein. Still all local data declared in "log2" are automatic; they live only from the call up to the return, and then vanish. On the other hand, all global data in "main_procedure" are also static. See Example 13-2.

```
 1                  |WITH text_io; USE text_io;
 2                  |FUNCTION log2( arg : integer ) RETURN integer IS
 3        11   1    | count, temp : integer; -- automatic
 4        13   1    |BEGIN -- log2
 5             1    | temp := ABS arg;
 6    5        1  1 | count := 0;
 7    8        1  1 | WHILE temp > 1 LOOP
 8   12        1  1 |  count := count + 1;
 9   17        1  2 |  temp := temp / 2;
10   22        1  2 | END LOOP;
11   23        1  1 | RETURN count;
12   28        1  1 |END log2;
13   28             |PRAGMA main;
14   28             |PROCEDURE main IS
15   30        1    | a : integer; -- static
16   30   11   1    |BEGIN -- main
17   30        1    | a := 16;
18   34        1  1 | put_line( log2( a ) );
19   41        1  1 |END main;
```

Example 13-2 Global Data in Ada That Are Automatic and Static

"Count" and "temp" declared on line 3 are automatic. They are reincarnated each time "log2" is called. But "a" declared on line 15 is static. All of them are global to their respective scopes.

PL/I

PL/I has two ways of defining variables as static. All variables in the main program are static for the same reason already observed in Ada and Pascal. In addition it is possible to declare explicitly that local variables be static. See Example 13-3.

```
SDEMO: PROC OPTIONS( MAIN );
 DCL S1 BIN FIXED;  /* IMPLICITLY STATIC */
NEST:  PROC;
 DCL S2 BIN FIXED STATIC;
 IF S1 = 1 THEN
  S2 = 1;
 ELSE
  DO
   IF S2 = S1-1 THEN
    PUT SKIP LIST( ' S2 RETAINED OLD VALUE' );
   ELSE
    PUT SKIP LIST( ' S2 IS NOT STATIC' );
   S2 = S1;
  END;
END NEST;

/* MAIN PROGRAM */
 DO S1 = 1 TO 5;
  CALL NEST;
 END;
END SDEMO;
```

Example 13-3   Explicit Static Attribute in PL/I

Initialization of Static Storage

For most cases the initialization of static storage is not different from the initialization of other data. But local data must be initialized each time the defining scope is entered, while static data are initialized just once. Pascal allows no initialization at the place of declaration, so some code sequence must be executed to assign a first value.

Since the environments of static data become active only once per program execution in Pascal, the issue of initialization is without problem. Special attention must be directed only to PL/I with its explicit STATIC attribute and the INIT Clause. If we have an understanding of initialization and of the storage attribute "static," we should be able to predict the results of the two almost identical PL/I programs in Examples 13-4 and 13-5. So we challenge the reader to analyze the two following PL/I source programs "STAT1" and "STAT2" and predict their outputs before reading on.

```
0    1    0         STAT1: PROC OPTIONS( MAIN );
     2    1          NEST:  PROC;
     3    2                   DCL LOCAL BIN FIXED INIT( 199 );
     4    2                   LOCAL = LOCAL + 1;
     5    2                   PUT LIST( ' LOCAL = ', LOCAL );
     6    2                   PUT SKIP;
     7    2                 END NEST;
                        /* MAIN PROGRAM */
     8    1                 CALL NEST;
     9    1                 CALL NEST;
    10    1               END STAT1;
```

Example 13-4 "Local" Is AUTOMATIC

```
0    1    0         STAT2: PROC OPTIONS( MAIN );
     2    1          NEST:  PROC;
     3    2                   DCL LOCAL BIN FIXED STATIC INIT( 199 );
     4    2                   LOCAL = LOCAL + 1;
     5    2                   PUT LIST( ' LOCAL = ', LOCAL );
     6    2                   PUT SKIP;
     7    2                 END NEST;
                        /* MAIN PROGRAM */
     8    1                 CALL NEST;
     9    1                 CALL NEST;
    10    1               END STAT2;
```

Example 13-5 "Local" Is STATIC

STAT1 in Example 13-4 contains a local procedure named "nest." Nest is called twice, and the integer variable "local" comes to life at both calls with the initial value 199. Since 1 is added before the printing, 200 is output twice.

Things are quite different in program STAT2 in Example 13-5. At first glance, it may look like only the name has changed; but notice that the local variable "local" has received the storage attribute STATIC by explicit declaration. The initialization, therefore, is effective only once when "nest" is called the first time. Due to the static attribute, "local" retains its old value and upon second invocation yet another 1 is added to the previous value. The point is, the previous value is not lost; since it is still 200, the two lines of output this time around are 200 and 201. This is quite a subtle difference, but it is one that we must be aware of in order to understand "static."

13.2 Automatic Storage

Data that start living upon subprogram entry and that cease to exist upon subprogram exit are *automatic* data. The storage area from which they receive space is the automatic storage, usually the system stack. Automatic here means that acquisition and release are controlled by the system without the user's intervention. Automatic is a technical term borrowed from the PL/I subculture. Some languages use the term *dynamic* for the same storage allocation policy. Since another meaning of the word dynamic implies a change in size of the same data structure from one moment to the next, we use the PL/I term here for the sake of clarity.

Fortran and Cobol have no automatic storage. All their data are static. In Ada, Pascal, Modula-2, and PL/I the default storage attribute is automatic. A data structure, or more generally, one possible implementation of a data structure, from which automatic storage is allocated, is the run time stack. Whenever a subprogram is entered, this stack grows by the amount of automatic storage needed for the new context. When a return is executed, that portion of the stack is freed again. The exact amount of space per context, meticulously computed by the compiler, consists of space for local variables, parameters, which are nothing but a special form of local variables, and user-transparent information for bookkeeping and temporaries.

The great advantage of automatic storage is space economy. Subprograms consume space for locals only as long as they are still active. When a subprogram is not alive, its local variables consume zero bits of space. Such economy cannot be surpassed. Additionally this stack or last-in/first-out policy is the natural data structure for implementation of recursion, which some languages offer as well.

The great disadvantage of automatic storage allocation is the "intentional blindness" of one invocation of a subprogram with respect to other invocations of the same subprogram. This tunnel vision per se is not a handicap, but there are inherent limitations following from the reallocation of local data. The reallocation implies that the previous value of the same local variable, having come to life in a different environment, is inaccessible to the current environment. It is equally impossible in such an environment to know whether the current invocation is the first or last one that will occur. If the program logic requires keeping track of such knowledge, then outside environments must explicitly manage this information. This is demonstrated with the Ada subprograms "fact" and "outside," in Example 13-6.

Function "fact" is our old acquaintance, the factorial function, chosen here solely for the sake of simplicity. Inside of this subprogram we cannot know whether the current environment exists because of a self-recursive call or due to some call from the outside world. The one piece of intelligence that "fact" can keep track of is the counter "num_of_calls," a global object. Each time "fact" is called, "num_of_calls" is incremented.

Keeping track of the number of calls to "fact" from the outside cannot be done from within "fact." Therefore the global variable "num_of_fact" must be managed by that outside environment.

```
 1                  |WITH text_io; USE text_io;
 2                  |
 3                  |PROCEDURE outside IS
 4            1      | total,            -- all factorials added together
 5      10   1      | average,          -- total / num_of_fact
 6      10   1      | num_of_calls,     -- total number of calls to fact
 7      10   1      | temp,
 8      10   1      | num_of_fact       -- number of factorials
 9      10   1      |                       : integer;
10      15   1      |
11      15   1      | FUNCTION fact( arg : integer ) RETURN integer IS
12      11   2      | BEGIN -- fact
13            2      |   num_of_calls := num_of_calls + 1;
14   6       2   1  |   IF arg <= 1 THEN
15  10       2   1  |     RETURN 1; -- fact(0) is also 1
16  15       2   2  |   ELSE
17  15       2   1  |     RETURN arg * fact( arg - 1 );
18  29       2   2  |   END IF;
19  29       2   1  | END fact;
20  29       1      |
21  29       1      |BEGIN -- outside
22  31       1      | total := 0;
23  35       1   1  | num_of_calls := 0;
24  38       1   1  | num_of_fact := 0;
25  41       1   1  | FOR i IN 0 .. 7 LOOP
26  45       1   1  |   num_of_fact := num_of_fact + 1;
27  50       1   2  |   temp := fact( i );
28  56       1   2  |   put_line( temp );
29  59       1   2  |   total := total + temp;
30  64       1   2  | END LOOP;
31  65       1   1  | put( " Total number of calls:  " );
32  67       1   1  | put_line(integer' image( num_of_calls ));
33  70       1   1  | average := total / num_of_fact;
34  75       1   1  | put( " Average factorial    :  " );
35  77       1   1  | put_line( integer' image( average ));
36  80       1   1  |END outside;
```

Example 13-6 The Limitation of Automatic, Local Variables

13.3 Controlled Storage

Programmers have always been an immodest breed, but this sometimes has its benefits. Programmers are never satisfied with the processing power of their machine—running, alas, with only finite speed—and are never content with the available storage space. Programmers always want more! But when they can't get more storage space, these insatiable tinkerers invent more intelligent storage access policies. This way, their immodesty leads them to overcome yet one more frontier.

The storage classes we have discussed thus far, static and automatic, are historically the oldest ones. Static space is allocated once and forever as far as program execution is concerned. Naturally even static storage is recycled for other purposes once the owning program has terminated. Automatic storage springs to life when the environment containing the declaration becomes active. It too is recycled as soon as that environment returns to its caller.

The immodest programmers want more. Sometimes, they think, it would be helpful if they could free some portion of a complex data structure without having to leave the currently working subprogram. Other times it would be nice to have the option of leaving a subprogram and maintaining data structures without having to declare them as static. This leads to explicit control over allocating and freeing of data space, and that is exactly the reason why *controlled data space* was invented. Controlled storage allows the programmer to allocate any number of objects when needed and to free any subset of these when they are obsolete.

The system data structure, from which programs are granted such controlled space in a transparent fashion is called the *heap.* While the allocation and freeing policy from the stack can be characterized by the simple last-in/first-out strategy, there is no such discipline and order for heap allocation. Space acquisitions from and releases to the heap space are as wild as we can imagine: from this we can conclude that there is no easy, optimal allocation policy for heap space.

We deliberately choose the PL/I term controlled for this useful storage policy to avoid confusion. Confusion could have been caused had we chosen the terminology of the old, de facto Pascal standard, the precious monograph by Jensen and Wirth [1978]. There we find the attribute dynamic used again, this time to classify controlled storage, introducing yet one more interpretation of the overused term *dynamic.*

Pointers

With the exception of PL/I's nonbased, controlled variables, all other controlled data space is accessible via pointers. Conceptually, pointers are just addresses of other data structures. Pointers then can be used (dereferenced) in order to make the respective object accessible. Initially, all pointers are (or should be) null, which only says that they are pointing to no data at all.

Ada and PL/I use the keyword NULL for that purpose, while Pascal and Modula-2 use NIL. Speaking of subtle differences in Pascal NIL is a reserved keyword and cannot be used for any other purpose. Modula-2 is thrifty with its use of reserved keywords and predefines the identifier NIL for the null pointer. NIL is not a reserved keyword. Therefore, it is perfectly legal in a Modula-2 program to declare a pointer variable (or any other object) named NIL, and write a most confusing program. Fortran, as we should have suspected due to its old age, has no controlled storage class and no pointers at all. Ada postulates that all pointers have the initial value NULL, even when lacking such explicit initialization in the pointer declaration. Pascal, Modula-2, and PL/I make no such safe demands.

Heap Access in Ada

Access to the controlled storage area of Ada's run time system requires that two type marks be defined. One type mark specifies the type detail of the objects to be allocated; the second is a pointer to the objects of such type. Pointers are denoted by the reserved word ACCESS in Ada. If the pointer type is recursive, an incomplete type declaration is also involved, and the general pattern of declarations is as shown in Example 13-7.

```
TYPE node_type; -- incomplete type
TYPE node_pin_type IS ACCESS node_type; -- use of incomplete
TYPE node_type IS -- resolve incomplete
 RECORD
  ... use of node_pin_type
 END RECORD;
```

Example 13-7 Recursive Types in Ada

During the translation time the compiler maps pointer variables onto static or automatic space. The heap objects themselves do not exist yet. They will spring to life only when explicitly so instructed via allocators. Ada allocators are identified by the reserved keyword NEW, followed by the type mark that defines the type of space needed, as shown here:

```
node := NEW node_type;
```

Before this assignment to "node" is executed, the only space consumed during the program's execution is the space for the variable "node" itself. This is only a minimal amount; addresses are simple objects. But each time the allocator "NEW node_type" is invoked, a whole record is granted from the system heap.

Usually many of these objects will be allocated, and then linked together in the fashion of a list or a tree.

Heap Access in Pascal

Again we must define two type identifiers: one for the heap object, the other for a pointer to such objects. Note that Pascal pointer types are introduced by the symbol ^, here named "up arrow." The built-in Pascal function "new" allocates heap space of the type as indicated by the pointer object, passed as an actual parameter. This is shown as follows:

```
new( pointer_type_object );
```

Heap Access in PL/I

In PL/I the allocatable objects are also tied to a pointer. Below we show the declaration of the structure "ELEMENT," associated with the pointer "PIN." The structure is only used as a template to characterize the object that "PIN" will point to. At run time no space for the actual structure is consumed, no matter how complex it is; only "PIN" consumes enough space to hold an address. Hence, it is comparable to an anonymous type declaration in Pascal-like languages. Space will only be consumed when explicitly so requested via an Allocate Statement. The argument of the Allocate Statement must be the structure name, here "ELEMENT." As an invisible side-effect, the associated pointer variable "PIN" is set to point to the allocated object. See the Allocate Statement on line 8 in Example 13-8.

```
1       /* DECLARATIONS */
2       DECLARE 1 ELEMENT BASED( PIN ),
3                 2 DATA BIN FIXED( 31 ),
4                 2 LINK POINTER;
5       DECLARE FIRST POINTER;
6
7       /* STATEMENTS */
8       ALLOCATE ELEMENT; /* SIDE EFFECT ON PIN */
9       FIRST = PIN;
10      FIRST -> LINK = NULL;
```

Example 13-8 Sample PL/I Pointer Declaration and Heap Allocation

The second declaration on line 5, defines "FIRST" to be a pointer type variable. In our example we let "FIRST" also point to the allocated structure. It is interesting to notice that in PL/I, pointers are not tied to a specific type.

In another portion of the program, "FIRST" could be assigned to point to a data structure of different type than "ELEMENT." The Assignment Statement on line 10 above marks the field "LINK" to point to nowhere. Precisely speaking, in PL/I "NULL" is a built-in function that returns the pointer value null. In reality, this is only linguistic hair-splitting, and "NULL" is nothing but a pointer type literal of predefined value.

We also notice that the "DATA" field portion of the structure does consume its portion of space after the allocation, but holds no value yet. A possible initialization could be accomplished by the sample input statement as follows:

```
GET LIST( PIN -> DATA ); /* FULLY QUALIFIED */
```

Next we show the PL/I program "LLIST" which creates a linked list of elements shown in Example 13-8. The pointer variable "FIRST" points to its first, and "LAST" to its last element.

```
LLIST: PROC OPTIONS( MAIN );
         DCL 1 ELEMENT BASED( PIN ),
                2 DATA BIN FIXED( 31 ),
                2 LINK POINTER,
              ( FIRST, LAST ) POINTER;
         ON ENDFILE( SYSIN ) STOP;
         FIRST = NULL; LAST = NULL;
         DO WHILE( '1'B ); /* PL/I INFINITE LOOP */
          ALLOCATE ELEMENT;
          GET LIST( DATA ); /* INCOMPLETE QUALIFICATION O.K. */
          IF FIRST = NULL THEN
           FIRST = PIN;
          ELSE
           LAST -> LINK = PIN;
          PIN -> LINK = NULL;
          LAST = PIN;
         END; /* WHILE */
        END LLIST;
```

Example 13-9 PL/I Program to Build Linked List in Heap

The program in Example 13-9 allocates nodes of type "ELEMENT" off the system heap, as long as new data are found on the standard input file "SYSIN." The nodes are chained backwards, and the pointer variable "LAST" is necessary not only for building the chain, but also for having access to all elements of the list. The program in Example 13-9 does nothing with the linked list after building it. Next we demonstrate a similar solution in Ada, then the same in Pascal; but in these solutions we make use of the information stored in the linked lists.

The programs read an unknown number of integers from the standard input file. Unknown here means, at the time of compilation, the program has no idea how many numbers will come in. The appropriate data structure for storing all these data is a linked list of records. Each record has one data field for holding the integer value and one pointer field which addresses the next record of identical type. Space for each record element is allocated off the system heap.

```
 1                        | WITH text_io; USE text_io;
 2                        | PROCEDURE pointers IS
 3              1          |   PACKAGE int_io IS NEW integer_io(integer); USE int_io;
 4              1          |   TYPE  node_type;
 5              1          |   TYPE  node_pin    IS ACCESS node_type;
 6              1          |   TYPE  node_type   IS
 7              1          |     RECORD
 8              1          |       data          : integer;
 9              1          |       next          : node_pin;
10              1          |     END RECORD;
11              1          |   node             : node_pin; -- initially NULL
12        11    1          |   number           : integer;
13        12    1          |
14        12    1          |   PROCEDURE allocate(
15              2          |       data     : integer;
16        11    2          |       node     : IN OUT node_pin ) IS
17        12    2          |       temp     : node_pin;
18        13    2          |   BEGIN -- allocate
19              2          |       temp := node;
20    4         2   1  |       node := NEW node_type;
21    7         2   1  |       node.data := data;
22    11        2   1  |       node.next := temp;
23    14        2   2  |
24    14        2   1  |     WHEN storage error =>
25    19        2   2  |       put_line( " system has no more heap space." );
26    24        2   2  |       RAISE;
27    24        2   1  |   END allocate;
28    24        1          |
29    24        1          |   PROCEDURE printall(
30    26        2          |       node     : IN OUT node_pin ) IS
31    26    11  2          |   BEGIN -- printall
32    26        2          |     WHILE node /= NULL LOOP
33    31        2   1  |       put_line( node.data );
34    36        2   2  |       node := node.next;
35    42        2   2  |     END LOOP;
36    43        2   1  |   END printall;
37    43        1          |
38    43        1          | BEGIN -- pointers
39    45        1          |   node := NULL; -- not necessary
```

```
40   49        1  1 |   put_line( " enter line full of numbers." );
41   52        1  1 |   WHILE NOT end_of_line( input ) LOOP
42   55        1  1 |    get( number );
43   57        1  2 |    allocate( number, node );
44   62        1  2 |   END LOOP;
45   63        1  1 |   printall( node );
46   67        1  1 |  END pointers;
```

Example 13-10 Controlled Storage Allocation in Ada

Immediately we make an interesting observation about lines 4 through 6 of the Ada source. Line 4 is a so-called incomplete type declaration. All incomplete type declarations can do is to promise that a full type will come. Ada demands that the announcement must be resolved by a complete type declaration in the same declarative part that contains the incomplete type. For packages, the complete type declaration may come in the PRIVATE part. And just a few lines further we see that indeed the announced type mark "node_type" is fully defined as a record. In between the incomplete and complete declarations, we discover an access type declaration. Type mark "node_pin" is a pointer to an object of type "node_type," which is in the process of being defined.

This is Ada's skillful way of avoiding forward references to any name. A problem is nicely solved, as the careful reader may already have noticed, for another variant of the old "chicken and egg" problem. We wish to define a type mark that is a pointer to an object of some other type. The object of that other type, however, contains itself a reference to the very type mark we are trying to define. Thus we have a problem of circularity, unless the programming language allows the forward referencing of names. Who comes first, that is the question? PL/I does allow forward references of names, but Ada and Modula-2 do not. Pascal grants an interesting exception here, creating one of its few language inconsistencies. See Example 13-11, in particular lines 2 and 3. Here we show the general pattern first.

```
TYPE
 nodepin    = ^ nodetype; { forward use of "nodetype" }
 nodetype   =
  RECORD
   ... use of "nodepin"
  END {RECORD};
```

Example 13-11 Pascal Forward Reference

With the exception of label literals, type identifiers for the exclusive use of pointer type declarations are the only instance in Pascal, where a name may be used before its declaration. See Example 13-12.

```
 1   1  0  0      PROGRAM pointers( input, output );
 2   2  0  0       TYPE
                    nodepin   = ^ nodetype;
 3   4  0  0        nodetype  =
                     RECORD
 3   6  0  1          data     : integer;
 4   7  0  1          next     : nodepin;
 5   8  0  1         END; {RECORD}
 6   9  0  0       VAR
                    node       : nodepin;
 7  11  0  0        number     : integer;

 8  13  0  0       PROCEDURE allocate(
 8  14  1  0         data      : integer;
                    VAR
                     node      : nodepin );
 9  17  1  0        VAR
                     temp      : nodepin;
10  19  1  0        BEGIN { allocate }
10  20  1  1         temp := node;
11  21  1  1         new( node );
12  22  1  1         IF node = NIL THEN
13  23  1  1          writeln( ' system has no more heap space.' )
                     ELSE
14  25  1  1          BEGIN
14  26  1  2           node^.data := data;
15  27  1  2           node^.next := temp;
16  28  1  2          END;
18  29  1  1         {END IF}
                    END; { allocate }

19  32  0  0       PROCEDURE printall(
19  33  1  0         node      : nodepin );
20  34  1  0        BEGIN { printall }
20  35  1  1         WHILE node <> NIL DO
21  36  1  1          BEGIN
21  37  1  2           writeln( ' next node contains: ', node^.data );
22  38  1  2           node := node^.next;
23  39  1  2          END;
25  40  1  1         {END WHILE}
                    END; { printall }

26  43  0  0       BEGIN { pointers }
26  44  0  1        node := NIL;
27  45  0  1        writeln( ' enter line full of numbers.' );
28  46  0  1        WHILE NOT eoln( input ) DO
29  47  0  1         BEGIN
29  48  0  2          read( input, number );
```

```
30    49  0  2              allocate( number, node );
31    50  0  2            END;
33    51  0  1          {END WHILE}
                        printall( node );
                      END { pointers }.
```

Example 13-12 Controlled Storage Allocation in Pascal

Lines 3 through 4 in Example 13-12 solve the same interesting, circular problem just described for Ada. Again we attempt to define a pointer type to an object, whose type already contains a reference to the type we are currently defining. Pascal circumvents this issue by allowing, on this very exceptional basis, the forward reference of a name.

Now let us run the program in Example 13-12. To our surprise we will see that the numbers entered come out in the reverse order. Once we analyze the simple "allocate" subprogram, we shall understand why. Allocate does two things. First, it acquires heap space for a record of type "nodetype," and then it ties the new node to the existing linked list. Initially the linked list is empty, and global variable "node" is properly initialized to NIL. The head of the linked list is remembered in "temp." See the assignment "temp := node" on lines 19 and 20 in "allocate." Then the newly allocated node is put at the head of the linked list. So the value that is read last will be accessible in the linked list first. Hence the reversed order.

When Do We Need Controlled Storage?

Expressed in a nutshell, controlled storage is an adequate allocation method, when the storage area needed cannot be computed beforehand, neither at compilation time, nor at the start of execution time. Let's look at a detailed rationale for this assertion. Imagine that we need to hold a single record. If we use controlled storage allocation, we really have no advantage over automatic allocation. We could do nothing with the pointer and the single record object pointed at that we could not also do with a local, automatically allocated variable. Even if we would eventually free the object pointed at, then reallocate it and move new data into the data portion of that record, with automatic storage we can achieve the same thing easier and without the run time overhead for allocating and freeing. And if we are concerned about preserving the last value of the data pointed at, beyond the lifetime of the allocating subprogram, a global static variable can do this for us.

Since there is no clear advantage in using controlled storage for single records, (except maybe for handling very large structures of different shapes) perhaps we might need it for storing multiple records, say 100 elements of a record type. But here, of course, an Array of 100 elements of that record type will be the appropriate data structure.

It is only when the number of objects to be stored is unknown at the time of compilation and at the time of using the first element that the appropriate data structure is a list or a tree allocated off the system heap. We'll support this claim with some examples which should also show just how useful controlled storage can be. The Pascal program in Example 13-13, which we call "tree," builds and then outputs a binary tree.

"Tree" reads an arbitrary sequence of characters from the input file and sorts them in the usual lexicographical order. The sorted structure is represented via a binary tree, each node of which contains the character and two pointers to the subtrees. During the read operation, the tree is built, and when no more input is available, the tree is printed using preorder, postorder, and inorder traversal. A NIL pointer is printed as the '.' character. The same input character is stored only once. If the input contains duplicate characters, then a message from the tree builder should indicate this and throw the duplicate away. See Figures 13-1 and 13-2.

```
Input:       xam

Tree:           x
               / |
              a  .
             / |
            /  |
           .   m
              / |
             .  .

Output:     xa.m...     in Preorder
            ...ma.x     in Postorder
            .a.m.x.     in Inorder
```

Figure 13-1 Sample 1 for Alphabetic Tree "XAM"

```
Input:        mayer
Tree:             m
                 /|
                / |
               /  |
              a   y
             /|  /|
            . e r .
              | |
              . .
Output:    ma.e..yr...      in Preorder
           ...ea..r.ym      in Postorder
           .a.e.m.r.y.      in Inorder
```

Figure 13-2 Sample 2 for Alphabetic Tree "MAYER"

In Example 13-13 we show the partial listing of the Pascal program "tree" that builds a binary tree of characters from an input line of text, and then prints the tree in preorder, inorder, and postorder.

```
program tree( input, output );
  const
    dot         = '.';
  type
    nodepin     = ^ nodetype;
    nodetype    =
      record
        data      : char;
        left,
        right     : nodepin;
      end; {record}
  var
    root          : nodepin;
    c             : char;

  procedure preorder( pin : nodepin );
    begin { preorder }
      if pin = nil then
        write( output, dot )
      else
        begin
          write( output, pin^.data );
          preorder( pin^.left );
          preorder( pin^.right );
        end;
      {end if}
    end { preorder };
```

```
procedure postorder( pin : nodepin );
 ...
procedure entersorted(
 var
  root  : nodepin;
  c     : char );
 begin { entersorted }
  if root = nil then
   begin
    new( root );
    root^.data := c;
    root^.left := nil;
    root^.right := nil;
   end
  else if root^.data = c then
   writeln( output, c, ' already in tree' )
  else if root^.data > c then
   entersorted( root^.left, c )
  else
   entersorted( root^.right, c );
  {end if}
 end { entersorted };

begin { tree }
 root := nil;
 writeln( output, ' Enter Tree. Terminate with .' );
 read( input, c );
 while ( c <> dot ) and not eoln( input ) do
  begin
   entersorted( root, c );
   read( input, c );
  end;
 {end while}
 preorder( root );
 ...
end { tree }.
```

Example 13-13 Binary Tree Allocated in Pascal Heap

13.4 Summary

We have analyzed the scope attributes local and global, and the storage attributes static, automatic, and controlled. Since the storage attributes refer to physically disjoint areas of memory, a frequently used memory allocation scheme lets stack and heap space grow toward one another. Since the static area of a program does not change, it is possible to position it at either end.

See the sketch of a memory map in Figure 13-3.

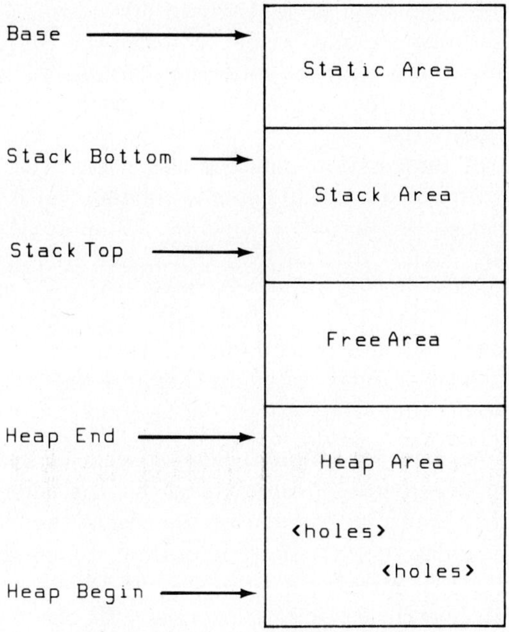

Figure 13-3 Storage Layout

Chapter 5 is related to storage classes. While the former took a close look at the different types of operands, the current chapter has analyzed how such operands fit into a program as a whole. In particular we have tried to explain the different storage and scope attributes and to emphasize that they are indeed separate programming language issues. The most abused terms in this context are dynamic and global, both of which were explained here. Even if the reader is not happy with our interpretation of terms, we have achieved our goal if the storage and scope attributes are understood to be orthogonal issues.

13.5 Exercises

1. The problem is to simulate a simple heap manager. The heap is a data structure from which consecutive blocks of storage will be granted to requesting programs. Included in a request for allocation must be the size of space needed. When we free an area no longer used, the same program must be friendly enough to return the block of storage to the heap. Address and size must be included in this "free" request. Initially the

simulator is only responsible for the allocation of heap storage; freeing will be done in the related Exercise 2.

Simulate the heap by a large Array of 10,000 integers, named "mem." Use the globally known name "avail" to index the first block of available storage. Initially there will be only one free block, which is the total memory space. At that moment a greedy program could request the whole heap for its exclusive use.

Two fields of information must be associated with any free block in the linked list. One field must indicate the amount of free space, including the overhead fields; the second should be a link to the next free block. This link will be NULL for the first block. All links must be in strictly ascending order.

The function "first_fit" is called with one integer argument called "size," which must indicate the number of elements in the desired block. "First_fit" returns the index into the heap if the free block is found; otherwise, it returns "nilval."

2. Simulate the "free_mem" function of heap space. Procedure "free_mem" is called with two arguments. "Addr" must be the index into the Array, simulating the heap, and "size" must be the size of the block to be returned to the heap at index "addr." It is important to combine adjacent free blocks. To make this merging easy, it should be assumed that the linked list elements described in Exercise 1 are in strictly ascending order.

3. Write a Pascal program that tests if the "dispose" built-in procedure truly recycles data objects that are returned to the heap. A Pascal implementation may choose not to perform garbage collection and simply set the pointer to NIL that is passed as the parameter in the "dispose" call. Hint: To actually execute the program it would be best to be alone on a system. The test program can be very simple, but it may request all available heap space.

4. The listing of program "tree" includes the procedure "preorder." "Preorder" tree traversal interprets the data in the current node first, and then traverses the left and right subtrees in preorder. In this exercise we add the procedures "postorder" and "inorder." As the names imply, "postorder" traverses the left and right subtrees first, and then interprets the current node, while "inorder" traverses the binary tree in order, that is, the left subtree first, the current node next, and the right subtree last.

5. Rewrite program "tree" in Ada.

6. You are using a program that stores integer values in a binary tree. Each tree node consists of a "data" field for the integer value and two pointer fields for the left and right subtrees. Assume for simplicity that the space for the pointers is the same as for an integer. How much total space is required to store "n" integer values?

14

Type Equivalence and Type Conversions

Was sich überhaupt sagen läßt,
läßt sich klar sagen;
und wovon man nicht reden kann,
darüber mußman schweigen.

Ludwig Wittgenstein
Quoted from the "Report on the Algorithmic Language ALGOL 60"

Be specific!

Free Interpretation of Wittgenstein's phrase in English

Strong typing, even more than recursion or Gotos, has stimulated quite a controversy. Many programmers find it not only superfluous, but a handicap to their artistic freedom as well. The fact is, however, that newer, high level languages tend more and more toward strong typing.

What does this mean to programmers? The stricter the type rules of a language, the fewer operations are allowed on objects of nonidentical types. Hence, the writing of a program becomes more difficult when a programmer must mix types. Such a mix is not always by choice—it may be imposed by outside requirements.

In this chapter we will define type and type equivalence, present some advantages and shortcomings of strict typing, and show how an object of one type can be converted into another object of a different type but with the same value. Our ultimate goal is to give a programming language designer sufficient information to make a sound decision about the inclusion or exclusion of strict typing.

14.1 Type Equivalence

A *type* defines a range of values and a set of operations permissible on objects of such a type. Usually the range is ordered, but there are types without implied order, such as the SET type in Modula-2 or Pascal. Some languages have no explicit type definition and rely on a small number of predefined, elementary types and a few type constructors such as ARRAY. Other languages allow explicit type declarations for the purpose of associating objects with such types. The type declaration defines a type mark that can be referenced. See, for example, Ada and Modula-2.

The issue of *type equivalence* arises when two objects enter into a common operation. As long as the two object types are identical, there is no problem. When the objects are only closely related, we need to know whether they are compatible with one another. This leads us to the question, when are two types compatible? The answer varies with the language, but we observe two principles, known as *structural equivalence* and *named equivalence.*

Structural Equivalence

Structural equivalence is more permissive but less clear than named equivalence. It defines two types to be compatible if they have the same "logical" structure. Sometimes logical equivalence is easy to recognize, as in Example 14-1; other times it is subject to arbitrary preferences.

```
TYPE
 range1    = 1 .. 100;
 range2    = 1 .. 100;
VAR
 r1         : range1;
 r2         : range2;
BEGIN
 r1 := r2;
```

Example 14-1 Sample of "Obvious" Structural Equivalence in Pascal

Type equivalence according to the "structural" principle is, unfortunately, not always this easy to decide. For example, are two records that only differ in one single field-name equivalent? Are two records equivalent if the order of two otherwise identical fields is exchanged? Are arrays and strings of different lengths equivalent? These are just a few questions that demonstrate that structural equivalence is a collective term for a complete range of different equivalence principles.

Named Equivalence

Named equivalence is more rigid and simpler to explain. Ada, for example, applies the named type equivalence that requires that two objects are compatible only if they are declared by the same type mark. This is easy to check at translation time. The biggest advantage of named equivalence is increased security. Moreover, the principle is simple to learn and simple to verify by a compiler. A disadvantage is the need to define more type marks than in a more loosely typed language. In Example 14-2 we show a sample Assignment Statement that would pose no problem in Pascal, Modula-2, or PL/I, but which is erroneous in Ada.

```
 TYPE meter_type IS NEW integer;
 TYPE yard_type  IS NEW integer;
 meters : meter_type;
 yards  : yard_type;
BEGIN--named equivalence
 meters := 1600;
 yards := meters;--illegal in Ada
```

Example 14-2 Are Yards and Meters Compatible?

Readers who are not familiar with Ada might become outraged about the simple-mindedness of language rules that make this Assignment Statement illegal. It is so clear to them that all operations legal with meters can also be performed on yards. Moreover, yards has the same set of permissible values that meters has. Why then is the statement wrong?

Advocates of strict typing retaliate that the program designer obviously wanted meters and yards to mean different things; otherwise, the two NEW type marks would not have been introduced. In other words, the user asks the compiler for help in verifying the consistent separation of two distinct concepts that happen to have something in common. An Ada compiler will always flag the Assignment Statement in Example 14-2.

When objects are not compatible, but we need them to be, one of them must be coerced to the other type. This coercion is also know as type conversion. Why do type conversions exist at all, and how are they used? The next section will address this question. And to help the reader grasp the true cost involved in using this construct, we will analyze some actual code sequences that have been generated for type conversions. We shall also see that many of these conversions incur no run time cost at all.

14.2 Type Conversion, An Artifact

We don't find type conversions in the abstract world of mathematics, and yet, mathematicians handle all kinds of numbers without problems. Most mathematical models are complete enough to treat what programmers call integer, rational, irrational, and imaginary numbers; but the abstract laws seem to find no need to distinguish between different types. Hence, no type conversions are needed! Why then do programming languages need them?

Whether type conversions are a vice or a virtue depends on one's standpoint. In the best of all possible worlds, programming languages would not need such constructs. Computers in such a perfect world would instead provide data types that are as convenient and unlimited as our natural numbering system.

Unfortunately, we live in a much more restricted real world. Our present-day computers have just a few natural data types, all with hard-nosed, physical restrictions. Typical operations assume the data to be of type integer, floating point, fixed point, or some other rigid type the machine understands well. If we adhere to this assumption, the machine executes operations correctly and quickly—no questions asked. If we violate the assumption, the computed results will be incorrect, because the machine will interpret the data in a way different from their intent.

What can we do though, if we must perform an integer type operation on a character type object? The easy work-around is to use type conversions. It is possible to build radically diverse computers that have no integer data type, and that perform arithmetic operations on strings of numeric digits, just as we have done since high school arithmetic. Those computers would work without type conversions for all arithmetic processing, but they would lose every race for speed with our current binary computers.

By now we should understand that type conversion is a kind of artifact that we would like to live without. But, given that computers behave the way they do, and given that we like to take advantage of their processing power and speed, we must resort to conversions when operations involve operands of dissimilar types.

Whenever an object is to be interpreted differently from the declared type, *implicit type conversion* lets the compiler do the work. PL/I and Fortran are advocates of this convenience. Ada, Pascal, and Modula-2, however, choose the more rigid philosophy of *explicit type conversion,* which holds the programmer responsible for the divergent types. In the following we look closer at explicit and implicit type conversions.

14.3 Explicit Type Conversion

We start out with the syntax rules for explicit type conversion in Ada and in Pascal. We shall also demonstrate that Pascal is neither strictly typed, nor complete in its functionality as far as type conversion is concerned. Ada, on the other hand, is quite complete, but a considerable body of language rules must be mastered for the full use of type conversions.

Explicit Type Conversion in Ada

We have already encountered Ada's type conversion proper in Chapter 6. The syntax is remarkably simple, but the functionality very limited. If we need to perform a genuine conversion to a different type in Ada, we must use attributes. Type conversions, ironically, will not convert an object from one to a radically different type. In Example 14-3 we list the grammar fragments for "ada_type_conversion" and "attribute"; samples follow.

```
ada_type_conversion     ::= type_mark ( expression )
attribute               ::= prefix ' attribute_designator
attribute_designator    ::= simple_name [ ( static_expression ) ]
```

Example 14-3 Grammar Fragment for Ada Type Conversion

A type mark in Ada type conversions classifies the desired target type, while the expression yields the value to be converted to that target type. It would be ideal if the expression could be of any type that can meaningfully be converted to the target type. This is not possible in Ada. Ada instead requires the types to be "closely related." And the interpretation of this phrase is very rigid. For example, it is not possible via type conversions in the Ada sense to generate the corresponding integer value of a character object, as is easily done in Pascal. In Ada's philosophy those types are not "closely related."

But Ada provides other tools that in a strict sense accomplish the same task as type conversions. These are the attributes, comparable to built-in functions of other languages. With type conversions, Ada only permits the reinterpretation of, say, integer type objects as objects of other integer types; but the intervention of attributes allows direct conversion to character, boolean or enumerative types. The instances in Example 14-4 illustrate conversions between integers and characters in either direction. Again, note that these are not type conversions in the sense of the Ada syntax construct "type conversions." They are attribute references.

```
PROCEDURE demo IS
 c : character;
 i : integer;
BEGIN -- demo
 c := 'A';
 i := character'pos( 'A' );
 i := integer'succ( 49 ); -- i := 50;
 c := character'val( character'pos( 'A' ) + 1 ); -- c = 'B';
END demo;
```

Example 14-4 Sample Ada Type Conversions

The major attributes that perform the type conversion functions are listed in Table 14-1.

Table 14-1 Ada Attributes Performing Type Conversion

Attribute	Target Type	Arg. Type	Sample Source
Image	String	Scalars	"=" & integer'image(i)
Pos	Integer	Scalars	i:=character'pos('0');
Val	Scalars	Integer	c:=character'val(i);
Value	Scalars	String	i:=integer'value("50")

The sample program in Example 14-5 illustrates a variety of operands that have dissimilar types. The operations adhere to the language's type rules, guaranteed so by the attributes used, which deliver the desired target types. Only a few of the procedures use "type conversion" in the literal sense of the Ada syntax.

Procedure "charint" presents in a practical way the possible conversions between integer and character type data. Attribute "pos" converts from character to integer, line 29, and attribute "val" on line 34 from integer to character. Subprogram "enumint" does the same for integer and enumeration types. Again we use attributes to perform the desired conversion. If readers study this sample very carefully, they will notice later just how awkward it is in Pascal to achieve the same results. Procedures "floatint" and "mixed" are the only samples of proper Ada type conversions.

```
                 |WITH text_io; USE text_io;
                 |PROCEDURE ada_type_conversion IS
            1    |
            1    | PROCEDURE floatint IS
            2    |   r  : float;
       11   2    |   i  : integer;
       12   2    |  BEGIN--floatint
            2    |   i := 12345;
   4        2  1 |   r := float( i );
   8        2  1 |   IF r /= 12345.0 THEN
  13        2  1 |    put_line( " integer->float error" );
  16        2  2 |   END IF;
  16        2  1 |   r := 23456.7;
  20        2  1 |   i := integer( r );
  24        2  1 |   IF i /= 23456 THEN
  28        2  1 |    put_line( " float->integer TRUNC error" );
  31        2  2 |   END IF;
  31        2  1 |   i := integer( r + 0.5 );
  38        2  1 |   IF i /= 23457 THEN
  42        2  1 |    put_line( " float->integer ROUND error" );
  45        2  2 |   END IF;
  45        2  1 |  END floatint;
  45        1    |
  45        1    | PROCEDURE charint IS
  47        2    |   i  : integer;
  47   11   2    |   c  : character;
  47   12   2    |  BEGIN--charint
  47        2    |   c := '5';
  51        2  1 |   i := character'pos( c );
  54        2  1 |   IF i /= 53 THEN
  58        2  1 |    put_line( " char->integer error" );
  61        2  2 |   END IF;
  61        2  1 |   i := 54;
  64        2  1 |   c := character'val( i );
  67        2  1 |   IF c /= '6' THEN
  71        2  1 |    put_line( " integer->char error" );
  74        2  2 |   END IF;
  74        2  1 |  END charint;
  74        1    |
  74        1    | PROCEDURE enumint IS
  76        2    |  TYPE light_type IS ( green, yellow, red );
  76        2    |   light      : light_type;
  76   11   2    |   i          : integer;
  76   12   2    |  BEGIN--enumint
  76        2    |   light := red;
  80        2  1 |   i := light_type'pos( light );
  83        2  1 |   IF i /= 2 THEN
  87        2  1 |    put_line( " enum->integer error" );
```

```
49    90       2   2  |   END IF;
50    90       2   1  |   i := 1;--light: YELLOW
51    93       2   1  |   light := light_type'val( i );
52    96       2   1  |   IF light /= yellow THEN
53   100       2   1  |     put_line( " direct integer->enum error." );
54   103       2   2  |   END IF;
55   103       2   1  | END enumint;
56   103       1      |
57   103       1      | PROCEDURE boolint IS
58   105       2      |   i   : integer;
59   105   11  2      |   b   : boolean;
60   105   12  2      | BEGIN--boolint
61   105       2      |   b := true;
62   109       2   1  |   i := boolean'pos( b );
63   112       2   1  |   IF i /= 1 THEN
64   116       2   1  |     put_line( " bool->integer error" );
65   119       2   2  |   END IF;
66   119       2   1  |   i := 0;
67   122       2   1  |   b := i >= 0 AND i MOD 2 /= 0;
68   133       2   1  |   IF b THEN
69   135       2   1  |     put_line( " integer->bool error" );
70   138       2   2  |   END IF;
71   138       2   1  | END boolint;
72   138       1      |
73   138       1      | PROCEDURE mixed IS
74   140       2      |   i   : integer;
75   140   11  2      |   c   : character;
76   140   12  2      |   r   : float;
77   140   13  2      | BEGIN--mixed
78   140       2      |   c := '5';
79   144       2   1  |   r := float( character'pos( c ) );
80   148       2   1  |   IF r /= 53.0 THEN
81   153       2   1  |     put_line( " char->integer->float error" );
82   156       2   2  |   END IF;
83   156       2   1  |   r := float( 54 );--explicit integer->float
84   160       2   1  |   c := character'val( integer( r ) );
85   164       2   1  |   IF c /= '6' THEN
86   168       2   1  |     put( " float->integer->char error. C = '" );
87   170       2   2  |     put( c );
88   172       2   2  |     put_line( "'" );
89   175       2   2  |   END IF;
90   175       2   1  |   i := boolean'pos( true );--should be 1
91   178       2   1  |   r := float( character'pos('6' ) + i );
92   184       2   1  |   IF r /= 55.0 THEN
93   189       2   1  |     put_line( " bool->int/char->int->float error" );
94   192       2   2  |   END IF;
95   192       2   1  | END mixed;
96   192       1      |
```

```
192     1     | BEGIN--ada_type_conversion
194     1     |  put_line( " START Type Conversions" );
198     1   1 |  floatint;
201     1   1 |  charint;
204     1   1 |  enumint;
207     1   1 |  boolint;
210     1   1 |  mixed;
213     1   1 |  put_line( " *END* Type Conversions" );
216     1   1 | END ada_type_conversion;
```

Example 14-5 Ada Type Conversion Program

The program "ada_type_conversion" in Example 14-5 uses predefined attributes to perform a few conversions between the most primitive types. The conversions are truly necessary, and the attributes provide a legal path. A typical application for this kind of conversion is the writing of input and output routines that deal with numeric values on one side, and with strings of characters on the other. Also the lexical analysis portion of compilers and assemblers requires the conversion from character to integer.

Explicit Type Conversion in Pascal

Pascal's solution to type conversions is simpler than Ada's, but it is not complete. To convert types where the language provides no explicit tool can become a cumbersome task. A few built-in functions are provided in Pascal for doing what is most often required. Also some implicit type conversions, those between integer and real type data, are permitted. Other type conversions are not directly supported and must be "kludged" via dirty programming tricks, as shown in the Pascal procedure "enumint" in Example 14-6. The trick is straightforward and usually workable, but it introduces a machine dependency that is hard to trace.

The "chr" function in "pascaltypeconversion" in Example 14-6 takes a single argument of integer type and returns the character whose ordinal number is that integer value. Since there are more integers than values in a character set, the potential for error exists. Hence a good implementation of "chr" should always check the value of the argument.

"Ord" returns the ordinal number of the argument value. The type of the argument may be char, boolean, or enumerative type. No range error is possible here, since there are many more integers than values in the other primitive types. The "round" built-in function returns the value of the real type argument, rounded to the closest integer. Errors are possible on machines whose real type data span a wider range of numbers than their natural integers do. "Trunc" only returns the integral portion of the real type argument.

Implicit Type Conversions in Pascal, the Exception

Integer-to-real conversion is performed implicitly in Pascal. The rationale behind this convenience, which actually introduces some inconsistency, reduces the chances for errors. All integer numbers can be accurately represented as real numbers, except on systems that provide the same number of bits for floating point and integer type objects. If the conversion goes the other way (i.e., real to integer), a change in numeric value is usually involved, unless, by chance, the value of the real type number happens to be an integer that can be represented by a natural integer object. Therefore the programmer must explicitly state which type of approximation is intended. Rounding searches for the closest integer value, while truncation simply drops any fractional part. Such laxness in type checking violates the consistency principle, cannot be found in Ada. As a general rule in programming language design we should consider a reverse function each time we propose any new function. Pascal violates this sound rule for conversions between integer and enumeration types. While the "ord" function yields the integer of an enumerative type argument, we cannot directly assign an integer to enumerative type variables. The trick for overcoming this limitation is shown in procedure "enumint" in Example 14-6. We have already shown the simple, consistent way that Ada handles this case.

```
program pascaltypeconversion( output );
 procedure realint;
  var r  : real; i : integer;
  begin { realint }
   i := 12345;
   r := i;
   if r <> 12345.0 then
    writeln( output, ' integer->real error' );
   {end if}
    r := 23456.7;
    i := trunc( r );
    if i <> 23456 then
     writeln( output, ' real->integer TRUNC error' );
    {end if}
    i := round( r );
    if i <> 23457 then
     writeln( output, ' real->integer ROUND error' );
    {end if}
   end { realint };

  procedure charint;
   var i  : integer; c : char;
   begin { charint }
    c := '5';
```

```
  i := ord( c );
  if i <> 53 then
   writeln( output, ' char->integer error' );
  {end if}
  i := 54;
  c := chr( i );
  if c <> '6' then
   writeln( output, ' integer->char error' );
  {end if}
 end { charint };

procedure enumint;
 type
  lighttype = ( green, yellow, red );
  tricktype =
   record
    case boolean of
     true:  ( i : integer );
     false: ( l : lighttype );
    {end case}
   end; {record}
 var light  : lighttype;
  trick     : tricktype;
  i         : integer;
 begin { enumint }
  light := red;
  i := ord( light );
  if i <> 2 then
   writeln( output, ' enum->integer error' );
  {end if}
  trick.i := 1;
  light := trick.l;
  if light <> yellow then
   writeln( output, ' integer->enum error' );
  {end if}
 end { enumint };

procedure boolint;
 var i  : integer; b : boolean;
 begin { boolint }
  b := true;
  i := ord( b );
  if i <> 1 then
   writeln( output, ' bool->integer error' );
  {end if}
  i := 0;
  b := ( i >= 0 ) and ( i mod 2 <> 0 );
  if b then
```

```
      writeln( output, ' integer->bool error' );
     {end if}
   end { boolint };

 procedure mixed;
  var i   : integer;
   c      : char;
   r      : real;
  begin { mixed }
   c := '5';
   r := ord( c );
   if r <> 53.0 then
    writeln( output, ' char->integer->real error' );
   {end if}
   r := 54; { implicit integer->real }
   c := chr( trunc( r ) );
   if c <> '6' then
    writeln( output, ' real->integer->char error' );
   {end if}
   i := ord( true ); { should be 1 }
   r := ord( '6' ) + i;
   if r <> 55.0 then
    writeln( ' bool->int/char->int->real error' );
   {end if}
  end { mixed };

begin { pascaltypeconversion }
 realint;
 charint;
 enumint;
 boolint;
 mixed;
end { pascaltypeconversion }.
```

Example 14-6 Pascal Type Conversion Program

The Ada and Pascal programs in Example 14-6 are designed to execute without problems. We have not planned any type conversions that cause errors. Our next sample program, however, causes an execution time error.

Ada Type Conversion Exception

Ada defines that the exception "constraint_error" must be raised if the argument of an attribute is out of range. Similarly, in Pascal, a program is wrong if its type conversion argument does not hold a legal value of the target type. Such is the case in the program in Example 14-7. The integer value

1000 is "converted" to a character, but we know that there is no Ascii character with the ordinal number 1000. There exist only 128 different character values. Even the Ebcdic character set knows only 256 distinct values.

So the program "wrong_int_to_char" does something illegal. During the program execution the Ada run time system detected the error and caused an exception.

```
                |WITH text_io; USE text_io;
                |PROCEDURE wrong_int_to_char IS
          1     | c : character;
     11   1     | i : integer;
     12   1     |
     12   1     | PROCEDURE print IS
          2     | BEGIN--print
          2     |   put_line( " i = " & integer'image( i ) );
 6        2  1  |   put_line( " c = " & character'image( c ) );
11        2  1  | END print;
11        1     |
11        1     |BEGIN--wrong_int_to_char
13        1     | i := 1000;
17        1  1  | c := 'A';
20        1  1  | print;
23        1  1  | c := character'val( i );
26        1  1  | print;
29        1  1  |END wrong_int_to_char;

i =      1000
c = A
```

Example 14-7 Exception Condition for "wrong_int_to_char"

Cost of Explicit Type Conversion

In this section we prove false the rumor that explicit type conversion is more costly in terms of code size and execution time than implicit type conversion. We also establish some rules that help us determine the conditions under which conversions do generate extra code.

14.4 Conversion Versus Reinterpretation

Whenever the bit string that holds the target type differs from the bit string of the source type, the compiler must generate code. The code performs a true conversion on the object level; it effectively informs the machine about the nature of the operation. In all other cases, where the type conversion is merely a reinterpretation of one and the same bit string, no object code is necessary.

If the machine is expected to interpret a sequence of bits differently from the way it normally would, it must be told to do so. This information must be supplied by somebody. It does not matter whether the language compiler emits these instructions based on its own judgment when encountering implicit conversions, or whether the programmer requests this by writing down type conversions explicitly. Therefore, it is not the explicit type conversion that affects the amount of generated code space. This is invariant for implicit and explicit conversion over the same operation. The distinguishing point between implicit and explicit conversion lies elsewhere—in the subtle area of program readability. A cost in terms of execution time (or generated code size) incurs only if bits must be changed. We distinguish two cases explained below.

Case 1: Pure Reinterpretation

When we ask the machine just to reinterpret data of some type as objects of another type we do not want to impose any interpretation on the meaning of the original value. We wish to see the raw data exactly as it is stored in the machine. For example, when we ask for the ordinal value of a character, we just want an integer. If the receiving integer type has a wide enough range to hold all possible values from 0 to 127, then of course no code for a type conversion is necessary. Or if we fetch a integer object but interpret it as an floating point, regardless of the value, no code need be emitted. See the sample Fortran program in Example 14-8, in particular lines 4 and 7.

```
1          program typecv
2           i = 53
3     10    format( a1 )
4           write( 6, 10 ) i
5           i = 999999.99
6     20    format( f7.3 )
7           write( 6, 20 ) i
8          end

5
11.938
```

Example 14-8 "Brute Force" Reinterpretation

Line 4 in Example 14-8 reinterprets an integer as a character, and line 7 reinterprets (or deliberately misinterprets?) the same integer but with a higher value as a piece of floating point data. The printed values are machine dependent and turned out to be character '5' and the floating point number '11.938'. This floating point result is particularly interesting, since it seems it should be closer to '999999.99'. But line 5 silently converts this into the integer value 999999, which then is reinterpreted with floating point format.

Case 2: True Type Conversion

Line 5 in in Example 14-8 is a genuine type conversion. On most machines the operation involves a change in data representation; bits will change. In Fortran and PL/I this conversion is performed implicitly by the compiler. In Ada, Modula-2, and Pascal the language type rules require the programmer to state the conversion.

There is yet another case. Even if no change of bits is involved, it can still happen that the receiving variable cannot hold all receiving values. But this may not be detectable at compile time. In this situation code is generated to perform run time range checks. Hence this case has really nothing to do with type conversion but with range checking. Had no type conversion taken place, then the range check would still be generated. Example 14-9 is the listing of an Ada program that performs type conversion between integer and floating point objects. Even though we have not shown the code generated by this program, we have checked and found that the compiler generated instructions 3 and 7 to inform the machine of the necessary conversions.

```
1                    |PROCEDURE int_float IS
2            1       | i : integer;
3        11  1       | f : float;
4        12  1       |BEGIN--int_float
5            1       | f := float( 1 );
6    5       1   1   | i := integer( f );
7    9       1   1   |END int_float;
```

Example 14-9 Explicit Code for Type Conversion

14.5 Implicit Type Conversion

This section points out a few implicit type conversions in Ada and Pascal. We shall learn that some implicit conversions appear attractive to the casual observer, since less typing is involved. But the lack of a general conversion capability requires some obscure programming practices. PL/I's implicit type conversions are more complete than Fortran's, but they are also full of mean surprises.

Implicit Type Conversions in Ada

Ada could not exist without at least a few implicit type conversions, because of its "named equivalence" principle. For example, an uncomplicated Assignment Statement like "i := 2;" does involve an implicit type conversion. Literal "2" is of type "universal_integer," while variable "i" has presumably been declared by the standard type mark "integer." So the universal_integer must be coerced into type integer. Even though the conversion is provided implicitly, Ada also permits the petty explicit conversion "i:=integer(2);," with the same semantics as the Assignment Statement just described. Code will not be generated in either case.

Situations like the implicit type conversion just explained, and in particular the notion of the type "universal_integer," are contained in Ada's definition to make the philosophy of strict typing work consistently. Compared with Ada, even Pascal is loosely typed. Such artificial sounding, implicit Ada type conversions don't need to concern the casual programmer; they exist solely for fixing a few loopholes in a contradictory model. With this additional philosophical overhead the model works completely.

More Implicit Type Conversions in Pascal

Pascal is more lax about type equivalence. Two types are equivalent if they are structurally equivalent. It does not matter how this is expressed. Even some different types are compatible. Integer and real types, though considered different, are still compatible in one direction; the language translator generates an implicit type conversion. The resulting type is always real. This happens in Assignment Statements like "r := i;" and in arithmetic expressions. Implicit conversion from real to integer never occurs in Pascal. If it is nevertheless desired, it must be stated explicitly and generates conversion code on most computers. This liberty is only granted for scalars; composites of type integer cannot be converted to their equivalent real structure. See the Pascal program in Example 14-10.

```
 1    program typeequiv( output );
 2     var
 3      a1   : array[ 1 .. 10 ] of integer;
 4      a2   : array[ 1 .. 10 ] of real;
 5      i    : integer;
 6     begin { typeequiv }
 7      for i := 1 to 10 do
 8       begin
 9        a1[ i ] := i*i;
10        a2[ i ] := a1[ i ];
11       end;
12      {end for}
13      a2 := a1;
E 13 - Type clash: nonidentical array types
14      for i := 1 to 10 do
15       writeln( a2[ i ] );
16      {end for}
17     end { typeequiv }.
```

Example 14-10 Implicit Type Conversion for Scalars, not for Arrays

Line 10 shows that an integer element is coerced into a real element, but the same operation is not permitted for a complete array; see line 13.

Implicit Type Conversion in Fortran

The sample program "ada_type_conversion" in Example 14-5 has been recoded in Fortran in Example 14-11. Fortran-77 is reasonably safe because it does not permit conversions that could cause errors. Lines 36 and 57 in Example 14-11 show two such forbidden cases. Both source lines have been transformed into comments, because the compiler would not accept them as they are stated. The danger in both cases is the larger numeric range of "integer" type data versus "character" or "logical" type data. On the other hand, the Fortran-77 compiler or language designers must have thought that it is too much to ask a compiler to generate the necessary checks that would make such a conversion possible again.

Although safety is always important, it is carried too far when Fortran-77 does not allow the assignment of a "logical" type object to an "integer" variable. There is no chance for a safety violation! See line 47 in Example 14-11.

```
      PROGRAM TYPECV
       WRITE( 6, * ) ' START Type Conversion'
       CALL RI
       CALL CI
       CALL LI
       CALL MIXED
       WRITE( 6, * ) ' *END* Type Conversion'
      END

      SUBROUTINE RI
       INTEGER I
       REAL    R
       I = 12345
       R = I
       IF ( R .NE. 12345.0 ) THEN
        WRITE( 6, * ) ' R Should be 12345.0, but is = ', R
       END IF
       R = 23456.7
       I = R
       IF ( I .NE. 23456 ) THEN
        WRITE( 6, * ) ' I Should be 23456, but is = ', I
       END IF
      END

      SUBROUTINE CI
       INTEGER I, J
       CHARACTER C
       EQUIVALENCE ( C, J )
       C = '5'
       I = C
       IF ( I .NE. 53 ) THEN
        WRITE( 6, * ) ' I Should be 53, but is = ', I
       END IF
       I = 54
       J = I
C------ C = I   Illegal Conversion
C------         Achieved anyway via equivalence
       IF ( C .NE. '6' ) THEN
        WRITE( 6, * ) ' C Should be "6", but is = ', C
       END IF
      END

      SUBROUTINE LI
       LOGICAL L
       INTEGER I
       L = .TRUE.
C------ I = L   Illegal Conversion
       IF ( L ) THEN
```

```
          I = 1
         ELSE
          I = 0
         END IF
         IF ( I .NE. 1 ) THEN
          WRITE( 6, * ) ' I Should be 1, but is =', I
         END IF
         I = 0
C------  L = I    Illegal Conversion
         IF ( I .EQ. 1 ) THEN
          L = .TRUE.
         ELSE IF ( I .EQ. 0 ) THEN
          L = .FALSE.
         ELSE
          WRITE( 6, * ) ' I out of range for logical = ', I
         END IF
         IF ( L ) THEN
          WRITE( 6, * ) ' L Should be false, but is .TRUE.'
         END IF
        END

        SUBROUTINE MIXED
         CHARACTER C
         INTEGER   I
         C = '5'
         I = C
         R = I
         IF ( R .NE. 53.0 ) THEN
          WRITE( 6, * ) ' R Should be 53.0, is = ', R
         END IF
        END
```

Example 14-11 Fortran Type Conversion Program

Since Fortran has no enumeration type, no conversion to or from this type is possible. Hence the original Ada procedure "enumint" has not been recoded. But overall, we recognize the same idea in the Fortran program "TYPECV" as in the previous programs. PL/I, on the other hand, has many unique quirks.

Implicit Type Conversion in PL/I

Consistent with PL/I's misdirected generosity, type conversions are usually implicit, thus saving some time during data entry. But they do cause great debugging problems. Program "TYPECV" in Example 14-12 has interesting illustrations in procedures "CTOI," "LOOPS," and "CONVERT." We encourage the reader to study the listing.

```
0    1  0        TYPECV: PROC OPTIONS(MAIN);
     2  1                 DCL I BIN FIXED; /* DEFAULT PRECISION */
     3  1                 DCL D DEC FIXED; /* DEFAULT PRECISION */
     4  1                 DCL C CHAR;      /* DEFAULT LENGTH */
     5  1         INIT:   PROC;
     6  2                  C = '5';
     7  2                  D = 5.0;
     8  2                  I = 5;
     9  2                 END INIT;
    10  1         PRINT:  PROC;
    11  2                  PUT LIST( ' I = ', I ); PUT SKIP;
    13  2                  PUT LIST( ' D = ', D ); PUT SKIP;
    15  2                  PUT LIST( ' C = ', C ); PUT SKIP;
    17  2                 END PRINT;
    18  1         CTOI:   PROC;
    19  2                  DCL I BIN FIXED INIT( 9 ); /* NO SIDE EFFECT */
    20  2                  I = '0'; /* CHAR -> INTEGER */
    21  2                  PUT LIST( ' I = "0", I = ', I ); PUT SKIP;
    23  2                 END CTOI;
    24  1         LOOPS:  PROC;
    25  2                  DCL I BIN FIXED; /* AVOID SIDE EFFECT */
    26  2                  DO I = 0, I = 1;
    27  2    1              PUT LIST( ' VAL OF I = ', I ); PUT SKIP;
    29  2    1             END;
    30  2                 END LOOPS;
    31  1         CONVERT:PROC;
    32  2                  C = 53; /* Ascii '5' */
    33  2                  PUT LIST( ' C = 53, = ', C ); PUT SKIP;
    35  2                  I = D / 3;
    36  2                  PUT LIST( ' I = D / 3, = ', I ); PUT SKIP;
    38  2                  D = 25 + 1 / 3;
    39  2                  PUT LIST( ' D = 25 + 1/3, = ', D ); PUT SKIP;
    41  2                 END CONVERT;
    42  1                 CALL INIT;
    43  1                 CALL PRINT;
    44  1                 CALL CTOI;
    45  1                 CALL LOOPS;
    46  1                 CALL CONVERT;
    47  1                END TYPECV;
I =          5
D =          5
C =          5
I = '0', I =0
VAL OF I =  0
VAL OF I =  0
```

Example 14-12 PL/I Type Conversion Program

The goal of "CTOI" is to convert a character literal into an integer value. It just so happens that the character is a decimal digit, and after the conversion the integer value should be that of the digit. Integer variable "I" is declared locally in "CTOI" and is initialized to 9. Then the character '0' is assigned to I. The result is a compiler writer's dream, since the final integer value corresponds exactly to the digit represented by that character, zero. This is very convenient when converting numbers from string form into binary form and conversely. Most other languages require the addition or subtraction of some offset.

But there is again a hidden monster lurking behind this convenience. The PL/I D subset compiler, while also permitting this type conversion, simply creates a different result. It treats the character '0' just like any other character, not as a special character that incidentally represents a decimal digit. The D compiler is blind to such special treatment. As a result, programs that run fine in the full PL/I dialect, are not portable to the subset. This kind of policy is even worse than forcing different languages upon a programmer community that wishes to share programs. It creates the illusion of compatibility, only to disappoint later!

The control variable "I" in procedure "LOOPS" in Example 14-12 appears to span the values 0 to 1. This too is an illusion. In reality we have two distinct ranges for the loop control variable, separated from one another by a comma. Both ranges span only one single value. The first part covers only the value 0. The second range requires some computation involving a type conversion. "I" is tested for equality with 1. Since "I" was set to zero, it will still have that value and the equality test with 1 fails. The result is the bit string value '0'B. This bit string is then converted into the corresponding integer value, clearly 0, and therefore the second iteration sets "I" again to 0. The program will emit two "0" values, not a "0" and "1," as the casual PL/I programmer might have suspected. Admittedly this is extremely tricky, but that is precisely the point: implied type conversions have the tendency to make programs difficult to understand.

The example procedure "CONVERT" includes three type conversions. The first one is not too surprising. Assigning integer 53 to character variable "C" does not set "C" to '5', as would happen in most other languages. It is possible that the PL/I compiler and run time system use the Ebcdic character set, so the correspondence of integer 53 and character '5' no longer holds. To set "C" to '5' via an integer value involving type conversion, we must instead use the value 5 in PL/I. If this seems natural, it is nevertheless inconsistent. For all other values outside 0 to 9 the type conversions from integer to character have a different effect. In statement 35 in Example 14-12, the conversion from the decimal fixed variable "D" to I is complex in terms of code and execution time, but it works without problem. Then comes the surprise in statement 38. Assigning the sum of literals "25" and "1/3" to "D" causes a run time abort. If the PL/I run time system had not crashed, we would also have been surprised by the result we got! The language requires that "D" must have the value 5 after assignment of 25+1/3, not 25 or 25.333, as one might hope.

Type Conversions in Modula-2, a Strict Policy

In general, Modula-2 and Pascal are quite similar. Also the built-in type conversion functions of Modula-2 are similar to the ones we know already from Pascal. But implicit type conversions from integer to real, allowed in Pascal, are not permitted in Modula-2. Modula-2 is one notch closer to the stricter philosophy behind Ada's design. If we still wish to perform "mixed mode" arithmetic between integers and reals, we have to use the built-in conversion functions. This way the target type is well defined, visible, and can be chosen by the programmer. In Pascal the target type of mixed mode arithmetic is always real. In Modula-2, integers can be transformed into reals by the FLOAT function, and reals can be converted to CARDINAL with the TRUNC function. The ROUND function is not predefined by the language, but individual implementations are likely to offer this and many other extensions. See Example 14-13.

```
VAR
 i    : CARDINAL;
 r    : REAL;
 c    : CHAR;
BEGIN (* TYPE CONVERSION *)
 i := 50;
 r := FLOAT( i ) + 0.5;
 i := TRUNC( r );
 c := CHR( i );
```

Example 14-13 Built-In Modula-2 Type Conversion Functions

In Example 14-13 we have also used the CHR function, returning a character type value from the CARDINAL argument, just as we do in Pascal. The inverse function is ORD, again known from Pascal. If "i" and "c" are defined as in the example, then the following identities hold in (Pascal and) Modula-2:

```
CHR( ORD( c ) ) = c
ORD( CHR( i ) ) = i
```

14.6 Summary

In this chapter we have defined *type* and explained *strict typing.* Also we have presented various principles of type equivalence. We also justified type conversions and saw that occasionally these can become costly in terms of emitted code. A higher and less tangible cost incurs from implicit type conversions, which more often than not causes the running program to perform differently than expected. If the reader can assert at the end of this chapter that the higher effort in writing explicit type conversions is well worth the time, then we have achieved our primary goal for a critical subject. But all our efforts of computing are fruitless if we cannot see the accomplishments. Therefore, programming languages must provide a communications means between the machine and the user. This is why we have IO, explained in the following chapter.

4.7 Exercises

1. Write an Ada program that converts Ascii characters to integers. The program should include a function named "ascii_to_int," which reads one string of digits from the input file. Function "ascii_to_int" should have no parameters. It should use the global character variable "nextchar" to get the next input character. These characters are assumed to be digits. "Ascii_to_int" must convert these digits into integer values and this way compose a number, one digit at a time. This is one form of lexical analysis typically performed by language compilers and assemblers.

   When the function is called, the current character is the first digit of the next number. Assume that characters are either digits or white space. "Ascii_to_int" returns the constructed value as an integer. On the input file the single number is followed by one blank or some illegal character as terminator. Unrealistically, we will assume perfect input. No integer overflow will occur, and the input file holds no bad characters, except maybe to the right of the number. But the program will never read this.

2. Write an extended Ada function "new_ascii_to_int" that is safe. Assume that Ada is implemented on a two's complement, byte-addressable machine with a word width of 16 bits.

   This time the function is called repeatedly, so that it reads one number at a time from the input file until the last number read was zero. If the source contains wrong input before the number, this is interpreted as white space, and an error message must be emitted. Assume the hardware ignores integer overflow. So if the scanned number is too large, the software function must detect the overflow before it actually happens and issue a warning.

3. Write an Ada procedure "average" that reads all numbers from a text file by calling "new_ascii_to_int" and then prints the average value. The whole program should use only integer variables, no "real" types. Other types like "character" are, of course, permitted. Procedure "average" is only concerned with an accuracy of two places to the right of the decimal point.

4. Explain why the conversion from integer to real (or vice versa) requires a genuine conversion on most Pascal run time systems. It is somewhat counterintuitive, since it doesn't matter in arithmetic whether we represent the value one by 1.0 or by 1. Why would it matter on a machine?

15

Input, Output

... that we are interested in the actual execution of a process
will nearly always imply
that we are also interested in the results.
in the description of the process to be carried out
we therefore wish to be able to indicate
which results the computer must deliver to the outside world.
On this matter, the official Algol 60 report is as silent as the grave,
and with very good reason.

Edsger W. Dijkstra
A Primer of ALGOL 60 Programming

Find a computer to print me a fact,
to multiply, add, to divide and subtract.
But the output can be
never more than debris
if the input is short of exact.

Free after /USR/GAMES/FORTUNE on Unix

Input and Output (hereafter abbreviated as IO) are neglected, second-class citizens in the world of programming languages. Machine instructions usually have no IO operations, but even some high level programming languages pretend as if IO is not an integral part or programming. Intrinsic functions, of which IO operations are only a special case, are also considered an extralinguistic device in some languages and are, therefore, not defined as part of the language proper. This chapter and Chapter 16 address this issue and present languages with a different philosophy. We define and give numerous examples for IO. To treat this subject exhaustively would require a volume in itself, so we have restricted ourselves to the rather narrow portion of IO called "Text input output," and particularly interactive Text IO. We focus on the language rules for Text IO rather than the programming design aspect of IO.

Without IO, all computing would be senseless. Should the computations ever get started, an activity already assuming input, we would never be able to see the fruits of our program's and the processor's endeavors unless the machines create output. Therefore we would have no motivation to ever build computers. IO is necessary for the interaction of machines and persons, and programming languages are the medium through which we communicate our instruction to the computer.

When the "Mission Control" computer in Houston receives a spacecraft signal about Jupiter's temperature, measured by some infrared sensor, this is a form of input. The subsequent plotting of an isothermic map with six colour pens is a form of output. Or when a process controller reads an assembly line part's distance from a soldering machine, this is input, while moving the robot's arm to ignite the electric welding arch is output.

Input can be defined very broadly as the flow of information from the outside world into a computer's memory. This is a physical viewpoint. Since in this text we are concerned about programming languages and their abstract manipulation of data, we also give a definition of input from a logical viewpoint: input is the flow of information from the outside world into the data area of a running program.

Output flows the other way. It is the transfer of data from the internal storage area of a computer to a peripheral device. Or, expressed in the more logical view, output makes the state of a program's data visible to the user. Based on this broad definition, we can imagine quite a variety of input and output operations.

One good programming language, Algol-60, never received universal acceptance, partly because it lacked a definition for IO. Though the language provides some farsighted concepts, it never took programming shops by storm, because each implementor of Algol-60 was forced to add the particular compiler's view of IO. Thus all source was inherently nonportable. Referring to the quote at the head of this chapter, we should see Dijkstra's strong defense for Algol-60's lack of IO in this light, and take it with a big grain of salt. No matter how good the reasons were for being "silent as the grave" on the IO issue, the absence of IO surely contributed to the failure of Algol-60. The world continued with Cobol and Fortran for a good reason: IO was defined!

On the other hand, absence of IO is no guarantee for failure. Ada, C, Jovial, and Modula-2 are all defined without IO. Jovial has had a successful history as the preferred language in U.S. Air Force applications; but Jovial's longevity is more a consequence of the Air Force's push for standardization than of its inherent design qualities. C is gaining more and more acceptance. It overcomes the lack of IO by wise INCLUDE conventions. As long as programmers strictly adhere to these conventions, the effect is the same as accepting a standard. Ada proposes a perfect compromise: the language proper includes no IO, but each compiler is required to make available a minimum set of IO functions, which then are uniform over all Ada compilers. This set of functions is quite powerful and supports a wide diversity of IO operations that include sequential-, direct-, and Text IO. In the Ada standard, ANSI [1983a], the chapter defining IO, Chapter 14, is one of the longest of all.

15.1 Text IO

Text IO is a special form of input output, where the objects being sent and received are readable (or printable) characters. These characters form lines of text, terminated by information that indicates the end of a line and the start of the next line. In low level languages the programmer has to be concerned about the exact nature of these "line end" indicators, while in higher level languages the translator shields the user from such detail. A higher level language only provides the logical concept of line end by functions that interrogate for the line end condition and by statements that cause this condition to yield true. Other related functions of text processing include checking for the "end of file" condition, the overprinting and underlining of characters, and the selection of different printing fonts. Most of these we shall not cover here. We shall instead focus our attention on interactive IO of plain text. This is one of the simplest, though most used and useful forms of IO.

In the batch form of Text IO, programs run without letting the programmer interfere in any intermediate step. Only the final output is of interest to the user. Naturally, for correct program execution, the programmer must provide a full set of input data to cover the anticipated course of execution. For the same reason the program must provide an execution path for all anticipated sets of input data. It is essential for batch IO that once a program starts execution, the programmer can no longer influence the flow of control.

Interactive Text IO

In interactive Text IO we imagine the user and the system to be involved in a dialogue. The executing machine acts like an intelligent conversation partner. The programmer knows, of course, that this apparent intelligence has been preprogrammed and is nothing but human intelligence, not the machine's. Typically the programmer sits in front of a CRT (Cathode Ray Tube) or monitor, reads the responses of the active program (output), and supplies new information for the program (input). An outside observer might get the impression that another person sits behind the CRT and invents the output on the fly. Therefore, this form of interaction is called program dialogue: each new input token depends on the most recent output; each output token is the result of the previous input.

Let's start with a typical scenario of interactive IO. The user issues a command to start program execution. Eventually the system loads the program identified and transfers execution control to the first piece of object code in the program. Usually this is the initialization phase, followed by a request for input. It is crucial for the user to know that input is expected. To clearly indicate this situation, the program should emit a corresponding request or prompt.

Some systems provide a prompt automatically for each element of interactive input. Other systems leave this responsibility exclusively in the hands of the programmer. Either approach has its advantages and shortcomings. In the section entitled "Iterative, Interactive IO" we present one regrettable situation, showing some disadvantages of a system without automatic prompts. Note that this is only an arbitrary sample. It is not meant to provide evidence that automatic prompting would be superior.

Infinite loops are quite a nuisance to say the least. There is one class of problems, typically confronting novices in a new programming language, that appears to be an infinite loop. In reality it is just a program waiting for input, while the programmer sits waiting for output. Since the prompt does not come, the programmer supplies no input, and both sit there, facing each other, making no progress. This situation occurs quite often, and we shall discuss various sample programs that perform interactive IO where this problem surfaces.

In the first program we present an extremely simple case where the program asks the user to input a number. The plan is to let the user input a number on the same line as the request. Then, on a new line, the program should repeat this number. We warn the reader that the program does not always function as planned due to language or implementation peculiarities that we shall point out.

Then in the following section, entitled "Iterative, Interactive IO," we shall present a second set of IO examples that use IO repeatedly. In these examples the algorithmic action depends on the "end of file" condition that is tested via a built-in function. Data are read and output is produced as long as there is further information available on the input file.

Simple, Interactive IO

Simple Ada IO

Our first programming task, to be written in Ada, Fortran, Pascal, PL/I, and Modula-2, is quite simple. The reader is advised to study only those sections that cover unfamiliar languages. During execution time the program will write a line of text. This text calls upon the user to enter a number on the same line and to terminate the line by a carriage return. After this, the program will print the message "The Number Was = " and will repeat the number to the right of this text. Example 15-1 is the Ada program listing that performs the specified task.

```
WITH text_io; USE text io;
PROCEDURE simple_ada io IS
 i : integer;
 BEGIN--simple_ada io
  put( " enter number " );
  get( i );
  put_line( " The Number Was = " & integer'image( i ) );
 END simple_ada io;

enter number 11111
The Number Was =        11111
```

Example 15-1 Simple, Interactive IO in Ada

We conclude from the two lines of generated output that program "simple_ada io" does what we planned. Number "11111" has been entered on the same line on which the system asks for input. The single blank preceding the first digit "1" has not been input by the user. It is the trailing character of the program's first text output. The second line of IO contains both the system's text message and the repeated integer number. The user could just as well have entered the number "11111" with a few leading blanks. During Text IO the integer numbers are interpreted as lexical tokens in free format. Leading blanks and line ends are silently swallowed. Here the line end after the string "11111" served as terminator of a lexical token.

Simple Fortran IO

In our second example we try to achieve the same result using Fortran. See Example 15-2.

```
      PROGRAM SFIO
       INTEGER I
       WRITE( 6, * ) ' enter next number'
       READ( 5, * ) I
       WRITE( 6, * ) ' The Number Was = ', I
      END

enter next number
22222
The Number Was =       22222
```

Example 15-2 Simple, Interactive IO in Fortran

Fortran program "SFIO," however, does not behave exactly as we intended. An implicit line end, automatically generated after the first output, precedes the input string 22222. As we see, the first output message and the first input appear on two distinct lines, contrary to what we wanted. But the Fortran implementation is correct. A Write Statement always terminates the generated output with a newline.

Simple Pascal IO

The Pascal sample "simplepascalio" in Example 15-3 performs as specified.

```
PROGRAM simplepascalio( input, output );
 VAR
  i : integer;
 BEGIN { simplepascalio }
  write( output, ' enter integer number' );
  readln( input, i );
  writeln( output, ' The Number Was = ', i );
 END. { simplepascalio }

enter integer number33333
The Number Was = 33333
```

Example 15-3 Simple, Interactive IO in Pascal

The Pascal program works very much like the Ada program with one minor exception, which was built in purposely to illustrate the difference in the two implementations. Here the first system message does not include a trailing blank character as it does in the Ada program. Therefore, the generated prompt and the entered number form a continuous line.

Simple PL/I IO

In the PL/I program in Example 15-4 we encounter a curious, illogical behaviour that can probably only be blamed on the particular implementation we used. Notice that it offers us what looks like a friendly implicit prompt in the form of the ? character. But then, despite our correct program, the system does not behave as expected. We want the prompt " ENTER NUMBER =" to be the first IO action, but because of the implicit prompt, the request for input comes after the input itself! We know that input is required only because of the implicit prompt.

```
0      1    0          SIMPLE_PLI IO: PROC;
       2    1           DCL I BIN FIXED;
       3    1           PUT LIST( ' ENTER NUMBER = ' );
       4    1           GET LIST( I );
       5    1           PUT LIST( ' THE NUMBER WAS = ', I );
       6    1           PUT SKIP;
       7    1          END SIMPLE_PLI IO;
? 44444
1 ENTER NUMBER =    THE NUMBER WAS =         44444
```

Example 15-4 Simple, Incorrect, Interactive IO in PL/I

Even though the circumstances in Example 15-4 are quite reversed from the way they should be, we should not conclude prematurely that the PL/I language is so silly. This is only an implementation quirk; the language specification is more reasonable. According to the language definition, first the message "ENTER NUMBER =" should have appeared. The user would have entered the number on that same line, presumably terminated by a carriage return, which the PL/I IO routines recognize as a delimiter for an integer number. On the following line this number would have been repeated, after the text string "THE NUMBER WAS =." This is what our intuition tells us when we read the source in Example 15-4; this is also what PL/I defines ought to happen.

The second PL/I program in Example 15-5 shows a way to overcome this situation and get us closer to an acceptable form of dialogue with the system. But the "way around" is to change our specification!

```
1    0          BETTER_PLI IO: PROC;
2    1           DCL I BIN FIXED;
3    1           PUT LIST( ' ENTER NUMBER = ' );
4    1           PUT SKIP;
5    1           GET LIST( I );
6    1           PUT LIST( ' THE NUMBER WAS = ', I );
7    1           PUT SKIP;
8    1          END BETTER_PLI IO;
1 ENTER NUMBER =
? 55555
THE NUMBER WAS =          55555
```

Example 15-5 Better, Interactive IO in PL/I

We have added a "PUT SKIP" Statement on line 4. Then the interactive IO sequence is equivalent to the one observed in Fortran, hence not exactly as specified, but at least input and output are not reversed.

The digit '1' output at the start of each interactive PL/I execution is also supplied implicitly by the system. It is meant to cause a page eject, in case the output is sent to a line printer. On a CRT screen this only causes a minor cosmetic nuisance. At the time PL/I was defined, the line printer was the standard output device, and the card reader the standard input peripheral.

Simple Modula-2 IO

Our next example will acquaint us with IO in Modula-2. Modula-2, like Ada, does not provide IO as part of the language definition. Different from Ada, a Modula-2 implementation does not guarantee to provide a common, well-defined set of IO primitives. The language has not (yet) been standardized, and the user community will be subjected to individually chosen implementor conventions. We can only hope that despite the odds, the Modula-2 world will experience the same miracle we observe with C. All C systems include a useful, common set of IO primitives together with the compiler. A C program then can "Include" these primitives. In Modula-2 the same facility will be accomplished in a clean way by "Importing" modules. Example 15-6 imports selected IO routines from the predefined Module "InOut."

```
 1            MODULE SimpleModula2IO;
 2             FROM InOut IMPORT ReadInt, WriteString, WriteInt, WriteLn;
 3             VAR  i : INTEGER;
 4             BEGIN
 5              WriteString( " enter number " );
 6              ReadInt( i );
 7              WriteString( " The Number Was = " );
 8              WriteInt( i, 10 );
 9              WriteLn;
10             END SimpleModula2IO.
```

```
enter number +1946
The Number Was =        1946
```

Example 15-6 Simple, Interactive IO in Modula-2

The invitation to enter a number and the value actually input appear on the same line. That is intended, since the WriteString Statement on line 5 only prints a partial line; it does not emit a line end. If that were desired, we would have to add a WriteLn Statement. Our input number has a legal though redundant leading + sign, which is gracefully swallowed. The ReadInt procedure recognizes the end of the input number "+1946" by the EOL character after the '6'. Therefore the next output message appears on a new line. The following section shows a more complex pattern of IO operations.

Iterative, Interactive IO

Iterative Ada IO

Our next IO examples are a bit more sophisticated. This time we read integers from standard input until the end of the file is reached. Each time input is expected, the system prompts the user with a message. A solution in Ada is shown in Example 15-7.

```
WITH text_io; USE text io;
PROCEDURE iterative_ada io IS
 i : integer;
 BEGIN--iterative_ada io
  WHILE NOT end_of file( input ) LOOP
   put( " enter number " );
   get( i );
   put_line( " number was" & integer'image( i ) );
  END LOOP;
 END iterative_ada io;

enter number 22
number was         22
enter number 33
number was         33
enter number
**Abort**
```

Example 15-7 Iterative, Interactive IO in Ada

It is hard to see, but the program's first request to "enter number" comes after the user has hit the return key. In other words, the user had to enter an empty line before the programmed prompt was printed. This is exactly the regrettable situation mentioned earlier, where the user sits in front of a terminal, waiting for output, while the program idles, expecting some input. Here the user broke the tie by entering an empty line. Why does this happen?

Algorithm "iterative_ada io" clearly defines that all program messages will be printed and all input will be read, as long as the "end_of file" condition is false. The question then arises, how can the running program know if the next input token will be an "end_of file" indicator? If the program could read the user's mind, there would be no problem. But since it cannot know in advance whether the user intends to stop or continue, an empty line must be entered to signal that there will be some input. This way the system knows there is action to come and prints the prompt for a number.

From then on, however, the program will always request more input. Only after receiving a special control character indicating end of processing will the program terminate. This is not a very graceful way of terminating! But there is a cleaner way of handling IO that depends on an "end of file" condition. We shall see such a clean way in a moment, when we cover Fortran. If the input comes from a disk file, the "end_of file" condition can be tested cleanly, and the issue of undecidability ("will the user now stop entering data or not?") cannot arise. Disk files have a special marker that explicitly states: "here is the end of the file." The lesson to learn from the Ada example is that iterative, interactive IO which is controlled by a While Statement does not always execute as our intuition would have it.

Interactive Fortran IO

The Fortran solution coming next works correctly, but we should notice a very subtle difference in the problem specification. See Example 15-8.

```
1          PROGRAM IOTST2
2           INTEGER I, EOF
3   10      WRITE( 6, * ) ' enter next number'
4           READ( 5, *, IOSTAT = EOF ) I
5           IF ( EOF .GE. 0 ) THEN
6            WRITE( 6, * ) ' value is', I
7            GOTO 10
8           END IF
9          END
```

```
enter next number
777
value is 777
enter next number
888
value is 888
enter next number
Interrupt
```

Example 15-8 Iterative, Interactive IO in Fortran

Fortran program "IOTST2" executes as it should. The request "enter next number" appears on the CRT screen right away. A closer look at the program listing shows us, however, that the Fortran program is driven by a repeat loop. The test for termination is at the end of the loop body. So "IOTST2" is not an exact translation of the Ada program in Example 15-7.

Also, it is interesting to observe how Fortran checks for the "end of file" condition. The predefined input output specifier "iostat" is referenced in the Read Statement (line 4) with the following meaning: iostat sets the integer variable to the right of the assignment operator to 0, if neither an error condition nor an end of file condition is encountered by the system. An error condition would set variable "eof" to a positive, integer value, while an end of file condition will set "eof" to a negative value. Note the reverse direction of the assignment operation. Conventionally, the receiving variable is on the left of the = operator (see, for example, the Assignment Statement), but here it is on the right. This is a counterexample to the programming language design principle of uniformity: when two constructs have the same meaning, they should have the same syntax.

Interactive Pascal IO

The Pascal program "iterativepascalio" in Example 15-9 is more of a success story.

```
PROGRAM iterativepascalio( input, output );
 VAR
  i : integer;
 BEGIN { iterativepascalio }
  WHILE NOT eof( input ) DO
   BEGIN
    write( output, ' enter integer number: ' );
    readln( input, i );
    writeln( output, ' number is = ', i );
   END;
  {END WHILE}
  END. { iterativepascalio }

enter integer number: 55
number is =           55

enter integer number: 66
number is =           66

enter integer number:
```

Example 15-9 Iterative, Interactive IO in Pascal

The Pascal version of the iterative IO program is a true transliteration of the Ada solution. Both the system output and user input are controlled by the While Statement, which tests for the end of file condition via the predefined function "eof." As with program "iterative_ada io," the user must first press the return key on the keyboard to break the impasse of the mutual "after you, after you" situation. Then the IO function testing for end of file knows that the user intends to input yet another number. So the While Loop is executed for the n-th time, which could be the first iteration, and the message "enter integer number:" shows up on the CRT screen.

After the program has printed the short text message and displayed the number, the mutual wait situation is back. This is why we see one empty line on the output screen after each iteration through the loop. The final end of file condition for interactive IO is established by hitting the "delete" key. This is an implementation specific solution and may vary from one system to another. On the system used here the "delete" key takes over the special function of an "end of file" marker, otherwise implemented for input files that reside on disk.

Interactive PL/I IO

PL/I program "ITERATIVE_PLI IO" in Example 15-10 behaves just as we wish. The program prompt "ENTER NEXT NUMBER:" comes out without delay, and the user knows that the system expects input.

```
0    1   0       ITERATIVE_PLI IO: PROC OPTIONS(MAIN);
     2   1        DCL I BIN FIXED;
     3   1        LOOP:
                   PUT LIST( ' ENTER NEXT NUMBER: ' ); PUT SKIP;
     5   1         ON ENDFILE( SYSIN ) GOTO END_LOOP;
     7   1         GET LIST( I );
     8   1         PUT LIST( ' THE NUMBER WAS = ', I ); PUT SKIP;
    10   1         GOTO LOOP;
    11   1        END_LOOP:
                  PUT LIST( ' ** EOF **' ); PUT SKIP;
    13   1       END ITERATIVE_PLI IO;
```

```
1 ENTER NEXT NUMBER:
? 12345
THE NUMBER WAS =          12345
ENTER NEXT NUMBER:
? 23456
THE NUMBER WAS =          23456
ENTER NEXT NUMBER:
?
** EOF **
```

Example 15-10 Iterative, Interactive IO in PL/I

In addition to the user prompt in the form of a readable message, the system also supplies the default prompt, ?, each time input is expected. Let us analyze the program body more carefully. Again we have not used a proper While Loop. Instead we constructed a hand-manufactured "loop-and-a-half." At first glance it seems that the termination condition is checked for in the middle of the loop body: if true, a Goto Statement transfers control to the point of termination. This is not entirely accurate. In reality the On Condition named "Endfile," checks for the indicated situation. If true, an interrupt is generated. In Ada we would say an exception is raised. Then the interrupt is serviced. The service action is the one specified as part of the On Condition, which must be a simple PL/I statement. The interesting point here is that the On Condition could have been specified anywhere, where the label END_LOOP is accessible, even before the actual loop body. The interrupt will be generated as soon as the Get List Statement (or any other input statement) encounters the end of the input file. We chose the loop-and-a-half construct here, because it is the natural loop for the problem. We always want to see the message "ENTER NEXT NUMBER:"; then we want to decide whether our input sequence should terminate or not.

Interactive Modula-2 IO

In addition to the numerous IO primitives, the predefined module "InOut" exports the character type constant "EOL" and the boolean variable "Done." "Done" indicates whether or not the previous IO operation was successful and hence can take over the function of the end of file condition. When single characters are being read, "Done" should not be used to detect the "end of line" condition. Instead our program should check for equality with the character "EOL." In the program in Example 15-11 we choose to terminate a line by explicitly writing an "EOL" character, just to familiarize the reader with the alternative to the "WriteLn" procedure.

```
MODULE IterativeModula2IO;
 FROM InOut
 IMPORT ReadInt, WriteString, WriteInt, Done, EOL;
 VAR  i : INTEGER;
 BEGIN
 WriteString( " enter number " );
 ReadInt( i );
 WHILE Done DO
  WriteString( " The Number Was = " );
  WriteInt( i, 10 );
  Write( EOL );
  WriteString( " enter number " );
  ReadInt( i );
 END;
END IterativeModula2IO.
```

Example 15-11 Iterative, Interactive IO in Modula-2

This concludes our short introduction to interactive IO. In the following sections we explain the main rules of Text IO.

15.2 Text IO in Ada

Input and output in Ada is provided by means of predefined packages; it is not part of the language proper. These packages must be supplied by each Ada implementation in order to have the compiler validated.

There are three classes of IO: sequential, direct, and Text IO with the respective predefined packages "sequential_io," "direct_io," and "text_io." The first two are generic and hence need a type mark as a parameter upon instantiation; we shall not cover these here. Also the Ada concepts of generic packages and their instantiation are too advanced to receive a more detailed treatment than the short explanation in the following.

Package text_io operates on objects of globally known type, which are strings of characters. Therefore no instantiation is needed; importing via a context clause is sufficient. We have seen the Ada mechanism for importing several times already in sample programs. The Context Clause "WITH text_io;" tells the compiler to import all names that are defined in the Package "text_io." It will still be necessary to fully qualify all names so imported by the prefix "text_io.," unless we explicitly request the abbreviated form. "USE text_io;" accomplishes the abbreviation. If Text IO on integer type objects is desired, an implicit conversion to and from type string is provided by the generic package "integer_io." In that case a declaration of the following form is required.

```
PACKAGE my_int_io IS NEW integer_io( integer );
```

Text output for integers can also be produced by explicit conversion with the "image" attribute, as we have shown various times in sample programs.

Text IO operations read from and write to text files. An Ada file is a sequence of pages, a page is a sequence of lines, and a line is a sequence of characters. Each page, each line, and each character on a line has a distinct number associated with it. This number can be set and interrogated via predefined Ada functions and procedures. For example, the procedure "set_page_length" allows the user to define the number of lines per page in the file that is passed as the first parameter; the function "page_length" returns this number. Procedure "set_line_length" sets the maximum line length of the specified output file, while the function "line_length" retrieves it. And procedure "set_col" specifies the column position for the next character to be read or written; function "col" returns the current column number of the passed file name. These are only a few of the numerous, predefined IO services. For more detail see ANSI [1983a], Chapter 14.

"Get" and "put" are the overloaded, predefined procedures that perform the actual Text IO. Either statement comes in two forms, with and without an explicit file specifier. If the file is not explicitly given in the IO Statement, input is read from the standard input file, and output is written to the standard output file. Again Ada permits the setting and interrogating of these standard files. Procedures "set_input" and "set_output" provide for the control of the default files that are used when a file parameter is omitted in "get" or "put" Statements. The argument is the input or output file, respectively. Functions "standard_input" and "standard_output" return the standard input and output files, while "current_input" and "current_output" do so for the current default files.

Line Ends in Ada

A sequence of put statements writes strings onto the same line of output, concatenated from left to right, in the order of execution. To specify that the end of a line is desired, the last Output Statement can either be a "put_line" Statement, or the sequence of Put Statements may be followed by a "new_line" Statement. To test whether the currently read line is at its end, the predefined function "end_of_line" is provided. During reading the rest of the current line can be skipped via the "skip_line" Statement. This rest may be empty. A "get_line" Statement with an argument may be used instead of the "skip_line."

Explicit Width of Ada IO Arguments

After instantiation of the generic package "integer_io," it is possible to read or write objects of all primitive types, as specified in the types passed during instantiation. The number of character positions consumed on text files is dependent on the type, but is predefined by defaults for each type. This number of characters is named the *field width.* Another form of overloaded IO Statements permits the explicit setting of that field width. This is done by supplying a third argument to the "get" or "put" procedures. An example follows.

```
put( my_file, 1943, 12 );
```

This Text Output Statement prints the integer literal "1943" onto file "my_file" and consumes exactly 12 positions. No leading zeros are printed, hence only four positions are absorbed by the literal. Eight leading blanks precede the integer literal.

5.3 Text IO in Fortran

Fortran defines two types of IO: formated and unformated. *Formated* is the Fortran term for human-readable Text IO; all other types of IO are *unformated.* Fortran does not support the use of logical, mnemonic file names; it can be simulated through PARAMETER declarations, which are comparable to the CONST declarations known from Pascal. Numeric unit numbers are used in place of file names. By convention the unit number 6 specifies the default output file, and unit number 5 the default input file. We have shown examples of this numerous times, including the program called "IOTST2" in Example 15-8.

There are nine IO-related statements in Fortran. These are the Read, Write, Print, Open, Close, Inquire, Backspace, Endfile, and Rewind Statements. In conjunction with a substantial number of status and format specifiers, Fortran permits considerable IO flexibility. A partial syntax for Read and Write Statements is given in Example 15-12.

```
fortran_read statement   ::= READ ( cilist ) [ iolist ]
                           | READ form [ , iolist ]

fortran_write statement  ::= WRITE ( cilist ) [ iolist ]

cilist                   ::= ci_element { ci_element }

ci_element               ::= [ UNIT = ] unit_specifier
                           | [ FMT = ] form
                           | REC = integer_expression
                           | IOSTAT = integer_variable
                           | ERR = s
                           | END = s

iolist                   ::= io_element { io_element }

io_element               ::= variable
                           | fortran_expression

unit_specifier           ::= integer_expression
                           | *

form                     ::= statement_label

s                        ::= statement_label
```

Example 15-12 Grammar Fragment for Fortran Read-Write Statement

The complete set of syntax rules for Fortran IO Statements is quite complex; refer to ANSI [1978] Chapters 12 and 13.

A *unit specifier* is optionally preceded by the keyword UNIT and the = symbol. There can be at most one unit specifier per IO Statement. If the unit specifier is an integer expression, its value must be zero or positive. An asterisk in its place identifies a particular processor-dependent external file unit that is connected for sequential Text IO.

The statement label is optionally preceded by the keyword FMT and the = symbol. There can be at most one format specifier per IO Statement, which may be one of the following: the label of a Format Statement, an integer variable that has been assigned a Format Statement label, or an asterisk. For a complete set of rules refer to ANSI [1978] page 12-8. If an asterisk is given as the format specifier, then list-directed IO is provided. List-directed IO views the text input or output as a sequence of pages, each of which is logically tabulated into six vertical columns. During each IO operation the operand is written to the next available column. See for comparison and more detail our explanation of list-directed IO in the PL/I discussion in Section 15-5.

15.4 Text IO in Pascal

Pascal has binary files and text files. Text files are files of characters. These files have a small set of predefined procedures, which operate on lines of text. Binary files consist of a sequence of primitive types or Records that may be arbitrarily complex. A single IO Statement can, therefore, read or write a complete structure. There is one exception to this generality: the element of a file cannot again be of type file. In other words, it is impossible to nest the file concept in Pascal. With the exception of this meaningful restriction, files are just one instance of a type in Pascal. Consequently, files can be Record fields or Array elements. Such a level of orthogonality and the absence of special rules constitute the "good part" of Pascal's IO and its file concept; the "bad part" is its excessive simplicity. Later in this section we shall analyze an interesting anomaly with Arrays of files that has been observed by Stadel [1984a].

Where are Pascal's limitations regarding IO? First, only sequential files exist in Pascal. Second, standard Pascal has only the notion of a "logical" file name. It ignores the important fact that files do have a "physical" representation on a storage medium and, therefore, have a "physical" name as well. The association between logical and physical file name is implementation-dependent and is not included as part of the language. In particular, the standard language permits no explicit association between the two names. Most implementations extend the language by permitting a second argument of string type in the "reset" and "rewrite" procedures. The language designer can derive a rule-of-thumb here: whenever implementors consistently extend some language facility, that facility is apparently inadequate.

On the good side, all IO Statements are defined as part of the language proper. Read and Write Statements have an optional logical file name, followed by any number of read or write arguments. If the file name is omitted, the standard input file is assumed for read operations and the standard output file for write operations. Otherwise, the specified logical file name is affected. In place of the predefined statements "read" and "write," an equivalent pair of statements involving "get" and "put" may be used. See Example 15-13.

```
read( input, i )         same as:      i := input^;
                                       get( input );

write( output, 1234 )    same as:      output^ := 1234;
                                       put( output );

read( i, k )             same as:      i := input^;
                                       get( input );
                                       k := input^;
                                       get( input );
```

Example 15-13 Pascal Text IO

This type of sequential Text IO uses *file windows,* which means the program can peek into a small subsection of a file without impact on the file. The advantage of the "File Window IO" shown in Example 15-13 is subtle though important. Splitting the actual IO operation into an assignment and file pointer advancement allows the program to inspect the next element on the file. This information then can steer subsequent actions, and the program may choose not to read because the current input data are untouchable. This liberty is not possible with "read" (or "write") statements.

A list of predefined IO functions and procedures follows: Readln, Writeln, Read, Write, Get, Put, Eof, Eoln, Reset, and Rewrite. The Writeln Statement has the effect of a Write Statement with the same arguments, but in addition a line terminator is emitted. A Readln Statement has the same effect as a Read Statement with identical arguments, but after completion of the read operation the rest of the current line of text (if any) is skipped and reading will proceed on the subsequent line.

Opening Files

To open a file for input, a Reset Statement must be executed first. This establishes the connection between the existing physical file and the logical file in the Pascal source. Both names are the same or subject to implementation-specific conventions. To open a file for output, a Rewrite Statement is executed. Execution of this statement creates the file with a physical name, again controlled by a local convention. It is not possible in Pascal to read from and write to a file simultaneously without intervening Reset or Rewrite Statements.

End of Line, End of File

The predefined boolean function "eof" returns true if the current input file has been completely read. It is not meaningful to test an output file for the "eof" condition, because for output it is universally true. Also, we have shown in Example 15-9 that the "eof" function is not always meaningful for interactive IO. The predefined function "eoln" returns true, if the specified input text file is at the end of a line. Otherwise, false is returned.

Arrays of Files

Stadel points out an interesting aspect of Pascal's Text IO that is based on a very delicate side effect. This side effect shows up in an Array of files, an element of which is referenced in a Read Statement with multiple arguments. We reuse Stadel's sample program in Example 15-14 with a minor variation.

```
PROGRAM confusing( output );
 VAR
  textarray : ARRAY[ 1 .. 2 ] OF text;
  i, n      : integer;
 BEGIN { confusing }
  i := 1;
  rewrite( textarray[ 1 ] );
  write( textarray[ 1 ], 2, 5 );
  rewrite( textarray[ 2 ] );
  write( textarray[ 2 ], 3, 9 );
  reset( textarray[ 1 ] );
  reset( textarray[ 2 ] );
  read( textarray[ i ], i, n );
  writeln( n );
 END. { confusing }
```

Example 15-14 A Confusing Pascal Program

Upon first inspection of the "confusing" program in Example 15-14 we believe that the Read Statement will read two values from file "textarray[1]." No input should come from file "textarray[2]," since variable "i" holds the value 1 and indexes the Array of files. It turns out that the compiler used to run this test behaves just as intuition tells us. Indeed the value 5 is printed onto standard output. We must conclude that variable "n" receives its value from the second element on file "textarray[1]," which is 5.

Unfortunately, both our intuition and the particular compiler are wrong. The Pascal standard defines that a Read Statement with multiple arguments is equivalent to multiple Read Statements with one argument. Hence, "read(

textarray[i], i, n)" is equivalent to: "read(textarray[i], i); read(textarray[i], n)." We notice that "i" changes along the way. After the first read operation, the second Read Statement refers to a different file, since "textarray" is now indexed by 2. Therefore, the next element to be read should come from "textarray[2]." So the correct program behaviour would have been to print a 3 instead.

15.5 Text IO in PL/I

PL/I has three classes of Text IO: list-directed, edit-directed, and data-directed. List-directed IO is the simplest form. It assumes all IO to be done in text form, and that text to be arranged on pages in a fixed columnar form. The format of each IO item is specified by system defaults according to its data type. Edit-directed IO requires explicit format specifiers for each item read or written. The format list is given after the argument list in the edit-directed IO Statement. In data-directed IO the name of written variables is printed in conjunction with the value. We shall not go into the details of data-directed IO.

Syntax for PL/I Get and Put Statements

The keyword LIST, EDIT, or DATA is generally included as part of a PL/I IO Statement in order to specify the desired class of IO. If it is omitted, PL/I assumes LIST by default. Also the file name may be omitted, just as we have observed for other languages. In this case PL/I assumes the default input and output files. In Example 15-15 we give a sample PL/I Output Statement for each class and the corresponding generated character string; variable "I" is assumed to be 44. In the remainder of this section we shall not cover data-directed IO any further, because it is too esoteric an IO capability and specific only to PL/I.

```
+----------------------------+-----------------------------------+
|  PUT LIST( I, I );         |  44                    44         |
|  PUT EDIT( I, I )( F(2) ); |  4444                             |
|  PUT DATA( I, I );         |  I  =     44         I  =     44; |
+----------------------------+-----------------------------------+
```

Example 15-15 PL/I Output Statements

List-Directed IO

List-directed IO in PL/I is simple and convenient, but also inflexible. Input files are scanned for lexical tokens in sequence. Tokens are separated from one another by at least one blank or by a comma. The separator comma may also be surrounded by blanks. Note, if the input variable is a string type, then commas and blanks are interpreted as input text as long as they are embedded in single quotes.

Output files hold the printed items in a tabular form, with a fixed number of columns per page or per line. This should not be confused with character columns, which naturally consume exactly one position or "column" per character. List-directed IO has a fixed number of logical columns per page. This is illustrated with two Output Statements in Example 15-16.

```
+-----------------------------+-----------------------------------+
| PUT LIST( I, I, I );        |    55            55           55  |
| PUT LIST( '''','A',''''     |    '             A             '  |
+-----------------------------+-----------------------------------+
```

Example 15-16 List-Directed IO Statements

We might disagree with PL/I about the generated output for the second statement that emits merely three characters. Each of these consumes one logical column. Therefore, the character "A," to be embedded in single quotes, stands alone on the output line. The surrounding single quotes are to the far left and right. We can, however, apply list-directed IO to create the desired output by concatenating the three partial strings. The correct statement, using the concatenation operator || twice, is

```
PUT LIST( '' || 'A' || '' );.
```

The latter Put List Statement will emit the string 'A', with single quotes around the A. The statement now has only one argument.

Edit-Directed IO

Edit-directed IO grants the programmer precise control over each character position on a line, and over the complete layout of lines and pages as a coherent text. This increased flexibility does cost something. The price is increased complexity in writing source programs. Not only does the user have to define which objects have to be input or output, but it is also necessary to provide a so-called format list with each IO Statement. The format specifiers in the format list correspond with the objects on a one-to-one basis, left to right with wrap around. Should the format list be longer than the object list, then the right tail is ignored. If the format list is too short, then it is elaborated again from left to right for the subsequent IO objects.

Format specifiers define the nature of conversions to and from string, and allow explicit control over the number of character positions consumed in each step. Further specifiers allow explicit control over the space between objects. The most frequent format specifiers are listed as follows with a brief explanation of their function.

A(w)
For input, interpret the next "w" characters as input string. For output, emit a string of length "w" onto the output file. If the width is not given, then the current length of the printed object is taken.

E(w,d)
Interpret the next "w" characters as a floating point number. The total length is exactly "w," rounded to "d" digits to the right of the decimal point. The so-called "scientific notation" is assumed with no explicit sign for positive arguments. For example, if E(9,4) were the format specifier, the string -1.6500E1 would correspond to -16.5.

X(w)
If another token is to be read or written, skip exactly "w" blanks. Otherwise, if the last IO token was the last on the list of IO tokens, then the format specifier X is ignored.

COL(c)
For input, read the next character from position "c." If there is any number of characters between the current column position and position "c," then skip the remaining characters. Should the current position on the current line already be greater than "c," then skip the rest of the current line completely and read from column "c" of the next line. Output works analogously, except that blanks are printed, not skipped, during read operations.

F(w[,d])
The next argument is a fixed point number with "w" characters of precision, of which "d" digits are for the fraction. If "d" is missing it defaults to zero.

15.6 Text IO in Modula-2

Predefined Module "InOut"

Text IO in Modula-2 is arranged as in Ada. The language has no intrinsic IO functions, but each Modula-2 implementation is expected to provide a certain set of IO Modules. The most commonly used module for Text IO is "InOut." The main procedures that can be imported from "InOut" are listed as follows.

Table 15-1 Ten Procedures

Modula 2	Meaning of Procedures
Read	reads one character
ReadString	reads a character string
ReadInt	read an integer
ReadCard	read cardinal number
Write	write one character
WriteString	write a character string
WriteLn	write end of line, same as Write(EOL)
WriteInt	write an integer value
WriteCard	write a cardinal number
WriteOct	write an integer, base 8
WriteHex	write an integer, base 16

The system-provided module "InOut" supplies all primitives necessary to perform sequential Text IO. Routines that perform automatic conversion from and to CARDINAL and INTEGER are also given. The "ReadInt" procedure has only one parameter, which is an integer type variable. The exact number of characters read to construct an integer value is not fixed and depends instead on the lexical rules for an integer literal. A leading - or + sign is legal with the conventional meaning. Leading blanks are simply ignored. Then ReadInt reads all characters that are digits until an overflow occurs or until the next character is no longer a digit. A blank, a line end, or the end of a file are legal, possible delimiters. The WriteInt procedure, on the other hand, needs a second parameter, which is the minimum number of character positions for the integer argument to be printed. In our program in Example 15-11 we chose 10 positions. A leading + is not printed for positive values, but negative integers are preceded by the - character.

The WriteString and WriteLn procedures append characters to the end of the current output file. WriteLn is functionally equivalent to the statement "Write(EOL)," where EOL is a predefined language constant that denotes the end of a line. Write appends one single character to the output file. WriteString appends as many characters as specified in the actual string parameter.

We need to emphasize one more interesting similarity with Ada. Module "InOut" offers the procedures "OpenInput" and "OpenOutput," which allow the redefinition of the standard input and output text files. If the standard files are not explicitly assigned the keyboard is the standard input device, and the CRT screen the standard output device. When used, the standard Text IO files can be any files. After calling "CloseInput" and "CloseOutput" standard input and output revert to keyboard and CRT screen.

Another important module, "RealInOut," which should be furnished with each implementation, provides IO for real type arguments. The supplied procedures are listed as follows.

ReadReal	read a floating point number
WriteReal	write a floating point number
WriteRealOct	write a floating point number, base 8

15.7 Number Guessing Game

How can IO be explained better than by real examples? In this section we shall play some interactive games, during which various Text IO statements will be executed. First, the Ada program "find_numbers" in Example 15-17 asks for numbers to be thought up by the programmer. It then tries to read the user's mind. More precisely, the program guesses the number within just a few mistrials. This process requires heavy IO interaction, exactly what we are trying to demonstrate.

```
                       |WITH text_io; USE text io;
                       |PROCEDURE find_number IS
                1      | min : CONSTANT integer := 1;
          10    1      | max : CONSTANT integer := 1_000;
          10    1      | low,    --true number not below low
          10    1      | high,   --true number not greater than high
          10    1      | guess       : integer;
          13    1      | PACKAGE my_io IS NEW integer_io( integer ); USE my_io;
          13    1      | PROCEDURE enter IS
                2      | BEGIN--enter
                2      |  put_line( " Think up a number in range 1 .. 1 000" );
    4           2   1  |  put_line( " I shall guess your number swiftly." );
    7           2   1  |  new_line( output );
    8           2   1  | END enter;
    8           1      |
    8           1      | FUNCTION too_high RETURN boolean IS
   10           2      |  answer : character;
   10     11    2      | BEGIN--too_high
```

```
10    2     |  put( " Is my guess too high? Answer y or n." );
13    2  1  |  put( integer'image( guess ) );
16    2  1  |  get( answer );
18    2  1  |  RETURN answer = 'y';
25    2  1  | END too_high;
25    1     |
25    1     |BEGIN--find_number;
27    1     | low := min;
31    1  1  | high := max;
34    1  1  | enter;
37    1  1  | LOOP
37    1  1  |  guess := integer( float( low + high ) / 2.0 + 0.5 );
50    1  2  |  IF too_high() THEN
54    1  2  |   high := guess - 1;
59    1  3  |  ELSE
59    1  2  |   low := guess;
63    1  3  |  END IF;
63    1  2  |  EXIT WHEN low = high;
68    1  2  | END LOOP;
69    1  1  | put( " the guessed number is: " );
71    1  1  | put_line( integer'image( low ) );
74    1  1  |END find_number;
```

Example 15-17 Number Guessing Game in Ada

In this game the user and the computer (program) play together. The user thinks up a number in some range, without telling the program, while the computer attempts to guess that number. In this implementation the range is between 1 and 1000 inclusively.

Naturally there exists a trivial solution. If the computer would just ask for all numbers in sequence, then sooner or later the secret will be unveiled. The purpose of the game is to let the program ask the user the minimum number of questions that can be answered with a yes or no that guarantee a correct guess. This listing of Ada program "find_number" offers one solution to the problem. Readers are invited to implement the game themselves and to enjoy playing it. After all, if we couldn't play, programming would only be half as much fun.

The Game of Nimm

Now let us play with more sophistication! The famous "nimm_game" is a bit involved, but playing it offers quite a challenge. Here the human programmer plays against the cold, emotionless machine, which is only following the instructions of the program. Both the inspiration for this game and its solution come from Knuth [1973], page 85.

Computer and programmer compete in the following way: there is an imaginary pile of chips, the exact number of which can be entered at the keyboard by the human player. To convey the impression of fairness, the programmer is allowed to decide this number. The programmer also chooses who is to make the first move. From then on, machine and programmer alternate in their moves. In the very first step any number of (but not all) chips may be taken; taking all chips would render the game pointless.

Each player must remove at least one chip during each subsequent step, but nobody is permitted to remove more than twice the amount most recently taken. The player who removes the last chip is the winner.

If it is legal in the current move to take all remaining chips, this is the natural step to win. Otherwise, a player tries to place the opponent into a losing situation as follows: take so many chips in the legal range that the number of chips left in the pile is a Fibonacci number and the leftover pile is greater than twice what is currently removed. Fibonacci numbers have been covered in Chapter 11. This leaves the opponent in a "losing position." Once a player is in a losing position, there is nothing that can be done to win unless the other side makes a mistake. Again, a player is in a losing position if upon drawing the number of chips is a Fibonacci number, and not all chips can be grabbed at once.

In other words, this is not really a game driven by chance and luck, because the outcome is predetermined right from the start. As soon as the number of chips in the pile has been determined and the beginner is chosen, then it is clear who will win, assuming nobody makes a mistake. Why then is it still interesting to play this game? Simply because most players do not know the solution, and, therefore, will make nonoptimal moves. So it appears as if the opponent, the computer, were extremely intelligent, making wiser choices than the human player. But as soon as the human counterpart has "cracked" the algorithm and knows about the "losing situation" when faced with a Fibonacci number, the true riddle of the game is solved—and that's where the fun lies. However, after this revelation, playing the game becomes pointless. See Example 15-18.

```
            |WITH text_io; USE text io;
            |
            |PROCEDURE nimm_game IS
        1   |  my_turn          : boolean;
 11     1   |  chips_left       : integer;
 12     1   |
 12     1   | FUNCTION fibo_less( n : integer ) RETURN integer IS
 11     2   |   old_fibo,
 11     2   |   next_fibo,
 11     2   |   new_fibo   : integer;
 14     2   |  BEGIN--fibo_less
        2   |   old_fibo := 0;
```

```
13    4        2  1  |   new_fibo := 1;
14    7        2  1  |   next_fibo := 1;
15   10        2  1  |   WHILE next_fibo <= n LOOP
16   14        2  1  |     next_fibo := old_fibo + new_fibo;
17   19        2  2  |     old_fibo := new_fibo;
18   22        2  2  |     new_fibo := next_fibo;
19   25        2  2  |   END LOOP;
20   26        2  1  |   RETURN old_fibo;
21   31        2  1  | END fibo_less;
22   31        1     |
23   31        1     | PROCEDURE enter IS
24   33        2     |   answer  : character;
25   33   11   2     | BEGIN--enter
26   33        2     |   put( " enter number of chips in game: " );
27   36        2  1  |   get( chips_left );
28   38        2  1  |   IF chips_left < 0 THEN
29   42        2  1  |     put_line( " I ignore minus sign. " );
30   45        2  2  |     chips_left := -chips_left;
31   49        2  2  |   END IF;
32   49        2  1  |   IF chips_left > 1000 THEN
33   53        2  1  |     put_line( " getting too big. I set 1000" );
34   56        2  2  |     chips_left := 1000;
35   59        2  2  |   END IF;
36   59        2  1  |   put( " If you want to start, enter 'y' or 'Y': " );
37   61        2  1  |   get( answer );
38   63        2  1  |   new_line( output );
39   64        2  1  |   my_turn := answer /= 'y' AND answer /= 'Y';
40   73        2  1  | END enter;
41   73        1     |
42   73        1     | FUNCTION you_take(last_take:integer) RETURN integer IS
43   75   11   2     |   n : integer;
44   75   12   2     | BEGIN--you_take
45   75        2     |   put( " You take: " );
46   78        2  1  |   get( n );
47   80        2  1  |   IF n < 1 THEN
48   84        2  1  |     put_line( " you took not enough, I enforce 1" );
49   87        2  2  |     n := 1;
50   90        2  2  |   ELSIF n > 2 * last_take OR n > chips_left THEN
51  101        2  1  |     put_line( " you took too many, I enforce 1" );
52  104        2  2  |     n := 1;
53  107        2  2  |   END IF;
54  107        2  1  |   RETURN n;
55  112        2  1  | END you_take;
56  112        1     |
57  112        1     | FUNCTION i_take(
58  114        2     |   chips_left,
59  114        2     |   last_take  : integer ) RETURN integer IS
60  114   12   2     |   max,
```

```
114   12   2      |   try : integer;
114   14   2      |  BEGIN--i_take
114        2      |   max := fibo_less( chips left );
122        2   1  |   try := chips_left - max;
127        2   1  |   IF last_take * 2 >= chips_left THEN--take all
133        2   1  |    RETURN chips_left;
138        2   2  |   ELSIF try > last_take * 2 THEN--take less
145        2   1  |    RETURN i_take( try, last_take );
155        2   2  |   ELSIF chips_left - 3 * try <= 0 THEN--losing
164        2   1  |    RETURN i_take( try, try / 3 );
176        2   2  |   ELSIF max = chips_left THEN--loser position
181        2   1  |    RETURN 1;
186        2   2  |   ELSE--good chance
186        2   1  |    RETURN try;
192        2   2  |   END IF;
192        2   1  |  END i_take;
192        1      |
192        1      | PROCEDURE play IS
194        2      |   last_take  : integer;
194   11   2      |  BEGIN--play
194        2      |   last_take := ( chips_left - 1 ) / 2;
202        2   1  |   WHILE chips_left > 0 LOOP
206        2   1  |    IF my_turn THEN
208        2   2  |     put( chips_left );
210        2   3  |     put( " chips left. " );
212        2   3  |     last_take := i_take( chips_left, last_take );
220        2   3  |     put( " I take:" );
222        2   3  |     put_line( last_take );
225        2   3  |     chips_left := chips_left - last_take;
230        2   3  |     IF chips_left = 0 THEN
234        2   3  |      put_line( " I won." );
237        2   4  |     END IF;
237        2   3  |     my_turn := false;
240        2   3  |    END IF;
240        2   2  |    IF not my_turn and ( chips_left > 0 ) THEN
247        2   2  |     put( chips_left );
249        2   3  |     put( " chips left. " );
251        2   3  |     last_take := you_take( last_take );
258        2   3  |     chips_left := chips_left - last_take;
263        2   3  |     IF chips_left = 0 THEN
267        2   3  |      put_line( " you won" );
270        2   4  |     END IF;
270        2   3  |     my_turn := true;
273        2   3  |    END IF;
273        2   2  |   END LOOP;
274        2   1  |  END play;
274        1      |
274        1      | BEGIN--nimm_game
```

```
109  276        1     |  enter;
110  280        1  1  |  play;
111  283        1  1  | END nimm_game;
```

Example 15-18 Listing of Nimm Game in Ada

Apart from winning or losing, when we run the preceding program, we notice that each step involves several IO operations. The computer asks and responds, the user reads and enters. Only an interactive system with an appropriate set of IO primitives makes this game a delight to play. But all languages covered here provide a satisfactory set of primitives to express the program.

15.8 Summary

This chapter has familiarized the reader with the simplest rules of IO. We have concentrated on syntax and semantics of one small aspect of IO, Text IO, which is the most useful form for human interaction. Language design issues have been mentioned only in passing—as, for example, the disadvantages in not including IO as part of the language proper. Such questionable practices have been employed as early as Algol-60, and as recently as Ada. On the positive side we have experienced the conveniences of language-defined IO in Pascal and PL/I, which allow an arbitrary number of arguments in their IO routines. For a silver-tongued, though not fully convincing, rationalization, we recommend Niklaus Wirth's justification for excluding IO from Modula-2, Wirth [1982] page 27. Procedures and functions that perform IO can be considered special "intrinsic functions," which we shall cover in the next chapter.

15.9 Exercises

1. The following PL/I program fragment prints one line of text output. Analyze the Output Statement and all other necessary text and determine exactly, character by character, what the printed line looks like.

```
DCL ( I, J ) BIN FIXED( 31 );
I = 2;
J = 12;
PUT EDIT( 'MIN(', I, ',', J, ') = ', MIN(I,J) )
        ( COL( 13 ), A(4), F(2), A(1), F(2), A(4), F(2) );
```

2. The next PL/I program fragment looks like the previous one, but the format list is different. Write down the exact output string. Remember, when the format list is shorter than the number of IO elements, it is restarted from the left end.

```
DCL ( I, J ) BIN FIXED( 31 );
I = 2;
J = 12;
PUT EDIT( 'MIN(', I, ',', J, ') = ', MIN(I,J) ) ( A, F );
```

3. We wish to output the two string literals "Hello" and "World," separated from one another by a single blank, onto the standard output file via one single Ada "put" statement. How can we accomplish this?

4. How can we print the string literal " X = " and the value of the integer variable "x" via a single Ada "put" statement?

5. Assume the Procedure Call Statement "WriteInt(j)" references the Modula-2 Output Statement, imported from "InOut." Detect the syntax error in the WriteInt statement. What is disturbing from a language design standpoint about the rule that defines the statement to be wrong?

16

Intrinsic Functions

The abstract theory ... tells in no uncertain terms
that the machines' potential range is enormous,
and that its theoretical limitations are
of the subtlest and most elusive sort.
There is no reason to suppose
machines have any limitations not shared by man.

Marvin Minsky
Computation: Finite and Infinite Machines

Glaubt's nur, ihr gravitätischen Herrn!
Gescheite Leute narrieren gern.

Gottfried August Bürger
Freiherr von Münchhausen

This chapter explains the purpose of intrinsic functions and how their composition can create more powerful tools by building on simpler modules. It also shows the variant forms of functions in the different languages. Other names for intrinsic functions are *built-in functions, predefined-functions,* and *required functions.* We want to familiarize the reader only with the more important built-in functions in each of these languages. The previous chapter serves as an introduction to the current chapter, since IO is usually defined as a special case of predefined functions.

Functions in programming languages are close relatives to mathematical functions. A mathematical function expresses an algorithm that computes a value, usually based on given arguments, and then returns that value. Some programming languages model their definition of functions exactly after the mathematical original. This philosophy has created a special form of programming languages known as functional programming languages. The mathematical function concept is too restrictive to be adopted for programming languages because it requires the exclusion of side effects—that is, any change outside of the function proper. This includes setting global variables, reading from files, writing onto files, and causing aborts. Most practical programming languages find it overly restrictive to disallow all of the preceding, and, therefore, do permit side effects in functions.

Intrinsic functions are those functions that are already provided by the language and its implementation. Their primary purpose is to avoid the replication of commonly used functions. They also ease the writing of programs because all users already know that predefined set of functions. And they enhance reliability since intrinsic functions are usually well tested and debugged. They may be used anywhere in a program without explicit definition by the programmer. In addition, the languages covered in this text even permit the overwriting of intrinsic functions by user-defined functions.

Function Composition

By applying composition, the programmer can make built-in functions and explicitly declared functions the basis for more and more complex functions. *Composition,* also called *nesting,* is the application of one or more functions in succession on a given set of parameters. The return value provided by one function serves as parameter to the next function. It is interesting that multiparameter functions are not more general than single-parameter functions. See Machtey and Young [1978] for more detail and for proofs. Examples of function composition are shown in Example 16-1. Note that the composition can be applied to the function itself, as shown with "min" in the first instance, and with "one_more" various times in the second instance.

```
i := min( max( trunc( r + 0.1 ), min( ord( c ), ord( '0' ) ) ) );
i := one_more( one_more( one_more( 0 ) ) ); -- result is 3
```

Example 16-1 Function Composition

16.1 Intrinsic Functions in Ada

Ada has a small number of predefined packages that each implementation must provide. These packages—in conjunction with attributes, a few predefined operators, and type conversions—contribute to a set of operations that we collectively call intrinsic functions. Predefined operators are known from other languages, so we do not include their treatment here.

IO Packages

The predefined packages for IO are "sequential_io," "direct_io," and "text_io." The functions provided in these packages, though they are in some sense intrinsic functions, will also not be covered here, since they are directed specifically toward input and output. We refer the reader instead to Chapter 15, where that subject is handled in detail.

Package "standard," also mandatory for every implementation of Ada, provides a large collection of predefined, overloaded functions, all expressed in Ada. In the strict sense of the Ada language definition, all "conventional" operations like addition, expressed by +, or multiplication, expressed by *, are intrinsic functions. Note that a function name in Ada may be an identifier or a string literal, enclosed in double quotes, like "+," "*," or "<=." Referencing the string value without the double quotes is a way of invoking that function. It is just an additional convenience that the two arguments may be written textually to the left and to the right of the function name, thus using the function name as an infix operator. The resulting string may look like the following arithmetic expression.

```
a + 7 * b
```

In Ada's world this represents two function invocations. First the function "*" is called, yielding the right operand for addition; then "+" is called. Again, we will not dwell further on this quite unique form of intrinsic function. Instead, we will turn to the more "conventional" kind as found in Fortran, Modula-2, Pascal, and PL/I. In Ada these are separated into "attributes," "special operators," and "type conversions."

Attributes

The Ada definition of *attribute,* repeated here from section 4.1.4 of ANSI [1983a], is vague and evasive: "An attribute denotes a basic operation of an entity given by a prefix." Our less terse and more simplistic definition of attribute follows: Ada attributes are intrinsic functions, whose operations are determined by the Attribute_Designator. The Attribute_Designator also defines the return type. The Prefix plays only a minor role in qualifying the parenthetical argument. The syntax for Ada attributes is shown in Example 16-2.

```
attribute               ::= prefix ' attribute_designator
attribute_designator    ::= simple_name [ ( static_expression ) ]
prefix                  ::= type_mark
                          | variable
```

Example 16-2 Syntax Fragment for Ada Attributes

Depending on the attribute designator, the prefix is a type mark, a variable, a program unit, a label, or an entry. The attribute designator is usually an identifier, but in a few cases a reserved keyword is used in its place. Examples include DELTA, RANGE, or DIGITS. Due to the attribute syntax, no ambiguity can arise from the use of the overloaded keyword. More detail about the prefix must be extracted from the standard, Appendix A, which lists about 43 different, predefined attributes. Individual implementations may add further attributes but must describe these at a predefined place in the language specification. We list here some of the more frequently used attributes and include samples.

"First" Attribute

The prefix of the "first" attribute may be a variable or a type mark, designating a scalar type or the type array. For an array type the desired dimension may be specified; in this case, "first" is applied to the specified dimension. If none is given, "first" is applied to the first dimension. If the prefix denotes a scalar type, then the "first" attribute yields the lowest possible value of that type, while the return type is given by the prefix. Otherwise, if the prefix is an array type, then "first" returns the lower bound of the specified dimension. The return type is the index type of that array dimension. See Example 16-3.

```
my_colour := colour_type'first;
FOR colour IN colour_type'first .. colour_type'last LOOP ...
her_colour := rainbow_type'base'first;
```

Example 16-3 "First" Attributes

"Last" Attribute

The prefix of the "last" attribute may be a variable or a type mark that designates a scalar or array type. If an array type is designated and the dimension is not explicitly specified, the first dimension is assumed. Otherwise, "last" returns the upper bound of the specified dimension. If the prefix denotes a scalar type, then the "last" attribute returns its largest possible value. See Example 16-4.

```
my_colour := colour_type'last;
WHILE my_colour > colour_type'first LOOP
 operate;
 my_colour := colour_type'pred( my_colour );
END LOOP;
her_colour := rainbow_type'base'last;
```

Example 16-4 "Last" Attribute

"Pos" Attribute

The "pos" attribute has one parameter, which must be a value of the base type of the prefix. Pos returns the position number of the actual parameter. The returned type is universal integer. "Pos" is the inverse function of the "val" attribute explained in the next section. Hence the following identities hold. See Example 16-5.

```
character'pos( character'val( 65 ) )  = 65
character'val( character'pos( 'A' ) ) = 'A'

TYPE week_end_type IS ( Saturday, Sunday );
day : week_end_type := Sunday;
day_position : integer := week_end_type'pos( day );--is 1
```

Example 16-5 "Pos" Attribute

"Val" Attribute

"Val" can be considered the inverse function of "pos." The resulting type is the base type of the prefix. The result is the value whose position number is the integer value corresponding to the argument. An exception is raised if the argument's integer value is outside the bounds of the range TYP'POS(TYP'BASE'FIRST)..TYP'POS(TYP'BASE'LAST).

```
c := character'val( 65 );--c = 'A' in Ascii
b := boolean'val( 0 );--b = false
```

Example 16-6 "Val" Attributes

Special Operators

Formally, the special operators modulus and absolute value are not defined as intrinsic functions in Ada. Their definition follows the example set by Pascal: modulus is a binary operator, expressed by the reserved keyword MOD, and the absolute value function is represented by the unary operator ABS, also a reserved keyword. Semantically, however, there is, of course, no difference between intrinsic functions and predefined operators. The distinction is purely of syntactic nature. Admittedly, this level of language analysis is getting picky, but we need a full understanding of the tradeoffs, if we wish to be in the position of designing our own language. For more detail about the tradeoffs, consistent language design versus program reliability, revisit sections "MOD and REM Operators" and "Abs Unary Operator in Ada" in Chapter 6.

Type Conversions

In most languages type conversions are just another form of built-in function. In Pascal, for example, they are called transfer functions. Ada chooses to distinguish type conversions from other expressions both formally and syntactically. At first glance the type conversion syntax resembles the syntax for function calls, but the mandatory leading type mark for type conversions distinguishes this form of expression clearly from functions. See the grammar fragment in Example 16-7. For more information revisit Chapter 6.

```
type_conversion     ::= type_mark ( expression )
```

Example 16-7 Grammar Fragment for Ada Type Conversion

It is essential that the type of the parenthesized expression be closely related to the base type of the mandatory leading type mark. Typically it will be a subtype or a derived type of the base type.

.6.2 Intrinsic Functions in Fortran

Fortran's philosophy of intrinsic functions is uncomplicated, particularly when contrasted with Ada. There is no need to keep the syntactic construct of attribute separate from type conversion, or the predefined operator separate from the predefined "standard" function. The Fortran standard ANSI [1978], Table 5, lists 79 distinct built-in functions. The number is so large, because some of these functions have up to four variations for arguments of type integer, real, double, and complex. Knowing their exact name is the way of keeping them apart, and we certainly make no attempt here to list them all.

One of Fortran's strong sides is the choice of built-in functions. Not only is the square root function included, something we dearly miss in Ada, but we also find a wide complement of trigonometrical functions such as sine and cosine. The inverse functions, arcsine and arccosine and the hyperbolic functions are available as well. Fortran's range of intrinsic functions has in fact made obsolete the need for the large volumes of printed tables that engineers and scientists previously referred to at all times for performing computations. Perhaps this is why Fortran is so consistently called a "scientific" programming language.

The designers of languages that do not predefine such useful functions may argue that their implementation is a straightforward task, since their infinite series are so well-known. But this kind of thinking is extremely uneconomical. Programmers should reuse modules, not reinvent them, since the reinvention of even the simplest thing means a replication in cost. Fortran apparently stands behind this principle. It is preferable to have just one, complete, well-tested and reliable set of functions provided by the language than to have multiple copies of "almost" the same functions.

In Table 16-1 we list just a few Fortran intrinsic functions with their names, argument types and return types.

Table 16-1 Fortran Intrinsic Functions

Intrinsic Function Name	Fortran Name	Argument Type	Return Type
Remainder	MOD	Integer	Integer
Square Root	SQRT	Real	Real
Square Root, Double Prec.	DSQRT	Double	Double
Natural Logarithm	ALOG	Real	Real
Decimal Logarithm	ALOG10	Real	Real
Sine	SIN	Real	Real
Cosine	COS	Real	Real
Tangent	TAN	Real	Real
Arcsine	ASIN	Real	Real
Hyperbolic Sine	SINH	Real	Real
Lexically Greater Than	LGT	Character	Logical
Lexically Less Than	LLT	Character	Logical

16.3 Intrinsic Functions in Pascal

One of the goals in the design of Pascal was to keep the language simple. This goal is clearly reflected in the number of intrinsic functions. Other than the IO-related functions "eoln" and "eof," there are only 15 of these functions. In the Pascal standard, intrinsic functions are called "required functions." Some of these are type conversion functions like "trunc" or "round." Pascal again has its own terminology for this kind of functions calling them "transfer functions." Some trigonometric functions and arithmetic functions are also included. See section 6.6.6 in ANSI [1983b], the standard document, for more information and Pascal specific terminology.

Since the total number of intrinsic functions is so small, we list them all in Table 16-2. Notice there is not a single function, at least among the "transfer functions," that converts integer type arguments into their real type equivalent. This is not an oversight in Pascal. Conversion from integer to real is done implicitly whenever at least one operand of type real is involved.

There is only one built-in logarithmic function provided in Pascal, the natural logarithm. Does this limit programmers to logarithms of base "e," even if base 10 is needed? If we think back again to high school, we may remember that the natural logarithm can be used to find logarithms to any base. If we need, for example, another function to the base 10, we can use the following simple mathematical identity.

```
log_10(x) = ln(x) / ln(10)
```

By the same mechanism we can create logarithm functions to any base. The provided trigonometric functions "sin" and "cos" are also sufficient to compute related ones like tangent, cotangent, secant, and cosecant. Similarly, the missing "even(x)" function can be simulated in Pascal by "NOT odd(x)," but this is pushing the thriftiness a bit. "NOT odd(x)" is clearly less readable than "even(x)."

Table 16-2 Pascal Intrinsic Functions

Intrinsic Function Name	Pascal Name	Argument Type	Return Type
Absolute Value, Int, Real	abs	Int, Real	Same
Arctangent in Radians	arctan	Real	Real
Type Conversion to Char	chr	Integer	Char
Cosine	cos	Real	Real
E to Power of Argument	exp	Int, Real	Real
Natural Logarithm	ln	Real	Real
Is Argument Odd?	odd	Integer	Boolean
Ordinal Value of	ord	Scalar	Integer
Predecessor Function	pred	Scalar	Same
Round to Nearest Integer	round	Real	Integer
Sine	sin	Real	Real
Square of Argument	sqr	Int, real	Same
Square Root, Positive Arg.	sqrt	Int, Real	Real
Successor Function	succ	Scalar	Same
Truncate to Next Lower Int	trunc	Real	Integer

16.4 Intrinsic Functions in PL/I

PL/I provides a built-in function whenever there might be a good use for one. "Abs" and "mod" are provided as just two of many arithmetic functions; all trigonometrical functions, including the hyperbolic ones, are included. Parameters for the trigonometrical functions must be expressed in radians. Functions to perform arithmetic on complex types are supplied, as well as intrinsics to find the "hbound" and "lbound" of arrays. Function return values inherit their base, scale, and precision attributes from the arguments, unless they operate on strings. In that case the return type varies with the individual intrinsic function. With such a large array of intrinsic functions, PL/I probably deserves more than Fortran to be classified as a "scientific" language.

But that label was created for Fortran, and it has stuck. We describe only those intrinsic functions that are unconventional or particularly useful. These include "max," "index," "substr," and "translate."

The "Max" Function

Contrary to convention, the PL/I "max" built-in function may have any number of parameters, but it must have at least two. While other languages must resort to function composition, PL/I permits a simplified use of the same function. Two pairs are given in Example 16-8. Each pair consists of one PL/I call to the intrinsic function and one invocation to the explicitly coded "max" function in Pascal.

```
/*  PL/I  */                    { Pascal }
i = MAX( J, 77 );               i := max( j, 77 );
i = MAX( J, J-L, I*N );         i := max( max( j, j-l ), i*n );
```

Example 16-8 Max

The "Index" Function

"Index(a[,b])" operates on one or two arguments "a" and "b," and returns an integer type value. Both arguments must be of type string. If only argument "a" is specified, the function returns zero. We conjecture that the latter is included as a particularly clever or obscure way of generating zeros. The function searches whether the second string occurs as a substring in the first. If it is found, then "index" returns the start index of "b" in "a," starting the count with index 1 for the first character in "a." If "b" is not found, "index" returns zero. See Example 16-9.

```
DCL TOWN CHAR(7) INIT( 'KREFELD' );
DCL I     BIN FIXED;
I = INDEX( TOWN, 'FELD' );
/* VALUE OF I = 4 */
```

Example 16-9 PL/I Index

The "Substr" Function

"Substr(a,b[,c])" has two or three arguments; parameter "c" is optional or can be an asterisk. The first argument is a character or bit string. Parameter "b" specifies a start index in "a." If the third parameter is specified, it defines the length of the substring of "a," starting at index "b." If "c" is not specified, the whole substring, starting at "b" is referenced. Should the length "c" result in a substring that is outside the first argument, then the function result is undefined. See Example 16-10.

```
DCL BOY1 CHAR(9) VARYING INIT( 'ALEXANDER' );
DCL BOY2 CHAR(5) VARYING INIT( 'ANDRE' );
SUBSTR( BOY1, 5 )    = BOY2;                    /* SAME AS: */
SUBSTR( BOY1, 5, 5 ) = BOY2;                    /* SAME AS: */
SUBSTR( BOY1, 5 )    = SUBSTR( BOY2, 1 );       /* SAME AS: */
SUBSTR( BOY1, 5, 5 ) = SUBSTR( BOY2, 1, * );/* SAME AS: */
SUBSTR( BOY1, 5 )    = SUBSTR( BOY2, 1, 5 );
/* BOY1 = 'ALEXANDRE' */
```

Example 16-10 PL/I Substr

The "Translate" Function

The "translate(a,b,c)" intrinsic function is most likely a leftover from the IBM 360 instruction set that assembly language programmers were unwilling to give up. The assembler instruction was quite useful for translating one character set into another. With the "translate" intrinsic the same function can easily be coded in PL/I. The value returned by "translate(a,b,c)" is a character string with the length of "a." For each character "x" in "a," the following operation is done: if "x" occurs in "c," then the resulting string has "x" replaced by the corresponding character, extracted from "b." If this sounds confusing, Example 16-11 should help clarify how the "translate" function works.

```
DCL ( MOTTO, NEW_MOTTO ) CHAR(10) INIT( 'CARPE DIEM' );
DCL LOWER                CHAR(6)  INIT( 'aeimpr' );
DCL UPPER                CHAR(6)  INIT( 'AEIMPR' );
/* STATEMENTS */
NEW_MOTTO = TRANSLATE( MOTTO, LOWER, UPPER );
/* NOW: NEW_MOTTO = 'Carpe Diem' */
```

Example 16-11 PL/I Translate

6.5 Intrinsic Functions in Modula-2

Regarding intrinsic functions and procedures, Modula-2 pursues the same philosophy of thriftiness that we have seen in Ada. Very few functions and procedures are predefined. In particular such useful and common functions as sine, cosine, and logarithm are missing. The rationale is probably that any project can write its own library—and make the units exportable. Each user imports the trigonometric functions as needed. As stated before, this principle is shortsighted and causes replication of work.

Luckily, some functions cannot be written by the user, so the language is required to predefine them or else be very incomplete. Users cannot write some functions or procedures for various reasons: the number of arguments for the same procedure may vary (DEC); types for the same parameter of a function may vary (ABS); the argument of the function may be a type mark (VAL), or access to run time descriptors may be impossible (HIGH). A table of all Modula-2 intrinsic functions follows.

Table 16-3 Modula-2 Intrinsic Functions

Intrinsic Function Name	Modula-2 Name	Argument Type	Return Type
Absolute Value, INT, REAL	ABS	INT, REAL	Same
Capital Letter Function	CAP	CHARACTER	same
Type Conversion to Char	CHR	CARDINAL	CHARACTER
Convert CARDINAL to REAL	FLOAT	CARDINAL	REAL
High Bound of Array a	HIGH(a)	ARRAY	Index T
Is Argument Odd?	ODD	INTEGER	BOOLEAN
Ordinal Value of	ORD	Scalar	INTEGER
Truncate REAL to INTEGER	TRUNC	REAL	INTEGER
Value with ordinal Number	VAL(T,x)	Any Discr	Same

The HIGH function returns the upper bound of the Array-type argument. It is useful for "Open Array Parameters," whose bounds are not specified at compilation time. An associated LOW function is not needed, because in Modula-2 all Open Array Parameters have the lower bound zero. If an actual array parameter, passed to a formal Open Array Parameter, has the bounds [m..n], the value of HIGH is n-m.

The VAL function is very similar to Ada's VAL attribute and effectively is the inverse of the ORD function. Notice that its first argument is a type mark, which defines the type of the resulting expression. In Ada this type mark is specified by the prefix, while in Pascal the whole function is missing.

In Table 16-4 we list all Modula-2 intrinsic procedures. Their purpose and syntax can easily be derived from the information in the table. We see that some are merely conveniences that can be expressed by the user directly (DEC, INC), but others are not under user control (HALT). The conveniences, however, occur frequently and provide an easy way for a compiler to produce very good code without costly optimization passes.

Table 16-4 Modula-2 Intrinsic Procedures

Intrinsic Procedure Name	Modula-2 Name	Description of Procedure
Decrement Argument	DEC(x)	x := x - 1
Subtract n from Argument	DEC(x,n)	x := x - n
Exclude Element from Set	EXCL(s,i)	s := s - {i} Set Diff
Halt Procedure	HALT	Terminate Program
Increment Argument	INC(x)	x := x + 1
Add n to Argument	INC(x,n)	x := x + n
Include Set Element	INCL(s,i)	s := s + {i} Set Incl

16.6 Summary

In this chapter we have given a rationale for intrinsic functions. Their purpose is not only to reduce the overall programming effort by providing solutions to commonly needed functions, but also to provide services that otherwise are impossible to get. For example, in a strictly typed language it is illegal to use objects of one type in the context of another type, even though this can be meaningful. Type conversion functions are the communications vehicle for getting permission from the compiler to overrule the type checking. Also, if dynamic (open) arrays are provided, the language must allow generic access to their bounds. Otherwise, the programmer has to explicitly pass the lower and upper bounds as additional parameters, thus cluttering up the source and introducing a new source of error.

We have become acquainted with some specific intrinsic functions in the languages treated here. Fortran has a rich set of these, and PL/I an overly rich set. Ada, Modula-2, and Pascal almost shortchange the language user by not providing functions that are definitely needed.

16.7 Exercises

1. The following Assignment Statement is a PL/I statement, which uses the intrinsic function "min" with four parameters. Rewrite this PL/I statement with a single Ada assignment, preserving the semantics by using only the user-implemented Ada function "min." "Min" expects two actual parameters. Use all arguments in exactly the same order as in the original PL/I statement.

```
I = MIN( J, 5, I, -K ); /* PL/I */
```

2. How many ways are there to express the preceding PL/I statement in Ada using the same explicitly coded function "min," when only one single Ada statement is used? Do not rearrange the order of the four actual parameters of the original PL/I statement.

3. How can the reader (and compiler) distinguish between an Ada type conversion and an Ada function call?

4. Use only intrinsic Pascal functions to compute the value for the base-2 logarithm of the value 55.

5. Use only built-in Pascal functions to compute the value of tan(x). Assume that "tan" means the trigonometrical tangent function, and the argument "x" is of proper type and value.

6. What is wrong with the following PL/I statement. "SUBSTR" may be used as a built-in function and as pseudo-variable, hence it may be used on the left-hand side of an Assignment Statement.

```
SUBSTR( 'ABC', 1, 1 ) = SUBSTR( 'ABC', 3, * );
```

7. What is the value of the PL/I string variable "A" after the following correct second Assignment Statement?

```
A = 'SDSU';
SUBSTR( A, 1, 2 ) = SUBSTR( A, 3 );
```

8. Which values do PL/I variables "I" and "J" have after the following two Assignment Statements?

```
I = INDEX( 'Good Morning', 'od' );
J = INDEX( 'Good Morning', 'odd' );
```

17

Language Peculiarities

Although correct, it hurts me,
for I don't like to crack an egg with a sledgehammer,
no matter how effective the sledgehammer is for doing so.

Edsger W. Dijkstra
A Discipline of Programming

This chapter lists lexical and syntactical rules that not only strike the language novice as unusual, but can surprise a seasoned programmer as well. Often these rules are meaningful in the context of the full language definition. Therefore, this chapter is presented toward the end of this book, after the reader has been exposed to numerous facets of each language. From a less forgiving position, the purpose of this chapter is to present counterexamples to good programming language design principles. Likewise, Chapter 18 will present counterexamples to good programming practices.

17.1 Lexical Peculiarities

Each programming language has certain lexical peculiarities or rules for putting strings together. Regardless of how many languages we already know, past experience in these cases may hinder rather than help us. This section is dedicated to warning the programmer of some of the surprising lexical rules in each of the languages we have discussed.

Peculiar Lexical Rules in Ada

Ada Single Quotes

In Ada, character type literals are enclosed within single quotes and are precisely three characters long. The format—leading single quote, character, ending single quote—is as follows:

```
'x'      -- x is any character, including '
```

This format also holds when the character enclosed between the single quotes is the single quote character. This is unusual, since most other languages require "quote stuffing," the repetition of the enclosed quote. The following sample illustrates how this character literal looks in other languages and then how it looks in Ada.

```
in most languages: ''''
in Ada:            '''
```

Ada Apostrophe

Ada also uses the single quote character as a separate lexical token. When used this way, however, the character is called an apostrophe. In contrast to the single quote characters used to enclose character literals, the apostrophe occurs by itself, not in pairs. Its function is to separate type marks and identifiers in attributes, or to separate qualifiers and expressions in qualified expressions.

Despite their obvious differences, the two functions of this particular character can be easily confused, even if the program text is not particularly long. The following short source substring illustrates the kind of ambiguity that can occur:

```
'('='..
```

Without looking at more context around this substring, it is impossible to tell whether the open parenthesis symbol is a character literal enclosed between single quotes or the first character is an apostrophe token followed by some parenthetical expression.

To decipher the meaning of the ' character in this example, the reader (and compiler) will need to know whether the token immediately preceding the ' character was an identifier. If so, the ' is an apostrophe. If not, it is the opening quote of a character literal. Naturally we assume that the string is not part of a comment and not part of a string literal. We show two possible expansions of the preceding fractional string.

```
ascii'('=')
```

This substring represents the character literal '=', qualified by "ascii." However,

```
IF '('=')' THEN
```

is the beginning of a boolean expression after the reserved keyword IF, yielding false. See Goodenough [1980], Chapter 2, for more information.

Ada String Literals

String literals are denoted by a leading " and an ending ", and they behave just like character literals in other languages. The " can be substituted by the % character. Any length from zero up to the total length of a text line is allowed. If string literals longer than one line are required, these must be concatenated by the & operator. Any enclosed " must be specified twice. See Example 17-1.

```
""                  -- empty string
"Hi"                -- Hi
""""                -- "
"L""A"              -- L"A
" a long" &
" string "          -- still one string literal
```

Example 17-1 Strings in Ada

The "'" and ''' literals, for example, have the same value but different types. The first one is a string that happens to have the length one; the latter is of type character, which always has the length one.

Ada Numeric Literals

Numeric literals in Ada are unique because of their explicit base in the range 2 to 16 inclusive. If no base is given, then a decimal number is assumed. Otherwise, the given base must itself be in decimal notation. Once the base is defined, a pair of # characters encloses the actual numeric literal. Naturally all digits must be less than the base. For bases larger than 10, the extended digits from the conventional hexadecimal notation are used. Digit A stands for 10, B for 11, and so on.

Lower- and uppercase letters for extended digits are equivalent. A fractional part as well as an exponent part are permitted for based numbers. Isolated underline characters are also allowed to increase readability. See Example 17-2.

16#fffF#	means	4,095
12#1_000_000#	means	2,985,984
4e5	means	400,000
10#123.456#e+3	means	123,456.0
999_999_999	means	999,999,999

Example 17-2 Ada Numbers

Ada Identifiers

Ada identifiers must start with a letter. Allowed are letters, digits, and isolated underlines. In PL/I the underline may occur more than once in a row and may be the last character of an identifier, neither of which is legal in Ada. Lower- and uppercase may be used interchangeably anywhere except inside string and character literals. See Examples 17-3 and 17-4.

```
good_id, i_d_e_n_t, same_as, Good_Id, I_D_E_N_T, P_000_000
```

Example 17-3 Good Identifier Samples

```
_not_at_start, not_at_end_, not__two, not_#_ok, 3_start_with_digit
```

Example 17-4 Wrong Identifier Samples

The wrong identifiers in Example 17-4 have the following flaws: one identifier starts with an underline, which is not a letter. Another name ends with an underline, which is also outlawed by Ada. The third wrong identifier has two underlines in a row, and the next one includes a # character, which is never permitted in names. Finally, the last wrong name starts with the digit 3, certainly not a letter. The case of a letter does not matter for reserved words either. Therefore, the keyword BEGIN, for example, may be spelled: Begin, begin, or BEGIn.

Ada Comments

An Ada comment is introduced by two contiguous hyphens and stops at the end of the same line. As in Fortran, no specific terminator is needed. In contrast to Fortran, an Ada comment may start anywhere within a line of text. Note that Ada does not permit multiple unary operators, and also no unary operators in the middle of an expression. Hence, the string --12 can only be an Ada comment, not the literal +12.

Ada Unprintable Characters

Unprintable characters can be spelled in the source by referencing their symbolic names from the predefined package Ascii; for example, ascii.ack references the acknowledge character.

Ada Labels

Labels are marked via the unusual << and >> tokens that stick out like sore thumbs. Labels are quite distinct from statement names: the former may be targets of Goto Statements, while the latter may not. Names merely serve as documentation and can be referenced in Exit Statements.

Ada Pointer Dereference

Ada pointer types are declared with the reserved keyword ACCESS. Dereferencing a pointer variable is done implicitly. Normally the pointer variable addresses a Record, hence name qualification takes over the role of dereference and qualification. Then how can we access a Record as a whole, if it is described via a Pointer? Ada has to introduce a phantom-field "ALL," expressed by a reserved keyword, to guarantee that users never choose this name as a real field. See Example 17-5.

```
    TYPE element_type IS
    RECORD
      data1   : integer;
      data2   : character;
    END RECORD;
    TYPE element_pin_type IS ACCESS element_type;
    element_pin : element_pin_type := NEW element_type;
    element     : element_type;
  BEGIN -- body
    element_pin.data1 := 12;     -- Access one Field
    element_pin.data2 := 'A';    -- Access one Field
    element := element_pin.ALL;  -- Access the whole Record
```

Example 17-5 Pointers and Records

Peculiar Lexical Rules in Fortran

Insignificant Blank Rule

Fortran is very unusual in one regard. Even though the language needs separators, and the blank would be a perfect candidate, Fortran does not give the blank this role. Only inside of character string literals does Fortran acknowledge the significance of a blank. Compiler and reader alike have some unnecessary difficulty if a programmer really chooses to use this unconventional rule. For example, take the string:

```
DO10I=5..
```

The compiler cannot know at the digit 5 what this statement means. The two dots indicate that more source text may follow. If no other token follows after the 5, and if no continuation character appears on the next line, it is an Assignment Statement and variable DO10I receives the new value 5. But if a comma comes after the 5, we have the start of a Do Statement, like

```
DO 10 I = 5,10
```

Upon finding the comma, the compiler can at least guess that it has found a Fortran Do Statement. But this guess must be verified. To this end, the presumed variable, in this case "DO10I," must be analyzed and bisected into subcomponents that yield the keyword DO and a numeric label. Then a variable must come before the assignment operator. In these cases the compiler and reader will succeed.

Fortran Comments

Fortran comments are marked by a C character in column one. The complete line (and only this line) is interpreted as a comment. Empty lines are a special form of comment.

One Line, One Statement in Fortran

Everything in Fortran is a "statement"—be it a declaration or a statement. Fortran specifies that one line holds exactly one statement. This can be overruled only by a continuation marker that virtually extends the length of a line by wrapping around multiple lines.

No Reserved Keyword in Fortran

Fortran does have keywords, but these are not reserved. As long as no other rule is violated, the programmer may freely choose keywords as names for any Fortran object. A subroutine, therefore, may have the name "CALL," and must be called via the statement "CALL CALL." This may also be spelled "CALLCALL," without the supporting blank. Also an Assignment Statement like IF=THEN+ENDIF*DO is perfectly legal, as long as the variables THEN, DO, and ENDIF hold proper values.

The Period Character in Fortran

The "insignificant blank" rule mentioned earlier brings occasional trouble for the Fortran syntax. Relational and boolean operators are designated by special identifiers in Fortran, not by special symbols. This alone would cause language ambiguity. For example, the string "A OR B" cannot be a logical expression. The only legal interpretation outside of character strings is the identifier "AORB." To mark "OR" as the logical operator it must be separated from the rest. Fortran chose embedding dots; this is also true for all other logical and all relational operators. So the correct logical expression is "A .OR. B." This can, however, create an unusual proliferation of dots, as Example 17-6 shows.

```
L=0..GT..4.OR..4.LT..5+.7
```

Example 17-6 Assignment to Logical Variable L

Fortran Identifiers

Fortran identifiers may be at most six characters long. This harsh rule helps explain the cryptic, assembly-languagelike names found in numerous Fortran programs. It is hard to invent good names when they can be no longer than six characters. No underline character is allowed to make programs more readable. It is understandable that many Fortran compilers extend the language and permit more characters, which then becomes an indirect reflection on unreasonable restrictions and a suggestion to language designers of what not to do.

Peculiar Lexical Rules in Pascal

Pascal Comments

Pascal comments are delimited at both ends by special symbols. They start with either the { or (* symbol, and end with either the } or *) symbol. Such explicit enders terminate a comment unconditionally, independent of how it starts. As a consequence, comments cannot be nested. Most Pascal compilers do not respect this standard rule.

Pascal Array Subscripts

Typical for a language in the Algol family, Pascal's array subscripts are enclosed by paired square bracket symbols [and]. Other languages use the (and) symbols for subscript notation. Pascal implementations with non-Ascii character sets usually simulate the [and] characters by composing the special symbols (. and .) in their place.

Pascal Pointer Symbol

Fortran has no pointers. Ada has implicit pointer dereferencing and, therefore, needs no symbol to indicate this operation. Pascal uses the ^ character for both the definition of a pointer type, and the dereferencing of a pointer type object. This is a worthwhile documentation aid, which gives the compiler and, more importantly, the reader of the source a clear hint about the type of referenced variables. When designing a language, we should consider the advantages of the style that Modula-2 and Pascal have chosen.

Peculiar Lexical Rules in PL/I

PL/I Identifiers

PL/I identifiers must start with a letter and may contain up to 32 letters, digits, and underlines. PL/I is unique in defining the $, @, and # characters as letters. Therefore, names like $, $, $##@@@, $ # @, and $100 000 are all perfectly legal, though not very mnemonic. Contrary to Ada, a PL/I name may end with an underline and have multiple underlines in a row.

No Reserved Keyword in PL/I

PL/I has a large number of keywords. These are not reserved. So the PL/I compiler and reader will have to extract from context which of the following tokens is the keyword IF and which is the identifier "if." The first line shows the source as it appears to a compiler; underneath we have rewritten the same silly source string with modifications that suggest the difference between keyword and user-defined name.

```
IF THEN=ELSE THEN ELSE=IF;ELSE IF=THEN;
IF then = else THEN
 else = if;
ELSE
 if = then;
/*END IF*/
```

Example 17-7 PL/I Keywords

PL/I Default Declarations

It is impossible in PL/I to get the infamous error message, so often issued by Pascal or Ada compilers, "Undeclared Identifier." This is because PL/I adds a default declaration to any name that has no explicit declaration. The type definition for variables declared by default is derived from the first letter. Letters I through N indicate FIXED BINARY with 15 bits precision. All other first letters imply DECIMAL FLOAT with 6 digits precision. These ingenious rules are historically grounded in Fortran.

If an unknown name is referenced in a nested block, the compiler has to go into outside lexical scopes in order to find the name. If the name is declared in an intermediate level, between the current and external scope, then the current identifier refers to that global name. Otherwise the compiler has to add the default declaration on the outermost level. The name becomes a global name with a relatively long life span. All intentional or accidental spellings of that name refer to the same secretly created variable and can cause hideous side effects.

Peculiar Lexical Rules in Modula-2

Modula-2 String Literals

String literals start with the ' or " character and must end with that same start character. It is, for no apparent reason, not possible to write a single string literal that contains both the ' and a " character. Instead such an outcast must be constructed by concatenation in Modula-2. See Example 17-8.

```
'Double " o.k.'
"Single ' o.k."
"Single ' and" & ' double " not o.k.'
```

Example 17-8 Modula-2 Quotes

Modula-2 Identifiers

In his Turing Award lecture Niklaus Wirth [1985] puts off complaints about lexical rules regarding case sensitivity in identifiers as ephemeral. We wholeheartedly disagree. Such rules are critical for readability as well as portability, and can be made perfect with so little effort. Why then make them less than perfect? Identifiers in Modula-2 are case sensitive, hence "FirstmeanVal" is different from "FirstMeanVal." Moreover, the underline character is not allowed, even though it so nicely enhances readability.

Octal and Hexadecimal Numbers in Modula-2

Integer and real literals are decimal numbers. Integers are taken as octal numbers if followed by the capital letter B, or as hexadecimal numbers if followed by an uppercase H. For octal numbers the digits 8 and 9 are illegal, while for hexadecimal numbers the extended digits A through F are included. So far the rules don't strike us as unusual, but now we ask the reader to identify whether FFFH is a hexadecimal literal or the (presumably declared) identifier FFFH. Modula-2 is missing a rule for making unambiguous the cases where a hexadecimal literal consists exclusively of extended digits. We imply that Modula-2 requires a leading 0 digit if the literal is meant. See Example 17-9.

```
1984
1984H
0FFFH
177B
```

Example 17-9 Modula-2 Numbers

Numbers in a small range followed by the character C are really character type literals. The number selects the position in the character collating sequence and hence provides a tool to express otherwise unprintable characters in the

Modula-2 source program. See Example 17-10.

```
65C    (* means 'A' *)
127C   (* means "del" character *)
```

Example 17-10 Modula-2 Characters

17.2 Syntax Peculiarities

This section lists syntax rules that warrant special mention due to their advantage, disadvantage, or just eccentricity.

Peculiar Syntax Rules in Ada

No Forward Reference
Data structures for linked lists and trees can be mutually recursive or directly recursive. This makes it necessary to reference object descriptions before these objects are completely known. Pascal solves this problem via an exceptional rule; pointer type declarations may reference type identifiers forward. Ada invents the incomplete type declaration for this purpose. The associated complete type declaration may then appear textually after a reference to the incomplete one. It must, however, come in the same declarative section.

The analogous problem surfaces in the declaration of mutually recursive subprograms. Again Pascal solves the problem via an exceptional form of declaration, the FORWARD announcement. Ada introduces the subprogram specification, terminated by a semicolon. In contrast, Ada subprogram bodies have the reserved keyword IS in place of the semicolon and include the complete body.

Quite unusually, if a parameter list is specified, it must be presented in identical, lexical notation both at the specification and in the body. For example, if a formal integer type parameter is initialized by the expression 2+3, then in the repeated parameter declaration of the subprogram body this may not be replaced by 5 even though the values are clearly identical. Only the textual layout of the parameter lists may differ. In other words they may differ in a few extra blanks and newlines.

No Dangling Else in Ada
Pascal, PL/I, and all languages without forced closure but with optional Else Clause suffer from the dangling else problem. Due to its required closure, END IF, this well-known ambiguity does not come up in Ada's If Statements.

Overloading in Ada

Subprograms and enumeration type literals may be overloaded in Ada. Overloading permits two or more names of the same spelling in one and the same scope, as long as the context supplies sufficient information to distinguish the names clearly. In Pascal it is not possible to declare two enumeration types with the colours "red" and "green," as the Ada sample in Example 17-11 allows:

```
TYPE prime_colours IS ( red, yellow, blue );
TYPE traffic_light IS ( green, yellow, red );
```

Example 17-11 Overloaded Enumeration Literals in Ada

We may also use character literals in enumeration types. This can be quite helpful in the definition of the type "character" itself; printable characters are listed, while unprintable ones can be named.

Ada Default Parameters

Ada's formal in Parameters have an optional initialization clause serving as a default value. If the option is used and in the Call Statement the number of actual parameters is less than the number of formals, then the default value is passed. This makes the source slightly less readable, since the reader is either under the misconception that the actual parameter list is already complete, or it will be necessary to cross-reference to find the default values at the place of declaration. This unusual feature does, however, reduce the program writer's burden in rare cases.

To enhance readability Ada provides named parameter association, a nice facility for long parameter lists. It alleviates the incidental order dependency. See Example 17-12.

```
motion( x_val => 100.0, y_val => 0.0, z_val => 0.0 );--readable
motion( 100.0. 0.0, 0.0 );--less documentary
```

Example 17-12 Ada Default Parameters

Peculiar Syntax Rules in Fortran

Implied-Do in Fortran IO Statements

IO Statements in Fortran may have an implied do loop as part of the data list. This implied do loop is parenthesized and may be nested. The syntax is shown in Example 17-13:

```
implied_do          ::= ( dlist , loop_var = e1 , e2 [ , e3 ] )
loop_var            ::= implicitly_declared_variable
```

Example 17-13 Grammar Fragment for Fortran Implied-Do

The semantics for expressions e1 through e3 in Example 17-13 are the same as those in Fortran's For Statement. Implied Do Variables live only inside the paired parentheses and may not be referenced in the "dlist" of Read Statements. Otherwise they would receive two conflicting values in the same statement. See Example 17-14. The two Write Statements are correct, but the Read Statement uses the implied Do Variable illegally.

```
program impldo
 write( 6, * )( i**2, i = 1, 5 )
 write( 6, * )( ( i*100 + j**2, i = 1, 3 ), j = 1, 3 )
 read( 5, * )( i, i = 1, 5 )
end
```

Example 17-14 Legal and Illegal Uses of Implied Do Variables

Parenthesized Expression in Fortran If Statement

As a consequence of the dubious rule that blanks are insignificant, Fortran must sweeten its If Statement by adding "syntactic sugar." The logical expression after the keyword IF must be parenthesized. If this rule did not exist, the language would be ambiguous. A sample piece of source code in Example 17-15, which references the logical variable "L," should clarify this assertion.

```
C------Correct Fortran
      IF(L)A=0

C------Wrong Without parens: If statement?
      IF L A = 0

C------Wrong Without parens: Assignment Statement?
      IFLA=0
```

Example 17-15 Justification for Parens in If Statement

No Records, No Pointers in Fortran

Programmers can live without pointers in quite a large range of applications. Pointers can be simulated to some degree by indices into arrays. Another class of programs, typically systems programs, does need pointers and, therefore, cannot be expressed in Fortran.

Fortran also lacks records. Again it is possible to simulate these in a primitive way with parallel arrays, and then use the same subscript for each array element reference that the programmer interprets as part of the same record.

Fortran Operator Associativity

Multiple occurrences of operators with the same priority in one expression are evaluated from left to right. The only exception to this is the ** operator for exponentiation. Two or more exponentiations are evaluated right to left. The purpose here is clear; the language semantics refer to what is already familiar to us. We know from high school the meaning of 10**10**10. This expression is interpreted from right to left, meaning 10**(10**10), rather than (10**10)**10. The latter value is substantially smaller than the former.

Peculiar Syntax Rules in Pascal

Pascal Labels

Pascal has no variables or parameters of type label. Labels must be predeclared as integer numbers, usually in the small range of 1 through 9999. Many compilers add mnemonic label names to Pascal.

Pascal Permanent Files

The names of permanent files must be announced in the PROGRAM declaration. Later, in the variable declaration part of the main program, the same file names must be declared together with their associated types. This unusual double declaration is, so we speculate, a leftover from a machine requirement of Pascal's first implementation. It is a common convention on large-scale CDC Cyber machines to preannounce all permanent files even in higher level languages. The original Zürich Pascal implementation was hosted on a Cyber system.

One Single Compilation in Pascal

Pascal's greatest weakness is the absence of a multicompilation unit facility. Some programming problems can be modularized physically in Pascal by separating them into distinct programs. Eventually these programs communicate with one another via files. But programming tasks that cannot be separated this way result in huge Pascal source files.

Pascal Fixed Declaration Order

Pascal scopes are divided into two sections—one for declarations and one for statements. The declarative section may contain Label, Const, Type, Var, and subprogram declarations in exactly that order. Any of these classes of declarations may be omitted; even an empty declaration section is allowed in Pascal. This stiff ordering of declarations may appear overly rigorous to the language novice, but due to other limitations in Pascal, it really imposes no new hardship. Notice, however, we only say that this strictness imposes no new limitations, not that it is an advantage. Other limitations, such as the lack of general constant expressions, have already severely cut down the usefulness of an otherwise great language.

Peculiar Syntax Rules in PL/I

PL/I Structures

PL/I structures have explicit level numbers in the formal declaration. These numbers are historical leftovers from the model language Cobol, from which PL/I borrowed the idea. The absolute value of these level numbers is not relevant; only the relative values matter.

Incomplete Qualification of Record Fields

As long as field names are unique, it is not necessary in PL/I to fully qualify them. Unique substructure names are sufficient. If other fields in any structure of the same scope have the same name, then a more complete qualification is necessary. This principle of partial qualification is used in a recursive fashion in PL/I. If the major structure of an ambiguous field is unique, then the partial qualification is sufficient. For the sake of open-endedness in program design, it is preferable to use full qualification. Otherwise, the subsequent introduction of a few more fields in an existing structure, or the addition of further structures, may cause sudden error messages on existing, partial qualifications. All in all, the "partial qualification feature" is a nice present that the PL/I language designers intended to offer to the programming community, but it is such an unsafe construct that we had best forget it ever existed. See Example 17-16 which shows partial qualification.

```
DECLARE
  1  CAR,
    2  NAME CHARACTER(10),
    2  YEAR FIXED, /* YEAR OF MANUFACTURE */
      3  ENGINE,
        4  CYLINDERS FIXED,
        4  HORSEPOWER FIXED,
      3  OWNER,
        4  FIRST CHAR(10),
        4  LAST  CHAR(10);
DECLARE
1  PERSON,
  2  NAME,
    3  FIRST CHAR(10),
    3  LAST  CHAR(10),
    3  MID   CHAR(1),
  2  YEAR  FIXED, /* OF BIRTH */
  2  SSN   CHAR(11);

/* program statements */
YEAR = 1980; /* AMBIGUOUS */
```

```
PERSON.YEAR = 1955; /* ONLY ONE CHOICE */
FIRST = 'MARGARETE'; /* AMBIGUOUS */
NAME.FIRST = 'HANNAH'; /* CLEAR */
PERSON.NAME.LAST = 'SCHWARTZ'; /* FULLY QUALIFIED */
NAME = 'FORD'; /* AMBIGUOUS, CAR OR PERSON? */
```

Example 17-16 Incomplete Qualification

PL/I "By Name Clause"

PL/I has borrowed the "Corresponding Clause" from Cobol under the alias "By Name Clause." Adding the BY NAME specification right after any statement that references a structure is sufficient to specify the name of the outermost structures. All subfields with identical names in the structures are affected. We give two equivalent instances in Example 17-17. The first program segment uses the "by name" clause, which makes the source short and concise. The second version uses the spelled-out form of structure references and is much longer.

```
DECLARE
  1  ACCOUNT(N),
    2  NAME,
      3  FIRST CHAR(10),
      3  LAST  CHAR(10),
    2  OLD_BALANCE DEC FIXED(12,2),
    2  NEW_BALANCE DEC FIXED(12,2);
DECLARE
  1  TOTAL,
    2  OLD_BALANCE DEC FIXED(12,2),
    2  NEW_BALANCE DEC FIXED(12,2);
/* STATEMENTS */
TOTAL = 0.0; /* sets both fields to zero */
DO I = 1 TO N;
  TOTAL = TOTAL + ACCOUNT(I), BY NAME;
END;
/* SHORT WITH BY NAME CLAUSE */
/* SAME AS */
TOTAL = 0.0;
DO I = 1 TO N;
  TOTAL.OLD_BALANCE = TOTAL.OLD_BALANCE + ACCOUNT(I).OLD_BALANCE;
  TOTAL.NEW_BALANCE = TOTAL.NEW_BALANCE + ACCOUNT(I).NEW_BALANCE;
END;
/* LONG, SPELLED OUT FORM */
```

Example 17-17 PL/I "By Name" Clause

Identifying the Main Program in PL/I

PL/I has a crystal clear way of identifying the main procedure. The added option MAIN in the formal declaration of a nonnested procedure defines where execution will start. In Pascal the problem does not surface, since there is only one compilation unit. Fortran has one special compilation unit, named PROGRAM, which identifies the main entry point. Ada leaves this point unclear; individual implementors will probably add a MAIN PRAGMA to select the main procedure. Unfortunately, this leaves a few variations open that make some programs nonportable. For example, will the PRAGMA precede or follow the procedure so identified? Can such a procedure be nested, or must it lie on the outermost level? Maybe later Ada language revisions will fix such a glaring omission and, incredible, adopt a language convention set by PL/I.

PL/I Pseudo-Variables

In PL/I there are three built-in functions that can also be used as variables. These are called *pseudo-variables* and can be used on the left-hand side of an assignment operator. We demonstrate this in Example 17-18 with the sample function SUBSTR. Used in an expression, SUBSTR yields a substring of the first argument. Used as a pseudo-variable, SUBSTR allows the selected string argument to be set just as any other variable.

```
DECLARE
 SHORT CHAR(3) INIT ( 'ADA' );
DECLARE
 LONG  CHAR(6) INIT ( 'ADAGIO' );
/* STATEMENTS */
SUBSTR( LONG, 4 ) = SHORT; /* pseudo-variable */
/* LONG = 'ADAADA' */
SHORT = SUBSTR( LONG, 2, 3 ); /* function */
/* NOW SHORT EQUALS 'DAG' */
```

Example 17-18 SUBSTR, Used as Pseudo-Variable and as Function

This construct is an invention to patch up a situation which was faulty to begin with—namely, PL/I's lack of a clean mechanism for substring. Any powerful language will allow substring references on either side of the assignment operator. Principally, this same freedom is already known from array references. Thus there is no need to create special cases when the object happens to be an array of characters. Compare, for example, Ada's slices. A few pseudo-variables have been covered in Chapter 16.

17.3 Summary

This chapter is a collection of curious language rules. All too often such curiosities stem from exceptions or from two conflicting principles. Many examples presented here are meant to provide programmers with an educational form of entertainment and to give language designers a chance to review the effect of exceptions. Other examples, such as the explicit ^ symbol for pointer dereferencing in Pascal and the MAIN attribute in PL/I, are peculiar but enhance readability in a strongly positive way and have been included as a suggestion to language designers.

Except for a few lexical glitches, the total lack of the Goto Statement, and the incomplete forced closure, we could find no rules in Modula-2 that would need improvement. This is a subjective observation, especially since it implies that we perceive Modula-2 as "close to perfect," which is exactly how we feel, particularly when we weigh the size of the language definition with the expressive power of the described object. Ada, by contrast, also an excellently designed language, is slightly more powerful, but significantly more complicated to learn.

17.4 Exercises

1. The following string is a piece of Ada source that is not inside a string literal and also not part of a comment. It is syntactically correct. Is the first single quote an apostrophe (a full lexical token by itself), or is it the start of an Ada character literal, which needs the matching second quote? The two dots indicate that more source text is following.

```
:= min_val'('..    --Partial Ada source string
```

2. What is the decimal value of the following Ada numeric literal?

```
2#0111_1111_1111_1111#
```

3. Represent the value of the following Ada numeric literal as another numeric literal, to the base 3.

```
10#2700#e-2
```

4. How many comments are on the single line of Ada source text?

```
-- A comment, -- and some more -- maybe even a third??
```

5. We wish to write two Fortran statements, assigning "B" to "A," and "D" to "C." What is wrong with the following fortran source, and how can it be corrected?

```
A = B C = D
```

6. Is it a good idea to let the programmer redefine keywords of a programming language? What advantages would this freedom offer? Would there be any disadvantages?

7. Pascal requires the ^ symbol for pointer dereferencing. Does this additional writing effort have any advantage?

8. What is the Ada syntax rule for dereferencing Access type objects?

9. Could the following source string possibly be a correct PL/I statement?

```
@ =$  -$  +$ *@$ -$   ;
```

10. What is the value of the PL/I variable "I" after the following Assignment Statement?

```
I = 3**3**3;
```

18

Aliases, Side Effects, and Other Bad Things

Many languages do not require the programmer
to declare his variables at all.
Instead they define complex default rules
which the compiler must apply to undeclared variables.
But this can only encourage sloppy program design and documentation,
and nullify many of the advantages
of block structure and type checking;
the default rules soon get so complex
that they are very likely to give results
not expected by the programmer,
and as ludicrously or subtly inappropriate to his intentions
as a machine code program which contains a type error.

Of course, wise programmers have learned
that it is worthwhile to expend the effort to avoid these dangers.
They eagerly scan the compiler listings to ensure
that every variable has been declared,
and that all the characteristics assigned to it are acceptable.
What a pity that the designers of these languages take such trouble
to give such trouble to their users and themselves.

C. A. R. Hoare
Hints On Programming Language Design

This chapter points out a family of programming errors that cannot be caught by language translators, since the mistakes are not of syntactic nature. Quite often, when errors of this kind are made, the programmer is under the mistaken impression of having designed something particularly clever. In fact, these constructions tend to become so clever that even the original designer cannot comprehend anymore what they mean and why things go wrong. We group these mistakes into the subclasses aliases, side effects, and default actions. Among the defaults are implicit type conversions and implicit substitutions for syntax elements not stated explicitly.

Admittedly, the title of this chapter has been phrased with the intent to catch the reader's attention. If the guidelines proposed in this section are respected by the reader, the benefit in saved debugging time can be substantial. But this chapter in conjunction with the previous has a double mission. Not only do we try to make the readers better programmers by urging them to abstain from the dangerous constructs expounded here, we also sharpen the skills of programming language designers by persuading them to avoid the inclusion of dangerous traps exhibited there.

Not all aliasing and not all side effects are necessarily wrong. It is the goal of this chapter to give the reader some understanding and control over these hard-to-handle tools.

18.1 Aliases

A program object that is known under more than one name is an *alias.* Aliasing as a concept can be quite helpful at times, even necessary in some contexts. For example, Pascal's variant records offer a controlled way of accessing the same storage areas under new names. The intent here is usually clear: it is necessary to interpret the same storage locations as having different types. With Pascal's relatively strict typing rules this would otherwise be impossible. By using aliases, some shortcomings of the language can be bypassed as well. For instance, Pascal has no conversion function for assigning an integer type object to another variable of enumerative type, even though the converse function is provided. With variant records and a controlled way of "cheating," this can be solved. Ada's discriminant records, the Fortran EQUIVALENCE declarations, and PL/I's DEFINED attribute all perform this same function. All "rich" languages allow the reinterpretation of the same storage area under dissimilar types.

In this chapter we are not concerned about these controlled uses of aliasing. The kind of alias treated here is of slightly different, less intentional nature. Here, rather than interpreting the same object under a new type, the programmer has created aliased objects of identical type but each with distinct names. Usually this kind of aliasing happens by accident, when the same object is available as a global variable and as a parameter. "Aliasdemo1" in Example 18-1 is an instance of this kind of accident.

```
 1 program aliasdemo1( output );
 2  var global : integer;
 3  procedure alias1( var local : integer );
 4   var temp : integer;
 5   begin { alias1 }
 6    temp := global;
 7    local := local + 1;
 8    if temp <> global then
 9     writeln( ' What happened?' );
10    {end if}
11   end { alias1 };
12  begin { aliasdemo1 }
13   global := 5;
14   alias1( global );
15  end { aliasdemo1 }.
```

Example 18-1 Aliasing of Local and Global Variables in Pascal

The reader should be astonished when studying lines 6 and 8. Line 6 assigns "temp" its initial value; but two lines later, when we check if "temp" still equals "global," the check fails. It is in no way apparent that the only statement in between could have changed "temp" or "global." And still it did! The variable "local" is simply an alias for "global," hence "global" receives a new value on line 7. This only demonstrates that using global variables can be dangerous. But we should not be fooled into believing that abstaining from using globals would cure this problem.

Unintentional aliasing can also happen when two apparently distinct formal out (reference) parameters designate the same object. In this case aliasing is caused by passing the same variable more than once as an actual parameter in a subprogram call. Some languages explicitly forbid this (Jensen and Wirth [1978] p.71). But as we can see in the Pascal program "aliasdemo2" in Example 18-2, a compiler cannot always detect this error. Subprogram "alias2" on line 18 is called with two array elements. Such subscripts are not always known before execution time.

The lesson we should learn from these two programs is this: the relevant procedures "alias1" and "alias2" respectively access two supposedly disparate names. In "alias1" these names are "local" and "global," both integer type variables. When a value is assigned to the one, there is no reason to believe that the other one should change as well. However, this obvious "fact" turns out to be fallacy when aliases are involved. Line 7 in the Pascal program "aliasdemo1" increments "local," but there is no assignment whatsoever to "global." Why does variable "global" change anyway? Because it is an alias of "local" and that variable is altered.

The same thing happens with "local1" and "local2" in the Pascal procedure "alias2." Analyzing "alias2" in a modular fashion, without considering the surrounding scopes, will make us believe in mysteries.

```
1  program aliasdemo2( output );
2   var i : integer; a : array[ 1 .. 2 ] of integer;
3   procedure alias2(
4    var local1, local2 : integer );
5    var temp           : integer;
6    begin { alias2 }
7     temp := local1;
8     local2 := local2 + 1;
9     if temp <> local1 then
10     writeln( ' Another surprise?' );
11    {end if}
12   end { alias2 };
13  begin { aliasdemo2 }
14   i := 1;
15   a[ 1 ] := 1;
16   a[ 2 ] := 1;
17   alias2( i, i );
18   alias2( a[ i ], a[ i ] ); { pass a[2] twice }
19  end { aliasdemo2 }.
```

Example 18-2 Aliasing Two Out (Reference) Parameters in Pascal

Program "aliasdemo2" above has the same quirk as shown before. Only the cause is different. Here we have passed the same variable twice as an actual parameter to two formal out parameters. This, too, is a cardinal sin in programming particularly if out parameters are implemented by address passing. Well-designed languages recommend against this, but, unfortunately, a compiler cannot check for such sins within reasonable cost. See lines 17 and 18, both acting in bad faith.

18.2 Side Effects Revisited

Side effects are usually unwanted changes in a program's state. Each time an instruction or a statement is executed, the state of the overall program changes. It is the sole purpose of that statement to cause that change. Upon reading a program's source we should be able to keep track of which effect a statement will have during execution. Side effects are the "fringe benefits" that come in addition to the visible effects and can have various causes.

The three most common causes of side effects are changes of nonlocal variables in subprogram bodies, assignments to parameters passed by other means than by value, and exception conditions.

In this section we have various implementations of a trivial function named "one." "One" always returns the integer value 1, but also increments a global variable. This increment is a deliberate side effect. When "one" is used in certain contexts—as, for example, in array subscripts—then its side effect may become critical. This critical situation arises when the affected global variable, in this case "i," is also part of the index expression itself.

We demonstrate this lingering threat in "ada_side_effect" and "pascalsideeffect" in Examples 18-3 and 18-4 by using a seemingly trivial Assignment Statement. Line 15 in program "ada_side_effect" in Example 18-3 seems to achieve nothing but to move the value of array element a(one+i) into itself. Line 18 in "pascalsideeffect" in Example 18-4 works analogously. But here comes the interesting surprise! The array subscript produces a side effect. Depending on the particular language definition and implementation, either the left-hand side is evaluated first, as is the case with this Ada run time system, or the right-hand side is executed first. The Pascal compiler used here generated code with the latter meaning. This very subtle language rule causes the result to be different from language to language. We urge the reader to carefully study the two programs and follow our explanation to understand why the outputs are different.

What do the languages require? In this particular instance, Ada and Pascal agree in philosophy. Both languages specify that the evaluation order of left- and right-hand side in an Assignment Statement is undefined. This is a positive step toward safe programming. Any program that requires the right-hand side to be evaluated first (or last) promotes side effects. The Ada and Pascal language rules discourage such obscure programming.

As soon as we note that "one" has a side effect on "i," we sense that we are in for trouble. But we do not know exactly what the overall effect of the Assignment Statement will be. Again, we encourage the reader to fully understand program "ada_side_effect" in Example 18-3 before reading on.

```
                 | WITH text_io; USE text_io; USE integer_io;
                 | PROCEDURE ada_side_effect IS
             1   |  i  :  integer;
       11    1   |  a  :  ARRAY( 1 .. 10 ) OF integer;
       21    1   |  FUNCTION one RETURN integer IS
             2   |   BEGIN--one
             2   |    i := i + 1;
   6         2 1 |    RETURN 1;
  11         2 1 |   END one;
  11         1   |  BEGIN--ada_side_effect
  13         1   |   FOR j IN 1 .. 10 LOOP
  18         1 1 |    a( j ) := j ** 2;
  26         1 2 |   END LOOP;
  28         1 1 |   i := 5;
  31         1 1 |   a( one + i ) := a ( one + i );--trivial ??
  49         1 1 |   FOR j IN 1 .. 10 LOOP
  53         1 1 |    put_line( a( j ) );
  60         1 2 |   END LOOP;
  62         1 1 |  END ada_side_effect;
```

Example 18-3 Side Effect in Ada Assignment Statement

We know for certain that after execution of the critical Assignment Statement, global variable "i" will have the value 7; "i" has been incremented twice. What we do not know is whether the left- or right-hand side is executed first. In the former case array element "a(7)" will change and assume the value of "a(8)"; in the latter the element "a(8)" receives a new value from "a(7)." In the Ada program "ada_side_effect" in Example 18-3 the variable on the left-hand side is evaluated first. Then the expression is computed and assigned to the receiving variable. Consequently, elements 7 and 8 have the same value, 64, which will be printed twice. Since Ada does not specify the order of evaluation of left-hand side and right-hand side this is in conformance with the standard, see ANSI [1983a] section 5.2.

The run time behaviour of the Pascal program "pascalsideeffect" in Example 18-4 is also correct. We know from the standard ([3], p.77) that the evaluation order for Assignment Statements is "implementation-dependent." The results show that the right-hand side has been evaluated first. Index "one+i" results in 7, and array element a[7] is assigned to "a[one+i]," which maps into "a[8]." Consequently, both "a[7]" and "a[8]" have the value 49.

The danger of side effects rests on the programmer's relying in an object like "i" being invariant over a certain range of source lines. That trust is based on the absence of any visible assignment. If a side effect breaks that trust, the programmer made a wrong assumption and the system malfunctions.

```
 1    1  0  0     PROGRAM pascalsideeffect( output );
 2    2  0  0       VAR
                      i   :   integer;
 3    4  0  0         a   : ARRAY[ 1 .. 10 ] OF integer;
 4    6  0  0       FUNCTION one : integer;
 5    7  1  0         BEGIN { one }
 5    8  1  1           i := i + 1;
 6    9  1  1           one := 1;
 7   10  1  1         END; { one }
 8   12  0  0       BEGIN { pascalsideeffect }
 8   13  0  1         writeln( output, ' START Pascal side effect' );
 9   14  0  1         FOR i := 1 TO 10 DO
10   15  0  1           a[ i ] := i * i;
11   16  0  1         {END FOR}
                        i := 5;
12   18  0  1         a[ one + i ] := a [ one + i ];
13   19  0  1         FOR i := 1 TO 10 DO
14   20  0  1           writeln( output, a[ i ] );
15   21  0  1         {END FOR}
                      writeln( output, ' END   Pascal side effect' );
16   23  0  1       END. { pascalsideeffect }
```

Example 18-4 Side Effect in Pascal Assignment Statement

8.3 Defaults

The *default* principle is a two sided sword. One side is dull and not worth very much, while the other is sharp and can hurt tremendously. It is the goal of defaults to save programming time, or more precisely, to reduce the number of keystrokes necessary to enter the program text. Language translators then provide the default action in place of an explicit specification. The assumption is that this default action is precisely what the programmer intended in the first place.

A Catastrophe

Here we show a correct Fortran program fragment that uses a default action. This beauty can be found in Horning [1979]. As is the case so often, the Fortran compiler assumes that a particular default is desired, even if in fact it is not. In this hair-raising example, the saving of a few keystrokes, or actually a recompilation, cost the American taxpayer many million dollars. We repeat Horning's illustrative example:

The first American Venus probe was lost due to a program fault caused by the inadvertent substitution of a statement of the form

```
DO 3 I = 1.3
```

for one of the form

```
DO 3 I = 1,3
```

The first thing to observe about this unfortunate incident is that the punishment exceeded the crime.

What is wrong here? A simple keystroke error made the programmer write 1.3 instead of 1,3. The intent was to let the Do Statement iterate from 1 to 3, expressed in Fortran as 1,3 and not as 1.3. The intent was to let the control variable "I" in the Do Statement assume the values 1 through 3, thus executing the loop three times. Unfortunately, the unintended program with the error is also a correct program, but what a different one! The Fortran compiler sees no loop here at all, instead it recognizes a correct Assignment Statement. Variable "DO3I," implicitly declared with default attributes, is assigned the decimal value 1.3 without type conversion. The default type for "DO3I" is extracted from the starting letter "D." Needless to say, the Venus probe was lost without accomplishing its mission.

Default PL/I Types (Attributes)

It is sometimes annoying to see our Modula-2 or Pascal compiler listing and notice that we misspelled a few names. The compiler is unforgiving and scolds us with the message "Undeclared Identifier." So we correct the source and initiate another compilation until the compiler is content. This will not happen in PL/I. There are no misspellings! If a name is mistyped by accident, the compiler implicitly declares it with default attributes. These are DECIMAL and FLOAT. Numeric literals, on the other hand, are always of type FIXED DECIMAL. Chances are that all operations involving literals and implicitly declared variables cause type conversions. It just turns out that type conversions with FIXED DECIMAL data are the most obscure. We challenge the reader and write a simple DECIMAL FIXED type expression as follows; guess the value before reading on!

```
25 + 1/3
```

It is hard to believe, but the default conversions that apply here cause the expression to yield 5.33333333333333. A truncation is necessary, since the intermediate result is clearly too long. Unfortunately, the default action is to cut off the most significant digit, rather than one of the trailing fractional digits. We speculate that most our readers believe the expression to yield 25.333333, different from what PL/I yields.

18.4 Summary

This chapter exposes the unexpected side of programming devices that are legal but usually cause errors. Three of the most dangerous devices are aliases, side effects, and program defaults. Ironically, the defaults have been invented—and in some languages developed to a high level of sophistication—with the intent to make programming easy. It turned out to be a terrible trap instead! When we understand these dangers, we can avoid them and become better programmers.

More importantly, we try to convince the programming language designer to abstain from defining defaults and from specifying every nook and cranny of the language. It is all right to leave some items undefined. The example set by Ada and Pascal in leaving open the evaluation order of Assignment Statement parts is a good reference point. The example set by Modula-2 and Pascal to let the control variable be undefined after a For Statement is a positive step toward safe programming. When we define languages in this spirit, we discourage programmers from relying on program interplay that is incomprehensible.

8.5 Exercises

1. Analyze the Assignment Statement on line 15 of "ada_side_effect" in Example 18-3. Which output will be generated if both index expressions are "i+one"?

2. Do the same for program "pascal_side_effect" in Example 18-4. Which output will be generated with the compiler used, if both index expressions on line 18 are "i+one"?

3. Which advantages does Fortran's implicit declaration of variables provide? List also disadvantages, and weigh the two against one another.

4. To execute an Assignment Statement the variable on the left-hand side and the expression to the right must be evaluated. Ada defines that the order of these evaluations is unspecified. What is the reason for leaving this subtle aspect open?

5. If a programming language has only value parameters, one type of side effect is thus eliminated. Discuss whether it is a good language design decision to exclude reference parameters for this reason.

6. Write a PL/I program that contains the following statements and interpret the output. Before the program executes, predict what the output should be.

```
DO I = 1 TO 32/2;
  PUT LIST( ' I = ', I );
  PUT SKIP;
END;
```

19

Concurrent Programming

The aim of Concurrent Pascal is to do for operating systems what Sequential Pascal has done for compilers: to reduce the programming effort by an order of magnitude.

Per Brinch Hanson
The Architecture of Concurrent Programs

So far all our discussions about programming languages have implied the limitation that processing would proceed in a sequential fashion on a single processor. This restriction is quite understandable, since practically all conventional systems are sequential monoprocessors. In this chapter we drop the limitation and address architectures and programming language facilities that support concurrent programming. We shall explain the relevant terminology, give a motivation for multiprocessing, and show simple programming examples in Ada and Modula-2. This will lead us into the chapter on Prolog, a programming language with great potential for parallel execution on a multiprocessing system.

Legend has it that Julius Caesar could simultaneously give orders to his officers while listening to a messenger reporting the current status; his orders were clear and the news was accurately perceived. If legend is true, Caesar must have had a multiprocessing system, different from the conventional single-brain unit the rest of his fellows and opponents had to live with. Or Caesar must have multiplexed (time-shared) his single processor so fast that the outside world perceived it as multiple units working simultaneously. The current section introduces the attractive side of concurrent processing and the very closely related topics of parallel processing, better known as multiprocessing. Until we explain the terms in detail in Section 19-2, we can pretend that all three are synonyms.

19.1 A Parallel Processing Example

Multiprocessing is by no means new nor is it restricted to computer applications. Imagine how long it would have taken to complete the Empire State Building, if only one single person had constructed it! With this example we have a motivation for multiprocessing: it's simply faster. *Multiprocessing* is a frequently used and heavily abused term. The associated terminology has become equally indistinct as a result of commercial abuse. Before we straighten out the vocabulary, we offer a motivation for multiprocessing through a more detailed example.

If we had to construct a new aircraft, how would we go about it? After having identified all requirements, we would first design the overall system, then build the major subcomponents such as fuselage, navigation system, wings, and engines. Naturally we would have to specify the interface between engines and wings, and wings and fuselage. After building all subcomponents in parallel, we ensure proper integration of the navigation system with the fuselage, and of the engines with the wings. Finally we would test the complete assembly. This top level model is probably so shallow that an aircraft designer would chuckle, but our modest aim is only to demonstrate the advantage of working in parallel. We can express the identified steps in a *dependency graph,* as shown in Figure 19-1. Such graphs are acyclic and directed, typically with one entry and one exit node.

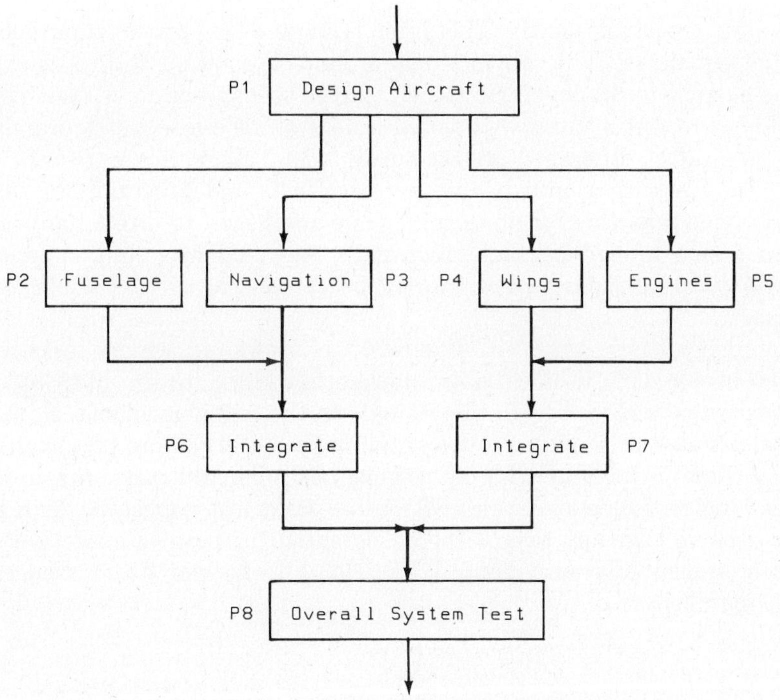

Figure 19-1 Dependency Graph for Aircraft Design

Without being operations research experts or aircraft architects we can see that tasks P2 to P5 and later P6 and P7 can be done simultaneously. The subtasks can be performed in parallel. The logical dependencies, reflected in the graph by directed vertices, make it impossible for P2 to be started before P1 is reasonably complete. Similarly, it is not possible to start the integration step P6 before P2 and P3 are both complete. But, if we have a sufficiently large work force available, P2 through P5 can be done simultaneously, and later on P6 and P7 will be performed at the same time. It is conceivable that not all workers involved in P2 through P5 can be used in P6 and P7, so they can play cards, or better even, start the construction of the next specimen, conveniently injecting a new dimension of multiprocessing into this model.

What does this all have to do with programming languages? Practically all present-day computers are single processor systems; tasks are executed in a strictly sequential fashion. For many time-critical (real-time) applications the execution speed of single processors is too slow, and for some not time-critical applications the computations are so complex that a sufficiently accurate answer takes too long to be of interest. The obvious way around this dilemma is to build faster machines of the kind we have always constructed. But, much to our chagrin, there is a stubborn, physical limitation to how far we can increase the processor speed. This limit is imposed by propagation delay and by cooling problems. The "obvious way around" is soon pushed to its extremes with the current technology. How then can we still speedup our systems? One possibility is to forget our self-imposed limitation of sequential processing and invent radically different architectures that allow more work to be accomplished per time unit. Computer architects and programming language designers have seen this for quite some time and begun to direct hardware and software design toward parallel processing. Ada and Modula-2 support such architectures in varying degrees, as will be demonstrated by samples later in this chapter.

The dependency graph in Figure 19-1 shows us which tasks *can* be executed in parallel; it does not impose that these tasks *must* indeed be performed simultaneously. If only a single work crew is available, all subtasks can be elaborated in sequence. It just will take longer. More importantly, the execution order (the schedule) of parallel tasks is arbitrary; any order will work, as long as the dependencies with other tasks are respected. As a general rule we observe that any task with the potential for parallel execution can be processed sequentially, but not all sequential tasks can be rearranged into multiple, parallel tasks.

19.2 Terminology

Multiprogramming is the concurrent execution of two or more tasks on a single processor. Generally, these tasks are independent from one another. Multiprogramming is an old, third generation computer concept. Motivated by (then relatively) high processor speed and manufacturing cost, system designers developed multiprogramming as a way to share an expensive resource among multiple users. Every user received the service of a full, virtual machine that just happened to be much slower than the real processor, but sufficiently fast to satisfy each user's need. In some sense the different users on a multiprogramming system represent one macroscopic task each. If multiple machines were available, each task (user) could be serviced by a dedicated processor. Because of the slow human response in an assumed interactive environment, most of the time the processors would sit idle, so it made sense to multiplex one processor. In the absence of resource sharing (files, data) scheduling the competing (concurrent) tasks is easy.

Multiprocessing is the simultaneous execution of one or more tasks by two or more processors. The "one or more" portion in this definition should strike us as counter-intuitive. How could we possibly process one task on multiple processors? The reader should be puzzled because we have been vague in our discussion so far; we have not defined *task.* A task is any form of service we wish to have performed by a computer system. This is still vague, but we can work with it. Quite often a task can be broken into smaller tasks, called subtasks, which could be serviced in parallel. The multiprocessed execution of a single task is indeed the most desirable mode of operation, since it provides the potential for the shortest possible execution time. Since we are not discussing operating systems, we ignore the critical issue of overhead cost. Firing off another processor, bringing multiple execution streams back together, imposes some overhead that we do not consider in our introductory discussion.

Concurrent Processing is the sequential execution of multiple tasks that have the potential for parallel execution. Their sequential elaboration is a consequence of the underlying hardware that has only one processor. *Concurrent* is the preferred term in Modula-2, probably because its designer assumes the language to run on single processors. We can use it as a synonym to *parallel. Concurrent Programming* is a form of programming that permits software to execute on a multiprocessor system. If the target machine truly has multiple processing elements, the run time will be short. Otherwise, if there is only a single processor, the same software will also run correctly but take longer.

Overlapped IO in second-generation computer systems was already a form of multiprocessing, though very restricted. One of the processors, the IO channel, could perform just IO operations. Multiple arithmetic processing units on large CDC systems also represent a special type of parallel processing, but again each processor could perform only one specific type of operation. Furthermore, array processors such as the old Solomon computer, the Illiac-IV, and the Burroughs BSP system are restricted multiprocessors. The restriction was that at any moment only one instruction could be executed on a large matrix of data. Other architects proposed radically different languages with the restriction that no statement would have any data dependency on other statements of a program. This would allow only one single assignment to any variable, hence the name Single Assignment Languages. Architectures for such languages can perform many tasks in parallel. For more information about the software aspect see D. D. Chamberlin's Ph. D. Thesis [1971]. Single Assignment Language systems were developed in France in the early 1970s. The problem with these is the severe limitation of the software tool.

Lastly, pipelined architectures do more than one operation in parallel. But again, these multiple operations are restricted to cracking different portions of instructions in an interleaved fashion; only the instructions in turn are assumed to be executed strictly in sequence. These older forms are only first attempts of multiprocessing; they are not the general kind of parallel processor we need to achieve a quantum leap in performance improvement.

Parallelism is the potential of tasks to be processed at the same time. When this parallelism is expressed by the user in a source program, we say the parallelism is explicit. Otherwise the parallelism is implicit. Parallelism requires that the tasks to be performed at the same time share no data. If data are to be shared, then their access must be monitored via *locks* (also called semaphores), which enforce sequentialization. Implied parallelism is our greatest hope for future breakthroughs in execution speed enhancements. Let us illustrate this by a sample Ada Assignment Statement.

```
a := b * c + d * e;
```

Our conventional interpretation of the preceding statement is that two multiplications take place in sequence, then an addition, and lastly an assignment; we count four individual steps. On many real systems the multiplication steps are more costly than the other steps. If this statement were executed on a parallel processor, and its Ada compiler were so intelligent to discover implied parallelism, then the execution would proceed in three steps: two simultaneous multiplications, followed by one addition and the assignment. In Chapter 6 we have seen that in Ada the order of operand fetching is undefined, hence the simultaneous creation of the values for "b" through "e" causes no semantic problem. We observe the same kind of potential on the statement level; see the Modula-2 source in Example 19-1.

```
Count := Count + 1;
Buffer[ in ] := NextChar;
Index := Index MOD Max + 1;
```

Example 19-1 Data Dependency

If we assume all involved objects to be of appropriate type—in particular "NextChar" and "Max" to be simple variables, not functions with side effects—then all three Modula-2 statements can be executed simultaneously. Never mind that they are written in sequence. Better even, we observe the same potential for parallelism on the procedure level. To exploit implied parallelism we need new computer architectures with multiple processing elements, and very intelligent compilers that generate multiple code streams for the parallel processors and schedulers. To exploit explicit parallelism we need multiprocessing systems and appropriate schedulers. The load on the language translators is much lighter. In the following sections we explain the steps taken by the language designers for Ada and Modula-2 to support explicit parallelism.

19.3 Parallel Tasks without Data Sharing

The potential speed improvement caused by multiprocessing is sufficient to have stimulated programming language designers to include explicit control for parallel (concurrent) processing. Algol-68, for example, defines the "collateral clause," a sequence of expressions that are separated from one another by a comma. The semantics associated with the comma separator is that each such clause may be executed in parallel. Other languages have invented more conspicuous constructs -- for example, the Parallel Compound Statement embraced by the keywords COBEGIN and COEND in Concurrent Pascal; see Hansen [1973]. Any statement in between these brackets can be executed in parallel per language definition.

Ada provides Tasks. A *Task* is a specific object, identified by the reserved keyword TASK. To distinguish it from the general term *task,* we shall capitalize the Ada object. Any Task represents an independently executing environment. If a program declares "n" Task objects, all of them start simultaneously before the first statement of the rest of the declaring unit is initiated. Ada even allows Tasks to share data in a well-controlled fashion. Modula-2 defines concurrent processes for simultaneous execution. To initiate these processes that look like regular procedures, the predefined "Init" and "StartProcess" system calls are provided. To synchronize those processes that share data, Modula-2 provides Monitors. A Monitor is simply a module with an explicit priority. We shall explore these in more detail in the following sections.

Ada Tasks without Data Sharing

In Ada, objects that execute in parallel with other objects, are called Tasks. A Task cannot be a compilation unit and must therefore be nested in a subprogram or a package. In general, a Task is an object like any other, and may be declared as a formal parameter, a record field, or even an access type. But Tasks are "limited private," which means they cannot be compared or assigned. The explicit initiation of a Task is not possible in Ada; a Task is fired off as soon as the declarative part that contains its formal declaration has been elaborated. See the BNF grammar fragment in Example 19-2.

```
task_declaration     ::= task_specification ;
task_specification   ::= TASK [ TYPE ] identifier [ IS
                           { entry_declaration }
                           { representation_clause }
                         END [ identifier ] ]
task_body            ::= TASK BODY identifier IS
                           [ declarative_part ]
                         BEGIN
                            sequence_of_statements
                          [ EXCEPTION
                            exception_handler
                          { exception_handler } ]
                         END [ identifier ] ;
```

Example 19-2 Skeleton of Grammar For Ada Task Declaration

If the optional keyword TYPE is used, the task identifier is a type mark, not an object. Type marks are of interest only at compile time, hence Task type marks have no associated execution. However, Task type marks are necessary for the formal declaration of Task type parameters, mode IN only, and of Task access types (Pointers). If the TYPE keyword is not used, the defined Task object becomes active as soon as the declarative part containing the Task declaration has been elaborated.

The formal Task Specification defines the logical interface of a Task, while the separate Task Body establishes what the Task does. The Body can subsequently be used for the execution of all tasks of that type. But the Task Body is optional. If none is given, a Body with a Null Statement is assumed.

It is critical to understand that in Ada Tasks are fired off as soon as the declarative part has been elaborated. The associated sequence of statements of the subprogram may long have finished; if one or more local Tasks are still active, the subprogram will not return. It has to wait until all local tasks have terminated. This waiting for Task completion is a trivial form of Ada's Rendez-Vous concept, which will be illustrated in this chapter. First, let's analyze a simple model. See Example 19-3.

```
PROCEDURE build_components IS
 TASK fuselage;
 TASK BODY fuselage IS
  BEGIN -- fuselage
  -- statement of "fuselage"
  END fuselage;
 TASK navigation;
 TASK BODY navigation IS
  BEGIN -- navigation
  -- statements of "navigation"
  END navigation;
 BEGIN -- build_components
  NULL; --
  -- both tasks are implicitly initiated
 END build_components;
```

Example 19-3 Sample Ada Task Declarations and Task Bodies

As soon as procedure "build_components" is called, presumably after completion of "design_aircraft," the Tasks "fuselage" and "navigation" are initiated. This means that both start running at the same time without explicit initiation. Even though the body of procedure "build_components" contains no real statement, the Null Statement generates no code; it cannot return until both "fuselage" and "navigation" have terminated. In Example 19-3 we have left out the Tasks "wings" and "engines" to keep the code short.

Modula-2 Tasks Without Data Sharing

So far nothing is difficult or hard to grasp. We just have to accept that according to the Ada language definition a Task is initiated implicitly. If the target machine is a single processor, the different Tasks are run in an unpredictable order. Ada's solution to the simultaneous Task problem is not overly complicated, so it is hard to believe that Modula-2 provides yet a simpler solution. Modula-2 doesn't even introduce a specific Task object. Tasks are declared just like regular procedures, but they can be fired off explicitly as parallel tasks via the predefined system procedure "StartProcess." This system call is defined in Module "Processes" and requires two parameters. The first is the name of the procedure to be started, and the second is the amount of work space needed. See the formal declaration in Example 19-4.

```
PROCEDURE StartProcess( P : PROC; n : CARDINAL );
(* Start Procedure "P" as a parallel process *)
(* and give it "n" elements of work space *)
```

Example 19-4 Interface to Predefined Modula-2 Process Initiator

Once we have learned how to write procedures in Modula-2, the writing of parallel processes is easy; there is just one more item we need to know, the preceding system call "StartProcess." Later we shall show the complete interface for the system Module "Processes," but here we must explain that PROC is a type mark that accepts all procedures that have no parameters. We now know enough to rewrite the Ada Task Example 19-3 in Modula-2. An implementation follows in Example 19-5.

```
PROCEDURE BuildComponents;
  PROCEDURE Fuselage;
    BEGIN (* Fuselage *)
      ...
    END Fuselage;
  PROCEDURE Navigation;
    BEGIN (* Navigation *)
      ...
    END Navigation;
  BEGIN (* BuildComponents *)
    StartProcess( Fuselage,   100 ); (* 100 words work space *)
    StartProcess( Navigation, 250 ); (* 250 words work space *)
  END BuildComponents;
```

Example 19-5 Sample Concurrent Processes in Modula-2

If the actual hardware has multiple processors, the Modula-2 program executes "Fuselage" and "Navigation" at the same time. Otherwise, they are executed in sequence, probably "Navigation" after "Fuselage." So far the language design overhead in Modula-2 is less than in Ada, but the same is accomplished. Hence Modula-2 offers a better solution; it is simpler. Now we need to analyze the more interesting and difficult aspect of multiprocessing where data are shared.

19.4 Parallel Tasks with Data Sharing

Let us consider that two tasks T1 and T2 execute simultaneously and share a data structure D. If T1 is ready to update D, it could happen that T2 wishes to read D. Will it read the old value before, or the new one after the update? More critical is the possibility that T2 wishes to update D at the same time T1 writes into D. If T2 fetches the old value of D just before T1 had a chance to write its new result, the fruits of T1's work may be lost forever. It is clear that some synchronization is in place. One of the tasks has to wait until the other has completed the update. This means the simultaneous mode of operation has to be interrupted for a moment and be replaced by a mutually exclusive sequence. Notice that the task that causes another to wait may not abort or perform an infinite loop; it would cause the dependent task to wait forever.

To guarantee such mutual exclusion, and to guarantee that indeed one of the tasks acquires priority over the others, special guards have to be provided. Such guards (or semaphores) have been introduced long ago with the advent of multiprogramming. Is this a striking coincidence? It turns out that it does not matter whether data-sharing tasks are executed simultaneously on a multiprocessor or sequentially in a multiplexed fashion on a single-processor system. The design requirements to implement such guards correctly are identical. In this text we shall not explain the detail but refer the interested reader to the literature Hanson [1973] and Haberman [1976]. We only show how the problem is solved in high level languages, with the Rendez-Vous concept in Ada and Signals in Modula-2.

Parallel Tasks in Ada with Data Sharing

In Example 19-6 we list the Task portion of an Ada program that has two parallel Tasks, "producer" and "consumer," which read from and write into the same buffer. The buffer is managed by a third task.

```
 TASK producer;
 TASK BODY producer IS
  next_char : character;
  BEGIN
   LOOP
   -- generate next_char;
    buffer_manager.write_buffer( next_char );
   END LOOP;
  END producer;

TASK consumer;
TASK BODY consumer IS
 next_char : character;
 BEGIN
  LOOP
   buffer_manager.read_buffer( next_char );
  -- consume next_char
  END LOOP;
 END consumer;

```

```
TASK buffer_manager IS
 ENTRY read_char( next_char : OUT character );
 ENTRY write_char( next_char : IN character );
END buffer_manager;

TASK BODY buffer_manager IS
 max_size  : CONSTANT integer := 1000;
 TYPE buffer_range IS RANGE 1 .. max_size;
 buffer    : ARRAY( buffer_range ) OF character;
 count     : integer RANGE 0 .. max_size := 0;
 in_index,
 out_index : buffer_range := 1;
BEGIN -- buffer_manager
 LOOP
  SELECT
   WHEN count < max_size =>
    ACCEPT write_buffer( next_char : IN character ) DO
     buffer( in_index ) := next_char;
    END;
    in_index := in_index MOD max_size + 1;
    count := count + 1;
   OR WHEN count > 0 =>
    ACCEPT read_buffer( next_char : OUT character ) DO
     next_char := buffer( out_index );
    END;
    out_index := out_index MOD max_size + 1;
    count := count - 1;
   OR
    TERMINATE;
  END SELECT;
 END LOOP;
END buffer_manager;
```

Example 19-6 Listing of Ada Buffer Manager with Data Sharing

The Tasks "producer" and "consumer" can in general run at the same time. The former creates an unbounded sequence of data structures, in this model mere characters. The latter consumes them in the order they are generated. Both Tasks can execute with radically different speeds. Maybe consuming is much more involved than producing; maybe the consumer runs on a slower processor than the producer. The difference in speed should not matter and is ironed out by the "buffer_manager."

The "producer" and "consumer" Tasks can only see the specification of the "buffer_manager." The interface to the shared "buffer" is defined by Entry Declarations, and the actual handling of a request for "read_buffer" and "write_buffer" is accomplished in the called Task by Accept Statements. This is explained in the next section.

Entry Declarations and Accept Statements

Entry calls and their associated Accept Statements are the primary means for synchronizing and communicating values between Tasks in Ada. An *Entry Declaration* looks similar to a procedure declaration and is allowed only in a Task Specification. For the syntax rules of Entry Declarations see the grammar fragment in Example 19-7. When an Entry is called the action to be performed is expressed by the corresponding Accept Statement. Ada permits Arrays of Entries, named *Families of Entries.* Each distinct family member can be accessed by its index. The rules for Entry parameters are the same as for subprograms, and the syntax for Entry Calls is the same as that for Procedure Call Statements.

An Accept Statement defines the action to be performed at an Entry Call and may include any Ada statement. The formal parameter part of an Accept Statement must be identical to the formal parameter part of the Entry Declaration named by the Accept Statement. See the grammar in Example 19-7.

Rendez-Vous Concept

The execution of an Accept Statement begins with the evaluation of the Entry Index, if any, and execution of an Entry Call Statement starts with the evaluation of the actual parameters in the same manner as for Procedure Call Statements. Now comes the crucial point for Ada: the execution of an Accept Statement and its associated Entry Call statement are synchronized based on the following cases.

If the calling Task issues an Entry Call Statement before the corresponding Accept Statement is reached by the Task owning the Entry, the calling Task is suspended. There may be several such calls that need acceptance, in which case they are queued in a first-in/first-out fashion. Otherwise, if a Task reaches an Accept Statement before a call to that Entry has been issued, the Task is suspended until a call will be received. In other words, if the queue for an Entry is empty, the Task must wait until the next Entry call. And if several Entry Calls arrive before they can be serviced, they will be queued. Each Entry and each member of a Family of Entries has its own queue.

Generally, one of the two cases will happen. When an Entry has been called and the associated Accept Statement has been reached, the calling Task remains suspended until the sequence of statements of the Accept Statement has finished executing. Thereafter, the calling Task continues in parallel with the called Tasks. This synchronization is called the “Rendez-Vous.”

```
entry_declaration    ::= ENTRY identifier [ ( discrete_range ) ]
                            [ formal_part ] ;
entry_call           ::= entry_name [ actual_parameter_part ] ;
accept_statement     ::= ACCEPT entry_name [ ( entry_index ) ]
                            [ formal_part ] [ DO
                            sequence_of_statements
                         END [ entry_name ] ] ;
select_statement     ::= selective_wait
                       | other choices not discussed here
selective_wait       ::= SELECT
                            [ WHEN condition => ]
                                select_alternative
                            { OR [ WHEN condition => ]
                                select_alternative }
                            [ ELSE
                                sequence_of_statement ]
                         END SELECT;
select_alternative   ::= [ WHEN condition => ]
                             selective_wait_alternative
selective_wait       ::= accept_alternative
                       | delay_alternative
                       | TERMINATE
accept_alternative   ::= accept_statement { sequence_of_statements }
delay_alternative    ::= DELAY simple_expression
```

Example 19-7 Ada Grammar Fragment for Rendez-Vous

To evaluate the language design choices taken in Ada and Modula-2 we implement the same problem in Modula-2 in the next section. But first we shall list the complete interface of the system Module "Processes." See Example 19-8.

Parallel Tasks in Modula-2 with Data Sharing

```
DEFINITION MODULE Processes;
TYPE SIGNAL;
PROCEDURE StartProcess( P : PROC; n : CARDINAL );
  (* Start procedure P as parallel process *)
  (* Give P a workspace of n elements *)
PROCEDURE SEND( VAR s : SIGNAL );
  (* If one process is waiting for s, that process *)
  (* will resume activity again *)
PROCEDURE WAIT( s : SIGNAL );
  (* Wait until other process sends s *)
PROCEDURE Awaited( s : SIGNAL ) : BOOLEAN;
  (* Awaited(s) := at least one entry in Queue of s *)
PROCEDURE Init( VAR s : SIGNAL );
  (* mandatory initialization *)
END Processes.
```

Example 19-8 Listing of Predefined Module "Processes"

For our level of understanding we can pretend that the type "Signal," defined in Module "Processes," is a boolean variable. Objects of type "Signal" control whether a processes can run or whether it has to wait. This synchronization via Signals is one method of controlling safe data sharing. To initiate a process we issue a call to "StartProcess," as explained before. "SEND" can awaken the next process in a queue of suspended processes that are waiting for the signal "s," while "WAIT" will suspend a process, until its signal "s" will be sent. In addition to Signals, a safe way of handling shared data in Modula-2 is to use Monitors. A Monitor is solely responsible and authorized to access shared data; this is easily accomplished by declaring the data local to the Monitor. A Monitor is defined by specifying the optional priority for a Module. This is the total overhead we need to learn in Modula-2 to be able to run parallel processes. Now we have sufficient knowledge to program the buffer manager in Modula-2. See Example 19-9.

```
MODULE Main;
 (* IMPORTs, global data, etc. *)
 PROCEDURE Producer;
  VAR
   NextChar : CHAR;
  BEGIN (* Producer *)
   LOOP
    (* Produce NextChar *)
    WriteBuffer( NextChar );
```

```
    END;
   END Producer;

  PROCEDURE Consumer;
   VAR
    NextChar : CHAR;
   BEGIN (* Consumer *)
    LOOP
     ReadBuffer( NextChar );
     (* and consume NextChar *)
    END;
   END Consumer;
  BEGIN (* Main *)
   (* Initialization if any *)
   StartProcess( Consumer, 200 );
   StartProcess( Producer, 200 );
  END Main.

MODULE BufferManager[ 10 ];
 (* Explicit Priority makes Module a Monitor *)
 EXPORT ReadBuffer, WriteBuffer;
 IMPORT SIGNAL, SEND, WAIT, Init;

 CONST
  MaxSize      = 1000;
 TYPE
  BufferRange = [ 1 .. MaxSize ];
 VAR
  Count        : [ 0 .. MaxSize ];
  NonFull      : SIGNAL; (* means Count < MaxSize *)
  NonEmpty     : SIGNAL; (* means Count > 0 *)
  InIndex,
  OutIndex     : BufferRange;
  Buffer       : ARRAY[ BufferRange ] OF CHAR;

 PROCEDURE WriteBuffer( NextChar : CHAR );
  BEGIN (* WriteBuffer *)
   IF Count = MaxSize THEN
    WAIT( NonFull );
   END (* IF *);
   (* Count < MaxSize *)
   Count := Count + 1;
   Buffer[ InIndex ] := NextChar;
   InIndex := InIndex MOD MaxSize + 1;
   SEND( NonEmpty );
  END WriteBuffer;

 PROCEDURE ReadBuffer( VAR NextChar : CHAR );
```

```
58          BEGIN (* ReadBuffer *)
59           IF Count = 0 THEN
60            WAIT( NonEmpty );
61           END (* IF *);
62           (* Count > 0 *)
63           Count := Count - 1;
64           NextChar := Buffer[ OutIndex ];
65           OutIndex := OutIndex MOD MaxSize + 1;
66           SEND( NonFull );
67          END ReadBuffer;
68
69          BEGIN (* BufferManager *)
70           Count := 0;
71           InIndex := 1; (* pick any in range *)
72           OutIndex := 1; (* must equal InIndex *)
73           Init( NonFull );
74           Init( NonEmpty );
75          END BufferManager.
```

Example 19-9 Listing of Modula-2 Buffer Manager Using Parallel Processes

The Modula-2 program in Example 19-9 has numerous parallel tasks (in Modula-2 called "concurrent"), among them "ReadBuffer" and "WriteBuffer." For these there will be two wait situations. The first arises when "ReadBuffer" tries to fetch "NextChar," but the buffer is empty; the second, when "WriteBuffer" wants to store, but the buffer is already full. See the corresponding calls to "WAIT" on lines 48 and 60. If a Modula-2 tasks has to wait, it sends itself to sleep via a call to "WAIT" with an appropriate signal, here "NonFull" or "NonEmpty." Just as we have seen for Ada Entries, each Modula-2 signal has an associated FIFO queue. As long as the queue is empty, all tasks that wait for this signal have to sleep. The purpose of "SEND" is to wake up the next element in the queue.

9.5 Summary

In this chapter we have given a motivation for multiprocessing, also called concurrent processing in Modula-2. We have exhibited two types of parallel processing. One form is explicitly programmed, the other implicitly resident in an algorithm. Ada and Modula-2 provide language facilities to capitalize on the former type, while the latter is possibly a rewarding future research area, with applications in Prolog and similar languages.

To demonstrate the different ways of expressing explicit parallelism, we have solved the same problem in Ada and in Modula-2. The Modula-2 solution is a bit longer than the Ada equivalent, partly because Modula-2 initializes its variables via Assignment Statement, partly because of the direct calls to "SEND" and "WAIT." Except for this hand coding of the synchronization the solutions are quite similar.

19.6 Exercises

1. Evaluate the relative language complexities in Ada and Modula-2 for the facility of explicit parallel processing.
2. Explain why tasks that can be executed in parallel may be scheduled in any order on a single processor system.

20

Logic Programming

LOGIC, the systematic study
of the methods and principles
used in distinguishing
correct from incorrect reasoning.
Here reasoning is the process
by which one proposition,
the conclusion,
is affirmed on the basis
of one or more other propositions,
the premises,
which are accepted
as the starting point of the process.
The logician investigates the evidential relations
that may hold between premises
and conclusions in arguments.
If the conclusion follows from,
or is implied by, the premises,
then the reasoning is correct;
otherwise, it is incorrect.

New Age Encyclopedia
Volume 11, 1982

Up to this point most of our discussions have been dedicated to the restricted class of procedural programming languages. Ada, Fortran, Modula-2, Pascal, and PL/I are all members of this class. Procedural languages require the programmer to express in detail which action has to be taken and how it must be executed. The "how" includes in particular the precise specification of individual steps in the form of Assignment, Control, and Iterative Statements.

In this chapter we make a 90-degree turn and discuss a functional language, more specifically a logic programming language. This is Prolog. Prolog is covered only briefly, but hopefully enough to stir up the reader's curiosity to explore further. Since it is so different from the classical procedural languages, it does not fit naturally into the pattern that we have used so far. But Prolog is too important to be omitted altogether, so we have dedicated a separate chapter to it. In the previous chapter we have given a short introduction into a new form of computer architecture that may enter into happy marriage with Prolog by executing large program portions in parallel and thus yield fast execution.

20.1 Prolog

Prolog is already a middle-aged language. It was designed in 1972 at the University of Marseille in southern France and has since then created little pockets of vivid enthusiasm at various schools, notably the Universities of Leuven in Belgium, Budapest in Hungary, Edinburgh in Scotland, and New South Wales in Australia. Prolog stands for Programming in Logic. For many of those who know and use the language, Prolog is "the best invention since sliced bread."

Our Prolog tutorial is again centered around small sample programs. These were run on the Prolog interpreter provided by the University of New South Wales. Both the language and the interpreter are a joy to use. First, we provide a general introduction to Prolog, then follow numerous examples. It will become clear during the presentation that substantial portions of Prolog can be executed in any order, not necessarily in the sequence as written. Hence, execution on a multiprocessor system will be possible, but it requires an intelligent Prolog interpreter that exhibits the implied parallelism.

20.2 Characterization of Prolog

Readers who are accustomed to procedural languages, may find a resemblance between Prolog and the query language of a Data Base Management system. And we shall see that there are in fact quite a few similarities. Programmers who learn Prolog as their "Mother Language" may never notice anything peculiar or eccentric about it, since they are not yet biased by their own past. But almost everybody who picks up Prolog after exposure to procedural languages is baffled by the strangeness of the language. As a case in point, the "flow of control" concept is missing in Prolog. A Prolog session is a dialogue between the user and the system. First, the user establishes a list of "Facts" and "Rules," which forms a database for Prolog to work with. From then on the user may ask Prolog "Questions" based upon this list. Prolog, in turn, will do its best to derive a logically correct answer to the Question, but only based on the Rules and Facts stated so far. Further Facts and Rules can be added at any moment during a session. This means that the same Question asked at different times can generate different answers. Throughout this chapter we capitalize Fact, Rule, and Question if these terms refer to the specific Prolog syntax constructs.

The best way to give the reader a feeling for Prolog's unique character is to personify the language and describe it just as we would draw another human being. For example, when interacting with Prolog, we feel at times like we are working with a partner, a servant, and still a distinct individualist all at the same time! As our partner, Prolog is devoted, meticulously accurate, and logical. This partner not only tries to find an answer to each of our questions, but also gives us *all* correct answers. Prolog is our servant because it behaves as if fulfilling our requests were its sole reason for being. And it leaves us no doubt that it is an individualist because it insists upon dictating its own methods for finding answers. The user has nothing to say about it!

For these reasons, we shall continue throughout this discussion to refer to the Prolog system simply as "Prolog"—our partner in dialogue.

0.3 The Structure of Prolog Programs

Prolog programs consist only of "Facts," "Rules," and "Questions" in any order. As long as we are stating our Facts and Rules, Prolog silently accumulates this knowledge and stores it in its data base. As soon as we ask a Question, Prolog responds by producing output. If we enter a Fact that is already known, Prolog is meticulous enough to remember the repetition. We shall see this in some of our examples. Facts, Rules, and Questions must all be terminated by a period. If the premises of a Rule are complicated, they can be separated from one another by a comma. But be careful! Such a comma means Logical And. It is a good recommendation when reading a source program to think AND when we encounter commas. If we wish multiple premises to be combined by the Logical Or, we must use a semicolon. We shall see program examples of these rules later in this chapter.

When Prolog responds to our Questions, it supplies *all* answers. If there are two or more, it is a convention in the UNSW interpreter to list them beneath one another. But this is done differently depending on the implementation. Clocksin and Mellish [1981] describe that the Edinburgh Prolog system writes one answer at a time, terminated by a semicolon. The user who wishes to see another answer just presses the return key. In order to know all answers in that system, one must press the return key until the final answer is "no."

"Facts"

The syntax for Facts is as simple as in English, but a bit more rigid. For example, if we wish to express that "Helen is beautiful," we have to state this Fact in Prolog as "beautiful_is(helen)." This form of syntax should be quite familiar already from mathematical functions. Prolog believes our Facts, so it does not question the beauty of Helen; it does not even bring to our attention that beauty lies in the eye of the beholder! For Prolog, Facts simply provide the premises from which it will derive logical answers. Not all Facts are so simple in nature; some Facts may involve more parties. For example, the relationship of "mother" typically involves two or more people, who in sober Prolog terminology are referred to as objects. If we wish to express in Prolog that "the mother of Helen was Leda," we can write "mother_of(helen, leda)." It would have been equally correct to say "mother_of(leda, helen)," just as the English phrase "Leda was the mother of Helen" is identical in meaning to the first. For consistency, we must remember the exact direction of the relationship and then stick with the convention. The Prolog system cannot help us here with type checking. All objects are of the same type.

We hope it has not gone unnoticed that Helen is consistently spelled with an uppercase H in our English sentences, but with lowercase in Prolog. This has a good reason. Prolog literals, of which the proper name Helen is one instance, must start with a lowercase letter. Variables, on the other hand, must start with an uppercase letter. Some Prolog implementations have this the other way around, a minor disadvantage of not having standardized the language.

"Rules"

The form for Prolog Rules is only a generalization of that for Facts. Rules are bound by a condition or premise. If the condition holds, the Rule yields true; otherwise it is false. Let us clarify this with an example. Two people, Romeo and Juliet, get married only if they love one another. In Prolog this can be expressed as shown in Example 20-1.

```
get_married( Romeo, Juliet ) :-
  loves( Romeo, Juliet ), loves( Juliet, Romeo ).
```

Example 20-1 Prolog "Rules"

The only novelty in this Rule is the ":-" operator, which we can pronounce "IF." In some Prolog cultures it is also called "neck." Another subtle, though not new, change has been introduced in this example. Romeo and Juliet are in this case variables, meaning that their names stand generically for all true lovers. As such they may assume the names of many different people during the execution of a Prolog program. But whoever these real people are, as far as Prolog is concerned, they get married only if they love each other. The Rule is too long to fit conveniently onto a single line, but Prolog has no restrictions in this regard. We may write our source free from any physical format or layout considerations.

"Questions"

Prolog Questions are introduced by the "?-" operator, followed by a clause that looks just like a Rule. Like all clauses, a Question must be terminated by a period. Since we have already learned a relatively large portion of Prolog, we can write a program and try our luck.

The program in Example 20-2 starts with a few Facts and uses the "get_married" Rule shown earlier. We are then free to ask whatever Questions we like. Prolog will answer them to the best of its knowledge. When Prolog answers "yes," it really means "based on the facts that are available to me, I must conclude that the statement is true." And similarly, a "no" answer is also based on current Facts and the rules of logic. If we were to ask, for example, if Prolog is a fine language, Prolog's response will be a cool "no," unless we have explicitly told it otherwise. Now we shall analyze a very simple sample program, summarizing what we have learned so far.

```
1     loves( helen, menelaus ).
2     loves( menelaus, helen ).
3     get_married( Man, Woman )
       :- loves( Man, Woman ), loves( Woman, Man ).
4     ?-get_married( menelaus, helen ).
5     ** yes
6     ?-get_married( socrates, xanthippe ).
7     ** no
```

Example 20-2 Sample Prolog Program with Facts, Rules, and Questions

Line 4 in the program in Example 20-2 is a Prolog Question. The premises, leading to an answer of this Question, are already complex. See line 3 for details. First, the Facts are established that Menelaus loves Helen, and Helen loves Menelaus as well. Then a Rule for getting married is defined for all pairs Man and Woman. Finally, we can ask whether Menelaus and Helen get married. Based on the premises given, Prolog's positive answer is correct. On the other hand, Prolog knows nothing about the severe marital problems Socrates and his wife had, so it answers "no" to the Question whether this couple ever got married.

The Prolog syntax so far poses no difficulty, but everything looks a bit unconventional, not like a "real" programming language. Can we compute arithmetic functions, solve the Towers of Hanoi, and write compilers in Prolog? In all cases the answer is positively "yes," but we won't go into detail about how to write a compiler! If our readers are suspicious or lost, we plead for patience and ask them to go on reading. In the remaining sections of this chapter we shall elaborate on Prolog syntax and get into more complicated sample programs so that all of the traditional things we do with programming languages will pose no problem for even the most inexperienced Prolog programmer. We shall introduce simple Questions that lead to more complicated ones; we shall expose "correct" answers in Prolog which actually make no sense in common English; and we will introduce the "Cut" operator and explain why it is needed. We will use the "anonymous" variable when we discuss list processing, and finally, we'll end up with a sample program that can find all safe paths through a complicated maze. So read on! By the time we've done all this, solving the Towers of Hanoi will be so simple that we'll hardly need an explanation!

20.4 Analysis of Prolog Programs

In the program in Example 20-3 we show the reader once more how to state Facts, establish Rules, and ask Questions. We start out by creating a small data base that holds objects, which fulfill the attribute "person." Based on a general Rule that defines "person," we ask Prolog whether various "objects" satisfy this criterion.

```
1    person( mary ).
2    person( X )       :- mother_of( Y, X ).
3    mother_of( mary, alexander ).
4    mother_of( mary, andre ).
5
6    : ?-person( mary ).
7    ** yes
8    : ?-person( alexander ).
9    ** yes
10   : ?-person( andre ).
11   ** yes
12   : ?-person( carmen ).
13   ** no
```

Example 20-3   First Prolog Program, of "Facts," "Rules," and "Questions"

Line 1 states that "mary" is a "person." Remember that since "mary" begins with a lowercase letter, it represents a particular person, and in Prolog such specific values are called literals, as opposed to variables. Line 2 defines a Rule: it generalizes what makes a person. The Rule defines any variable X as a person, if there exists another object Y such that Y is the mother of X. We happen to know that motherhood also implies the person quality, but Prolog is blind to such implicit wisdom.

On lines 3 and 4 we see two more Facts. Here we learn that Mary is the mother of Alexander and Andre. Again, all three names start with lowercase letters, so they are literals. Then come three Questions, all of which Prolog answers correctly. Three times Prolog answers positively, and for obvious reasons. But why does Prolog believe that Carmen is not a person? She may well be a very sweet girl, but Prolog is ignorant of her existence. It is our program's responsibility to fill the data base with all Facts that we wish Prolog to consider; the program has failed to do so for Carmen.

Before analyzing more Prolog semantics, we should explain the special characters in our source listings. First, our Prolog programs have a numeric left column. This column holds the line numbers, and has been added only for reference. In no way are line numbers part of the program proper. The colons we encounter on all even-numbered lines, starting with line 6, are Prolog prompts. Such prompts are requests for input. In Example 20-3 our inputs are Questions, all starting with the ?- symbol. Finally, the two asterisks on all odd-numbered lines starting with 7 are part of Prolog's "yes" answer.

Now let's look more closely at line 6, our first Question. We ask, is Mary a "person," and Prolog responds positively. How does Prolog know this? Does it conclude from Mary's being the mother of two boys that she is a "person"? Clearly not, since Prolog has never been informed of such implications. Prolog knows, because the first Fact states Mary is a "person."

Example 20-4 reverses this order. Lines 1 and 2 establish the Rule that motherhood implies the person attribute to both the mother and the child. We should notice that this is a very compact way of saying that everybody who has a mother, is a person, and every mother is a person, too. Lines 3 to 5 list three children of the mother Mary, then Questions follow.

```
1     person( X )      :- mother_of( Y, X ).
2     person( Y )      :- mother_of( Y, X ).
3     mother_of( mary, carmen ).
4     mother_of( mary, alexander ).
5     mother_of( mary, andre ).
6
7     : ?-person( carmen ).
8     ** yes
9     : ?-person( alexander ).
10    ** yes
11    : ?-person( andre ).
12    ** yes
13    : ?-person( mary ).
14    ** yes
15    ** yes
16    ** yes
17    : ?-person( herb ).
18    ** no
```

Example 20-4 Multiple Answers to One Question

The reader should have no problem with the first three Questions and find the answers obvious. Having a mother implies that Carmen, Alexander, and Andre are persons. But why are there three "yes" answers when we ask if Mary is a person? This happens because Prolog remembers everything it is told. Mary's being a person is implied by her being a mother, but this implication holds three times, once for every child. So Prolog dutifully answers "yes" three times.

In the next program in Example 20-5 we shall discover that logic and intuition can contradict one another. Prolog believes that Carmen is a sister of herself, quite contrary to our normal understanding. Once we are a bit more advanced in Prolog, we shall learn how to avoid these cases. And at the same time, we shall see how to get only a single answer for the fourth Question in Example 20-4.

Below we establish the characteristics "male," "female," "parent," and "sister," and their relationships with one another. Lines 1 through 6 enumerate Facts. Line 7 defines a relatively complex Rule, but if we read it aloud, we shall understand it immediately, since it corresponds exactly to our conventional understanding. This is how the Rule should sound: "X is a sister of Y, if X is female, and the parents of X are the same as the parents of Y."

Except for the unemotional names "X" and "Y," this sounds just like everyday language, not like a programming language!

```
1     female( carmen ).
2     male( alexander ).
3     male( andre ).
4     parent( carmen, herb, mary ).
5     parent( alexander, herb, mary ).
6     parent( andre, herb, mary ).
7     sister( X, Y ) :- female( X ), parent( X, F, M ), parent( Y, F, M ).
8
9     : ?-sister( carmen, alexander ).
10     ** yes
11    : ?-sister( carmen, andre ).
12    ** yes
13    : ?-sister( carmen, mary ).
14    ** no
15    : ?-sister( mary, herb ).
16    ** no
17    : ?-sister( carmen, carmen ).
18    ** yes
```

Example 20-5 Carmen Is a Sister of Herself?

Prolog's answers to the first four Questions are clear after the explanation of the sister Rule given earlier. In particular we understand why Carmen is not a sister of Mary. Mary was defined to be one of Carmen's parents on line 4. Only the final answer should puzzle us. Is Carmen a sister of Carmen? Prolog says "yes." This does not follow our intuition, so what is wrong here?

Let us analyze line 17 carefully. When we ask "sister(carmen,carmen).," Prolog checks its data base for information about the characteristic of a sister. If it finds none, the answer will be clearly "no." But Prolog retrieves the definition and sees that sister has two formal parameters, "X" and "Y," which are both associated with the literal "carmen." So Prolog tests, if "carmen" is female. To this end, Prolog must again search the data base, this time for the "female" characteristic, which it finds. It can infer that the specific object Carmen is indeed female. Then Prolog determines the parents of Carmen as well as those for the second formal parameter, which is again Carmen. Clearly both parent pairs are identical; therefore, the whole AND condition is true. Prolog states "yes," Carmen is the sister of Carmen, because our own logic in establishing the Facts and Rules was not precise enough. If we want the definition of "sister" to match our intuitive understanding, we must propose a more complete definition of sister. Fortunately, this is easy. We make sure that the two persons under consideration are not identical. In the language of Prolog, we must ensure that the two formal parameters are different. For this we add another premise to the definition of "sister," demanding that X/=Y.

The "/=" operator is a test for unequality, as we know it from Ada or PL/I. A more correct definition of "sister" is given in Example 20-6.

```
sister( X, Y ) :-
female( X ), parent( X, F, M ), parent( Y, F, M ), X /= Y.
```

Example 20-6 Complete Sister Definition

If we replace the rule for "sister" in Example 20-5 with this more complete Rule definition, we no longer get a silly answer from Prolog. We can see from this example just how helpful a partner Prolog can be by forcing us to be more specific and logical. And truly, if we ask this time whether Carmen is a sister of herself, Prolog will correctly answer "no."

20.5 Prolog Arithmetic

Originally, computers were invented as "number crunching" machines. Parallel to the development of faster and more powerful machines, has been the evolution of high level languages and their compilers that allow programmers to express data and formulae in a convenient form. But number crunching always remains a driving force. Can Prolog perform arithmetic and evaluate complex expressions? In this section we provide a short introduction into Prolog's arithmetic operations, just enough to assure the reader that "Programming in Logic" can handle such elementary tasks.

Built-In Operators

We have already seen the /= operator, well known from other languages. Prolog provides a whole list of conventional operators. Formally these are just predefined functions that allow a higher degree of freedom for positioning the parameters than the typical Prolog Rules do. Often these are named "Functors," but nothing new hides behind such a scientific name; they are just predefined operators. Like so many other new models of thought, Prolog could not resist the temptation of introducing its own new vocabulary. So many philosophies seem to need this as a trick to support their claim to uniqueness. Fortunately, Prolog did not carry this so far as to create its own subculture.

In Prolog we end up with exactly the set of conventional arithmetic operators. The predefined operators +, -, *, /, and MOD have the usual meanings and priorities, and + and - are overloaded as unary and binary operators. Furthermore, all six relational tests are included, but some are spelled a bit backward. The test for "less than or equal" is expressed as =<.

In some Prolog implementations, the /= operator is spelled with a backslash instead of the slash. In addition, the factorial operator is built-in, expressed by the conventional ! to the right of its operand. Finally, assignment is performed by the IS operator. We shall try some of these operators in the next sample program.

Summation of First N Integers

In Example 20-7 we list a Prolog program that adds the first "N" integer numbers. "N" is passed as a parameter to function "sum_to," and a second parameter, "Res," returns the result. The algorithm we chose is taken from Clocksin and Mellish [1981], and represents a clear instance of "cracking an egg with a sledge hammer"; we apply recursion in place of iteration. "Sum_to" calls itself recursively, with the next smaller argument, just as we have shown with our various factorial sample programs. See Example 20-7 which uses the + and - operators and assignment.

```
1      sum_to( 1, 1 ) .
2      sum_to( N, Res ) :-
3        N1 is N-1,
4        sum_to( N1, Res1 ),
5        Res is Res1+N.
6
7      : ?-sum_to( 1, X ).
8
9      X = 1
10
11     STACK OVERFLOW
```

Example 20-7 Recursive Summation, Causing Program Abort

Line 1 sets an initial condition, comparable to the initialization of variables in procedural languages. The meaning is as follows: if "sum_to" is ever called with the first parameter set to 1, then return the value 1 in the second parameter. We secretly assume throughout our discussion that "sum_to" will never be called with a negative argument. This assumption is a key point, and the reader should keep it in mind. Lines 2 through 5 represent the now familiar definition of a Rule. This Rule is named "sum_to" and has two parameters, "N" and "Res." The first one is an IN parameter, as we know it from Ada, while "Res" is an OUT parameter, again exactly as in Ada. Prolog parameters are all potentially IN-OUT parameters. No parameter mode or type is declared formally. The mode is implied by the way the parameter is used in the program body.

Line 3 defines a new, local variable, named "N1," and initializes this local to N-1. So line 3 is quite innovative. It demonstrates a formal parameter reference to produce a value, shows assignment and subtraction, and introduces the declaration of local data. This declaration is again implicit. Line 4 calls "sum_to" recursively and declares a new local variable on the fly, named "Res1." "Res1" is expected to hold the sum of the first "N1" integers, when returning from the call. On line 5 this return value is added to "N," and the sum total is assigned to "Res."

Finally, on line 7 we ask a Question: Please Prolog system, sum up all integers from 1 to 1. The computation is trivial; the result X=1 on line 9 is correct, but then comes the bitter surprise. Prolog reports a STACK OVERFLOW. It is almost impossible to guess why Prolog would use any stack space at all, unless we know a bit more about its internal working. We need to explore these internals in some detail, because it will assist our understanding the "Cut" operator, introduced in the next sample program in Example 20-8.

Multiple Answers

Just because Prolog finds an answer, this does not mean it will stop searching for more. Prolog doesn't know we are satisfied once we have found the one and only numeric result to a numeric problem.

In our program in Example 20-7, Prolog immediately finds an answer to "?-sum_to(1,X).," since we explicitly provided one in the Fact on line 1. But Prolog continues to search and finds that there exists yet another definition for "sum_to." So line 2 is also processed. Soon the local variable "N1" is set to N-1, which is zero, and we have a terrible violation of the secret assumption that the first parameter would never be less than 1.

20.6 Backtracking and Cut

In this section we shall introduce a new operator called "Cut." Using Cut, we can rewrite "sum_to" so that the infinite recursion will no longer occur. This is only a special application for Cut. Generally, Cut is used to inform Prolog that we wish it to stop searching for more answers. These further searches are activated by Prolog's backtracking mechanism.

Prolog's search for a positive answer is, in the general case, a complex operation. Frequently, the result depends on the logical AND of multiple Rules. In such a situation it may happen that the currently processed Rule yields false. This does not necessarily mean that the total answer is "no." So Prolog "backtracks." *Backtracking* means to go back to a previously tried Rule and look up another possible combination of parameter values, one that has not yet been tried. The new combination of previous Rule and current Rule may still yield a "yes."

In order to backtrack, Prolog must keep a little notepad for each Rule in its data base. Each time a Rule reports a positive response, Prolog must remember this. It could be that during the backtracking process, execution comes back to the current Rule, demanding "another positive" response. To avoid infinite looping, Prolog keeps a log of all positive responses for each Rule. Naturally, once all positive answers of a Rule have been exhausted, even backtracking cannot find a new answer, and Prolog must report "no."

There are cases where we wish to limit or completely eliminate backtracking. This is the purpose of the "Cut" operator, represented by the exclamation mark. When Prolog encounters the ! symbol, it must stop. This is exactly what we want for the first "sum_to" Rule. We inform Prolog that once it has found the result for the initial case, it should not look for more results. So line 1 of the program in Example 20-7 is rewritten as follows:

```
1      sum_to( 1,1 ) :- ! .
```

Pronounced in conventional English, line 1 now says "Prolog, if you want to find the sum of the first 1 integer numbers, report that the result is 1, and look for no additional results." The complete program performing the correct summation is listed in Example 20-8.

```
1      sum_to( 1, 1 ) :- ! .
2      sum_to( N, Res ) :-
3        N1 is N-1,
4        sum_to( N1, Res1 ),
5        Res is Res1+N.
6
7      : ?-sum_to( 1, X ).
8      X = 1
9      : ?-sum_to( 10, X ).
10     X = 55
11     : ?-sum_to( 100, X ).
12     X = 5050
```

Example 20-8 The Prolog "Cut" Operator

Lines 1 through 8 are not much different from the previous solution; only the Cut for the first Rule is new. But this minor change is sufficient to let the Rule work properly, as the remaining Questions demonstrate. With this body of knowledge we can easily write the factorial function in Prolog, which we do in Example 20-9.

```
1   factorial( 0, 1 ) :- !.
2   factorial( Arg, Res ) :-
3    Arg1 is Arg-1,
4    factorial( Arg1, Res1 ),
5    Res is Res1 * Arg.
6
7   : f( X, Y ) :- factorial( X, Y ).
8   : ?-f( 5, X ).
9   X = 120
10  : ?-f( 10, X ).
11  X = 3628800
```

Example 20-9 Factorial Function in Prolog

The "factorial" program closely resembles "sum_to." Line 1 provides the initial case, and the remaining program is the definition of a recursive Rule, exactly following the previous pattern. The only new aspect is the use of the multiplication operator on line 5. Thus far, we have only encountered abnormally simple data. In the next section we shall widen our understanding of more typical Prolog data structures, which are lists.

20.7 List Objects

In this section we get acquainted with the most powerful data structure of Prolog, the list. We also introduce the built-in mechanism of breaking a list into its head and tail. Two sample programs will give us a feeling for why list processing is so meaningful.

A *list* is an ordered collection of zero or more elements, which can be primitive data objects or more lists. The simplest list is the empty list, having no element at all. It is spelled [] in Prolog. Since the elements of lists can be lists, a general Prolog datum can be viewed as an arbitrarily complex tree. The sole, explicit list operator is the vertical bar | that breaks a list into head and tail. But built-in functions, notably the "name" function, are also available. A few list examples are shown in Table 20-1.

Table 20-1 Prolog List with Head and Tail

Prolog List	Head	Tail(Is List)
[andrej, rublev]	andrej	[rublev]
[eros]	eros	[]
[[a, b], c]	[a, b]	[c]
[a+b, a-b]	a+b	[a-b]

The Built-In Function "Name"

The Prolog function "name" is a conversion vehicle between strings and lists of characters. It works in either direction, depending on which of its two parameters is used as an OUT parameter. If the first parameter is a string expression and the second one the variable "X," then "X" will return a list of characters. If the first parameter is a variable "X," and the second one a list of characters, then "X" will return a string. We demonstrate this with three samples in Example 20-10.

```
: ?-name( X, [ herb ] ).
X = herb
: ?-name( X, [ h, e, r, b ] ).
X = herb
: ?-name( herb, X ).
X = [ 'h', 'e', 'r', 'b' ]
```

Example 20-10 Sample Uses of the "Name" Function

Alphabetical Sorting in Prolog

Now we have sufficient Prolog expertise to write a small program that sorts text strings in lexicographic order. Our program will have two parameters, both of type string, and will determine whether the first parameter is "less than" the second one. In lexicographic ordering we say "comes before" rather than "less," but for the sake of brevity we give our rule the name "less" anyway. Since both parameters are of string type, we must break the strings into lists of characters and perform the "less than" test on the list elements. We know how to break the string into its character components; the function "name" does this for us. But how can we determine if one string is less than another? We do this by performing the same procedure we go through when we look up a word in a dictionary. Let the two strings be X and Y.

Three Principles for Alphabetical "Less Than" Ordering

If parameter X has been completely exhausted, every letter in it has been compared to one in Y, no unequality has shown up, and there is at least one more character in Y, then $X<Y$ holds. Or, if no unequality has shown up, and the next letter of the first parameter X is less then the next letter of the second parameter Y, then $X<Y$ holds. Otherwise, if during previous tests no unequality has emerged, and the next character in X equals the next in Y, then $X<Y$ holds if the rest of X is less than Y. In all other cases $X<Y$ is false. Initially, no unequality can be assumed. This is expressed in Prolog by the three Rules for "alpha_less" in Example 20-11, in lines 2 through 4.

```
1     less( X, Y )      :- name( X, L ), name( Y, R ), alpha_less( L, R ).
2     alpha_less( [], [_|_] ).
3     alpha_less( [ A | _ ], [ B | _ ] ) :- A < B.
4     alpha_less( [ A | X ], [ B | Y ] ) :- A = B, alpha_less( X, Y ).
5
6     : ?-less( a, b ).
7     ** yes
8     : ?-less( x, w ).
9     ** no
10    : ?-less( abracadabra, ibricidibri ).
11    ** yes
12    : ?-less( ibricidibri, abracadabra ).
13    ** no
```

Example 20-11 Alphabetical Sorting in Prolog

Line 1 defines "less" in the following way. The first parameter "X" is broken into a list of characters. The list is named "L." Then "Y" is decomposed into its characters, again by using the built-in function "name." This list has the name "R." The boolean value of "name" is always true, so the result for Rule "less" depends only on the result for Rule "alpha_less." "Alpha_less" incorporates the three tests for lexicographical "less than," as just defined. What does the cryptic-looking line 2 do? If we read aloud what is expressed so concisely, we shall understand immediately the meaning of this Rule, so let's do that.

Start of Reading Aloud: If the first parameter is the empty list (or a null string), then it is always alphabetically less than the second nonempty parameter. In that case, it does not matter what the head or what the tail of the second parameter is. The first one is less! In fact, the tail of the second parameter may also be empty, and the "less than" condition still holds. *Stop Reading Aloud.*

This is the meaning of line 2, expressed in loudly spoken English. For line 3 we shall explain its meaning in more formal-sounding Prolog terminology first. This goes as follows: Let "A" be the head (one character) and the anonymous variable "_" be the tail of the first parameter. Let "B" be the head (one character) of the second parameter, and its tail be anonymous as well. Then "alpha_less" is true if A<B is true. The "less than" relational test for single characters is trivial. Now let us spell out line 3 in conventional English as well, and we will probably recognize the second of the three principles for the lexicographical "less than" relation: if the first letter of the first parameter is less than the first letter of the second, then the complete first parameter is "less than" the second. Line 4 is nothing but the last of our principles, expressed in Prolog. Four sample tests on lines 6 through 12 reinforce our confidence that the algorithm for "alpha_less" is indeed correct. All four printed answers correlate with our intuition. Now we have sufficient language understanding to grasp the more interesting membership test in Example 20-12.

In Example 20-12 we write a Prolog program that tests whether the first parameter, named "X," is a member of the second parameter. This second parameter must be a list. The idea is extremely simple and goes as follows: if "X" is equal to the head of the second parameter, then the membership relation is true. Otherwise, if "X" is a member of the tail of the second parameter, then again the membership relation holds. Otherwise, the result is false.

```
1    member( X, [ X | _ ] ).
2    member( X, [ _ | Y ] )   :- member( X, Y ).
3    m( X, Y )                :- member( X, Y ).
4
5    : ?-m( a, [ c, d, e, a, f, y, i, a, l ] ).
6    ** yes
7    ** yes
8    : ?-m( [ a, b ], [ a, b, f, [ a, b ], o, a, b ] ).
9    ** yes
```

Example 20-12 List Membership Operator, Implemented in Prolog

Lines 1 and 2 are only Prolog's way of rephrasing the two tests just described. Line 3 is a permissible definition for lazy typists. The name "m" is introduced as a synonym for the name "member"; functionally they are identical. As we can see in the Questions asked on lines 5 and 8, Prolog understands this aliasing. There are two "yes" answers for the first Question. This is because the character "a" appears twice in the list, passed as the second parameter. The next Question shows us that the membership test is also performed correctly if the first argument is a list.

We understand now how to state Facts, how to define Rules, and how to pose Questions in Prolog. We also have some feeling for arithmetic and list processing. In the next section we will let Prolog perform a task that seems completely different. We will try to find a possible passage through a maze.

20.8 Finding Paths Through a Maze

Greek mythology tells us an interesting story about a maze and the ingenious hero, Theseus, who used a thread to find his way back, after finally killing the monstrous Minotaur with his man-eating habits. The proper, old-fashioned term then was labyrinth, not maze, but if we are inclined to believe that labyrinths are things of the past, we would be entirely wrong! Mazes today play an important role in the automated process of designing computers.

Typically a PCB (Printed Circuit Board) is inhabited by components with pins that need connections. The emerging, interesting field of Computer Aided Engineering provides so-called "Placement" and "Routing" tools that generate the physical layout of PC Boards automatically. And many of these routing algorithms are based on precisely the kind of problem solved in this section.

The problem is to find all possible paths through a maze. A maze has doors that represent legal access, and closed walls, which are impenetrable. In the PCB world, the path is a conducting route from one pin to another and the impenetrable walls are already existing copper lines. If any route crosses or even touches such an existing connection, an illegal short-circuit would result. Finally, the open doors in the maze stand symbolically for those areas of PC Board space that have neither a copper conductor nor a "no touch" pin. If the "perfect" maze algorithm cannot find such a route, the circuit represents a nonplanar graph. Such a design cannot be mapped onto a single layer board and requires instead special treatment such as jump wires—something which is referred to with distaste as "patches"—or a completely new placement of components on the board. Unfortunately, sometimes none of these new placement strategies brings the desired success. In such a worst case the computer designer must decide for a multilayer board. But we are not interested in these aspects; we just wish to use Prolog to find a windy alley through the maze.

To this goal we shall write three programs, each leading us closer to the solution we need. We shall start with a very simple maze, as shown in Figure 20-1, for which we design a simple-minded program that does indeed find a legal way. As we shall notice later, the algorithm succeeds only by chance. Worse even, the first solution to this problem will have several undesirable properties that will be shown by Prolog's responses. In the second attempt the algorithm used will be identical, so the anomalies will remain. But we shall broaden the scope of our understanding. Not until the third program will we have a properly working Prolog solution that can find all possible routes through the maze. After we have achieved this and seen that our algorithm is both correct and powerful, we shall present a more complicated maze.

Figure 20-1 is a simple maze with nine rooms, arranged as a three-by-three square. The start room is "a1," and the final goal room is "b1."

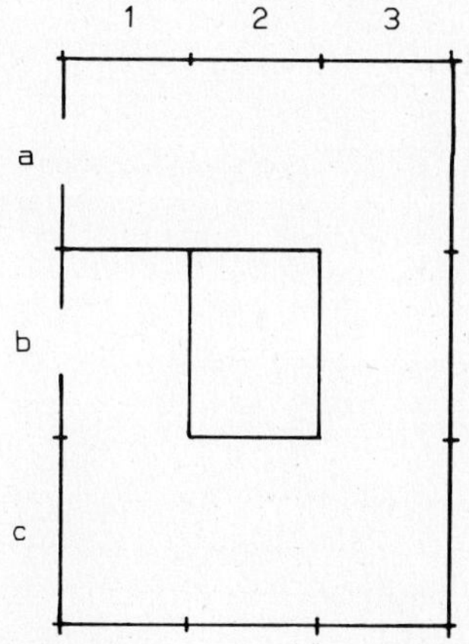

Figure 20-1 A Simple Maze

It is our goal to find a path in this maze from room "a1" to "b1." Since this "beginners maze" is so simple, the picture shows us the only possible path immediately. When we issue a Question to Prolog of the form ?-path(a1,b1) we wish to see the answer ** yes. In a moment we will list the first solution.

If we wish to ask Prolog Questions about possible paths through this simple maze, we must first tell Prolog what a "path" is. Second, we must tell Prolog what *our* maze looks like. Only the combination of both pieces of information makes it possible to determine an answer. This is exactly what the program in Example 20-13 does.

```
1       path( X, Y )  :- door( X, Y ).
2       path( X, Y )  :- door( X, Z ), path( Z, Y ).
3
4       door( a1, a2 ).   door( a2, a3 ).   door( a3, b3 ).
5       door( b3, c3 ).   door( c3, c2 ).   door( c2, c1 ).
6       door( c1, b1 ).
7
8       : ?-path( a1,b1 ).
9       ** yes
10      : ?-path( a1, X ).
11       X = a2
12       X = a3
13       X = b3
14       X = c3
15       X = c2
16       X = c1
17       X = b1
18      : ?-path( b1, a1 ).
19      ** no
20      : ?-path( a1, a1 ).
21      ** no
22      : ?-path( X, X ).
23      ** no
```

Example 20-13 Solution 1: Prolog Maze Program with Anomalies

Lines 1 and 2 define the idea of a "path." A path exists from room "X" to room "Y," if there is a door from room "X" to "Y." This is a trivial path, requiring no intermediate steps. Otherwise, and this is expressed on line—we can find a path from room "X" to "Y" if there is some other room "Z" such that a door exists between "X" and "Z" and a path from "Z" to "Y." The Rule for "path" is used recursively, but consistent with our understanding of recursion, we see that the recursive use of "path" involves a simpler problem. We are exactly one room closer than in the previous problem. Lines 4 to 6 inform Prolog which of the rooms have doors. It is not necessary to mention rooms that have no doors; that information is always implied and understood. Finally, on line 8 we ask Prolog if there is a way from room "a1" to room "b1." Prolog uses the algorithm outlined on lines 1 and 2 and responds correctly.

On the previous pages we have made a sneaky attempt to bias the mind of the reader into believing that room "b1" has some special meaning; for example, that it is the "one and only" final room. But Prolog has no concept of "final goal" for any of the rooms. If we ask whether there is a path from "a1" to "a3," the response has to be positive. Prolog has no idea that we project a special meaning onto room "b1."

On line 10 in Solution 1 we ask the general question: which are all values of variable "X" such that "X" can be reached from "a1"? Lines 11 through 17 give all correct answers. But what a disappointment: the remaining Questions on lines 18, 20, and 22 are all answered with "no," contrary to our intuition. We know, for example, that if there is a way of going from "a1" to "b1," there is also a path from "b1" to "a1": we need only to reverse our steps. And if we are in room "a1" already, there must be a way of getting there: we simply remain where we are. Prolog would also know these things if we had informed it; but we have not, and until we correct these oversights, our algorithm will not be satisfactory.

Example 20-14 is identical in function, but it sheds more light on Prolog variables and very subtle rules. In the second sample we have added one more Fact, called "final." "Final" qualifies one special room in the maze as the ultimate destination. This allows us to ask for "paths" that are reachable *and* that end up in a particular room.

```
1     path( X, Y )  :- door( X, Y ).
2     path( X, Y )  :- door( X, Z ), path( Z, Y ).
3
4     final( b1 ).
5
6     door( a1, a2 ).    door( a2, a3 ).    door( a3, b3 ).
7     door( b3, c3 ).    door( c3, c2 ).    door( c2, c1 ).
8     door( c1, b1 ).
9
10    : ?-path( a1, b1 ).
11    ** yes
12    : ?-path( a1, X ), final( X ).
13    X = b1
14    : ?-path( a1, X ). final( X ).
15    X = a2
16    X = a3
17    X = b3
18    X = c3
19    X = c2
20    X = c1
21    X = b1
22    : ?-path( a1, X ), final( X ).
23    X = a2
24    X = a3
25    X = b3
26    X = c3
27    X = c2
28    X = c1
29    X = b1
30    X = b1
```

Example 20-14 Solution 2: Side Effects on Prolog Variables

On line 12 we ask for all legal values of a variable "X," such that there exists a path from "a1" to "X," and that "X" is the "final" destination. Correctly, Prolog prints "X = b1."

The next Question on line 14 looks strikingly similar, but let us inspect it closer. The comma after the first half of the clause, which has the meaning of a logical AND function, has been replaced by a period. Now the Question has quite a different meaning. Now Prolog is to print all values of variable "X," such that there is a path from "a1" to "X," and then to add these values to the "final" property. So each destination reachable from "a1" will be made a "final" room. And truly, when we later ask on line 22 which final destinations can be reached from "a1," the variety of answers has grown substantially. This sample is intended to show us the effects of Questions that are asked in combination with Facts, as done on line 14. This subtle syntactic difference with such a radical change in semantics confirms the language design principle that "things which are different ought to look different"; Prolog does not think much of this principle.

Our next program is a modified version of the preceding two algorithms with the anomalies finally removed. A complete solution must correct the two irregularities with our previous algorithms. Prolog must recognize that it is always possible to find a way from within a room to the same room, and to run through the hallways of a maze in either direction.

From a Room to Itself

Line 4 in Example 20-15 expresses the Fact that there always exists a way from any room to itself. Even though this clause has three parameters, the third parameter plays no role in this fact and has, consequently, been replaced by the anonymous " " parameter.

Pass Doors Either Direction

Why couldn't Prolog figure out in the previous two programs that a path can lead through a door in either direction? Because in our programs we explicitly stated that doors can be passed one way, but we have mentioned nothing about the other way. An obvious method of rectifying this is to add more Facts for "door." Whenever we state "door(a,b).", we could add the complementary Fact "door(b,a)." This method is simple and correct, but clumsy. The number of Facts suddenly would double, something we can't ignore with a good-sized labyrinth.

Another method of correcting this undesirable one-way constraint is to introduce a more general Rule, one that states there is a path from "a" to "b" if "door(a,b)." is true, *or* if "door(b,a)." is true. This method is simple and correct, but also quite short and elegant. All we add is one clause, which will work no matter how complicated the maze may be. This is the approach taken on line 5.

```
1     member( Head, [ Head | _ ] ).
2     member( Head, [ _ | Tail ] ) :- member( Head, Tail ).
3
4     path( Start, Start, _ ).
5     path( Start, Goal, Trace ) :- ( door( Start, X ); door( X, Start ) ),
6                                    not( member( X, Trace ) ),
7                                    path( X, Goal, [ X | Trace ] ).
8
9     door( a1, a2 ).   door( a2, a3 ).   door( a3, b3 ).
10    door( b3, c3 ).   door( c3, c2 ).   door( c2, c1 ).
11    door( c1, b1 ).
12
13    : ?-path( a1, b1, [] ).
14    ** yes
15    : ?-path( b1, a1, [] ).
16    ** yes
17    : ?-path( b2, b2, [] ).
18    ** yes
```

Example 20-15 Solution 3: A Better Maze Program in Prolog

Use a Thread to Find the Way Back

The idea of the Greek hero to use a thread for finding his way back in the bewildering labyrinth was not so bad after all. Not only would the thread guarantee him a quick escape route if the situation demanded a fast return, but it also prevented the problem of circularity: if the hero should come to a room that has his thread passing through, he would immediately know that he has been there before, so he would retract his decision of trying to enter that room a second time. Our algorithm must have the same capability. The thread in the Greek myth can be nicely simulated via a Prolog list. Or, if we don't like the idea of the thread, we can imagine holding a clipboard, onto which we write every room number through which we have passed. If the next room under consideration is already on the list, the algorithm does not consider it anymore. This is what the third parameter of "path" is for! It is a list that is initially empty. Each time the route grows one step, the list grows by this same element.

What foresight that in the previous section we have covered the "member" relationship! This is what we have to use now. For each room we intend to enter, we check that it is *not* a member of the current list. If it is, we don't enter the room, since it would lead to a circular path. Otherwise, we are free to enter and attempt to find a route through it. With this knowledge we understand lines 5, 6, and 7 in solution 3 in Example 20-15. A path from "Start" to "Goal" along a "Trace" is defined as follows. If there is a door from "Start" to any adjacent room "X," either direction, so that "X" is not yet on the "Trace," and if there exists any way from "X" to the "Goal," then this is a successful path. We would have to add "X" to the "Trace."

Once this is understood, the whole program becomes clear. The remaining lines define doors as in the previous examples, and the preceding lines define the familiar "member" condition. All three Questions can, therefore, be answered correctly by Prolog. Notice that we have initialized the "Trace" list to the empty list. If, for some reason, we wish Prolog to find a passage that does NOT go through any particular room, we just initialize "Trace" to that room (or that list of rooms) and Prolog will exclude all these paths from the array of solutions. With so much expertise about mazes at hand, we can now enjoy a more complex problem and its solution.

Figure 20-2 shows a more interesting labyrinth. It has been designed by a very orderly architect, who arranged the rooms like a two-dimensional array, with six rows, named "a" through "f," and ten columns, named "1" to "10." So room "a1," which happens to be our start room, means the first room in row "a." Analogously, the final room is "f10."

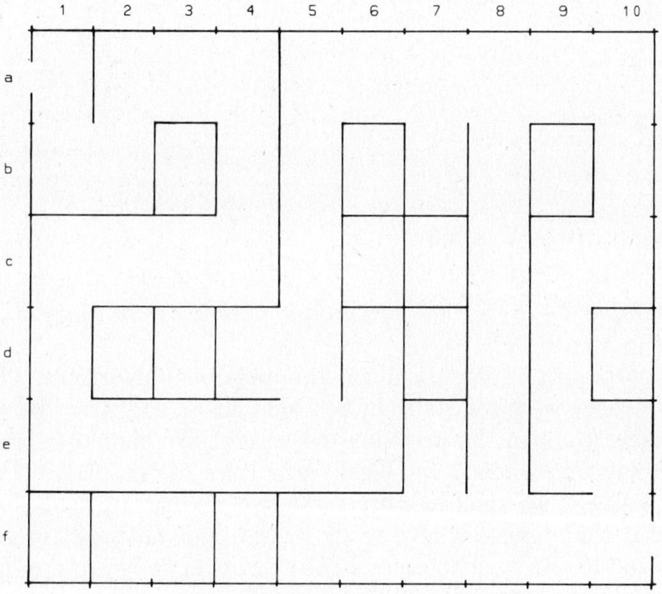

Figure 20-2 A Complicated Maze

The goal is to design a Prolog program that finds all passages from "a1" to "f10." The program in Example 20-16 is such a solution.

```
member( Head, [ Head | _ ] ).
member( Head, [ _ | Tail ] ) :- member( Head, Tail ).

path( Start, Start, Trace ).
path( Start, Goal, Trace )    :- ( door( Start, X ); door( X, Start ) ),
                                 not( member( X, Trace ) ),
                                 path( X, Goal, [ X | Trace ] ).

door( a1, b1 ).   door( a2, b2 ).   door( a2, a3 ).   door( a3, a4 ).
door( a4, b4 ).   door( a5, b5 ).   door( a5, a6 ).   door( a6, a7 ).
door( a7, b7 ).   door( a7, a8 ).   door( a8, b8 ).   door( a8, a9 ).
door( a9, a10 ). door( a10, b10 ). door( b1, b2 ).   door( b4, c4 ).
door( b5, c5 ).   door( b8, c8 ).   door( b10, c10 ). door( c1, d1 ).
door( c1, c2 ).   door( c2, c3 ).   door( c3, c4 ).   door( c5, d5 ).
door( c8, d8 ).   door( c9, d9 ).   door( c9, c10 ).  door( d1, e1 ).
```

```
door( d4, d5 ).   door( d5, e5 ).   door( d6, e6 ).   door( d8, e8 ).
door( d9, e9 ).   door( e1, e2 ).   door( e2, e3 ).   door( e3, e4 ).
door( e4, e5 ).   door( e5, e6 ).   door( e7, f7 ).   door( e8, f8 ).
door( e9, e10 ).  door( e10, f10 ). door( f2, f3 ).   door( f5, f6 ).
door( f6, f7 ).   door( f7, f8 ).   door( f8, f9 ).   door( f9, f10 ).

: ?-path( a1, f10, [] ).
** yes
** yes
: ?-path( b7, f10, [] ).
** yes
** yes
: ?-path( f10, a1, [ d9 ] ).
** yes
```

Example 20-16 Prolog Program for Complicated Maze

Logically, this program is identical to the previous algorithm. The only difference is that here we have many more Facts about doors, so the data base for Prolog is larger than in the previous two cases. We should be satisfied to observe that Prolog finds indeed two legal paths from “a1” to “f10.” If we follow Figure 20-2 attentively, we shall identify these two routes. In the last Question Prolog is asked if there exists a reverse path that does not lead through room “d9.” There is exactly one such route and the algorithm states so appropriately.

20.9 Prolog IO

The last Prolog program in Example 20-17 represents a solution to the Towers of Hanoi. Since the algorithm is clear, and since the Prolog constructs except IO have been treated before, we will use this program as an opportunity to introduce Prolog IO.

```
hanoi(N) :- move( N, start, finish, buffer ).

move( 0, _, _, _ ) :- !.
move( N, Start, Finish, Buffer ) :- M is N-1,
        move( M, Start, Buffer, Finish ),
        pr( Start, Finish, N ),
        move( M, Buffer, Finish, Start ).

pr( From, To, Disk ) :-
    write( [ move_disk, Disk, from, From, to, To ] ), nl.

: ?-hanoi( 0 ).
```

```
13      ** yes
14      : ?-hanoi( 1 ).
15      [move_disk, 1, from, start, to, finish ]
16      ** yes
17      : ?-hanoi( 3 ).
18      [move_disk, 1, from, start, to, finish]
19      [move_disk, 2, from, start, to, buffer]
20      [move_disk, 1, from, finish, to, buffer]
21      [move_disk, 3, from, start, to, finish]
22      [move_disk, 1, from, buffer, to, start]
23      [move_disk, 2, from, buffer, to, finish]
24      [move_disk, 1, from, start, to, finish]
25      ** yes
```

Example 20-17 The Towers of Hanoi in Prolog

Writing

The program in Example 20-17 uses the built-in routine "write" for text output. "Write" has one argument, which may be a list. Any element that is a literal will be printed as spelled. If any argument of the "write" procedure is a variable, its current value will be printed. The short built-in procedure "nl," also referenced on line 10, performs the same function as the Pascal "writeln" statement. It has no arguments and emits line-feed and carriage return.

Reading

The predefined Prolog Rule "read" has one parameter that will be initialized when the "read" is executed. By default all input comes from the standard input file. The related Rule "get" also has one argument, but expects to read just a single character. All nonprintable characters on standard input will be skipped before the "get" operation is satisfied.

Changing Files

Prolog IO interacts also with files other than standard input and standard output. To do so, the predefined Rule "tell(X)" must be executed. Argument "X" specifies the file to or from which IO is expected to be performed. If we wish to return back to standard IO files, the previous file "X" must be explicitly closed. This is achieved by the parameterless Rule "told."

20.10 Summary

We started this book with a history of computers and programming languages. Then we covered much material about procedural languages, most of which made implicit assumptions about their sequential execution. Chapter 19 introduced the idea of Concurrent Programming. We hedge some hope that the speed advantage of Concurrent Programming together with Prolog's potential for parallel execution will create the perfect symbiosis for new programming environments. If we have stimulated the reader's curiosity about future developments or if we succeeded in conveying some language design principles derived from more classical languages, we feel satisfied and happy with the effort expended while working on this text.

20.11 Exercises

1. Read the following Prolog program and predict the answers.

```
person( X )  :- mother_of( Y, X ).
person( Y )  :- mother_of( Y, X ).
mother_of( mary, carmen ).
mother_of( mary, alexander ).
mother_of( mary, andre ).
: ?-person( X ).
```

2. Analyze the following Prolog program below. Which answers will the system give for the three questions? We only add the hint that the answers are "yes" or "no" answers.

```
member( X, [ X |   ] ).
member( X, [   | Y ] ).
: ?-member( [ a ], [ a, b, [ a ] ] ).
: ?-member( [ [ a ] ], [ b, [ [ a ] ], c ] ).
: ?-member( [ [ a ] ], [ a, b, [ a, b, [ a ], c ], c ] ).
```

3. Analyze the following Prolog program and derive the same answers Prolog must determine.

```
path( X, Y )  :- door( X, Y ).
path( X, Y )  :- door( Y, X ).
path( X, Y )  :- door( X, Z ), path( Z, Y ).
path( X, Y )  :- door( Z, X ), path( Z, Y ).

door( a1, a2 ).   door( a2, a3 ).   door( a3, b3 ).
door( b3, c3 ).   door( c3, c2 ).   door( c2, c1 ).
door( c1, b1 ).
: ?-path( a1, b1 ).
: ?-path( b1, a1 ).
```

Appendix A

Glossary

Algorithm A sequence of precise instructions that are guaranteed to terminate. The instructions produce output data and normally require input. Most of the sample programs used in this text require no input, only because they are designed as demonstration programs.

Assembler A software package that translates an assembly language source program into an equivalent object program.

Automatic storage One kind of storage space for variables local to a subprogram. This space is automatically allocated by the system when a subprogram is entered, and it is freed when the subprogram terminates. Data space is typically granted from and returned to a stack, since the order of request and free operations proceeds in LIFO fashion.

BNF Backus Naur Form (or Backus Normal Form) is a concise symbolism used to describe the syntax of programming languages. The symbolism is used as a *metalanguage* and is a tool for describing the syntax of languages. BNF became popular with the introduction of Algol-60 in the Algol-60 Report, but it was rediscovered later that the principles of the BNF form had already been applied centuries earlier by an Indian linguistic researcher.

Cast In Algol-68 and C, a synonym for explicit type conversion.

Code A sequence of executable machine instructions.

Common A Fortran term for static storage with the scope attribute external.

Compiler A software package that translates a high level language source program into an equivalent, executable object program.

Compiler Compiler A software package whose input is a language definition and whose output is a compiler in source or object form for that language. In most existing implementations, however, compiler compilers are not what the label promises. In reality they are only parser generators.

Constant A data object that does not change its value. Thus it may be a literal, which cannot take on any value other than the one it represents, or it may be a *variable* that just happens not to be reassigned.

Context Free Grammar (CFG) A grammar that allows only a single nonterminal symbol on the left-hand side of a production.

Controlled storage A PL/I synonym for storage allocation off the system heap.

Data Typed objects that hold values. These objects come in two flavors, variables and constants.

Declaration That portion of a source program that associates an object with a name and a type. The type implies the kind of operations that may be performed on the named object.

Dummy parameter Fortran's and PL/I's term for formal parameter.

Exporting Making a name available in scopes outside of the defining one. This breaks conventional scope rules in a well-controlled fashion. An exportable name must be explicitly imported before it becomes accessible in another scope.

Expression A combination of operands (data) and operators that yields a value. The arrangement of operators must adhere to the syntax rules; they typically come in different binding strengths or priorities.

Expression language A class of programming languages in which the smallest complete executable unit is an expression. In contrast to statement-oriented languages, these languages do not require that a full statement be specified in order for a complete action to take place. Algol-68 and C are examples of expression languages.

External A name has the scope attribute external if it is known systemwide. For example, the name of a Fortran compilation unit is external. The storage attribute for external data is inherently static.

Fixed point Numeric data that may have a fractional part. The difference between any two adjacent fixed point values is constant.

Floating point Numeric data that may have a fractional part. The difference between any two adjacent floating point values increases with the absolute value of the data.

Fonts Assortment of sizes and styles for printed characters.

Forced closure Required lexical token at end of a syntactic unit such as a statement or declaration. Ada example: IF condition THEN dothis; END IF;. The END IF keywords close the If Statement and are enforced by the compiler.

Formal parameter Used in a subprogram declaration to specify the parameter name, position, and type. A formal parameter is the place holder for its associated actual parameter for the duration of a call.

Forward reference Use (or reference) of a name in a source program before the declaration of that name. The term *before* implies a sequential processing of source from top to bottom, left to right. Note that external names are usually exempt from this ordering constraint.

Function A logical module or subprogram that returns a value. The module is activated when the function name is referenced in an expression.

Global The scope attribute for a name that is known in multiple blocks due to the nesting structure of the blocks. This has nothing to do with the name's storage attribute, which can in fact be static, automatic, or controlled.

Heap Data structure from which storage parts are allocated and freed in the order of incoming requests. That order does not follow a regular pattern.

Identifier The character string representation of the name for an object. Often confused with variable.

Importing Making named objects that are defined in one module accessible in another. Usually the defining module must mark such names as exportable. The purpose of importing is to have actions or data structures available through the imported objects without having to reimplement them in the referencing module.

Information hiding Modularization principle, in which only invariant information of a common action is publicized in an interface. Any number of modules may reference or import such interfaces. Incidental detail, on the other hand, is hidden and is available only to the module that performs the agreed-upon action.

Integer Numeric data type that can hold only integral or whole values.

Interpreter A software package that translates and immediately executes a source program. In contrast to a compiler, an interpreter emits no object program corresponding to the source.

Literal A character string denoting a direct value of type integer, character, string, boolean, or the like. A literal's value is always constant, but not every constant is a literal.

Logical module A complete entity within a source program with a well-defined logical function. Typically it has local data that are invisible to the outside of the module. A logical module can communicate with the outside world via return value, certain parameters, or global variables in decreasing order of safeness.

Metalanguage A language used to describe a language. English, for example, is used frequently as the metalanguage for the description of programming languages.

Multiprocessing Simultaneous execution of one or more tasks on two or more processors. In its most general form, a multiprocessing system needs just one single task, which is then broken into independent subtasks (if possible). These subtasks are executed simultaneously on a multitude of processors.

Multiprogramming Concurrent execution of two or more tasks on one single processor.

Multitasking Synonym for *Multiprocessing.*

Nonterminal symbol A grammar symbol appearing on the left-hand side of a production.

Object Synonym for *data.*

Object program Source program converted into a form intelligible to a computer. Object code is emitted during the Code Generation phase of a compiler or assembler.

Physical module A sequence of one or more logical modules on a file that can be completely compiled.

Procedure A sequence of precise instructions. A procedure is almost identical to an algorithm, except that it is not guaranteed to terminate. This interpretation of procedure should not be confused with the syntactic entity PROCEDURE explained next, but they are closely related.

PROCEDURE A syntactical way of expressing a logical module, in some languages by choosing the keyword PROCEDURE or SUBROUTINE.

Production Rule of a CFG, having a nonterminal on the left-hand side followed by a production operator, and a string of terminal and nonterminal symbols to the right of the production operator. Often the production operator is spelled ::=. The string on the right is derived from the left nonterminal.

Program A set of physical modules cooperating on one common task. One of the program's logical modules, called the MAIN procedure, initiates execution.

Recursion Principle of expressing an algorithm by using the same algorithm in the explanation. When done incorrectly (i.e., it is *not* recursion), this principle deteriorates into infinite circularity with no solution. Done properly, each recursive step guarantees some progress toward the solution of a finite problem.

Scope A domain of source text over which a name is well defined. Thus, the term describes a static aspect of a source program, relevant at compilation time. The term scope is often misused as synonym for block. *Block* addresses more the run time allocation of space that is associated with a scope.

Semantics Rules that define the meaning of operations in a source program. One of the hard problems in the design of programming languages is the unambiguous definition of the language semantics.

Source A string of text holding a program. This string is the output of the text-editing phase. The source is read as input by a compiler to be converted into equivalent object form.

Stack Data structure from which parts of storage are allocated and released in a last-in/first-out (LIFO) fashion.

Stack frame Run time data structure associated with each incarnation of a block. It holds the data space for all automatic variables of this block including parameters and additional control information. Such control information allows the currently active block to reset the stack to its state before the call and to have the program continue execution at the place after the call, and it permits access to nonlocal data during the call.

Statement-oriented language A class of programming languages in which the smallest, complete syntactical unit is the statement. Ada, Fortran, Modula-2, Pascal, and PL/I are sample statement-oriented languages. In contrast to expression languages, it is not sufficient to merely specify an expression for a complete action to take place; instead a full statement has to be written. For example, to return a value, the body of a function in a statement-oriented language must execute a Return Statement. In an expression language an arithmetic expression is sufficient.

Static storage That part of a system's storage that is active as long as the main program lives.

Syntax Rules for forming correct source programs. For that subclass of languages that is interesting for programming, the precise definition of syntax is well understood.

Terminal symbols Those elements of a grammar's vocabulary that are literals standing for themselves. Terminals cannot derive any other string; thus they can never appear on the left-hand side of a production operator.

Type conversion (explicit) Transformation of a value from one type to another. Usually the actual bit strings, representing the value, do not change. It is the interpretation of these bits that changes. Hence this class of explicit type conversion causes no object code generation. It is simply a way of informing a compiler for a strongly typed language "Yes sir, I know what I am doing, and please let me do it!" There are also cases, where the explicit (and implicit as well) type conversion does, in fact, alter the bits holding the value.

Typemark Ada term for *type name.*

Type name Name that identifies a type. Some languages provide only a limited set of predefined type names. Fortran, for example, includes the type name *LOGICAL.* In other languages the programmer can define new type names.

Variable A data object that receives different values at different moments of time during program execution.

Appendix B

Introduction to Ada

This introduction should be studied by those readers who have no previous knowledge of Ada. Here we show only a few of the simplest Ada programming constructs. The purpose of the programs explained here is to give the language novice sufficient knowledge to understand the discussions in Chapter 4. Readers who are very familiar with Pascal and Modula-2 may feel free to skip this explanation. These two languages are sufficiently close to Ada in syntax for the reader to understand what is covered in the text.

All sample programs included in this section are full compilation units. This enables an Ada compiler to read and translate each program to the extent that it can be executed without relying on other program parts that must be written by the user. There are two kinds of compilation units in Ada: Procedures and Packages. Since Packages require a more advanced understanding of Ada, they do not fit into this introduction.

First we shall explain the simplest possible Ada program, the "emptyprogram," which has the special virtue of doing nothing. For an assembly language programmer this would be a NOOP. Next, in two programs called "greetings1" and "greetings 2," we shall cover Ada text output by letting the program tell us a few words of ancient wisdom. In the programs named "variables" and "structured," we shall introduce the declaration of variables in primitive and structured form, and present Assignment Statements with Type Conversion. Finally, we shall discuss Array declarations and various Ada loop constructs that access these Arrays one element at a time.

B-1 The Empty Program

The sample Ada program in Example B-1 expresses in the smallest number of lexical tokens how to do nothing except consume a few cycles of machine time during execution. Such cleverness is not all we intend to convey to the reader; a discussion of important syntax rules follows, but first we should carefully read the following four-line program.

```
1                  |PROCEDURE empty_program IS
2           1      |BEGIN -- empty_program
3           1      | NULL;
4    1      1  1   |END;
```

Example B-1 The Empty Ada Program

The "emptyprogram" teaches us a number of important Ada syntax constructs. Most importantly, here we see the outline of how to declare a PROCEDURE. We cannot say that Ada is free from layout constraints, but, in fact, the same program without comment could also have been written on a single line.

Procedure Head

Procedures are introduced by the reserved keyword, followed by the procedure name. Unlike in Pascal, another reserved keyword, the token IS, follows the procedure name. Imagine—one full keystroke more than the conventional semicolon! But the reader should not be overly concerned about this waste in data entry time. Ada also provides a form of Procedure Declaration with the semicolon in place of the IS keyword. But that construct addresses a more sophisticated programming area, the forward declaration, which will not be covered here.

Procedure Skeleton

The head of a Procedure Declaration is followed by a body that looks like a conventional Compound Statement. We are assuming that the reader is familiar with the Compound Statement from Modula-2, Pascal, or PL/I. Together, head and body form a skeleton of an Ada Procedure. The Ada Procedure body permits one minor variation to the Compound Statement in this context. It is the repetition of the procedure name after the END keyword. Although we have not used this option in Example B-1, we do use it in all of the following sample programs, because it provides a nice documentary aid.

Null Statement, Semicolon, and Comment

The only statement used in this program is the Null Statement, explicitly denoted by the reserved keyword NULL. The trailing semicolon after NULL on line 3 is mandatory. Every Ada statement must be terminated by a semicolon.

Also for documentation, we have included a short comment. The procedure name is repeated after the keyword BEGIN in the form of a comment. To identify source text as a comment, it must be introduced by two hyphens. All subsequent characters, up the the end of the line, are commentary.

B-2 Output Statement

The next two Ada procedures are not much more complicated than the preceding empty program. We have only replaced the Null Statement by an Output Statement, so we learn how to let our Ada programs communicate with the outside world. See Example B-2.

```
 1                  |WITH text_io;
 2                  |PROCEDURE greetings_1 IS
 3             1    |BEGIN -- greetings_1
 4             1    | text_io.put_line( " Mot de jour # 1 : 'CARPE DIEM'" );
 5    4        1  1 |END greetings_1;
 6    4             |
 7    4             |WITH text_io; USE text_io;
 8    4             |PROCEDURE greetings_2 IS
 9    6        1    |BEGIN -- greetings_2
10    6        1    | put_line( " Mot de jour # 2 : 'PER ASPERA AD ASTRA'" );
11   10        1  1 |END greetings_2;
```

Example B-2 Text Output Messages in Ada

Algol-60 set the classical precedent that turned out to be one of the reasons for its failure. This was the omission of IO from the language definition. Numerous other programming languages followed suit. Such an omission is not particularly meaningful although in its pure form it will render a language completely useless. It certainly provides a nice political argument: everything else being equal, a language without IO must be simpler than a language that does have IO. So if a language would be criticized for excessive complexity, the same criticism may be refuted if IO is missing. But we trust that the Ada language designers had a better, more technical motivation for omitting IO from the definition. It would be nice, however, to communicate such reasons to the programming community as well!

To avoid repeating Algol-60's fate, however, Ada included a definition of compiler-supplied Packages that perform IO. The programmer must only remember each time that these predefined Packages are additions to the language, not part of it.

One of these IO Packages is called for on line 1 of program "greetings1" in Example B-2, via a With Clause. The Package name is "textio." The Ada With Clause looks similar to the Pascal With Statement, and its semantics is, therefore, often confused with this most troublesome Pascal construct. But the purpose of the With Clause in Ada is to make all names defined in the referenced Package known to the including scope. Therefore, after having specified "WITH textio;," the programmer can freely reference all names defined in that Package without getting compiler warnings about undeclared identifiers. It is, however, still necessary to spell out the fully qualified name. So the Output Statement on line 4 in Example B-2 must reference the Package name first, and then the particular IO procedure of that Package. This is the reason for the wordy name "textio.put line."

The "putline" procedure prints one single string onto the standard output file, and then terminates this line with a carriage return and newline. So the semantics is similar to the sequence of the Modula-2 statements "WriteString" and "WriteLn." It is also comparable to Pascal's "writeln" statement with the additional restriction that there is only a single argument and that argument is of type string.

If the programmer does not always wish to spell out this lengthy name, Ada provides a shortcut in the the Use Clause. This clause has a similar meaning to Pascal's With Statement. The Use Clause, seen on line 7 in program "greetings2" in Example B-2, allows the short reference to IO routines, as shown on line 10. Repeating the Package name is no longer required.

B-3 Variable Declarations, Type Conversions, and Assignment Statements

In Example B-3 we introduce variable declarations, Assignment Statements, type conversions, and the declaration of a structured type.

```
 1                    |WITH text_io; USE text_io;
 2                    |PROCEDURE variables IS
 3            1        | c : character;
 4        11  1        | i : integer;
 5        12  1        |BEGIN -- variables
 6            1        | put ( " enter character: " );
 7    3      1  1      | get ( c );
 8    5      1  1      | i := character'pos ( c );
 9    8      1  1      | i := i + 2;
10   13      1  1      | put_line ( character'val ( i ) );
11   16      1  1      |END variables;
12   16               |
13   16               |PROCEDURE structured IS
14   18      1        | TYPE complex_type IS
15   18      1        |  RECORD
16   18      1        |    real,
17   18      1        |    imag : integer;
18   18      1        |  END RECORD;
19   18      1        | complex : complex_type;
20   18  12  1        |BEGIN -- structured
21   18      1        | complex.real := 5566;
22   22      1  1      | complex.imag := 7788;
23   26      1  1      | put ( integer'image ( complex.real ) & '.' &
                                integer'image ( complex.imag ) );
24   38      1  1      |END structured;
```

Example B-3 Variable Declarations in Ada

Variable Declaration

Lines 3 and 4 are sample variable declarations, for which the proper Ada term is "object declaration." In this case, variables "c" and "i" are defined by predefined type marks. Ada provides a few of these, including "boolean," "character," and "integer." These are quite similar to the predefined Pascal types, except for the longer spelling of "character." After such a declaration without an initialization clause, the variable remains undefined at run time.

Type Compatibility

Two Ada objects are type compatible only if they are declared by the same type mark. Structural equivalence is *not* sufficient in Ada for two types to be compatible. This sounds like a severe limitation, but in reality such strict typing enhances program reliability. Also, the conversion between structurally equivalent types is provided and is simple in Ada. We have used something reminiscent of type conversions in the sample program "variables," but the exact syntax construct used is "Attribute." The difference between attributes and type conversions is clarified in Chapter 6.

Type Conversion

To allow for the assignment of a character value to an integer variable and vice versa, Ada provides the "pos" and "val" attributes, used on lines 8 and 10 in B-3. Attribute "pos" returns the integer equivalent of character variable "c," while attribute "val" returns the character value of the included integer expression, in this case "i." Such conversions are not restricted to "integer" and "character" types; but they are the most frequently used conversions. However, the type mark before the "pos" attribute must fully specify the type of the converted expression, and the type mark before the "val" attribute yields the target type of the converted integer type expression.

Assignment Statement

The Assignment Statement is one of the most primitive and crucial constructs, the syntax of which is already familiar from Algol, Pascal, or Modula-2. The variable on the left side receives the value of the expression on the right. Ada does not define the order of evaluation. Under normal circumstances this does not matter anyway. We will not address here those tricky and subtle applications where it does matter.

Notice that Ada permits the assignment of full Arrays and Records to one another, provided that the types are compatible. Also slices of one Array can be assigned to slices of another Array. So the Ada Assignment Statement is quite general.

Records

In the short program "structured" in Example B-3, we see the declaration of a Record Type. Each type declaration in Ada is introduced by the reserved keyword TYPE followed by the defined type mark and the keyword IS. Then comes the type definition. In this case the type is still quite simple. "Complextype" is defined on line 14 as a Record type with two integer fields. The field names are "real" and "imag." We choose the name "real" to express clearly that it is not a predefined Ada type mark. However, Ada does allow us to redefine predefined identifiers. If we had preferred, we could have named one of the Record fields "float." This would not even have overwritten the predefined type mark "float," which is also permitted, because every Record effectively opens a new scope for identifiers. Pascal's "real" type identifier corresponds to Ada's "float" type mark, but Ada allows a considerably higher degree of control in defining exactly what a floating point number is.

Variable "complex," declared on line 19, is a Record variable. Its fields are referenced several times in the procedure body, and we should recognize a familiar pattern. Record fields are addressed as in Modula-2, Pascal, and PL/I, except that the incomplete qualification allowed in PL/I is not permitted in Ada. Every Ada Record field must be completely qualified by listing every single intermediate Record structure.

Single Argument for IO Statements

The argument of the "put" statement on line 23 of Example B-3 is a complicated expression. Its complexity is caused by the Ada rule that only one single argument may be printed via a "put" Statement. Since we wish to print three substrings, we have to concatenate them so that syntactically they form one string. The concatenation operator is represented by the ampersand character.

B-4 Ada Arrays, Procedure Calls, and Procedure Calls

Ada program "loopsarrays" in Example B-4 demonstrates the declaration of Array types and variables, and shows how Array elements can be referenced. The Array "table" is initialized to character expressions and then printed. Initialization and printing are accomplished by two Procedure Call Statements. The output, generated by the program during execution, follows after the source listing.

```
                 |WITH text_io; USE text_io;
                 |PROCEDURE loops_arrays IS
           1     | TYPE table_type IS ARRAY( 0..4, 0..4 ) OF character;
           1     | table : table_type;
       35  1     |
       35  1     | PROCEDURE init_table IS
           2     | BEGIN -- init_table
           2     |  FOR i IN 0 .. 4 LOOP
  5        2  1  |   FOR j IN 0 .. 4 LOOP
  9        2  2  |    table(i,j) := character'val(i+j+character'pos('A'));
 23        2  3  |   END LOOP;
```

```
12   24          2  2 |   END LOOP;
13   25          2  1 | END init_table;
14   25          1    |
15   25          1    | PROCEDURE print_table IS
16   27          2    |   j : integer;
17   27    11    2    | BEGIN -- print_table
18   27          2    |   FOR i IN 0 .. 4 LOOP
19   32          2  1 |     j := 0;
20   35          2  2 |     WHILE j <= 4 LOOP
21   39          2  2 |       put( table( i, j ), 2 );
22   50          2  3 |       j := j + 1;
23   55          2  3 |     END LOOP;
24   56          2  2 |     new_line( output );
25   57          2  2 |   END LOOP;
26   58          2  1 | END print_table;
27   58          1    |
28   58          1    |BEGIN -- loops_arrays
29   60          1    | init_table;
30   64          1  1 | print_table;
31   67          1  1 |END loops_arrays;

A B C D E
B C D E F
C D E F G
D E F G H
E F G H I
```

Example B-4 Ada Loops and Arrays

Array Declarations

Ada Arrays are declared just as they are in Pascal. "Tabletype" on line 3 is a two-dimensional Array of characters. As in Modula-2 and Pascal, the actual index ranges can be specified explicitly as shown here, or via range type marks. In addition, Ada permits unconstrained Arrays for procedure parameters. *Unconstrained Arrays* have their bounds fixed only at execution time, when the actual call is executed. Also, the null range, where the upper bound is less than the lower bound, is legal in Ada.

Procedure Calls

Lines 29 and 30 show Ada Procedure Call Statements. The syntax for these is again exactly as in Pascal. The first procedure call initializes "table," referenced as a global variable, while the second call causes the initialized "table" to be printed in tabular form. This output is displayed after the listing.

For Statements

A straightforward way of accessing Array elements is by using For Statements, one per dimension. We see two instances on lines 8 and 9 in Procedure "inittable." The For Statement control variables, called "loop parameters" in Ada, are declared implicitly. Their scope is limited to that of the For Statement itself. Such implicit declarations make it unnecessary to define variables "i" and "j" in the Procedure "inittable." In fact, had we defined two integer type variables with these names, then in the scope of the For Statement the implicit declaration of the control variables would have temporarily overwritten the local variables.

To familiarize the reader with another loop construct, we have included a sample While Statement in "printtables." Notice that now an explicit declaration for the control variable "j" is necessary. "J" is initialized via the Assignment Statement on line 19, and incremented in the While Statement body on line 22. We should notice the common rules for loop bodies in both the For Statements and While Statements.

B-5 Summary

This short, informal introduction to Ada has obviously not offered a great deal of detail about Ada programming constructs. It has, however, reviewed the essential concepts, including Output Statements, variable declarations, type conversions, Assignment Statements, Records, and Arrays. This should enable the reader to understand the examples presented in Chapter 4.

Appendix C

Solutions to Exercises

Chapter 1

1. A left recursive grammar of the form "a ::= a A B" can be transformed into an equivalent grammar with the two rules "a ::= B a'" and "a' ::= A a' LAMBDA." A primitive string substitution algorithm is sufficient to solve the problem.

   Substituting "+E" in EG1 for "A" and "E" for "B" will generate the following grammar:

```
EG1':            s  ::= E s'
                 s' ::= + E s'  | LAMBDA
```

2. The start symbol in EG1' does not generate the empty string. Therefore the grammar can be completely translated into an equivalent one without lambda productions. Just systematically replace all references of nonterminals that do generate lambda with the empty string on the right-hand side of all productions. This will generate grammar EG1".

```
EG1'':            s  ::= E | E s'
                  s' ::= + E s' | + E
```

3. Every statement in language L(G5) must be terminated by a semicolon. Since there is no semicolon after the "1" in the Assignment Statement "i:=i+1," we have an error.

4. The shortest string in EG2 has a length of zero, since start symbol "s" can generate the empty string. The terminal symbols in L(EG2) are "(," ")," and lambda. The language defined by EG2 is the infinite set of all well-formed parentheses. Well-formed means that the number of open parentheses in any string equals the number of closing parentheses, and there are never more closing than open parentheses in the input during a left to right scan.

5. Base case: The empty string is trivially well-formed, hence the claim holds for strings of length zero. We assume inductively that the claim is also true for strings of length up to 2*n, for n >= 0. Then all strings of length 2*(n+1) must also be well-formed. Since the only production that adds more parentheses to a parse tree is the rule "s ::= (s) s," which is also well-formed, it follows that all strings of length 2*(n+1) fulfill the claim as well.

6. The set "t" of terminal symbols is t = AND, OR, FALSE, TRUE . The set "nt" of nonterminal symbols is nt = disj, conj, term . The only metasymbols used are ::= and .
   The ambiguousness of EG3 is caused by the lack of a priority structure of the two operands to the binary operators AND and OR. For any terminal string containing either the OR or AND operator, there are at least two parse trees.
   An equivalent, unambiguous grammar EG3' follows.

```
EG3':            disj ::= conj [ AND disj ]
                 conj ::= term [ OR  conj ]
                 term ::= FALSE | TRUE
```

7. The two languages are not equivalent. One of them has a symbol, lambda; the other one contains no symbol at all. It is the empty language. So there are more strings in one than in the other language.

8. The complete list can be generated systematically by using all possible leftmost derivations. The sentences are listed here, but we must remember that the grammar contains no meaning. So some sentences may sound silly.

```
THE WORLD WILL WELCOME LOVERS
    WORLD WILL WELCOME LOVERS
THE WORLD WILL WELCOME
    WORLD WILL WELCOME
THE TIME  WILL WELCOME LOVERS
    TIME  WILL WELCOME LOVERS
THE TIME  WILL WELCOME
    TIME  WILL WELCOME
THE WORLD FLIES LOVERS
    WORLD FLIES LOVERS
THE WORLD FLIES
    WORLD FLIES
THE TIME  FLIES LOVERS
    TIME  FLIES LOVERS
THE TIME  FLIES
    TIME  FLIES
```

9. The rail road diagram of the For Statement is listed as follows.

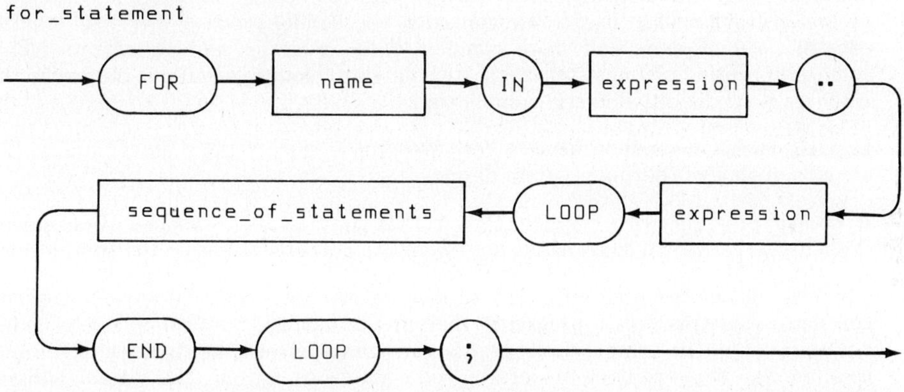

Chapter 2

1. From the standpoint of programming language design, Fortran's tendency to have exceptions is bad because it is in opposition to the orthogonality principle. Each programmer of such a language must learn two rules for expressions. In addition, the compiler must do special checking.

   Implementors always find things that can be added on cheaply, but their concept may not be good. Other language constructs may be costly to implement but extremely valuable. The need to work hard should not be a reason to exclude a good construct from a language. Also, maybe tomorrow a better implementation strategy will be found that reduces the cost of implementations.

2. Pascal's single compilation unit rule is probably its main flaw for real-life projects. For toy programs this restriction is tolerable. But when complex projects are written by independently working groups, the submodules must be tested out before the whole system is complete. In this situation multiple physical compilation units are highly desirable.

3. Clearly a good programming language should be rich enough to permit expressing complex programs in it. But simplicity is also a virtue. A simple language can be mastered and understood more easily than a complicated one. Ideally a programming language has a few concepts, the composition of which allows the constructions of more and more complex data structures and statements. This composition principle must be usable without introducing exceptions; otherwise the language is by definition overly complicated.

4. Implicit type conversions save a few keystrokes during data entry and a few seconds of thought during program design.

5. A source program with implicit type conversions is less readable. Conversely, explicitly written type conversions document the author's intent on the spot.

6. The class of source programs that cannot be compiled even by a very powerful translator contains "real" programs that are too long. For example, too many declarations fill the symbol table, or too many lines exceed the capacity of the line counter, too many statements create code addresses beyond the virtual address space of the target machine. Luckily, for realistic compilers, this infinitely large class of programs is uninteresting. Source programs of, say, more than 25,000 lines, are highly suspicious. They should probably have been broken into multiple compilation units.

7. These very, very long programs that can be easily handled by a compiler are again uninteresting. They are effectively "null" programs. In Pascal, this would be programs with nothing but semicolons, indicating empty statements. In Ada, this would be programs with only Null Statements.

8. Presumably, procedure "p" has been defined, because some statement would like to call "p." A call to "p" is legitimate in the scope that contains the definition of "p." Therefore, "p" must be preserved.

9. Generally, the "silent error" is the killer! If something goes wrong and nothing is indicated, the disastrous effect shows up after it is too late. The other kind of error, "false alarm," is only a nuisance that normally can be worked around.

10. Clearly, the compiler must enter implicitly declared names in the symbol table. So nothing is saved by implicit declarations, but clarity and readability are lost.

11. The : character is not always a colon. Pascal has an assignment operator that starts with the : character. The full token is :=.

12. Yes, the optimizer may safely replace the BRANCH 600 by a BRANCH 700. The only effect of this is that the code eventually executes a bit faster. The branch at location 600 can, in general, not be eliminated. Instructions between 500 and 600, indicated by dots, may very well end up at address 600 and expect a branch there.

Chapter 3

1. The explicit and recommended way of identifying the main program in a sequence of Fortran compilation units is via the PROGRAM statement. If the program statement is not used, then the one and only compilation unit not identified as a SUBROUTINE or FUNCTION is by definition the main program.

2. The option MAIN must be specified in the OPTIONS Clause in one of the PL/I compilation units.

3. Mutual recursion in Ada, Pascal, and PL/I:

```
-- in Ada
PROCEDURE a;
PROCEDURE b IS
 BEGIN -- b
  a;
  b;
 END b;

PROCEDURE a IS
 BEGIN -- a
  a;
  b;
 END a;
```

```
{ in Pascal }
PROCEDURE a; FORWARD;
PROCEDURE b;
 BEGIN { b }
  a;
  b;
 END; { b }

PROCEDURE b;
 BEGIN { a }
  a;
  b;
 END; { a }
```

```
/* in PL/I */
PROC a; RECURSIVE;
 CALL a;
 CALL b;
END;

PROC b; RECURSIVE;
 CALL a;
 CALL b;
END;
```

4. One way of solving a recursive algorithm in Fortran without using recursion is by finding an equivalent, nonrecursive algorithm. This works only in some cases. Another solution is the explicit simulation of a run time stack.

5. The <> symbol is used as the inequality operator in Pascal and as the box symbol in Ada. The box symbol is used, for example, to express that bounds are not specified at compile time.

6. Since correctness is assumed, the only context allowed is the start of an Assignment Statement. Hence END must be a user-defined name that is assigned a value.

7. The shortest possible Ada string literal is the empty string. It is two characters long, spelled “.” The shortest possible character literal in Ada is three characters long, as are ALL Ada character literals, e.g. ’”.

8. There are six distinct relational operators in PL/I. Their ten lexical denotations are =, >, <, >=, <=, ¬=, ¬<, ¬<=, ¬>, ¬ and >=.

9. The subprogram declaration, syntactically terminated by a semicolon, corresponds to Pascal’s FORWARD announcement.

10. The two types “character” and “ARRAY(1..1) of character” are quite distinct; hence any such assignment is illegal in Ada.

11. A variable used as an actual parameter determines that passing is done by reference. An expression used as an actual parameter determines passing by value. A variable can be used as an expression by embedding it in redundant parentheses or by modifying the variable via an identity operation. For example, the integer 0 can be added to a variable of type BIN FIXED; also the empty string can be concatenated to a string variable, thus creating an expression.

12. The first letter of the name determines the type by default if no explicit indication is included in the program. Letters "i" through "n" yield integer type declarations; all other first letters yield floating point objects.

13. The PL/I Begin block and the Ada Declare Statement may both hold local declarations and statements. There is no essential difference between them. There exists a minor difference, though. In Ada all declarations must be grouped together before the reserved keyword BEGIN, while in PL/I everything may be written down in a wild mix of statements and declarations.

14. Pascal does not allow local declarations in Begin Statements.

15. The storage attribute for local Pascal variables is "automatic."

16. Type marks are compile time entities; hence they have no storage attribute associated with them.

17. The obvious way to construct string literals longer than one source line is to concatenate several shorter string literals with the & string concatenation operator.

18. There are two scopes in Fortran: external and local.

19. The real issue in this discussion is consistency. The specific subissue is the "zero-one-infinity" principle, which is a guideline for language designers. The principle suggests that any syntax construct should either be required once, be optional, or be repeatable any number of times. All other restrictions, such as 3 dimensions, 9 continuations in Fortran-66, 19 continuations in Fortran-77, 32 characters per identifier in PL/I represent additional ballast that make learning a language more difficult than it should be.

20. Global is only a scope attribute. Ada type marks (or Pascal type identifiers), for example, have no associated storage but can be used globally.

21. Automatic is only a storage attribute.

Chapter 4

1. The solution idea developed here is simple but far from optimal. We leave the discovery of a good algorithm as an interesting challenge to the reader.

   Let the start position arbitrarily have the name "black" and the final position arbitrarily have the name "white." Our solution to the "annoy" algorithm then consists of two simple steps. Step one moves the subtower of (n-1) disks from "black" to "white," using the well-known mechanism of the "towers of hanoi." Step two calls the "annoy" algorithm recursively with (n-1) disks.

   Notice that after step one, the largest and lowest disk already rests on its final place; hence it never needs to be moved. When "annoy" is called recursively, this time with only (n-1) disks to be moved from position "white," then again that tower's lowest disk also sits on its final destination, and will never be moved. Towers with less than two disks are already completely sorted and no move is necessary. So the kernel of the recursive algorithm "annoy" is

```
IF disks > 1 THEN
 hanoi( disks - 1, black, white, buffer );
 annoy( disks - 1, white, black, buffer );
END IF;
```

The proposed solution with expected output is listed as follows. Notice that for a tower of three disks, the number of moves is four, while an optimum solution needs only three moves.

```
PROGRAM towers_of_annoy( output );
 TYPE
  string = ARRAY[ 1..5 ] OF char;
 VAR
  disks  : integer;

 PROCEDURE hanoi(
   disks  : integer;
   start,
   final,
   buffer   : string );
  BEGIN { hanoi }
   IF disks > 0 THEN
    BEGIN
     hanoi( disks-1, start, buffer, final );
     writeln( output, 'move disk ', disks:1,
       ' from ', start, ' to ', final );
     hanoi( disks-1, buffer, final, start );
    END;
   {END IF}
  END; { hanoi }

 PROCEDURE annoy(
   disks  : integer;
   black,
   white,
```

```
    buffer : string );
   BEGIN { annoy }
    IF disks > 1 THEN
     BEGIN
      hanoi( disks-1, black, white, buffer );
      annoy( disks-1, white, black, buffer );
     END
    {END IF}
   END; { annoy }

  BEGIN { towers_of_annoy }
   FOR disks := 2 TO 4 DO
    BEGIN
     writeln( output, ' moving ', disks, ' disks' );
     annoy( disks, 'black', 'white', 'buffr' );
     writeln( output );
    END;
   {END FOR}
  END. { towers_of_annoy }
```

Example C-4-1 Listing of "Annoy" Solution

```
 moving          2 disks
move disk 1 from black to white

 moving          3 disks
move disk 1 from black to buffr
move disk 2 from black to white
move disk 1 from buffr to white
move disk 1 from white to black

 moving          4 disks
move disk 1 from black to white
move disk 2 from black to buffr
move disk 1 from white to buffr
move disk 3 from black to white
move disk 1 from buffr to black
move disk 2 from buffr to white
move disk 1 from black to white
move disk 1 from white to buffr
move disk 2 from white to black
move disk 1 from buffr to black
move disk 1 from black to white
```

Output of "Annoy"

2. How many moves are necessary to sort a black-and-white tower into two strictly black-and-white subtowers, always adhering to the rules of the Towers of Hanoi puzzle? Let the function a(n) return the number of moves for n disks in the "annoy" game. Let h(n) be a function, returning the number of moves for the Towers of Hanoi problem with n disks. From the preceding Pascal solution we can see the recurrence relation:

```
a(n) = h(n-1) + a(n-1)  for n>0
```

Such an obvious recurrence relation does not convey much information, but it can be used handily in the following proof. Rather than expressing the number of moves a(n) as a recurrence formula, we prefer to reduce it to something more tangible—a formula yielding the result immediately. To this end we establish a table with values, deduce or guess a formula, and prove it to be correct.

Table C-4-1 Moves for Hanoi and Annoy

n	h(n)	a(n)
1	1	0
2	3	1
3	7	4
4	15	11
5	31	26

From Table C-4-1 we can see that a(n) = the sum of all h(i) for i=1 .. (n-1). In more fashionable jargon, this is expressed as: a(n) = Sigma(h(i)), for i=1..n-1. This could, of course, be a coincidence, and might not be true for some values of n>5. So we have to prove its correctness or try another deduction. Luckily the proof is easily done by induction.

The base case for n<=2 can be verified immediately. So we can assume inductively that a(n+1)=Sigma(h(i)) for i=1 to n.

```
Proof:          a(n+1) = Sigma( h(i) ), i=1..n
                a(n+1) = h(n) + Sigma( h(i) ) i=1..n-1
We know that
                a(n)   = Sigma( h(i) ), i=1..n-1, so it follows
                a(n+1) = h(n) + a(n)
```

The last identity is known to be correct; hence our assumption that the formula holds for all n is also correct. This concludes the proof.

3. For a tower of just one single disk, it is clear that "annoy" takes less moves. The tower does not need to be modified at all; both subtowers are already completely sorted by color. The first has by definition only one color, since we assume a single disk, and the second subtower is empty, so there is no mix of colors either.

   On the other hand, the "Hanoi" solution requires one move even with a single disk.

   For towers with more disks it is similar: Annoy always has at least some disk that can remain where it is, while Hanoi must move everything.

4. It is much better to test only for up to the square root of the test number. This transforms an algorithm requiring O(n) steps, with "n" being the number to be tested for primality by another algorithm that takes only O(sqrt(n)) steps.

   How can we prove that the root bound is sufficient? Let us assume to the contrary that divisions up to the root sqrt(n) are not sufficient for primality tests. Then for non-primes "n" there must exist some number "A," n>A>sqrt(n), which is the smallest integer to divide "n" evenly. However, since the division is even, there will also be an integer "B," which, when multiplied with "A," will yield "n," since

A*B=n. Now it follows that "B" must be smaller than the square root, since "A" is already greater than the root and sqrt(n)**2 yields "n." Since "B" is smaller than the root and divides "n" evenly, "A" cannot be the smallest integer to divide "n" evenly. Hence we have a contradiction.

5. The famous Sieve of Eratosthenes is strikingly simple and correct. The disadvantage is the need to have at least one bit of storage per tested number. If we are testing primality for numbers in an interesting range, say a few million billion, then the storage requirement is excessive. Much larger prime numbers are really needed for practical applications in encryption programs. Even prime numbers with one hundred decimal positions may still be too small.

6. The following sample solution "slowprime" is written in Ada. The compiler is implemented on a 16-bit computer; hence large numbers like 250,000 cannot be handled naturally. However, rehosting the algorithm on a "real" computer should involve no changes except increasing the values for "maxpindex" and "max primes."

   Maxpindex is the index of the last prime number that must be stored. All elements in "primes" and only those are used as divisors. Since we know that the largest divisor for "n" is O(sqrt(n)), the index of that prime number is rather small. To find the first 250,000 primes we have stored only 300 prime numbers.

   The kernel of "slowprime" is the short procedure "testforprime." Global variable "test" is analyzed for primality, and the result is returned via the global boolean "isprime." Everything else is only of cosmetic nature, meant to place the numerous prime numbers into a nice, tabular form. Unfortunately, we have to include a hand-coded version of the integer "sqrt" function, since such luxuries are not predefined in Ada.

```
                 |WITH text_io; USE text_io;
                 |
                 |PROCEDURE slowprime IS
           1     | max_pindex       : CONSTANT integer :=    100;
      10   1     | max_primes       : CONSTANT integer :=  32000;
      10   1     | SUBTYPE prange IS integer RANGE 0 .. max_pindex;
           1     | test,            -- number tested for primality
      10   1     | found,           -- so many primes found
      10   1     | pages,           -- so many pages printed
      10   1     | max,             -- no need to divide beyond max
      10   1     | cand             -- divide test by cand
      10   1     |                  : integer;
      15   1     | primes           : ARRAY( prange ) of integer;
     116   1     | primeindex       : integer; -- init to -1
     117   1     | isprime          : boolean;
     118   1     |
     118   1     | PROCEDURE printprime IS
           2     |  BEGIN -- printprime
           2     |   put( test );
 3         2  1  |   put( "  " );
 5         2  1  |  END printprime;
 5         1     |
 5         1     | PROCEDURE printpage IS
 7         2     |  BEGIN -- printpage
 7         2     |   new_line( output );
```

```
26    9       2  1 |    new_page( output );
27   10       2  1 |    pages := pages + 1;
28   15       2  1 |    put( " Table of PRIMES, indexed from ".);
29   17       2  1 |    put( found + 1 );
30   21       2  1 |    put( " .. " );
31   23       2  1 |    put( found + 500 );
32   27       2  1 |    put( "                    PAGE :" );
33   29       2  1 |    put_line( pages );
34   32       2  1 |    new_line( output );
35   33       2  1 |  END printpage;
36   33       1    |
37   33       1    | PROCEDURE printmargin( arg : integer ) IS
38   35   11  2    | BEGIN — printmargin
39   35       2    |   new_line( output );
40   37       2  1 |   put( arg );
41   39       2  1 |   put( ".)   " );
42   41       2  1 | END printmargin;
43   41       1    |
44   41       1    | PROCEDURE initialize IS
45   43       2    | BEGIN — initialize
46   43       2    |   found := 0; — so first header line o.k.
47   47       2  1 |   pages := 0;
48   50       2  1 |   printpage;
49   54       2  1 |   found := 1; — 2 already found as prime
50   57       2  1 |   printmargin( 1 );
51   62       2  1 |   test := 2;
52   65       2  1 |   printprime;
53   69       2  1 |   primeindex := -1;
54   73       2  1 |   test := 3; — next number to be tested
55   76       2  1 | END initialize;
56   76       1    |
57   76       1    | PROCEDURE testforprime IS
58   78       2    |   candindex : prange;
59   78   11  2    |
60   78   11  2    |   FUNCTION sqrt( arg : integer ) RETURN integer IS
61   78   11  3    |   old_root,
62   78   11  3    |   new_root  : integer;
63   78   13  3    |   BEGIN — sqrt
64   78       3    |     old_root := arg;
65   82       3  1 |     new_root := 1;
66   85       3  1 |     WHILE ABS ( new_root - old_root ) > 1 LOOP
67   92       3  1 |       old_root := new_root;
68   95       3  2 |       new_root := ( old_root + ( arg / old_root ) ) / 2;
69  104       3  2 |     END LOOP;
70  105       3  1 |     RETURN new_root;
71  110       3  1 |   END sqrt;
72  110       2    |
73  110       2    |   BEGIN — testforprime
74  112       2    |     max := sqrt( test );
75  119       2  1 |     candindex := 0;
76  124       2  1 |     cand := 3;
77  127       2  1 |     isprime := true;
```

```
 78  130         2  1 |   WHILE isprime and cand <= max LOOP
 79  136         2  1 |    isprime := test MOD cand /= 0;
 80  143         2  2 |    candindex := candindex + 1;
 81  150         2  2 |    cand := primes( candindex );
 82  157         2  2 |   END LOOP;
 83  158         2  1 |  END testforprime;
 84  158         1    |
 85  158         1    | PROCEDURE first_max_primes IS
 86  160         2    |  BEGIN -- first_max_primes
 87  160         2    |   WHILE found < max_primes LOOP
 88  165         2  1 |    testforprime;
 89  169         2  2 |    IF isprime THEN
 90  171         2  2 |     IF found MOD 10 = 0 THEN
 91  177         2  3 |      IF found MOD 500 = 0 THEN
 92  183         2  4 |       printpage;
 93  187         2  5 |      END IF;
 94  187         2  4 |      printmargin( found + 1 );
 95  194         2  4 |     END IF;
 96  194         2  3 |     printprime;
 97  198         2  3 |     IF found <= max_pindex + 1 THEN
 98  204         2  3 |      -- primes has max_pindex+1 elements, 2 not stored
 99  204         2  3 |      primeindex := primeindex + 1;
100  209         2  4 |      primes( primeindex ) := test;
101  215         2  4 |     END IF;
102  215         2  3 |     found := found + 1;
103  220         2  3 |    END IF; -- isprime
104  220         2  2 |    test := test + 2;
105  225         2  2 |   END LOOP;
106  226         2  1 |  END first_max_primes;
107  226         1    |
108  226         1    | PROCEDURE finish IS
109  228         2    |  BEGIN -- finish
110  228         2    |   new_line( output );
111  230         2  1 |   new_page( output );
112  231         2  1 |   put( " largest prime found = " );
113  233         2  1 |   put_line( test - 2 );
114  238         2  1 |   put( " largest stored prime= " );
115  240         2  1 |   put_line( primes( max_pindex ) );
116  247         2  1 |  END finish;
117  247         1    |
118  247         1    | BEGIN -- slowprime
119  249         1    |  initialize;
120  253         1  1 |  first_max_primes;
121  256         1  1 |  finish;
122  259         1  1 | END slowprime;
```

Example C-4-2   A "Good" Prime Number Generator in Ada

7. Example C-4-3 shows a "better" implementation, written in Pascal. We have run both algorithms on a 32-bit computer, and measured the execution times in a fairly crude way. In either case only the first 100,000 prime numbers have been computed and printed. The times measured are listed in Table C-4-2.

Table C-4-2 Time Measurements for "Good" and "Better" Prime Finders

good	21:17	Ada
better	18:22	Pascal

We describe here why the Pascal implementation runs faster than the previous one, shown in Ada.

The Pascal program "fastprime" is effectively the same algorithm as Ada program "slowprime," except for three minor hand optimizations. First, the various calls to "printprime" and "printmargin" in the Ada program are replaced by inline expansion. Rather than calling the procedures, the Pascal program expands the bodies of these fairly simple procedures "inline" at the place of the calls. This only saves the time for call and return but increases the code size marginally.

The second improvement splits the single, overall while loop into two distinct loops. One loop finds prime numbers and places them into Array "primes," so they can be used as candidate denominators in subsequent tests for primality. Loop number two assumes the Array "primes" to be complete and never bothers writing anything into it. Consequently, since we have implicit knowledge available, the "better" algorithm saves one If Statement during each outer loop execution.

Improvement number three is the substitution of the inner loop by a hand-coded loop. Where is the inner loop? Since the original prime finder has no recursive calls and also no Goto Statement, the inner loop is swiftly identified. On source line 87 in "slowprime" we have the beginning of a While Statement. Line 88 calls "testforprime," which contains the second and last while loop of the whole program. Hence, "testforprime" contains the inner, critical loop. This improvement again performs inline expansion but then replaces the While Statement by a hand-coded loop via Goto Statements. The brute force power of the Goto Statement also eliminates the need for boolean variable "isprime." This speeds up the inner loop body *and* simplifies the termination condition. To our surprise we don't need an If Statement after the inner while loop.

Local procedure "firstprimes" has been left clean and readable; no Goto Statement is used, since its inner loop is executed only a few hundred times. So we can see the clear structure of the algorithm: the inner while loop on lines 51 through 57 of the Pascal program "fastprime" sets the boolean variable "isprime," and the following If Statement tests it.

The inner loop in procedure "lastprimes" is executed orders of magnitudes more often. Therefore, we committed the sin of writing less readable code. Our reward is a 14% time improvement over the slower but more readable version. We also ran the same algorithm to compute the first quarter million prime numbers.

Our two sample solutions have pretentious names alluding to some inherent quality in the algorithm, but do not be deluded by such illusionary names. For pinpointing practical prime numbers, these algorithms are useless, since the running time is too long. We need to be aware that the detection of new primes will necessarily be in the rather large range of integers; consequently, they cannot be processed by the natural arithmetic units of computers. String manipulation simulation must substitute the fast natural arithmetic, thus making each operation, even a simple addition, quite an expensive operation. Worse even, the number of steps per prime would be gargantuan, if we choose to reuse our "good" or "better" programs. But we are lucky; much better algorithms than those are available. For stimulating literature see Knuth [1981], especially pages 389 and following.

```
 1    1  0  0        PROGRAM fastprime( input, output );
 2    2  0  0         CONST
                       max_pindex    =   100;
 3    4  0  0          max_primes    = 32000;
 4    5  0  0         TYPE
                       prange       = 0 .. max_pindex;
 5    7  0  0         VAR
                       test,         { number tested for primality }
                       found,        { so many primes found }
                       pages,        { so many pages printed }
                       max,          { no need to divide beyond max }
                       cand          { divide test by cand }
                                     : integer;
 6   14  0  0          primes        : ARRAY[ prange ] OF integer;
 7   15  0  0          primeindex    : integer; { initialize to -1 }

 8   17  0  0         PROCEDURE printpage;
 9   18  1  0          BEGIN { printpage }
 9   19  1  1           writeln( output );
10   20  1  1           page( output );
11   21  1  1           pages := pages + 1;
12   22  1  1           writeln(' Table of PRIMES,indexed from ',found+1:1,
                         ' .. ',found+500:1,'               PAGE :',pages );
13   24  1  1           writeln( output );
14   25  1  1          END; { printpage }

15   27  0  0         PROCEDURE initialize;
16   28  1  0          BEGIN { initialize }
16   29  1  1           found := 0; { for page eject }
17   30  1  1           pages := 0;
18   31  1  1           printpage;
19   32  1  1           writeln( output );
20   33  1  1           write( output, 1 : 6, '.)' ); { print margin }
21   34  1  1           write( output, 2 : 8 ); { print first prime }
22   35  1  1           primeindex := -1; { prepare to fill first prime }
23   36  1  1           found := 1; { 2 has been found }
24   37  1  1           test := 3; { next number to be tested }
25   38  1  1          END; { initialize }

26   40  0  0         PROCEDURE firstprimes;
27   41  1  0          VAR
                        candindex : prange;
28   43  1  0           isprime   : boolean;
29   44  1  0          BEGIN { firstprimes }
29   45  1  1           WHILE found <= max_pindex + 1 DO
30   46  1  1            BEGIN
```

```
30  47  1  2        max := trunc( sqrt( test ) );
31  48  1  2        candindex := 0;
32  49  1  2        cand := 3;
33  50  1  2        isprime := true;
34  51  1  2        WHILE isprime AND ( cand <= max ) DO
35  52  1  2         BEGIN
35  53  1  3          isprime := test MOD cand <> 0;
36  54  1  3          candindex := candindex + 1;
37  55  1  3          cand := primes[ candindex ];
38  56  1  3         END;
40  57  1  2        {END WHILE}
                    IF isprime THEN
41  59  1  2         BEGIN
41  60  1  3          IF found MOD 10 = 0 THEN
42  61  1  3           BEGIN
42  62  1  4            writeln( output );
43  63  1  4            write( output, found + 1 : 6, '.)' );
44  64  1  4           END;
46  65  1  3          {END IF}
                      write( output, test : 8 );
47  67  1  3          primeindex := primeindex + 1;
48  68  1  3          primes[ primeindex ] := test;
49  69  1  3          found := found + 1;
50  70  1  3         END;
52  71  1  2        {END IF}
                    test := test + 2;
53  73  1  2       END;
55  74  1  1      {END WHILE}
                 END; { firstprimes }

56  77  0  0    PROCEDURE lastprimes;
57  78  1  0     LABEL
                  1, 2, 3;
58  80  1  0     VAR
                  candindex : prange;
59  82  1  0     BEGIN { lastprimes }
59  83  1  1      WHILE found < max_primes DO
60  84  1  1       BEGIN
60  85  1  2        max := trunc( sqrt( test ) );
61  86  1  2        candindex := 0;
62  87  1  2        cand := 3;
63  88  1  2     1: IF cand > max THEN
64  89  1  2         GOTO 2 { is prime }
                    ELSE IF test MOD cand <> 0 THEN
66  91  1  2         BEGIN
66  92  1  3          { could be prime }
                      candindex := candindex + 1;
67  94  1  3          cand := primes[ candindex ];
68  95  1  3          GOTO 1;
69  96  1  3         END
70  97  1  2        ELSE
71  98  1  2         { cand <= max AND test MOD cand = 0, no prime }
```

```
                               GOTO 3;
72  100  1  2                 {END IF}
                          2: { is prime }
                              IF found MOD 10 = 0 THEN
73  103  1  2                  BEGIN
73  104  1  3                   IF found MOD 500 = 0 THEN
74  105  1  3                    printpage;
75  106  1  3                   {END IF}
                                writeln( output );
76  108  1  3                   write( output, found + 1 : 6, '.)' );
77  109  1  3                  END;
79  110  1  2                 {END IF}
                              write( output, test : 8 );
80  112  1  2                 found := found + 1;
81  113  1  2                 { END of logic, where test is prime }

                          3:  test := test + 2;
82  116  1  2                 IF test MOD 3 = 0 THEN
83  117  1  2                  test := test + 2;
84  118  1  2                 {END IF}
                             END;
86  120  1  1               {END WHILE}
                           END; { lastprimes }

87  123  0  0             PROCEDURE terminate;
88  124  1  0              BEGIN { terminate }
88  125  1  1               writeln( output );
89  126  1  1               page( output );
90  127  1  1               writeln( ' largest prime found = ', test - 2 );
91  128  1  1       writeln( ' largest stored prime= ', primes[ max_pindex ] );
92  129  1  1              END; { terminate }

93  131  0  0             BEGIN { fastprime }
93  132  0  1              initialize;
94  133  0  1              firstprimes;
95  134  0  1              lastprimes;
96  135  0  1              terminate;
97  136  0  1             END. { fastprime }
```

Example C-4-3 A Better Prime Number Generator in Pascal

8. These are some of the ways Modula-2 differs from Pascal, as observed in the programs listed up to Chapter 4:
Modula-2 has separate compilation units. Names can be exported from and imported to modules. IO routines must be explicitly imported from predefined system modules. Structured statements in Modula-2 are terminated by the reserved END keyword. Lowercase and uppercase letters are significant.

Chapter 5

It is good programming practice to explicitly define the type "integer" if there is a high likelihood that the source will be ported to another host.

1. Once the new compiler reads a declaration of the form

```
TYPE integer = -nnnnn .. +nnnnn;
```

it has the option of informing the programmer of host machine-specific restrictions. For example, the numbers represented symbolically by "nnnnn" could be too large for the new host. It is good to know this right away, with the first attempt to compile.

2. Symbolic constants are a valuable parameterization tool. Probably this is why Fortran calls its constant declaration a PARAMETER statement. Sometimes it is necessary to change an integer value that specifies some bound, say the upper bound of a range. Chances are that there is a number of For Statements, If Statements, and the like, which all reference the same number. If this number is expressed symbolically, we need to change just that Constant Declaration, nothing more. Otherwise, we have to search through the whole program, possibly other compilation units, and change the same number with the same meaning in all places. Notice that the same number can also occur in the same program with yet a different meaning. These other same numbers may, of course, not be changed. Again, two Constant Declarations make such program modifications easy.

3. The test "c IN ['A'..'Z']" is generally insufficient for the Ebcdic character set. Our program could be reading character data from a file, the contents of which is beyond our control. Certainly we have to suspect that all kinds of strange characters will come in. It is a good habit to program "defensively" and detect all errors early.

4. Use of the number 48 has two disadvantages. First, the reader will see a "magic number"; it takes a while before we understand that 48 also can mean "ord('0')." To make this understanding immediate, we should express it directly. Second, if the program is ever ported to another host with a different character set, the expression "-ord('0')" will still work, while "-48" will have to be modified into the new host-specific magic number.

5. The use of magic numbers in programming language rules is a poor design practice. A designer should instead employ a practice that is easy to remember. For example, it is much easier to remember rules that simply postulate zero, one, or any number of repetitions. MacLennan [1983] calls this principle the "zero-, one-, infinity principle," which is a name quite to the point.

6. The following is a memory map of the Fortran Array "X". The index pairs are written inside the elements, the position numbers above.

```
   1     2     3     4     5     6     7     8     9     10    11    12
+-----+-----+-----+-----+-----+-----+-----+-----+-----+-----+-----+-----+
| 2,3 | 3,3 | 4,3 | 2,4 | 3,4 | 4,4 | 2,5 | 3,5 | 4,5 | 2,6 | 3,6 | 4,6 |
+-----+-----+-----+-----+-----+-----+-----+-----+-----+-----+-----+-----+
                                          ^
                                  X(3,5) |
```

7. The memory map for the Modula-2 array "x" is shown here, again with the indices inside and the offset above.

```
   0     1     2     3     4     5     6     7     8     9     10    11
+-----+-----+-----+-----+-----+-----+-----+-----+-----+-----+-----+-----+
| 2,3 | 2,4 | 2,5 | 2,6 | 3,3 | 3,4 | 3,5 | 3,6 | 4,3 | 4,4 | 4,5 | 4,6 |
+-----+-----+-----+-----+-----+-----+-----+-----+-----+-----+-----+-----+
                                    ^
                            x[3,5] |
```

8. Instead of making functions with side effects inside subscripts illegal, a language designer has two more choices: Either allow side effects and leave the semantics unspecified, or allow side effects and specify exactly the evaluation order.

   If we choose the first alternative, we define a language in which correct object programs are nonportable. The side effect on one target computer might be different on a new target system. It is not a good design policy to give furtherance to nonportable programs.

   If we choose the second alternative, then we require the compiler to generate code that in some instances is inefficient or outright dumb. Rather than overspecifying the language and restricting the translator, we should put the responsibility back into the hand of the villain: a program that relies on side effects is very hard to read, obscure, and hard to maintain. Let it be wrong!

9a. The memory map for the Pascal declarations without rearranging is shown here. Addresses are shown over the memory cells, symbolic names inside. Question marks indicate "holes."

```
  0    1    2    3    4    5    6    7    8    9    10   11   12   13   14   15
+----+----+----+----+----+----+----+----+----+----+----+----+----+----+----+----+
| ?? | ?? | ?? | b1 |         i1          | ?? | ?? | ?? | b2 |         i2          |
+----+----+----+----+----+----+----+----+----+----+----+----+----+----+----+----+
```

9b. The memory map for the rearranged case shows that memory is used more prudently. Since the assumed target machine is not bit-addressable, the compiler had to allocate one byte per boolean. Otherwise, if the compiler had placed more than one boolean into the same byte, it would be necessary to generate shift and mask instructions. In that case the generated code sequence would be slower than in the preceding case 9a.

```
  0    1    2    3    4    5    6    7    8    9
+----+----+----+----+----+----+----+----+----+----+
|         i1          |         i2        | b1 | b2 |
+----+----+----+----+----+----+----+----+----+----+
```

10. The expression to reference the third data field assumes that there will, indeed, be two subsequent nodes. This cannot be checked. Hence the expression is unsafe. The correct syntax for this is: head^.next^.next^.data.

11. It is sufficient to remember the head of the list. Some iterative statement may be used to process the circular list. During each iteration, some temporary Pointer identifies the current node. If this temporary is equal to the head, then the iteration must terminate.

```
temp := head;
REPEAT
 temp := temp^.next;
 { process data, pointed at by "temp" }
UNTIL temp = head;
```

This solution assumes there is at least one element in the circular list.

Chapter 6

1. Mathematically speaking, there is no largest numeric value. Hence, adding any arbitrarily sized integer values cannot cause any logical problems. With physical machines this is different, because machines definitely do have the concept of a largest number. This is either the largest representable, natural integer value in a machine word, or it may be a symbolic string representation of a number, consuming some portion of memory. There is an end to representing values on computers. Once this end has been reached, further increases cause overflow and a loss of information.

2. x := ((a = b) OR (c > d)) OR (c <= e);

3. The original Ada expression cannot be interpreted as Pascal. Redundant parentheses as shown in solution 2 must be added in Pascal.

4. Expression (a+ +b) is only legal in PL/I.

5. Execution on a 32-bit machine would cause no problems, since initialization takes place via the literal 32767. A better programming practice would have been to use the predefined (Ada) symbolic constant "maxint" instead. In that case overflow will occur for the same reason. Corollary: It is a good programming practice to use symbolic constants rather than magic literals!

6. Operator evaluation order does not imply any operand evaluation order. Possible legal code sequences for expression (a*b*c) are

```
PUSH a      PUSH b      PUSH c
PUSH b      PUSH a      PUSH a
MULT        MULT        PUSH b
PUSH c      PUSH c      MULT
MULT        MULT        MULT
```

7. In PL/I, the same as NOT (a > b).

8. In Ada 71 MOD 20 MOD 7. The result yields 4.

9. There are eight levels of operators in Fortran. Sample operators on the eight different levels are listed here in increasing order: .EQV., .OR., .AND., .NOT., .LE., +, *, **.

10. The equivalent Pascal expressions are: i DIV j, and a / b.

11. pl1_expression ::= expression_7 ::= expression_6 ::= expression_5 ::= expression_4 ::= expression_3 ::= expression_2 ::= prefix_expression ::= prefix_op expression_2 ::= -expression_2 ::= -expression_1 ::= -primitive_expression ** expression_2 ::= -a ** expression_2 ::= -a ** prefix_expression ::= -a ** prefix_op expression_2 ::= -a ** -expression_2 ::= -a ** -primitive_expression ::= -a ** -b

12. Pascal has no short circuit operators, but the same logic can be achieved by nested If Statements.

```
IF a <> 0 THEN
 IF ( b / a ) > max THEN
  c := max;
 {END IF}
{END IF}
{ -- another example }
IF pin = NIL THEN
 invalid_data
ELSE IF pin^.value = 0.0 THEN
 invalid_data;
{END IF}
```

13. Adding redundant parentheses in a complex expression exposes the semantics. The operator hierarchy becomes visible, so the source is more readable.

14. The expression "integer(nextchar)" cannot be a qualified expression, since the required single quote mark is missing. But if we assume that the object "nextchar" is misleadingly of a subtype of integer, then the expression represents a legal type conversion.

15. Pascal has an obvious shortcoming here. A conversion function, ORD, is included, but the reverse function is not defined. There is a remedy here, even though "dirty programming" must be used. A sample variant Record declaration and references are shown.

```
TYPE
 trick_type =
  RECORD
   CASE boolean OF
    false: ( day  : work_day_type );
    true:  ( i    : integer );
   {END CASE}
  END; {RECORD}
 VAR
  trick  : trick_type;
 BEGIN { program part }
  i := ord( work_day );
  { other computations }
  trick.i := i;
  work_day := trick.day;
```

After the last assignment "workday" receives the proper value, if and only if the compiler that was used maps the integer field "i" in the variant Record of type "tricktype" in a certain way over the field "day." With some compilers this trick works; with others, a number of dummy fields must be specified as well until the mapping works. Since the solution depends on the compiler chosen, and on the programming language, we refer to this style as "dirty programming."

16. The associativities are as follows:

```
OP1 is left associative
OP2 is right associative
OP3 is not clear, should be defined via context condition
OP4 is left associative.
```

17. Procedure "operandorder" is rewritten in Pascal with minor modifications in output character strings. The changes are necessary, because the output should identify the source language, in this case Pascal.

```
 1    1 0 0        PROGRAM assoc( output );

 2    3 0 0         FUNCTION five( name : char ) : integer;
 3    4 1 0          BEGIN { five }
 3    5 1 1           write( output, name, ', ' );
 4    6 1 1           five := 5;
 5    7 1 1          END; { five }

 6    9 0 0         PROCEDURE operandorder;
 7   10 1 0          BEGIN { operandorder }
 7   11 1 1           write( output, ' Pascal + arg sequence ');
 8   12 1 1           IF five('1')+five('2')+five('3') <> 15 THEN
 9   13 1 1            writeln( ' wrong compiler ' )
                      ELSE
10   15 1 1            writeln;
11   16 1 1           {END IF}
                      write( output, ' Pascal - arg sequence ' );
12   18 1 1           IF five('1')-five('2')-five('3') <> -5 THEN
13   19 1 1            writeln( ' wrong compiler ' )
                      ELSE
14   21 1 1            writeln;
15   22 1 1           {END IF}
                      write( output, ' Pascal * arg sequence ' );
16   24 1 1           IF five('1') * five('2') * five('3') <> 125 THEN
17   25 1 1            writeln( ' wrong compiler ' )
                      ELSE
18   27 1 1            writeln;
19   28 1 1           {END IF}
                      write( output, ' Pascal / arg sequence ' );
20   30 1 1           IF five('1') DIV five('2') DIV five('3') <> 0 THEN
21   31 1 1            writeln( ' wrong compiler ' )
                      ELSE
22   33 1 1            writeln;
23   34 1 1           {END IF}
                     END; { operandorder }

24   37 0 0         BEGIN { assoc }
24   38 0 1          operandorder;
25   39 0 1         END { assoc }.
```

```
Pascal + arg sequence 3, 2, 1,
Pascal - arg sequence 3, 2, 1,
Pascal * arg sequence 3, 2, 1,
Pascal / arg sequence 3, 2, 1,
```

Example C-6-1 Order of Evaluation of Operands in Pascal

18. We assume that the Pascal procedure "operandorder" generates the output "Pascal + arg sequence 3, 2, 1." This may surprise us at first. Operands are evaluated in exactly the reversed order of their textual appearance in the source. The question now arises, does that Pascal compiler still implement the language correctly? We have to learn here to distinguish between operator associativity and operand evaluation. Pascal specifies that multiple dyadic operators are left associative. From this we cannot make any assumptions about operand evaluation. Evaluation order for dyadic OPERANDS is implementation-dependent. See the standard ANSI [1983b], section 6.7.2.1.
    In the following, we give a hypothetical stack machine instruction sequence, which a language translator may generate from source expression "1+2+3," an expression similar to the ones under discussion.

```
PUSH_LIT 3
PUSH_LIT 2
PUSH_LIT 1
ADD         -- 3 and (2+1) on top
ADD         -- (3+(2+1)) on top
```

Add Operator is Left Associative, Operands Emitted in Reversed Order

Chapter 7

1. Remember that Pascal has no WHEN OTHERS Clause. Also a Pascal program will abort if the case expression does not match any of the case selectors during run time. So the safest method is to enumerate all possible values. For integer types this is prohibitive. Instead an integer subrange type should be used.

2. Fortran is not limited in that sense. Any Case Statement can be simulated via nested If Statements. Note that also all If Statements can be simulated via Case Statements.

3. Since the THEN keyword is followed by a semicolon, the body of the Then Clause is empty. Consequently, the PUT LIST statement is executed each time the loop body is executed. So the message HELLO appears ten times.

4. The semicolon after procedure call "rest" is illegal.

5. Even in Fortran it is illegal to branch into the body of a block If Statement from the outside. So statement "GOTO 10" is illegal.

6. The idea of the more complicated grammar is to introduce two kinds of If Statements, those with an Else Clause and those without.

```
statement           ::= if_statement
                      | other_statement

if_statement        ::= IF condition THEN
                         statement
                      | IF condition THEN
                         nested
                        ELSE
                         statement

nested              ::= IF condition THEN
                         nested
                        ELSE
                         nested
                      | other_statement
```

Grammar for Unambiguous If Statement

7. Since the Case Statement is nothing but a special "case" of If Statement, the claim is trivially true. These restricted If Statements have the following form. In all conditions the "expression" is identical and assumed to have no side effect.

```
IF expression = literal_1 THEN
 do_action_1;
ELSIF expression = literal_2 THEN
 do_action_2;
ELSIF expression = literal_n THEN
 do_action_n;
ELSE
 catch_the_rest;
END IF;
```

Schema of Restricted If Statement

8. The equivalent If Statement is

```
IF nn >= 'a' AND nn <= 'z' THEN
 scan_ident;
ELSIF nn >= '0' AND nn <= '9' THEN
 get_base;
 scan_number( base );
ELSIF nn = ''' THEN
 scan_char_literal;
ELSIF nn = '"' THEN
 scan_string_literal;
ELSE
 scan_special_symbol;
END IF;
```

9. Formally speaking, it is correct that "all If Statements can be expressed by equivalent Case Statements." Since the type of the case expression can be boolean, the if condition can be copied literally, and then be compared with the case choices "true" and "false." In many situations the Case Statements so constructed will look ridiculously unreadable. For a demonstration see Exercise 10.

10. The equivalent, less readable Case Statement is

```
CASE a > b AND c /= d IS
 WHEN  true => do_action_1;
 WHEN false =>
  CASE e < f IS
   WHEN  true => do_action_2;
   WHEN false =>
    CASE func( a, g ) IS
     WHEN  true => do_action_3;
     WHEN false => do_action_4;
    END CASE;
  END CASE;
END CASE;
```

Chapter 8

1. When the program has completed execution, the values are as follows: I=11, J=10, K=6, L=5, and N=50.

2. After execution of the program SECOND, the values are as follows: I=11, J=10, K=5, N=0, and L is undefined.

3. Since it is not known exactly how many iterations will be necessary to compute the "sine" of argument "x," a While loop should be used.

4. Since at the start of the loop the number of iterations is computable, a For Loop is the appropriate statement to use. Note that the loop body clearly iterates from 1 to 10000.

5. Program "binarysearch" in Example C-8-1 includes the desired function "binsearch." All other Ada code provides "binsearch" with a functional environment. "Fillkey" initializes "key" in a trivial way, and "trace" prints the output conveniently.

   The binary search algorithm is quite simple. However, a couple of tricky spots are easily overlooked. Twice we are comparing "wanted" with a key element in the table. If we replace the <= or the >= operator with the < and > operators respectively, the whole algorithm becomes nonfunctional. "Binsearch" will loop infinitely. This represents quite a radical change for a minor difference!

   Also, if we replace the loop termination condition "first<=last" by a test for strictly less than, then the loop always terminates, but sometimes with the wrong value for "temp." So with this minor alteration "binsearch" would return an out-of-range index every once in a while.

```
                |WITH text_io; USE text_io; -- Solution exercise 5.
                |PROCEDURE binary_search IS
          1     |  min        : CONSTANT integer := 0;
     10   1     |  max        : CONSTANT integer := 200;
     10   1     |  TYPE span IS RANGE min .. max;
          1     |  key        : ARRAY( span ) OF integer;
    211   1     | PROCEDURE fillkey IS
          2     |  BEGIN -- fillkey
          2     |   FOR i IN min .. max LOOP
 5        2  1  |    key( i ) := i * 100;
13        2  2  |   END LOOP;
14        2  1  |  END fillkey;
14        1     |
14        1     | FUNCTION bin_search( wanted : integer ) RETURN integer IS
16   11   2     |   first,
16   11   2     |   last,
16   11   2     |   temp     : integer;
16   14   2     |  BEGIN -- bin_search
16        2     |   first := min;
20        2  1  |   last := max;
23        2  1  |   WHILE first <= last LOOP
27        2  1  |    temp := ( first + last ) / 2;
34        2  2  |    IF key( temp ) >= wanted THEN
```

```
24   42        2  2 |    last := integer'pred( temp );
25   46        2  3 |   END IF;
26   46        2  2 |   IF key( temp ) <= wanted THEN
27   54        2  2 |    first := integer'succ( temp );
28   58        2  3 |   END IF;
29   58        2  2 |  END LOOP;
30   59        2  1 |  RETURN temp;
31   64        2  1 | END bin_search;
32   64        1    |
33   64        1    | PROCEDURE trace( wanted : integer ) IS
34   66   11   2    | BEGIN -- trace
35   66        2    |  put( " index of " );
36   69        2  1 |  put( integer'image( wanted ) );
37   71        2  1 |  put( " is: " );
38   73        2  1 |  put_line( bin_search( wanted ) );
39   80        2  1 | END trace;
40   80        1    |
41   80        1    | BEGIN -- binary_search
42   82        1    |  fillkey;
43   86        1  1 |  trace( 500 );
44   90        1  1 |  trace( 9800 );
45   94        1  1 | END binary_search;
```

Example C-8-1 Binary Search in Ada

6. If the loop is to be executed only once for every four array elements, we have to look at four elements during each iteration. So the array must provide four "phantom" elements to ensure that no array bounds violations will occur during tests. A sample solution is listed in Example C-8-2.

```
1                      |WITH text_io; USE text_io;
2                      |PROCEDURE linear_search IS
3                1     | first    : CONSTANT integer := -3;
4         10     1     | last     : CONSTANT integer := 1000;
5         10     1     | a        : ARRAY( first .. last ) OF integer;
6         1014   1     | index    : integer;
7         1015   1     |
8         1015   1     | FUNCTION quadrupled(
9                2     |  wanted : IN integer ) RETURN integer IS
10        11     2     | i        : integer;
11        12     2     | BEGIN -- quadrupled
12               2     |  a( 0 ) := wanted;
13        7      2  1  |  i := last;
14        10     2  1  |  LOOP
15        10     2  1  |   IF a( i ) = wanted THEN
16        18     2  2  |    RETURN i;
17        23     2  3  |   ELSIF a( i - 1 ) = wanted THEN
18        34     2  2  |    RETURN i -1;
19        41     2  3  |   ELSIF a( i - 2 ) = wanted THEN
20        52     2  2  |    RETURN i - 2;
21        59     2  3  |   ELSIF a( i - 3 ) = wanted THEN
22        70     2  2  |    RETURN i - 3;
```

```
 77     2 3 |   ELSE
 77     2 2 |    i := i - 4;
 83     2 3 |   END IF;
 83     2 2 |  END LOOP;
 84     2 1 | END quadrupled;
 84     1   |
 84     1   |BEGIN -- linear_search
 86     1   | FOR i IN first .. last LOOP
 91     1 1 |  a( i ) := 2*last + 4*i; -- arbitrarily
103     1 2 | END LOOP; -- array initialized, ascending
104     1 1 | put_line( " quadrupled" );
107     1 1 | FOR i IN 1 .. 50 LOOP
111     1 1 |  index := quadrupled( i );
117     1 2 | END LOOP;
118     1 1 |END linear_search;
```

Example C-8-2 Linear Search in Ada

7. The Fortran solution listed in Example C-8-3 computes the square root of the passed argument "ARG" with a precision of 10**(-7).

```
         PROGRAM ROOT
10       FORMAT ( ' ROOT OF ', I3, ' = ', F15.12 )
         DO 20 I = 1, 10
          WRITE( 6, 10 ) I, SQROOT( I )
20       CONTINUE
         END

         REAL FUNCTION SQROOT( ARG )
         INTEGER ARG
         REAL OLD, NEW
         OLD = ARG
         NEW = 1.0
10       IF ( ABS( NEW - OLD ) .GT. 0.0000001 ) THEN
          OLD = NEW
          NEW = ( OLD + ( ARG / OLD ) ) / 2.0
          GOTO 10
         END IF
         SQROOT = NEW
         END
```

Example C-8-3 Newton's Square Root in Fortran

Chapter 9

1a. The language must be Fortran. CALL indicates that the choice is either PL/I or Fortran; the lack of the semicolon excludes PL/I.

1b. Again the CALL makes PL/I and Fortran candidate languages. Since the source contains a semicolon, the language must be PL/I.

1c. Possible choices are Pascal and Ada. Lack of the semicolon indicates Pascal. Note that there are some contexts in which even a Pascal procedure Call Statement must be followed by a semicolon, but in such cases it is not part of the Call Statement. In Ada, on the other hand, any statement must be terminated with the semicolon.

1d. Here the language is clearly Ada, visible by the named parameter substitution.

2. Since no arithmetic operation is performed on the arguments of "min," no side effects such as overflow are possible. Hence the two statements are equivalent.

3. The call to procedure "namedparameters" contains three kinds of passing IN parameters. Formal parameters "c1" and "c2" are associated with their actual parameters by position and receive the values 'P' and 'e' respectively. Parameters "c3" and "c6" are not associated with an actual parameters; but their declarations include the default values 'a' and '.'. So only "c4" and "c5" need to be initialized. We see in the Procedure Call Statement that they receive their initial value through named parameter association, even though the order in the call is a different permutation than in the declaration. The final value printed, included in double quotes here for clarity, is "Peace.."

4. All parameter passing in this program is by reference. The first Procedure Call Statement, on line 29, causes the formal parameter "x" to become an alias of "a" and "y" to become an alias of "b." The second call, "nested2refs(x,a);" on line 23, aliases "x" with "i" and "a" with "j." Since "x" is already an alias of "a" it follows that "i," "j," "a," and "x" are all aliases. The Assignment Statement "b:=j;" on line 13 now assigns the value of "j," which is -1 to "b" and to its alias "y." Hence all six variables hold the same value at the moment of printing. The output is listed as follows.

```
a =        -1
b =        -1
i =        -1
j =        -1
x =        -1
y =        -1
```

5. The explicit CALL keyword identifies the type of statement more directly. The absence of the CALL keyword eliminates the unnecessary distinction between user-defined procedures and system-predefined procedures. Notice that in Fortran the intrinsic Output Statement "WRITE" requires no CALL keyword for identification as a procedure call.

Chapter 10

1. To simplify matters, let us assume that I, J, K, TABLE[K], L, and TABLE[L] are not already aliases for one another. All are distinct variables. Statements a.) and b.) then perform the desired swap function. In the last statement the power of the by-name passing mechanism becomes suicidal. Rather than exchanging L with TABLE[L], statement c.) swaps L and TABLE[TABLE[L]].

2. There are four errors. An IN parameter cannot be assigned; hence the assignment to "a" is illegal. An OUT parameter cannot be referenced; so use of "b" is not possible. Also the unary minus operator may not be used in the middle of an expression. Hence b*-1.5 is incorrect. Additionally, the type of 1.5 is incompatible with the integer type operands.

3. While it is permissible in Pascal to assign new results to parameters passed by value, Ada does not permit any assignment to IN parameters.

4. While a Pascal implementation must copy all values of a complex value parameter, in Ada it is sufficient to pass an array, used as IN parameter, by address. No copying is required for Ada.

5. Since we wish to maintain the recursive algorithm, rather than replace the recursion via iteration, "arg" must be modified inside "fact." This modification must have the same effect as if "arg" had been passed as an actual parameter. Hence for each call "arg" must be decremented, while after the return the old value of "arg" must be preserved.

```
PROGRAM noparams( output );
 var
   arg  : integer;
 function fact : integer;
  begin { fact }
   if arg = 0 then
    fact := 1
   else
    begin
     arg := arg - 1;
     fact := fact * ( arg + 1 );
     arg := arg + 1;
    end;
   {end if}
  end { fact };
 begin { noparams }
  arg := 10;
  writeln( ' fact(', arg:1, ') = ', fact );
 end { noparams }.
```

Example C-10-1 Factorial without Parameters in Pascal

6. Actual parameters that correspond to formal name parameters are not evaluated at the place of call. For this reason the invocation of function "algolsum1" will not abort. Moreover, we see that the first reference of any of the parameters is the

assignment to "i" on line 11 via the statement "k: = 3;". Since the text of the actual parameter substitutes the formal parameter, the Assignment Statement is equivalent to setting "i" to 3. Subsequent references of "a[i]," therefore, are perfectly legal, because index 3 is within legal bounds.

7. The Pascal program in Example C-10-2 produces an output that indicates if reference parameters are passed by address or value result.

```
 1    1  0  0    PROGRAM byreferenceorvalueresult( output );
 2    2  0  0     VAR
                   a : integer;

 3    5  0  0     PROCEDURE reforvalueresult(
 3    6  1  0      VAR
                    x : integer );
 4    8  1  0     BEGIN { reforvalueresult }
 4    9  1  1      writeln( output, ' old x = ', x );
 5   10  1  1      x := 200;
 6   11  1  1      writeln( output, ' new x = ', x );
 7   12  1  1      writeln( output, ' global= ', a );
 8   13  1  1      IF ( x = 200 ) AND ( a = 200 ) THEN
 9   14  1  1       writeln( output, ' Ref param passing by address' )
                   ELSE IF ( x = 200 ) AND ( a = 100 ) THEN
11   16  1  1       writeln( output, ' Ref param pass by value/result' )
                   ELSE
12   18  1  1       writeln( output, ' Magic way to pass ref params' );
13   19  1  1     END; { reforvalueresult }

14   21  0  0    BEGIN { byreferenceorvalueresult }
14   22  0  1     a := 100;
15   23  0  1     writeln( output, ' old a = ', a );
16   24  0  1     reforvalueresult( a );
17   25  0  1     writeln( output, ' new a = ', a );
18   26  0  1    END { byreferenceorvalueresult }.
```

Example C-10-2 Check Reference Parameter Passing Method

Chapter 11

1. A sample listing of a recursive descent parser for language EL1 is shown in Example C-11-1. The implementation language is Pascal.

```
 1    1 0 0      PROGRAM el1( input, output );
 2    2 0 0       VAR
                   found  : char;

 3    5 0 0       PROCEDURE scan( wanted : char );
 4    6 1 0        BEGIN { scan }
 4    7 1 1         read( input, found );
 5    8 1 1         IF wanted <> found THEN
 6    9 1 1          writeln( output, ' wanted char=''', wanted, '''' );
 7   10 1 1         {END IF}
                   END; { scan }

 8   13 0 0       PROCEDURE t;
 9   14 1 0        BEGIN { t }
 9   15 1 1         { don't know, whether found 'A' or 'B' }
                    IF found = 'A' THEN
10   17 1 1          BEGIN
10   18 1 2           read( input, found ); { skip 'A' }
11   19 1 2           t;
12   20 1 2           scan( 'B' );
13   21 1 2          END;
15   22 1 1         {END IF}
                   END; { t }

16   25 0 0       PROCEDURE s;
17   26 1 0        BEGIN { s }
17   27 1 1         scan( 'A' ); { need at least 1 'A' }
18   28 1 1         read( input, found );
19   29 1 1         t;
20   30 1 1        END; { s }

21   32 0 0       BEGIN { el1 }
21   33 0 1        s;
22   34 0 1        IF not eoln( input ) THEN
23   35 0 1         writeln( output, ' garbage after source ignored' );
24   36 0 1        {END IF}
                  END { el1 }.
```

Example C-11-1 Recursive Descent Parser for EL1

2. Having an end indicator provides a convenient termination condition. Language L1 has such a terminator. With a minor rewrite of EG1, it is also easy to design a recursive descent parser. We choose the following, equivalent grammar.

```
s ::= AtB$
t ::= AtB | LAMBDA
```

Grammar EG1', Equivalent to EG1

Notice that the implementation of an iterative parser would be much more appropriate for the simple language L(EL1). Simply read all 'A' symbols and count. Then read all 'B' symbols and count. If both counts are at least one and equal, the string is accepted; otherwise, report an error.

3. The recursive definition for "power2" is borrowed from the ideas already encountered in program "factorial." If the argument is 0, then the result is 1. Otherwise, the result is 2*power2(argument-1). Note that it is implicitly assumed that arg is greater than or equal to zero; otherwise the scheme would be infinitely recursive.

4. A Pascal implementation of "recursivepower2" is listed in Example C-11-2. Function "power2" performs all checks necessary to verify implicit assumptions. Once they are verified, the nested function "pow2" is called. "Pow2" then does not check anything; the argument is guaranteed to be in the right range.

```
 1   1 0 0     PROGRAM recursivepower2( input, output );
 2   2 0 0      CONST
                 maxexponent    = 14; { 2**14=16384 on 16-bit }
 3   4 0 0      VAR
                 i              : integer;

 4   7 0 0      FUNCTION power2( arg : integer ) : integer;

 5   9 1 0       FUNCTION pow2( arg : integer ) : integer;
 6  10 2 0        BEGIN { pow2 }
 6  11 2 1         IF arg = 0 THEN
 7  12 2 1          pow2 := 1
                   ELSE
 8  14 2 1          pow2 := 2*pow2( arg-1 );
 9  15 2 1         {END IF}
                  END; { pow2 }

10  18 1 0       BEGIN { power2 }
10  19 1 1        IF arg < 0 THEN
11  20 1 1         power2 := 1
                  ELSE IF arg > maxexponent THEN
13  22 1 1         power2 := 1
                  ELSE
14  24 1 1         power2 := pow2( arg );
15  25 1 1        {END IF}
                 END; { power2 }

16  28 0 0      BEGIN { recursivepower2 }
16  29 0 1       FOR i := 1 TO 15 DO
17  30 0 1        writeln( ' 2**', i, ' = ', power2( i ) );
18  31 0 1       {END FOR}
                END { recursivepower2 }.
```

Example C-11-2 Recursive Power2 Program

5. Solution of fifth exercise:

```
                   |WITH text_io; USE text_io;
                   |PROCEDURE non_recursive_power2 IS
              1    |  maxstack  : CONSTANT integer := 14;
         10   1    |  i         : integer;
         11   1    |
         11   1    | FUNCTION power2( arg : integer ) RETURN integer IS
         11   2    |  TYPE stackrange  IS RANGE 0 .. maxstack;
         11   2    |  TYPE stackelem   IS
         11   2    |   RECORD
         11   2    |    val         : integer;
         11   2    |    ret         : integer;
         11   2    |   END RECORD;
         11   2    |  top          : stackrange;
         12   2    |  stack        : ARRAY( stackrange ) OF stackelem;
         42   2    |
         42   2    | BEGIN -- power2
              2    |  stack( 0 ).ret := 3;
    9         2  1 |  IF arg = 0 THEN
   13         2  1 |   stack( 0 ).val := 1;
   20         2  2 |  ELSE
   20         2  1 |   top := 0;
   26         2  2 |   stack( 0 ).val := arg;
   33         2  2 |<<label1>>
   33         2  2 |   top := integer'succ( top );
   39         2  2 |   stack( top ).val := stack( top - 1 ).val - 1;
   55         2  2 |   stack( top ).ret := 2; -- label 2
   63         2  2 |   IF stack( top ).val > 0 THEN
   72         2  2 |    GOTO label1; -- call recursively
   73         2  3 |   END IF;
   73         2  2 |   stack( top ).val := 1; -- for 2**0
   80         2  2 |<<label2>>
   80         2  2 |   top := integer'pred( top );
   86         2  2 |   stack( top ).val := stack( top + 1 ).val * 2;
  102         2  2 |   IF stack( top ).ret = 2 THEN
  112         2  2 |    GOTO label2;
  113         2  3 |   END IF;
  113         2  2 |  END IF;
  113         2  1 |<<label3>>
  113         2  1 |  RETURN stack( top ).val;
  123         2  1 | END power2;
  123         1    |
  123         1    | BEGIN -- non_recursive_power2
  125         1    |  FOR i IN 0 .. 14 LOOP
  130         1  1 |   put_line( power2( i ) );
  136         1  2 |  END LOOP;
  137         1  1 | END non_recursive_power2;
```

Example C-11-3 Non Recursive Power of 2 in Ada

C-11-3 is a sample solution for "nonrecursive power2," implemented in Ada. This program uses the same algorithm as does "recursivepower2," but without calling any subprogram recursively.

6. The special case Ackermann function a(x,2) is identical to the function "powerof 2(arg)," yielding two to the power of "arg."

7. Emitting the full name or full numeric value for an operand in "expressiong4" requires only a minor, cosmetic change. In procedure "numericliteral" of the Ada solution we insert "put(next);" after line 68 and remove line 75. Analogously, add "put(next);" after line 97 in procedure "name" of the Ada solution and remove line 100.

8. in either solution the associativity of the binary operator + and - is left to right, as required by the language definitions. This is guaranteed by the sequential nature of the While Statement used to parse any number of these binary operators. In other words, the second '+' is processed only after all work for the first '+' has been completed.

9. To replace left associativity by right associativity we use a modified grammar for the parser. The rule for "simpleexpression" is

```
simple_expression    ::= term [ + simple_expression ]
                       | term [ - simple_expression ]
```

which will be mapped into a recursive call. A partial programming solution to this follows:

```
PROCEDURE simple_expression IS
 remember : character := ' ';
 BEGIN -- simple_expression
  -- process unary operators
  term;
  IF next = '+' OR next = '-' THEN
   remember := next; -- for later semantics
   getnext( next );  -- skip + or -
   simple_expression;
   -- do semantics
  END IF;
 END simple_expression;
```

Example C-11-4

10. Following Flanders's solution blindly will indeed decrease the readability of the source program. The obvious solution to this side effect problem is to modularize again. Typically, the statement lists between the recursive calls can be relocated into new procedures, and the respective source code then be replaced by a call to the new procedure.

This way the readability is reinstated to almost the quality of the original programming solution with explicit forward declarations, but the additional procedures incur a new call and return overhead in terms of execution time.

11. A "hilbert" implementation in Ada follows in Example C-11-5.

```
                 |WITH text_io; USE text_io;
                 |PROCEDURE hilbert IS
             1   |  low          : CONSTANT :=  0;
        10   1   |  high         : CONSTANT := 32;
        10   1   |  TYPE screenrange IS RANGE low .. high;
             1   |  screen : ARRAY(screenrange, screenrange) OF character;
      1099   1   |  degree,      -- degree of current Hilbert curve
        10   1   |  unit,        -- unit length of plot line
        10   1   |  origx,       -- x-coordinate of origin
        10   1   |  origy,       -- y-coordinate of origin
        10   1   |  newx,        -- x-coordinate of new pin position
        10   1   |  newy,        -- y-coordinate of new pin position
        10   1   |  oldx,        -- x-coordinate of current pin position
        10   1   |  oldy,        -- y-coordinate of current pin position
        10   1   |  max_degree   -- we don't want curve of higher degree
        10   1   |               : integer;
      1108   1   |
      1108   1   | PROCEDURE init IS
             2   |  BEGIN -- init
             2   |   FOR i IN low .. high LOOP
  5          2 1 |    FOR j IN low .. high LOOP
  9          2 2 |     IF i=low OR i=high OR j=low OR j=high THEN
 25          2 3 |      screen( i, j ) := '.';
 35          2 4 |     ELSE
 35          2 3 |      screen( i, j ) := ' ';
 46          2 4 |     END IF;
 46          2 3 |    END LOOP;
 47          2 2 |   END LOOP;
 48          2 1 |  END init;
 48          1   |
 48          1   | PROCEDURE display( degree : integer ) IS
 50    11    2   |  BEGIN -- display
 50          2   |   FOR i IN low .. high LOOP
 55          2 1 |    put( "  " );
 57          2 2 |    FOR j IN low .. high LOOP
 61          2 2 |     put( screen( i, j ) );
 71          2 3 |    END LOOP;
 72          2 2 |    put_line( " " );
 75          2 2 |   END LOOP;
 76          2 1 |   put_line( " " );
 79          2 1 |   put_line( "    Hilbert  Curves  of  Degrees  1 .." &
                       integer'image( degree ) );
 84          2 1 |   put_line( " " );
 87          2 1 |  END display;
 87          1   |
 87          1   | PROCEDURE plot(
 89          2   |  newx, newy : IN integer;
 89    12    2   |  oldx, oldy : IN OUT integer ) IS
 89    14    2   |  BEGIN -- plot
 89          2   |   IF newx > oldx THEN
 94          2 1 |    FOR i IN oldx .. newx LOOP
 98          2 2 |     screen( newy, i ) := '*';
```

```
 52  108        2  3 |    oldx := newx;
 53  111        2  3 |    END LOOP;
 54  112        2  2 |   ELSIF newx < oldx THEN
 55  117        2  1 |    FOR i IN newx .. oldx LOOP
 56  121        2  2 |     screen( newy, i ) := '*';
 57  131        2  3 |     oldx := newx;
 58  134        2  3 |    END LOOP;
 59  135        2  2 |   ELSIF newy > oldy THEN
 60  140        2  1 |    FOR j IN oldy .. newy LOOP
 61  144        2  2 |     screen( j, newx ) := '*';
 62  154        2  3 |     oldy := newy;
 63  157        2  3 |    END LOOP;
 64  158        2  2 |   ELSIF newy < oldy THEN
 65  163        2  1 |    FOR j IN newy .. oldy LOOP
 66  167        2  2 |     screen( j, newx ) := '*';
 67  177        2  3 |     oldy := newy;
 68  180        2  3 |    END LOOP;
 69  181        2  2 |   END IF;
 70  181        2  1 |  END plot;
 71  181        1    |
 72  181        1    | PROCEDURE b( degree : integer );
 73  183    11  1    |
 74  183    11  1    | PROCEDURE c( degree : integer );
 75  183    11  1    |
 76  183    11  1    | PROCEDURE d( degree : integer );
 77  183    11  1    |
 78  183    11  1    | PROCEDURE a( degree : integer ) IS
 79  183    11  2    |  BEGIN -- a
 80  183        2    |   IF degree > 0 THEN
 81  188        2  1 |    d( degree - 1 ); newx := newx - unit;
 82  200        2  2 |    plot( newx, newy, oldx, oldy );
 83  208        2  2 |    a( degree - 1 ); newy := newy - unit;
 84  220        2  2 |    plot( newx, newy, oldx, oldy );
 85  228        2  2 |    a( degree - 1 ); newx := newx + unit;
 86  240        2  2 |    plot( newx, newy, oldx, oldy );
 87  248        2  2 |    b( degree - 1 );
 88  255        2  2 |   END IF;
 89  255        2  1 |  END a;
 90  255        1    |
 91  255        1    | PROCEDURE b( degree : integer ) IS
 92  257    11  2    |  BEGIN -- b
 93  257        2    |   IF degree > 0 THEN
 94  262        2  1 |    c( degree - 1 ); newy := newy + unit;
 95  274        2  2 |    plot( newx, newy, oldx, oldy );
 96  282        2  2 |    b( degree - 1 ); newx := newx + unit;
 97  294        2  2 |    plot( newx, newy, oldx, oldy );
 98  302        2  2 |    b( degree - 1 ); newy := newy - unit;
 99  314        2  2 |    plot( newx, newy, oldx, oldy );
100  322        2  2 |    a( degree - 1 );
101  329        2  2 |   END IF;
102  329        2  1 |  END b;
103  329        1    |
```

```
104  329        1    | PROCEDURE c( degree : integer ) IS
105  331   11   2    | BEGIN -- c
106  331        2    |   IF degree > 0 THEN
107  336        2  1 |     b( degree - 1 ); newx := newx + unit;
108  348        2  2 |     plot( newx, newy, oldx, oldy );
109  356        2  2 |     c( degree - 1 ); newy := newy + unit;
110  368        2  2 |     plot( newx, newy, oldx, oldy );
111  376        2  2 |     c( degree - 1 ); newx := newx - unit;
112  388        2  2 |     plot( newx, newy, oldx, oldy );
113  396        2  2 |     d( degree - 1 );
114  403        2  2 |   END IF;
115  403        2  1 | END c;
116  403        1    |
117  403        1    | PROCEDURE d( degree : integer ) IS
118  405   11   2    | BEGIN -- d
119  405        2    |   IF degree > 0 THEN
120  410        2  1 |     a( degree - 1 ); newy := newy - unit;
121  422        2  2 |     plot( newx, newy, oldx, oldy );
122  430        2  2 |     d( degree - 1 ); newx := newx - unit;
123  442        2  2 |     plot( newx, newy, oldx, oldy );
124  450        2  2 |     d( degree - 1 ); newy := newy + unit;
125  462        2  2 |     plot( newx, newy, oldx, oldy );
126  470        2  2 |     c( degree - 1 );
127  477        2  2 |   END IF;
128  477        2  1 | END d;
129  477        1    |
130  477        1    | BEGIN -- hilbert
131  479        1    | max_degree := 0;
132  483        1  1 | WHILE max_degree < 3 LOOP
133  487        1  1 |   max_degree := max_degree + 1;
134  492        1  2 |   degree := 0;
135  495        1  2 |   init;
136  498        1  2 |   unit := high;
137  501        1  2 |   origx := unit / 2;
138  506        1  2 |   origy := unit / 2;
139  511        1  2 |   WHILE degree < max_degree LOOP
140  515        1  2 |     degree := degree + 1;
141  520        1  3 |     unit := unit / 2;
142  525        1  3 |     origx := origx + unit / 2;
143  532        1  3 |     origy := origy + unit / 2;
144  539        1  3 |     oldx := origx;
145  542        1  3 |     oldy := origy;
146  545        1  3 |     newx := oldx;
147  548        1  3 |     newy := oldy;
148  551        1  3 |     a( degree );
149  555        1  3 |   END LOOP;
150  556        1  2 |   display( max_degree );
151  560        1  2 | END LOOP;
152  561        1  1 | END hilbert;
```

Example C-11-5 Listing of Hilbert Curve Plotter

The output generated by the program in Example C-11-5 follows. Notice that each plot draws all Hilbert curves on one screen, up the current, maximum degree. This is why we see intersecting curves; one Hilbert curve alone never intersects with itself. The two indications about unit length have been inserted into the curves manually; the program does not output these.

```
.................................
.                               .
.                               .
.                               .
.                               .
.       |<--- Unit ---->|       .
.       |               |       .
.       v               v       .
.       *****************       .
.       *                       .
.       *                       .
.       *                       .
.       *                       .
.       *                       .
.       *                       .
.       *                       .
.       *                       .
.       *                       .
.       *                       .
.       *                       .
.       *                       .
.       *                       .
.       *                       .
.       *                       .
.       *****************       .
.                               .
.                               .
.                               .
.                               .
.                               .
.                               .
.                               .
.................................
```

Hilbert Curves of Degrees 1 .. 1

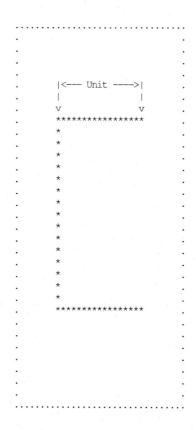

```
.................................
.           |< Unit>|           .
.           |       |           .
.           v       v           .
.   *****************       *   .
.   *               *       *   .
.   *               *       *   .
.   *               *       *   .
.   *   *****************   *   .
.   *   *           *       *   .
.   *   *           *       *   .
.   *   *           *       *   .
.   *********       *********   .
.       *   *                   .
.       *   *                   .
.       *   *                   .
.       *   *                   .
.       *   *                   .
.       *   *                   .
.       *   *                   .
.   *********       *********   .
.   *   *           *       *   .
.   *   *           *       *   .
.   *   *           *       *   .
.   *   *****************   *   .
.   *               *       *   .
.   *               *       *   .
.   *               *       *   .
.   *****************       *   .
.                               .
.                               .
.                               .
.................................
```

Hilbert Curves of Degrees 1 .. 2

```
.................................
.                               .
. *********   *********   ***** .
. *       *   *       *   *     .
. * ***************** *   * *   .
. * *     *   *     * *   * *   .
. *****   *****   *****   ***** .
.   * *           * *       * * .
.   * * *****************   * * .
.   * * *         * *       * * .
. ***** * *****   * * ***** * * .
. * *   * *   *   * * *   * * * .
. * ********* *   * ********* * .
. *     * * * *   *   *   *   * .
. ********* * *   *****   ***** .
.       *   * *                 .
.       *   * *                 .
.       *   * *                 .
. ********* * *   *****   ***** .
. *     * * * *   *   *   *   * .
. * ********* *   * ********* * .
. * *   * *   *   * * *   * * * .
. ***** * *****   * * ***** * * .
.   * * *         * *       * * .
.   * * *****************   * * .
.   * *           * *       * * .
. *****   *****   *****   ***** .
. * *     *   *     * *   * *   .
. * ***************** *   * *   .
. *       *   *       *   *     .
. *********   *********   ***** .
.                               .
.................................
```

Hilbert Curves of Degrees 1 .. 3

12. Listing of Sierpinski Plot Program

```
                  |WITH text_io; USE text_io;
                  |PROCEDURE sierpinski IS
              1   |  maxdegree    : CONSTANT integer :=      2;
        10    1   |  low          : CONSTANT integer :=      0;
        10    1   |  high         : CONSTANT integer :=     32;
        10    1   |  TYPE screenrange IS RANGE low .. high;
              1   |  screen : ARRAY(screenrange, screenrange) OF character;
      1099    1   |  degree,      -- degree of Sierpinski curve
        10    1   |  unit,        -- unit length of line segment
        10    1   |  origx,       -- x-coordinate of curve origin
        10    1   |  origy,       -- y-coordinate of curve origin
        10    1   |  newx,        -- x-coordinate of next pen position
        10    1   |  newy,        -- y-coordinate of next pen position
        10    1   |  oldx,        -- x-coordinate of current pen position
        10    1   |  oldy         -- y-coordinate of pen.
        10    1   |               : integer;
      1107    1   |
      1107    1   | PROCEDURE clear_screen IS
              2   |  BEGIN -- clear_screen
              2   |   FOR i IN low .. high LOOP
   5          2 1 |    FOR j IN low .. high LOOP
   9          2 2 |     IF i = low OR i = high OR j = low OR j = high THEN
  25          2 3 |      screen( i, j ) := '.';
  35          2 4 |     ELSE
  35          2 3 |      screen( i, j ) := ' ';
  46          2 4 |     END IF;
  46          2 3 |    END LOOP;
  47          2 2 |   END LOOP;
  48          2 1 |  END clear_screen;
  48          1   |
  48          1   | PROCEDURE display IS
  50          2   |  BEGIN -- display
  50          2   |   FOR i IN low .. high LOOP
  55          2 1 |    put( "  " );
  57          2 2 |    FOR j IN low .. high LOOP
  61          2 2 |     put( screen( i, j ) );
  71          2 3 |    END LOOP;
  72          2 2 |    put_line( " " );
  75          2 2 |   END LOOP;
```

```
40    76          2  1 |  END display;
41    76          1    |
42    76          1    | PROCEDURE plot(
43    78          2    |  oldx, oldy : IN OUT integer;
44    78     12   2    |  newx, newy : IN integer ) IS
45    78     14   2    | BEGIN -- plot
46    78          2    |  IF newx < oldx AND newy < oldy THEN --diag loleft
47    87          2  1 |   FOR i IN 0 .. oldx - newx LOOP
48    93          2  2 |    screen( oldx - i, oldy - i ) := '*';
49   107          2  3 |   END LOOP;
50   108          2  2 |   oldx := newx; oldy := newy;
51   114          2  2 |  ELSIF newx > oldx AND newy > oldy THEN --diag hiright
52   123          2  1 |   FOR i IN 0 .. newx - oldx LOOP
53   129          2  2 |    screen( oldx + i, oldy + i ) := '*';
54   143          2  3 |   END LOOP;
55   144          2  2 |   oldx := newx;
56   147          2  2 |   oldy := newy;
57   150          2  2 |  ELSIF newx > oldx AND newy < oldy THEN --diag loright
58   159          2  1 |   FOR i IN 0 .. newx - oldx LOOP
59   165          2  2 |    screen( oldx + i, oldy - i ) := '*';
60   179          2  3 |   END LOOP;
61   180          2  2 |   oldx := newx; oldy := newy;
62   186          2  2 |  ELSIF newx < oldx AND newy > oldy THEN --diag hileft
63   195          2  1 |   FOR i IN 0 .. oldx - newx LOOP
64   201          2  2 |    screen( oldx - i, oldy + i ) := '*';
65   215          2  3 |   END LOOP;
66   216          2  2 |   oldx := newx; oldy := newy;
67   222          2  2 |  ELSIF newx > oldx THEN -- horizontal right
68   227          2  1 |   FOR i IN oldx .. newx LOOP
69   231          2  2 |    screen( newy, i ) := '*';
70   241          2  3 |    oldx := newx;
71   244          2  3 |   END LOOP;
72   245          2  2 |  ELSIF newx < oldx THEN -- horizontal left
73   250          2  1 |   FOR i IN newx .. oldx LOOP
74   254          2  2 |    screen( newy, i ) := '*';
75   264          2  3 |    oldx := newx;
76   267          2  3 |   END LOOP;
77   268          2  2 |  ELSIF newy > oldy THEN -- vertical up
78   273          2  1 |   FOR j IN oldy .. newy LOOP
79   277          2  2 |    screen( j, newx ) := '*';
80   287          2  3 |    oldy := newy;
81   290          2  3 |   END LOOP;
82   291          2  2 |  ELSIF newy < oldy THEN -- vertical down
83   296          2  1 |   FOR j IN newy .. oldy LOOP
84   300          2  2 |    screen( j, newx ) := '*';
85   310          2  3 |    oldy := newy;
86   313          2  3 |   END LOOP;
87   314          2  2 |  END IF;
88   314          2  1 | END plot;
89   314          1    |
90   314          1    | PROCEDURE b( degree : integer ); -- forward dcl
91   316     11   1    | PROCEDURE c( degree : integer ); -- forward dcl
```

```
 92  316  11  1  | PROCEDURE d( degree : integer ); -- forward dcl
 93  316  11  1  | PROCEDURE a( degree : integer ) IS
 94  316  11  2  |   BEGIN -- a
 95  316      2  |    IF degree > 0 THEN
 96  321      2 1|      a( degree - 1 );
 97  328      2 2|      newx := newx + unit;
 98  333      2 2|      newy := newy - unit;
 99  338      2 2|      plot( oldx, oldy, newx, newy );
100  346      2 2|      b( degree - 1 );
101  353      2 2|      newx := newx + 2*unit;
102  360      2 2|      plot( oldx, oldy, newx, newy );
103  368      2 2|      d( degree - 1 );
104  375      2 2|      newx := newx + unit;
105  380      2 2|      newy := newy + unit;
106  385      2 2|      plot( oldx, oldy, newx, newy );
107  393      2 2|      a( degree - 1 );
108  400      2 2|    END IF;
109  400      2 1|   END a;
110  400      1  |
111  400      1  | PROCEDURE b( degree : integer ) IS
112  402  11  2  |   BEGIN -- b
113  402      2  |    IF degree > 0 THEN
114  407      2 1|      b( degree - 1 );
115  414      2 2|      newx := newx - unit;
116  419      2 2|      newy := newy - unit;
117  424      2 2|      plot( oldx, oldy, newx, newy );
118  432      2 2|      c( degree - 1 );
119  439      2 2|      newy := newy - 2*unit;
120  446      2 2|      plot( oldx, oldy, newx, newy );
121  454      2 2|      a( degree - 1 );
122  461      2 2|      newx := newx + unit;
123  466      2 2|      newy := newy - unit;
124  471      2 2|      plot( oldx, oldy, newx, newy );
125  479      2 2|      b( degree - 1 );
126  486      2 2|    END IF;
127  486      2 1|   END b;
128  486      1  |
129  486      1  | PROCEDURE c( degree : integer ) IS
130  488  11  2  |   BEGIN -- c
131  488      2  |    IF degree > 0 THEN
132  493      2 1|      c( degree - 1 );
133  500      2 2|      newx := newx - unit;
134  505      2 2|      newy := newy + unit;
135  510      2 2|      plot( oldx, oldy, newx, newy );
136  518      2 2|      d( degree - 1 );
137  525      2 2|      newx := newx - 2*unit;
138  532      2 2|      plot( oldx, oldy, newx, newy );
139  540      2 2|      b( degree - 1 );
140  547      2 2|      newx := newx - unit;
141  552      2 2|      newy := newy - unit;
142  557      2 2|      plot( oldx, oldy, newx, newy );
143  565      2 2|      c( degree - 1 );
```

```
144  572      2  2 |   END IF;
145  572      2  1 |  END c;
146  572      1    |
147  572      1    |  PROCEDURE d( degree : integer ) IS
148  574  11  2    |  BEGIN -- d
149  574      2    |   IF degree > 0 THEN
150  579      2  1 |    d( degree - 1 );
151  586      2  2 |    newx := newx + unit;
152  591      2  2 |    newy := newy + unit;
153  596      2  2 |    plot( oldx, oldy, newx, newy );
154  604      2  2 |    a( degree - 1 );
155  611      2  2 |    newy := newy + 2*unit;
156  618      2  2 |    plot( oldx, oldy, newx, newy );
157  626      2  2 |    c( degree - 1 );
158  633      2  2 |    newx := newx - unit;
159  638      2  2 |    newy := newy + unit;
160  643      2  2 |    plot( oldx, oldy, newx, newy );
161  651      2  2 |    d( degree - 1 );
162  658      2  2 |   END IF;
163  658      2  1 |  END d;
164  658      1    |
165  658      1    |  BEGIN -- sierpinski
166  660      1    |   clear_screen;
167  664      1  1 |   degree := 0;
168  667      1  1 |   unit := high / 4;
169  672      1  1 |   origx := unit * 2;
170  677      1  1 |   origy := unit * 3;
171  682      1  1 |   WHILE degree < maxdegree LOOP
172  686      1  1 |    degree := degree + 1;
173  691      1  2 |    origx := origx - unit;
174  696      1  2 |    unit := unit / 2;
175  701      1  2 |    origy := origy + unit;
176  706      1  2 |    oldx := origx;
177  709      1  2 |    oldy := origy;
178  712      1  2 |    newx := oldx;
179  715      1  2 |    newy := oldy;
180  718      1  2 |    a( degree );
181  722      1  2 |    newx := newx + unit;
182  727      1  2 |    newy := newy - unit;
183  732      1  2 |    plot( oldx, oldy, newx, newy );
184  739      1  2 |    b( degree );
185  743      1  2 |    newx := newx - unit;
186  748      1  2 |    newy := newy - unit;
187  753      1  2 |    plot( oldx, oldy, newx, newy );
188  760      1  2 |    c( degree );
189  764      1  2 |    newx := newx - unit;
190  769      1  2 |    newy := newy + unit;
191  774      1  2 |    plot( oldx, oldy, newx, newy );
192  781      1  2 |    d( degree );
193  785      1  2 |    newx := newx + unit;
194  790      1  2 |    newy := newy + unit;
195  795      1  2 |    plot( oldx, oldy, newx, newy );
```

```
802    1  2 |  END LOOP;
803    1  1 |  display;
806    1  1 | END sierpinski;
```

Example C-11-6   Listing of Sierpinski Curve Program

The output generated by the program of Example C-11-6 follows.

```
.................................
.                               .
.   *       *       *       *   .
.  * *     * *     * *     * *  .
. *   *****   *   *   *****   * .
.  *   * *   *     *   * *   *  .
.   * *   * *       * *   * *   .
.   **     **       **     **   .
.   *       *********       *   .
.   **      *       *      **   .
.   * *     *       *     * *   .
.  *   *     *     *     *   *  .
. *   *****   *****   *****   * .
.  * *  *  *         *  *  * *  .
.   *   *   *       *   *   *   .
.       *   *       *   *       .
.       *   *       *   *       .
.       *   *       *   *       .
.   *   *   *       *   *   *   .
.  * *  *  *         *  *  * *  .
. *   *****   *****   *****   * .
.  *   *     *     *     *   *  .
.   * *     *       *     * *   .
.   **      *       *      **   .
.   *       *********       *   .
.   **     **       **     **   .
.   * *   * *       * *   * *   .
.  *   * *   *     *   * *   *  .
. *   *****   *   *   *****   * .
.  * *     * *     * *     * *  .
.   *       *       *       *   .
.                               .
.................................
```

Sierpinski Curves of Degree 1 and 2 on Same Screen

13. In reality the successor function performs also an addition that is very primitive, since one of the operands is guaranteed to be 1. The idea is to replace general addition by repeated increments, and use recursion to do the iteration. A Pascal implementation follows.

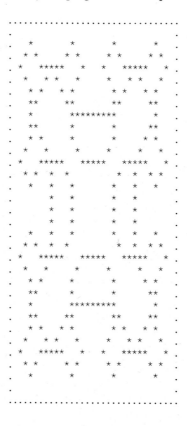

```
function add( a, b : integer ) : integer;
 begin
  if b = 0 then
   add := a
  else
   add := succ( add( a, pred( b ) ) );
  {end if}
 end { add };
```

Example C-11-7

Chapter 12

1. Absence of Goto Statements does not, of course, guarantee well-structured software. Structure and readability result from the quality of design, not from the way the design is expressed in a programming language. One can even write well-structured and maintainable programs in assembly language; this requires more discipline, however. The automatic translator cannot provide any help.

2. By the same argument made in Exercise 1, the presence of Goto Statements does not necessarily mean the software to be unstructured.

3. Any unconditional GOTO to a second unconditional branch can be replaced by a branch to the second target at the place of the first.

4. The unconditional GOTO to a conditional branch can be replaced by the same conditional branch even in the presence of side effects.

5. In the presence of side effects in the condition evaluation the answer is "no." But if both conditions are free of side effects, the first conditional branch can be replaced by the AND function of the two conditions.

6. Any code sequence after an unconditional Goto is "dead code" unless that branch is followed by a label. Dead code is a sequence of instructions that can never be executed.

Chapter 13

2. In the following program listing we have designed a simple, economical manager for a large heap named "mem." Included is an allocation function, named "firstfit," alluding to the simple method chosen. Also we list procedure "freemem," which returns an area of "size" consecutive elements in "mem" starting at address "addr." Naturally we would like to test the program with a realistic environment, which emits a random sequence of requests for allocation and freeing. This lets our sample solution grow a bit in size.

   Most importantly, after each request for allocation and freeing, the simulator will print a trace of the available blocks of free heap space. The conceptual pointer variable "Avail" points to the start of a linked list of free memory records. If Avail is NULL, then there is no free element. Initially the whole memory area is a single free block. In our implementation we arbitrarily locate Avail into element "Mem(0)."

   Each free block has two overhead fields named "size" and "link." "Size" indicates the size of the current free block, including the space for "size" and "link" as well. "Link" points to the beginning of the next free block of memory. If "link" is NULL, then the current block is the last one.

   Function "firstfit" is called with a "size" parameter holding the required number of memory elements. "Firstfit runs through the linked list of free elements, and returns the index to the first free block that is big enough to grant the request. If the free block is of the same size as required by the argument, then this block is removed from the free list. Note that this can result in "avail" being set to NULL.

   Otherwise, if the free block found is greater than the desired size, the current free block remains on the list, but the "size" field is decremented by the number of elements that was granted to the requesting function. Finally, "firstfit" returns the index of the first element of the granted block.

   Should "firstfit" not find a block large enough to fulfill the request, it returns a NULL index. See Example C-13-1.

```
  1 0 0        PROGRAM heapmanager( input, output );

  3 0 0        {

     memory Layout:  mem[0].link is used for AVAIL pointer.

  +---+                   +-----------+           +-----------+
  |   V                   |           V           |           V
+-|-+---+---+---+---+---+-|-+---+---+---+---+---+-|-+---+---+---+---+
| o | o |   |aaa|bbb|ccc| o |   |ddd| o |   |eee| o |   |fff| o |   |
+---+-|-+---+---+---+---+---+---+---+-|-+---+---+---+---+---+-|-+---+
      |                   ^           |           ^           |
      +-------------------+           +-----------+           -

              +---+---+--->
              |siz|lnk|data
              +---+---+--->

              Link of -1 means: NULL. Overhead for size and link.
              }
                CONST
                 nilval            =     -1;
```

```
 3   25  0  0        avail           =      0;
 4   26  0  0        minmem          =      0;
 5   27  0  0        maxmem          =  10000;
 6   28  0  0        overhead        =      2; { space for size and link }
 7   29  0  0       TYPE
                     memrange        = minmem .. maxmem;
 8   31  0  0       VAR
                     mem             : ARRAY[ memrange ] OF integer;
 9   33  0  0        totallinks      : integer;

10   35  0  0       FUNCTION getsize( addr : memrange ) : memrange;
11   36  1  0        { addr is assumed to point to free block }
                     { hence getsize always returns good value }
                     BEGIN { getsize }
11   39  1  1         getsize := mem[ addr ];
12   40  1  1        END { getsize };

13   42  0  0       PROCEDURE setsize( addr, size : memrange );
14   43  1  0        BEGIN { setsize }
14   44  1  1         mem[ addr ] := size;
15   45  1  1        END { setsize };
16   46  0  0
                    FUNCTION getlink( addr : memrange ) : integer;
17   48  1  0        { addr assumed to be pointer to mem, hence memrange }
                     { however, next link may be nilval, so integer }
                     BEGIN { getlink }
17   51  1  1         getlink := mem[ addr + 1 ];
18   52  1  1        END { getlink };

19   54  0  0       PROCEDURE setlink(
19   55  1  0         addr    : memrange;
                       link    : integer );
20   57  1  0        BEGIN { setlink }
20   58  1  1         mem[ addr + 1 ] := link;
21   59  1  1        END { setlink };

22   61  0  0       PROCEDURE tracefreemem;
23   62  1  0        VAR
                      link     : integer;
24   64  1  0        BEGIN { tracefreemem }
24   65  1  1         link := getlink( avail );
25   66  1  1         WHILE link <> nilval DO
26   67  1  1          BEGIN
26   68  1  2       writeln( ' avail block of:',getsize(link):4,' range:',
                          link : 5,' ..',link  - 1 + getsize( link ) : 5 );
27   70  1  2           link := getlink( link );
28   71  1  2          END;
30   72  1  1         {END WHILE}
                      { link = nilval }
                     END { tracefreemem };

31   76  0  0       PROCEDURE init;
```

```
32   77  1  0      BEGIN { init }
32   78  1  1       totallinks := 0;
33   79  1  1       mem[ 0 ] := 0;
34   80  1  1       mem[ 1 ] := 2;
35   81  1  1       mem[ 2 ] := maxmem + 1 - overhead; { +1 low = 0 }
36   82  1  1       mem[ 3 ] := nilval;
37   83  1  1      END { init };

38   85  0  0     PROCEDURE linkcount(
38   86  1  0      VAR
                    link,
                    oldlink : integer );
39   89  1  0      BEGIN { linkcount }
39   90  1  1       totallinks := totallinks + 1;
40   91  1  1       oldlink := link;
41   92  1  1       link := getlink( link );
42   93  1  1      END; { linkcount }
43   94  0  0
                  FUNCTION firstfit( size : integer ) : integer;
44   96  1  0      { When not found, return nilval, so integer type }
                   VAR
                    found    : boolean;
45   99  1  0       oldlink,
                    diffsize,
                    link     : integer;
46  102  1  0      BEGIN { firstfit }
46  103  1  1       IF size < overhead THEN
47  104  1  1        size := overhead;
48  105  1  1       {END IF}
                    writeln( output );
49  107  1  1       writeln( ' request to allocate block of: ', size );
50  108  1  1       oldlink := avail;
51  109  1  1       link := getlink( oldlink ); { may be nilval }
52  110  1  1       found := false;
53  111  1  1       WHILE ( link <> nilval ) AND NOT found DO
54  112  1  1        IF getsize( link ) >= size THEN
55  113  1  1         found := true
                     ELSE
56  115  1  1         linkcount( link, oldlink );
57  116  1  1        {END IF}
                    {END WHILE}
                    { link = nilval or found }
                    IF found THEN
58  120  1  1        BEGIN
58  121  1  2         diffsize := getsize( link ) - size;
59  122  1  2         IF diffsize = 0 THEN { exact fit, remove block }
60  123  1  2          BEGIN
60  124  1  3           setlink( oldlink, getlink( link ) );
61  125  1  3           firstfit := link;
62  126  1  3          END
63  127  1  2         ELSE
64  128  1  2          BEGIN
```

```
64  129  1  3              setsize( link, diffsize );
65  130  1  3              firstfit := link + diffsize;
66  131  1  3              setsize( link + diffsize, size );
67  132  1  3            END
68  133  1  2           {END IF}
                      END
69  135  1  1         ELSE
70  136  1  1          firstfit := nilval;
71  137  1  1         {END IF}
                      tracefreemem;
72  139  1  1        END; { firstfit }
73  140  0  0

                     PROCEDURE freemem( addr, size : integer );
74  142  1  0        VAR
                       oldlink,
                       link     : integer;
75  145  1  0        BEGIN { freemem }
75  146  1  1         writeln( output );
76  147  1  1         writeln( ' freeing memory at: ',addr,' size= ',size);
77  148  1  1         IF mem[ addr ] <> size THEN
78  149  1  1          writeln(' mem[',addr,']=',mem[ addr ],'size=',size);
79  150  1  1         {END IF}
                      IF ( addr < minmem ) or ( addr > maxmem ) THEN
80  152  1  1          writeln( ' * illegal free address: ', addr )
                      ELSE
81  154  1  1          BEGIN
81  155  1  2           oldlink := avail;
82  156  1  2           link := getlink( oldlink );
83  157  1  2           WHILE ( link <> nilval ) AND ( link <= addr ) DO
84  158  1  2            linkcount( link, oldlink );
85  159  1  2           {END WHILE}
                        { ( link=nilval ) OR ( link>addr ), oldlink<addr }
                        IF oldlink = addr THEN
86  162  1  2            { element is already free }
                         writeln( ' * illegal; block free, at', addr )
                        ELSE
87  165  1  2            BEGIN
87  166  1  3             IF addr + size = link THEN { link <> nilval }
88  167  1  3              BEGIN
88  168  1  4               size := size + getsize( link );
89  169  1  4               setlink( addr, getlink( link ) );
90  170  1  4              END
91  171  1  3             ELSE
92  172  1  3              setlink( addr, link );
93  173  1  3             {END IF}
                          IF oldlink + getsize( oldlink ) = addr THEN
94  175  1  3              BEGIN
94  176  1  4               setsize( oldlink, getsize( oldlink ) + size );
95  177  1  4               setlink( oldlink, getlink( addr ) );
96  178  1  4              END
97  179  1  3             ELSE
98  180  1  3              BEGIN
```

```
 98  181  1  4                setlink( oldlink, addr );
 99  182  1  4                setsize( addr, size );
100  183  1  4               END;
102  184  1  3              {END IF}
                            END;
104  186  1  2             {END IF}
                          END;
106  188  1  1           {END IF}
                         tracefreemem;
107  190  1  1          END; { freemem }
108  191  0  0
                       PROCEDURE processtransactions;
109  193  1  0          CONST
                         maxtrans    = 1000;
110  195  1  0          TYPE
                         transrange  = 0 .. maxtrans;
111  197  1  0           remtype     =
                          RECORD
111  199  1  1             size,
                           addr       : integer;
112  201  1  1           END;
113  202  1  0          VAR
                         transaction : integer;
114  204  1  0           rem         : ARRAY[ transrange ] OF remtype;

115  206  1  0          PROCEDURE nexttransaction;
116  207  2  0           VAR
                          transtype  : char;
117  209  2  0            i,
                          size       : integer;
118  211  2  0           BEGIN { nexttransaction }
118  212  2  1            read( input, transtype );
119  213  2  1            IF transtype = 'f' THEN
120  214  2  1             BEGIN
120  215  2  2              read( input, i );
121  216  2  2              IF ( i < 0 ) OR ( i > transaction ) THEN
122  217  2  2               writeln( ' * illegal trans # to free= ', i )
                             ELSE
123  219  2  2               freemem( rem[ i ].addr, rem[ i ].size );
124  220  2  2              {END IF}
                            END
125  222  2  1            ELSE IF transtype = 'a' THEN
127  223  2  1             BEGIN
127  224  2  2              read( input, size );
128  225  2  2              rem[ transaction ].addr := firstfit( size );
129  226  2  2              IF rem[ transaction ].addr = nilval THEN
130  227  2  2               writeln( ' * Unsuccessful. Size:', size );
131  228  2  2              {END IF}
                             rem[ transaction ].size := size;
132  230  2  2             END
133  231  2  1            ELSE
134  232  2  1             writeln( ' * illegal trans = ''',transtype,'''' );
```

```
135  233  2  1           {END IF}
                         readln( input );
136  235  2  1          END { nexttransaction };

137  237  1  0         BEGIN { processtransactions }
137  238  1  1          transaction := 0;
138  239  1  1          WHILE NOT eof( input ) DO
139  240  1  1           BEGIN
139  241  1  2            nexttransaction;
140  242  1  2            transaction := transaction + 1;
141  243  1  2           END;
143  244  1  1          {END WHILE}
                        END { processtransactions };

144  247  0  0        PROCEDURE finish;
145  248  1  0         BEGIN { finish }
145  249  1  1          writeln( output );
146  250  1  1          writeln( output, ' total  links = ', totallinks );
147  251  1  1         END { finish };

148  253  0  0        BEGIN { heapmanager }
148  254  0  1         init;
149  255  0  1         processtransactions;
150  256  0  1         finish;
151  257  0  1        END { heapmanager }.
```

Example C-13-1   Listing of Heap Manager in Pascal

3. To test whether the heap manager recycles data blocks that are disposed of, we try to grab the complete heap space. We are not using the heap for anything reasonable; we just ensure the heap manager cannot grant us any more.

   Then we dispose one element and subsequently ask for an element of the same size from the heap. If we get the new element, we can conclude that we must be recycling the block released previously. Otherwise, we may conclude that no recycling takes place. The program listed in Example C-13-2 does this.

```
program testdispose( output );
 type
  bigmatrixtype = array[ 0 .. 500, 0 .. 500 ] of integer;
  pblocktype    = ^ blocktype;
  blocktype     =
   record
    data        : bigmatrixtype;
    link        : pblocktype;
   end;
 var
  tail          : pblocktype;
 procedure graball;
  var blockno : integer;
  begin { graball }
   new( tail );
   blockno := 1;
```

```
  while tail <> nil do
   begin
    writeln( ' block: ', blockno, ' of 501*501 integers.' );
    new( tail ); { elements are not linked }
    blockno := succ( blockno );
   end;
  {end while}
 end { graball };

procedure freelast;
 begin { freelast }
  dispose( tail ); { free 1 element }
  new( tail );
  if tail = nil then
   writeln( ' didn''t collect garbage' )
  else
   writeln( ' Good, recycled last block.' );
  {end if}
 end { freelast };
begin { testdispose }
 graball;
 freelast;
end { testdispose }.
```

Example C-13-2   Pascal Test Program to Check DISPOSE Semantics

4. The bodies of procedure "postorder" and "inorder" look almost identical to the pattern set in "preorder"; only the order of calls and interpretation of the current node's data changes. See the listing in Example C-13-3.

```
procedure postorder( pin : nodepin );
 begin { postorder }
  if pin = nil then
   write( output, dot )
  else
   begin
    postorder( pin^.left );
    postorder( pin^.right );
    write( output, pin^.data );
   end;
  {end if}
 end { postorder };

procedure inorder( pin : nodepin );
 begin { inorder }
  if pin = nil then
   write( output, dot )
  else
   begin
    inorder( pin^.left );
    write( output, pin^.data );
    inorder( pin^.right );
   end;
  {end if}
 end { inorder };
```

Example C-13-3 Postorder and Inorder Tree Traversal in Pascal

5. A listing of the Ada program "tree" follows in Example C-13-4.

```
                   | WITH text_io; USE text_io;
                   | PROCEDURE tree IS
              1    |  dot          : CONSTANT character := '.';
        10    1    |  TYPE node_type;
              1    |  TYPE node_pin_type IS ACCESS node_type;
              1    |  TYPE node_type IS
              1    |   RECORD
              1    |    data       : character;
              1    |    left,
              1    |    right      : node_pin_type;
              1    |   END RECORD;
              1    |  root         : node_pin_type;
        11    1    |  c            : character;
        12    1    |
        12    1    | PROCEDURE preorder( pin : node_pin_type ) IS
        11    2    |  BEGIN -- preorder
              2    |   IF pin = NULL THEN
  5           2  1 |    put( dot );
  7           2  2 |   ELSE
  7           2  1 |    put( pin.data );
 12           2  2 |    preorder( pin.left );
 20           2  2 |    preorder( pin.right );
```

```
 28        2  2 |   END IF;
 28        2  1 |  END preorder;
 28        1    |
 28        1    | PROCEDURE postorder( pin : node_pin_type ) IS
 30   11   2    |  BEGIN -- postorder
 30        2    |   IF pin = NULL THEN
 35        2  1 |    put( dot );
 37        2  2 |   ELSE
 37        2  1 |    postorder( pin.left );
 46        2  2 |    postorder( pin.right );
 54        2  2 |    put( pin.data );
 58        2  2 |   END IF;
 58        2  1 |  END postorder;
 58        1    |
 58        1    | PROCEDURE inorder( pin : node_pin_type ) IS
 60   11   2    |  BEGIN -- inorder
 60        2    |   IF pin = NULL THEN
 65        2  1 |    put( dot );
 67        2  2 |   ELSE
 67        2  1 |    inorder( pin.left );
 76        2  2 |    put( pin.data );
 80        2  2 |    inorder( pin.right );
 88        2  2 |   END IF;
 88        2  1 |  END inorder;
 88        1    |
 88        1    | PROCEDURE entersorted(
 90        2    |   root   : IN OUT node_pin_type;
 90   11   2    |   c      : character ) IS
 90   12   2    |  BEGIN -- entersorted
 90        2    |   IF root = NULL THEN
 95        2  1 |    root := NEW node_type;
 98        2  2 |    root.data := c;
102        2  2 |    root.left := NULL;
107        2  2 |    root.right := NULL;
112        2  2 |   ELSIF root.data = c THEN
119        2  1 |    put_line( c & " already in tree" );
122        2  2 |   ELSIF root.data > c THEN
129        2  1 |    entersorted( root.left, c );
137        2  2 |   ELSE
137        2  1 |    entersorted( root.right, c );
146        2  2 |   END IF;
146        2  1 |  END entersorted;
146        1    |
146        1    | BEGIN -- tree
148        1    |  root := NULL;
152        1  1 |  put_line( " Enter tree, terminated with '.'" );
155        1  1 |  get( c );
157        1  1 |  WHILE c /= dot AND NOT end_of_line( input ) LOOP
164        1  1 |   entersorted( root, c );
169        1  2 |   read( input, c );
171        1  2 |  END LOOP;
172        1  1 |  preorder( root );
```

```
176        1  1 |  new_line;
179        1  1 |  postorder( root );
183        1  1 |  new_line;
186        1  1 |  inorder( root );
190        1  1 |  new_line;
193        1  1 |END tree;
```

Example C-13-4   Tree Traversal in Ada

6. By definition of the problem statement, each node consumes three units of storage. If the tree is empty the program requires only space for the root, which is one unit. For each stored number the program consumes three more units. Hence the formula for the total space, expressed as a function of "n" is:

```
space = 3*n + 1
```

Chapter 14

1. The solution for function "asciito int" follows in Example C-14-1.

```
 1                        |WITH text_io; USE text_io;
 2                        |PROCEDURE scan_number IS
 3              1          | temp        : integer;
 4         11   1          | curchar     : character;
 5         12   1          |
 6         12   1          | FUNCTION ascii_to_int RETURN integer IS
 7              2          |   inum      : integer;
 8         11   2          | BEGIN -- ascii_to_int
 9              2          |   inum := 0;
10    4        2  1        |   WHILE curchar IN '0' .. '9' LOOP
11    9        2  1        |     inum := inum * 10
12   12        2  2        |                 + character'pos( curchar )
13   14        2  2        |                 - character'pos( '0' );
14   18        2  2        |     get( curchar ); -- skip digit or ' '
15   20        2  2        |   END LOOP;
16   21        2  1        |   RETURN inum;
17   26        2  1        | END ascii_to_int;
18   26        1          |
19   26        1          |BEGIN -- scan_number
20   28        1          | put( " enter one number: " );
21   31        1  1        | get( input, curchar );
22   33        1  1        | WHILE curchar = ' ' LOOP
23   37        1  1        |   get( input, curchar );   -- skip blanks
24   39        1  2        | END LOOP;
25   40        1  1        | temp := ascii_to_int();
26   45        1  1        | put( " number was = " );
27   47        1  1        | put_line( temp );
28   50        1  1        |END scan_number;
```

Example C-14-1

2. Solution for function "newascii to int."

```
 1                        |WITH text_io; USE text_io;
 2                        |PROCEDURE scan_number IS
 3              1          | temp        : integer;
 4         11   1          | curchar     : character;
 5         12   1          |
 6         12   1          | FUNCTION new_ascii_to_int RETURN integer IS
 7              2          |   last_digit : CONSTANT character := '7'; -- last 32767
 8         10   2          |   zero       : CONSTANT integer := character'pos( '0' );
 9         10   2          |   maxintby10 : CONSTANT integer := 3276; -- 32767 / 10
10   10        2          |   inum       : integer;
11   11        2          | BEGIN -- new_ascii_to_int
12              2          |   inum := 0;
13    4        2  1        |   WHILE curchar IN '0' .. '9' LOOP
14    9        2  1        |     IF inum < maxintby10 THEN  -- o.k. to * and +
```

```
15  13      2 2 |    inum := inum * 10 + character'pos( curchar ) - zero;
16  22      2 3 |    ELSIF inum = maxintby10 THEN  -- only safe to add < 8
17  27      2 2 |     IF curchar > last_digit THEN
18  31      2 3 |      put_line( " integer overflow" );
19  34      2 4 |     ELSE -- safe
20  34      2 3 |      inum := inum * 10 + character'pos( curchar )-zero;
21  44      2 4 |     END IF;
22  44      2 3 |    ELSE  -- inum > maxintby10
23  44      2 2 |     put_line( " integer overflow" );
24  48      2 3 |    END IF;
25  48      2 2 |    get( curchar ); -- skip digit or ' '
26  50      2 2 |   END LOOP;
27  51      2 1 |   RETURN inum;
28  56      2 1 | END new_ascii_to_int;
29  56      1   |
30  56      1   |BEGIN -- scan_number
31  58      1   | put_line( " enter numbers" );
32  62      1 1 | LOOP
33  62      1 1 |  put( " Enter next number: " );
34  64      1 2 |  get( input, curchar );
35  66      1 2 |  WHILE NOT ( curchar IN '0' .. '9' ) LOOP
36  72      1 2 |   get( input, curchar );  -- skip blanks
37  74      1 3 |  END LOOP;
38  75      1 2 |  temp := new_ascii_to_int();
39  80      1 2 |  put( " number was = " );
40  82      1 2 |  put_line( temp );
41  85      1 2 |  EXIT WHEN temp = 0;
42  90      1 2 |  skip_line( input );
43  91      1 2 | END LOOP;
44  92      1 1 |END scan_number;
```

Example C-14-2

3. An Ada sample solution to the "average" program is shown in Example C-14-3.

```
1               |WITH text_io; USE text_io;
2               |PROCEDURE average_process  IS
3        1      | temp      : integer;
4    11  1      | total     : integer; -- sums it all up
5    12  1      | count     : integer; -- so many numbers entered
6    13  1      | average   : integer; -- total / count, logically
7    14  1      | curchar   : character;
8    15  1      |
9    15  1      | FUNCTION ascii_to_int RETURN integer IS
10       2      |  last_digit : CONSTANT character := '7'; -- last 32767
11   10  2      |  zero       : CONSTANT integer := character'pos( '0' );
12   10  2      |  maxintby10 : CONSTANT integer := 3276; -- 32767 / 10
13   10  2      |  inum       : integer;
14   11  2      | BEGIN -- ascii_to_int
15       2      |  inum := 0;
16    4  2 1    |  WHILE curchar IN '0' .. '9' LOOP
17    9  2 1    |   IF inum < maxintby10 THEN  -- o.k. to * and +
```

```
18   13    2  2 |    inum := inum * 10 + character'pos( curchar ) - zero;
19   22    2  3 |   ELSIF inum = maxintby10 THEN  -- only safe to add < 8
20   27    2  2 |    IF curchar > last_digit THEN
21   31    2  3 |     put_line( " integer overflow" );
22   34    2  4 |    ELSE -- safe
23   34    2  3 |     inum := inum * 10 + character'pos( curchar )-zero;
24   44    2  4 |    END IF;
25   44    2  3 |   ELSE  -- inum > maxintby10
26   44    2  2 |    put_line( " integer overflow" );
27   48    2  3 |   END IF;
28   48    2  2 |   get( curchar ); -- skip digit or ' '
29   50    2  2 |  END LOOP;
30   51    2  1 |  RETURN inum;
31   56    2  1 | END ascii_to_int;
32   56    1     |
33   56    1     | PROCEDURE initialize IS
34   58    2     | BEGIN -- initialize
35   58    2     |  put_line( " Enter numbers. I print average." );
36   62    2  1 |  total := 0;
37   65    2  1 |  count := 0;
38   68    2  1 | END initialize;
39   68    1     |
40   68    1     |BEGIN -- average_process
41   70    1     | initialize;
42   74    1  1 | LOOP
43   74    1  1 |  put( " Enter next number: " );
44   76    1  2 |  get( input, curchar );
45   78    1  2 |  WHILE NOT ( curchar IN '0' .. '9' ) LOOP
46   84    1  2 |   get( input, curchar );  -- skip blanks
47   86    1  3 |  END LOOP;
48   87    1  2 |  temp := ascii_to_int();
49   92    1  2 |  total := total + temp;
50   97    1  2 |  count := integer'succ( count );
51  101    1  2 |  EXIT WHEN temp = 0;
52  106    1  2 |  skip_line( input );
53  107    1  2 | END LOOP;
54  108    1  1 | average := ( total * 100 ) / ( count - 1 ); --1 for 0
55  117    1  1 | put( " The average was: " );
56  119    1  1 | put( average / 100 );
57  123    1  1 | put( '.' );
58  125    1  1 | put_line( average MOD 100, 2 );
59  131    1  1 |END average_process;
```

Example C-14-3

```
Enter numbers. I print average.
Enter next number: 13
Enter next number: 19
Enter next number: 199
Enter next number: 99
Enter next number: 1234
Enter next number: 8889
Enter next number: 98
Enter next number: 0
The average was:        1507.28
```

4. Integers and reals span two different subranges of the integral numbers in our mathematical system. Usually the range spanned by the reals is substantially larger. From this it follows already that there will be at least one number, which upon conversion to an integer value will require some form of truncation. But this does not yet explain why it must happen.
   Integers are represented differently than reals. Typically, reals are stored as floating point numbers; one fixed sequence of bits holds the mantissa, another sequence stores the exponent. The base is implied, and is 16 on many machines. Both, the mantissa and the exponent have a sign, the exponent's sign is implied on some machines by mapping the positive and negative number range onto a positive only range that is twice as large.

   Integers are usually represented by the bits of a machine word, with one bit standing for the sign. In other words, the algorithm to express a numeric value by machine bits differs for the different types. Hence it would be purely incidental if two bit patterns stand for the same value in both types.

Chapter 15

1. The first format specifier is COL(13), so the first character is printed in column 13. If necessary, the current line is terminated first. Then follows the string:

```
MIN( 2,12) =  2
```

The blank after the '(' symbol is printed, because the format specifier for "I" is F(2); so two character positions are provided for printing the "2."

2. The first character of the output statement is printed into the next available column. If by chance the current line to be printed is the first line, then the string "MIN.." will start in column 1. Similarly, if by chance a line end has been emitted, then again the "M" would be printed in column 1. The point to learn here is, since no specific column is indicated, the next string floats into whatever position is available. The exact string is:

```
MIN(2,12) = 2
```

Format specifier "A" receives the length from the object printed, since no explicit length is given. So string "MIN(" is allocated four character positions, and the short string ,"" is granted one. Both fixed point numbers are given as many character positions as necessary to hold the value.

3. The simplest way of printing the concatenation of three strings is to concatenate them. In Ada this is accomplished by the & operator. So a possible output statement is: put("Hello" & ' ' & "World").

   In this particular case the string value is already known at the time of compilation. So a "tricky" way to output the same string is by saying: put("Hello World").

4. Again the strings must be concatenated. Before this, the second argument must be converted to the type string via the "image "image" attribute. So the complete Ada Put Statement is: put(" X = " & integer'image(x)).

5. The predefined procedure "WriteInt" clearly requires two arguments. The first argument of type INTEGER is the value to be printed; the second of type CARDINAL specifies the number of character positions for the emitted character string. It certainly would be more convenient to have this second argument to be optional. If omitted, a reasonable number of default character positions could be consumed.

Chapter 16

1. One possible rewrite of the PL/I statement in Ada is the following.

```
i := min( min( j, 5 ), min( i, -k ) );
```

2. The question is equivalent to the following problem: "how many binary trees with four distinct end-nodes can be built such that the order of the nodes from left to right is invariant?" Here the question can be solved by enumeration. There are five such trees. The corresponding expressions are as follows.

```
min(min(min(1,2),3),4)
min(min(1,min(2,3)),4)
min(min(1,2),min(3,4))
min(1,min(2,min(3,4)))
min(1,min(min(2,3),4))
```

3. Lexically, type conversions and function calls with one argument look alike. Syntactically, the difference can be determined by the class of the leading name. If the name is a type mark, the string must be a type conversion or an error. Otherwise, if the leading name is a function name, the expression must be a function call or an error. Otherwise, the string is wrong.

4. Pascal has the intrinsic function "ln" for the natural logarithm. The logarithm to base two, here called log2, is defined by the identity

```
log2(55) = ln(55) / ln(2) = 5.7813597
```

5. Pascal does not provide the "tan(x)" built-in function. But the identity tan(x)=sin(x)/cos(x) can serve to find the tangent of any legal argument, except for the 90-degree and 180-degree angles.

6. When SUBSTR is used as a pseudo-variable, the first argument naturally must be a variable, not a literal.

7. After the assignment "A" equals "SUSU."

8. After the two assignments, I = 2, and J = 0.

Chapter 17

1. Since the Ada source string is correct, the first single quote must be an apostrophe. To the left of the apostrophe is a qualifier, and to the right must come a parenthesized expression. Incidentally the argument of the parenthetical expression is a character literal, as indicated by the second single quote. Contrast the language requirement for a parenthesized expression here with the rules for the ABS operator; ABS does not require parentheses, but they are allowed.

2. The decimal value of 2#01111111 1111 1111# is clearly 32767. It is the largest positive integer value representable on a two's complement machine with a word width of 16 bits.

3. The decimal value is 27, not exponent -2, applied to the base 10. The value 27 to the base 3 in Ada would be: 3#1000#.

4. Any Ada line can hold at most one single comment. Once the comment starts, the whole remainder of the line is interpreted as a comment.

5. A line of Fortran source text can hold only one statement. Therefore, the two statements must be split over two lines. The corrected source is

```
A = B
C = D
```

6. There is one advantage to letting the user redeclare keywords: of the limited number of identifiers, no name will be lost for use as keywords. But we must be aware that the total number of identifiers, even though limited, is enormous. In Ada, where the identifier length is only limited by the physical source length, say 80, the number of possible combinations is about 1.7869E+125, much larger than can ever be exhausted. Subtracting less than 100 reserved words from this list is no real limitation.

   The disadvantage of allowing keyword redeclaration is an increased chance for writing obscure programs. Usually it is better to have reserved keywords. But if this is the rule, the total number of keywords must be small. The number of reserved keywords in Cobol, for example, is too big to be remembered. In Ada the number of keywords is tolerable, but becoming dangerous.

7. The explicit ^ symbol for pointer object dereferencing is a helpful documentation for the reader.

8. Access type dereferencing in Ada is done implicitly. From this, in conjunction with the strict typing, follows a unique language rule. If we wish to refer to the object pointed to, rather than the pointer itself, the fictitious name-qualifier ."ALL" must be appended after the access type object.

9. Since PL/I defines the @, $, and # characters to be letters, and since the underline character is allowed inside of identifiers, the source string is a correct Assignment Statement. The variable names are $, $, $, @ , and @$. These are not very reasonable, but are legal.

10. The value of 3**3**3 in PL/I is a large number, approximately 7.6256*10**12. It is not 19683.

Chapter 18

1. Analysis of program "adaside effect" shows an interesting tidbit about Assignment Statements. Usually programming languages require the right-hand side to be evaluated before the left-hand side. This definition is made to avoid ambiguous interpretations in case of overlapping operands. For example, if the sending expression and receiving variable are substrings of the same string, the result differs depending on the order.

   Ada excludes those cases of obscure programming from the set of correct programs. Ada, therefore, permits either evaluation order in Assignment Statements. In our case the left-hand side is evaluated first. Given this policy and the rule that the evaluation order of operands of binary operators is also undefined, we cannot make a firm statement about the result if both expressions are "i + one()."

   There are two possible results: one as shown in the text, the second one duplicating the value 49 for indices 6 and 7.

2. Pascal requires the right-hand side of an Assignment Statement to be evaluated first. Also the compiler evaluates the left operand of a binary operator before the right operand. Therefore, the result will show 36 for indices 6 and 7.

3. The advantage and true motivation for the inclusion of default variable declarations is Fortran is clear. This default saves several characters of data entry time per variable. Assuming that a slow typist prints one character per second, a middle-sized Fortran program with 1000 lines and 100 variables can save approximately 10 minutes of typing.

   The main disadvantage of the default declaration is that typing errors cannot be caught by the compiler. Every misspelled variable causes a new default declaration to be added by the compiler. The intended operation does not take place; instead a similar operation, involving an undeclared and long unknown variable, takes place.

   On the average, a 1000-line program has at least two typing errors of this form, each of which causes from one hour to a day of debugging time. It is easy to weigh the advantages versus the disadvantages here.

4. Normally it does not matter whether the left or right side is evaluated first. The situations where it matters are usually obscure, and involve side effects in subscripts or overlapping string operands. Both should be discouraged. To discourage programmers from using any of these constructs that make programs hard to understand, the Ada designers leave the order unspecified.

5. The "denial of features" for the sake of security is not a good principle. In its extreme form this principle would make all programming languages absurd by allowing only the Empty Statement.

   Unconditional inclusion of features is also unsound, as demonstrated by PL/I's complexity. But a rule of thumb is that if the language is well designed, a construct should not be excluded for the sake of eliminating classes of side effects. Languages like Algol-68 and C that have only value parameters still can pass pointer values. The objects pointed to may be changed, thus still allowing the side effect that was planned to be abolished in the first place.

6. The naive user will believe that 16 lines of output will be generated, printing the values of "I" in the range 1 to 16. The default conversion involving the fixed point division causes the loop not to be executed at all.

Chapter 19

1. The language overhead in Ada to provide for the parallel execution of Tasks is substantially higher than that in Modula-2. Provided that the expressive power of Ada is similar to that in Modula-2 tasks, the Modula-2 solution is preferable due to its simplicity.

2. Multiple Tasks can be executed fully in parallel if they share no common data. We say their data dependency is empty. For this reason it does not matter in which sequence such tasks are executed in a monoprocessor.

Chapter 20

1. The Prolog Question is ?-person(X). We ask for all possible values of variable "X" such that "person" is satisfied. This has been answered in the text already; we have asked four Questions, and Prolog has responded to all of them. In this form of Question, only the format of the answer is a bit different.

```
X = carmen
X = alexander
X = andre
X = mary
X = mary
X = mary
```

   Again Mary appears three times as a person. The reason for this is still the same as explained in the text.

2. We repeat the three Questions here and list Prolog's answers underneath.

```
: ?-member( [ a ], [ a, b, [ a ] ] ).
** yes
: ?-member( [ [ a ] ], [ b, [ [ a ] ], c ] ).
**yes
: ?-member( [ [ a ] ], [ a, b, [ a, b, [ a ], c ], c ] ).
** no
```

   The first answer is obvious. List [a] is included as a member of the second parameter. Question two is identical in structure, only the list concept has been carried one level deeper. In the third case we have tried to lead the reader astray. The doubly nested list [[a]] is nowhere included in the second parameter of "member." The four elements of that list are "a," "b," "[a,b,[a,b,[a],c],c]," and "c," but not "[[a]]."

3. The first Question is ?-path(a1,b1). Prolog finds innumerably many passages, since cyclic paths are allowed in the given algorithm. Therefore Prolog answers with an endless list of "yes," until all stack space is exhausted, and the interpreter aborts.

   The second Question is ?-path(b1,a1). Again Prolog finds circular paths. But because of the way the Facts are arranged, Prolog tries so many unsuccessful cyclic paths that all stack space is exhausted before the first complete passage through the maze is constructed.

Appendix D

Bibliography

Aho, A. V., and Johnson, S. C. [1974]. "LR Parsing," ACM Computing Surveys, Vol. 6, No. 2.

Aho, A. V., and Ullman, J. D. [1979]. Principles of Compiler Design, Addison-Wesley, Reading, Mass.

ANSI [1976]. American National Standard Programming Language PL/I (ANS X3.53 - 1976), American National Standards Institute, New York, N. Y.

ANSI [1978]. American National Standard Programming Language Fortran (ANS X3.9 - 1978), American National Standards Institute, New York, N. Y.

ANSI [1983a]. Military Standard Ada Programming Language, (ANSI/MIL-STD-1815 A), American National Standards Institute, New York, N. Y.

ANSI [1983b]. American National Standard Pascal Computer Programming Language, (ANSI/IEEE 770X3.97 - 1983), American National Standards Institute, New York, N. Y.

Atkins, M. S. [1973]. "Mutual Recursion in Algol 60 Using Restricted Compilers," Comm. ACM Vol. 16, No. 1.

Bailey, C. [1983]. "Unix and the NS16000," Unix Review, December/January 1983.

Birtwistle, G. [1985]. "The Coroutines of Hanoi," ACM Sigplan Notices, Vol. 20, No. 1.

Brodie, L. [1981]. Starting Forth, Prentice-Hall, Englewood Cliffs, N. J.

Chamberlin, D. D. [1971]. Parallel Implementation of a Single Assignment Language, Stanford Electronics Laboratories, Technical Report 13, January 1971.

Christensen and Willett, [1980]. Computer Programming Manual for the Jovial (J73) Language, (1049 D-A009-8001) prepared for Softech Inc., by Christensen & Willett Associates, Melrose, Mass., January 1980.

CII Honeywell Bull [1979]. Reference Manual for the Green Programming Language, March 15, 1979.

Clocksin, W. F., and Mellish, C. S. [1981]. Programming in Prolog, Springer-Verlag, Berlin.

Conway, R. W., Gries, D., and Zimmerman, E. C. [1976]. A Primer on Pascal, Winthrop Publishers, Cambridge, Mass.

Dijkstra, E. W. [1968]. "Go To Statement considered harmful," Comm. ACM, Vol. 11, No. 3.

Flanders, H. [1983]. "Two Pascal Devices," Pascal & Modula2 News, No. 27, November 1983.

Franklin, W. R. [1984]. "A Simpler Iterative Solution to the Towers of Hanoi Problem," ACM Sigplan Notices, Vol. 19, No. 8.

Goodenough, J. B. [1980]. Ada Compiler Validation Implementors' Guide, Softech, Waltham, Mass.

Gries, D. [1971]. Compiler Construction for Digital Computers, John Wiley & Sons, New York, N. Y.

Habermann, A. N. [1976]. Introduction to Operating Systems Design, Science Research Associates, Palo Alto, Calif.

Halstead, M. H. [1979]. Elements of Software Science, The Computer Science Library, Elsevier North Holland, Third Printing.

Hansen, P. B. [1973]. Operating System Principles, Prentice-Hall Series in Automatic Computation, Englewood Cliffs, N. J.

Hoare, C. A. R. [1964]. "Case Expressions," Algol Bulletin, No. 18, October 1964.

Hoare, C. A. R. [1981]. "The Emperor's Old Clothes," Comm. ACM, Vol. 24, No. 2.

Holt, R. C. [1973]. "Teaching the Fatal Disease," ACM Sigplan Notices, Vol. 8, No. 5.

Hopcroft, J. E., and Ullman, J. D. [1979]. Introduction to Automata Theory, Languages, and Computation, Addison-Wesley, Reading, Mass.

Horning, J. J. [1979]. "A Note on Program Reliability," ACM Sigsoft, Software Engineering Notes, Vol. 4, No. 4.

Ingerman, P. Z. [1961]. "Thunks," Comm. ACM, Vol. 4, No. 1.

Jensen, K., and Wirth, N. [1978]. Pascal User Manual and Report, Springer-Verlag, Berlin.

Kaufman, R. E. [1978]. A Fortran Coloring Book, The MIT Press, Cambridge, Mass.

Knuth, D. E. [1973]. The Art of Computer Programming, Vol. 1, Fundamental Algorithms, Addison-Wesley, Reading, Mass.

Knuth, D. E. [1981]. The Art of Computer Programming, Vol. 2, Seminumerical Algorithms, Addison-Wesley, Reading, Mass.

Knuth, D. E. [1973]. The Art of Computer Programming, Vol. 3, Sorting and Searching, Addison-Wesley, Reading, Mass.

Knuth, D. E. [1964]. "Man or Boy," Letters to the Editor, Algol Bulletin, No. 17, July 1964, p. 7.

Knuth, D. E. [1974]. "Structured Programming with Go To Statements," ACM Computing Surveys, Vol. 6, No. 4.

Knuth, D. E., and Pardo, L. T. [1976]. "The Early Development of Programming Languages," STAN-CS-76-562, Stanford University, Computer Science Dept.

Machtey, M., and Young, P. [1978]. An Introduction to the General Theory of Algorithms, The Computer Science Library, Elsevier, North Holland.

MacLennan, B. J. [1983]. Principles of Programming Languages: Design, Evaluation, and Implementation, Holt, Rinehart and Winston, New York.

Mayer, H. G., and Perkins, D. [1984]. "Towers of Hanoi Revisited, a Nonrecursive Surprise," ACM Sigplan Notices, Vol. 19, No. 2.

Meyer, B. [1984]. "A Note on Iterative Hanoi," ACM Sigplan Notices, Vol. 19, No. 12.

Naur, P., et al. [1963]. Revised Report on the Algorithmic Language Algol 60, Comm. ACM, Vol. 5, No. 1.

Pascal, B. [1963]. Oeuvres Completes, Aux Editions du Seuil, 27 Rue Jacob, Paris-VIe.

Radin, G. [1978]. "The Early History and Characteristics of PL/I," ACM Sigplan Notices, Vol. 13, No. 8.

Raloff, J. [1984]. "Swift Mechanical Logic," Science News, Vol. 125, No. 22, June 2, 1984.

Randell, B., and Russell, L. J. [1971]. Algol 60 Implementation, Academic Press, London and New York, fifth printing.

Shore, B. [1984]. "Computer's Real Father Stands Up," The San Diego Union, Sunday, August 5, 1984.

Stadel, M. [1984a]. "A Remark on the ISO-Standard for Pascal," ACM Sigplan Notices, Vol. 19, No. 3.

Stadel, M. [1984b]. "Another Nonrecursive Algorithm for the Towers of Hanoi," ACM Sigplan Notices, Vol. 19, No. 9.

Webster [1981]. New Collegiate Dictionary 150th Anniversary Edition, Springfied, MA., G.&C. Merriam Co.

Wexelblat, R. L., Editor [1978]. History of Programming Languages Conference, Los Angeles, Calif., ACM Sigplan Notices, Vol. 13, No. 8.

Wirth, N. [1976]. Algorithms + Data Structures = Programs, Prentice-Hall Series in Automatic Computation, Englewood Cliffs, N. J.

Wirth, N. [1985]. "From Programming Language Design to Computer Construction," Comm. ACM, Vol. 28, No. 2.

Wirth, N. [1977]. "Modula, a Language for Modular Programming," Software - Practice and Experience, Vol. 7, p. 3-35.

Wirth, N. [1982]. Programming in Modula-2, Texts and Monographs in Computer Science, Springer-Verlag, second, corrected edition.

Zonnefeld, J. A. [1964]. "Man Compiler Needs Big Brother Machine," Letters to the Editor, Algol Bulletin, No. 18, July 1964.

Index